FOR DUMMIES
BESTSELLING
BOOK SERIES

SQL All-in-One Desk Reference For Dummies®

Cheat Sheet

The Phases of the System Development Life Cycle

- **Definition Phase:** Precisely define the problem to be solved, its magnitude, and who will work on it.

- **Requirements Phase:** Develop a detailed description of exactly what the development effort will produce. Gather all relevant information and put it into a requirements document (Statement of Requirements). Get client signoff.

- **Evaluation Phase:** Determine exactly how you will meet the requirements. What tools will you use? How will you deploy your development team? Determine whether the job is doable within time and budget constraints.

- **Design Phase:** Create a database model and then design a database and database application that satisfy the terms of the requirements document.

- **Implementation Phase:** Build the database and the database application. Include copious documentation within the code and in external documents.

- **Final Documentation and Testing Phase:** Give the database and application a tough workout. Hit the system with every conceivable input condition and a few inconceivable ones. Try to overload it. See where it breaks. When it breaks, send it back to the implementers or even back to the designers. Document everything.

- **Maintenance Phase:** Fix latent bugs as they arise. Provide updates and enhancements called for by the client.

Criteria for Normal Forms

First Normal Form (1NF)

Table must be two-dimensional, with rows and columns.

Each row contains data that pertains to one thing or one portion of a thing.

Each column contains data for a single attribute of the thing being described.

Each cell (intersection of row and column) of the table must be single-valued.

All entries in a column must be of the same kind.

Each column must have a unique name.

No two rows may be identical.

The order of the columns and of the rows does not matter.

Second Normal Form (2NF)

Table must be in first normal form (1NF).

All nonkey attributes (columns) must be dependent on all of the keys.

Third Normal Form (3NF)

Table must be in second normal form (2NF).

Table has no transitive dependencies.

Domain-Key Normal Form (DK/NF)

Every constraint on the table is a logical consequence of the definition of keys and domains.

WHERE Clause Predicates

Comparison Predicates

=	Equal
<>	Not equal
<	Less than
<=	Less than or equal
>	Greater than
>=	Greater than or equal

Other Predicates

BETWEEN	SOME, ANY
IN	EXISTS
NOT IN	UNIQUE
LIKE	OVERLAPS
NOT LIKE	MATCH
NULL	SIMILAR
ALL	DISTINCT

For Dummies: Bestselling Book Series for Beginners

SQL All-in-One Desk Reference For Dummies®

Value Functions

String Value Functions	Effect
SUBSTRING	Extracts a substring from a source string
UPPER	Converts a character string to all uppercase
LOWER	Converts a character string to all lowercase
TRIM	Trims off leading or trailing blanks
TRANSLATE	Transforms a source string from one character set to another
CONVERT	Transforms a source string from one character set to another
Numeric Value Functions	**Effect**
POSITION	Returns the starting position of a target string within a source string
CHARACTER_LENGTH	Returns the number of characters in a string
OCTET_LENGTH	Returns the number of octets (bytes) in a character string
EXTRACT	Extracts a single field from a datetime or interval
Datetime Value Functions	**Effect**
CURRENT_DATE	Returns the current date
CURRENT_TIME(p)	Returns the current time; (p) is precision of seconds
CURRENT_TIMESTAMP(p)	Returns the current date and the current time; (p) is precision of seconds

Set Functions

COUNT	Returns the number of rows in the specified table
MAX	Returns the maximum value that occurs in the specified table
MIN	Returns the minimum value that occurs in the specified table
SUM	Adds up the values in a specified column
AVG	Returns the average of all the values in the specified column

SQL Data Types

Exact Numerics	Character Strings	Intervals
INTEGER	CHARACTER	INTERVAL DAY
SMALLINT	CHARACTER VARYING (VARCHAR)	INTERVAL YEAR
BIGINT	NATIONAL CHARACTER	**Large Objects**
NUMERIC	NATIONAL CHARACTER VARYING	BLOB
DECIMAL	**Datetimes**	CLOB
Approximate Numerics	DATE	**Collection Types**
REAL	TIME	ARRAY
DOUBLE PRECISION	TIMESTAMP	MULTISET
FLOAT	TIME WITH TIMEZONE	**Other Types**
Boolean	TIMESTAMP WITH TIMEZONE	ROW
BOOLEAN		XML

For Dummies: Bestselling Book Series for Beginners

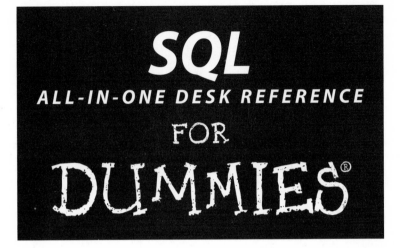

by Allen G. Taylor

Wiley Publishing, Inc.

SQL All-in-One Desk Reference For Dummies®
Published by
Wiley Publishing, Inc.
111 River Street
Hoboken, NJ 07030-5774
www.wiley.com

For general information on our other products and services, please contact our Customer Care Department within the U.S. at 800-762-2974, outside the U.S. at 317-572-3993, or fax 317-572-4002.

For technical support, please visit www.wiley.com/techsupport.

Wiley also publishes its books in a variety of electronic formats. Some content that appears in print may not be available in electronic books.

Library of Congress Control Number: 2007926383

ISBN: 978-0-470-11928-0

Manufactured in the United States of America

10 9 8 7 6 5 4 3 2 1

WILEY

About the Author

Allen G. Taylor is a 30-year veteran of the computer industry and the author of 25 books, including *SQL For Dummies, Crystal Reports 10 For Dummies, Database Development For Dummies, Access 2003 Power Programming with VBA,* and *SQL Weekend Crash Course.* He lectures internationally on databases, networks, innovation, and entrepreneurship. He also teaches database development through a leading online education provider and teaches microprocessor design at Portland State University. For the latest news on Allen's activities, check out `www.DatabaseCentral.Info`. You can contact Allen at `allen.taylor@ieee.org`.

Dedication

This book is dedicated to Joyce Carolyn Taylor, who still puts up with me after all these years.

Author's Acknowledgments

First and foremost, I would like to acknowledge the help of Jim Melton, editor of the ISO/ANSI specification for SQL. Without his untiring efforts, this book, and indeed SQL itself as an international standard, would be of much less value. Andrew Eisenberg has also contributed to my knowledge of SQL through his writing. I would also like to thank my project editor, Nicole Sholly, and my acquisitions editor, Kyle Looper, for their key contributions to the production of this book. Thanks also to my agent, Carole McClendon of Waterside Productions, for her support of my career.

Publisher's Acknowledgments

We're proud of this book; please send us your comments through our online registration form located at www.dummies.com/register/.

Some of the people who helped bring this book to market include the following:

Acquisitions, Editorial, and Media Development

Project Editor: Nicole Sholly

Acquisitions Editor: Kyle Looper

Copy Editor: Linda Morris

Technical Editor: Robert Schneider

Editorial Manager: Kevin Kirschner

Media Development and Quality Assurance: Angela Denny, Kate Jenkins, Steven Kudirka, Kit Malone

Media Development Coordinator: Jenny Swisher

Media Project Supervisor: Laura Moss-Hollister

Editorial Assistant: Amanda Foxworth

Sr. Editorial Assistant: Cherie Case

Cartoons: Rich Tennant (www.the5thwave.com)

Composition Services

Project Coordinator: Kristie Rees

Layout and Graphics: Carl Byers, Carrie A. Foster, Denny Hager, Stephanie D. Jumper, Heather Ryan

Proofreaders: Laura Albert, Aptara, John Greenough

Indexer: Aptara

Anniversary Logo Design: Richard Pacifico

Publishing and Editorial for Technology Dummies

   Richard Swadley, Vice President and Executive Group Publisher

   Andy Cummings, Vice President and Publisher

   Mary Bednarek, Executive Acquisitions Director

   Mary C. Corder, Editorial Director

Publishing for Consumer Dummies

   Diane Graves Steele, Vice President and Publisher

   Joyce Pepple, Acquisitions Director

Composition Services

   Gerry Fahey, Vice President of Production Services

   Debbie Stailey, Director of Composition Services

Contents at a Glance

Table of Contents

Introduction

SQL is the internationally recognized standard language for dealing with data in relational databases. Originally developed by IBM, SQL became an international standard in 1986. The standard was updated in 1989, 1992, 1999, and 2003. It continues to evolve and gain capability. Database vendors continually update their products to incorporate the new features of the ANSI/ISO standard. (ANSI is the American National Standards Institute, and ISO is the International Organization for Standardization.)

SQL is not a general-purpose language, such as C++ or Java. Instead, it is strictly designed to deal with data in relational databases. With SQL, you can

✦ Create a database, including all tables and relationships

✦ Fill database tables with data

✦ Change the data in database tables

✦ Delete data from database tables

✦ Retrieve specific information from database tables

✦ Grant and revoke access to database tables

✦ Protect database tables from corruption due to access conflicts or user mistakes

About This Book

This book is not just about SQL, but also about how SQL fits into the process of creating and maintaining databases and database applications. In this book, I cover how SQL fits into the larger world of application development and how it handles data coming in from other computers, which may be on the other side of the world, or even in interplanetary space.

Here are some of the things you can do with this book:

✦ Create a model of a proposed system and then translate that model into a database

✦ Find out about the capabilities and limitations of SQL

✦ Discover how to develop reliable and maintainable database systems

✦ Create databases

✦ Speed up database queries

✦ Protect databases from hardware failures, software bugs, and Internet attacks

✦ Control access to sensitive information

✦ Write effective database applications

✦ Deal with data from a variety of non-traditional data sources using XML

Foolish Assumptions

I know this is a . . . *For Dummies* book, but I don't really expect that you are a dummy. In fact, I assume that you are a very smart person. After all, you decided to read this book, which is a sign of high intelligence indeed. Therefore, I assume you may want to do a few things; for example, recreate some of the examples in the book. You may even want to enter some SQL code and execute it. To do that, you need at the very least an SQL editor, and more likely a database management system of some sort. Many choices are available, both proprietary and open-source. I mention several of these at various places throughout the book. I don't recommend any one in particular. Any product that complies with the ANSI/ISO international SQL standard should be fine.

However, take claims of ANSI/ISO compliance with a grain of salt. No database management system available today is 100% compliant with the ANSI/ISO SQL standard. For that reason, some of the code examples I give in this book may not work on the particular SQL implementation that you are using. The code samples I use in this book are consistent with the international standard rather than agreeing with the syntax of any particular implementation, unless I specifically specify that the code is for a particular implementation.

Conventions Used in This Book

By *conventions,* I simply mean a set of rules I've employed in this book to present information to you consistently. When you see a term *italicized,* look for its definition, which I've included so that you know what things mean in the context of SQL. Web site addresses and e-mail addresses appear in `monofont` so that they stand out from regular text. Many aspects of the SQL language, such as statements, data types, constraints, and keywords also appear in `monofont`. Code appears in its own font, set off from the rest of the text, like this:

```
CREATE SCHEMA RETAIL1 ;
```

What You Don't Have to Read

I've structured this book modularly — that is, it's designed so that you can easily find just the information you need — so you don't have to read whatever doesn't pertain to your task at hand. I include sidebars here and there throughout the book that contain interesting information that isn't necessarily integral to the discussion at hand; feel free to skip over these. You also don't have to read the Technical Stuff icons, which parse out über-techy tidbits (which you may or may not be your cup of tea).

How This Book Is Organized

SQL All-in-One Desk Reference For Dummies is split into eight minibooks. You don't have to read it sequentially; you don't have to look at every minibook; you don't have to review each chapter; and you don't even have to read all the sections in any particular chapter. (Of course, you can if you want to; it's a good read.) And the Table of Contents and the index can help you quickly find whatever information you need. In this section, I briefly describe what each minibook contains.

Book I: SQL Concepts

SQL is a language specifically and solely designed to create, operate on, and manage relational databases. I start with a description of databases and how relational databases differ from other kinds. I then move on to modeling business and other kinds of tasks in relational terms. How SQL relates to relational databases is covered next, along with a detailed description of the components of SQL and how to use them. The types of data that SQL deals with are described, as are constraints that restrict the data that can be entered into a database.

Book II: Relational Database Development

Many database development projects, like other software development projects, start in the middle rather than at the beginning as they should. This fact is responsible for the notorious tendency of software development projects to run behind schedule and over budget. Many self-taught database developers don't even realize that they are starting in the middle. They think they are doing everything right. This minibook introduces the System Development Life Cycle (SDLC), which shows what the true beginning of a software development project is, as well as the middle and the end.

Key to the development of an effective database that does what you want is an accurate model of the system you are abstracting in your database.

Modeling is described here, as is the delicate tradeoff between performance and reliability. The actual SQL code used to create a database rounds out the discussion.

Book III: SQL Queries

Queries sit at the core of any database system. The whole reason for storing data in databases is so that you can retrieve the information you want from them at a later time. SQL is above all a query language. Its specialty is enabling you to extract from a database the exact information you want, without cluttering up what you retrieve with a lot of stuff you don't want.

This book starts off with a description of values, expressions, and functions. It then gives detailed coverage to the powerful tools SQL gives you to zero in on the information you want, even if it is scattered across multiple tables.

Book IV: Data Security

Your data is one of your most valuable assets. Acknowledging that fact, I discuss ways to protect it from a diverse array of threats. One threat is outright loss due to hardware failures. Another is attack by hackers wielding malicious viruses and worms. I discuss how you can protect yourself from such threats, whether they are random or purposeful.

Other sources of error, such as the entry of bad data or the harmful interaction of simultaneous users, are extensively dealt with in this book. I also cover how to control access to sensitive data and how to handle errors gracefully when they occur, as they inevitably will.

Book V: SQL and Programming

SQL's primary use is as a component of an application program that operates on a database. Because SQL is a data language and not a general-purpose programming language, this means that SQL statements must be integrated somehow with the commands of a language such as Visual Basic, Java, C++, or C#. This book outlines the process with the help of a fictitious sample application, taking it from the beginning, when the need for a new application is perceived, to the final release of the finished application. Best practices are emphasized throughout.

Book VI: SQL and XML

XML is the language used to transport data between dissimilar data stores. The 2005 extensions to the SQL:2003 standard greatly expanded SQL's capacity to handle XML data. This book gives the basics of XML and how it relates to SQL. SQL functions that are specifically designed to operate on data in XML format are described as the operations of storing and retrieving data in XML format.

Book VII: Database Tuning Overview

Depending on how they are structured, databases can efficiently respond to requests for information or perform very poorly. Often the performance of a database degrades over time as its structure and the data in it change, or as the types of retrievals typically performed change. This book describes the parts of a database that are amenable to tuning and optimization. It also gives a procedure for tracking down bottlenecks that are choking the performance of the entire system.

Book VIII: Appendixes

Appendix A lists words that have a special meaning in SQL. You can't use these words as the names of tables, columns, views, or anything other than what they were meant to be used for. If you receive a strange error message to an SQL statement that you have entered, check to see if you have inadvertently used a reserved word inappropriately.

Appendix B is a glossary that gives brief definitions of many of the terms used in this book as well as many others that relate to SQL and databases, whether they are used in this book or not.

Icons Used in This Book

. . . *For Dummies* books are known for those helpful icons that point you in the direction of really great information. This section briefly describes each icon used in this book.

The Tip icon points out helpful information that is likely to make your job easier.

This icon marks a generally interesting and useful fact — something that you might want to remember for later use.

The Warning icon highlights lurking danger. When you see this icon, pay attention and proceed with caution.

This icon denotes that there's techie stuff nearby. If you're not feeling very techie, you can skip this info.

Where to Go from Here

Book I is the place to go if you are just getting started with databases. It explains why databases are useful and describes the different types. It focuses on the relational model and describes SQL's structure and features.

Book II goes into detail on how to build a database that is reliable as well as responsive. Unreliable databases are much too easy to create, and this book tells you how to avoid the pitfalls that lie in wait for the unwary.

Go directly to Book III if your database already exists and you just want to know how to use SQL to pull from it the information you want.

Book IV is primarily aimed at the database administrator (DBA) rather than the database application developer or user. It discusses how to build a robust database system that resists data corruption and data loss.

Book V is for the application developer. In addition to discussing how to write a database application, it gives an example that describes in a step-by-step manner how to build a reliable application.

If you are already an old hand at SQL and just want to know how to handle data in XML format in your SQL database, Book VI is for you.

Book VII gives you a wide variety of techniques for improving the performance of your database. This is the place to go if your database is operating, but not as well as you think it should. Most of these techniques are things that the DBA can do, rather than the application developer or the database user. If your database isn't performing the way you think it should, take it up with your DBA. There are things she can do that could help immensely.

Book VIII is a handy reference that helps you quickly find the meaning of a word you have encountered, or to see why an SQL statement you have entered did not work as expected. (Maybe you used a reserved word without realizing it.)

Book I

SQL Concepts

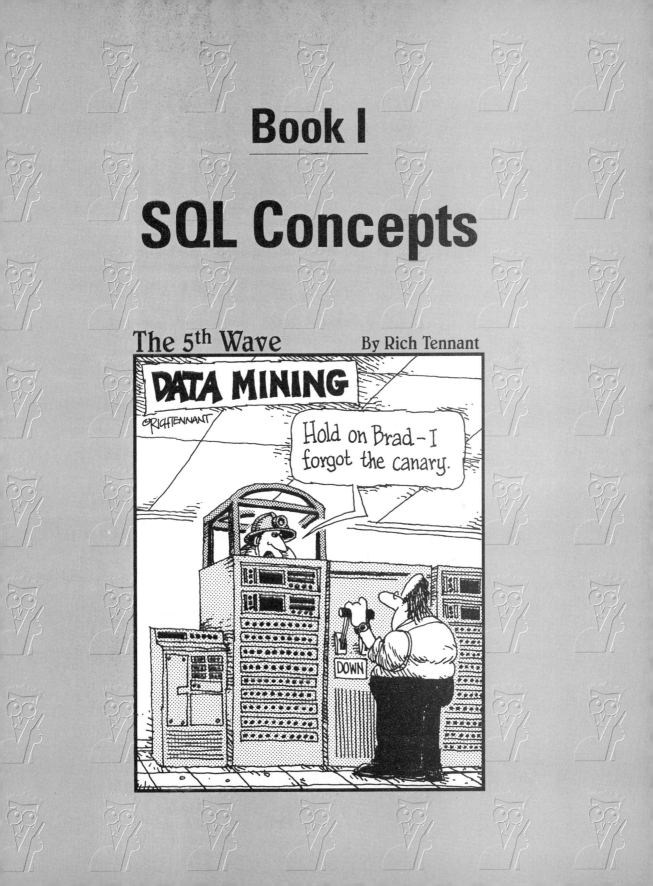

The 5th Wave — By Rich Tennant

DATA MINING

Hold on Brad – I forgot the canary.

DOWN

Contents at a Glance

Chapter 1: Relational Database Basics

In This Chapter

✓ Discovering data files and databases

✓ Finding out what makes a database relational

✓ Databases, queries, and database applications

✓ Understanding SQL and relational database management systems

✓ Capturing the users' data model

✓ Translating the users' data model to a relational model

✓ Getting to know the relational database hierarchy

✓ Building a database from a relational model

✓ Building a database application

*I*n order to understand why relational databases are the primary repositories for the data of both small and large organizations, you must first understand the various ways in which computer data can be stored, and how those ways relate to the relational database model. To help you gain that understanding, in this chapter, I go back to the earliest days of electronic computers and recap the history of data storage. The different data storage strategies that have been used over the years each have their own strengths and weaknesses. Ultimately, the strengths of the relational model overshadowed its weaknesses, and it became the most frequently used method of data storage. Shortly after that, SQL became the most frequently used method of dealing with data stored in a relational database.

Data Files and Databases

In the early days of computers, the concept of a database was more theoretical than practical. Vannevar Bush, the twentieth-century visionary, conceived the idea of a database in 1945, even before the first electronic computer was built. However, practical implementations of databases did not appear for a number of years after that. Initially, computer data was kept in files rather than in databases.

Irreducible complexity

Any software system that performs a useful function is going to be complex. The more valuable the function, the more complex its implementation will be. Regardless of how the data is stored, the complexity remains. The only question is where that complexity resides.

Any non-trivial computer application has two major components: the program and the data. Although an application's level of complexity depends on the task to be performed, developers have some control over the location of that complexity. The complexity may reside primarily in the program part of the overall system, or it may reside in the data part.

The complex program/simple data organization

In the earliest applications of computers to solve problems, all of the complexity resided in the program. The data consisted of one data record of fixed length after another, stored sequentially in a file. This is called a *flat file* data structure. The data file contains nothing but data. Information about where particular records are within the data file (one form of *metadata*) must be included in the program. Thus, for this type of organization, the complexity of managing the data is entirely in the program.

Here's an example of data organized in a flat file structure:

```
Harold Percival26262 S. Howards Mill Rd.Westminster CA92683
Jerry Appel     32323 S. River Lane Road Santa Ana   CA92705
Adrian Hansen   232   Glenwood Court     Anaheim     CA92640
John Baker      2222  Lafayette Street   Garden GroveCA92643
Michael Pens    77730 S. New Era Road    Irvine      CA92715
Bob Michimoto   25252 S. Kelmsley Drive  Stanton     CA92610
Linda Smith     444   S.E. Seventh StreetCosta Mesa  CA92635
Robert Funnell  2424  Sheri Court        Anaheim     CA92640
Bill Checkal    9595  Curry Drive        Stanton     CA92610
Jed Style       3535  Randall Street     Santa Ana   CA92705
```

There are fields for name, address, city, state, and ZIP code. Each field has a specific length, and data entries must be truncated to fit into that length. If entries don't use all the space allotted to them, storage space is wasted.

This organization has several consequences, some beneficial and some not. First the beneficial consequences:

✦ **Storage requirements are minimized.** Because the data files contain nothing but data, they take up a minimum amount of space on hard disks or other storage media. The code that must be added to any one program that contains the metadata is small compared to the overhead involved with adding a database management system (DBMS) to the data side of the system.

✦ **Operations on the data can be fast.** Because the program interacts directly with the data, with no DBMS in the middle, well-designed applications can run as fast as the hardware permits.

Wow! What could be better? A data organization that minimizes storage requirements and at the same time maximizes speed of operation seems like the best of all possible worlds. But wait a minute . . .

Flat file systems came into use in the 1940s. We have known about them for a long time, and yet today they have been almost entirely replaced by database systems. What's up with that? Perhaps it is the not-so-beneficial consequences:

✦ **Updating the data's structure can be a huge task.** It is common for an organization's data to be operated on by multiple application programs, with multiple purposes. If the metadata about the structure of data is in the program rather than attached to the data itself, *all* the programs that access that data must be modified whenever the data structure is changed. Not only does this cause a lot of redundant work (because the same changes must be made in all the programs), but it is an invitation to problems. All the programs must be modified in exactly the same way. If one is inadvertently forgotten, it will fail the next time it is run. Even if all the programs *are* modified, any that aren't modified exactly as they should be will fail, or even worse, corrupt the data without giving any indication that something is wrong.

✦ **Flat file systems provide no protection of the data.** Anyone who can access a data file can read it, change it, or delete it. A database management system restricts access to authorized users.

✦ **Portability becomes an issue.** If the specifics of retrieving a particular piece of data from a particular disk drive is coded into each program, what happens when your hardware becomes obsolete and you must migrate to a new system? All your applications will have to be changed to reflect the new way of accessing the data. This task is so onerous that many organizations have chosen to limp by on old, poorly performing systems rather than enduring the pain of transitioning to a system that would meet their needs much more effectively. Organizations with legacy systems consisting of millions of lines of code are pretty much trapped.

In the early days of electronic computers, storage was relatively expensive, so system designers were highly motivated to accomplish their tasks using as little storage space as possible. Also, in those early days, computers were much slower than they are today, so doing things the fastest possible way also had a high priority. Both of these considerations made flat file systems the architecture of choice, despite the problems inherent in updating the structure of a system's data.

The situation today is radically different. The cost of storage has plummeted and continues to drop on an exponential curve. The speed at which computations are performed has increased exponentially also. As a result, minimizing storage requirements and maximizing the speed with which an operation can be performed are no longer the primary driving forces that they once were. Because systems have continually become bigger and more complex, the problem of maintaining them has likewise grown. For all these reasons, flat file systems have lost their attractiveness, and databases have replaced them in practically all application areas.

The simple program/complex data organization

The major selling point of database systems is that the metadata resides on the data end of the system rather than in the program. The program doesn't have to know anything about the details of how the data is stored. It makes logical requests for data, and the DBMS translates those logical requests into commands that go out to the physical storage hardware to perform whatever operation has been requested. Here are the advantages of this organization:

✦ Because application programs only need to know what data they want to operate on, and not where that data is located, they are unaffected when the physical details of where data is stored changes.

✦ Portability across platforms, even when they are highly dissimilar, is easy as long as the DBMS used by the first platform is also available on the second. Generally, the programs need not be changed at all.

What about the disadvantages? They include the following:

✦ Placing a database management system in between the application program and the data slows down operations on that data significantly.

✦ Databases take up more space on disk storage than the same amount of data would take up in a flat file system. This is due to the fact that metadata is stored along with the data. The metadata contains information about how the data is stored, so that the application programs don't have to include it.

Which type of organization is better?

I bet you think you already know how I am going to answer this question. You are probably right, but the answer is not quite so simple. There is no one correct answer that applies to all situations. In the early days of electronic computing, flat file systems were the only viable option. To perform any reasonable computation in a timely and economical manner, you had to use whatever approach was the fastest and required the least amount of storage space. As more and more application software was developed for these systems, the organizations that owned them became locked in tighter and tighter to what they had. To change to a more modern database system requires rewriting all their applications from scratch and reorganizing all their data, a monumental task. As a result, we still have legacy flat file systems that continue to exist because switching to more modern technology isn't feasible, both economically and in terms of the time it would take to make the transition.

Databases, Queries, and Database Applications

What are the chances that a person could actually find a needle in a haystack? Not very good. Finding the proverbial needle is so hard because the haystack is a random pile of hay with individual pieces of hay going in every direction, and the needle is located at some random place among all that hay.

A flat file system is not really very much like a haystack, but it does lack structure, and in order to find a particular record in such a file, you must use tools that lie outside of the file itself. This is like applying a powerful magnet to the haystack to find the needle.

The first database system

The first true database system was developed by IBM in the 1960s in support of NASA's Apollo moon landing program. The number of components in the Saturn V launch vehicle, the Apollo Command and Service Module, and the Lunar Lander far exceeded anything that had been build up to that time. Every component had to be tested more exhaustively than anything had ever been tested before because they were all going to have to withstand the rigors of an environment that was more hostile and more unforgiving than any environment that humans had ever attempted to work in. Flat file systems were out of the question. IBM's solution, which it later transformed into a commercial database product named IMS, kept track of each individual component, as well its complete history.

When the ill-fated Apollo 13's main oxygen tank ruptured on the way to the Moon, engineers worked frantically to come up with a plan to save the lives of the three astronauts onboard. The engineers succeeded and transmitted a plan to the astronauts that worked. After the crew had returned safely to Earth, querying IMS about the oxygen tank that failed showed that somewhere between its manufacture and its installation in Apollo 13, it had been dropped on the floor. It was retested for its ability to withstand the pressure it would have to contain during the mission, and then replaced in stock after passing the test. In this case, the test did not detect the hidden damage to the tank, but at least the history stored in IMS showed that passing a pressure test is not enough to assure that a dropped tank is undamaged. No dropped tanks were ever used on subsequent Apollo missions.

Making data useful

For a collection of data to be useful, you must be able to easily and quickly retrieve the particular data you want, without having to wade through all the rest of the data. One way to make this happen is to store the data in a logical structure. Flat files don't have much structure, but databases do. Historically, the hierarchical database model and the network database model were developed before the relational model. Each one organizes data in a different way, but all three produce a highly structured result. As a result, starting in the 1970s, any new development projects were most likely to be done using one of three database models: either the hierarchical model, the network model, or the relational model. I explore database models further in the "Competing Database Models" section, later in this chapter.

Retrieving the data you want — and only the data you want

Of all the operations that people perform on a collection of data, the retrieval of specific elements out of the collection is the most important. This is because retrievals are performed more often than any other operation. Data entry is done only once. Changes to existing data are made infrequently, and data is deleted only once. Retrievals, on the other hand, are performed frequently, and the same data elements may be retrieved many times. Thus, if you could optimize only one operation performed on a collection of data, that one operation should be data retrieval. As a result, modern database management systems put a great deal of effort into making retrievals fast. Retrievals are performed by queries. A modern database management system analyzes a query that is presented to it and decides how best to perform it. Generally there are multiple ways of performing a query, some much faster than others. A good DBMS consistently chooses a near-optimal execution plan. Of course, it helps if the query is formulated in an optimal manner to begin with. I discuss this subject in depth in Book VII, which covers database tuning.

Competing Database Models

IBM's precursor to IMS, which first went "live" at an Apollo contractor's site on August 14, 1968, was the first functioning database system. Amazingly, IMS (Information Management System) is still in use today, almost 40 years later, because IBM has continually upgraded it in support of its customers.

If you are in the market for a database management system, you may want to consider buying it from a vendor that will be around and that is committed to supporting it, for as long as you will want to use it. IBM has shown itself to be such a vendor, and of course, there are others as well.

IMS is an example of a hierarchical database product. About a year after IMS was first run, the network database model was described by an industry committee. About a year after that, Dr. E. F. Codd, also of IBM, proposed the relational model. Within a short span of years, the three models that were to dominate the database market for decades were spawned. Quite a few years went by before the object-oriented database model appeared to address some of the deficiencies of the relational model. The object-relational model is a merger of the relational and object models that is designed to capture the strengths of both, while leaving behind their major weaknesses.

The hierarchical database model

The hierarchical database model organizes data into a hierarchy of levels, where each level contains a single category of data, and parent/child relationships are established between levels. Each parent item can have multiple children, but each child item can have one and only one parent. Thus all relationships in a hierarchical database are either one-to-one or one-to-many. Many-to-many relationships are not allowed.

A bill of materials application is well suited for a hierarchical database. An entire machine is composed of assemblies, which are each composed of sub-assemblies, and so on, down to individual components. As an example of such an application, consider the mighty Saturn V Moon rocket that sent American astronauts to the Moon in the late 1960s and early 1970s. Figure 1-1 shows a hierarchical diagram of major components of the Saturn V.

Three relationships can occur between objects in a database:

✦ **One-to-one relationship:** One object of the first type is related to one and only one object of the second type. In Figure 1-1, there are several examples of one-to-one relationships. One is the relationship between the S-2 stage LOX tank and the aft LOX bulkhead. Each LOX tank has one and only one aft LOX bulkhead, and each aft LOX bulkhead belongs to one and only one LOX tank.

✦ **One-to-many relationship:** One object of the first type is related to multiple objects of the second type. In the Saturn V's S-1C stage, the thrust structure contains five F-1 engines, but each engine belongs to one and only one thrust structure.

✦ **Many-to-many relationship:** Multiple objects of the first type are related to multiple objects of the second type. This kind of relationship is not handled cleanly by a hierarchical database. Attempts to do so tend to be kludgy. One example might be two-inch hex-head bolts. These bolts are not considered to be uniquely identifiable, and any one such bolt is interchangeable with any other. An assembly might use multiple bolts, and a bolt could be used in any of several different assemblies.

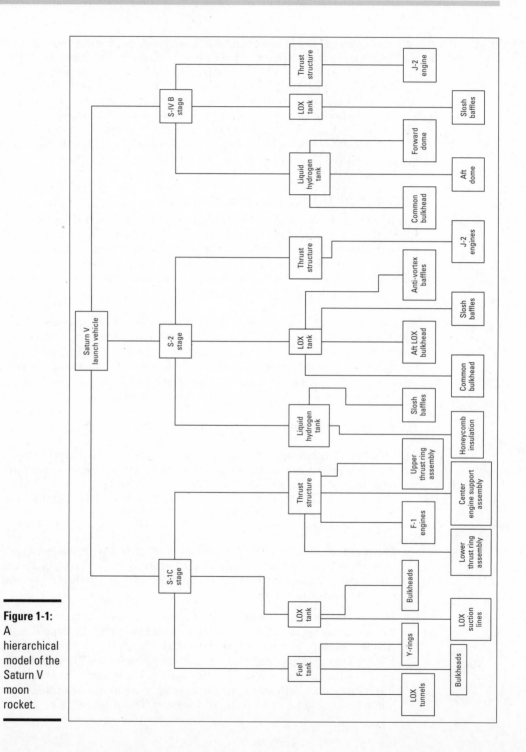

Figure 1-1:
A hierarchical model of the Saturn V moon rocket.

A great strength of the hierarchical model is its high performance. Because relationships between entities are simple and direct, retrievals from a hierarchical database that are set up to take advantage of the way the data is structured can be very fast. However, retrievals that don't take advantage of the way the data is structured are slow and sometimes can't be made at all. It's difficult to change the structure of a hierarchical database to address new requirements. This structural rigidity is the greatest weakness of the hierarchical model. Another problem with the hierarchical model is the fact that, structurally, it requires a lot of redundancy.

Not many organizations today are designing rockets capable of launching payloads to the Moon. The hierarchical model can also be applied to more common tasks, such as tracking sales transactions for a retail business. As an example, I use some sales transaction data from Gentoo Joyce's fictitious online store of penguin collectibles.

As shown in Figure 1-2, customers who have made multiple purchases show up in the database multiple times. This is a waste of storage space because one copy of the data about a customer is sufficient. Perhaps even more damaging than the wasted space that results from redundant data is the possibility of data corruption. Whenever multiple copies of the same data exist in a database, there is the potential for modification anomalies. A *modification anomaly* is an inconsistency in the data after a modification is made. Suppose you want to delete a customer who is no longer buying from you. If multiple copies of that customer's data exist, you must find and delete all of them to maintain data integrity. Suppose you want to update a customer's address information. If multiple copies of the customer's data exist, you must find and modify all of them in exactly the same way to maintain data integrity. This can be a time-consuming and error-prone operation.

The network database model

The network model, which appeared in 1969, is almost the exact opposite of the hierarchical model. Wanting to avoid the redundancy of the hierarchical model without sacrificing too much in the way of performance, the designers of the network model opted for an architecture that does not duplicate items, but instead increases the number of relationships associated with some items. Figure 1-3 shows this architecture for the same data that was shown in Figure 1-2.

The network model eliminates redundancy, but at the expense of more complicated relationships. This model can be better than the hierarchical model for some kinds of data storage tasks, but worse for others. Neither one is consistently superior to the other.

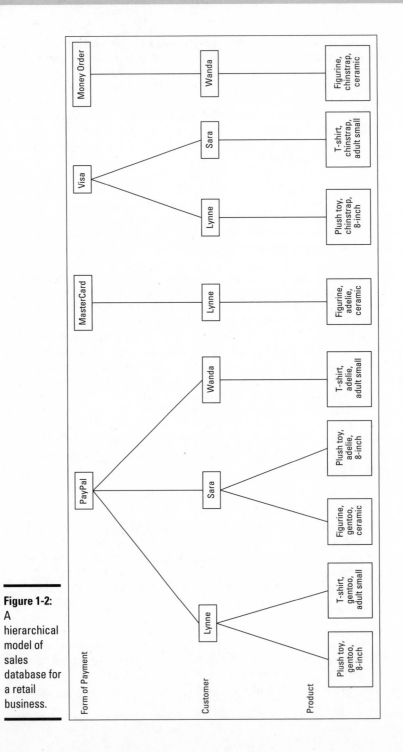

Figure 1-2:
A hierarchical model of sales database for a retail business.

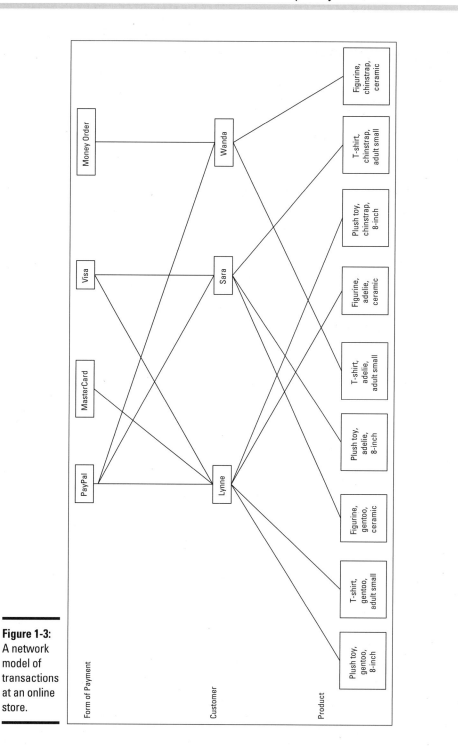

Figure 1-3:
A network model of transactions at an online store.

The relational database model

In 1970, Edgar F. (Ted) Codd of IBM published a paper introducing the relational database model. Initially, it was given little consideration by database experts. It clearly had an advantage over the hierarchical model in that data redundancy was minimal; it had an advantage over the network model with its relatively simple relationships. However, it had what was perceived to be a fatal flaw. Due to the complexity of the relational database engine that it required, any implementation would be much slower than a comparable implementation of either the hierarchical or the network model. As a result, it was almost ten years before the first implementation of the relational database idea hit the market. IBM delivered a relational DBMS integrated into the operating system of the System 38 in 1978, and Relational Software, Inc. delivered the first version of Oracle in 1979.

What makes a database relational?

The original definition of a relational database specified that it must consist of two-dimensional tables of rows and columns, where the cell at the intersection of every row and column contains an atomic value (where *atomic* means not divisible into subvalues). This definition is commonly stated by saying that a relational database table may not contain any *repeating groups*. The definition also specified that each row in a table be uniquely identifiable. Another way of saying this is that every table in a relational database must have a primary key. A *primary key* uniquely identifies a row in a database table. Figure 1-4 shows the structure of the online store database, built according to the relational model.

Codd's Rules

As the relational model gained in popularity, vendors of database products that were not really relational started to advertise their products as relational database management systems. To fight the dilution of his model, Codd formulated 12 rules that served as criteria for determining whether a database product was relational. Codd's idea was that a database must satisfy all 12 criteria in order to be considered relational.

Here are Codd's 12 rules:

1. **The information rule:** Data can be represented only one way, as values in column positions within rows of a table.

2. **The guaranteed access rule:** Every value in a database must be accessible by specifying a table name, a column name, and a row. The row is specified by the value of the primary key.

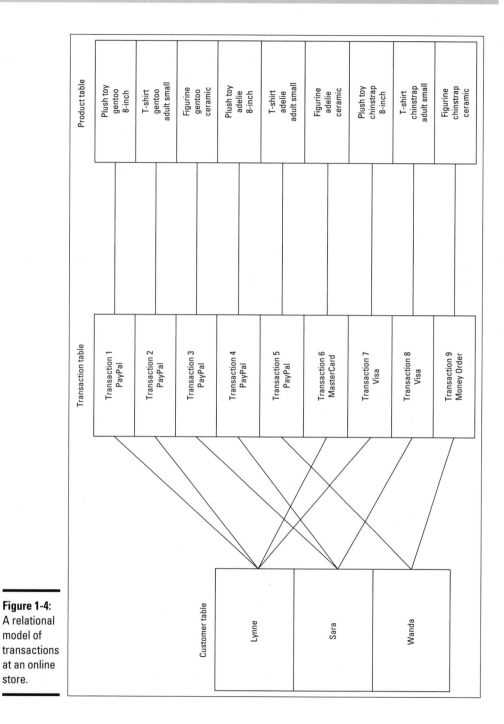

Figure 1-4:
A relational
model of
transactions
at an online
store.

3. **Systematic treatment of null values:** Missing data is distinct from specific values, such as zero or an empty string.

4. **Relational online catalog:** Authorized users must be able to access the database's structure (its catalog) using the same query language they use to access the database's data.

5. **The comprehensive data sublanguage rule:** The system must support at least one relational language that can be used both interactively and within application programs, that supports data definition, data manipulation, and data control functions. Today, that one language is SQL.

6. **The view updating rule:** All views that are theoretically updatable must be updatable by the system.

7. **The system must support set-at-a-time insert, update, and delete operations.** This means that the system must be able to perform insertions, updates, and deletions of multiple rows in a single operation.

8. **Physical data independence:** Changes to the way data is stored must not affect the application.

9. **Logical data independence:** Changes to the tables must not affect the application. For example, adding new columns to a table should not "break" an application that accesses the original rows.

10. **Integrity independence:** Integrity constraints must be specified independently from the application programs and stored in the catalog.

11. **Distribution independence:** Distribution of portions of the database to various locations should not change the way applications function.

12. **The nonsubversion rule:** If the system provides a record-at-a-time interface, it should not be possible to use it to subvert the relational security or integrity constraints.

Over and above the original 12 rules, in 1990, Codd added one more rule:

> **Rule Zero:** For any system that is advertised as, or claimed to be, a relational database management system, that system must be able to manage databases entirely through its relational capabilities, no matter what additional capabilities the system may support.

This was in response to the vendors of various database products who claimed their product was a relational DBMS, when it fact it was not primarily relational.

Codd's rules are so stringent, that even today, there is not a DBMS on the market that completely complies with all of them. However, they have provided a good goal toward which database vendors strive.

Inherent flexibility

You might wonder why it is that relational databases have conquered the planet and relegated hierarchical and network databases to niches consisting mainly of legacy customers who have been using them for more than 20 years. It's even more surprising in light of the fact that when the relational model was first introduced, most of the experts in the field considered it to be utterly uncompetitive with either the hierarchical or the network model.

One advantage of the relational model is its flexibility. It is much easier to restructure a relational database than it is to restructure either a hierarchical or network database. This is a tremendous advantage in dynamic business environments where requirements are constantly changing.

The reason database practitioners originally "dissed" the relational model is because the extra overhead of the relational database engine was sure to make any product based on that model so much slower than either hierarchical or network databases, as to be non-competitive. I say more about this later in this chapter.

The object-oriented database

Object-oriented database management systems (OODBMS) first appeared in 1980. They were developed primarily to handle non-text, non-numeric data such as graphical objects. Relational DBMS typically do not do a good job with such so-called complex data types. OODBMS use the same data model as object-oriented programming languages such as Java, C++, and C#, and work well with such languages. Although object-oriented databases outperform relational databases for selected applications, they do not do as well in most mainstream applications, and have not made much of a dent in the hegemony of the relational products.

The object-relational database

An object-relational database is a relational database that allows users to create and use new data types that are not part of the standard set of data types provided by SQL. User-defined types were added to the SQL:1999 specification and are available in current implementations of IBM's DB2, Oracle, and Microsoft SQL Server. Current relational database management systems are actually therefore object-relational database management systems rather than pure relational database management systems.

Why Did the Relational Model Win?

Throughout the 1970s and into the 1980s, hierarchical and network were the database technologies of choice for large organizations. Oracle, the first standalone relational database system to reach the market, did not appear until 1979, and initially met with limited success.

For the following reasons, as well as just plain old inertia, relational databases caught on slowly at first:

+ **The earliest implementations of relational database management systems were slow performers.** This was due to the fact that they required more computations to be made than other database systems did to perform the same operation.

+ **Most business managers were reluctant to try something new when they were already familiar with one or the other of the older technologies.**

+ **Data and applications that already existed for an existing database system would be very difficult to translate to work with a relational DBMS.** For most organizations with an existing hierarchical or network database system, it would be too costly to make a conversion.

+ **Employees would have to learn an entirely new way of dealing with data.** This would be very costly, too.

However, things gradually started to change.

Although databases structured according to the hierarchical and the network models had excellent performance, they were difficult to maintain. Structural changes to a database took a high level of expertise and a lot of time. In many organizations, backlogs of change requests grew from months to years. Department managers started putting their work on personal computers rather than going to the corporate IT department to ask for a change to a database. IT managers, fearing that their power in the organization was eroding, took the drastic step of considering relational technology.

Meanwhile, Moore's Law was inexorably changing the performance situation. In 1965, Gordon Moore of Intel noted that about every 18 months the price of semiconductor memory would be cut in half. He predicted that this exponential trend would continue. A corollary of the law was that the performance of integrated circuit processors would double every 18 months. Both of these laws have held true for more than 40 years, and the end is not yet in sight. In addition, the capacities and performance of hard disk storage devices have also improved at an exponential rate, paralleling the improvement in semiconductor chips.

The performance improvements in processors, memories, and hard disks combined to dramatically improve the performance of relational database systems, making them more competitive with hierarchical and network systems. When this improved performance was added to the relational architecture's inherent advantage in structural flexibility, relational database systems started to become much more attractive, even to large organizations with major investments in legacy systems. In many of these companies, although existing applications remained on their current platforms, new applications and the databases that held their data were developed using the new relational technology.

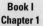

Book I
Chapter 1

Relational Database
Basics

Chapter 2: Modeling a System

In This Chapter

✔ Capturing the users' data model

✔ Translating the users' data model to a relational model

✔ Drawing entity-relationship diagrams

✔ The relational database hierarchy

*I*n order to have any hope of developing a database system that delivers the results, performance, and reliability that the users need, you must understand, in a highly detailed way, what those needs are. To understand the users' needs, you must create a model of what they have in mind. After perfecting the model through much dialog with the user, you need to translate the model into something that can be implemented with a relational database. This chapter takes you through the steps of taking what might be a vague and fuzzy idea in the minds of the users, and transforming it into something that can be converted directly into a robust and high-performance database.

Capturing the Users' Data Model

The whole purpose of a database is to hold useful data and to enable one or more people to selectively retrieve and use the data they want. Generally, before a database project is begun, interested parties have some idea of what data they want to store, and what subsets of the data they are likely to want to retrieve. More often than not, peoples' ideas of what should be included in the database and what they want to get out of it are not terribly precise. Vague and nebulous as it may be, the concepts each of these people have in their mind is their own individual user's data model. To have any hope of building a database system that meets the needs of the users, you must understand this data model. Beyond understanding it, you must help to clarify it so that it can become the basis for a database system that is useful.

Identifying and interviewing stakeholders

The first step in discovering the users' data model is to find out who the users are. This goes beyond the people who actually sit in front of a PC and run your database application. A number of other people usually have a stake in the development effort. Perhaps several people will be interacting directly with the system. They, of course, are very interested parties. So are their supervisors, and even higher management. If the database will deal with customer or vendor information, the customers and vendors are probably stakeholders too. The IT department, which is responsible for keeping systems up and running, is also a major stakeholder. There may be others, such as owners or major stockholders in the company. All of these people will have an image in their mind of what the system ought to be. You need to find these people, interview them, and find out how they envision the system, how they expect it to be maintained, and what they want it to produce.

Reconciling conflicting requirements

Just as the set of stakeholders will be diverse, so will their ideas of what the system should be and do. If not reconciled, this is a recipe for disaster. You run the risk of developing a system that is not satisfactory to anybody.

It is your responsibility as the database developer to develop a consensus. You are the only independent, outside party who does not have a personal stake in what the system is and does. Generally the stated requirements of the stakeholders will fall into three categories. They are

✦ A feature that is absolutely mandatory: The system would be of limited value without it.

✦ A feature that is important and that adds greatly to the value of the system.

✦ A feature that would be nice to have, but is not actually needed.

Database developers are like army doctors

Battleground field hospitals make use of a technique called *triage* to allocate their limited resources in the most beneficial way. When people are brought in for treatment, they are examined to determine the extent of their injuries. After the examination, they are placed into one of three categories:

✔ The person has critical wounds and must receive treatment immediately, or he will die.

✔ The person has serious wounds, but they are not immediately life-threatening. The doctors can afford to let this person wait while patients with more serious injuries are treated.

✔ The person is so badly wounded that no treatment available will save her.

Patients in the first category are treated immediately. Patients in the second category are treated as soon as circumstances permit. Patients in the third category are made as comfortable as possible, but treated only for pain.

Once you have appropriately categorized the want lists of the stakeholders, you are in a position to determine what is really required, and what is possible within the allotted budget and development time. Now comes the fun part. You must convince all the stakeholders that their cherished features that fall into the third category, must be deleted or changed if they conflict with someone else's first-category or second-category feature. Of course, politics also intrudes here. Some stakeholders have more "clout" than others. You must be sensitive to this. Sometimes the politically acceptable solution is not exactly the same as the technically optimal solution.

Obtaining stakeholder buy-in

One way or another, you will have to get all the stakeholders to agree on one set of features that will be included in the system you are planning to build. This is critical. If the system does not adequately meet the needs of all those for whom it is being built, it is not a success. You must get the agreement of everyone that the system you propose meets their needs. Get it in writing. Enumerate everything that will be provided in a formal Statement of Requirements, and then have every stakeholder sign off on it. This will potentially save you from much grief later on.

Translating the Users' Data Model to a Relational Model

After you have a coherent users' data model in a clear, concise, concrete form, the real work begins. Somehow, you must transform that model into a relational model that serves as the basis for a database. In most cases, a users' data model is not in a form that can be directly translated into a relational model. A helpful technique is to first translate it into one of several formal modeling systems that make the various entities in the users model and the relationships between them clear. Probably the most popular of those formal modeling techniques is the Entity-Relationship (E-R) model.

Entity-Relationship modeling techniques

In 1976, six years after Dr. Codd published the relational model, Peter Chen published a paper in the *ACM Transactions on Database Systems,* introducing the Entity-Relationship (E-R) model. The E-R model represented a conceptual breakthrough because it provided a means to translate a users' data model into a relational model. In 1976, the relational model was still nothing more than a theoretical construct. It would be three more years before the first standalone relational database product (Oracle) appeared on the market. The E-R model was an important factor in turning theory into practice.

One of the strengths of the E-R model is its generality. E-R models can be used to represent a wide variety of different systems. An E-R model can be used to represent a physical system as big and complex as a fleet of cruise ships, or as small as the livestock maintained by a gentleman farmer on his two acres of land.

Any entity-relationship model, big or small, consists of four major components: entities, attributes, identifiers, and relationships. I examine each one of these concepts in turn.

Entities

Dictionaries will tell you that an entity is something that has a distinct, separate existence. It could be a material entity, such as the Great Pyramid of Giza, or an abstract entity, such as a tetrahedron. Just about any distinct, separate thing that you can think of qualifies as being an entity. When used in a database context, an entity is something that the user can identify and that she wants to keep track of.

A group of entities with common characteristics is called an *entity class.* Any one example of an entity class is an *entity instance.* A common example of an entity class for most organizations would be the EMPLOYEE entity class. An *instance* of that entity class would be a particular employee, such as Duke Kahanamoku.

Attributes

Entities are things that users can identify and want to keep track of. However, the users probably don't want to use up valuable storage space keeping track of every conceivable aspect of an entity. Some aspects are of more interest than others. For example, in the EMPLOYEE model, you probably want to keep track of such things as first name, last name, and job title. You probably do not want to keep track of the employee's favorite surfboard manufacturer or favorite musical group. Figure 2-1 shows an example of an entity class, including typical attributes. Figure 2-2 shows an example of an instance of the EMPLOYEE entity class.

Figure 2-1: EMPLOYEE, an example of an entity class.

```
EMPLOYEE
    EmpID
    FirstName
    LastName
    JobTitle
    Exempt/Non-exempt
    HireDate
    Extension
    E-mail
    Department
```

Figure 2-2:
Duke
Kahanamoku,
an example
of an
instance
of the
EMPLOYEE
entity class.

EMPLOYEE
172850
Duke
Kahanamoku
Cultural ambassador
E
01/01/2002
10
duck@surfboardsrus.com
Public Relations

Identifiers

In order to do anything meaningful with data, you must be able to tell one piece of data from another. That means each piece of data must have an identifying characteristic that is unique. In the context of a relational database, a "piece of data" is a row in a two-dimensional table. For example, in the EMPLOYEE table, the row describing Duke Kahanamoku would be the piece of data, and the EmpID attribute would be the identifier. No other employee will have the same EmpID as the one that Duke has.

In the above example, EmpID is not just an identifier — it is a unique identifier. There is one and only one EmpID that corresponds to Duke Kahanamoku. Non-unique identifiers are also possible. For example, a FirstName of Duke does not uniquely identify Duke Kahanamoku. There might be another employee named Duke Snyder. Having an attribute such as EmpID is a good way to guarantee that you are getting the employee you want when you are searching for Duke Kahanamoku, the former Olympic swimming champion. Another way, however, is to use a composite identifier. A *composite identifier* is a combination of several attributes that is sufficient to uniquely identify a record. The combination of FirstName and LastName would be sufficient to distinguish Duke Kahanamoku from Duke Snyder, but would not be enough to distinguish the Olympic champion from his father, who had the same name. In such a case, a composite identifier consisting of FirstName, LastName, and BirthDate would suffice.

Relationships

Any non-trivial database contains more than one table. When you have more than one table, the question arises as to how the tables relate to each other. A company might have an EMPLOYEE table, a CUSTOMER table, and a PRODUCT table. These become related when an employee sells a product to a customer. Such a sales transaction can be recorded in a TRANSACTION table. Thus the EMPLOYEE, CUSTOMER, and PRODUCT tables are related to each other via the TRANSACTION table. Relationships such as these are key to the way relational databases operate. Relationships can differ in the number of entities that they relate.

Degree-two relationships

Degree-two relationships are ones that relate one entity directly to one other entity. EMPLOYEE is related to TRANSACTION by a degree-two relationship, also called a *binary* relationship. CUSTOMER is also related to TRANSACTION by a binary relationship, as is PRODUCT. Figure 2-3 shows a diagram of an example degree-two relationship.

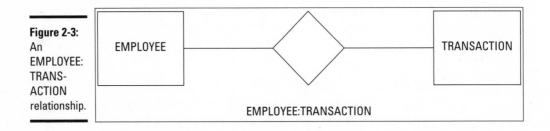

Figure 2-3: An EMPLOYEE: TRANSACTION relationship.

Degree-two relationships are the simplest possible, and, happily, just about any system that you are likely to want to model consists of entities connected by degree-two relationships, although more complex relationships are possible.

There are three kinds of binary relationships:

✦ A one-to-one (1:1) relationship relates one instance of one entity class to one instance of a second entity class.

✦ A one-to-many (1:N) relationship relates one instance of one entity class to multiple instances of a second entity class.

✦ A many-to-many (N:M) relationship relates multiple instances of one entity class to multiple instances of a second entity class.

Figure 2-4 is a diagram of an example of a one-to-one relationship between a person and that person's driver's license. A person can have one and only one driver's license, and a driver's license can apply to one and only one person.

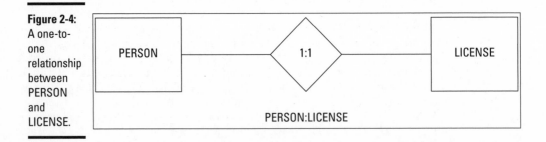

Figure 2-4: A one-to-one relationship between PERSON and LICENSE.

Figure 2-5 is a diagram of an example of a one-to-many relationship between a person and that person's traffic violation tickets. A person can be served with multiple tickets, but a ticket can apply to one and only one person.

Figure 2-5:
A one-to-many relationship between PERSON and TICKET.

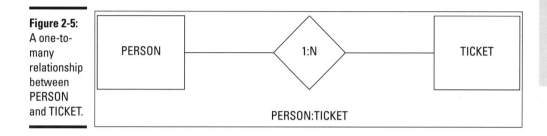

Figure 2-6:
A many-to-many relationship between PERSON and ROUTE.

Figure 2-6 is a diagram of an example of a many-to-many relationship between a person and the route she takes on her drive to work. A person can take one of several routes from home to work, and each one of those routes can be taken by multiple people.

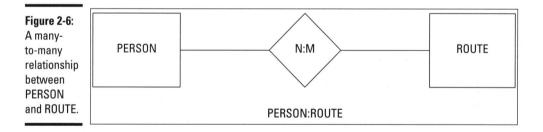

Complex relationships

Degree-three relationships are possible, but rarely occur in practice. Relationships of degree higher than three probably mean that you need to redesign your system to use simpler relationships. An example of a degree-three relationship would be the relationship between a musical composer, a lyricist, and a song. Figure 2-7 shows a diagram of this relationship.

Although it is possible to build a system with such relationships, it is probably better in most cases to restructure the system in terms of binary relationships.

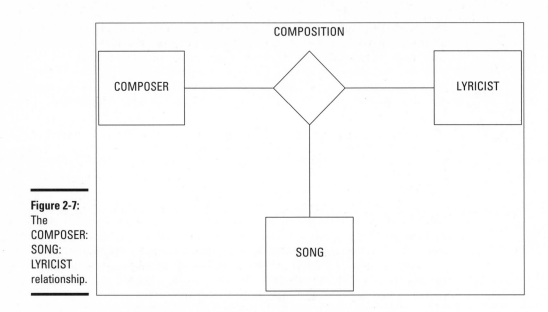

Figure 2-7:
The
COMPOSER:
SONG:
LYRICIST
relationship.

Drawing Entity-Relationship diagrams

I find it easier to understand relationships between things if I see a diagram instead of merely looking at sentences describing the relationships. Apparently a lot of other people feel the same way because systems represented by the E-R model are universally depicted in the form of diagrams. A few simple examples of E-R diagrams appear in the previous section. In this section, I introduce some concepts that add detail to the diagrams. One of those concepts is *cardinality*. In mathematics, cardinality is the number of elements in a set. In the context of relational databases, a relationship between two tables has two cardinalities of interest, the cardinality associated with the first table and the cardinality associated with the second table. We look at these cardinalities two primary ways: maximum cardinality and minimum cardinality.

Maximum cardinality

The E-R diagram's representation of maximum cardinality is shown in Figures 2-4, 2-5, and 2-6. The diamond between the two entities in the rela-tionship holds the two cardinality values. Figure 2-4 shows a one-to-one relationship. In the example, a person is related to that person's driver's license. One driver can have at most one license, and one license can belong at most to one driver. The maximum cardinality on both sides of the relationship is one.

Figure 2-5 illustrates a one-to-many relationship. When relating a person to the tickets he has accumulated, each ticket belongs to one and only one driver, but a driver may have more than one ticket. The number of tickets above one is indeterminate, so it is represented by the variable N.

Figure 2-6 shows a many-to-many relationship. The maximum cardinality on the PERSON side is represented by the variable N, and the maximum cardinality on the ROUTE side is represented by the variable M because although both the number of drivers and the number of routes are more than one, they are not necessarily the same. You might have seventeen different drivers that take any one of ten routes, for example.

Minimum cardinality

Just as the maximum cardinality of one side of a relationship shows the largest number of entities that can be on that side of the relationship, the minimum cardinality shows the least number of entities that can be on that side of the relationship. In some cases, the least number of entities that can be on one side of a relationship can be zero. In other cases, the minimum cardinality could be one or more.

Refer to the relationship in Figure 2-4 between a person and that person's driver's license. The minimum cardinalities in the relationship depend heavily on subtle details of the users' data model. Take the case where a person has been a licensed driver, but due to excessive citations, his driver's license has been revoked. The person still exists, but the license does not. If the users' data model stipulates that the person is retained in the PERSON table, but the corresponding row is removed from the LICENSE table, the minimum cardinality on the PERSON side is one, and the minimum cardinality on the LICENSE side is zero. Figure 2-8 shows how minimum cardinality is represented in this example.

Figure 2-8:
E-R diagram showing minimum cardinality, where a person must exist, but his corresponding license need not exist.

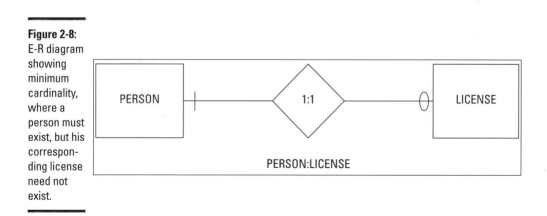

driver, but a driver may have more than one ticket. The number of tickets
PERSON:LICENSE

The slash mark on the PERSON side denotes a minimum cardinality of *mandatory,* meaning at least one instance must exist. The oval on the

LICENSE side denotes a minimum cardinality of *optional,* meaning at least one instance need not exist.

For this one-to-one relationship, a given person can correspond to at most one license, but may correspond to none. A given license *must* correspond to one person.

If only life were that simple . . . Remember that I said that minimum cardinality depends subtly on the users' data model? What if the users' data model were slightly different, based on another possible case? Suppose a person has a very good driving record and a valid driver's license in her home state of Washington. Next, suppose that she accepts a position as a wildlife researcher on a small island that has no roads and no cars. She is no longer a driver, but her license will remain valid until it expires in a few years. This is the reverse case of what is shown in Figure 2-8; a license exists, but the corresponding driver does not (at least as far as the state of Washington is concerned). Figure 2-9 shows this situation.

Figure 2-9:
E-R diagram
showing
minimum
cardinality,
where a
license must
exist, but its
correspond-
ing person
need not
exist.

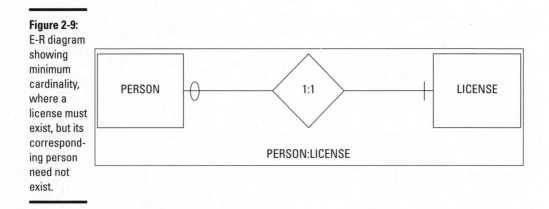

The lesson to take home from this example is that minimum cardinality is often difficult to determine. You will need to question the users very carefully and explore unusual cases such as those cited above before deciding how to model minimum cardinality.

If the minimum cardinality of one side of a relationship is mandatory, that means the cardinality of that side is at least one, but might be more. Suppose, for example, you were modeling the relationship between a basketball team and its players. A person cannot be a basketball player unless she is a member of a basketball team, so the minimum cardinality on the TEAM side is mandatory, and in fact is one. This assumes that the users' data model states that a player cannot be a member of more than one team. Similarly, it is not possible for a basketball team to exist unless it has at least five players. This means that the minimum cardinality on the PLAYER side is also mandatory, but in this case is five. Once again, depending on the users' data model, the rule might be that a team cannot exist unless it has at least five players. The minimum cardinality of the PLAYER side of the relationship is five.

Primarily you are interested in whether the minimum cardinality on a side of a relationship is either mandatory or optional and less interested in whether a mandatory minimum cardinality has a value of one or more than one. The difference between mandatory and optional is the difference between whether an entity exists or not. The difference between existence and non-existence is substantial. In contrast, the difference between one and five is just a matter of degree. Both cases refer to a mandatory minimum cardinality. For most applications, the difference between one mandatory value and another does not matter.

Advanced E-R model concepts

In the previous sections of this chapter, I talk about entities, relationships, and cardinality. I have pointed out that subtle differences in the way users model their system can modify the way minimum cardinality is modeled. These concepts are a good start, and are sufficient for many simple systems. However, more complex situations are bound to arise. These call for extensions of various sorts of the E-R model. So now I take a look at a few of these situations and at the extensions to the E-R model that have been made to deal with them.

Strong entities and weak entities

All entities are not created equal. Some are "stronger" than others. An entity that does not depend on any other entity for its existence is considered a strong entity. Consider the sample E-R model in Figure 2-10.

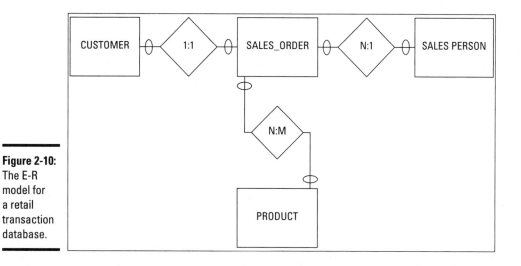

Figure 2-10:
The E-R model for a retail transaction database.

First consider maximum cardinality. A CUSTOMER can make multiple purchases, each one recorded on a SALES_ORDER. A SALESPERSON can make multiple sales, each one recorded on a SALES_ORDER. A SALES_ORDER can include multiple PRODUCTs, and a PRODUCT can appear on multiple SALES_ORDERs.

Minimum cardinality may be modeled a variety of ways, depending on how the users' data model views things. For example, a person might be considered a customer even before he buys anything because the store received his information in a promotional campaign. An employee might be considered to be a salesperson as soon as she is hired, even though she has not sold anything yet. A sales order might exist before it lists any products, and a product might exist on the shelves before any of them have been sold. According to this model, all the minimum cardinalities are optional. A different users' data model could mandate that some of these relationships be mandatory.

In a model such at the one described, where all the minimum cardinalities are optional, none of the entities depends on any of the other entities for its existence. A customer can exist without any associated sales orders. An employee can exist without any associated sales orders. A product can exist without any associated sales orders. A sales order can exist in the order pad without any associated customer, salesperson, or product. In this arrangement, all of these entities are classified as *strong entities.* They all have an independent existence.

Not all entities are strong, however. Consider the case shown in Figure 2-8. In this model, a driver's license cannot exist unless the corresponding driver exists. The license is *existence-dependent* upon the driver. Any entity that is existence-dependent on another entity is a *weak entity.* In an E-R diagram, a weak entity is represented with a box that has rounded corners. The diamond that shows the relationship between a weak entity and its corresponding strong entity also has rounded corners. Figure 2-11 shows this representation.

Figure 2-11:
A PERSON-
LICENSE
relationship,
showing
LICENSE as
a weak
entity.

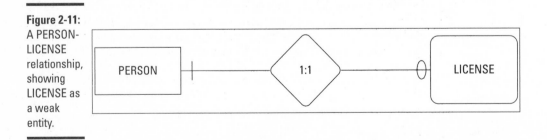

ID-dependent entities

A weak entity cannot exist without a relationship to a strong entity. A special case of a weak entity is one that depends on a strong entity not only for its existence, but also for its identity. One example of an ID-dependent entity is a seat on an airliner flight. Figure 2-12 illustrates the relationship.

Figure 2-12: The SEAT is ID-dependent on FLIGHT via the FLIGHT-SEAT relationship.

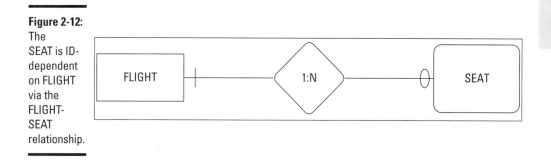

The seat number, for example 23-A, does not completely identify an airline seat. However, seat 23-A on Hawaiian Airlines flight 25 from PDX to HNL, on October 2, 2007 *does* completely identify a particular seat that a person can reserve. That additional information would all be attributes of the FLIGHT entity.

Supertype and subtype entities

In some databases, some entity classes might share attributes with other entity classes, rather than being as dissimilar as customers and products. One example might be an academic community. There are a number of people in such a community: students, faculty members, and non-academic staff. All of those people share some attributes, such as name, home address, home telephone number, and e-mail address. However, there are also attributes that are not shared. A student would also have attributes of grade point average, class standing, and advisor. A faculty member would have attributes of department, academic rank, and phone extension. A staff person would have attributes of job category, job title, and phone extension.

You can create an E-R model of this academic community by making STUDENT, FACULTY, and STAFF all *subtypes* of the *supertype* COMMUNITY. Figure 2-13 shows the relationships.

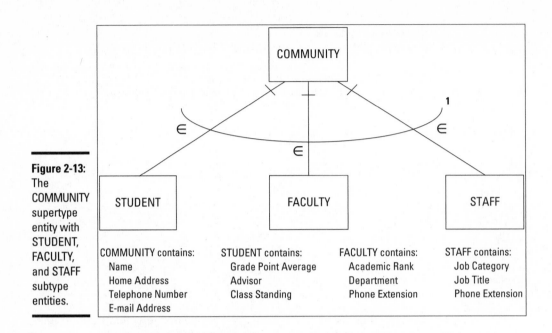

COMMUNITY contains:
  Name
  Home Address
  Telephone Number
  E-mail Address

STUDENT contains:
  Grade Point Average
  Advisor
  Class Standing

FACULTY contains:
  Academic Rank
  Department
  Phone Extension

STAFF contains:
  Job Category
  Job Title
  Phone Extension

Supertype/subtype relationships borrow the concept of *inheritance* from object-oriented programming. The attributes of the supertype entity are inherited by the subtype entities. Each subtype entity has additional attributes that it does not necessarily share with the other subtype entities. In the example, everyone in the community has a name, a home address, a telephone number, and an e-mail address. However, only students have a grade point average, an advisor, and a class standing. Similarly, only a faculty member can have an academic rank, and only a staff member can have a job title.

Some aspects of Figure 2-13 require a little additional explanation. The _ next to each relationship line signifies that the lower entity is a subtype of the higher entity, so STUDENT, FACULTY, and STAFF are subtypes of COMMU-NITY. The curved arc with a number 1 at the right edge represents the fact that every member of the COMMUNITY must be a member of one of the sub-type entities. In other words, you cannot be a member of the community unless you are either a student, or a faculty member, or a staff member. It is possible in some models that an element could be a member of a supertype without being a member of any of the subtypes. However, that is not the case for the community example.

Incorporating business rules

Business rules are formal statements about how an organization does business. Business rules typically differ from one organization to another. For example, one university may have a rule that a faculty member must hold a PhD degree. Another university could well have no such rule.

Sometimes you may not find important business rules written down anywhere. They may just be things that everyone in the organization understands. It is important to conduct an in-depth interview of everyone involved to fish out any business rules that people failed to mention when the job of creating the database was first described to you.

A simple example of an E-R model

In this section, as an example, I apply the principles of E-R models to a hypothetical Web-based business named Gentoo Joyce that sells apparel items with a penguin motif, such as T-shirts, scarves, and dresses. The business displays its products and takes credit card orders on its Web site. There is no "brick and mortar" store. Fulfillment is outsourced to a fulfillment house, which receives and warehouses product from vendors, and then, upon receiving orders from Gentoo Joyce, ships the orders to customers.

The Web site front end consists of pages that include descriptions and pictures of the products, a shopping cart, and a form for capturing customer and payment information. The Web site back end holds a database that stores customer, transaction, inventory, and order shipment status information. Figure 2-14 shows an E-R diagram of the Gentoo Joyce system. It is an example typical of a very small "boutique" business.

Gentoo Joyce buys goods and services from three kinds of vendors: product suppliers, Web hosting services, and fulfillment houses. In the model, VENDOR is a supertype of SUPPLIER, HOST, and FULFILLMENT_HOUSE. Some attributes are shared among all the vendors; these are assigned to the VENDOR entity. Other attributes are not shared and are instead attributes of the subtype entities.

A many-to-many relationship exists between SUPPLIER and PRODUCT because a supplier may provide more than one product, and a given product may be supplied by more than one supplier. Similarly, any given product will (hopefully) appear on multiple orders, and an order may include multiple products. Such many-to-many relationships can be problematic. I discuss how to handle such problems in Book II.

The other relationships in the model are one-to-many. A customer can place many orders, but each order comes from one and only one customer. A fulfillment house can stock multiple products, but each product is stocked by one and only one fulfillment house.

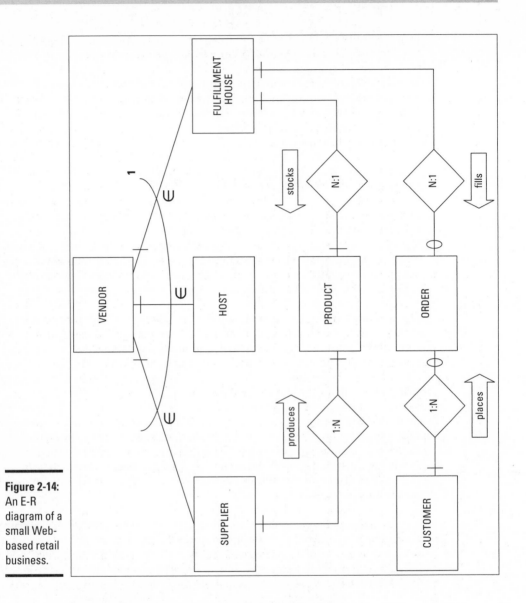

Figure 2-14:
An E-R
diagram of a
small Web-
based retail
business.

A slightly more complex example

The Gentoo Joyce system that I describe in the preceding section is an easy-to-understand example, similar to what you often find in database textbooks. Most real-world systems are much more complex. I don't try to show a genuine real-world system here, but to move at least one step in that direction, I'll model the hypothetical Clear Creek Medical Clinic (CCMC). As I discuss in

Book II, one of the first things to do when assigned the project of creating a database for a client is to interview everyone who has a stake in the system, including management, users, and anyone else who has a say in how things are run. Listen carefully to these people and discern how these people model in their minds the system they envision. Find out what information they need to capture and what they intend to do with it.

CCMC employs doctors, nurses, medical technologists, medical assistants, and office workers. The company provides medical, dental, and vision benefits to employees and their dependents. The doctors, nurses, and medical technologists must all be licensed by a recognized licensing authority. Medical assistants may be certified, but need not be. Neither licensure nor certification is required of office workers.

Typically, a patient will see a doctor, who will examine the patient, and then order one or more tests. A medical assistant or nurse may take samples of the patient's blood, urine, or both, and take the samples to the laboratory. In the lab, a medical technologist performs the tests that the doctor has ordered. The results of the tests are sent to the doctor who ordered them, as well as to perhaps one or more consulting physicians. Based on the test results, the primary doctor, with input from the consulting physicians, makes a diagnosis of the patient's condition and prescribes a treatment. A nurse then administers the prescribed treatment.

Based on the descriptions of the envisioned system, as described by the interested parties (called stakeholders), you can come up with a proposed list of entities. A good first shot at this is to list all the nouns that were used by the people you interviewed. Many of these will turn out to be entities in your model, although you may end up classifying some of those nouns as attributes of entities. For this example, say you generated the following list:

Employee

Office worker

Doctor (physician)

Nurse

Medical technologist

Medical assistant

Benefits

Dependents

Patients

Doctor's license

Nurse's license

Medical technologist's license

Medical assistant's certificate

Examination

Test order

Test

Test result

Consultation

Diagnosis

Prescription

Treatment

In the course of your interviews of the stakeholders, you found that one of the categories of things to track is employees, but there are several different employee classifications. You also found that there are benefits and that benefits apply to dependents. From this, you conclude that EMPLOYEE is an entity and it is a supertype of the OFFICE_WORKER, DOCTOR, NURSE, MEDTECH, and MEDASSIST entities. A DEPENDENT entity also should fit into the picture somewhere.

Although doctors, nurses, and medical technologists all must have current valid licenses, because a license applies to one and only one professional and each professional has one and only one license, it makes sense for those licenses to be attributes of their respective DOCTOR, NURSE, and MEDTECH entities rather than to be entities in their own right.

PATIENT clearly should be an entity, as should EXAMINATION, TEST, TESTORDER, and TESTRESULT. CONSULTATION, DIAGNOSIS, PRESCRIPTION, and TREATMENT also deserve to stand on their own as entities.

After you have decided what the entities are, you can start thinking about how they relate to each other. You may be able to model the relationships in one of several ways. This is where the interviews with the stakeholders are critical. The model you arrive at must be consistent with the organization's business rules, both those written down somewhere and those that are understood by everyone, but not usually talked about. Figure 2-15 shows one possible way to model this system.

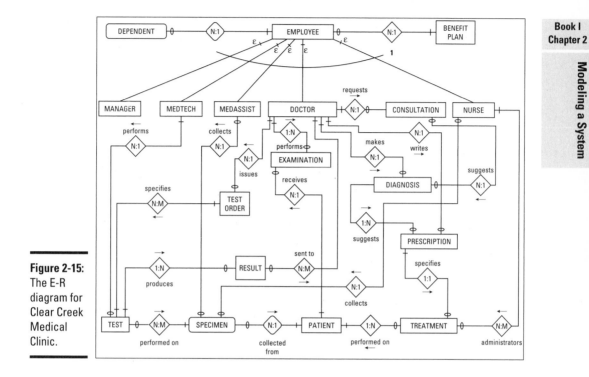

Figure 2-15:
The E-R
diagram for
Clear Creek
Medical
Clinic.

From this diagram, you can extract certain facts:

✦ An employee can have zero, one, or multiple dependents, but each
dependent is associated with one and only one employee. (Business
rule: If both members of a married couple work for the clinic, for insurance purposes, the dependents are associated with only one of them.)

✦ An employee must be either an office worker, a doctor, a nurse, a medical technologist, or a medical assistant. (Business rule: An office worker
cannot, for example, also be classified as a medical assistant. Only one
job classification is permitted.)

✦ A doctor can perform many examinations, but each examination is performed by one and only one doctor. (Business rule: If more than one
doctor is present at a patient examination, only one of them takes
responsibility for the examination.)

✦ A doctor can issue many test orders, but each test order can specify one
and only one test.

✦ A medical assistant or a nurse can collect multiple specimens from a patient, but each specimen is from one and only one patient.

✦ A medical technologist can perform multiple tests on a specimen, and each test can be applied to multiple specimens.

✦ A test may have one of several results; for example, positive, negative, below normal, normal, above normal, as well as specific numeric values. However, each such result applies to one and only one test.

✦ A test result can be sent to one or more doctors. A doctor can receive many test results.

✦ A doctor may request a consultation with one or more other doctors.

✦ A doctor may make a diagnosis of a patient's condition, based on test results and possibly on one or more consultations.

✦ A diagnosis could suggest one or more prescriptions.

✦ A doctor can write many prescriptions, but each prescription is written by one and only one doctor for one and only one patient.

✦ A doctor may order a treatment, to be administered to a patient by a nurse.

Often after drawing an E-R diagram, and then determining all the things that the diagram implies by compiling a list such as that given above, the designer finds missing entities or relationships, or that the model does not accurately represent the way things are actually done in the organization. Creating the model is an iterative process of progressively modifying the diagram until it reflects the desired system as closely as possible.

Problems with complex relationships

The Clear Creek Medical Clinic example in the preceding section contains some many-to-many relationships, such as the relationship between TEST and SPECIMEN. Multiple tests can be run on a single specimen, and multiple specimens, taken from multiple patients, can all be run through the same test. There is a problem in storing the relevant information. If the TEST entity is translated into a table in a relational database, how many columns should be set aside for specimens? Because you don't know how many specimens a test will be run on, and because the number of specimens could be quite large, it doesn't make sense to allocate space in the TEST table to show that the test was performed on a particular specimen.

Similarly, if the SPECIMEN entity is translated into a table in a relational database, how many columns should be set aside to record the tests that might be performed on it? That is unknown. It doesn't make sense to allocate space in the SPECIMEN table to hold all the tests that might be run on it. For these reasons, it is common practice to convert a many-to-many relationship into two one-to-many relationships, both connected to a new entity that lies between the original two. You can make that conversion with no loss of accuracy, and the problem of how to store things disappears. In Book II I go into detail on how to make this conversion.

Simplifying relationships using normalization

Even after you have eliminated all the many-to-many relationships in an E-R model, there can still be problems if you have not conceptualized your entities in the simplest way. The next step in the design process is to examine your model and see if operations of adding, changing, or deleting data can cause inconsistencies or even outright wrong information to be retained in your database. Such problems are called anomalies, and if they are possible, you will need to adjust your model to eliminate them. This process of model adjustment is called normalization and is covered in Book II.

Translating an E-R model into a relational model

After you are satisfied that your E-R model is not only correct, but economical and robust, the next step is to translate it into a relational model. The relational model is the basis for all relational database management systems. I go through that translation process in Book II.

The Relational Database Hierarchy

A relational database is organized in a hierarchical structure, where the highest level is the catalog. Generally only the largest, most complex databases will have multiple catalogs.

Catalogs: A database catalog only comes into play in large, complex databases that have multiple schemas.

Schemas: A database schema contains metadata. This metadata includes definitions of tables, views, value ranges, indexes, users, and user groups. It could also include stored procedures and triggers.

Tables: A database table is a set of elements organized as a two-dimensional table with horizontal rows and vertical columns. The columns correspond to the attributes in the E-R model of an entity. The rows hold the data about individual instances of the entity.

Columns: A column is a component of a database table. Each column in the table corresponds to one of the attributes in the E-R model of the entity that is being actualized by the table.

Chapter 3: SQL Overview

*I*n the early days of relational database management systems, as is true for the early days of just about anything, there was no standard language for performing relational operations on data. A number of companies came out with relational database management system products, and each had its own associated language. There were some general similarities among the languages because they all were performing essentially the same operations on the same kinds of data, structured in the same way. However, there were differences in syntax and in functionality that made it impossible for a person using the language of one RDBMS to operate on data that had been stored by another RDBMS. All the RDBMS vendors tried to gain dominant market share so that their particular proprietary language would prevail. The logic was that once developers learned a language, they would want to stick with it on subsequent projects. This steaming cauldron of ideas set the stage for the emergence of SQL. There was one company that had more market power than all the others combined, and had the additional advantage of being the employer of the inventor of the relational database model.

Where SQL Came From

It is interesting to note that even though Dr. Codd was an IBM employee when he developed the relational database model, IBM's initial support of that model was lukewarm at best. One reason might have been the fact that IBM already had a leading position in the database market with its IMS hierarchical DBMS. In 1978, IBM released System/38, a minicomputer that came with a RDBMS that was not promoted heavily.

As a result, in 1979, the world was introduced to a fully realized RDBMS by a small startup company named Relational Software, Inc. headed by Larry Ellison. Relational's product, called Oracle, is still the leading relational database management system on the market today.

Although Oracle had the initial impact on the market, other companies, including IBM, followed. In the process of developing the SQL/DS RDBMS product, IBM created a language code-named SEQUEL, which was an acronym for Structured English QUEry Language. This moniker was appropriate because SEQUEL statements looked like English-language sentences, but were more structured than most casual speech.

When it came time to actually release its RDBMS product, along with its associated language, IBM's legal department flagged a possible copyright issue with the name SEQUEL. In response, management elected to drop the vowels and call the language SQL (pronounced ess-cue-ell). The reference to Structured English was lost in the process. As a result, many people thought that SQL was an acronym for Structured Query Language. This is not the case. In computer programming, a structured language has some very well-defined characteristics. SQL does not share those characteristics and is thus not a structured language, query or otherwise.

What SQL Does

SQL does far more than just execute queries. Yes, of course you can use it to retrieve the data you want from a database, using a query. However, you can also use SQL to create and destroy databases, as well as modify their structure. In addition, you can add, modify, and delete database data with SQL. Even with all that capability, SQL is still considered only a data sublanguage. It does not have all the features of general-purpose programming languages such as C, C++, C#, or Java.

SQL is specifically designed for dealing with relational databases, and thus does not include a number of features that are needed for creating useful application programs. As a result, to create a complete application that accesses a database, you must write the code in one of the general-purpose languages, and embed SQL statements within the program whenever it communicates with the database.

SQL is a joke

There is a joke about the inappropriateness of saying SQL stands for Structured Query Language. It says that SQL is not structured, not restricted to performing queries, and is not a language. The language part refers to the fact that SQL is not Turing-complete, as are general-purpose programming languages. This joke echoes Voltaire's comment about the Holy Roman Empire, which he said was neither holy, Roman, nor an empire.

The ANSI/ISO SQL Standard

In the early 1980s, IBM started using SQL in its first relational database product, which was incorporated into the System/38 minicomputer. Smaller companies in the DBMS industry, in an effort to be compatible with IBM's offering, modeled their languages after SQL. In this way, SQL became a *de facto* standard. In 1986, the de facto standard became a standard *de jure* when the American National Standards Institute (ANSI) issued the SQL-86 standard. The SQL standard has been continually updated since then, with subsequent revisions named SQL-89, SQL-92, SQL:1999, and SQL:2003. SQL:2003 was updated in 2005 with a section called SQL/XML, which significantly enhances SQL's ability to deal with data in XML format.

What SQL Does Not Do

In the 1930s, Alan Turing defined a very simple machine that could perform any computation that could be performed by any computer imaginable, regardless of how big and complex. This simple machine has come to be known as a Universal Turing Machine. Any computer that can be shown to be equivalent to a Universal Turing Machine is said to be Turing-complete. All modern computers are Turing-complete. Similarly, a computer language that is capable of expressing any possible computation is said to be Turing-complete. Practically all popular languages, such as C, C#, C++, BASIC, Fortran, COBOL, Pascal, Java, and many others are Turing-complete. SQL, however, is not. It lacks flow of control structures that are needed for some classes of computations.

Because SQL is not Turing-complete, you cannot write an SQL program to perform a complex series of steps, as you can with a language such as C or Java. On the other hand, languages such as C and Java do not have the data manipulation facilities that SQL has, so you cannot write a program with them that will efficiently operate on database data. There are several ways to solve this dilemma:

✦ Combine the two types of language by embedding SQL statements within a program written in a host language such as C.

✦ Have the C program make calls to SQL modules to perform data manipulation functions.

✦ Create a new language that includes SQL, but also incorporates those structures that would make the language Turing-complete.

All three of these solutions are offered by one or another of the DBMS vendors.

What's a database?

There is a lot of confusion about what exactly someone is talking about when they mention the word *database*. I have mentioned database management systems (DBMSs), database applications, and databases. Some people lump these things together and call the whole lot databases. Loose usage of this sort just confuses everybody. To keep things clear in your own mind, remember the following distinctions:

✔ A *database* is a structured collection of integrated records. In other words, it is the data, but organized in a structured way.

✔ A *database application* is a computer program that operates on a database, that enables users to maintain the database and query it for needed information.

✔ A *database management system* is the engine that controls access to a database. Database applications must work through a DBMS in order to access the database. Conceptually, the DBMS lies between the database and the database application.

Available Implementations

A number of database management systems are currently available, and they all include a version of SQL that adheres more or less closely to the ANSI/ISO international standard for the SQL language. No SQL version available today is completely compliant with the standard, and probably none ever will be. The standard is updated every few years, adding new capability, putting the vendors in the position of always playing catch-up. In addition, in most cases, the vendors do not *want* to be 100% compliant with the standard. They like to include useful features that are not in the standard in order to make their product more attractive to developers. If a developer uses a vendor's non-standard feature, this has the effect of locking in the developer to that vendor. It makes it difficult for the developer to switch to a different DBMS.

Microsoft Access

Microsoft Access is an entry-level DBMS with which developers can build relatively small and simple databases and database applications. It is designed for use by people with little or no training in database theory. You can build databases and database applications using Access, without ever seeing SQL. Access does include an implementation of SQL, and you can use it to query your databases, but it is a severely limited subset of the language and Microsoft does not encourage its use. Instead, they prefer that you use the graphical database creation and manipulation tools and use the query-by-example (QBE) interface to ask questions of your database. "Under the covers" and beyond user control, the table creation tasks that the user specifies using the graphical tools are translated to SQL before being sent to the database engine, which is the part of the DBMS that actually operates on the database. Microsoft Access runs under any of the Microsoft Windows operating systems, but not under Linux, Apple's OS X, or any other non-Microsoft operating system.

To reach the SQL editor in Access, do the following:

1. **Open a database that already has tables and at least one query defined.**

You see a database window that looks something like Figure 3-1.

Figure 3-1:
A Microsoft Access 2003 database window.

2. **Select Queries from the menu on the left side of the database window, and then click on the Design icon at the top of the database window.**

This opens a window that resembles Figure 3-2.

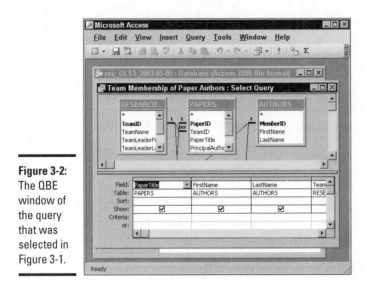

Figure 3-2:
The QBE window of the query that was selected in Figure 3-1.

3. **Drop down the View menu in the upper-left corner of the database window as shown in Figure 3-3.**

Figure 3-3:
The QBE window of the query that was selected in Figure 3-1, showing the View menu.

4. **Select SQL View from the View menu.**

As Figure 3-4 shows, this displays an SQL editor window, with the SQL statement selected that was generated by the query shown in the QBE window.

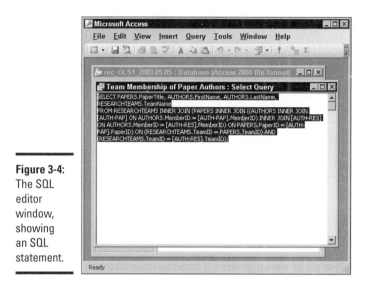

Figure 3-4:
The SQL
editor
window,
showing
an SQL
statement.

5. **You can now delete the existing SQL statement and type in your own.**

Figure 3-5 shows what this looks like.

Figure 3-5:
The SQL
editor
window,
showing a
newly
entered SQL
statement.

6. **Click the exclamation point icon to execute the statement.**

This produces the result shown in Figure 3-6.

Team Membership of Paper Authors : Select Query			
PaperTitle	FirstName	LastName	TeamName
Water at the Lunar Poles	Bob	McGoing	MBRT
Lava Tubes as Sites for Lunar Bases	Bryce	Thoreau	MBRT
Lava Tubes as Sites for Lunar Bases	Cheryl	Lancaster	MBRT
Lava Tubes on the Slopes of Martian Volcanoes	Tom	Charges	SIAM
Lava Tubes on the Slopes of Martian Volcanoes	Gus	Roderick	SIAM

Record: 1 of 5

Figure 3-6:
The result of
the query in
Figure 3-5.

Microsoft SQL Server

Microsoft SQL Server is Microsoft's entry into the enterprise database market. It runs only under one of the various Microsoft Windows operating systems. The latest version is SQL Server 2005. Unlike Microsoft Access, SQL Server requires a high level of expertise in order to use it at all. Users interact with SQL Server using Transact-SQL, also known as T-SQL. T-SQL adheres quite closely to the syntax of ANSI/ISO standard SQL and provides much of the functionality described in the standard. Additional functionality, not specified in the ANSI/ISO standard, provides the developer with usability and performance advantages that Microsoft hopes will make SQL Server more attractive than its competitors. Like Access, SQL Server runs only in Microsoft Windows environments. There is a free version of SQL Server 2005 called SQL Server 2005 Express Edition that you might think of as SQL Server on training wheels. Read *Microsoft SQL Server 2005 Express Edition For Dummies* (Wiley) by Robert Schneider to find out more about it.

IBM DB2

DB2 is a flexible product that runs on Windows and Linux PCs on the low end, all the way up to IBM's largest mainframes. As you would expect for a DBMS that runs on "big iron," it is a full-featured product. It incorporates key features that were added to the SQL standard in 1999, as well as numerous non-standard additions. Like Microsoft's SQL Server, to use DB2 effectively, a developer must have received extensive training and considerable hands-on experience.

Oracle

Oracle is another DBMS that runs on PCs, running either the Windows, Linux, or Mac OS X operating system, and also on very large, powerful computers. Oracle SQL is a superset of SQL:1999 and SQL Developer is a free graphical tool that developers can use to enter and debug Oracle SQL code. A free version of Oracle 10g, called Oracle 10g Express Edition, is available for download from the Oracle Web site. It provides a convenient environment for learning Oracle. Migration to the full Oracle 10g product is smooth and easy when you are ready to move into production mode. The enterprise-class edition of Oracle hosts some of the largest databases in use today. The same can be said for DB2 and SQL Server.

InterBase

InterBase is a relational DBMS produced by Borland Software Corporation. Its capabilities are similar to those of the other proprietary databases listed above, but it has a significantly smaller resource footprint, requiring both less RAM and less hard disk space. It is also easier to configure and run. InterBase's sophisticated handling of concurrency control can give it performance advantages in environments where both short and long transactions are common. InterBase runs in both Windows and Linux environments, as well as under the Sun Solaris operating system.

MySQL

MySQL is the most widely used open-source DBMS. Actually, there are four different versions of MySQL, each with a different database engine and different capabilities. The most feature-rich of these is MySQL InnoDB. People often use one or another of the MySQL versions as the back ends for a large number of data-driven Web sites. The level of compliance with the ANSI/ISO SQL standard differs between versions, but the compliance of MySQL InnoDB is comparable to that of the proprietary DBMS products mentioned above. MySQL is particularly noted for its speed. MySQL runs under Windows and Linux, but not under IBM's proprietary mainframe operating systems. It is supported by a large and dedicated user community.

PostgreSQL

PostgreSQL is another open source DBMS, that is generally considered to be more robust than MySQL, and more capable of supporting large enterprise-wide applications. It is also supported by an active user community. PostgreSQL runs under Linux, Unix, Windows, and IBM's z/OS mainframe operating system.

Chapter 4: SQL and the Relational Model

In This Chapter

✔ Relating SQL to the relational model

✔ Figuring out functional dependencies

✔ Discovering keys, views, users, privileges, schemas, and catalogs

✔ Checking out connections, sessions, and transactions

✔ Understanding routines and paths

The relational database model, as I mention in Chapter 1 of this minibook, existed as a theoretical model for almost a decade before the first relational database product appeared on the market. The first commercial implementation of the relational model, from the company that later became Oracle Corporation, did not use SQL, which had not yet been released by IBM. In those early days, there were a number of competing data sublanguages. Gradually, SQL became a de facto standard, thanks in no small part to IBM's dominant position in the market, and the fact that Oracle started offering it as an alternative to its own language early on.

Although SQL was developed to work with a relational database management system, it's not entirely consistent with the relational model. However, it is close enough, and, in many cases, it even offers capabilities that are not present in the relational model. Some of the most important aspects of SQL are direct analogs of some aspects of the relational model. Others are not. This chapter gives a brief introduction to some of these concepts and terms.

Sets, Relations, Multisets, and Tables

The relational model is based on the mathematical discipline known as *set theory*. In set theory, a set is defined as a collection of unique objects — duplicates are not allowed. This carries over to the relational model. A relation is defined as a collection of unique objects called *tuples* — no duplicates are allowed among tuples.

In SQL, the equivalent of a relation is a table. However, tables are not exactly like relations in that a table can have duplicate rows. For that reason, tables in a relational database are not modeled on the sets of set theory, but rather on multisets, which are similar to sets except they allow duplicate objects.

Although a relation is not exactly the same thing as a table, the terms are often used interchangeably. Because relations were defined by theoreticians, they have a very precise definition. The word *table,* on the other hand, is in general use and is often much more loosely defined. When I use the word *table* in this book, I use it in the more restricted sense, as being an alternate term for *relation.* The attributes and tuples of a relation are strictly equivalent to the columns and rows of a table.

So, what's a relation? Formally, a relation is a two-dimensional table that has the following characteristics:

✦ Every cell in the table must contain a single value, if it contains any value at all. Repeating groups and arrays are not allowed as values.

✦ All the entries in any column must be of the same kind. For example, if a column contains an employee name in one row, it must contain employee names in all rows that contain values.

✦ Each column has a unique name.

✦ The order of the columns doesn't matter.

✦ The order of the rows doesn't matter.

✦ No two rows may be identical.

If and only if a table meets all these criteria, it is a relation. You might have tables that fail to meet one or more of these criteria. For example, a table might have two identical rows. It is still a table in the loose sense, but it is not a relation.

Functional Dependencies

Functional dependencies are relationships between or among attributes. Consider the example of two attributes of the CUSTOMER relation, Zipcode and State. If you know the customer's ZIP Code, the state can be obtained by a simple lookup because each ZIP Code resides in one and only one state. You say that State is *functionally dependent* on Zipcode or that Zipcode *determines* state. Zipcode is called a *determinant.* The reverse is not true. State does not determine Zipcode because states can contain multiple Zipcodes. You denote functional dependencies as follows:

```
Zipcode ⇨ State
```

A group of attributes may act as a determinant. Consider the relation INVOICE (Inv#, CustID, W/R, ProdID, Quantity, Price, Extprice). Assuming that products have both a wholesale and a retail price, the W/R attribute tells whether this is a wholesale or a retail transaction. ProdID identifies the product. Extprice is extended price, derived by multiplying Quantity by Price.

```
(W/R, ProdID) ⇨ Price
(Quantity, Price) ⇨ Extprice
```

ProdID shows which product you are considering. W/R tells you whether you are charging the wholesale price or the retail price. Thus the combination of W/R and ProdID determines Price. Similarly, the combination of Quantity and Price determines Extprice. Neither W/R nor ProdID by itself determines Price; they are both needed to determine Price. Both Quantity and Price are needed to determine Extprice.

Keys

Keys are groups of one or more attributes that uniquely identify a tuple in a relation. One of the characteristics of a relation is that no two rows (tuples) are identical. You can guarantee that no two rows are identical if at least one field (attribute) is guaranteed to have a unique value in each row, or if some combination of fields is guaranteed to be unique for each row. Table 4-1 shows an example of the PROJECT relation. It lists researchers affiliated with the Gentoo Institute's Penguin Physiology Lab, the projects they are working on, and the locations at which they are conducting their research.

Table 4-1	PROJECT Relation	
ResearcherID	*Project*	*Location*
Pizarro	Why penguin feet don't freeze	Bahia Paraiso
Whitehead	Why penguins don't get the bends	Port Lockroy
Shelton	How penguin eggs stay warm in pebble nests	Peterman Island
Nansen	How penguin diet varies by season	Peterman Island

In this table, each researcher is assigned to only one project. Is this a rule? Must a researcher be assigned to only one project, or is it possible for a researcher to be assigned to more than one? If a researcher can be assigned to only one project, ResearcherID is a key. It guarantees that every row in the PROJECT table is unique. What if there is no such rule? What if a researcher may work on several projects at the same time? Table 4-2 shows this situation.

Table 4-2	PROJECTS Relation	
ResearcherID	*Project*	*Location*
Pizarro	Why penguin feet don't freeze	Bahia Paraiso
Pizarro	How penguin eggs stay warm in pebble nests	Peterman Island
Whitehead	Why penguins don't get the bends	Port Lockroy
Shelton	How penguin eggs stay warm in pebble nests	Peterman Island
Shelton	How penguin diet varies by season	Peterman Island
Nansen	How penguin diet varies by season	Peterman Island

In this scenario, Dr. Pizarro works on both the cold feet and the warm eggs projects, whereas Professor Shelton works on both the warm eggs and the varied diet projects. Clearly, ResearcherID cannot be used as a key. However, the combination of ResearcherID and Project is unique and is thus a key.

You are probably wondering how you can reliably tell what is a key and what isn't. Looking at the relation in Table 4-1, it looks like Researcher ID is a key because every entry in that column is unique. However, this could be due to the fact that you are looking at a limited sample, and any minute now someone could add a new row that duplicates the value of ResearcherID in one of the existing rows. How can you be sure that won't happen? Ask the users.

The relations you build are models of the mental images that the users have of the system they are dealing with. You want your relational model to correspond as closely as possible to the model the users have in their minds. If they tell you that in their organization researchers never work on more than one project at a time, you can use ResearcherID as a key. On the other hand, if it is even remotely possible that a researcher might be assigned to two projects simultaneously, you have to revert to a composite key made up of both ResearcherID and Project.

A question that might arise in your mind is, "Is it possible for a relation to exist that has no key?" By the definition of a relation, the answer is no. Every relation *must* have a key. One of the characteristics of a relation is that no two rows may be exactly the same. That means that you are always able to distinguish rows from each other, although you may have to include all the relation's attributes in the key to do it.

Views

Although the most fundamental constituent of a relational database is undoubtedly the table, another important concept is that of the virtual table or *view*.

Unlike an ordinary table, a view has no physical existence until it is called upon in a query. There is no place on disk where the rows in the view are stored. The view exists only in the metadata as a definition. The definition describes how to pull data from tables and present it to the user in the form of a view.

From the user's viewpoint (no pun intended), a view looks just like a table. You can do almost everything to a view that you can do to a table. The major exception is that you cannot always update a view the same way that you can update a table. The view may contain columns that are the result of some arithmetic operation on the data in columns from the tables upon which the view is based. You can't update a column that doesn't exist in your permanent storage device. Despite this limitation, views, after they're formulated, can save you considerable work: You don't need to code the same complex query every time you want to pull data from multiple tables. Create the view once, and then use it every time you need it.

Users

Although it may seem a little odd to include them, the users are an important part of any database system. After all, without the users, no data would be written into the system, no data would be manipulated, and no results would be displayed. When you think about it, the users are mighty important. Just as you want your hardware and software to be of the highest quality you can afford, in order to produce the best results, you want the highest quality people too, for the same reason. To assure that only the people who meet your standards have access to the database system, you should have a robust security system that enables authorized users to do their job and at the same time prevents access to everyone else.

Privileges

A good security system not only keeps out unauthorized users, but also provides authorized users with access privileges that are tailored to their needs. The night watchman has different database needs from those of the company CEO. One way of handling privileges is to assign every authorized user an authorization ID. When the person logs on with his authorization ID, the privileges associated with that authorization ID become available to the user. This could include the ability to read the contents of certain columns of certain tables, the ability to add new rows to certain tables, delete rows, update rows, and so on.

A second way to assign privileges is with roles, which were introduced in SQL:1999. Roles are particularly valuable in large organizations where a number of people have essentially the same job and thus the same needs for data. For example, the night watchman noted above might have the same data needs as other security guards. A suite of privileges could be granted to the SECURITY_GUARD role. From then on, whenever a new guard is hired, by assigning him to the SECURITY_GUARD role, all the privileges appropriate for that role are automatically assigned to him. When a person leaves or changes jobs, revocation of his role can be just as easy.

Schemas

Relational database applications typically make use of multiple tables. As a database grows to support multiple applications, it becomes more and more likely that an application developer will try to give one of her tables the same name as a table that already exists in the database. This can cause problems and frustration. To get around this problem, SQL has a hierarchical namespace structure. A developer can define her tables as being members of a *schema*. With this structure, one developer can have a table named CUSTOMER in her schema, whereas a second developer can also have an entirely different table, also named CUSTOMER, but in a different schema.

Catalogs

These days, organizations can be so big that if every developer had a schema for each of her applications, the number of schemas itself could be a problem. Someone might inadvertently give a new schema the same name as an existing schema. To head off this possibility, an additional level was added at the top of the namespace hierarchy. A *catalog* can contain multiple schemas, which in turn can contain multiple tables. The smallest organizations don't have to worry about either catalogs or schemas, but those levels of the namespace hierarchy are there if they're needed. If your organization is big enough to worry about duplicate catalog names, it is big enough to figure out a way to deal with the problem.

Connections, Sessions, and Transactions

A database management system is typically divided into two main parts, a client side, which interfaces with the user, and a server side, which holds the data and operates on it. To operate on a database, a user must establish a *connection* between her client and the server that holds the data she wants to access. Generally the first thing you must do, if you want to work on a database at all, is to establish a connection to it. You can do this with a CONNECT statement that specifies your authorization ID and names the server you want to connect to. The exact implementation of this varies from one DBMS to another. Most people today would use the DBMS's graphical user interface to connect to a server rather than using the SQL CONNECT statement.

A *session* is the context in which a single user executes a sequence of SQL statements, using a single connection. A "user" can either be a person entering SQL statements at the client console, or a program running on the client machine.

A *transaction* is a sequence of SQL statements that is atomic with respect to recovery. This means that if a failure occurs while a transaction is in progress, the effects of the transaction are erased so that the database is left in the state it was in before the transaction started. *Atomic* in this context means indivisible. Either the transaction runs to completion or it aborts in such a way that any changes it made before the abort are undone.

Routines

Routines are procedures, functions, or methods that can be invoked either by an SQL CALL statement, or by the host language program that the SQL is operating with. Methods are a kind of function used in object-oriented programming.

Because either a host language program or SQL can invoke a routine, and because the routine being invoked can be either written in SQL or in host language code, routines can cause confusion. A few definitions help to clarify the situation:

✦ **Externally invoked routine:** A procedure, written in SQL, residing in a module located on the client, which is invoked by the host language program

✦ **SQL-invoked routine:** Either a procedure or a function, residing in a module located on the server, which could be written in either SQL or the host language, that is invoked by SQL code

✦ **External routine:** Either a procedure or a function, residing in a module located on the server, which is written in the host language, but is invoked by SQL

✦ **SQL routine:** Either a procedure or a function, residing in a module located on either the server or the client, which is written in SQL and invoked by SQL

Routines enable SQL code to take advantage of calculations performed by host language code, and enable host language code to take advantage of data operations performed by SQL code.

Paths

A *path* in SQL, similar to a path in operating systems, tells the system what order to search locations in to find a routine that has been invoked. For a system with several schemas (perhaps one for testing, one for QA, and one for production), the path tells the executing program where to look first, where to look next, and so on, to find an invoked routine.

Chapter 5: The Major Components of SQL

In This Chapter

✔ The Data Definition Language (DDL)

✔ The Data Maintenance Language (DML)

✔ The Data Control Language (DCL)

*Y*ou can view SQL as being divided into three distinct parts, each of which has a different function. With one part, the Data Definition Language (DDL), you can create the structure (the metadata) of a database. With the second part, the Data Manipulation Language (DML), you can operate on the data contained in the database, and with the third part, the Data Control Language (DCL), you can maintain a database's security and reliability. Throughout this chapter, I look at each of these SQL components in turn.

The Data Definition Language (DDL)

The Data Definition Language (DDL) is the part of SQL that you use to create a database and all of its structural components. It is also the tool that you use to modify the structure of an existing database or to destroy it after you no longer need it.

The containment hierarchy

The defining difference between databases and flat files is that databases are structured. As I've shown you in previous chapters, the structure of relational databases differs from the structure of other database models, such as the hierarchical model and the network model. However, there is a definite hierarchical aspect to the structure of a relational database. Like Russian nesting dolls, one level of structure contains another, which in turn contains yet another, as shown in Figure 5-1.

Not all databases use all the available levels, but larger databases tend to use more of them. The top level is the database itself. As you would expect, every part of the database is contained within the database. A database can have one or more *catalogs*. Each catalog can have one or more *schemas*. Each schema can include one or more tables. Each table may consist of one or more columns.

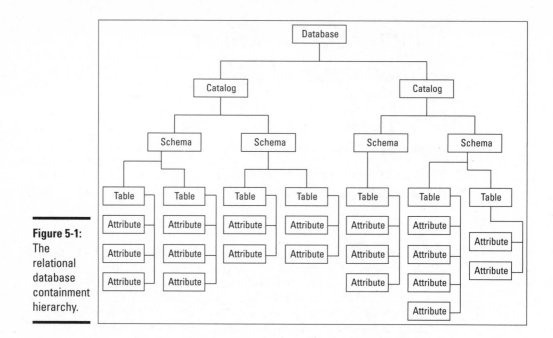

Figure 5-1:
The relational database containment hierarchy.

For small to moderately large databases, you need concern yourself only with tables and the columns they contain. Schemas and catalogs are invoked only when you have multiple unrelated collections of tables in the same database. To keep these groups separate, you can put them into separate schemas. If there is any danger of confusing unrelated schemas, you can put them in separate catalogs.

Creating tables

At its simplest, a database is a collection of two-dimensional tables, each of which has a collection of closely related attributes. The attributes are stored in columns of the tables. You can use SQL's CREATE statement to create a table, with its associated columns. Later, using SQL's Data Manipulation Language, you can add data to the table in the form of rows.

Specifying columns

The two dimensions of a table are its columns and rows. Each column corresponds to a specific attribute of the entity being modeled. Each row contains one specific instance of the entity. You can create a table with an SQL CREATE statement. Following is an example. Like all examples in this book, the code uses ANSI/ISO standard syntax:

```
CREATE TABLE CUSTOMER (
     CustomerID      INTEGER,
     FirstName       CHARACTER (15),
     LastName        CHARACTER (20),
     Street          CHARACTER (30),
     City            CHARACTER (25),
     Region          CHARACTER (25),
     Country         CHARACTER (25),
     Phone           CHARACTER (13) ) ;
```

In the CREATE TABLE statement, you specify the name of each column and the type of data that column contains. In the preceding example, the CustomerID column contains data of the INTEGER type, and the other columns contain character strings. The maximum lengths of the strings are also specified. Most implementations accept the abbreviation CHAR in place of CHARACTER.

Specifying constraints

It is important to keep erroneous data out of your databases. One way to do this is to prevent incorrect values from being entered in the first place. You can prevent the entry of invalid data with a constraint. There are several kinds of constraints, which I look at in more detail shortly. For now, I discuss a simple but very important constraint: the NOT NULL constraint.

SQL is different from many other computer languages in that in SQL, null values are legal. It is important to distinguish a null value from some other value that might be confused with it. A *null value* is a value that is either not known or not specified. It could be anything or nothing. This is quite a different thing from, for example, zero, which is a very definite numeric value. It is also quite different from a blank space, which is a very definite character value.

Although in SQL, a null value is legal, there may be columns in a table where you want to insist that a value is always present. You can enforce that requirement by adding a NOT NULL constraint to the table definition. Here's an example:

```
CREATE TABLE CUSTOMER (
     CustomerID      INTEGER          NOT NULL,
     FirstName       CHARACTER (15),
     LastName        CHARACTER (20) NOT NULL,
     Street          CHARACTER (30),
     City            CHARACTER (25),
     Region          CHARACTER (25),
     Country         CHARACTER (25),
     Phone           CHARACTER (13) ) ;
```

In any business's customer table, you want to be able to distinguish one customer from another, even if they have the same name. A good way to do this is to assign a unique ID number to each customer when that customer is first entered into the database. You can enforce uniqueness by adding a NOT NULL constraint to the CustomerID line of the table definition. In this example, a NOT NULL constraint has also been applied to the LastName column. This reflects a business rule that every customer must have at least one name, and that name is to be recorded in the LastName column. Other organizations may have different business rules. When you are interviewing the users, you must find out what those business rules are, so that you can enforce them with constraints.

Column constraints

The NOT NULL constraint is an example of a column constraint. As the name implies, column constraints apply to a single column in a table. You can gain more control over constraints by naming them. For example, you could name the NOT NULL constraints in the previous example as follows:

```
CREATE TABLE CUSTOMER (
    CustomerID   INTEGER
          CONSTRAINT Customer_not_null   NOT NULL,
    FirstName     CHARACTER (15),
    LastName      CHARACTER (20)
          CONSTRAINT LastName_not_null   NOT NULL,
    Street        CHARACTER (30),
    City          CHARACTER (25),
    Region        CHARACTER (25),
    Country       CHARACTER (25),
    Phone         CHARACTER (13) ) ;
```

Naming a constraint makes it easier to change or delete at a later time. You can do that with an ALTER TABLE statement, described below.

Constraints more complex than the NOT NULL constraint can be described by an expression. Such constraints use the keyword CHECK. Suppose, due to government export restrictions, that you do not want to accept any new customers who do not reside in the USA. You can enforce that policy with a CHECK constraint.

```
CREATE TABLE CUSTOMER (
    CustomerID   INTEGER
          CONSTRAINT Customer_not_null        NOT NULL,
    FirstName     CHARACTER (15),
    LastName      CHARACTER (20)
          CONSTRAINT LastName_not_null        NOT NULL,
    Street        CHARACTER (30),
    City          CHARACTER (25),
    Region        CHARACTER (25),
```

```
    Country         CHARACTER (25)
CONSTRAINT USA_only CHECK (Country = 'USA'),
    Phone           CHARACTER (13) ) ;
```

With these constraints, the DBMS doesn't allow a new record to be added to
the CUSTOMER table unless the CustomerID column contains a value, the
LastName column contains a value, and the Country column contains the
value USA.

Table constraints

Whereas some constraints apply to a single column or to a selected subset
of the columns in a table, a constraint may apply to an entire table. The
PRIMARY KEY constraint is an example of such. A table can have one and
only one primary key. Here's an example of such a usage:

```
CREATE TABLE CUSTOMER (
    CustomerID    INTEGER                    PRIMARY KEY,
    FirstName     CHARACTER (15),
    LastName      CHARACTER (20)
        CONSTRAINT LastName_not_null       NOT NULL,
    Street        CHARACTER (30),
    City          CHARACTER (25),
    Region        CHARACTER (25),
    Country       CHARACTER (25)
        CONSTRAINT USA_only CHECK (Country = 'USA'),
    Phone         CHARACTER (13) ) ;
```

Every table should have a primary key. A primary key uniquely identifies a row
in a table. It is a stronger constraint than the NOT NULL constraint, which
prevents one kind of duplication (two or more rows with the same null value
for an attribute), but not others (two or more rows with the same specific
value for an attribute). The DBMS will not allow you to add a row to a table if
the new row has the same primary key as a row that already exists in the table.

Assertions

Constraints that apply to more than one table are called *assertions*. Suppose
a small bookstore wants to control its exposure to dead inventory by not
allowing total inventory to grow beyond 20,000 items. Suppose further that
stocks of books and DVDs are maintained in different tables. An assertion
can guarantee that the maximum is not exceeded.

```
CREATE TABLE BOOKS (
    ISBN          INTEGER,
    Title         CHAR (50),
    Quantity      INTEGER ) ;
```

```
CREATE TABLE DVD (
    BarCode      INTEGER,
    Title        CHAR (50),
    Quantity     INTEGER ) ;

CREATE ASSERTION
    CHECK ((SELECT SUM (Quantity)
              FROM BOOKS)
         + (SELECT SUM (Quantity)
              FROM DVD)
         < 20000)
```

Most popular implementations do not support assertions. For example, SQL Server 2005, DB2, Oracle 10g, Borland InterBase, MySQL, and PostgreSQL do not. Assertions may become available in the future, since they are a part of SQL:2003, but it would not be wise to hold your breath until this functionality appears.

Creating other objects

Tables aren't the only things you can create with a CREATE statement. A few other possibilities are views, schemas, and domains.

Views

Sometimes what is stored in database tables is not exactly in the form that you want users to see. Perhaps a table containing employee data has address information that the social committee chairperson needs, but also contains salary information that should be seen only by authorized personnel in the human resources department. How can you show the social committee chairperson what she needs to see without spilling the beans on what everyone is earning? In another scenario, perhaps the information a person needs is spread across several tables. How do you deliver what is needed in one convenient result set? The answer to both questions is the view.

A *view* is a virtual table that has no physical existence apart from the tables that it draws from. Some views draw selected columns from one table. Others, called multi-table views, draw selected columns from multiple tables.

Single-table view

Consider a single-table view. Consider the social committee chairperson's requirement, which I mention in the preceding section. She needs the contact information for all employees, but is not authorized to see anything else. You can create a view based on the EMPLOYEE table that includes only the information she needs.

```
CREATE VIEW EMP_CONTACT AS
    SELECT EMPLOYEE.FirstName,
           EMPLOYEE.LastName,
           EMPLOYEE.Street,
           EMPLOYEE.City,
           EMPLOYEE.State,
           EMPLOYEE.Zip,
           EMPLOYEE.Phone,
           Employee.Email
    FROM EMPLOYEE ;
```

This `CREATE VIEW` statement uses an embedded `SELECT` statement to pull from the EMPLOYEE table only the columns desired. Now all you need to do is grant `SELECT` rights on the EMP_CONTACT view to the social committee chairperson. The right to look at the records in the EMPLOYEE table continues to be restricted to duly authorized human resources personnel and upper-management types.

Most implementations assume that if only one table is listed in the `FROM` clause, the columns being selected are in that same table. You can save some typing by eliminating the redundant references to the EMPLOYEE table.

```
CREATE VIEW EMP_CONTACT AS
    SELECT FirstName,
           LastName,
           Street,
           City,
           State,
           Zip,
           Phone,
           Email
    FROM EMPLOYEE ;
```

There is a danger in using the abbreviated format, however. A query may use a join to pull some information from this view and other information from another view or table. If the other view or table has a field with the same name, the database engine doesn't know which to use. It's always safe to use a fully qualified column name, but don't be surprised if you see the abbreviated form in somebody else's code. I discuss joins in Book III, Chapter 4.

Multi-table view

Although there are occasions when you might want to pull a subset of columns from a single table, a much more common requirement is to pull together selected information from multiple related tables and present the result in a single report. You can do this with a multi-table view. Creating multi-table views involves joins, so to be safe you should use fully qualified column names.

Suppose, for example, that you are tasked to create an order entry system for a retail business. The key things involved are the products that are ordered, the customers who order them, the invoices that record the order, and the individual line items on each invoice. It makes sense to separate invoices and invoice lines because an invoice can have an indeterminate number of invoice lines that varies from one invoice to another. You can model this system with an E-R diagram. Figure 5-2 shows one way to model the system.

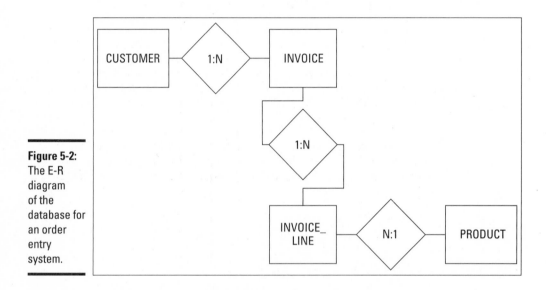

Figure 5-2:
The E-R diagram of the database for an order entry system.

The entities relate to each other through the columns they have in common. Here are the relationships:

✦ The CUSTOMER entity bears a one-to-many relationship to the INVOICE entity. One customer can make multiple purchases, generating multiple invoices. Each invoice, however, applies to one and only one customer.

✦ The INVOICE entity bears a one-to-many relationship to the INVOICE_LINE entity. One invoice may contain multiple lines, but each line appears on one and only one invoice.

✦ The PRODUCT entity bears a one-to-many relationship to the INVOICE_LINE entity. A product may appear on more than one line on an invoice, but each line deals with one and only one product.

The links between entities are the attributes they hold in common. Both the CUSTOMER and the INVOICE entities have a CustomerID column. It is the primary key in the CUSTOMER entity and a foreign key in the INVOICE entity. I discuss keys in detail in Book II, Chapter 4. The InvoiceNumber attribute connects the INVOICE entity to the INVOICE_LINE entity, and the ProductID attribute connects PRODUCT to INVOICE_LINE.

The first step in creating a view is to create the tables upon which the view is based. These tables are based on the entities and attributes in the E-R model. I discuss table creation in detail in Book II, Chapter 4. For now, I just show how to create the tables in the sample retail database.

```
CREATE TABLE CUSTOMER (
     CustomerID          INTEGER         PRIMARY KEY,
     FirstName           CHAR (15),
     LastName            CHAR (20)       NOT NULL,
     Street              CHAR (25),
     City                CHAR (20),
     State               CHAR (2),
     Zipcode             CHAR (10),
     Phone               CHAR (13) ) ;
```

The first column in the code contains attributes; the second column contains data types, and the third column contains constraints. I touch on primary key constraints in Book II, Chapter 2 and then describe them more fully in Book II, Chapter 4. For now, all you need to know is that good design practice requires that every table have a primary key. The NOT NULL constraint means that the LastName field must contain a value. I say more about null values in Book I, Chapter 6.

```
CREATE TABLE PRODUCT (
     ProductID           INTEGER     PRIMARY KEY,
     Name                CHAR (25),
     Description         CHAR (30),
     Category            CHAR (15),
     VendorID            INTEGER,
     VendorName          CHAR (30) ) ;

CREATE TABLE INVOICE (
     InvoiceNumber       INTEGER     PRIMARY KEY,
     CustomerID          INTEGER,
     InvoiceDate         DATE,
     TotalSale           NUMERIC (9,2),
     TotalRemitted       NUMERIC (9,2),
     FormOfPayment       CHAR (10) ) ;

CREATE TABLE INVOICE_LINE (
     LineNumber          Integer     PRIMARY KEY,
     InvoiceNumber       INTEGER,
     ProductID           INTEGER,
     Quantity            INTEGER,
     SalePrice           NUMERIC (9,2) ) ;
```

You can create a view containing data from multiple tables by joining tables in pairs until you get the combination you want. Suppose you want a display showing the first and last names of all customers along with all the products they have bought. You can do it with views.

```
CREATE VIEW CUST_PROD1 AS
    SELECT FirstName, LastName, InvoiceNumber
    FROM CUSTOMER JOIN INVOICE
    USING (CustomerID) ;

CREATE VIEW CUST_PROD2 AS
    SELECT FirstName, LastName, ProductID
    FROM CUST_PROD1 JOIN INVOICE_LINE
    USING (InvoiceNumber) ;

CREATE VIEW CUST_PROD AS
    SELECT FirstName, LastName, Name
    FROM CUST_PROD2 JOIN PRODUCT
    USING (ProductID) ;
```

The CUST_PROD1 view combines the customer's first and last name with
the invoice numbers of all the invoices generated for that customer. The
CUST_PROD2 view combines the customer's first and last name from the
CUST_PROD1 view with the ProductID from the INVOICE_LINE table. Finally,
the CUST_PROD view combines the customer's first and last name from the
CUST_PROD2 view with the Name of the product from the PRODUCT table.
This gives the display that we want. Figure 5-3 shows the flow of information
from the source tables to the final destination view. I discuss joins in detail in
Book III, Chapter 5.

Figure 5-3:
Creating a
multi-table
view using
joins.

There will be a row in the final view for every purchase. Customers who bought multiple items will be represented by multiple lines in CUST_PROD.

Schemas

In the containment hierarchy, the next level up from the one that includes tables and views is the schema level. It makes sense to place tables and views that are related to each other in the same schema. In many cases, a database may have only one schema, the default schema. This is the simplest situation, and when it applies, you don't need to think about schemas at all. However, more complex cases do occur. In those cases, it is important to keep one set of tables separated from another set. You can do this by creating a named schema for each set. Do this with a CREATE SCHEMA statement. I won't go into the detailed syntax for creating a schema here because it may vary from one platform to another, but you can create a named schema in the following manner:

```
CREATE SCHEMA RETAIL1 ;
```

There are a number of clauses that you can add to the CREATE SCHEMA statement, specifying the owner of the schema and creating tables, views and other objects. However, you can create a schema as shown above, and create the tables and other objects that go into it later. If you do create a table later, you must specify which schema it belongs to:

```
CREATE TABLE RETAIL1.CUSTOMER (
    CustomerID          INTEGER          PRIMARY KEY,
    FirstName           CHAR (15),
    LastName            CHAR (20)        NOT NULL,
    Street              CHAR (25),
    City                CHAR (20),
    State               CHAR (2),
    Zipcode             CHAR (10),
    Phone               CHAR (13) ) ;
```

This customer table will go into the RETAIL1 schema and will not be confused with the customer table that was created in the default schema, even though the table names are the same.

Domains

A domain is the set of all values that a table's attributes can take on. Some implementations of SQL allow you to define domains within a CREATE SCHEMA statement. You can also define a domain with a standalone CREATE DOMAIN statement, such as

```
CREATE DOMAIN Color CHAR (15)
    CHECK (VALUE IS "Red" OR "White" OR "Blue") ;
```

When a table attribute is defined as of type `Color`, only `Red`, `White`, and `Blue` will be accepted as legal values. Domains can save you a lot of typing, since you have to specify constraints only once, rather than every time you define a corresponding table attribute.

Modifying tables and other objects

After you create a table, complete with a full set of attributes, you may not want it to remain the same for all eternity. Requirements have a way of changing, based on changing conditions. The system you are modeling may change, requiring you to change your database structure to match. SQL's Data Definition Language gives you the tools to change what you have brought into existence with a `CREATE` statement. The primary tool is the `ALTER` statement. Here's an example of a table modification:

```
ALTER TABLE CUSTOMER
    ADD COLUMN Email CHAR (50) ;
```

This has the effect of adding a new column to the CUSTOMER table without affecting any of the existing columns. You can get rid of columns that are no longer needed in a similar way:

```
ALTER TABLE CUSTOMER
    DROP COLUMN;
```

I guess we don't want to keep track of customer e-mail addresses after all.

The `ALTER TABLE` statement also works for adding and dropping constraints.

Removing tables and other objects

It's really easy to get rid of tables, views, and other things that you no longer want. Here's how easy:

```
DROP TABLE CUSTOMER ;
DROP VIEW EMP_CONTACT ;
```

When you drop a table, it simply disappears, along with all of its data.

The Data Manipulation Language (DML)

Just as the DDL is that part of SQL that you can use to create database structural elements such as schemas, tables, and views, the Data Manipulation Language (DML) is the part of SQL that operates on the data that inhabits that structure. There are four things that you want to do with data:

✦ Store the data in a structured way that makes it easily retrievable.

✦ Change the data that is stored.

✦ Selectively retrieve information that responds to a need that you currently have.

✦ Remove data from the database that is no longer needed.

SQL statements that are part of the DML enable you to do all of these things. Adding, updating, and deleting data are all relatively straightforward operations. Retrieving the exact information you want out of the vast store of data that is not relevant to your current need can be more complicated. I give you only a quick look at retrieval here and go into more detail in Book III, Chapter 2.

Retrieving data from a database

The one operation that will be performed on a database more than any other is the retrieval of needed information. Data is placed into the database only once. It may never be updated, or at most only a few times. However, retrievals will be made constantly. After all, the main purpose of a database is to provide you with information when you want it. The SQL SELECT statement is the primary tool for extracting whatever information you want. Because the SELECT statement inquires about the contents of a table, it is called a *query*.

In its simplest form, a SELECT statement returns all the data in all the rows and columns in whatever table you specify. Here's an example:

```
SELECT * FROM PRODUCTS ;
```

The asterisk (*) is a wildcard character that means 'everything.' In this context, it means return data from all the columns in the PRODUCTS table. Because there is no restriction on which rows to return, all the data in all the rows of the table will be returned in the result set of the query.

I suppose there may be times when you want to see all the data in all the columns and all the rows in a table, but usually you will have a more specific question in mind. Perhaps you are not interested in seeing all the information about all the items in the PRODUCTS table right now, but are only interested in seeing the quantities in stock of all the guitars. You can restrict the result set that is returned by specifying the columns you want to see and by restricting the rows returned with a WHERE clause.

```
SELECT ProductID, ProductName, InStock
    FROM PRODUCTS
    WHERE Category = 'guitar' ;
```

This statement will return the product ID number, product name, and number in stock of all products in the guitar category, and nothing else. An ad hoc query such as this is a good way to get a quick answer to a question. Of course, there is a lot more to retrieving information than what I have covered briefly here. In Book III, Chapter 2, I will have a lot more to say on the subject.

Adding data to a table

Somehow, you have to get data into your database. This data may be records of sales transactions, employee personnel records, instrument readings coming in from interplanetary spacecraft, or just about anything you care to keep track of. The form that the data is in determines how it gets entered into the database.

Adding data the dull and boring way (typing it in)

If the data to be kept in the database was originally written down on paper, in order to get it into the database, it will have to be transcribed from the paper to computer memory by keying it in with a computer keyboard. This used to be the most frequently used method for entering data into a database because most data was initially captured on paper. People called data entry clerks worked from nine to five, typing data into computers. What a drag! It was pretty mind-deadening work. More recently, rather than first writing things down on paper, when a transaction occurs, it is entered directly into a point of sale terminal or computer. This is not nearly so bad because entering the data is only a small part of the total task.

The dullest and most boring way to enter data into a database is to enter one record at a time, using SQL INSERT statements. It works, if you have no alternative way to enter the data, and all other methods of entering data ultimately get translated into SQL INSERT statements, but after entering one or two records into the database this way, you will probably have had enough. Here's an example of such an INSERT operation:

```
INSERT INTO CUSTOMER (CustomerID, FirstName, LastName,
    Street, City, State, Zipcode, Phone)
    VALUES (:vcustid, 'Abe', 'Lincoln', '1600 Pennsylvania
    Avenue NW', 'Washington', 'DC', '20500', '202-555-1414') ;
```

The first value listed, :vcustid, is a variable that gets incremented each time a new record is added to the table. This guarantees that there will be no duplication of a value in the CustomerID field, which serves as the table's primary key. In a more realistic situation, all the values would be variables rather than the actual data items as shown. Rather than entering an INSERT statement into SQL, the data entry person would enter data values into fields on a form. The values would be captured into variables, which would then be used, out of sight of humans, to populate the VALUES clause of an INSERT statement.

Adding incomplete data

Sometimes you might want to add a record to a table before you have data for all the record's columns. As long as you have the primary key and data for all the columns that have a NOT NULL or UNIQUE constraint, you can enter the record. Because SQL allows null values in other columns, you can enter such a partial record now and fill in the missing information later. Here's an example of how to do it:

```
INSERT INTO CUSTOMER (CustomerID, FirstName, LastName)
    VALUES (:vcustid, 'Abe', 'Lincoln') ;
```

Adding data in the fastest and most efficient way: Bypassing typing altogether

Keying in a succession of SQL INSERT statements is the slowest and most tedious way to enter data into a database table. Entering data into fields on a video form on a computer monitor is not as bad because there is less typing and you probably have other things to do, such as talking to customers, checking in baggage, or consulting patient records.

Fast food outlets make matters even easier by giving you a special data entry panel rather than a keyboard. You can enter a double cheeseburger and a root beer float just by touching a couple of buttons. The correct information gets translated to SQL and put into the database and also gets sent back to the kitchen to tell the culinary staff what to do next.

If a business' data is inputted via a bar code scanner, the job is even faster and easier for the clerk. All he has to do is slide the merchandise past the scanner and listen for the beep that tells him the purchase has been registered. He doesn't have to know that besides printing the sales receipt, the data from the scan is being translated into SQL and then sent to a database.

Although the clerks at airline ticket counters, fast food restaurants, and supermarkets don't need to know anything about SQL, somebody does. In order to make the clerks' life easier, someone has to write programs that process the data coming in from keyboards, data entry pads, and bar code scanners, and send it to a database. Those programs are typically written in a general-purpose language such as C, Java, or Visual Basic, and incorporate SQL statements that are used in the actual 'conversation' with the database.

Updating data in a table

The world in the twenty-first century is a pretty dynamic place. Things are changing constantly, particularly in areas that involve technology. Data that was of value last week may be irrelevant tomorrow. Facts that were inconsequential a year ago may be critically important now. In order for a database to be useful, it must be capable of rapid change to match the rapidly changing piece of the world that it models. This means that in addition to the ability to add new records to a database table, you also need to be able to update the records that it already contains. With SQL, you do this with an UPDATE statement. With an UPDATE statement, you can change a single row in a table, a set of rows that share one or more characteristics, or all the rows in the table. Here's the generalized syntax:

```
UPDATE table_name
    SET column_1 = expression_1, column_2 = expression_2,
    ..., column_n = expression_n
    [WHERE predicates] ;
```

The SET clause specifies which columns will get new values and what those new values will be. The optional WHERE clause (square brackets indicate that the WHERE clause is optional) specifies which rows the update applies to. If there is no WHERE clause, the update is applied to all rows in the table.

Now for some examples. Consider the PRODUCT table shown in Table 5-1.

Table 5-1	PRODUCT Table		
ProductID	*Name*	*Category*	*Cost*
1664	Bike helmet	Helmets	20.00
1665	Motorcycle helmet	Helmets	30.00
1666	Bike gloves	Gloves	15.00
1667	Motorcycle gloves	Gloves	19.00
1668	Sport socks	Footwear	10.00

Now suppose the cost of bike helmets has gone up to $22.00. You can make that change in the database with the following UPDATE statement:

```
UPDATE PRODUCT
    SET Cost = 22.00
    WHERE Name = 'Bike helmet' ;
```

This statement makes a change in all rows where Name is equal to Bike helmet (Table 5-2).

Table 5-2	PRODUCT Table		
ProductID	*Name*	*Category*	*Cost*
1664	Bike helmet	Helmets	22.00
1665	Motorcycle helmet	Helmets	30.00

ProductID	Name	Category	Cost
1666	Bike gloves	Gloves	15.00
1667	Motorcycle gloves	Gloves	19.00
1668	Sport socks	Footwear	10.00

Because there is only one such row, only one is changed. If there is a possibility that more than one product might have the same name, you might erroneously update a row that you did not intend, along with the one that you did. To avoid this problem, assuming you know the ProductID of the item you want to change, you should use it in your WHERE clause. In a well-designed database, ProductID would be the primary key and thus guaranteed to be unique.

```
UPDATE PRODUCT
    SET Cost = 22.00
    WHERE ProductID = 1664 ;
```

You may want to update a select group of rows in a table. Suppose management decides that the Helmets category should be renamed as Headgear, to include hats and bandannas. You can change all the rows in the table that have a category of Helmets:

```
UPDATE PRODUCT
    SET Category = 'Headgear'
    WHERE Category = 'Helmets' ;
```

This would give you what is shown in Table 5-3:

Table 5-3	PRODUCT Table		
ProductID	Name	Category	Cost
1664	Bike helmet	Headgear	22.00
1665	Motorcycle helmet	Headgear	30.00
1666	Bike gloves	Gloves	15.00
1667	Motorcycle gloves	Gloves	19.00
1668	Sport socks	Footwear	10.00

Now suppose management decides it would be more efficient to lump headgear and gloves together into a single category named Accessories. Here's the UPDATE statement that will do that:

```
UPDATE PRODUCT
    SET Category = 'Accessories'
    WHERE Category = 'Headgear' OR Category = 'Gloves' ;
```

The result would be what is shown in Table 5-4:

Table 5-4	PRODUCT Table		
ProductID	*Name*	*Category*	*Cost*
1664	Bike helmet	Accessories	22.00
1665	Motorcycle helmet	Accessories	30.00
1666	Bike gloves	Accessories	15.00
1667	Motorcycle gloves	Accessories	19.00
1668	Sport socks	Footwear	10.00

All the headgear and gloves items are now considered accessories, but other categories, such as footwear, are unaffected.

Now suppose management sees that considerable savings have been achieved by merging the headgear and gloves categories. The decision is made that the company is actually in the active-wear business. To convert all company products to the new Active-wear category, a really simple UPDATE statement will do the trick:

```
UPDATE PRODUCT
    SET Category = 'Active-wear' ;
```

This produces the table shown in Table 5-5:

Table 5-5	PRODUCT Table		
ProductID	*Name*	*Category*	*Cost*
1664	Bike helmet	Active-wear	22.00
1665	Motorcycle helmet	Active-wear	30.00
1666	Bike gloves	Active-wear	15.00
1667	Motorcycle gloves	Active-wear	19.00
1668	Sport socks	Active-wear	10.00

Deleting data from a table

After you become really good at collecting data, your database starts to fill up with the stuff. With hard disk capacities getting bigger all the time, this may not seem like much of a problem. However, although you may never have to worry about filling up your new 2TB (that's 2,000,000,000,000 bytes) hard disk, the larger your database gets, the slower retrievals will become. If much of that data consists of rows that you will probably never need to access again, it makes sense to remove it. Financial information from the previous fiscal year after the books have been closed on it does not need to be in your active database. You may have to keep such data for a period of years to meet government regulatory requirements. If so, you can keep it in an off-line archive rather than burdening your active database with it. Additionally, data of a confidential nature may present a legal liability if compromised. If you no longer need it, get rid of it. With SQL, this is easy to do. First, decide whether you need to archive the data that you are about to delete. After that is taken care of, deletion can be as simple as this:

```
DELETE FROM TRANSACTION
    WHERE TransDate < '2007-01-01' ;
```

Poof! All of last year's transaction records are gone, and your database is speedy again. You can be as selective as you need to be with the WHERE clause, and delete all the records you want to delete and only the records you want to delete.

Updating views

Although ANSI/ISO standard SQL makes it possible to update a view, it rarely makes sense to do so. Recall that a view is a virtual table. It does not have any existence apart from the table or tables that it draws columns from. If you want to update a view, updating the underlying table will accomplish your intent and avoid problems in the process. Problems? What problems? Consider a view that draws salary and commission data from the SALES-PERSON table:

```
CREATE VIEW TOTALPAY (EmployeeName, Pay)
    AS SELECT EmployeeName, Salary + Commission AS Pay
    FROM SALESPERSON ;
```

The view TOTALPAY has two columns, EmployeeName and Pay. The Pay column is created by adding together the values in the Salary and the Commission columns in the SALESPERSON table. This is fine, as long as you don't ever need to update the virtual Pay column, like this:

```
UPDATE TOTALPAY SET PAY = PAY + 100
```

You may think you are giving all the salespeople a hundred dollar raise. Instead, you are just generating an error message. The data in the TOTALPAY view isn't stored as such on the system. It is stored in the SALESPERSON table, and the SALESPERSON table does not have a Pay column. Salary + Commission is an expression, and you cannot update an expression.

Another source of potential problems is views that draw data from more than one table. If you try to update such a view, even if expressions are not involved, the database engine may get confused about which of the underlying tables to apply the update to.

The lesson here is that although it is possible to update views, it is generally not a good practice to do so. Update the underlying tables instead, even if it causes you to make a few more keystrokes. You will have fewer problems in the long run.

The Data Control Language (DCL)

The third major component of SQL performs a function that is just as important as the functions performed by the DDL and the DML. The Data Control Language consists of statements that protect your precious data from misuse, misappropriation, corruption, and destruction. It would be a shame to go to all the trouble of creating a database and filling it with data that is critical to your business, and then have the whole thing destroyed. It would be even worse to have the data end up in the possession of your fiercest competitor. The DCL gives you the tools to address all those concerns. I discuss the DCL in detail in Book IV, Chapter 3. For now, here's an overview.

Granting access privileges

Most organizations have several different kinds of data with several different levels of sensitivity. Some data, such as the retail price list for your company's products, doesn't cause any problems even if everyone in the world can see it. In fact, you probably want everyone out there to see your retail price list. Somebody might buy something. On the other hand, you don't want unauthorized people to be making changes to your retail price list. You might find yourself giving away product for under your cost. Data of a more confidential nature, such as personal information about your employees or customers, should be accessible to only those who have a legitimate need to know about it. Finally, some forms of access, such as the ability to erase the entire database, should be restricted to a very small number of highly trusted individuals.

You have complete control over who has access to the various elements of a database, as well as what level of access they have, by using the GRANT statement. The GRANT statement gives you a fine-grained ability to grant specific privileges to specific individuals or to well-defined groups of individuals.

One example might be

```
GRANT SELECT ON PRICELIST TO PUBLIC ;
```

The PUBLIC keyword means everyone. No one is left out when you grant access to the public. The particular kind of access here, SELECT, enables people to retrieve the data in the price list, but not to change it in any way.

Revoking access privileges

If it is possible to grant access to someone, it better be possible to revoke those privileges too. People's jobs change within an organization, requiring different access privileges than those that were appropriate before the change. An employee may even leave the company and go to a competitor. Privilege revocation is especially important in such cases. The REVOKE statement does the job. Its syntax is almost identical to the syntax of the GRANT statement. Only its action is reversed.

```
REVOKE SELECT ON PRICELIST FROM PUBLIC ;
```

Now the pricelist is no longer accessible to the general public.

Preserving database integrity with transactions

Two problems that can damage database integrity are

✦ **System failures:** Suppose you are performing a complex, multi-step operation on a database when the system goes down. Some changes have been made to the database, and others have not. After you get back on the air, the database is no longer in the condition it was in before you started your operation, and it is not yet in the condition you hoped to achieve at the end of your operation. It is in some unknown intermediate state that is almost surely wrong.

✦ **Interactions between users:** When two users of the database are operating on the same data at the same time, they can interfere with each other. This interference can slow them both down or, even worse, the changes each makes to the database can get mixed up, resulting in incorrect data being stored.

The common solution to both these problems is to use transactions. A *transaction* is a unit of work that has both a beginning and an end. If a transaction is interrupted between the beginning and the end, after operation resumes, all the changes to the database made during the transaction are reversed in a ROLLBACK operation, returning the database to the condition it was in before the transaction started. Now the transaction can be repeated, assuming whatever caused the interruption has been corrected.

Transactions can also help eliminate harmful interactions between simultaneous users. If one user has access to a resource such as a row in a database table, other users cannot access that row until the first user's transaction has been completed with a COMMIT operation. In Book IV, Chapter 2, I discuss these important issues in considerable detail.

Chapter 6: SQL Characteristics

In This Chapter

✔ Executing SQL statements

✔ Using (and misusing) reserved words

✔ Working with SQL's data types

✔ Handling null values

✔ Applying constraints

*I*n this chapter, I get into the nitty-gritty of SQL. This is background knowledge you need to master before you embark on actually writing SQL statements. SQL has some similarities to computer languages you may already be familiar with, and some important differences. I touch on some of these similarities and differences in this chapter. I discuss others later when I get to the appropriate points in a complete discussion of SQL.

Executing SQL Statements

SQL is not a complete language, but a data sub-language. As such, you cannot write a "program" in the SQL language like you can with C or Java. There are several ways that you *can* use SQL. If you have a query editor up on your screen and all you want is the answer to a simple question, you can type an SQL query into your keyboard, and the answer, in the form of one or more lines of data, appears on your screen. This mode of operation is called *interactive SQL.*

If your needs are more complex, you have two additional ways of making SQL queries:

✦ You can write a program in a "host" language, such as C or Java, and embed single SQL statements here and there in the program as needed. This mode of operation is called *embedded SQL.*

✦ You can write a module containing SQL statements in the form of procedures. Call these procedures from a program written in a language such as C or Java. This mode of operation is called *module language.*

Interactive SQL

Interactive SQL consists of entering SQL statements into a database management system such as SQL Server, Oracle, or DB2. The DBMS then performs the commands specified by the statements. You could build a database from scratch this way, starting with a CREATE DATABASE statement, and building everything from there. You could fill it with data, and then type queries to selectively pull information out of it.

Although it is possible to do everything you need to do to a database with interactive SQL, this approach has a couple of disadvantages:

✦ It can get awfully tedious to enter everything in the form of SQL statements from the keyboard.

✦ Only people fluent in the SQL language can operate on the database, and most people have never even heard of SQL, let alone are able to use it effectively.

SQL *is* the only language that most relational databases understand, so there is no getting around using it. However, the people who interact with databases the most, those that ask questions of the data, do not need to be exposed to naked SQL. They can be protected from that intimidating prospect by wrapping the SQL in a blanket of code written in another language. With that other language, a programmer can generate screens, forms, menus, and other familiar objects for the user to interact with. Ultimately, those things translate the user's actions to SQL code that the DBMS understands, the desired information is retrieved, and the user sees the result.

Challenges to combining SQL with a host language

SQL has some fundamental differences from host languages that you might want to combine it with:

✦ **SQL is non-procedural.** One basic feature of all common host languages is that they are procedural, meaning that programs written in those languages execute procedures in a step-by-step fashion. They deal with data the same way, one row at a time. Because SQL is non-procedural, it does whatever it is going to do all at once and deals with data a set of rows at a time. Procedural programmers coming to SQL for the first time need to adjust their thinking in order to use SQL effectively as a data manipulation and retrieval tool.

✦ **SQL recognizes different data types than does whatever host language you are using with it.** Because there are a large number of languages out there that could serve as host languages for SQL, and the data types of any one of them do not necessarily agree with the data types of any other, the committee that created the ANSI/ISO standard defined the data types for SQL that they thought would be most useful, without referring to the data types recognized by any of the potential host languages. This data type incompatibility presents a problem if you want to perform calculations with your host language on data that was retrieved from a database with SQL. The problem is not serious; you just need to be aware of it. SQL provides the CAST statement for translating one data type into another.

Embedded SQL

By far, the most common form of SQL is embedded SQL. This method uses a general-purpose computer language such as C, Java, or Visual Basic to write the bulk of an application. Such languages are great for creating an application's user interface. They can create forms with buttons and menus. They can format reports. They can perform calculations. They can do all the things that SQL cannot do. In a database application, however, sooner or later, the database must be accessed. That is a job for SQL.

It makes sense to write the application in a host language, and, when needed, drop in SQL statements to interact with the data. It is the best of both worlds. The host language does what it is best at, and the embedded SQL does what it is best at. The only downside to the cooperative arrangement is that the host language compiler will not recognize the SQL code when it encounters it and will issue an error message. To avoid this problem, a pre-compiler processes the SQL before the host language compiler takes over. When everything works, this is a great arrangement. Before everything works, however, debugging can be tough because a host language debugger doesn't know how to handle any SQL that it encounters. Nevertheless, embedded SQL remains the most popular way to create database applications.

For example, look at a fragment of C code that contains embedded SQL statements. This particular fragment is written in Oracle's Pro*C dialect of the C language. It is code that might be found in an organization's human resources department, which authenticates and logs on a user, and then enables the user to change the salary and commission information for an employee.

```
EXEC SQL BEGIN DECLARE SECTION;
     VARCHAR uid[20];
     VARCHAR pwd[20];
     VARCHAR ename[10];
     FLOAT salary, comm;
     SHORT salary_ind, comm_ind;
EXEC SQL END DECLARE SECTION;
main()
{
     int sret;              /* scanf return code */
```

```
      /* Log in */
      strcpy(uid.arr,"Mary");     /* copy the user name */
      uid.len=strlen(uid.arr);
      strcpy(pwd.arr,"Bennett");    /* copy the password */
      pwd.len=strlen(pwd.arr);
      EXEC SQL WHENEVER SQLERROR STOP;
      EXEC SQL WHENEVER NOT FOUND STOP;
      EXEC SQL CONNECT :uid;
      printf("Connected to user: percents \n",uid.arr);
      printf("Enter employee name to update:  ");
      scanf("percents",ename.arr);
      ename.len=strlen(ename.arr);
      EXEC SQL SELECT SALARY,COMM INTO :salary,:comm
              FROM EMPLOY
              WHERE ENAME=:ename;
    printf("Employee: percents salary: percent6.2f comm:
percent6.2f \n",
          ename.arr, salary, comm);
    printf("Enter new salary:  ");
    sret=scanf("percentf",&salary);
    salary_ind = 0;
    if (sret == EOF !! sret == 0)    /* set indicator */
        salary_ind =-1;      /* Set indicator for NULL */
    printf("Enter new commission:  ");
    sret=scanf("percentf",&comm);
    comm_ind = 0;    /* set indicator */
    if (sret == EOF !! sret == 0)
        comm_ind=-1;         /* Set indicator for NULL */
    EXEC SQL UPDATE EMPLOY
            SET SALARY=:salary:salary_ind
            SET COMM=:comm:comm_ind
            WHERE ENAME=:ename;
    printf("Employee percents updated. \n",ename.arr);
    EXEC SQL COMMIT WORK;
    exit(0);
}
```

Here's a closer look at what the code does:

✦ First comes an SQL declaration section, where variables are declared.

✦ Next, C code accepts a user name and password.

✦ A couple of SQL error traps follow, and then a connection to the database is established.

✦ C code prints out some messages and accepts the name of the employee whose record will be changed.

✦ SQL retrieves that employee's salary and commission data.

+ C displays the salary and commission data and solicits new salary and commission data.

+ SQL updates the database with the new data.

+ C displays a successful completion message.

+ SQL commits the transaction.

+ C terminates the program.

Note that every SQL statement is introduced with an EXEC SQL directive. This is a clue to the compiler not to try to compile what follows, but instead to pass it directly to the DBMS' database engine.

Module language

Module language is similar to embedded SQL in that it combines the strengths of SQL with those of a host language. However, it does it in a slightly different way. All the SQL code is stored in a module that is separate from the host language program. The SQL is in the form of procedures. Whenever the host language program needs to perform a database operation, it calls a procedure from the SQL module to do the job. With this arrangement, there is no SQL in the main program, so the host language compiler has no problem and neither does the debugger. All they see is host language code, including the procedure calls. The procedures themselves cause no difficulty because they are in a separate module and the compiler and debugger just skip over them.

Another advantage of module language over embedded SQL is due to the fact that the SQL code is separated from the host language code. Because high skill in both SQL and any given host language is rare, it is difficult to find good people to program embedded SQL applications. Because a module language implementation separates the languages, you can hire the best SQL programmer to write the SQL and the best host language programmer to write the host language code. Neither one has to be an expert in the other language.

You can declare a module with the following syntax:

```
MODULE [module-name]
   [NAMES ARE character-set-name]
   LANGUAGE {ADA|C|COBOL|FORTRAN|MUMPS|PASCAL|PLI|SQL}
   [SCHEMA schema-name]
   [AUTHORIZATION authorization-id]
   [temporary-table-declarations...]
   [cursor-declarations...]
   [dynamic-cursor-declarations...]
   procedures...
```

The MODULE declaration is mandatory, but the module name is not. It is a good idea to name your modules anyway, just to reduce the confusion. With the optional NAMES ARE clause, you can specify a character set. The default character set will be used if you don't include a NAMES ARE clause. You must specify a host language. Each language has different expectations about what the procedure will look like, so the LANGUAGE clause determines the format of the procedures in the module.

Although the SCHEMA clause and the AUTHORIZATION clause are both optional, you must specify at least one of them. The AUTHORIZATION clause is a security feature. If your authorization ID does not carry sufficient privileges, you will not be allowed to use the procedures in the module.

If any of the procedures use temporary tables, cursors, or dynamic cursors, they must be declared before they are used. I talk about cursors in Chapter 5 of Book III.

Using Reserved Words Correctly

SQL has command words such as CREATE and ALTER. Clearly, it's unwise to use these same words at the names of tables or variables. To do so is a guaranteed way to confuse your DBMS. In addition to such command words, a number of other words also have a special meaning in SQL. These *reserved words* should also not be used for any purpose other than the one for which they are designed. Consider the following SQL statement:

```
SELECT CustomerID, FirstName, LastName
    FROM Customer
    WHERE CustomerID < 1000;
```

SELECT is a command word, and FROM and WHERE are reserved words. SQL has hundreds of reserved words, and you must be careful not to inadvertently use any of them as the names of objects or variables. Appendix A of this book contains a list of reserved words in ANSI/ISO standard SQL.

SQL's Data Types

SQL is capable of dealing with data of many different types. From the beginning, SQL has been able to handle the common types of numeric and character data. More recently, new types have been added that enable SQL to deal with non-traditional data types. At present, there are 11 major categories of data types. Within each category, one or more specific types may exist. Some implementations of SQL may include data types not mentioned here.

These additional types are not mentioned in the ANSI/ISO standard and thus are not guaranteed to be available in other implementations. To maximize portability for your applications, stick to the standard types. Here's a brief description of each of the categories and the standard types they include.

Exact numerics

Because computers store numbers in registers of finite size, there is a limit to how large or small a number can be and still be represented exactly. There is a range of numbers centered on zero that can be represented exactly. The size of that range depends on the size of the registers that the numbers are stored in. Thus a machine with 64-bit registers can exactly represent a range of numbers that is wider than the range that can be exactly represented on a machine with 32-bit registers. There are six standard exact numeric data types. They are

✦ INTEGER

✦ SMALLINT

✦ BIGINT

✦ NUMERIC

✦ DECIMAL

✦ BINARY LARGE OBJECT (BLOB)

INTEGER

Data of the INTEGER type is numeric data that has no fractional part. Any given implementation of SQL will have a limit to the number of digits that an integer can have. If for some reason, you want to specify a maximum size for an integer that is less than the default maximum, you can restrict the maximum number of digits by specifying a *precision* argument. By declaring a variable as having type INTEGER (10), you are saying numbers of this type can have no more than ten digits, even if the system you are running on is capable of handling more digits. Of course, if you specify a precision that exceeds the maximum capacity of the system, you will not get it. You cannot magically expand the sizes of the hardware registers in a machine with an SQL declaration.

If there is a possibility that sometime in the future, your application may be ported to a system that has a different default precision for exact numeric numbers, you should specify a precision. That way, the precision you have planned on will carry over to the new system. If you rely on the default precision, and the default precision of the system you port to is different, your operations may produce different results from those produced by your original system.

SMALLINT

The SMALLINT data type is similar to the INTEGER type, but how it differs from the INTEGER type is implementation-dependant. It may not differ from the INTEGER type at all. The only constraint on the SMALLINT type is that its precision may be no larger than the precision of the INTEGER type.

For systems where the precision of the SMALLINT type actually is less than the precision of the INTEGER type, it may be advantageous to specify variables as being of the SMALLINT type if you can be sure that the values of those variables will never exceed the precision of the SMALLINT type. This saves you some storage space. If storage space is not an issue, or if you cannot be absolutely sure that the value of a variable will never exceed the precision of the SMALLINT type, you may be better off specifying it as being of the INTEGER type.

BIGINT

The BIGINT type is similar to the SMALLINT type. The only difference is that the precision of the BIGINT type can be no *smaller* than the precision of the INTEGER type. As is the case with SMALLINT, the precision of the BIGINT type could be the same as the precision of the INTEGER type.

If the precision of the BIGINT type for any given implementation is actually larger than the precision of the INTEGER type, a variable of the BIGINT type will take up more storage space than a variable of the INTEGER type. Only use the BIGINT type if there is a possibility that the size of a variable may exceed the precision of the INTEGER type.

NUMERIC

Data of the numeric type *does* have a fractional part. This means the number contains a decimal point and zero or more digits to the right of the decimal point. For NUMERIC data, you can specify both precision and scale. The *scale* of a number is the number of digits to the right of the decimal point. For example, a variable declared as of type NUMERIC (10, 2) would have a maximum of ten digits, with two of those digits to the right of the decimal point. The largest number you can represent with this type is 99,999,999.99. If the system you are running on happens to be able to handle numbers with precision greater than ten, only the precision you specify will be used.

DECIMAL

Data of the DECIMAL type is similar to data of the NUMERIC type with one difference. For data of the DECIMAL type, if the system you are running on happens to be able to handle numbers with larger precision than what you have specified, the extra precision will be used.

The NUMERIC data type is better if portability is a possibility. When you use the NUMERIC type, you can be sure the precision you specify will be the precision that is used, regardless of the capabilities of the system. This ensures consistent results across diverse platforms.

BINARY LARGE OBJECT (BLOB)

The BINARY LARGE OBJECT (BLOB) type is not normally considered an exact numeric type. However, that is what it essentially is. It is a large binary number. That large binary number may represent a graphical image, or something else that doesn't seem to be a number. However, at the most fundamental level, it is a number.

The BLOB type is a relatively recent addition to the ANSI/ISO standard that was added to reflect the reality that more and more of the things that people want to store in databases do not fall into the classical categories of being either numbers or text. You cannot perform arithmetic operations on BLOB data, but at least you can store it in a relational database and perform some elementary operations on it.

Approximate numerics

The approximate numeric types exist so you can represent numbers that are either too large or too small to be represented by an exact numeric type. If, for example, a system has 32-bit registers, the largest number that can be represented with an exact numeric type is the largest number that can be represented with 32 binary digits. That number is composed of 32 binary ones, or 4,294,967,295 in decimal. If you have to deal with numbers larger than that, you must move to approximate numerics. This may not be much of a hardship: For most applications, after you get above 4 billion, approximations are good enough.

Similarly, values that are very close to zero cannot be represented with exact numerics either. The smallest number that can be represented exactly on a 32-bit machine has a one in the least significant bit position and zeros everywhere else. This is a very small number, but there a lot of numbers of interest, particularly in science, that are smaller. For such numbers, you must also rely on approximate numerics.

REAL

The REAL data type is what you would normally use for single-precision floating-point numbers. The exact meaning of the term *single precision* depends on the implementation. This is hardware-dependent, and a machine with 64-bit registers will, in general, have a larger precision than a machine with 32-bit registers. How much larger may vary from one implementation to another.

A floating-point number is a number that contains a radix point. In the case of decimal numbers, that means a decimal point. The decimal point could appear anywhere in the number, which is why it is called floating. 2.7, 2.73, 27.3, and 2735.53894 are all examples of floating-point numbers. Although we humans are accustomed to seeing numbers expressed in this form, approximate numerics are expressed as a combination of a mantissa and an exponent. This form is a little less user friendly, but enables the approximate representation of very large and very small numbers in a compact form. 6.626×10^{-34} is an approximation of Planck's constant, a very small number. 6.626 is the mantissa, and -34 is the exponent. It would not be possible to represent a number that small exactly with any currently existing hardware.

DOUBLE PRECISION

A double-precision number on any given system has greater precision than a real number on the same system. However, despite the name, a double-precision number does not necessarily have twice the precision of a real number. The most that can be said in general is that a double-precision number on any given system has greater precision than does a real number on the same system. On some systems, a double-precision number may have a larger mantissa than does a real number. On other systems, a double-precision number may support a larger exponent (absolute value). On yet other systems, both mantissa and exponent of a double-precision number may be larger than for a real number. You will have to look at the specifications for whatever system you are using to find out what is true for you.

FLOAT

The FLOAT data type is very similar to the REAL data type. The difference is that with the FLOAT data type you can specify a precision. With the REAL and DOUBLE PRECISION data types, the default precision is your only option. Because the default precision of these data types can vary from one system to another, porting your application from one system to another could be a problem. With the FLOAT data type, specifying the precision of an attribute on one machine guarantees that the precision will be maintained after porting the application to another machine. If a system's hardware supports double-precision operations and the application requires double-precision operations, the FLOAT data type will automatically use the double-precision circuitry. If single-precision is sufficient, it will use that.

Character strings

After numbers, the next most common thing to be stored is strings of alphanumeric characters. SQL provides several character string types, each with somewhat different characteristics from the others. The three main types are CHARACTER, CHARACTER VARYING, and CHARACTER LARGE OBJECT. These three types are mirrored by NATIONAL CHARACTER, NATIONAL CHARACTER VARYING, and NATIONAL CHARACTER LARGE OBJECT, which deal with character sets other than the default character set, which is usually the character set of the English language.

CHARACTER

A column defined as being of type CHARACTER or CHAR can contain any of the normal alphanumeric characters of the language being used. A column definition also includes the maximum length allowed for an item of the CHAR type. Consider this example:

```
Name      CHAR (15)
```

This field can hold a name that is up to 15 characters long. If the name is less than 15 characters long, the remaining spaces are filled with blank characters to bring to total length up to 15. Thus a CHARACTER field always takes up the same amount of space in memory, regardless of how long the actual data item in the field is.

CHARACTER VARYING

The CHARACTER VARYING or VARCHAR data type is like the CHARACTER type in all respects except that short entries are not padded out with blanks to fill the field to the stated maximum.

```
Name      VARCHAR (15)
```

The VARCHAR data type doesn't add blanks on the end of a name. Thus if the Name field contains 'Joe', the length of the field that is stored will be only three characters rather than fifteen.

CHARACTER LARGE OBJECT (CLOB)

Any implementation of SQL has a limit to the number of characters that are allowed in a CHARACTER or CHARACTER VARYING field. For example, the maximum length of a character string in Oracle 10g is 1,024 characters. If you want to store text that goes beyond that limit, you can use the CHARACTER LARGE OBJECT data type. The CLOB type is much less flexible than either the CHAR or VARCHAR types in that it does not allow you to do many of the fine-grained manipulations that you can do in those other types. You can compare two CLOB items for equality, but that is about all you can do. With CHARACTER type data you can, for instance, scan a string for the first occurrence of the letter W, and display where in the string it occurs. This type of operation is not possible with CHARACTER LARGE OBJECT data. Here's an example of the declaration of a CHARACTER LARGE OBJECT:

```
Dream    CLOB (8721)
```

Another restriction on CLOB data is that a CLOB data item may not be used as a primary key or a foreign key. Furthermore, you cannot apply the UNIQUE constraint to an item of the CLOB type. The bottom line is that the CLOB data type enables you to store and retrieve large blocks of text, but not to do much with them beyond that.

NATIONAL CHARACTER, NATIONAL CHARACTER VARYING, and NATIONAL CHARACTER LARGE OBJECT

Different languages use different character sets. For example, Spanish and German have letters with diacritical marks that change the way the letter is pronounced. Other languages, such as Russian, have an entirely different character set. To store character strings that contain these different character sets, the National character types have been added to SQL. If the English character type is the default on your system, as it is for most people, you can designate a different character set as your national character set. From that point on, when you specify a data type as NATIONAL CHARACTER, NATIONAL CHARACTER VARYING, or NATIONAL CHARACTER LARGE OBJECT, items in columns so specified use the national character set rather than the default character set.

In addition to whatever national character set you specify, you can use multiple other character sets in a table definition, by specifying them explicitly. Here's an example where the national character set is Russian:

```
CREATE TABLE BOOK_TITLE_TRANSLATIONS (
    English      CHARACTER (40),
    Greek        VARCHAR (40)            CHARACTER SET GREEK,
    Russian      NATIONAL CHARACTER (40),
    Japanese     CHARACTER (40)          CHARACTER SET KANJI
) ;
```

Some implementations may not support all the character sets. For example, MySQL does not currently support Kanji.

Booleans

A column of the BOOLEAN data type, named after nineteenth-century English mathematician George Boole, will accept any one of three values: TRUE, FALSE, and UNKNOWN. The fact that SQL entertains the possibility of NULL values expands the traditional restriction of Boolean values from just TRUE and FALSE to TRUE, FALSE, and UNKNOWN. If a Boolean TRUE or FALSE value is compared to a NULL value, the result is UNKNOWN. Of course, comparing a Boolean UNKNOWN value to any value also gives an UNKNOWN result.

Datetimes

You often need to store either dates, times, or both, in addition to numeric and character data. ANSI/ISO standard SQL defines five datetime types. Because considerable overlap exists among the five types, not all implementations of SQL include all five types. This could cause problems if you try to migrate a database from a platform that uses one subset of the five types to a platform that uses a different subset. There is not much you can do about this except deal with it when it arises.

DATE

The DATE data type is the one to use, if you care about the date, but not the time of day within a date. The DATE data type stores a year, month, and day in that order, using ten character positions in the form yyyy-mm-dd. If you were recording the dates that humans have landed on the Moon, the entry for Apollo 11 would be 1969-07-20.

TIME WITHOUT TIME ZONE

Suppose you want to store the time of day, but don't care which day, and furthermore, don't even care which time zone the time refers to? In that case the TIME WITHOUT TIME ZONE data type is for you. It stores hours, minutes, and seconds. The hours and minutes data occupies two digits apiece. The seconds data also occupies two digits, but in addition may include a fractional part for fractions of a second. If you specify a column as being of TIME WITHOUT TIME ZONE type, with no parameter, it will hold a time that has no fractional seconds. An example would be: 02:56:31, which is fifty-six minutes and thirty-one seconds after two in the morning.

For greater precision in storing a time value, you can use a parameter to specify the number of digits beyond the decimal point that will be stored for seconds. Here's an example of such a definition:

```
Smallstep          TIME WITHOUT TIME ZONE (2),
```

In this example, there are two digits past the decimal point, so time is measured down to a hundredth of a second. It would take the form of 02:56:31.17.

TIME WITH TIME ZONE

The TIME WITH TIME ZONE data type gives you all the information that you get in the TIME WITHOUT TIME ZONE data type, and adds the additional fact of what time zone the time refers to. All time zones around the Earth are referenced to Universal Time (UTC), formerly known as Greenwich Mean Time (GMT). Universal Time is the time in Greenwich, UK, which was the place where people first started being concerned with highly accurate timekeeping. Of course, the United Kingdom is a fairly small country, so UTC is in effect throughout the entire UK. In fact, a huge "watermelon slice" of the Earth, running from the North Pole to the South Pole, is also in the same time zone as Greenwich. There are 24 such slices that girdle the Earth. Times around the earth range from 11 hours and 59 minutes behind UTC to 12 hours ahead of UTC (not counting Daylight Savings Time). If Daylight Savings Time is in effect, the offset from UTC could be as much as -12:59 or +13:00. The International Date Line is theoretically exactly opposite Greenwich on the other side of the world, but is offset in spots so as to keep some countries in one time zone.

TIMESTAMP WITHOUT TIME ZONE

Just as sometimes you will need to record dates, and other times you will need to record times, it's certain that there will also be times when you need to store both times and dates. That is what the TIMESTAMP WITHOUT TIME ZONE data type is for. It is a combination of the DATE type and the TIME WITHOUT TIMEZONE type. The one difference between this data type and the TIME WITHOUT TIMEZONE type is that the default value for fractions of a second is six digits rather than zero. You can, of course specify zero fractional digits, if that is what you want. Suppose you specified a database table column as follows:

```
Smallstep        TIMESTAMP WITHOUT TIME ZONE (0),
```

A valid value for Smallstep would be 1969-07-21 02:56:31. That was the date and time in Greenwich when Neil Armstrong's foot first touched the lunar soil. It consists of ten date characters, a blank space separator, and eight time characters.

TIMESTAMP WITH TIME ZONE

If you have to record the time zone that a date and time refers to, use the TIMESTAMP WITH TIME ZONE data type. It is the same as the TIMSESTAMP WITHOUT TIME ZONE data type, with the addition of an offset that shows the time's relationship to Universal Time. Here's an example:

```
Smallstep        TIMESTAMP WITH TIME ZONE (0),
```

In this case, Smallstep might be recorded as 1969-07-20 20:56:31-05:00. That is the date and time in Houston when Neil Armstrong's foot first touched the lunar soil. Houston time is normally six hours ahead of Greenwich time, but, in July, it is only five hours ahead due to Daylight Savings Time.

Intervals

An interval is the difference between two dates, two times, or two datetimes. There are two different kinds of intervals, the year-month interval and the day-hour-minute-second interval. A day always has 24 hours. An hour always has 60 minutes. A minute always has 60 seconds. However, a month may have 28, 29, 30, or 31 days. Because of that variability, you cannot mix the two kinds of intervals. A field of the INTERVAL type can store the difference in time between two instants in the same month, but cannot store an interval such as two years, seven months, thirteen days, five hours, six minutes, and forty-five seconds.

XML type

The SQL/XML:2003 update to the ANSI/ISO SQL standard introduced the XML data type. Values in the XML type are XML values, meaning you can now manage and query XML data in an SQL database. SQL/XML:2006 moves to the XQuery Data Model. This means that any XML value is also an XQuery sequence. The details of the XQuery Data Model are beyond the scope of this book. Refer to *Querying XML* by Jim Melton and Stephen Buxton (published by Morgan Kaufmann) for detailed coverage of this topic.

In SQL/XML:2006, three subtypes of the XML type were defined. They are XML(SEQUENCE), XML(CONTENT), and XML(DOCUMENT). The three subtypes are related to each other hierarchically. An XML(SEQUENCE) is any sequence of XML nodes, XML values, or both. An XML(CONTENT) is an XML(SEQUENCE) that is an XML fragment wrapped in a document node. An XML(DOCUMENT) is an XML(CONTENT) that is a well-formed XML document.

Every XML value is at least an XML(SEQUENCE). An XML(SEQUENCE) that is a Document node is an XML(CONTENT). An XML(CONTENT) that has legal Document children is an XML(DOCUMENT).

XML types may be associated with an XML Schema. There are three possibilities:

✦ UNTYPED: There is no associated XML Schema

✦ XMLSCHEMA: There is an associated XML Schema

✦ ANY: There may or may not be an associated XML Schema

So a document of type XML(DOCUMENT(ANY)) may or may not have an associated XML Schema. If you specify a column as being of type XML with no modifiers, it must be either `XML(SEQUENCE)`, `XML(CONTENT(ANY))`, or `XML(CONTENT(UNTYPED))`. Which of those it is depends on the implementation.

Row types

Row types, introduced in the 1999 version of the ANSI/ISO SQL standard (SQL:1999), represent the first break of SQL away from the relational model, as defined by its creator, E. F. Codd. With the introduction of this type, SQL databases can no longer be considered pure relational databases. One of the defining characteristics of Codd's First Normal Form (1NF) is the fact that no field in a table row may be multi-valued. Multi-valued fields are exactly what the `ROW` type introduces. The `ROW` type enables you to place a whole row's worth of data into a single field, effectively nesting a row within a row. To see how this works, create a `ROW` type:

```
CREATE ROW TYPE address_type (
    Street      VARCHAR (25),
    City        VARCHAR (20),
    State       CHAR (2),
    PostalCode  VARCHAR (9)
    ) ;
```

This code effectively compresses four attributes into a single type. After you have created a Row type, you can use it in a table definition:

```
CREATE TABLE VENDOR (
    VendorID     INTEGER PRIMARY KEY,
    VendorName   VARCHAR (25),
    Address      address_type,
    Phone        VARCHAR (15)
) ;
```

If you have tables for multiple groups, such as vendors, employees, customers, stockholders, or prospects, you have to declare only one attribute rather than four. That may not seem like much of a savings, but you are not limited to putting four attributes into a Row type. What if you had to type in the same forty attributes into a hundred tables?

First appearing in SQL:1999, the `ROW` type, like many other aspects of SQL that have been added relatively recently, has not yet been included into many of the most popular implementations of SQL. Even Oracle, which is one of the closest implementations to the ANSI/ISO standard, does not support the `ROW` type.

Collection types

The introduction of ROW types in SQL:1999 was not the only break from the ironclad rules of relational database theory. In that same standard, the ARRAY type was introduced. Then in SQL:2003 the MULTISET type was added. Both of these collection types violate 1NF and thus take SQL databases a couple of steps further away from relational purity.

ARRAY

The ARRAY type violates 1NF, but not in the same way that the ROW type does. The ARRAY type enables you to enhance a field of an existing type by putting more than one entry into it. This creates a repeating group, which was demonized in Codd's original formulation of the relational model, but now reappears as a desirable feature. Arrays are ordered in the sense that each element in the array corresponds to exactly one ordinal position in the array.

As an example, suppose you want to have alternate ways of contacting your vendors in case the main telephone number does not work for you. Perhaps you would like the option of storing as many as four telephone numbers, just to be safe. A slight modification to the code shown above will do the trick.

```
CREATE TABLE VENDOR (
    VendorID     INTEGER PRIMARY KEY,
    VendorName   VARCHAR (25),
    Address      address_type,
    Phone        VARCHAR (15)  ARRAY [4]
) ;
```

When he created the relational model, Dr. Codd made a conscious decision to sacrifice some functional flexibility in exchange for enhanced data integrity. The addition of the ARRAY type, along with the ROW type and later the MULTISET type, takes back some of that flexibility in exchange for added complexity. That added complexity could lead to data integrity problems if it is not handled correctly.

Multiset

Whereas an array is an ordered collection of elements, a multiset is an unordered collection. You cannot reference individual elements in a multiset because you don't know where they are located in the collection.

REF types

REF types are different from distinct data types such as INTEGER or CHARACTER. Rather than holding values, they reference locations that hold values. Furthermore, REF types are not a part of core SQL. This means that database vendors can claim compliance with the SQL standard without implementing REF types. An item of the REF type is a pointer to a data item, row type, or abstract data type that resides in a site in a table. Dereferencing the pointer can retrieve the value stored at the target site.

The REF type is an aspect of the object-oriented nature of SQL since the SQL:1999 standard. If object-oriented programming seems obscure to you, as it does to many programmers of a more traditional bent, you can probably survive quite well without ever needing the REF type.

User-defined types

User-defined types (UDTs) are another addition to SQL imported from the world of object-oriented programming. If the data types that I have enumerated above are not enough for you, you can define your own data types. To do so, use the principles of abstract data types (ADTs) that are major features of such object-oriented languages as C++.

SQL is not a complete programming language, and as such must be used with a host language that is complete, such as C. One of the problems with this arrangement is that the data types of the host language often do not match the data types of SQL. User-defined types come to the rescue here. You can define a type that matches the corresponding type in the host language.

The object-oriented nature of UDTs becomes evident when you see that a UDT has attributes and methods encapsulated within it. The attribute definitions and the results of the methods are visible to the outside world, but the ways the methods are implemented are hidden from view. You can declare attributes and methods to be public, private, or protected. A *public* attribute or method is available to anyone who uses the UDT. A *private* attribute or method may be used only by the UDT itself. A *protected* attribute or method may be used only by the UDT itself and its subtypes. If this sounds familiar to you, don't be surprised. An SQL UDT is much like a class in object-oriented programming. There are two kinds of UDTs: distinct types and structured types.

Distinct types

A *distinct* type is very similar to a regular predefined SQL type. In fact, a distinct type is derived directly from a predefined type, called the *source* type. You can create multiple distinct types from a single source type, each one distinct from all the others and from the source type. Here's how to create a distinct type from a predefined type:

```
CREATE DISTINCT TYPE USdollar AS DECIMAL (10,2) ;
```

This definition creates a new data type for U.S. dollars, based on the predefined `DECIMAL` type. You can create additional distinct types in the same way:

```
CREATE DISTINCT TYPE Euro AS DECIMAL (10,2) ;
```

Now you can create tables that use the new types:

```
CREATE TABLE USinvoice (
    InvoiceNo   INTEGER      PRIMARY KEY,
    CustomerID  INTEGER,
    SalesID     INTEGER,
    SaleTotal   USdollar,
    Tax         USdollar,
    Shipping    USdollar,
    GrandTotal  USdollar
    ) ;

CREATE TABLE Europeaninvoice (
    InvoiceNo   INTEGER      PRIMARY KEY,
    CustomerID  INTEGER,
    SalesID     INTEGER,
    SaleTotal   Euro,
    Tax         Euro,
    Shipping    Euro,
    GrandTotal  Euro
    ) ;
```

The `USdollar` type and the `Euro` type are both based on the `DECIMAL` type, but you cannot directly compare a `USdollar` value to a `Euro` value, nor can you directly compare either of those to a `DECIMAL` value. This is consistent with reality because one U.S. dollar is not equal to one Euro. However, it is possible to exchange dollars for Euros and vice versa when traveling. You can make that exchange with SQL too, but not directly. You must use a `CAST` operation, which I describe in Book III, Chapter 1.

Structured types

Structured types are not based on a single source type as are the distinct types. Instead, they are expressed as a list of attributes and methods. When you create a structured UDT, the DBMS automatically creates a constructor function, a mutator function, and an observer function. The *constructor* for a UDT is given the same name as the UDT. Its job is to initialize the UDT's attributes to their default values. When you invoke a *mutator* function, it changes the value of an attribute of a structured type. You can use an *observer* function to retrieve the value of an attribute of a structured type. If you include an observer function in a SELECT statement, it will retrieve values from the database.

Subtypes and supertypes

A hierarchical relationship can exist between two structured types. One structured type can be a "child" or subtype of a "parent" or supertype. Consider an example involving books. Suppose you have a UDT named BookUDT, which has a subtype named NovelUDT and another subtype named TechBookUDT. BookUDT is a supertype of both subtypes. Suppose further that TechBookUDT has a subtype named DatabaseBookUDT. DatabaseBookUDT is not only a subtype of TechBookUDT, but also a subtype of BookUDT. Because Database BookUDT is a direct child of TechBookUDT it is considered a *proper subtype* of TechBookUDT.

A structured type that has no supertype is considered a *maximal supertype*, and a structured type that has no subtypes is considered a *leaf subtype*.

Structured type example

Here's how you can create structured UDTs:

```
/* Create a UDT named BookUDT */
CREATE TYPE BookUDT AS
/* Specify attributes */
   Title       CHAR (40),
   Author      CHAR (40),
   MyCost      DECIMAL (9,2),
   ListPrice   DECIMAL (9.2)
/* Allow for subtypes */
   NOT FINAL ;

/* Create a subtype named TechBookUDT */
CREATE TYPE TechBookUDT UNDER BookUDT NOT FINAL ;

/* Create a subtype named DatabaseBookUDT */
CREATE TYPE DatabaseBookUDT UNDER TechBookUDT FINAL ;
```

Now that the types are defined, we can create tables that use them.

```
CREATE TABLE DATABASEBOOKS (
    StockItem    DatabaseBookUDT,
    StockNumber INTEGER
    ) ;
```

Now that the table exists, we can add data to it.

```
BEGIN
    /* Declare a temporary variable x */
    DECLARE x = DatabaseBookUDT;
    /* Execute the constructor function */
    Set x = DatabaseBookUDT() ;
    /* Execute the first mutator function */
    SET x = x.Title('SQL for Dummies') ;
    /* Execute the second mutator function */
    SET x = x.Author('Allen G. Taylor') ;
    /* Execute the third mutator function */
    SET x = x.MyCost(22.55) ;
    /* Execute the fourth mutator function */
    SET x = x.ListPrice(24.95) ;
    INSERT INTO DATABASEBOOKS VALUES (x, 271828) ;
END
```

Data type summary

Table 6-1 summarizes the SQL data types and gives an example of each.

Table 6-1	Data Types
Data Type	*Example Value*
CHARACTER (20)	'Amateur Radio '
VARCHAR (20)	'Amateur Radio'
CLOB (1000000)	'This character string is a million characters long . . .'
SMALLINT, BIGINT or INTEGER	7500
NUMERIC or DECIMAL	3425.432
REAL, FLOAT, or DOUBLE PRECISION	6.626E-34
BLOB (1000000)	'100100111010101101010101010101. . .'
BOOLEAN	'true'
DATE	1957-08-14
TIME WITHOUT TIME ZONE (2)[1]	12:46:02.43
TIME WITH TIME ZONE (3)	12:46:02.432-08:00

[1]*Argument specifies number of fractional digits.* *(continued)*

Table 6-1 *(continued)*

Data Type	Example Value
TIMESTAMP WITHOUT TIME ZONE (0)	1957-08-14 12:46:02
TIMESTAMP WITH TIME ZONE (0)	1957-08-14 12:46:02-08:00
INTERVAL DAY	INTERVAL '4' DAY
ROW	ROW (Street VARCHAR (25), City VARCHAR (20), State CHAR (2), PostalCode VARCHAR (9))
ARRAY	INTEGER ARRAY [15]
MULTISET	No literal applies to the MULTISET type.
REF	Not a type, but a pointer
USER DEFINED TYPE	Currency type based on DECIMAL

Your SQL implementation may not support all the data types that I describe in this section. Furthermore, your implementation may support nonstandard data types that I don't describe here.

Handling Null Values

SQL is different from practically any computer language that you may have encountered up to this point in that it allows null values: Other languages don't. Allowing null values gives SQL a flexibility that other languages lack, but also contributes to the "impedance mismatch" between SQL and host languages that it must work with in an application. If an SQL database contains null values that the host language does not recognize, provision must be made to handle that difference in a consistent way.

A *null value* is a non-value. If you are talking about numeric data, a null value is not the same as zero. Zero is a definite value. It is one less than one. If you are talking about character data, a null value is not the same as a blank space. A blank space is also a definite value. If you are talking about Boolean data, a null value is not the same as FALSE. A false Boolean value is a definite value too.

A null value is the absence of a value. It reminds me of the Buddhist concept of emptiness. I almost feel that if I ever come to understand null values completely I will have transcended the illusions of this world and achieved a state of enlightenment.

A field may contain a null value for several reasons:

+ A field may have a definite value, but the value is currently unknown.

+ A field may not yet have a definite value, but it may gain one in the future.

+ For some rows in a table, a particular field in that row may not be applicable.

+ The old value of a field has been deleted, but it has not yet been replaced with a new value.

In any situation where knowledge is incomplete, null values are possible. Because in most application areas, knowledge is never complete, null values are very likely to appear in most databases.

Applying Constraints

Constraints are one of the primary mechanisms for keeping the contents of a database from turning into a misleading or confusing mess. By applying constraints to tables, columns, or entire databases, you prevent the addition of invalid data or the deletion of data that is required to maintain overall consistency. A constraint can also identify invalid data that already exists in a database. If an operation that you perform in a transaction causes a constraint to be violated, the DBMS will prevent the transaction from taking effect (being committed). This protects the database from being put into an inconsistent state.

Column constraints

You can constrain the contents of a table column. In some cases, that means constraining what the column *must* contain and in other cases what it *may not* contain. There are three kinds of column constraints: the NOT NULL, UNIQUE, and CHECK constraints.

NOT NULL

Although SQL allows a column to contain null values, there are times when you want to be sure that a column always has a distinct value. In order for one row in a table to be distinguished from another, there must be some way of telling them apart. This is usually done with a primary key, which must have a unique value in every row. Because a null value in a column could be anything, it might match the value for that column in any of the other rows. Thus it makes sense to disallow a null value in the column that is used to distinguish one row from the rest. You can do this with a NOT NULL constraint, as shown in the following example:

```
CREATE TABLE CLIENT (

    ClientName       CHARACTER (30)      NOT NULL,
    Address1         CHARACTER (30),
    Address2         CHARACTER (30),
    City             CHARACTER (25),
    State            CHARACTER (2),
    PostalCode       CHARACTER (10),
    Phone            CHARACTER (13),
    Fax              CHARACTER (13),
    ContactPerson    CHARACTER (30)
    ) ;
```

When entering a new client into the CLIENT table, you must make an entry in the ClientName column.

UNIQUE

The NOT NULL constraint is a fairly weak constraint. You can satisfy the constraint as long as you put anything at all into the field, even if what you put into it would allow inconsistencies into your table. For example, suppose you already had a client named David Taylor in your database, and someone tried to enter another record with the same client name. If the table was only protected by a NOT NULL constraint, the entry of the second David Taylor would be allowed. Now when you go to retrieve David Taylor's information, which one will you get? How will you tell whether you have the one you want? A way around this problem is to use the stronger UNIQUE constraint. The UNIQUE constraint will not only disallow the entry of a null value in a column, but it will also disallow the entry of a value that matches a value already in the column.

CHECK

Use the CHECK constraint for preventing the entry of invalid data that goes beyond maintaining uniqueness. For example, you can check to make sure that a numeric value falls within an allowed range. You can also check to see that a particular character string is not entered into a column. Here's an example that ensures that the charge for a service falls within the acceptable range. It ensures that a customer is not mistakenly given a credit rather than a debit, and that she is not charged a ridiculously high amount either.

```
CREATE TABLE TESTS (
    TestName           CHARACTER (30)        NOT NULL,
    StandardCharge    NUMERIC (6,2)
        CHECK (StandardCharge >= 0.00
            AND StandardCharge <= 200.00)
    ) ;
```

The constraint is only satisfied if the charge is positive and less than or equal to $200.

Table constraints

Sometimes a constraint applies not just to a column, but to an entire table. The PRIMARY KEY constraint is the principal example of a table constraint. The primary key applies to an entire table. Although a primary key *may* consist of a single column, it could also be made up of a combination of two or more columns. Because a primary key must be guaranteed to be unique, multiple columns may be needed if one column is not enough to guarantee uniqueness. Here's an example of a table with a single-column primary key:

```
CREATE TABLE PROSPECT (
    ProspectName       CHARACTER (30)        PRIMARY KEY,
    Address1           CHARACTER (30),
    Address2           CHARACTER (30),
    City               CHARACTER (25),
    State              CHARACTER (2),
    PostalCode         CHARACTER (10),
    Phone              CHARACTER (13),
    Fax                CHARACTER (13)
    ) ;
```

This may cause a problem. Some people have rather common names. It is quite possible that two people with the same name might both be prospects of your business. You could overcome that problem by using more than one column for the primary key. Here's one way to do that:

```
CREATE TABLE PROSPECT (
    ProspectName       CHARACTER (30)        NOT NULL,
    Address1           CHARACTER (30)        NOT NULL,
    Address2           CHARACTER (30),
    City               CHARACTER (25),
    State              CHARACTER (2),
    PostalCode         CHARACTER (10),
    Phone              CHARACTER (13),

    CONSTRAINT prospect_pk PRIMARY KEY
        (ProspectName, Address1)
    ) ;
```

A composite primary key is made up of both ProspectName and Address1.

You might ask, "What if a father and son have the same name and live at the same address?" The more such scenarios you think up, the more complex things tend to get. In many cases, it's best to make up a unique ID number for every row in a table and let that be the primary key. If you use an auto-incrementer to generate the keys, you can be sure they are unique. This keeps things relatively simple:

```
CREATE TABLE PROSPECT (
    ProspectID          INTEGER                 PRIMARY KEY,
    ProspectName        CHARACTER (30),
    Address1            CHARACTER (30),
    Address2            CHARACTER (30),
    City                CHARACTER (25),
    State               CHARACTER (2),
    PostalCode          CHARACTER (10),
    Phone               CHARACTER (13)
    ) ;
```

Many database management systems will automatically create auto-incrementing primary keys for you as you enter new rows into a table.

Foreign key constraints

Relational databases are named as they are because the data is stored in tables that are related to each other in some way. The relationship occurs because a row in one table may be directly related to one or more rows in another table. For example, in a retail database, the record in the CUSTOMER table for customer Lisa Mazzone is directly related to the records in the INVOICE table for purchases that Ms. Mazzone has made. To establish this relationship, one or more columns in the CUSTOMER table must have corresponding columns in the INVOICE table.

The primary key of CUSTOMER uniquely identifies each customer. The primary key of INVOICE uniquely identifies each invoice. In addition, the primary key of CUSTOMER acts as a foreign key in INVOICE to link the two tables. The foreign key in each row of the INVOICE table identifies the customer who made this particular purchase. Here's an example:

```
CREATE TABLE CUSTOMER (
    CustomerID          INTEGER                 PRIMARY KEY,
    CustomerName        CHARACTER (30),
    Address1            CHARACTER (30),
    Address2            CHARACTER (30),
    City                CHARACTER (25),
    State               CHARACTER (2),
    PostalCode          CHARACTER (10),
    Phone               CHARACTER (13)
    ) ;
```

```
CREATE TABLE SALESPERSON (
    SalespersonID      INTEGER                PRIMARY KEY,
    SalespersonName    CHARACTER (30),
    Address1           CHARACTER (30),
    Address2           CHARACTER (30),
    City               CHARACTER (25),
    State              CHARACTER (2),
    PostalCode         CHARACTER (10),
    Phone              CHARACTER (13)
    ) ;

CREATE TABLE INVOICE (
    InvoiceNo          INTEGER                PRIMARY KEY,
    CustomerID         INTEGER,
    SalespersonID      INTEGER,

    CONSTRAINT customer_fk FOREIGN KEY (CustomerID)
        REFERENCES CUSTOMER (CustomerID),
    CONSTRAINT salesperson_fk FOREIGN KEY (SalespersonID)
        REFERENCES SALESPERSON (SalespersonID)
    ) ;
```

Each invoice is related to the customer who made the purchase and the sales person who made the sale.

Assertions

Sometimes a constraint may apply not just to a column or a table, but to multiple tables or even an entire database. A constraint with such broad applicability is called an *assertion*. None of the currently popular implementations support assertions, so I will say no more about them here. They may be included in some future edition of one or more of the popular database management systems.

Book II

Relational Database Development

The 5th Wave   By Rich Tennant

"They're pushing the company into a new, hip direction and asked if we would pimp the storage system."

Contents at a Glance

Chapter 1: System Development Overview

Databases don't exist in isolation. They are part of a system that is designed to perform some needed function. To create a useful and reliable database system, you must be aware of all the parts of the system and how they work together. You must also follow a disciplined approach to system development to have any hope of delivering an effective and reliable product on time and on budget. In this chapter, I lay out the component parts of such a system, and then break down the steps you must go through to successfully complete a database system development project.

The Components of a Database System

A database containing absolutely critical information would not be of much use if there was no way to operate on the data or retrieve the particular information that you wanted. Between the database and the user are several intermediate components that translate the user's requests into a form that the database understands and then returns the requested information to the user in a form that the user understands. Figure 1-1 shows the information flow from the user to the database and back again, through the intermediate components.

Figure 1-1:
Information
flow in a
database
system.

Users   Database Application (The user interface)   Database Front End (Code)   Database Engine (Back End) (Code)   Database

I examine each of these components one by one, starting with the database itself.

The database

The core component of a database system is the database itself. It is the place where the data is stored. It is stored in a structured way, which is what makes it a database rather than a random pile of data items. The structure enables the efficient retrieval of specific items. A database may be stored in one place, or it could be distributed across multiple locations. Regardless of its physical form, logically it behaves as a single, unified repository of data.

The database engine

The database engine, also called the *back end* of a DBMS, is where the processing power of the database system resides. The database engine is that part of the system that acts upon the database. It responds to commands in the form of SQL statements and performs the requested operations on the database. In addition to its processing functions, it is a two-way communications channel, accepting commands from the DBMS front end and translating them into actions on the database. Results of those actions are then passed back to the front end for further processing by the database application and ultimate presentation to the user.

The DBMS front end

Whereas the back end is that portion of a DBMS that interfaces directly with the database, the *front end* is the portion that communicates with the database application or directly with the user. It translates instructions it receives from the user or the user's application into a form that the back end can understand. On the return path, it translates the results it receives from the back end into a form the user or the user's application can understand. The front end is what you see after you click an icon to launch a DBMS such as Access, SQL Server, or Oracle. Despite appearances, what you see is not the database. It is not even the database management system. It is just a translator, designed to make it easier for you to communicate with the database.

The database application

Although it is possible for a person to interact directly with the DBMS front end, this is not the way database systems are normally used. Most people deal with databases indirectly through an application. An application is a program, written in a combination of a host language such as C or Java, and SQL, which performs actions that are required on a repeating basis. The application provides a friendly environment for the user, with helpful screens, menus, command buttons, and instructive text, to make the job of dealing with the database more understandable and easier. Although it may take significant time and effort to build a database application, after it's built, it can be used multiple times. It also makes the user's job much easier, so that high-level understanding of the database is not needed in order to effectively maintain and use it.

The user

The user is a human being, but one who is typically not you, dear reader. Because you are reading this book, I assume that your goal is to learn to use SQL effectively. The user in a database system typically does not use SQL at all and may be unaware that it even exists. The user deals with the screens, menus, and command buttons of the database applications that you write. Your applications shield the user from the complexities of SQL.

It is possible for a user, in interactive SQL mode, to enter SQL statements directly into a DBMS and receive result sets or other feedback from the DBMS. This however is not the normal case. Usually a database application developer such as you operates in this manner, rather than the typical user.

The System Development Life Cycle

Producing both a reliable database and an easy-to-use application that fills a real need is a complex task. If you take the task too lightly and build a system without careful preparation, you are likely to produce something that is neither reliable nor adequately functional.

The best way to accomplish a large, complex task is to break it down into steps, each one of which you can do and do well. To develop a robust and reliable database system, you must go through the seven phases of the System Development Life Cycle (SDLC):

- ✦ Definition
- ✦ Requirements
- ✦ Evaluation
- ✦ Design
- ✦ Implementation
- ✦ Final documentation and testing
- ✦ Maintenance

Each one of these phases is important. Sometimes schedule pressure may tempt you to shortchange or even skip one of the phases. To do so invites costly errors or a final product that does not meet the needs of the users.

Definition phase

At the beginning of a project, the person who is assigning you the task of building a system, the client, has some idea of what is needed. That idea may be very specific, sharp, and concise, or it may be vague, nebulous, and ill-defined. Your first task is to generate and put into writing a detailed description of exactly what the end result of the project, called *the deliverables,* should be. This is the primary task of the definition phase, but this phase also includes the following tasks:

+ **Define the task to be performed.** Define the problem to be solved by your database and associated application as accurately as possible. Do this by listening carefully to your client as she describes what she envisions the system to be. Ask questions to clarify vague points. Often, the client will not have thought things through completely. She will have a general idea of what she wants, but no clear idea of the specifics. You must come to an agreement with her on the specifics before you can proceed.

+ **Determine the project's scope.** How big a job will it be? What will it require in terms of systems analyst time, programmer time, equipment, and other cost items? Is there a deadline?

+ **Perform a feasibility analysis.** Ask yourself, "Is it possible to do this job within the time and cost constraints placed on it by the client?" To answer this question, you must do a feasibility analysis. After you complete the analysis, you may decide that the project is not feasible as currently defined, and you must either decline it or convince the client to reduce the scope to something more manageable.

+ **Form a project team.** Decide who will work on the project. You may be able to do a small job all by yourself, but most development efforts will require a team of several individuals. Finding people who have the requisite skills and who are also available to work on the project when you need them can be just as challenging as any other part of the total development effort.

+ **Document the task definition, the project scope, the feasibility analysis, and the membership of the project team.** Carefully document the project definition, its scope, the feasibility analysis, and the development team membership. This documentation will be a valuable guide for everything that follows.

+ **Get the client to approve the definition phase document.** Make sure the client sees and agrees with everything recorded in the definition phase document. It is best to have her sign the document, signifying that she understands and approves of your plan for the development effort.

Requirements phase

In the definition phase, you talk with the client. This is the person who has the authority to hire you, or, if you are already an employee, to assign you to this development task. This person is not, however, the only one with an interest in the project. Chances are, someone other than the client will be using the system on a daily basis. Even more people may depend on the results generated by the system. It is important to find out what these people need and what they prefer because your primary client may not have a complete understanding of what would serve them best.

The amount of work you must do in the requirements phase depends on the client. It can be quick and easy if you are dealing with a client who has prior experience with similar database development projects. Such a client has a clear idea of what he wants and, equally important, what is feasible within the time and budget constraints that apply.

Book II
Chapter 1

**System
Development
Overview**

On the other hand, this phase can be difficult and drawn-out if the client has no experience with this kind of development, only a vague idea of what she wants, and an even vaguer idea of what can reasonably be done within the allotted time and budget.

Aside from your primary client, the one who hired you, other stakeholders in the project, such as various users, managers, executives, and board members, also have ideas of what they need. These ideas often conflict with each other. Your job at this point is to come up with a set of requirements that everyone can agree on. This will probably not meet everyone's needs completely. It will represent a compromise between conflicting desires, but will be the solution that gives the most important functions to the people who need them.

Establishing requirements: An example

I once created a database application for an adoption agency. First I talked to the manager who had overall charge of the agency. She had very definite ideas about how she wanted the system to perform. The agency already had a computerized adoption application, but it was becoming progressively less satisfactory as its business grew. The company had many facts to track to be able to match children with the best prospective adoptive parents and to meet stringent government requirements.

The manager wanted a system with expanded capacity, additional features, and higher performance compared to its existing system. However, she wanted the user interface to be as close as possible to that of its current system to minimize the confusion of users and the retraining time that they would require.

After talking to the manager, I talked to the users, each one specializing on a specific segment of the overall process. These people, who would be using the system every day, each had their own perspective on what was needed for them to do their jobs most effectively. I had to find a way to come up with a set of requirements that met the needs of the users and the desires of the manager, and at the same time one that specified a system that was feasible to build.

After considerable dialog with all concerned, I crafted a set of requirements that everyone could endorse. At every succeeding stage of development, I went back to the same people and kept them informed of progress. This way, they all felt they had a personal stake in the final product. These follow-up meetings also helped me to be sure that I had a good understanding of what they had in mind when they told me what they wanted.

The users' data model

After you have consensus among the stakeholders, you can use their requirements to construct a users' data model. The users' data model includes all the items of interest and how they relate to each other. It also incorporates any business rules that you may have been able to infer from people's comments. Business rules place restrictions on the items that can be included in a database and on what can be done with those items.

Statement of Requirements

After you have constructed the users' data model and verified its accuracy with your client, you can write a formal Statement of Requirements. The Statement of Requirements is an explicit statement of the database application's display, update, and control mechanisms. It will answer such questions as

✦ What will the display look like? What arrangement of items? What color scheme?

✦ What items will need to be updated, and how will that be done?

✦ How will navigation between screens be done?

✦ Will selections be made by key depressions? If so, which keys will do what?

✦ Will operations be initiated by mouse clicks? If so, which operations?

✦ What will the maximum acceptable response time to a query be?

The Statement of Requirements must be as detailed as possible because it is essentially a contract between you and your client. You are agreeing on exactly what will be delivered and when it will be delivered. To seal the arrangement, both you and your client should sign the Statement of Requirements, signifying agreement on what you will be responsible for delivering. This step may seem rather formal, but it protects both parties. There can never be any question later as to what was agreed upon.

Here's a summary of what you must do in the requirements phase:

✦ Interview typical members of all classes of stakeholders in the project.

✦ Provide leadership in getting stakeholders to agree on what is needed.

✦ Create a users' data model of the proposed system.

✦ Create the Statement of Requirements, which describes in detail what the system will look like and what it will do.

✦ Obtain client approval of the Statement of Requirements, indicated by a signature and date.

Evaluation phase

Upon completion of the requirements phase (see the preceding section), it is a good idea to do some serious thinking about what you will need to do in order to meet the requirements. This thinking is the main task of the evaluation phase, in which you address the issues of scope and feasibility more carefully than you have up to this point. You know more now. You know who all the stakeholders are and what they want. You know who is on your team and what their skills are. The Statement of Requirements document tells you exactly what you are expected to deliver.

Important considerations for the evaluation phase:

✦ **Determine the project's scope.** This step includes several tasks, including

• Selecting the best DBMS for the job, based on all relevant considerations.

• Selecting the best host language.

• Writing job descriptions for all team members.

✦ **Reassess the feasibility of the project and adjust project scope, deadlines, or budget if needed.**

✦ **Document all the decisions made in this phase and the reasoning for them.**

Determining project scope

Now that you know what you need to do, it is time to decide on exactly how you are going to do it. You have to choose what development tools you will use. What is the best DBMS to accomplish this particular project? To determine this, you need to consider these several factors:

✦ All DBMS products have limitations in terms of number of tables and records they will support, supported data types, and number of users. Considering the size and complexity of the task, which DBMS products will support the current project and any reasonable extensions to it that might be required in the years to come?

✦ Has the client standardized on a specific DBMS for all development? If so, will it work for the current project?

✦ Is your development team proficient with the selected DBMS? If not, what will it take for them to climb the learning curve and become proficient?

✦ Is the DBMS you choose supported by a strong company or developer community that will be able to provide upgrades and other services in the coming years?

✦ Is the best DBMS from a performance standpoint affordable to the client from a financial standpoint?

✦ Does the DBMS have a track record of reliable operation in applications similar to the one you are planning?

Another consideration is the language that you will use to develop the application. You can develop some database applications without writing a single line of program code. These tend to be simple applications that are useful in small organizations. More complex applications require at least some programming. For those more complex applications, you must choose the computer language that they will be written in. Some of the same considerations that apply to the selection of a DBMS apply here:

✦ Languages have limitations. Choose one that has all the functionality you need.

✦ Clients sometimes have a language standard. Is their standard language adequate?

✦ Is your development team familiar with the chosen language?

✦ Is the language popular enough to have a large number of practitioners? Ongoing maintenance of your code depends on the availability of people who are able to understand it.

With a clear idea of your task and the tools you will use to perform it, you can now write detailed job descriptions for everyone who will have a part in the development effort. This important step eliminates any confusion and finger-pointing about who is responsible for what.

Reassessing feasibility

At this stage in the process, you probably have a clearer idea than ever of the assigned task and what it will take to accomplish it. This is a good time to reassess the feasibility of the project. Is it really doable, or are your client and you both too optimistic in thinking that you can achieve everything in the Statement of Requirements, given the DBMS, language, team, budget, and time that you have decided upon?

If the job is not really feasible, it is much better to speak up now than to plunge ahead, burn through your budget and your scheduled time, only to fail to deliver a satisfactory product. At this point, when not much has been invested, you still have some flexibility. You may be able to reduce the scope of the project by deferring until later or even eliminating elements of the project that are not crucial. You may be able to negotiate for a schedule that is not quite so tight, or for a larger budget. You may even decide that the best course for all concerned would be to abandon the project.

At this point, you can bow out relatively gracefully. It will not cost either you or the client very much. If instead, you push ahead with a project that is doomed from the start, you could both suffer substantial loss, both monetarily and in terms of reputation. Making the correct decision here is of critical importance.

Documenting the evaluation phase

As you should do for every phase, document the steps you took in evaluating development tools such as DBMSs and languages. Place the job descriptions with the documentation. Document the feasibility analysis, the conclusions you came to, and the adjustments to the task scope, budget, and schedule that you made, if any.

Design phase

Up until this point, the project has primarily been analysis. Now you can enter the design phase and make the transition from analysis to design. You most likely know everything you need to know about the problem and can now start designing the solution.

Here's an overview of what you do in the design phase:

+ Translate the users' data model into an E-R model.

+ Convert the E-R model into a relational model.

+ Design the user interface.

+ Design the logic that performs the database application's functions.

+ Determine what might go wrong and design in safeguards to avoid problems.

+ Document the database design and the database application design thoroughly.

+ Obtain client signoff of the complete design.

Designing the database

Database design is all about models. Now you have the users' data model, which captures the users' concept of the structure of the database. It includes all the major types of objects, as well as the characteristics of those objects, and how the objects are related to one another. This is great as far as it goes. However, it's not sufficiently structured to be the basis for a database design. For that, you need to convert the users' data model into a model that conforms to one of the formal database modeling systems that have been developed over the past few decades.

The most popular of the formal modeling systems is the entity-relationship model, commonly referred to as the E-R model. In the next chapter, I describe the E-R model in detail. With this model, you can capture what the users have told you into a well-defined form that you can then easily translate into a relational database.

As you convert the users' data model into an E-R model, you need to make decisions that affect how that conversion is made. Make sure you document your reasoning for why you do things the way you do. At some later time, someone is going to have to modify, update, or add to the database you are building. That person will need all possible information about why the system is designed the way it is. Take the time to document your reasoning as well as documenting the model itself.

After you have the system in the form of an E-R model, it is easy to convert into a relational model. The relational model is something that your DBMS understands, and you can create the database directly from it.

The database application

After you have designed the database, the design task is only half done. You have a structure that you can now fill with data, but you do not yet have a tool for operating on that data. The tool you must design now is the database application.

The database application is the part of the total system that interacts with the user. It creates everything that the user sees on the screen. It senses and responds to every time the user presses a key or uses the mouse. It prints every report that is read by the user's coworkers. From the standpoint of the user, the database application *is* the system.

In designing the database application, you must ensure that it enables the users to do everything that the Statement of Requirements promises that they will be able to do. It must also present a user interface that is understandable and easy to use. The functions of the system must appear in logical positions on the screen. The user must easily grasp how to perform all the functions that the application provides.

What functions must the application perform? Using the DBMS and language that you chose, or that was chosen for you by the client, how will you implement those functions? At this point, you must conceive of and map out the logical flow of the application. Make sure you know exactly how each function will be performed.

Aside from mapping out all the functions that the application will perform, you must also think about protecting the database from inadvertent or intentional harm. People make mistakes. Sometimes they press the wrong key and perform an operation they really didn't want to perform. Sometimes they enter incorrect data. Sometimes they want to mess up the database on purpose. You need to design the application in such a way that minimizes the damage that such actions cause. Anticipate that someone might make an inappropriate keystroke, or enter a wrong value, or delete something that should not be deleted. If you anticipate such problems, you can incorporate recovery procedures that will restore things to their proper state.

Documenting the design phase

The final part of the design phase is — you guessed it — to document everything carefully and completely. The documentation should be so complete that a new development team could come in and implement the system without asking you a single question about the analysis and design efforts that you have just completed. Take the completed design document to the client and get them to sign it, signifying that they understand your design and authorize you to build it.

It is critically important to keep the client informed of what you are doing, every step of the way. This gives the client a sense of ownership in the decisions that have been made, and makes it less likely that they will experience an unpleasant surprise when you deliver the final product. They will know in advance what they are getting and will feel as if they had a major part in shaping its development and its final form.

Implementation phase

Many non-developers believe that developing a database and application is synonymous with writing the code to implement them. By now, you should realize that there is much more to developing a database system than that. In fact, writing the code is only a minor fraction of the total effort. However, it is a very important minor fraction! The best planning and design in the world would not be of much use if they did not lead to the building of an actual database and its associated application.

In the implementation phase, you

+ **Build the database structure.** In the following chapters of Book II, I describe how to create a relational model, based on the E-R model that you derive from the users' data model. The relational model consists of major elements called *relations,* which have properties called *attributes* and are linked to other relations in the model. You build the structure of your database by converting the model's relations to tables in the database, whose columns correspond to the relation's attributes. You implement the links between tables that correspond to the links between the model's relations, using constraints.

+ **Build the database application.** Building the database application consists of constructing the screens that the user will see and interact with. It also involves creating the formats for any printed reports and writing program code to make any calculations or to perform database operations such as adding data to a table, changing the data in a table, deleting data from a table, or retrieving data from a table.

+ **Generate user documentation and maintenance programmer documentation.** I'm repeating myself, but I can't emphasize enough the importance of creating and updating documentation at each phase.

Final documentation and testing phase

Documenting the database is relatively easy because most DBMS products do it for you. You can retrieve the documentation they create at any time, or print it out to add to the project records. You definitely need to print out at least one copy for that purpose.

Documenting a database application calls for some real work on your part. Application documentation comes in two forms, aimed at two potential audiences:

✦ You must create user documentation that describes all the functions the application is capable of and how to perform them.

✦ You must create maintenance documentation aimed at the developers who will be supporting the system in the future. Typically, those maintenance programmers will be people other than the members of your team. You must make your documentation so complete that a person completely unfamiliar with the development effort will be able to understand what you did and why you did it that way. Program code must be heavily documented in addition to the descriptions and instructions that you write in documents that are separate from the program code.

The testing and documentation phase includes the following tasks:

✦ Giving your completed system to an independent testing entity to test it for functionality, ease of use, bugs, and compatibility with all the platforms it is supposed to run on.

✦ Generating final documentation.

✦ Delivering system to client and receiving signed acceptance.

✦ Celebrating!

Testing the system with sample data

After you have built and documented a database system, it may seem like you are finished and you can enjoy a well-deserved vacation. I'm all in favor of vacations, but you're not quite finished yet. The system needs to be rigorously tested, and that testing needs to be done by someone who does not think the same way you do. After the system becomes operational, users will do things to it that you never imagined. They will make combinations of selections that you did not foresee. They will enter values into fields that make no sense. They will do things backwards and upside down. There is no telling what they will do. Whatever unexpected thing the user does, you want the system to respond in a way that protects the database and that guides the user into making appropriate input actions.

It is hard to build into a system protections against problems that you can't foresee. For that reason, before you turn the system over to your client, you must have an independent tester try to make it fail. The tester performs a functional test to see that the system does everything it is supposed to do. Also the tester runs it on all the types of computers and all the operating systems that it is supposed to run on. If it is a Web-based application, it needs to be tested for compatibility with all popular browsers. In addition, the tester needs to do illogical things that a user might do to see how the system reacts. If it crashes, or responds in some other unhelpful way, you will have to modify your implementation so it will prompt the user with helpful responses.

Quite often, when you modify a database or application to fix a problem, the modification will cause another problem. So after such a modification, the entire system must be retested to make sure that no new problems have been introduced. You might have to go through several iterations of testing and modification before you have a system that you can be very confident will operate properly under all possible conditions.

Finalizing the documentation

While the independent tester is trying everything conceivable (and several things inconceivable) to make your product fail, you and your team are still not ready to take that well-deserved vacation. Now is the time for you to put your documentation into final form. You have been carefully documenting every step along the way of every phase. At this time, you need to organize all that documentation because it is an important part of what you'll deliver to the client.

User documentation will probably consist of both context-sensitive help that is part of the application and a printed user's manual. The online help is best for answers to quick questions that arise when a person is in the middle of trying to perform a function. The printed manual is best as a general reference and as an overview of the entire system. Both are important and deserve your full attention.

Delivering the results (and celebrating)

When the testing and documentation phase is complete, all that is left to do is to formally deliver the system, complete with full documentation, to your client. This usually triggers the client's final payment to you if you are an independent contractor. If you are an employee, it will most likely result in a favorable entry in your personnel file that may help you get a raise at your next review.

Now you and your team can celebrate!

Maintenance phase

Just because you have delivered the system on time and on budget, have celebrated, and have collected your final payment for the job does not mean that your responsibilities are over. Even if the independent tester has done a fantastic job of trying to make the system fail, after delivery it may still harbor latent bugs that show up weeks, months, or even years later. You may be obligated to fix those bugs at no charge, depending on your contractual agreement with the client.

Even if no bugs are found, you may still have some ongoing responsibility. After all, no one understands the system as well as you do. As time goes on, your client's needs will change. Perhaps she will need additional functions. Perhaps she will want to migrate to newer, more powerful hardware. Perhaps she will want to upgrade to a newer operating system. All of these possibilities may require modifications to the database application, and you are in the best position to do those modifications, based on your prior knowledge.

This kind of maintenance can be good because it is revenue that you don't have to go out hunting for. It can also be bad because it ties you down to technology that, over time, you may consider obsolete and no longer of interest. Be aware that you may have at least an ethical obligation to provide this kind of ongoing support.

Every software development project that gets delivered has a maintenance phase. You may be required to provide the following services during that phase:

✦ Fix latent bugs that are discovered after the client has accepted the system. Often the client doesn't pay you any extra for this work on the assumption that the bugs are your responsibility. However, if you write your contract correctly, their signoff at acceptance protects you from perpetual bug fixing.

✦ Provide enhancements and updates requested by the client. This is a good, recurring income source.

Chapter 2: Building a Database Model

In This Chapter

✓ Finding and listening to interested parties

✓ Building consensus

✓ The Entity-Relationship modeling method

✓ Building a relational model

✓ Knowing the dangers of anomalies

✓ Avoiding anomalies with normalization

✓ Denormalizing with care

A successful database system must satisfy the needs of a diverse group of people. This group includes the people who will actually be entering data and retrieving results. It also includes others, though. People at various levels of management may rely on reports generated by the system. People in other functional areas, such as sales, or manufacturing, may use the products of the system, such as reports or bar code labels. The information technology (IT) people who set overall data processing standards for the organization may also weigh in on how the system is constructed and the form of the outputs it will produce. You must consider the needs of all these groups, and possibly others, when designing your system. You will have to combine all these inputs into a consensus called the users' data model.

Finding and Listening to Interested Parties

When you are assigned the task of building a database system, one of the first things that you must do is determine who all the interested parties are and what their levels of involvement are.

Human relations is an important part of your job here. When the views of different people in the organization conflict with each other, as they often do, you have to decide on a path to follow. You cannot simply take the word of the person with the most impressive title. Often unofficial lines of authority in an organization (which are the ones that really count) differ significantly from what the official organization chart might show.

Your immediate supervisor

Generally, if you are dealing with a medium- to large-sized organization, the person who contacts you about doing the development project is a middle manager. This person typically has the authority to find and recommend a developer for a needed application, but may not have the budget authority to approve the total development cost.

The person who hired you is probably your closest ally in the organization. She wants you to succeed because it will reflect badly on her if you don't. Be sure that you have a good understanding of what she wants and how important her stated desires are to her. It could be that she has merely been tasked with obtaining a developer and does not have strong opinions about what is to be developed. On the other hand, she may be directly responsible for what the application delivers and may have a very specific idea of what is needed. In addition to hearing what she tells you, you must also be able to "read between the lines" and determine how much *importance* she ascribes to what she is saying.

The users

After the manager who hires you, the next group of people you are likely to meet are the future hands-on users of the system you will build. They enter the data that populates the database tables. They run the queries that answer questions that they and others in the organization may have. They generate the reports that are circulated to coworkers and managers. They are the ones who come into closest contact with what you have built.

In general, these people are already accustomed to dealing with the data that will be in your system, or data very much like it. They are either using a manual system, based on paper records, or a computer-based system that your system will replace. In either case, they have become comfortable with a certain look and feel for forms and reports.

To ease the transition from the old system to the new one you are building, you will probably want to make your forms and reports look as much like the old ones as possible. Your system may present new information, but if it is presented in a familiar way, the users will accept it more readily and start making effective use of it sooner.

The people who will be using your system probably have very definite ideas about what they like and what they don't like about the system they are currently using. In your new system, you want to eliminate the aspects of the old system that they don't like, and retain the things they do like. It is critical for the success of your system that the hands-on users like it. Even if your system does everything that the Statement of Requirements specifies, it will be a failure if the everyday users don't like it. Aside from providing them with what they want, it is also important to build rapport with these people during the development effort. Make sure they agree with what you are doing, every step along the way.

The standards organization

Large organizations with existing software applications have probably standardized on a particular hardware platform and operating system. These choices can constrain which DBMS you use because not all database management systems are available on all platforms. The standards organization may even have a preferred DBMS. This is almost certain to be true if they already support other database applications.

Supporting database applications on an ongoing basis requires a significant infrastructure. That infrastructure includes DBMS software, periodic DBMS software upgrades, training of users, and training of support personnel. If the organization already supports applications based on one DBMS, it makes sense to leverage that investment by mandating that all future database applications use the same DBMS. If the application you have been brought in to create would best be built upon a foundation of a different DBMS, you will have to justify the increased support burden. Often this can only be done if the currently supported DBMS is downright incapable of doing the job.

Aside from your choice of DBMS, the standards people might also have something to say about your coding practices. They might have standards requiring structured programming and modular development, as well as very specific documentation guidelines. Where such standards and guidelines exist, they are usually all to the good. You will have to make sure that you comply with all of them. Your product will doubtless be better for it anyway.

Smaller organizations probably will *not* have any IT people enforcing data processing standards and guidelines. In those cases, you must act as if *you* were the IT people. Try to understand what would be best for the client organization in the long term. Make your selection of DBMS, coding style, and documentation with those long-term considerations in mind, rather than what would be most expedient for the current project. Be sure that your clients are aware of why you make the choices you do. They may want to participate in the decision, and at any rate, will appreciate the fact that you have their long-term interests at heart.

Upper management

Unless you are dealing with a very small organization, the manager who hired you for this project is not the highest-ranking person who has an interest in what you will be producing. It is likely that the manager with whom you are dealing must carry your proposals to a higher level for approval. It is important to find out who that higher-up is and to get a sense of what he wants your application to accomplish for the organization. Be aware that this person may not carry the most prestigious title in the organization and may not even be on a direct line to the person who hired you on the company organization chart. Talk to the troops on the front line, the people who will actually be using your application. They can tell you where the real power resides. After you find out what is most important to this key person, make sure that it is included in the final product.

Building Consensus

The interested parties in the application you are developing are called *stakeholders,* and you must talk to at least one representative of each group. After you talk to them, you are likely to be confused. Some people insist that one feature is crucial and not care about a second feature. Others insist that the second feature is very important and not even mention the first. Some will want the application to look and act one way, and others will want an entirely different look and feel. Some people consider one particular report to be the most important thing about the application, and other people don't care about reports at all, but only about the application's *ad hoc* query ability. It is just not practical to expect everyone in the client organization to want the same things and to ascribe the same levels of importance to those things. Your job is to bring some order out of this chaos. You will have to transform all these diverse points of view into a consensus that everyone can agree upon. This requires compromise on the part of the stakeholders. You want to build an application that meets the needs of the organization in the best possible way.

What do people want, and how badly do they want it?

As the developer, it should not be your job to resolve conflicts among the stakeholders regarding what the proposed system should do. However, as the technical person who is building it and has no vested interest in exactly what it should look like or what it should do, you may be the only person who can break the gridlock. This means that negotiating skills are a valuable addition to your toolkit of technical know-how.

Find out who cares passionately about what the system will provide, and whose opinions carry the most weight. The decisions that are ultimately made about project scope, functionality, and appearance will affect the amount of time and budget that will be needed to complete development.

Arriving at a consensus

Somehow, the conflicting input you receive from all the stakeholders must be combined into a uniform vision of what the proposed system should be and do. You may need to ask disagreeing groups of people to sit down together and arrive at a compromise that is at least satisfactory to all, if not everything they had wished for.

To specify a system that can be built within the time and budget constraints that have been set out for the project, some people may have to give up features they would like to have, but which are not absolutely necessary. As an interested but impartial outsider, you may be able to serve as a facilitator in the discussion.

After the stakeholders have agreed upon what they want the new database system to do for them, you need to transform this consensus into a model that represents their thinking. The model should include all the items that are of interest. It should describe how these items relate to each other. It should also describe in detail the attributes of the items of interest. This *users' data model* will be the basis for a more formal entity-relationship (E-R) model that you will then convert into a relational model. I cover these models and transformations later in this chapter.

Book II
Chapter 2

Building a Database Model

The three-option proposal

Sometimes it is not easy to get all the stakeholders to agree on what they want. Some might want more features, and others might want lower cost. One way to break this logjam is to come up with three proposals for the project rather than just one. Present the three proposals to your clients and let them decide which one they want. Here's what the three proposals should be:

✦ A minimal project that includes all the elements that everyone agrees are absolutely mandatory. This is also the lowest cost option in terms of time and dollars.

✦ A medium project that includes everything in option 1, plus additional features that most of the stakeholders believe would be valuable. This is a medium cost option in terms of time and dollars.

✦ A maximum project that includes everything that everyone wants.

Typically, option 3 is rejected immediately because it is too expensive and takes too long to complete. Next, option 1 is usually rejected because it is not really satisfactory to anybody. The stakeholders will then most likely agree to go ahead with option 2, perhaps with some minor modifications. Be sure to recalculate the time and cost estimates for any such changes to your original proposal. At this point, you are on your way. The project can start in earnest.

The Entity-Relationship Modeling Method

After you have constructed a users' data model that all stakeholders can support, you must put that model into a more formal structure that you can map directly into a relational model, which is the foundation of a relational database. A number of formalisms are available to give you such a structure, but the most widely used is the Entity-Relationship (E-R) model.

The E-R model is used to represent a wide variety of systems that people want to track in some detailed manner. The system being tracked could be physical, such as a jet airliner or the human genome, or it could be conceptual, such as the accounts receivable of a manufacturing company. One of the strengths of the E-R model is that even the largest and most complex systems can be modeled using just four basic elements:

✦ Entities

✦ Attributes

✦ Identifiers

✦ Relationships

Entities

In the context of the E-R model, an entity is something that the user can identify and wants to keep track of. An example might be an employee named Tracy Stein. Entities of a given type are grouped together into *entity classes*. EMPLOYEE is an instance of an entity class, and Tracy Stein is an example of an instance of an entity class, an *entity instance*. Figure 2-1 shows an example of the EMPLOYEE entity class, and Figure 2-2 shows an example of an instance of the EMPLOYEE entity class.

Figure 2-1:
EMPLOYEE,
an example
of an entity
class.

```
EMPLOYEE
    EmpID
    FirstName
    LastName
    JobTitle
    HireDate
    Extension
    E-mail
    Department
```

Figure 2-2:
Tracy Stein,
an instance
of the
EMPLOYEE
class.

801385
Tracy
Stein
IT Manager
10-15-2006
Information Tech
503-555-1234
Fred@xyz.com

Attributes

Entities have attributes, which are characteristics of the entity, that you want to know about. Most entities have lots of characteristics, most of which you don't want to know about. Take the example of the EMPLOYEE entity class shown in Figure 2-1. An employer probably wants to know every employee's first name, last name, home address, and home telephone number. These are attributes that are relevant to the employer's relationship with the employee. However, the employer probably does not want to keep track of each employee's hair color, shoe size, or favorite baseball team. These are attributes of the employee that are not relevant to the employer's relationship with the employee.

Identifiers

In a database, it is pretty important that you be able to distinguish one entity instance from another. For example, consider the CUSTOMER entity class. It is bad form to send a bill to a customer for an item that the customer did not order. It is an even bigger mistake to fail to bill a customer who has taken delivery on the most expensive product that you sell.

You must be able to identify individual instances of an entity class. You can do this with attributes or combinations of attributes called *identifiers:*

- ✦ A *unique identifier* identifies one and only one instance of an entity class.

- ✦ A *non-unique identifier* identifies a set of instances that share some common characteristic or group of characteristics.

- ✦ An identifier that is composed of two or more attributes is called a *composite identifier.*

Often, a single attribute serves as a unique identifier for an entity class. At other times, however, no single attribute narrows things down enough. In such cases, you can add additional attributes, making up a composite identifier, until the combination of attributes uniquely identifies every instance of the entity class. As an example, a Social Security Number (SSN) is a single-attribute unique identifier of a resident of the United States. A person's last name is typically a non-unique identifier of a resident of the United States. A composite identifier that includes a person's first name and street, city, state, and ZIP code, as well as last name, might still not constitute a unique identifier if, for example, a mother and daughter with the same first and last names lived in the same house.

Relationships

Entities are associated with other entities through *relationships. Relationship classes* are associations among entity classes. *Relationship instances* are associations among entity instances.

Relationships can exist in varying degrees. A degree-2 relationship is one between two entity classes or two entity instances. A degree-3 relationship relates three entity classes or entity instances to each other. An example of a degree-2 relationship would be that between a major league baseball team and its players. Each team has a set of players, none of whom are members of any other major league baseball team. Figure 2-3 is an E-R diagram of this relationship.

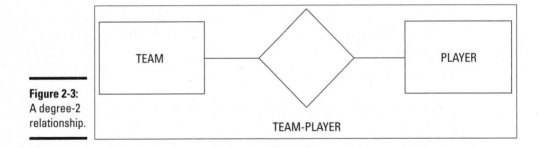

Figure 2-3:
A degree-2
relationship.

The rectangles represent the entities and the lines between them represent the relationships. The diamond in the middle of a relationship is used to represent maximum cardinality, which I discuss in a later section.

A degree-3 relationship would be one between three entities, such as that between a composer, a librettist, and an opera. In an opera, the composer writes the musical score, and the librettist writes the words that are sung. Together, they create a work of art called an opera. Figure 2-4 is an E-R diagram of this degree-3 relationship.

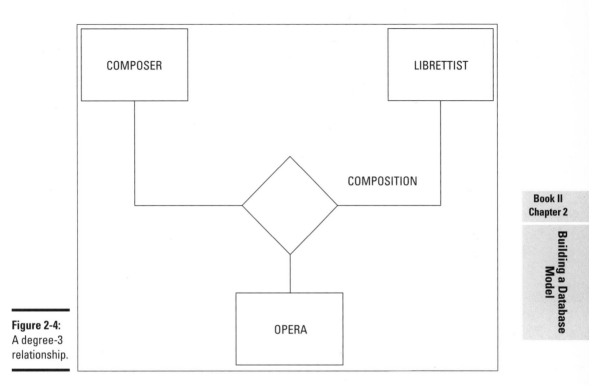

**Book II
Chapter 2**

Building a Database Model

Figure 2-4:
A degree-3
relationship.

Degree-2 relationships are sometimes called *binary relationships.* They are easier to work with than are relationships of higher degree. Fortunately, most of the systems that people want to build can be modeled quite effectively with binary relationships.

The three kinds of binary relationships are

+ A one-to-one relationship relates one instance of one entity class to one instance of a second entity class.

+ A one-to-many relationship relates one instance of one entity class to multiple instances of a second entity class.

+ A many-to-many relationship relates multiple instances of one entity class to multiple instances of a second entity class.

Figure 2-5 is an E:R diagram of a one-to-one relationship. A traveler who is a citizen of one and only one country can have one and only one passport. A passport is an official document that corresponds to one and only one person.

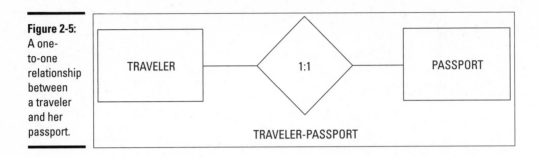

Figure 2-5:
A one-to-one relationship between a traveler and her passport.

Figure 2-6 shows an example of a one-to-many relationship. A traveler to foreign lands typically takes many photographs and then saves them later in an archive. A photographer can take many photographs, but each photograph was taken by one and only one photographer.

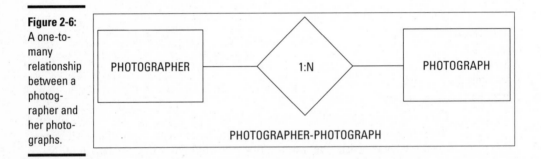

Figure 2-6:
A one-to-many relationship between a photographer and her photographs.

Figure 2-7 shows a many-to-many relationship. A traveler can visit many countries, and each country can be visited by many travelers.

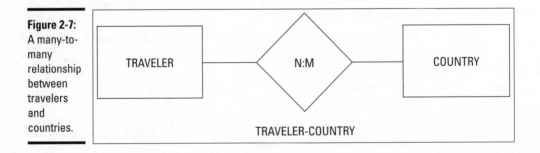

Figure 2-7:
A many-to-many relationship between travelers and countries.

Maximum cardinality

In an E-R diagram, the diamond at the center of the relationship line shows the maximum cardinality of each side of the relationship. The *maximum cardinality* is the maximum number of instances on each side of the relationship. For example, in a one-to-one relationship, the 1:1 designation means that a single instance of the entity on the left is related to a single instance of the entity on the right. In a 1:N relationship, a single instance of the entity on the left is related to multiple instances of the entity on the right. Finally, in an N:M relationship, multiple instances of the entity on the left are related to multiple instances of the entity on the right, and the maximum number of instances on the left is not necessarily equal to the maximum number of instances on the right.

Minimum cardinality

Just as maximum cardinality is the maximum number of instances of an entity on each side of a relationship, *minimum cardinality* is the minimum number of instances of an entity on each side of a relationship. In some cases, the minimum number of instances of an entity might be zero. For example, in the TRAVELER-PASSPORT relationship, a person traveling only within the United States does not need a passport and may not have one. In this case, an instance of the TRAVELER entity class may have no corresponding instance in the PASSPORT entity class, so the minimum cardinality of the PASSPORT side of the relationship is zero. On the other hand, every instance of the PASSPORT entity class corresponds to the person in the TRAVELER entity class to whom that passport was issued, so the minimum cardinality on the TRAVELER side is one.

Figure 2-8 shows the same relationship as Figure 2-5, but here minimum cardinality is indicated. The oval on the PASSPORT side of the relationship means that the minimum cardinality of PASSPORT is zero. The slash on the TRAVELER side means that the minimum cardinality is one or more. Another way of saying this is that existence of a passport is *optional,* but existence of the traveler is *mandatory.*

Book II
Chapter 2

Building a Database Model

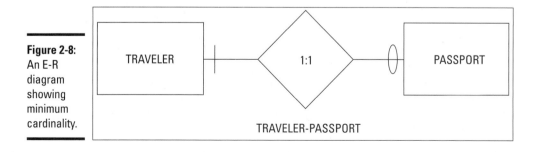

Figure 2-8:
An E-R
diagram
showing
minimum
cardinality.

TRAVELER   1:1   PASSPORT

TRAVELER-PASSPORT

Now that I have just told you that the minimum cardinality of the TRAVELER-PASSPORT relationship is mandatory to optional, get ready for a shock. It's not necessarily true. In fact, the minimum cardinality of that relationship might well be optional to mandatory. Suppose a traveler is issued a passport and then, through an unfortunate circumstance, passes away. The passport still exists and will continue to exist until it expires. However the traveler is no longer with us. The passport exists but the traveler does not. In this case, the relationship would be as shown in Figure 2-9, optional to mandatory. How can this be?

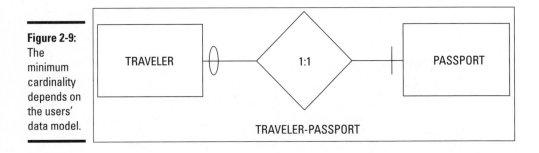

Figure 2-9:
The minimum cardinality depends on the users' data model.

The structure of an E-R model depends critically on the users' data model. How the users view the system determines how it is modeled. The TRAVELER-PASSPORT example shows that the way you model a system depends not only on the physical facts of the system, but also on the way the users view the facts. This is why capturing the users' data model accurately is so important. If your model does not match their expectations, your database application will not deliver them the information they are expecting. It may well mislead them into making bad decisions. This is why the very beginning stages of a database development project are the most important.

In most cases, the minimum cardinality of one side of a relationship will be either zero or one. It is zero if the existence of at least one instance of the entity on that side is *not* required, and it is one if the existence of at least one instance of the entity on that side *is* required. In some cases, however, the minimum cardinality of an entity may be more than one. For example, a baseball team must have at least nine players in order to compete in a baseball game. Any collection of athletes that consists of fewer than nine players is therefore not a baseball team. This fact argues that the minimum cardinality for PLAYER in the TEAM-PLAYER relationship is nine. Depending on the users' data model, you could also argue otherwise. It all depends on how the users see the system.

Don't spend too much time agonizing over whether the minimum cardinality for an entity in a relationship is one or nine or ten or any other non-zero number. The difference between zero and one is huge. It is the difference between whether something must exist or not. However, the difference between one and nine is just a matter of degree. The fact of existence is firmly established. The exact magnitude of the minimum cardinality on the mandatory side of a relationship generally has little effect on the design of the system.

Business rules

In addition to the entities and relationships that form the basis for the database application that you are constructing, another important element is the organization's *business rules.* Business rules may show up in formal policy statements or they may be unwritten rules that are generally understood by the people in the organization. In either case, you need to know what those rules are, and how they will affect the system you are designing. Business rules can differ drastically between two organizations that seem on the outside to be practically identical. There is no substitute for time spent in face-to-face meetings with stakeholders, asking probing questions, to tease out all the important business rules.

Building a Relational Model

Database modeling consists of a progression from the abstract to the concrete. The users' data model is a high-level description of what the users envisage the system to be and do. When you convert the users' data model to an entity-relationship model, you are solidifying things a little, but there is still more to do. In order to have a model that can be directly applied to the database management system, you need to make one more conversion, from the E-R model to a relational model.

Different worlds, different terminology

Newcomers to database sometimes get confused when listening to old-timers talk. This is due to the historical fact that those old-timers come out of three distinct traditions, each with its own set of terms for things. The three traditions are the relational tradition, the flat file tradition, and the personal computer tradition.

The relational tradition

The relational tradition had its beginnings in a paper published in 1970 by E. F. Codd, who was at that time employed by IBM. In that paper, Dr. Codd gave names to the major constituents of the relational model. The major elements of the relational model correspond closely to the major elements of the E-R model, making it fairly easy to translate one into the other.

In the relational model, items that people can identify and that they consider important enough to track are called *relations.* Relations in the relational model are similar to entities in the E-R model. Relations have certain properties, called *attributes,* which correspond to the attributes in the E-R model.

Relations can be represented in the form of two-dimensional tables. Each column in the table holds the information about a single attribute. The rows of the table are called *tuples.* Each tuple corresponds to an individual instance of a relation. Figure 2-10 shows an example of a relation, with attributes and tuples. Attributes are the columns: Title, Author, ISBN, and Pub. Date. The tuples are the rows.

Title	*Author*	*ISBN*	*Pub. Date*
The Road To Reality	Roger Penrose	0679454438	2004
Saturn Rukh	Robert L. Forward	0312863217	1997
Red Mars	Kim Stanley Robinson	0553092049	1993
The Artful Universe	John D. Barrow	0198539967	1995

Figure 2-10: The BOOK relation.

I mentioned that current database practitioners come out of three different traditions, the relational tradition being one of them. A second group consists of people who were dealing with flat files before the relational model became popular. Their terms *files, fields,* and *records* correspond to what Codd called *relations, attributes,* and *tuples.* The third group, the PC community, came to databases by way of the electronic spreadsheet. They used the spreadsheet terms *tables, columns,* and *rows,* to mean the same things as *files, fields,* and *records.* Table 2-1 shows how to translate what they are saying when database veterans talk about databases.

Table 2-1	**Describing the Elements of a Database**		
Relational community says	Relation	Attribute	Tuple
Flat-file community says	File	Field	Record
PC community says	Table	Column	Row

Don't be surprised if you hear database veterans mix these terms in the course of explaining or describing something. They may use them interchangeably within a single sentence. For example, one might say, "The value of the TELEPHONE attribute in the fifth record of the CUSTOMER table is Null."

What exactly is a relation?

Despite the casual manner in which database old-timers use the words *relation, file,* and *table* interchangeably, a relation is not exactly the same thing as a file or table. Relations were defined by a database theoretician, and thus the definition is very precise. The words *file* and *table,* on the other hand, are in general use and are often much more loosely defined. When I use these terms in this book, I mean them in the strict sense, as alternates for relation. That said, what's a relation? A *relation* is a two-dimensional table that must satisfy all of the following criteria:

✦ Each cell in the table must contain a single value, if it contains a value at all.

✦ All the entries in any column must be of the same kind. For example, if a column contains a telephone number in one row, it must contain telephone numbers in all rows that contain a value in that column.

✦ Each column has a unique name.

✦ The order of the columns is not significant.

✦ The order of the rows is not significant.

✦ No two rows can be identical.

A table qualifies as a relation if and only if it meets all the above criteria. A table that fails to meet one or more of them might still be considered a table in the loose sense of the word, but it is not a relation, and thus not a table in the strict sense of the word.

Functional dependencies

Functional dependencies are relationships between or among attributes. For example, two attributes of the VENDOR relation are State and Zipcode. If you know a vendor's ZIP code, you can determine the vendor's state by a simple table lookup because each ZIP code appears in only one state. Therefore, State is *functionally dependent* on Zipcode. Another way of describing this situation is to say that Zipcode *determines* State, thus Zipcode is a *determinant* of State. Functional dependencies are shown diagrammatically as follows:

```
Zipcode ⇨ State      (Zipcode determines State)
```

Sometimes, a single attribute may not be a determinant, but when it is combined with one or more other attributes, the group of them collectively is a determinant. Suppose you receive a bill from your local department store. It would list the bill number, your customer number, what you bought, how many you bought, the unit price, and the extended price for all of them. The bill you receive represents a row in the BILLS table of the store's database. It would be of the form

```
BILL(BillNo, CustNo, ProdNo, ProdName, UnitPrice, Quantity, ExtPrice)
```

The combination of UnitPrice and Quantity determines ExtPrice.

```
(UnitPrice, Quantity) ⇨ ExtPrice
```

Thus, ExtPrice is functionally dependent upon UnitPrice and Quantity.

Keys

A *key* is a group of one or more attributes that uniquely identify a tuple in a relation. For example, VendorID is a key of the VENDOR relation. VendorID determines all the other attributes in the relation. All keys are determinants, but not all determinants are keys. In the BILL relation, (UnitPrice, Quantity) is a determinant because it determines ExtendedPrice. However, (UnitPrice, Quantity) is not a key. It does not uniquely identify its tuple because another line in the relation might have the same values for Price and Quantity. The key of the BILL relation is BillNo. BillNo identifies one particular bill.

Sometimes it is hard to tell whether a determinant qualifies as a key. In the BILL case, we consider BillNo to be a key, based on the assumption that bill numbers are not duplicated. If this assumption is valid, BillNo is a unique identifier of a bill and qualifies as a key. When you are defining the keys for the relations that you build, you must make sure that your keys uniquely identify each tuple (row) in the relation.

Being Aware of the Danger of Anomalies

Just because a database table meets the qualifications to be a relation does not mean that it is well designed. In fact, bad relations are incredibly easy to create. By a bad relation, I mean one that is prone to errors or that is confusing to users. The best way to illustrate a bad relation is to show you an example.

Suppose an automotive service shop specializes in transmissions, brakes, and suspension systems. Tyson is the lead mechanic for transmissions, Dave is the lead mechanic for brakes, and Keith is the lead mechanic for suspension systems. Tyson works out of the Alabama Avenue location, Dave works at the Perimeter Road shop, and Keith operates out of the Main Street garage. You could summarize this information with a relation MECHANICS, as shown in Figure 2-11.

Figure 2-11:
The
MECHANICS
relation.

Mechanic	*Specialty*	*Location*
Tyson	Transmissions	Alabama Avenue
Dave	Brakes	Perimeter Road
Keith	Suspensions	Main Street

This table qualifies as a relation. Each cell contains only one value. All entries in each column are of the same kind, all names, or all specialties, or all locations. Each column has a unique name. The order of the columns and rows is not significant. If the order were changed, no information would be lost. And finally, no two rows are identical.

So what's the problem? Problems can arise when things change, and things always change, sooner or later. Problems caused by changes are known as *modification anomalies* and come in different types, two of which I describe here:

✦ **Deletion anomaly:** Suppose that Dave decides to go back to school and study computer science. When he quits his job, you can delete the second row in the table shown in Figure 2-11. If you do however, you lose more than the fact that Dave is the brakes mechanic. You also lose the fact that brake service takes place at the Perimeter Road location. This is a *deletion anomaly*. It is called a deletion anomaly because you lose information that you don't want to lose, as a result of a deletion operation.

✦ **Insertion anomaly:** Suppose you want to start working on engines at the Alabama Avenue facility. You cannot record that fact until an engine mechanic is hired to work there. This is an *insertion anomaly*. Because Mechanic is the key to this relation, you cannot insert a new tuple into the relation unless it has a value in the Mechanic column.

If modification anomalies are possible in a database, they will probably occur. If they occur, they can seriously degrade a database's usefulness. They may even cause users to draw incorrect conclusions from the results of queries they pose to the database.

Eliminating anomalies

When Dr. Codd created the relational model, he recognized the possibility of data corruption due to modification anomalies. To address this problem, he devised the concept of *normal forms*. Any table that satisfies the requirements for being a relation is in First Normal Form (1NF). As I discuss in the preceding section, tables in 1NF are subject to certain modification anomalies. Codd's Second Normal Form (2NF) removes these anomalies, but the possibility of others still remains. Codd foresaw some of those anomalies and defined Third Normal Form (3NF) to deal with them. Subsequent research uncovered the possibility of progressively more obscure anomalies and a succession of normal forms was devised to eliminate them. Boyce-Codd Normal Form (BCNF), Fourth Normal Form (4NF), Fifth Normal Form (5NF), and Domain/Key Normal Form (DKNF) provide increasing levels of protection against modification anomalies.

It is instructive to look at the normal forms in order to gain an insight into the kinds of anomalies that can occur, and how normalization eliminates the possibility of such anomalies. To start, consider the Second Normal Form. Suppose Tyson receives certification to repair brakes and spends some of his time at the Perimeter Road garage fixing brakes as well as continuing to do his old job repairing transmissions at the Alabama Avenue shop. This leads to the table shown in Figure 2-12.

Figure 2-12:
The
modified
MECHANICS
relation.

Mechanic	Specialty	Location
Tyson	Transmissions	Alabama Avenue
Tyson	Brakes	Perimeter Road
Dave	Brakes	Perimeter Road
Keith	Suspensions	Main Street

This table still qualifies as a relation, but the Mechanic column no longer is a key because it does not uniquely determine a row. However, the combination of Mechanic and Specialty does qualify as a determinant and as a key.

(Mechanic, Specialty) ⇨ Location

This looks fine, but there is a problem. What if Tyson decides to work full time on brakes, and not fix transmissions any longer. If we delete the Tyson/Transmissions/Alabama row, we not only remove the fact that Tyson works on transmissions, but we also lose the fact that transmission work is done at the Alabama shop. This is a deletion anomaly. This problem is caused by the fact that Specialty is a determinant, but is not a key. It is only part of a key.

Specialty ⇨ Location

REMEMBER

For a relation to be in Second Normal Form, every non-key attribute must be dependent on the entire key.

We can meet that requirement by breaking up the MECHANICS relation into two relations. This is illustrated in Figure 2-13.

Figure 2-13:
The
MECHANICS
relation has
been broken
into two
relations,
MECH-
SPEC and
SPEC-LOC.

Mechanic	Specialty
Tyson	Transmissions
Tyson	Brakes
Dave	Brakes
Keith	Suspensions

Table MECH-SPEC

Specialty	Location
Transmissions	Alabama Avenue
Brakes	Perimeter Road
Suspensions	Main Street

Table SPEC-LOC

The old MECHANICS relation had problems because it dealt with more than one idea. It dealt with the idea of the specialties of the mechanics, and it also dealt with the idea of where various specialties are performed. By breaking the MECHANICS relation into two, each one of which deals with only one idea, the modification anomalies disappear. Mechanic and Specialty together comprise a composite key of the MECH-SPEC relation and all the non-key attributes depend on the entire key because there are no non-key attributes. Specialty is the key of the SPEC-LOC relation and all of the non-key attributes (Location) depend on the entire key, which in this case is Specialty. Now if Tyson decides to work full time on brakes, the Tyson/Transmissions row can be removed from the MECH-SPEC relation. The fact that transmission work is done at the Alabama garage is still recorded in the SPEC-LOC relation.

A relation in Second Normal Form could still harbor anomalies. Suppose you are concerned about your cholesterol intake and want to track the relative levels of cholesterol in various foods. You might construct a table such as the one shown in Figure 2-14.

Figure 2-14:
The
LIPIDLEVEL
relation.

FoodItem	FoodType	Cholesterol
apple	fruit	none
beefsteak	red meat	high
hen's egg	egg	very high
salmon	fish	medium

This relation is in First Normal Form, and because it has a single attribute key (FoodItem), it is automatically in Second Normal Form also. All non-key attributes are dependent on the entire key. Nonetheless, there is still the chance of an anomaly. What if you decide to eliminate all beef products from your diet? If you delete the 'Beefsteak' row from the table, you not only eliminate beefsteak, but you also lose the fact that red meat is high in cholesterol. This fact might be important to you if you are considering substituting some other red meat such as pork, bison, or lamb for the beef you no longer eat. This is a deletion anomaly. There is a corresponding insertion anomaly. You cannot add a FoodType of Poultry, for instance, and assign it a Cholesterol value of High until you actually enter in a specific FoodItem of the Poultry type.

The problem this time is once again a matter of keys and dependencies. FoodType depends on FoodItem. If the FoodItem is Apple the FoodType must be Fruit. If the FoodItem is Salmon, the FoodType must be Fish. Similarly, Cholesterol depends on FoodType. If the FoodType is Egg, the Cholesterol value will be Very High. This is a *transitive dependency.*

FoodItem ⇨ FoodType ⇨ Cholesterol

Transitive dependencies are a source of modification anomalies. You can eliminate the anomalies by eliminating the transitive dependency. Breaking the table into two tables, each one of which embodies a single idea, does the trick. Figure 2-15 shows the resulting tables, which are now in Third Normal Form.

Figure 2-15:
The ITEM-TYPE relation and the TYPE-CHOL relation.

FoodItem	FoodType
apple	fruit
beefsteak	red meat
hen's egg	egg
salmon	fish

Table ITEM-TYPE

FoodType	Cholesterol
fruit	none
red meat	high
egg	very high
fish	medium

Table TYPE-CHOL

Now if you delete the Beefsteak row from the ITEM-TYPE relation, the fact that red meat is high in cholesterol is retained in the TYPE-CHOL relation. You can add poultry to the TYPE-CHOL relation, even though you don't have a specific type of poultry in the ITEM-TYPE relation.

The higher normal forms

Boyce-Codd Normal Form, Fourth Normal Form, and Fifth Normal Form each eliminate successively more obscure types of anomalies. In all likelihood, you might never encounter the types of anomalies they remove. There is one higher normal form, however, that is worth discussing: the Domain/Key Normal Form. DKNF is the only normal form that *guarantees* that a database contains no modification anomalies. If you want to be absolutely certain that your database is anomaly-free, put it into DKNF.

Happily, Domain/Key Normal Form is easier to understand than most of the other normal forms. You need to understand only three things: constraints, keys, and domains.

A relation is in Domain/Key Normal Form if every constraint on the relation is a logical consequence of the definition of keys and domains:

✦ A *constraint* is a rule that restricts the static values that attributes may assume. The rule must be precise enough for you to tell whether the attribute follows the rule. A static value is one that does not vary with time.

✦ A *key* is a unique identifier of a tuple.

✦ The *domain* of an attribute is the set of all values that the attribute can take.

If enforcing key and domain restrictions on a table causes all constraints to be met, the table is in DKNF. It is also guaranteed to be free of all modification anomalies.

As an example of putting a table into DKNF, look again at the LIPIDLEVEL relation in Figure 2-14. You can analyze it as follows:

LIPIDLEVEL(FoodItem, FoodType, Cholesterol)

Key: FoodItem

Constraints: FoodItem ⇨ FoodType

FoodType ⇨ Cholesterol

Cholesterol in ('none', 'low', 'medium', 'high', 'very high')

This relation is not in DKNF. It is not even in 3NF. However, you can put it into DKNF by making all constraints a logical consequence of domains and keys. We can make the Cholesterol constraint a logical consequence of domains by defining the domain of Cholesterol to be ('none', 'low', 'medium', 'high', 'very high'). The constraint 'FoodItem⇨FoodType' is a logical consequence of keys because FoodItem is a key. Those were both easy. One more constraint to go! We can handle the third constraint by making FoodType a key. The way to do this is to break the LIPIDLEVEL relation into two relations, one having FoodItem as its key and the other having FoodType as its key. This is exactly what we did in Figure 2-15. What we did to put LIPIDLEVEL into 3NF put it into DKNF at the same time.

Here is the new description for this system:

Domain Definitions:

FoodItem in CHAR(30)

FoodType in CHAR(30)

Cholesterol in ('none', 'low', 'medium', 'high', 'very high')

Relation and Key Definitions:

ITEM-TYPE (FoodItem, FoodType)

Key: FoodItem

TYPE-CHOL (FoodType, Cholesterol)

Key: FoodType

All constraints are a logical consequence of keys and domains.

The Database Integrity versus Performance Tradeoff

In the previous section, we saw some of the problems that can arise with database relations, and how they can be solved through normalization. We saw that the ultimate in normalization is Domain/Key Normal Form, which provides solid protection from the data corruption that can occur due to modification anomalies. It might seem that whenever you create a database, you should always put all its tables into DKNF. This, however, is not true.

When you guarantee a database's freedom from anomalies by putting all its tables into DKNF, you do so at a cost. Why? When you made your original unnormalized design, you grouped attributes together into relations because they had something in common. If you normalize some of those tables by breaking them up into multiple tables, you are separating attributes that would normally be grouped together. This can degrade your performance on retrievals if you want to use those attributes together. You will have to combine these now-separated attributes again before proceeding with the rest of the retrieval operation.

Consider an example. Suppose you are the secretary of a club made up of people located all around the United States who share a hobby. It is your job to send them a monthly newsletter as well as notices of various sorts. You have a database consisting of a single relation, named MEMBERS.

> MEMBERS(MemID, Fname, Lname, Street, City, State, ZIP)
>
> Key: MemID
>
> Functional Dependencies:
>
> MemID ⇨ all non-key attributes
>
> ZIP ⇨ State

Book II
Chapter 2

This relation is not in DKNF because State is dependent on ZIP and ZIP is not a key. If you know a person's ZIP code, you can do a simple table lookup and you will know what state he lives in.

You could put the database into DKNF by breaking the MEMBERS table into two tables as follows:

> MEM-ZIP(MemID, Fname, Lname, Street, City, ZIP)
>
> ZIP-STATE(ZIP, State)

MemID is the key of MEM-ZIP, and ZIP is the key of ZIP-STATE. The database is now in DKNF, but consider what you have gained and what you have lost:

✦ **What you have gained:** In MEMBERS, if we delete the last club member in ZIP code 92027, we lose the fact that ZIP code 92027 is in California. However, in the normalized database, that information is retained in ZIP-STATE when the last member with that ZIP code is removed from MEM-ZIP.

In MEMBERS, if you want to add the fact that ZIP code 07110 is in New Jersey, you can't, until you have a member living in that ZIP code. The normalized database handles this nicely by allowing you to add that state and ZIP code to ZIP-STATE, even though there are no members who live there in the MEM-ZIP table.

✦ **What you have lost:** Because the primary purpose of this database is to facilitate mailings to members, every time a mailing is made, the MEM-ZIP table and the ZIP-STATE table have to be joined together to generate the mailing labels. This is an extra operation that would not be needed if the data were all kept in a single MEMBERS table.

✦ **What you care about:** Considering the purpose of this database, the club secretary probably doesn't care what state a particular ZIP code is in if the club has no members in that ZIP code. She also probably doesn't care about adding ZIP codes where there are no members. In this case, both of the gains from normalization are of no value to the user. However, the cost of normalization is a genuine penalty. It will take longer for the address labels to print out based on the data in the normalized database than it would if they were stored in the unnormalized MEMBERS table. For this case, and others like it, normalization to DKNF does not make sense.

Chapter 3: Balancing Performance and Correctness

In This Chapter

✔ Designing a database

✔ Maintaining database integrity

✔ Avoiding data corruption

✔ Speeding data retrievals

✔ Indexes

✔ Data structures

✔ Reading execution plans

✔ Optimizing execution plans

✔ Load balancing

There is a natural conflict between the performance of a database and its correctness. If you want to minimize the chance that incorrect or inappropriate data will appear in a database, you must include safeguards against it. These safeguards take time and thus slow down operation.

Configuring a database for the highest possible performance may make the data it contains unreliable to the point of being unacceptable. Conversely, making the database as immune to corruption as possible could reduce performance to the point of being unacceptable. A database designer must aim for that "sweet spot" somewhere in the middle where performance is high enough to be acceptable, and the few data errors that occur do not significantly affect the conclusions that are drawn from information that is retrieved. Some applications put the sweet spot closer to the performance end; others put it closer to the reliability end. Each situation is potentially different, and depends on what is most important to the stakeholders. To illustrate the considerations that apply when designing a database system, in this chapter, I show you a fictional example, as well as discuss other factors you must consider when you're navigating the delicate balance between correctness and performance.

Designing a Sample Database

Imagine a local auto repair business located in the small town of Springfield, owned and operated by the fictional Abraham "Abe" Hanks. Abe employs mechanics who perform repairs on automobiles brought in by Abe's corporate customers. Repair jobs are recorded in invoices, which include charges for parts and labor. Charges are itemized on separate lines on the invoices. The mechanics hold certifications in such specialty areas as brakes, transmissions, electrical systems, and engines. Abe buys parts from multiple suppliers. Multiple suppliers could potentially supply the same part.

The E-R model for Honest Abe's

Figure 3-1 shows the E-R model for Honest Abe's Fleet Auto Repair.

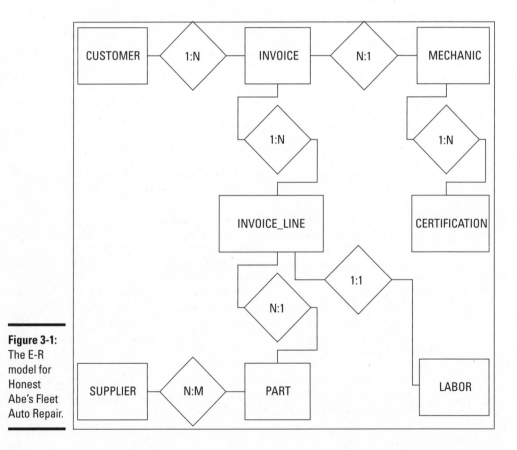

Figure 3-1:
The E-R model for Honest Abe's Fleet Auto Repair.

Take a look at the relationships.

✦ A customer can make purchases on multiple invoices, but each invoice deals with one and only one customer.

✦ An invoice can have multiple invoice lines, but each invoice line appears on one and only one invoice.

✦ A mechanic can work on multiple jobs, each one represented by one invoice, but each invoice is the responsibility of one and only one mechanic.

✦ A mechanic may have multiple certifications, but each certification belongs to one and only one mechanic.

✦ Multiple suppliers can supply a given standard part, and multiple parts can be sourced by a single supplier.

✦ One and only one part can appear on a single invoice line, and one and only one invoice line on an invoice can contain a particular part.

✦ One and only one standard labor charge can appear on a single invoice line, and one and only one invoice line on an invoice can contain a particular standard labor charge.

After you have an E-R model that accurately represents your target system, the next step is to convert the E-R model into a relational model. The relational model is the direct precursor to a relational database.

Converting an E-R model into a relational model

The first step in converting an E-R model into a relational model is to understand how the terminology used for one relates to the terminology used for the other. In the E-R model, we speak of *entities, attributes, identifiers,* and *relationships.* In the relational model, the primary items of concern are *relations, attributes, keys,* and *relationships.* How do these two sets of terms relate to each other?

In the E-R model, an *entity* is something we have identified as being important: Entities are physical or conceptual objects that we want to keep track of. This sounds a lot like the definition of a relation. The difference is that for something to be a relation, it must satisfy the requirements of First Normal Form. An entity might translate into a relation, but you have to be careful to assure that the resulting relation is in First Normal Form (1NF).

If you can translate an entity into a corresponding relation, the attributes of the entity translate directly into the attributes of the relation. Furthermore, an entity's identifier translates into the corresponding relation's key. The relationships between entities correspond exactly with the relationships between relations. Based on these correspondences, it's not too difficult to translate an E-R model into a relational model. The resulting relational model is not necessarily a good relational model, however. You may have to normalize the relations in it to protect it from modification anomalies. You may also have to decompose any many-to-many relationships to simpler one-to-many relationships. After your relational model is appropriately normalized and decomposed, the translation to a relational database is straightforward.

Normalizing a relational model

A database is fully normalized when all the relations in it are in Domain/Key Normal Form. As I mention in Chapter 2 of this minibook, at times, you may not want to normalize all the way to DKNF. As a rule, however, it is best to normalize to DKNF, and then check performance. Only if performance is unacceptable should you consider selective denormalization to speed things up.

Consider the example system shown in Figure 3-1, and then focus on one of the entities in the model. An important entity in the Honest Abe model is the CUSTOMER entity. Figure 3-2 shows a representation of the CUSTOMER entity (top) and the corresponding relation in the relational model (bottom).

Figure 3-2:
The
CUSTOMER
entity
and the
CUSTOMER
relation.

CUSTOMER
    CustID
    CustName
    StreetAddr
    City
    State
    PostalCode
    ContactName
    ContactPhone
    ContactEmail

CUSTOMER (CustID, CustName, Street Addr, City, State, PostalCode, ContactName, ContactPhone, ContactEmail)

The attributes of the CUSTOMER entity are listed in Figure 3-2. Figure 3-2 also shows the standard way of listing the attributes of a relation. The CustID attribute is underlined to signify that it is the key of the CUSTOMER relation. Every customer has a unique CustID number.

One way to determine whether CUSTOMER is in DKNF is to see whether all constraints on the relation are the result of the definitions of domains and keys. An easier way, one that works well most of the time, is to see if the relation deals with more than one idea. It does, and thus cannot be in DKNF. One idea is the customer itself. CustId, CustName, StreetAddr, and City are primarily associated with this idea. Another idea is the geographic idea. As we saw earlier, if you know the postal code of an address, you can find the state or province that contains that postal code. Finally, there is the idea of the contact person at the customer. ContactName, ContactPhone, and ContactEmail are the attributes that cluster around this idea.

You can normalize the CUSTOMER relation by breaking it into three relations as follows:

Book II
Chapter 3

Balancing Performance and Correctness

> CUSTOMER (CustID, CustName, StreetAddr, City, PostalCode, ContactName)
>
> POSTAL (PostalCode, State)
>
> CONTACT (ContactName, ContactPhone, ContactEmail)

These three relations are in DKNF. They also demonstrate a new idea about keys. The three relations are closely related to each other because they share attributes. The PostalCode attribute is contained in both the CUSTOMER and the POSTAL relations. The ContactName attribute is contained in both the CUSTOMER and the CONTACT relations. CustID is called the *primary key* of the CUSTOMER relation. It must uniquely identify each tuple in the relation. Similarly, PostalCode is the primary key of the POSTAL relation and ContactName is the primary key of the CONTACT relation.

In addition to being the primary key of the POSTAL relation, PostalCode is a *foreign key* in the CUSTOMER relation. It provides a link between the two relations. In the same way, ContactName is a foreign key in the CUSTOMER relation as well as being the primary key of the CONTACT relation. An attribute need not be unique in a relation where it is serving as a foreign key, but it must be unique on the other end of the relationship where it is the primary key.

After you have normalized a relation into DKNF, as we did above with the original CUSTOMER relation, you should ask yourself whether full normalization makes sense in this specific case. Depending on how you plan to use the relations, you may want to denormalize somewhat to improve performance. In this example, you may want to fold the POSTAL relation back into the CUSTOMER relation if you frequently need to access your customers' complete address. On the other hand, it might make sense to keep CONTACT as a separate relation, if you frequently refer to customer address information without specifically needing your primary contact at that company.

Handling binary relationships

In Chapter 2 of this minibook, I describe the three kinds of binary relationships: one-to-one, one-to-many, and many-to-many. The simplest of these is the one-to-one relationship. In the Honest Abe model earlier in this chapter, I use the relationship between a part and an invoice line to illustrate a one-to-one relationship. Figure 3-3 shows the E-R model of this relationship.

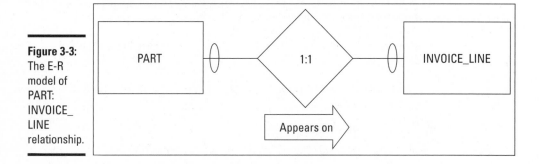

Figure 3-3:
The E-R
model of
PART:
INVOICE_
LINE
relationship.

The maximum cardinality diamond explicitly shows that this is a one-to-one relationship. The relationship is, "one PART connects to one INVOICE_LINE." The minimum cardinality oval at both ends of the PART:INVOICE_LINE relationship shows that it is possible to have a PART without an INVOICE_LINE, and it is also possible to have an INVOICE_LINE without an associated PART. A part on the shelf has not yet been sold, so it would not appear on an invoice. In addition, an invoice line could hold a labor charge rather than a part.

A relational model corresponding to the E-R model shown in Figure 3-3 might look something like the model in Figure 3-4. Figure 3-4 is an example of a *data structure diagram*.

PartNo is the primary key of the PART relation, and InvoiceLineNo is the primary key of the INVOICE_LINE relation. PartNo also serves as a foreign key in the INVOICE_LINE relation, binding the two relations together. Similarly, InvoiceNo, the primary key of the INVOICE relation, serves as a foreign key in the INVOICE_LINE relation.

Note: For a business that sells only products, the relationship between products and invoice lines might be different. In such a case, the minimum cardinality on the products side might be mandatory. That is not the case for the fictitious company in this example. It is important that your model reflect accurately the system you are modeling. You could model very similar systems for two different clients and end up with very different models. You need to account for differences in business rules and standard operating procedure.

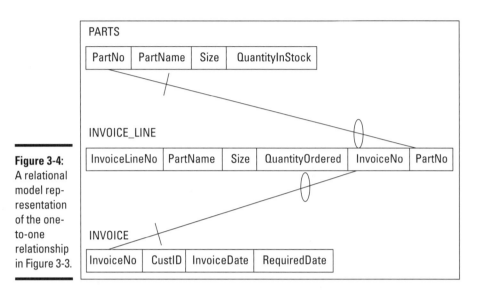

Figure 3-4:
A relational model representation of the one-to-one relationship in Figure 3-3.

 A one-to-many relationship is somewhat more complex than a one-to-one relationship. One instance of the first relation corresponds to multiple instances of the second relation. An example of a one-to-many relationship in the Honest Abe model would be the relationship between a mechanic and his or her certifications. A mechanic can have multiple certifications, but each certification belongs to one and only one mechanic. The E-R diagram shown in Figure 3-5 illustrates that relationship.

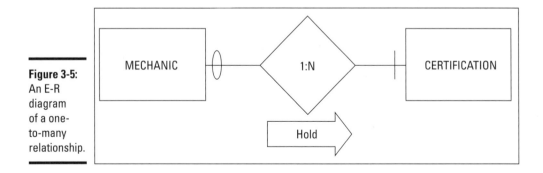

Figure 3-5:
An E-R diagram of a one-to-many relationship.

The maximum cardinality diamond shows that one mechanic may have many certifications. The minimum cardinality slash on the CERTIFICATIONS side indicates that a mechanic must have at least one certification. The oval on the MECHANICS side shows that a certification may exist that is not held by any of the mechanics.

You can convert this simple E-R model to a relational model and illustrate the result with a data structure diagram, as shown in Figure 3-6.

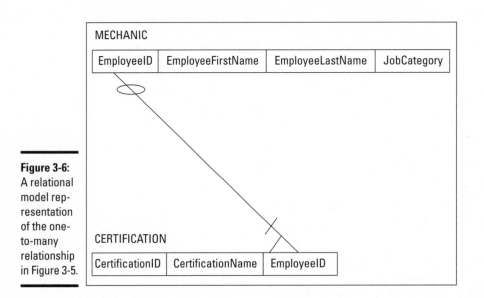

Many-to-many relationships are the most complex of the binary relationships. Two relations that are connected by a many-to-many relationship can have serious integrity problems, even if both relations are in DKNF. To illustrate the problem and then the solution, consider a many-to-many relationship in the Honest Abe model.

The relationship between suppliers and parts is a many-to-many relationship. A supplier may be a source for multiple different parts and a specific part may be obtainable from multiple suppliers. Figure 3-7 is an E-R diagram that illustrates this relationship.

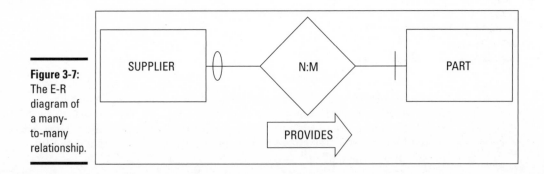

The maximum cardinality diamond shows that one supplier can supply different parts, and one specific part can be supplied by multiple suppliers. The fact that N is different from M shows that the number of suppliers that can supply a part does not have to be equal to the number of different parts that a single supplier can supply. The minimum cardinality slash on the SUPPLIER side of the relationship indicates that a part must come from a supplier. Parts don't materialize out of thin air. The oval on the PART side of the relationship means that a company could have qualified a supplier before it has supplied any parts.

So, what's the problem? The difficulty arises with how you use keys to link relations together. In the MECHANIC:CERTIFICATION one-to-many relationship, I linked MECHANIC to CERTIFICATION by placing EmployeeID, the primary key of the MECHANIC relation, into CERTIFICATION as a foreign key. I could do this because there was only one mechanic associated with any given certification. However, I can't put SupplierID into PART as a foreign key because any part can be sourced by multiple suppliers, not just one. Similarly, I can't put PartNo into SUPPLIER as a foreign key. A supplier can supply multiple parts, not just one.

To turn the E-R Model of the SUPPLIER:PART relationship into a robust relational model, decompose the many-to-many relationship into two one-to-many relationships by inserting an *intersection relation* between SUPPLIER and PART. The intersection relation, which I name SUPPLIER_PART, contains the primary key of SUPPLIER and the primary key of PART. Figure 3-8 shows the data structure diagram for the decomposed relationship.

Book II
Chapter 3

Balancing
Performance and
Correctness

Figure 3-8: The relational model representation of the decomposition of the many-to-many relationship in Figure 3-7.

SUPPLIER

| SupplierID | SupplierName | Street | City | State | PostalCode | ContactPerson | ContactTelephone |

SUPPLIER_PART

| SupplierID | PartNo |

PART

| PartNo | PartName | Size | QuantityInStock |

The SUPPLIER relation has a record (row, tuple) for every qualified supplier. The PART relation has a record for every part that Honest Abe uses. The SUPPLIER_PART relation has a record for every part that is supplied by every supplier. Thus there are multiple records in the SUPPLIER_PART relation for each supplier, depending on the number of different parts supplied by that supplier. Similarly, there are multiple records in the SUPPLIER_PART relation for each part, depending on the number of suppliers that supply each different part. If five suppliers are supplying N2457 alternators, there are five records in SUPPLIER_PART corresponding to the N2457 alternator. If Roadrunner Distribution supplies 15 different parts, 15 records in SUPPLIER_PART will relate to Roadrunner Distribution.

A sample conversion

Figure 3-9 shows the E-R diagram constructed earlier for Honest Abe's Fleet Auto Repair.

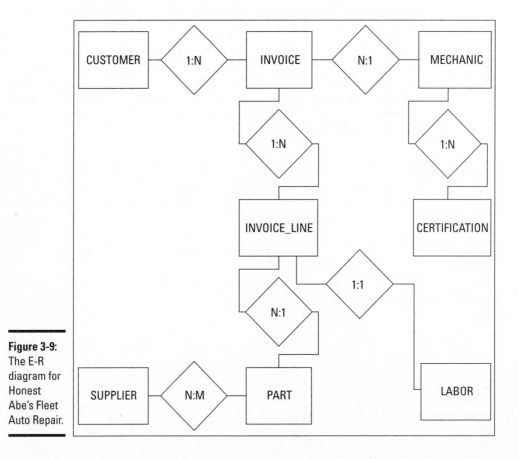

Figure 3-9:
The E-R diagram for Honest Abe's Fleet Auto Repair.

The many-to-many relationship tells you that you have to decompose it by creating an intersection relation. First, however, look at the relations that correspond to the pictured entities and their primary keys:

Relation	Primary Key
CUSTOMER	CustomerID
INVOICE	InvoiceNo
INVOICE_LINE	Invoice_Line_No
MECHANIC	EmployeeID
CERTIFICATION	CertificationNo
SUPPLIER	SupplierID
PART	PartNo
LABOR	LaborChargeCode

Book II
Chapter 3

Balancing
Performance and
Correctness

In each case, the primary key uniquely identifies a row in its associated table.

There is one many-to-many relationship, SUPPLIER:PART, so you need to place an intersection relation between these two relations. As shown in Figure 3-8, call it SUPPLIER_PART. Figure 3-10 shows the data structure diagram for this relational model.

This relational model includes eight relations that correspond to the eight entities in Figure 3-9, plus one intersection relations that replaces the many-to-many relationship. There are two one-to-one relationships and six one-to-many relationships. Minimum cardinality is denoted by slashes and ovals. For example, in the SUPPLIER:PART relationship, in order for a part to be in Honest Abe's inventory, that part must have been provided by a supplier. Thus there is a slash on the SUPPLIER side of that relationship. However, a company can be considered a qualified supplier without ever having sold Honest Abe a part. That is why there is an oval on the PART side of the relationship. Similar logic applies to the slashes and ovals on the other relationship lines.

When you have a relational model that accurately reflects the E-R model and contains no many-to-many relationships, construction of a relational database is straightforward. You have identified the relations, the attributes of those relations, the primary and foreign keys of those relations, and the relationships between those relations.

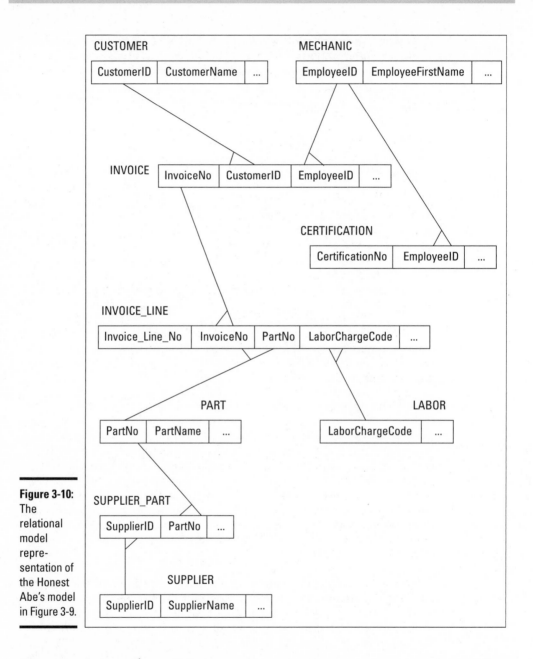

Figure 3-10: The relational model representation of the Honest Abe's model in Figure 3-9.

Maintaining Integrity

Probably the most important characteristic of any database system is that it takes good care of the data. There is no point in collecting and storing data if you cannot rely on its accuracy. Maintaining the integrity of data should be one of your primary concerns as either a database administrator or database application developer. There are three main kinds of data integrity to consider — entity, domain, and referential — and, in this section, I look at each in turn.

Entity integrity

An entity is either a physical or conceptual object that you deem to be important. *Entity integrity* just means that our database representation of an entity is consistent with the entity it is modeling. Database tables are representations of physical or conceptual entities. Although the tables are in no way copies or clones of the entities they represent, they capture the essential features of those entities and do not in any way conflict with the entities they are modeling.

An important requisite of a database with entity integrity is that every table has a primary key. The defining feature of a primary key is that it distinguishes any given row in a table from all the other rows. We can enforce entity integrity in a table by applying constraints. We have already seen that the NOT NULL constraint protects against one kind of duplication because one row with a null value for the primary key may not be distinguishable from another row that also has a primary key with a null value. This is not sufficient, however, because it does not prevent two rows in the table from having duplicate non-null values. One solution to that problem is to apply the UNIQUE constraint. Here's an example:

```
CREATE TABLE CUSTOMER (
    CustName          CHAR (30),
    Address1          CHAR (30),
    Address2          CHAR (30),
    City              CHAR (25),
    State             CHAR (2),
    PostalCode        CHAR (10),
    Telephone         CHAR (13),
    Email             CHAR (30),

    UNIQUE (CustName) ) ;
```

The UNIQUE constraint prevents two people with the exact same name from being entered into the database. In some businesses, it is likely that two customers will have the same name. In that case, using an auto-incrementing integer as the primary key is the best solution: It leaves no possibility of duplication.

Although the UNIQUE constraint guarantees that at least one column in a table contains no duplicates, you can achieve the same result with the PRIMARY KEY constraint, which applies to the entire table rather than just one column of the table. Below is an example of the use of the PRIMARY KEY constraint:

```
CREATE TABLE CUSTOMER (
    CustName            CHAR (30)    PRIMARY KEY,
    Address1            CHAR (30),
    Address2            CHAR (30),
    City                CHAR (25),
    State               CHAR (2),
    PostalCode          CHAR (10),
    Telephone           CHAR (13),
    Email               CHAR (30) ) ;
```

A primary key is an attribute of a table. It could comprise a single column or a combination of columns. In some cases, every column in a table must be part of the primary key in order to guarantee that there are no duplicate rows.

Domain integrity

The set of values that an attribute of an entity can have is that attribute's *domain*. For example, say that a manufacturer identifies its products with part numbers that all start with the letters *GJ*. Any time a person tries to enter a new part number that doesn't start with GJ into the system, a violation of domain integrity occurs. *Domain integrity* in this case is maintained by adding a constraint to the system that all part numbers must start with the letters GJ. You can specify a domain with a domain constraint, as follows:

```
CREATE DOMAIN PartNoDomain CHAR (15)
    CHECK (SUBSTRING (PartNo FROM 1 FOR 2) = 'GJ') ;
```

After a domain has been created, you can use it in a table definition:

```
CREATE TABLE PRODUCT (
    PartNo              PartNoDomain          PRIMARY KEY,
    PartName            CHAR (30),
    Cost                Numeric,
    QuantityStocked     Integer;
```

The domain is specified instead of the data type.

Referential integrity

Entity integrity and domain integrity apply to individual tables. Relational databases depend not only on tables but also on the relationships between tables. Those relationships are in the form of one table referencing another. Those references must be consistent in order for the database to have *referential integrity.* Problems can arise when data is added to or changed in a table and that addition or alteration is not reflected in the related tables. Consider the sample database created by the following code:

```
CREATE TABLE CUSTOMER (
    CustomerName        CHAR (30)       PRIMARY KEY,
    Address1            CHAR (30),
    Address2            CHAR (30),
    City                CHAR (25)       NOT NULL,
    State               CHAR (2),
    PostalCode          CHAR (10),
    Phone               CHAR (13),
    Email               CHAR (30)
    ) ;

CREATE TABLE PRODUCT (
    ProductName         CHAR (30)       PRIMARY KEY,
    Price               CHAR (30)
    ) ;

CREATE TABLE EMPLOYEE (
    EmployeeName        CHAR (30)       PRIMARY KEY,
    ADDRESS1            CHAR (30),
    Address2            CHAR (30),
    City                CHAR (25),
    State               CHAR (2),
    PostalCode          CHAR (10),
    HomePhone           CHAR (13),
    OfficeExtension     CHAR (4),
    HireDate            DATE,
    JobClassification   CHAR (10),
    HourSalComm         CHAR (1)
    ) ;

CREATE TABLE ORDERS (
    OrderNumber         INTEGER             PRIMARY KEY,
    ClientName          CHAR (30),
    TestOrdered         CHAR (30),
    Salesperson         CHAR (30),
    OrderDate           DATE,
    CONSTRAINT NameFK FOREIGN KEY (CustomerName)
       REFERENCES CUSTOMER (CustomerName)
          ON DELETE CASCADE,
    CONSTRAINT ProductFK FOREIGN KEY (ProductOrdered)
       REFERENCES PRODUCT (ProductName)
          ON DELETE CASCADE,
    CONSTRAINT SalesFK FOREIGN KEY (Salesperson)
       REFERENCES EMPLOYEE (EmployeeName)
          ON DELETE CASCADE
    ) ;
```

In this system, the ORDERS table is directly related to the CUSTOMER table, the PRODUCT table, and the EMPLOYEE table. One of the attributes of ORDERS serves as a foreign key by corresponding to the primary key of CUSTOMER. The ORDERS table is linked to PRODUCT and to EMPLOYEE by the same mechanism.

The ON DELETE CASCADE clause is included in the definition of the constraints on the ORDERS table to prevent deletion anomalies, which I cover in the next section.

Some implementations do not yet support the ON DELETE CASCADE syntax, so don't be surprised if it doesn't work for you. In such cases, you will have to cascade the deletes to the child tables by hand.

Avoiding Data Corruption

Databases are susceptible to corruption. It is possible, but extremely rare, for data in a database to be altered by some physical event, such as the flipping of a one to a zero by a cosmic ray. In general, only three occasions cause the data in a database to be corrupted:

✦ Adding data to a table

✦ Changing data in a table

✦ Deleting data from a table

If you don't allow changes to be made to a database (in other words, if you make it a read-only database), it can't be modified in a way that adds erroneous and misleading information (although it can still be destroyed completely). However, read-only databases are of limited use. Most things that you want to track change over time, and the database needs to change too. Changes to the database can lead to inconsistencies in its data, called *anomalies.* By careful design, you can minimize the impact of these anomalies, or even prevent them from ever occurring.

As discussed in Chapter 2 of this minibook, anomalies can be largely prevented by normalizing a database. This can be done by ensuring that each table in the database deals with only one idea. The E-R model of the Honest Abe database shown earlier in Figures 3-1 and 3-9 is a good example of a model where each entity represents a single idea. The only problem with it is the presence of a many-to-many relationship. As in the relational model shown in Figure 3-10, you can eliminate that problem in the E-R model by inserting an intersection relation between the SUPPLIERS entity and the PARTS entity to convert the many-to-many relationship to two one-to-many relationships. Figure 3-11 shows the result.

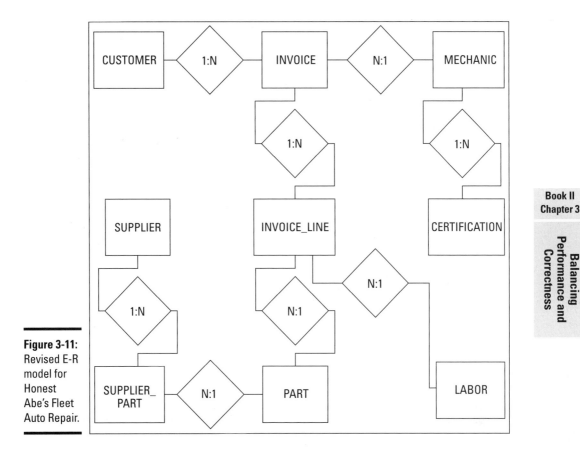

Book II
Chapter 3

Balancing
Performance and
Correctness

Figure 3-11:
Revised E-R
model for
Honest
Abe's Fleet
Auto Repair.

Speeding Data Retrievals

Clearly, maintaining the integrity of a database is of vital importance. A database is worthless, or even worse than worthless, if erroneous data in it leads to bad decisions and lost opportunities. However, the database must also allow needed information to be retrieved in a reasonable amount of time. Sometimes late information causes just as much harm as no information. The speed with which information is retrieved from a database depends on a number of factors. The size of the database and the speed of the hardware it is running on are obvious factors. Perhaps most critical, however, is the method used to access table data, which depends on the way the data is structured on the storage medium.

Hierarchical storage

How quickly a system can retrieve desired information depends on the speed of the device that stores it. Different storage devices have a wide range of speeds, spanning many orders of magnitude. For fast retrievals, the information you want should reside on the fastest devices. Because it is difficult to predict which data items will be needed next, you can't always make sure the data you are going to want next will be contained in the fastest storage device. Some storage allocation algorithms are nonetheless quite effective at making such predictions.

There is a hierarchy of storage types, ranging from the fastest to the slowest. In general, the faster a storage device is, the smaller its capacity. As a consequence, it is generally not possible to hold a large database entirely in the fastest available storage. The next best thing is to store that subset of the database that is most likely to be needed soon in the faster memory. If this is done properly, the overall performance of the system will be almost as fast as if the entire memory was as fast as the fastest component of it. Here are the components of a typical memory system, starting with the fastest part:

✦ **Registers:** The registers in a computer system are the fastest form of storage. They are integrated into the processor chip, which means they are implemented with the fastest technology and the delay for transfers between the processing unit and the registers is minimal. It is not feasible to store any portion of a database in the registers, which are limited in number and in size. Instead, registers hold the operands that the processor is currently working on.

✦ **L1 cache:** Level 1 cache is typically also located in the processor chip, but is not as intimately integrated with the processor as are the registers. It is the fastest form of storage that can store a significant fraction of a database.

✦ **L2 cache:** Level 2 cache is generally located on a separate chip from the processor. It has greater capacity and is usually somewhat slower than the L1 cache.

✦ **Hard disk:** Hard disk storage has orders of magnitude more capacity than does cache and is orders of magnitude slower. This is where databases are stored. Registers, L1 cache, and L2 cache are all volatile forms of memory. The data is lost when power is removed. Hard disk storage, on the other hand, is non-volatile. The data is retained even when the system is turned off. Because hard disk systems can hold a large database and retain it when power is off or interrupted, such systems are the normal home of all databases.

✦ **Offline storage:** It is not necessary to have immediate access to databases that are not in active use. They can be retained on storage media that are slower than hard drives. A sequential storage medium such as magnetic tape is fine for such use. Data access is exceedingly slow, but acceptable for data that is rarely if ever needed. Huge quantities of data can be stored on tape. Tape is the ideal home for archives of obsolete data that nevertheless need to be retained against the day when they might be called upon again.

Full table scans

The simplest data retrieval method is the *full table scan,* which entails reading a table sequentially, one row after another. Sooner or later, all the rows that satisfy the retrieval criteria will be reached, and a result set can be returned to the database application. If you are retrieving just a few rows from a large table, this method can waste a lot of time accessing rows that you don't want. If a table is so large that most of it does not fit into cache, this retrieval method can be so slow as to make retrievals impractical. The alternative is to use an index.

How indexes work

Indexes speed access to table rows. An index is a data structure consisting of pointers to the rows in a data table. Data tables are typically not maintained in sorted order. Re-sorting a table every time it is modified is time-consuming, and sorting for fast retrieval by one retrieval key guarantees that the table is not sorted for all other retrieval keys. You can have an index for every potential retrieval key, keeping each index sorted by its associated retrieval key. For example, in a CUSTOMER table, one index might be sorted in CustID order and another index sorted in PostalCode order. This would enable rapid retrieval of selected records by CustID or all the records with a given range of postal codes.

Creating the right indexes

A major factor in maximizing performance is choosing the best columns to index in a table. Because all the indexes on a table must be updated every time a row in the table is added or deleted, maintaining an index creates a definite performance penalty. This penalty is negligible compared to the performance improvement provided by the index if it is frequently used, but is a significant drain on performance if the index is rarely or never used to locate rows in the data table.

Analyze the way the tables in your database will be used and build indexes accordingly. Primary keys should always be indexed. Other columns should be indexed if they will frequently be used as retrieval keys. Columns that will not be frequently used as retrieval keys should not be indexed. Removing unneeded indexes from a database can often significantly improve performance.

Indexes and the ANSI/ISO Standard

The ANSI/ISO SQL standard does not specify how indexes should be constructed. This leaves the implementation of indexes up to each DBMS vendor. That means that the indexing scheme of one vendor may differ from that of another. If you want to migrate a database system from one vendor's DBMS to another's, you may have to recreate all the indexes.

Index costs

There are costs to excessive indexing that go beyond updating them whenever changes are made to their associated tables. If there are multiple indexes, the DBMS's optimizer may choose the wrong one when making a retrieval. This could impact performance in a major way. Updates to indexed columns are particularly hard on performance because the old index value must be deleted and the new one added. The bottom line is that you should index only columns that will frequently be used as retrieval keys or that are used to enforce uniqueness, such as primary keys.

Query type dictates the best index

For a typical database, the number of possible queries that could be run is huge. In most cases, however, a few specific types of queries are run frequently, others are run infrequently, and many are not run at all. You want to optimize your indexes so that the queries you run frequently gain the most benefit. There is no point in adding indexes to a database to speed up query types that are never run. This just adds system overhead and results in no benefit. To help you understand which indexes work best with which query types, I describe the most frequently used query types.

Point query

A point query returns at most one record. The query includes an equality condition.

```
SELECT FirstName FROM EMPLOYEE
    WHERE EmployeeID = 31415 ;
```

There is only one record in the database where EmployeeID is equal to 31415 because EmployeeID is the primary key of the EMPLOYEE table.

Multipoint query

A multipoint query may return more than one record, using an equality condition.

```
SELECT FirstName FROM EMPLOYEE
    WHERE Department = 'Advanced Research' ;
```

There are probably multiple people in the Advanced Research department. The first names of all of them will be retrieved by this query.

Range query

A range query returns a set of records whose values lie within an interval or half interval.

```
SELECT FirstName, LastName FROM EMPLOYEE
    WHERE AGE >= 55
    AND < 65 ;

SELECT FirstName, LastName FROM EMPLOYEE
    WHERE AGE >= 65 ;
```

A range where both lower and upper bound are specified is an interval. A range where only one bound is specified is a half interval.

Prefix match query

A prefix match query is one in which only the first part of an attribute or sequence of attributes is specified.

```
SELECT FirstName, LastName FROM EMPLOYEE
    WHERE LastName LIKE 'Sm%' ;
```

This query returns all the Smarts, Smetanas, Smiths, and Smurfs.

Extremal query

An extremal query returns the extremes, the minima and maxima.

```
SELECT FirstName, LastName FROM EMPLOYEE
    WHERE Age = MAX(SELECT Age FROM EMPLOYEE) ;
```

This query returns the name of the oldest employee.

Ordering query

An ordering query is one that includes an ORDER BY clause. The records returned are sorted by a specified attribute.

```
SELECT FirstName, LastName FROM EMPLOYEE
    ORDER BY LastName, FirstName ;
```

This query returns a list of all employees in ascending alphabetical order, sorted first by last name and within each last name, by first name.

Grouping query

A grouping query is one that includes a GROUP BY clause. The records returned are partitioned into groups.

```
SELECT FirstName, LastName FROM EMPLOYEE
    GROUP BY Department ;
```

This query returns the names of all employees, with the members of each department listed together as a group.

Equi-join query

Equi-join queries are common in normalized relational databases. The condition that filters out the rows you don't want to retrieve is based on an attribute of one table being equal to a corresponding attribute in a second table.

```
SELECT EAST.EMP.FirstName, EAST.EMP.LastName
    FROM EAST.EMP, WEST.EMP
    WHERE EAST.EMP.EmpID = WEST.EMP.EMPID ;
```

One schema (EAST) holds the tables for the eastern division of a company, and another schema (WEST) holds the tables for the western division. Only the names of the employees who appear in both the eastern and western schemas are retrieved by this query.

Data structures used for indexes

Closely related to the types of queries that are typically run on a database is the way the indexes are structured. Because of the huge difference in speed between semiconductor cache memory and online hard disk storage, it makes sense to keep the indexes you are most likely to need soon in cache. The less often you must go out to hard disk storage, the better.

A variety of data structures are possible. Some of these structures are particularly efficient for some types of queries, whereas other structures work best with other types of queries. The best data structure for a given application depends on the types of queries that will be run against the data.

B+ trees

Most popular data structures for indexes have a tree-like organization where one master node (the root) connects to multiple nodes, each of which in turn connects to multiple nodes, and so on. The B+ tree, where B stands for "balanced," is a good index structure for queries of a number of types. B+ trees are particularly efficient in handling range queries. They also are good in databases where inserts are frequently made.

Hash structures

Hash structures use a key and a pseudo-random hash function to find a location. They are particularly good at making quick retrievals of point queries and multipoint queries, but perform poorly on range, prefix, and extremal queries. If a query requires a scan of all the data in the target tables, hash structures are less efficient than B+ tree structures.

Indexes, sparse and dense

The best choice of indexes depends largely on the types of queries to be supported and on the size of the cache that is available for data, compared to the total size of the database.

Data is shuttled back and forth between the cache and the disk storage in chunks called *pages*. In one table, a page may hold many records; in another, it may contain few. Indexes are pointers to the data in tables, and if there is at most one such pointer per page, it is called a *sparse index*. At the other end of the scale, a *dense index* is one that points to every record in the table. A sparse index entails less overhead than a dense index does, and if there are many records per page, for certain types of queries, it can perform better. Whether that performance improvement materializes depends on clustering.

Index clustering

The rationale for maintaining indexes is that it is too time-consuming to maintain data tables in sorted order for rapid retrieval of desired records. Instead, we keep the index in sorted order. Such an index is said to be *clustered*. A clustered index is organized in a way similar to the way a telephone book is organized. In a telephone book, the entries are sorted by a person's last name, and secondarily by his or her first name. This means that all the Smiths are together and so are all the Taylors. This organization is good for partial match, range, point, multipoint, and general join queries. If you pull up a page that contains one of the target records into cache, it's likely that other records that you want are on the same page and are pulled into cache at the same time.

A database table can have multiple indexes, but only one of them can be clustered. The same is true of a telephone book. If the entries in the book are sorted by last name, the order of the telephone numbers is a random jumble. This means that if you must choose one table attribute to assign a clustered index, choose the attribute that is most likely to be used as a retrieval key. Building unclustered indexes for other attributes is still of value, but isn't as beneficial as the clustered index.

Composite indexes

Composite indexes are, as the name implies, based on a combination of attributes. In certain situations, a composite index can give better performance than can a combination of single attribute indexes. For example, a composite index on last name and first name zeroes in on the small number of records that match both criteria. Alternatively, if last name and first name are separately indexed, first all the records with the desired last name are retrieved, and then these are scanned to find the ones with the correct first name. The extra operation takes extra time and makes extra demands on the bandwidth of the path between the database and the database engine.

Although composite indexes can be helpful, you must be careful when you craft your query to call for the components of the index in the same order that they exist in the index itself. For example, if you have an index on LastName, FirstName, the following query would perform well:

```
SELECT * FROM CUSTOMER
    WHERE LastName = 'Smith'
    AND FirstName = 'Bob' ;
```

This efficiently retrieves the records for all the customers named Bob Smith. However, the following seemingly equivalent query doesn't perform as well:

```
SELECT * FROM CUSTOMER
    WHERE FirstName = 'Bob'
    AND LastName = 'Smith' ;
```

The same rows are retrieved, but not as quickly. A DBMS with an intelligent query optimizer would examine the query and reverse the order of retrieval in order to deliver the best performance. You can check how smart your optimizer is by coding a sample retrieval both ways and noting the retrieval time. If it is the same in both instances, your query optimizer has passed the test.

Index effect on join performance

As a rule, joins are expensive in terms of the time it takes to construct them. If the join attribute in both tables is indexed, the amount of time needed is dramatically reduced. (I discuss joins in Book III, Chapter 4.)

Table size as an indexing consideration

The amount of time it takes to scan every row in a table becomes an issue as the table becomes large. The larger the table is, the more time indexes can save you. The corollary to this fact is that indexes of small tables don't do much good. If a table has no more than a few hundred rows, it doesn't make sense to create indexes for it. The overhead involved with maintaining the indexes overshadows any performance gain you might get from having them.

Indexes versus full-table scans

The point of using indexes is to save time in query and join operations by enabling you to go directly to the records you want rather than having to look at every record in a table to see whether it satisfies your selection conditions. If you can anticipate the types of queries that are likely to be run, you can configure indexes accordingly to maximize performance. There will still likely be queries of a type that you did not anticipate. For those, full-table scans are run. Hopefully, these queries won't be run often and thus won't have a major effect on overall performance. Full-table scans are the preferred retrieval method for small tables that are likely to be completely contained in cache.

Reading SQL Server Execution Plans

When you enter an SQL query into a database, the DBMS decides how to execute it by developing an execution plan. In most cases, the execution plan the DBMS develops is the best possible, but sometimes it could do with a little tuning to make it better. In this section, I look at how Microsoft SQL Server develops an execution plan, and then I apply the Database Engine Tuning Advisor to determine whether the plan can be improved.

Robust execution plans

Any non-trivial query draws data from multiple tables. How you reach those tables, how you join them, and the order in which you join them determines, to a large extent, how efficient your retrieval will be. The order in which you

**Book II
Chapter 3**

**Balancing
Performance and
Correctness**

do these things is called an *execution plan.* For any given retrieval, there is a myriad of possible execution plans. One of them is optimal, and a small number are near-optimal.

The optimal plan may be hard to find, but in many cases the near-optimal plans, called *robust execution plans,* are quite adequate. You can identify a robust execution plan by noting its characteristics. All major DBMS products include a query optimizer that takes in your SQL and comes up with an execution plan to implement it. In many cases, plans derived in this manner are satisfactory. Sometimes, however, for complex queries involving many joins, manual tuning significantly improves performance.

Query performance largely depends on the number of rows that are touched by the query — the fewer the better. This means that with a query involving multi-table joins, it is a good practice for the execution plan to start with the table with the best filter ratio. A table's *filter ratio* is the number of rows remaining after a condition is applied divided by the total number of rows in the table. The lower the filter ratio, the fewer rows that are joined to the next table in line in a join. For best performance in most cases, construct the join from the many side to the one side of one-to-many relationships, choosing the table on the one side that has the lowest filter ratio.

A sample database

The Northwinds database is a sample database that Microsoft supplies along with SQL Server. Look at the Northwinds database schema shown in Figure 3-12.

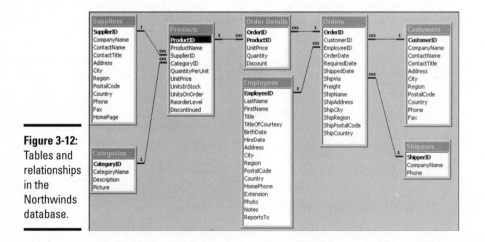

Figure 3-12:
Tables and relationships in the Northwinds database.

There is a one-to-many relationship between Customers and Orders, a one-to-many relationship between Shippers and Orders, and a one-to-many relationship between Employees and Orders. Furthermore, there is a one-to-many relationship between Orders and Order Details and a one-to-many relationship between Products and Order Details. Similarly, there is a one-to-many relationship between Suppliers and Products, and a one-to-many relationship between Categories and Products.

You might have a number of questions about the Northwinds business, as modeled by this database. In the following section, I build a query to answer one of those questions.

A typical query

Suppose you want to know if any of Northwind's salespeople are promising more than Northwind can deliver. We can get an indication of this by seeing which employees took orders where the ShippedDate was later than the RequiredDate. An SQL query will give us the answer to that question.

```
SELECT Employees.LastName
From Employees, Orders
    WHERE Employees.EmployeeID = Orders.EmployeeID
    AND Orders.ShippedDate > Orders.RequiredDate ;
```

Figure 3-13 shows the result. Late shipments were spread around among the orders of quite a few salespeople. No single one seems particularly prone to over-promising. There were 37 late shipments out of a total of 772 total shipments. To some companies, that might be an acceptable number; to others, it would not.

The execution plan

Figure 3-14 shows the execution plan for the query in the preceding section. An index scan, a clustered index scan, and a hash match consumed processor cycles, with the hash match taking up more than half of the time used.

The hash match, representing the formation of the inner join of the Employees and the Orders tables, takes up more time than do the index scans of the two tables involved.

Running the Database Engine Tuning Advisor

Although the answer to this query came back pretty fast, one might wonder whether it could have been faster. Executing the Database Engine Tuning Advisor may find a possible improvement. Run it to see.

Figure 3-13: SQL Server 2005 Management Studio execution of an SQL query.

Figure 3-14: The execution plan for the delivery time query.

Wow! The Tuning Advisor estimates that the query could be speeded up by 65% by creating some new indexes, as shown in Figure 3-15. Not surprisingly, the fields it suggests indexing in the Orders table are EmployeeID, RequiredDate, and ShippedDate. There is no recommendation for improvement of the Employees table.

Figure 3-15:
The
recommen-
dations
of the
Database
Engine
Tuning
Advisor.

Hot Tables and Load Balancing

A *hot table* is one that is accessed by many transactions at the same time. For such a table, you may get a performance improvement by locating the non-clustering indexes on a different disk from the one that contains the data and the clustering index. This form of load balancing enables the parallel execution of tasks that would otherwise be contending for the same resource. In Book VII, Chapter 3, I go into detail about balancing the load on the storage system to improve performance.

Chapter 4: Creating a Database with SQL

In This Chapter

✔ **Building tables**

✔ **Setting constraints**

✔ **Establishing relationships between tables**

✔ **Altering table structure**

✔ **Deleting tables**

A s stated in Chapter 5 of Book I, SQL is functionally divided into three components: the Data Definition Language (DDL), the Data Manipulation Language (DML), and the Data Control Language (DCL). The DDL consists of three statements: CREATE, ALTER, and DROP. You can use these statements to create database objects (such as tables), change the structure of existing object, or delete an object. After you have designed a database, the first step in bringing it into reality is to build a table with the DDL. After you have built the tables, the next step is to fill them with data. That is the job of the DML. With the DCL, you can preserve data integrity. In this chapter, I discuss the functions of the DDL.

First Things First: Planning Your Database

Before you can start constructing a database, you need to have a clear idea of the real-world or conceptual system that you are modeling. Some aspects of the system are of primary importance. Other aspects are subsidiary to the ones you have identified as primary. Additional aspects may not be important at all, depending on what you are using the database for. Based on these considerations, you will build an E-R model of the system, with primary aspects identified as *entities,* and subsidiary aspects identified as *attributes* of those entities. Unimportant aspects don't appear in the model at all.

After you have finalized your E-R model, you can translate it into a normalized relational model. The relational model is your guide for creating database tables and establishing the relationships between them.

Building Tables

The fundamental object in a relational database is the table. Tables correspond directly to the relations in a normalized relational model. Table creation can be simple or quite involved. In either case, it is accomplished with a CREATE TABLE statement.

In Chapter 3 of this minibook, I take you through the creation of a relational model for Honest Abe's Fleet Auto Repair. Using that sample design, you can take it to the next step by creating database tables based on the model. Table 4-1 shows the tables and their attributes.

Table 4-1	Tables for Honest Abe
Table	*Column*
CUSTOMER	CustomerID
	CustomerName
	StreetAddr
	City
	State
	PostalCode
	ContactName
	ContactPhone
	ContactEmail
MECHANIC	EmployeeID
	FirstName
	LastName
	StreetAddr
	City
	State
	PostalCode
	JobTitle
CERTIFICATION	CertificationNo
	CertName
	Expires
INVOICE	InvoiceNo
	Date
	CustomerID
	EmployeeID
INVOICE_LINE	Invoice_Line_No
	PartNo
	UnitPrice
	Quantity
	Extended Price
LABOR	LaborChargeCode
	TaskDescription
	StandardCharge

Table	Column
PART	PartNo
	Name
	Description
	CostBasis
	ListPrice
	QuantityInStock
SUPPLIER	SupplierID
	SupplierName
	StreetAddr
	City
	State
	PostalCode
	ContactName
	ContactPhone
	ContactEmail
SUPPLIER_PART	SupplierID
	PartNo

You can construct the DDL statements required to build the database tables directly from the enumeration of tables and columns in Table 4-1, but first you should understand the important topic of *keys,* which I discuss in the next section.

Locating table rows with keys

Keys are the main tool used to locate specific rows within a table. Without a key that guarantees that a row in a table is not a duplicate of any other row in the table, ambiguities arise. The row you want to retrieve may be indistinguishable from one or more other rows in the table. You wouldn't be able to tell which one was the right one. There are several different terms you may see in discussions of keys that uniquely identify rows in a table.

✦ **Candidate keys:** Ideally, at least one column or combination of columns within a table contains a unique entry in every row. Any such column or combination of columns is a candidate key. Perhaps your table has more than one such candidate. If your table has multiple candidate keys, select one of them to be the table's primary key.

✦ **The primary key:** A table's primary key has the characteristic of being a unique identifier of all the rows in the table. It is specifically chosen from among the candidate keys to serve as the primary identifier of table rows.

✦ **Composite keys:** Sometimes no single column uniquely identifies every row in a table, but a combination of two or more columns does. Together, those columns comprise a composite key, which can collectively serve as a table's primary key.

Using the CREATE TABLE statement

If you understand one of the functions of keys (see the preceding bulleted list), you can create tables using the CREATE TABLE statement:

```
CREATE TABLE CUSTOMER (
      CustomerID        INTEGER       PRIMARY KEY,
      CustomerName      CHAR (30),
      StreetAddr        CHAR (30),
      City              CHAR (25),
      State             CHAR (2),
      PostalCode        CHAR (10),
      ContactName       CHAR (30),
      ContactPhone      CHAR (13),
      ContactEmail      CHAR (30) ) ;

CREATE TABLE MECHANIC (
      EmployeeID        INTEGER       PRIMARY KEY,
      FirstName         CHAR (15),
      LastName          CHAR (20),
      StreetAddr        CHAR (30),
      City              CHAR (25),
      State             CHAR (2),
      PostalCode        CHAR (10),
      JobTitle          CHAR (30) ) ;

CREATE TABLE CERTIFICATION (
      CertificationNo   INTEGER       PRIMARY KEY,
      CertName          CHAR (30),
      Expires           Date ) ;

CREATE TABLE INVOICE (
      InvoiceNo         INTEGER       PRIMARY KEY,
      Date              DATE,
      CustomerID        INTEGER,
      EmployeeID        INTEGER ) ;

CREATE TABLE INVOICE_LINE (
      Invoice_Line_No   INTEGER       PRIMARY KEY,
      PartNo        INTEGER,
      UnitPrice         NUMERIC (9,2),
      Quantity          INTEGER,
      ExtendedPrice  NUMERIC (9,2) ) ;

CREATE TABLE LABOR (
      LaborChargeCode   INTEGER       PRIMARY KEY,
      TaskDescription   CHAR (40),
      StandardCharge    NUMERIC (9,2) ) ;
```

```
CREATE TABLE PART (
    PartNo              INTEGER      PRIMARY KEY,
    Name                CHAR (30),
    Description         CHAR (40),
    CostBasis           NUMERIC (9,2),
    ListPrice           NUMERIC (9,2),
    QuantityInStock     INTEGER ) ;

CREATE TABLE SUPPLIER (
    SupplierID          INTEGER      PRIMARY KEY,
    SupplierName        CHAR (30),
    StreetAddr          CHAR (30),
    City                CHAR (25),
    State               CHAR (2),
    PostalCode          CHAR (10),
    ContactName         CHAR (30),
    ContactPhone        CHAR (13),
    ContactEmail        CHAR (30) ) ;

CREATE TABLE SUPPLIER_PART (
    SupplierID          INTEGER NOT NULL,
    PartNo              INTEGER NOT NULL ) ;
```

**Book II
Chapter 4**

**Creating a
Database with SQL**

All the tables except SUPPLIER_PART have a single attribute as their primary key. In the SUPPLIER_PART table, no single attribute uniquely identifies a row, so the table has a composite key made up of both SupplierID and PartNo. Those two attributes together *do* uniquely identify each row in the table. Not all suppliers supply all parts, but there is a row in SUPPLIER_PART for every case where a specific supplier supplies a specific part.

Setting Constraints

One way to protect the integrity of your data is to add constraints to your table definitions. There are several different kinds of constraints, including column constraints, table constraints, check constraints, and foreign key constraints. In this section, I cover column constraints and table constraints. Other types of constraints will pop up here and there in the book as we go along.

Column constraints

Column constraints determine what may or may not appear in a column of a table. For example, in the SUPPLIER_PART table, NOT NULL is a constraint on the SupplierID column. It guarantees that the SupplierID column must contain a value. It doesn't say what that value must be, as long as it is *some* value.

Table constraints

A table constraint is not restricted to a particular column, but applies to an entire table. The PRIMARY KEY constraint is an example of a table constraint. A primary key may consist of one column, multiple columns, or even all the columns in the table — whatever it takes to uniquely identify every row in the table. Regardless of how many columns are included in the primary key, the primary key is a characteristic of the entire table.

Keys and Indexes

Because primary keys uniquely identify each row in a table, they are ideal for indexes. The purpose of an index is to point to a row or set of rows that satisfies a condition. Because a primary key identifies one and only one row in a table, an index on a table's primary key provides the fastest, most direct access to the row it points to. Less selective indexes give access to multiple rows that all satisfy the selection condition. Thus, although CustomerID may take you directly to the record of the customer you want, you may not remember every customer's CustomerID. A search on LastName might return several records, but you can probably determine pretty quickly which one is the one you want. In such a case, you may want to create an index on the LastName column as well as on CustomerID. Any column that you frequently use as a retrieval condition should probably be indexed. If a table's primary key is a composite key, the index would be on the combination of all the columns that make up the key. Composite keys that are not a table's primary key can also be indexed.

Ensuring Data Validity with Domains

Although you, as a database creator, can't guarantee that the data entry operator always enters the correct data, at least you can assure that the data entered is *valid* — that it excludes values that cannot possibly be correct. Do this with a CREATE DOMAIN statement. For example, in the LABOR table definition given in "The CREATE TABLE statement" section, the StandardCharge field holds currency values that are of the NUMERIC type. Suppose you want to assure that a negative value is never entered for a StandardCharge. You can do so by creating a domain, as in the following example:

```
CREATE DOMAIN CurrencyDom NUMERIC (9,2)
    CHECK (VALUE >= 0);
```

The definition of the LABOR table is altered correspondingly:

```
CREATE TABLE LABOR (
    LaborChargeCode     INTEGER  PRIMARY KEY,
    TaskDescription     CHAR (40),
    StandardCharge      CurrencyDom ) ;
```

The data type of StandardCharge is replaced by the new domain. With a domain, you can constrain an attribute to assume only those values that are valid.

Establishing Relationships between Tables

After you have created tables for a database, the next step is to establish the relationships between the tables. A normalized relational database has multiple tables, perhaps hundreds of them. Most queries or reports require data from more than one table. In order to pull the correct data from the tables, you must have a way of relating the rows in one table to corresponding rows in another table. This is accomplished with links consisting of columns in one table that correspond to columns in a related table.

Earlier in this chapter, I talk about primary keys and composite keys (which are a kind of primary key). Another kind of key that is important is the *foreign key*. Unlike primary keys, foreign keys do not uniquely identify a row in a table. Instead, they serve as links to other tables.

Relational databases are characterized by having multiple tables that are related to each other. Those relationships are established by columns that are shared between two tables. In a one-to-one relationship, one row in the first table corresponds to one and only one row in the second table. For a given row, one or more columns in the first table match a corresponding column or set of columns in the second table. In a one-to-many relationship, one row in the first table matches multiple rows in the second table. Once again, the match is made by columns in the first table that correspond to columns in the second table.

Consider the Honest Abe sample database of Book II, Chapter 3. It has a one-to-many link between CUSTOMER and INVOICE, mediated by the shared CustomerID column, and there is also a one-to-many link between MECHANIC and INVOICE mediated by the EmployeeID column. To create these links, you have to add a little more SQL code to the definition of the INVOICE table. Here's the new definition:

```
CREATE TABLE INVOICE (
    InvoiceNo       INTEGER     PRIMARY KEY,
    Date            DATE,
    CustomerID      INTEGER,
    EmployeeID      INTEGER,
```

```
         CONSTRAINT CustFK FOREIGN KEY (CustomerID)
            REFERENCES CUSTOMER (CustomerID),
         CONSTRAINT MechFK FOREIGN KEY (EmployeeID)
            REFERENCES MECHANIC (EmployeeID)
     ) ;
```

Adding the foreign key constraints to the table on the many side of a one-to-many relationship creates the links. For a one-to-one relationship, it doesn't matter which of the two tables you add the foreign key constraint to.

To tie the Honest Abe database together, add foreign key constraints to establish all of the relationships. Here's the result:

```
CREATE TABLE CUSTOMER (
    CustomerID          INTEGER      PRIMARY KEY,
    CustomerName        CHAR (30),
    StreetAddr          CHAR (30),
    City                CHAR (25),
    State               CHAR (2),
    PostalCode          CHAR (10),
    ContactName         CHAR (30),
    ContactPhone        CHAR (13),
    ContactEmail        CHAR (30) ) ;

CREATE TABLE MECHANIC (
    EmployeeID          INTEGER      PRIMARY KEY,
    FirstName           CHAR (15),
    LastName            CHAR (20),
    StreetAddr          CHAR (30),
    City                CHAR (25),
    State               CHAR (2),
    PostalCode          CHAR (10),
    Specialty           CHAR (30),
    JobTitle            CHAR (30) ) ;

CREATE TABLE CERTIFICATION (
    CertificationNo     INTEGER      PRIMARY KEY,
    CertName            CHAR (30),
    MechanicID          INTEGER,
    Expires             Date,
    CONSTRAINT CertMechFK FOREIGN KEY (MechanicID)
        REFERENCES MECHANIC (EmployeeID)
) ;

CREATE TABLE INVOICE (
    InvoiceNo           INTEGER      PRIMARY KEY,
    Date                DATE,
    CustomerID          INTEGER,
    EmployeeID          INTEGER,
```

```
        CONSTRAINT CustFK FOREIGN KEY (CustomerID)
            REFERENCES CUSTOMER (CustomerID),
        CONSTRAINT MechFK FOREIGN KEY (EmployeeID)
            REFERENCES MECHANIC (EmployeeID)
) ;

CREATE TABLE INVOICE_LINE (
        Invoice_Line_No    INTEGER       PRIMARY KEY,
        InvoiceNo          INTEGER,
        LaborChargeCode    INTEGER,
        PartNo             INTEGER,
        UnitPrice          NUMERIC (9,2),
        Quantity           INTEGER,
        ExtendedPrice      NUMERIC (9,2),
        CONSTRAINT InvFK FOREIGN KEY (InvoiceNo)
            REFERENCES INVOICE (InvoiceNo),
        CONSTRAINT LaborFK FOREIGN KEY (LaborChargeCode)
            REFERENCES LABOR (LaborChargeCode),
       CONSTRAINT PartFK FOREIGN KEY (PartNo)
            REFERENCES PART (PartNo)
) ;

CREATE DOMAIN CurrencyDom NUMERIC (9,2)
   CHECK (VALUE >= 0);

CREATE TABLE LABOR (
        LaborChargeCode     INTEGER       PRIMARY KEY,
        TaskDescription     CHAR (40),
        StandardCharge      CurrencyDom ) ;

CREATE TABLE PART (
        PartNo              INTEGER       PRIMARY KEY,
        Name                CHAR (30),
        Description         CHAR (40),
        CostBasis           NUMERIC (9,2),
        ListPrice           NUMERIC (9,2),
        QuantityInStock     INTEGER ) ;

CREATE TABLE SUPPLIER (
        SupplierID          INTEGER       PRIMARY KEY,
        SupplierName        CHAR (30),
        StreetAddr          CHAR (30),
        City                CHAR (25),
        State               CHAR (2),
        PostalCode          CHAR (10),
        ContactName         CHAR (30),
        ContactPhone        CHAR (13),
        ContactEmail        CHAR (30) ) ;
```

```
CREATE TABLE SUPPLIER_PART (
    SupplierID          INTEGER       NOT NULL,
    PartNo       INTEGER       NOT NULL,
    CONSTRAINT SuppFK FOREIGN KEY (SupplierID)
        REFERENCES SUPPLIER (SupplierID),
    CONSTRAINT PartSuppFK FOREIGN KEY (PartNo)
        REFERENCES PART (PartNo)
) ;
```

Note that the CERTIFICATION table has a column named MechanicID, which corresponds to the column named EmployeeID in the MECHANIC table. This is to show that a foreign key need not have the same name as the corresponding column in the table that it links to. Note also that additional columns that serve as foreign keys have been added to some of the tables on the many sides of relationships. These are required in addition to the constraint clauses.

A database that is properly linked together using foreign keys is said to have *referential integrity.* The key to assuring referential integrity is to make sure that the E-R diagram of the database is accurate and that it is properly translated into a relational model, which is then converted into a relational database.

Altering Table Structure

In the real world, requirements tend to change. Sooner or later this is bound to affect the databases that model some aspect of that world. SQL provides a means to change the structure of a database that has already been created. Structural changes can either be adding a new column to a table or deleting an existing one. The SQL to perform these tasks is pretty straightforward. Here is an example of adding a column:

```
ALTER TABLE MECHANIC
    ADD COLUMN Birthday DATE ;
```

Here's an example of deleting a column:

```
ALTER TABLE MECHANIC
    DROP COLUMN Birthday ;
```

I guess Honest Abe decided not to keep track of employee birthdays after all.

Deleting Tables

It's just as easy to delete an entire table as it is to delete a column in a table. Here's how:

```
DROP TABLE CUSTOMER ;
```

Uh-oh. Be really careful about dropping tables. When it's gone, it's gone, along with all its data.

Book III

SQL Queries

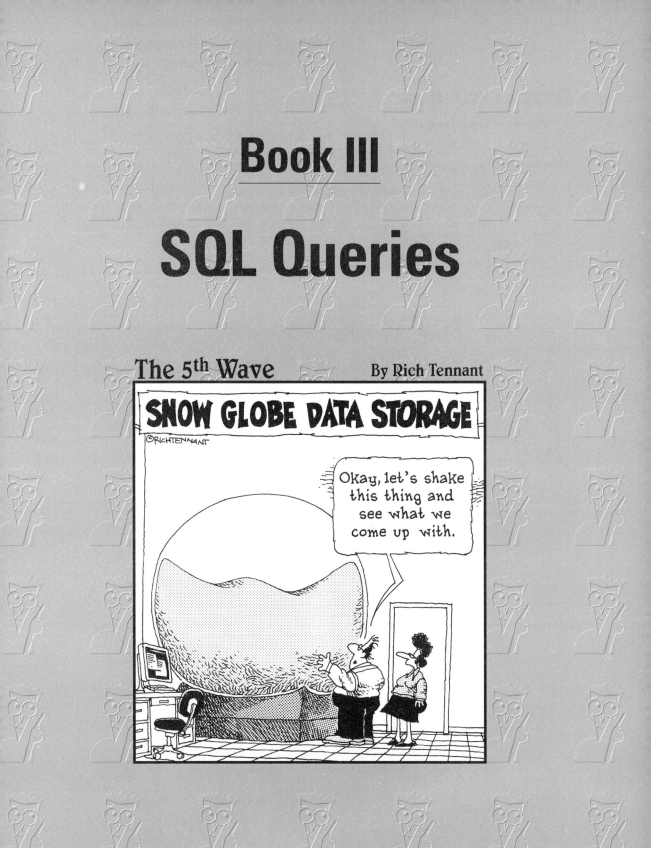

The 5th Wave By Rich Tennant

SNOW GLOBE DATA STORAGE

Okay, let's shake this thing and see what we come up with.

Contents at a Glance

Chapter 1: Values, Variables, Functions, and Expressions

*T*his chapter describes the tools that SQL provides to operate on data. In addition to specifying the value of a data item, you can slice it and dice it in a variety of ways. Rather than just retrieving raw data as it exists in the database, you can preprocess it to deliver just the information you want, in the form that you want it.

Entering Data Values

After you have created a database table, the next step is to enter data into it. SQL supports a number of different data types. Refer to Book I, Chapter 6 for coverage of those types. The five different kinds of values that can appear in table rows are

✦ Row values

✦ Literal values

✦ Variables

✦ Special variables

✦ Column references

I discuss each in turn throughout this section.

Row values have multiple parts

A *row value* includes the values of all the data in all the columns in a row in a table. It is actually multiple values rather than just one. The intersection of a row and a column, called a field, contains a single, so-called "atomic" value. All the values of all the fields in a row, taken together, are that row's row value.

Identifying values in a column

Just as you can specify a row value consisting of multiple values, you can specify the value contained in a single column. For illustration, consider this example from the Honest Abe database shown in Book II, Chapter 3:

```
SELECT * FROM CUSTOMER
   WHERE LastName = 'Smith' ;
```

This query returns all the rows in the CUSTOMER table where the value in the LastName column is `Smith`.

Literal values don't change

In SQL, a value can either be a constant, or it can be represented by a variable. Constant values are called *literals*. Table 1-1 shows sample literals for each of the SQL data types.

Table 1-1	Sample Literals of Various Data Types
Data Type	*Sample Literal*
BIGINT	8589934592
INTEGER	186282
SMALLINT	186
NUMERIC	186282.42
DECIMAL	186282.42
REAL	6.02257E23
DOUBLE PRECISION	3.1415926535897E00
FLOAT	6.02257E23
CHARACTER(15)	'GREECE '
Note: Fifteen total characters and spaces are between the quote marks above.	
VARCHAR (CHARACTER VARYING)	'lepton'
NATIONAL CHARACTER(15)	'ΕΛΛΑΣ '[1]
Note: Fifteen total characters and spaces are between the quote marks above.	
NATIONAL CHARACTER VARYING	'λεπτον'[2]
CHARACTER LARGE OBJECT (CLOB)	(A really long character string)

[1] This term is the word that Greeks use to name their own country in their own language. (The English equivalent is 'Hellas.')

[2] This term is the word 'lepton' in Greek national characters.

Data Type	Sample Literal
BINARY LARGE OBJECT (BLOB)	(A really long string of ones and zeros)
DATE	DATE '1969-07-20'
TIME(2)	TIME '13.41.32.50'
TIMESTAMP(0)	TIMESTAMP '2007-07-25-13.03.16.000000'
TIME WITH TIMEZONE(4)	TIME '13.41.32.5000-08.00'
TIMESTAMP WITH TIMEZONE(0)	TIMESTAMP '2007-07-25-13.03.16.0000+02.00'
INTERVAL DAY	INTERVAL '7' DAY

Numeric literals are just the values that they represent. Non-numeric literals are enclosed in single quotes.

Variables Vary

Literals, which explicitly hold a single value, are fine if that value appears only once or twice in an application. However, if a value appears multiple times, and if there is any chance that value might change in the future, you should represent it with a variable. That way, if changes are necessary, you have to change the code in one place only, where the value is assigned to the variable, rather than in all the places in the application where that value appears.

For example, suppose in an application dealing with a table containing the archives of a magazine, there are numerous spots where retrievals are made on various sections of the current issue. One such retrieval might look like this:

```
SELECT Editorial FROM PENGUINLIFE
    WHERE Issue = 47 ;
```

Another could be

```
SELECT LeadStory FROM PENGUINLIFE
    WHERE Issue = 47 ;
```

There could be many more like these two in the application. When next week rolls around and you want to run the application again for the latest issue, you must go through the program by hand and change all the instances of 47 to 48. Computers are supposed to rescue us from such boring, repetitive tasks, and they do. Rather than using literals in such cases, use variables instead, like this:

```
SELECT Editorial FROM PENGUINLIFE
   WHERE Issue = :IssueNumber ;
```

You have to change the IssueNumber variable in one place only, and the change affects all the places in the application where the variable appears.

Special Variables Hold Specific Values

SQL has a few special variables that hold information about system usage. In multiuser systems, you often need to know who is using the system at any given time. This information can be captured in a log file, using the special variables. The special variables are

✦ SESSION_USER holds a value that's equal to the user authorization identifier of the current SQL session. If you write a program that performs a monitoring function, you can interrogate SESSION_USER to find out who is executing SQL statements.

✦ CURRENT_USER stores a user-specified authorization identifier. If a module has no such identifier, CURRENT_USER has the same value as SESSION_USER.

✦ SYSTEM_USER contains the operating system's user identifier. This identifier may differ from that user's identifier in an SQL module. A user may log on to the system as ANDREW, for example, but identify himself to a module as DIRECTOR. The value in SESSION_USER is DIRECTOR. If he makes no explicit specification of the module identifier and CURRENT_USER also contains DIRECTOR, SYSTEM_USER holds the value ANDREW.

One use of the SYSTEM_USER, SESSION_USER, and CURRENT_USER special variables is to track who is using the system. You can maintain a log table and periodically insert into that table the values that SYSTEM_USER, SESSION_USER, and CURRENT_USER contain. The following example shows how:

```
INSERT INTO USAGELOG (SNAPSHOT)
   VALUES ('User ' || SYSTEM_USER ||
      ' with ID ' || SESSION_USER ||
      ' active at ' || CURRENT_TIMESTAMP) ;
```

This statement produces log entries similar to the following example:

```
User ANDREW with ID DIRECTOR active at 2007-08-07-23.50.00
```

Working with Functions

Functions perform computations or operations that are more elaborate than what you would expect a simple command statement to do. SQL has two kinds of functions: set functions and value functions. *Set functions* are so named because they operate on a set of rows in a table rather than on a single row. *Value functions* operate on the values of fields in a table row.

Summarizing data with set functions

When dealing with a set of table rows, often what you want to know is some aggregate property that applies to the whole set. SQL has five such aggregate or set functions: COUNT, AVG, MAX, MIN, and SUM. To see how these work, consider the example data in Table 1-2. It is a price table for photographic papers of various sizes and characteristics.

Table 1-2	Photographic Paper Price List per 20 Sheets	
Paper Type	*Size8*	*Size11*
Dual-sided matte	8.49	13.99
Card stock dual-sided matte	9.49	16.95
Professional photo gloss	10.99	19.99
Glossy HW 9M	8.99	13.99
Smooth silk	10.99	19.95
Royal satin	10.99	19.95
Dual-sided semi-gloss	9.99	17.95
Dual-sided HW semi-gloss	--	--
Universal two-sided matte	--	--
Transparency	29.95	--

The fields that contain dashes do not have a value. The dash in the table represents a null value.

COUNT

The COUNT function returns the number of rows in a table, or the number of rows that meet a specified condition. In the simplest case, we have

```
SELECT COUNT (*)
   FROM PAPERS ;
```

This returns a value of 10 because there are ten rows in the PAPERS table. You can add a condition to see how many types of paper are available in Size 8:

```
SELECT COUNT (Size8)
   FROM PAPERS ;
```

This returns a value of 8 because of the ten types of paper in the PAPERS table, only eight are available in size 8. You might also want to know how many different prices there are for papers of size 8. That is also easy to determine:

```
SELECT COUNT (DISTINCT Size8)
   FROM PAPERS ;
```

This returns a value of 6 because there are three instances of 10.99, only one of which gets counted. Null values are ignored.

AVG

The AVG function calculates and returns the average of the values in the specified column. It works only on columns that contain numeric data.

```
SELECT AVG (Size8)
   FROM PAPERS ;
```

This returns a value of 12.485. If you wonder what the average price is for the Size 11 papers, you can find out this way:

```
SELECT AVG (Size11)
   FROM PAPERS ;
```

This returns a value of 17.539.

MAX

As you might expect, the MAX function returns the maximum value found in the specified column. Find the maximum value in the Size8 column:

```
SELECT MAX (Size8)
   FROM PAPERS ;
```

This returns 29.95, the price for 20 sheets of Size8 transparencies.

MIN

The MIN function gives you the minimum value found in the specified column.

```
SELECT MIN (Size8)
   FROM PAPERS ;
```

Here the value returned is 8.49.

SUM

In the case of the photographic paper example, it doesn't make much sense to calculate the sum of all the prices for the papers being offered for sale, but in other applications, this type of calculation can be valuable. Just in case you wanted to know what it would cost to buy 20 sheets of every Size11 paper being offered, you could make the following query:

```
SELECT SUM (Size11)
   FROM PAPERS ;
```

It would cost 122.77 to buy 20 sheets of each of the seven kinds of Size11 paper that are available.

Dissecting data with value functions

A number of data manipulation operations come up fairly frequently. SQL provides value functions to perform these tasks. There are four types of value functions:

+ String value functions

+ Numeric value functions

+ Datetime value functions

+ Interval value functions

In the following subsections, I look at the functions that are available in each of these categories.

String value functions

String value functions take one character string as input and produce another character string as output. There are eight string value functions.

+ SUBSTRING (FROM)

+ SUBSTRING (SIMILAR)

- ✦ UPPER
- ✦ LOWER
- ✦ TRIM
- ✦ TRANSLATE
- ✦ CONVERT
- ✦ OVERLAY

SUBSTRING (FROM)

The operation of SUBSTRING (FROM) is similar to substring operations in many other computer languages. Here's an example:

```
SUBSTRING ('manual transmission' FROM 8 FOR 4)
```

This returns trans, the substring that starts in the eighth character position and continues for four characters. You want to make sure that the starting point and substring length you specify locate the substring entirely within the source string. If part or all of the substring falls outside the source string, you could receive a result you are not expecting.

Some implementations do not adhere strictly to the ANSI/ISO standard syntax for the SUBSTRING function, or for the other functions that follow. Check the documentation of the implementation you are using if the code samples given here do not work for you.

SUBSTRING (SIMILAR)

SUBSTRING (SIMILAR) is a regular expression substring function. It divides a string into three parts and returns the middle part. Consider this example:

```
SUBSTRING ('antidisestablishmentarianism'
          SIMILAR 'antidis\"[:ALPHA:]+\"arianism'
          ESCAPE '\' )
```

The original string is the first operand. The operand following the SIMILAR keyword is a character string literal that includes a regular expression in the form of another character string literal, a separator (\"), a second regular expression that means "one or more alphabetic characters," a second separator (\"), and a third regular expression in the form of a different character string literal. The value returned is

```
establishment
```

UPPER

The UPPER function converts its target string to all uppercase.

```
UPPER ('ChAoTic')                returns 'CHAOTIC'
```

The UPPER function has no effect on character sets, such as Hebrew, that do not distinguish between upper- and lowercase.

LOWER

The LOWER function converts its target string to all lowercase.

```
LOWER ('INTRUDER ALERT!')        returns 'intruder alert!'
```

As is the case for UPPER, LOWER has no effect on character sets that do not include the concept of case.

TRIM

The TRIM function enables you to crop a string, shaving off characters at either the front or the back of the string or both. Here are a few examples:

```
TRIM (LEADING ' ' FROM ' ALERT ')     returns 'ALERT '
TRIM (TRAILING ' ' FROM ' ALERT ')    returns ' ALERT'
TRIM (BOTH ' ' FROM ' ALERT ')        returns 'ALERT'
TRIM (LEADING 'A' FROM 'ALERT')       returns 'LERT'
```

If you don't specify what to trim, the blank space (" ") is the default.

TRANSLATE and CONVERT

The TRANSLATE and CONVERT functions take a source string in one character set and transform the original string into a string in another character set. Examples might be Greek to English or Katakana to Norwegian. The conversion functions that specify these transformations are implementation-specific, so I don't give any details here.

These functions do not really translate character strings from one language to another. All they do is translate a character from the first character set to the corresponding character in the second character set. In going from Greek to English, it would convert 'Ελλασ' as 'Ellas' rather than translating it as "Greece." "Ελλασ" is what the Greeks call their country. I have no idea why English speakers call it "Greece."

OVERLAY

The OVERLAY function is a SUBSTRING function with a little extra functionality. As with SUBSTRING, it finds a specified substring within a target string.

However, rather than returning the string that it found, it replaces it with a different string. For example:

```
OVERLAY ('I Love Paris' PLACING 'New York' FROM 8 FOR 5)
```

This changes the string to

```
I Love New York
```

Numeric value functions

Numeric value functions can take a variety of data types as input, but the output is always a numeric value. SQL has 13 types of numeric value functions:

- ✦ Position expression (POSITION)
- ✦ Extract expression (EXTRACT)
- ✦ Length expression (CHAR_LENGTH, CHARACTER_LENGTH, OCTET_LENGTH)
- ✦ Cardinality expression (CARDINALITY)
- ✦ Absolute value expression (ABS)
- ✦ Modulus expression (MOD)
- ✦ Natural logarithm (LN)
- ✦ Exponential function (EXP)
- ✦ Power function (POWER)
- ✦ Square root (SQRT)
- ✦ Floor function (FLOOR)
- ✦ Ceiling function (CEIL, CEILING)
- ✦ Width bucket function (WIDTH_BUCKET)

POSITION

POSITION searches for a specified target string within a specified source string and returns the character position where the target string begins. The syntax is as follows:

```
POSITION (target IN source)
```

Table 1-3 shows a few examples.

Table 1-3	Sample Uses of the POSITION Statement
This Statement	*Returns*
POSITION ('T' IN 'Transmission, automatic')	1
POSITION ('Tra' IN 'Transmission, automatic')	1
POSITION ('au' IN 'Transmission, automatic')	15
POSITION ('man' IN 'Transmission, automatic')	0
POSITION (" IN 'Transmission, automatic')	1

If the function doesn't find the target string, the POSITION function returns a zero value. If the target string has zero length (as in the last example), the POSITION function always returns a value of one. If any operand in the function has a null value, the result is a null value.

EXTRACT

The EXTRACT function extracts a single field from a datetime or an interval. The following statement, for example, returns 12:

```
EXTRACT (MONTH FROM DATE '2007-12-04')
```

CHARACTER_LENGTH

The CHARACTER_LENGTH function returns the number of characters in a character string. The following statement, for example, returns 20:

```
CHARACTER_LENGTH ('Transmission, manual')
```

This function is not particularly useful if its argument is a literal like 'Transmission, manual'. I can write 20 just as easily as I can write CHARACTER_LENGTH ('Transmission, manual'). In fact, writing 20 is easier. This function is more useful if its argument is an expression rather than a literal value.

OCTET_LENGTH

In music, a vocal ensemble made up of eight singers is called an *octet*. Typically, the parts that the ensemble represents are first and second soprano, first and second alto, first and second tenor, and first and second bass. In computer terminology, an ensemble of eight data bits is called a *byte*. The word *byte* is clever in that the term clearly relates to *bit* but implies something larger than a bit. A nice wordplay — but, unfortunately, nothing in the word *byte* conveys the concept of "eightness." By borrowing the musical term, a more apt description of a collection of eight bits becomes possible.

**Book III
Chapter 1**

**Values, Variables,
Functions, and
Expressions**

Practically all modern computers use eight bits to represent a single alphanumeric character. More complex character sets (such as Chinese) require 16 bits to represent a single character. The OCTET_LENGTH function counts and returns the number of octets (bytes) in a string. If the string is a bit string, OCTET_LENGTH returns the number of octets you need to hold that number of bits. If the string is an English-language character string (with one octet per character), the function returns the number of characters in the string. If the string is a Chinese character string, the function returns a number that is twice the number of Chinese characters. The following string is an example:

```
OCTET_LENGTH ('Brakes, disc')
```

This function returns 12 because each character takes up one octet.

Some character sets use a variable number of octets for different characters. In particular, some character sets that support mixtures of Kanji and Latin characters use *escape* characters to switch between the two character sets. A string that contains both Latin and Kanji may have, for example, 30 characters and require 30 octets if all the characters are Latin; 62 characters if all the characters are Kanji (60 characters plus a leading and trailing shift character); and 150 characters if the characters alternate between Latin and Kanji (because each Kanji character needs two octets for the character and one octet each for the leading and trailing shift characters). The OCTET_LENGTH function returns the number of octets you need for the current value of the string.

CARDINALITY

Cardinality deals with collections of elements such as arrays or multisets, where each element is a value of some data type. The cardinality of the collection is the number of elements that it contains. One use of the CARDINALITY function is something like this:

```
CARDINALITY (TeamRoster)
```

This function would return 12, for example, if there were 12 team members on the roster. TeamRoster, a column in the TEAM table, can be either an array or a multiset. An array is an ordered collection of elements, and a multiset is an unordered collection of elements. For a team roster, which changes frequently, multiset makes more sense.

ABS

The ABS function returns the absolute value of a numeric value expression.

```
ABS (-273)
```

This returns 273.

MOD

The MOD function returns the modulus of two numeric value expressions.

```
MOD (6,4)
```

This function returns 2, the modulus of six divided by four.

LN

The LN function returns the natural logarithm of a numeric value expression.

```
LN (6)
```

This function returns something like 1.791759469. The number of digits beyond the decimal point is implementation-dependent.

EXP

This function raises the base of the natural logarithms e to the power specified by a numeric value expression:

```
EXP (2)
```

This function returns something like 7.389056. The number of digits beyond the decimal point is implementation-dependent.

POWER

This function raises the value of the first numeric value expression to the power of the second numeric value expression:

```
POWER (3,7)
```

This function returns 2187, which is three raised to the seventh power.

SQRT

This function returns the square root of the value of the numeric value expression:

```
SQRT (9)
```

This function returns 3, the square root of nine.

FLOOR

This function rounds the numeric value expression to the largest integer not greater than the expression:

```
FLOOR (2.73)
```

This function returns 2.0.

CEIL or CEILING

This function rounds the numeric value expression to the smallest integer not less than the expression.

```
CEIL (2.73)
```

This function returns 3.0.

WIDTH_BUCKET

The WIDTH_BUCKET function, used in online application processing (OLAP), is a function of four arguments, returning an integer between the value of the second (minimum) argument and the value of the third (maximum) argument. It assigns the first argument to an equiwidth partitioning of the range of numbers between the second and third arguments. Values outside this range are assigned to either the value of zero or one more than the fourth argument (the number of buckets).

For example:

```
WIDTH_BUCKET (PI, 0, 10, 5)
```

Suppose PI is a numeric value expression with a value of 3.141592. The example partitions the interval from zero to ten into five equal *buckets*, each with a width of two. The function returns a value of 2 because 3.141592 falls into the second bucket, which covers the range from two to four.

Datetime value functions

SQL includes three functions that return information about the current date, current time, or both. CURRENT_DATE returns the current date; CURRENT_TIME returns the current time; and CURRENT_TIMESTAMP returns both the current date and the current time. CURRENT_DATE doesn't take an argument, but CURRENT_TIME and CURRENT_TIMESTAMP both take a single argument. The argument specifies the precision for the seconds part of the time value that the function returns. Datetime data types and the precision concept are described in Chapter 6 of Book I.

The following table offers some examples of these datetime value functions.

This Statement	Returns
CURRENT_DATE	2007-05-31
CURRENT_TIME (1)	08:36:57.3
CURRENT_TIMESTAMP (2)	2007-05-31 08:36:57.38

The date that CURRENT_DATE returns is DATE type data. The time that CURRENT_TIME (p) returns is TIME type data, and the timestamp that CURRENT_TIMESTAMP(p) returns is TIMESTAMP type data. Because SQL retrieves date and time information from your computer's system clock, the information is correct for the time zone in which the computer resides.

In some applications, you may want to deal with dates, times, or timestamps as character strings to take advantage of the functions that operate on character data. You can perform a type conversion by using the CAST expression, which I describe later in this chapter.

Using Expressions

An *expression* is any combination of elements that reduces to a single value. The elements could be numbers, strings, dates, times, intervals, Booleans, or more complex things. What they are doesn't matter, as long as after all operations have taken place, the result is a single value.

Numeric value expressions

The operands in a numeric value expression can be numbers of an exact numeric type or of an approximate numeric type. Operands of different types can be used within a single expression. If at least one operand is of an approximate type, the result is of an approximate type. If all operands are of exact types, the result is of an exact type. The SQL specification does not specify exactly what type the result of any given expression will be, due to the wide variety of platforms that SQL runs on.

Here are some examples of valid numeric value expressions:

✦ –24

✦ 13+78

✦ 4*(5+8)

✦ Weight/(Height*Height)

✦ Miles/5280

String value expressions

String value expressions can consist of a single string or a concatenation of strings. The concatenation operator (| |) is the only one you can use in a string value expression. Table 1-4 shows some examples of string value expressions and the strings that they produce.

Table 1-4	Examples of String Value Expressions
String Value Expression	*Resulting String*
'nanotechnology'	'nanotechnology'
'nano' || 'technology'	'nanotechnology'
'nano' || " || 'technology'	'nanotechnology'
'Isaac' || ' ' || 'Newton'	'Isaac Newton'
FirstName || ' ' || LastName	'Isaac Newton'
B'10101010' || B'01010101	B'1010101001010101'

Datetime value expressions

Datetime value expressions perform operations on dates and times. Such data is on the DATE, TIME, TIMESTAMP, or INTERVAL type. The result of a Datetime value expression is always of the DATE, TIME, or TIMESTAMP type. Intervals are not one of the datetime types, but an interval can be added to or subtracted from a datetime to produce another datetime. Here's an example datetime value expression:

```
CURRENT_DATE + INTERVAL '2' DAY
```

This expression evaluates to the day after tomorrow.

Datetimes can also include time zone information. The system maintains times in Universal Time Coordinated (UTC), which until recently was known as Greenwich Mean Time (GMT). (I guess the feeling was that Greenwich was too provincial and a more general name for world time was called for.) You can specify a time as being either at your local time, or as an offset from UTC. An example is

```
TIME '13:15:00' AT LOCAL
```

for 1:15 PM local time. Another example is

```
TIME '13:15:00' AT TIME ZONE INTERVAL '-8:00' HOUR TO MINUTE
```

for 1:15 PM Pacific Standard Time. (Pacific Standard Time is eight hours earlier than UTC.)

Interval value expressions

An *interval* is the difference between two datetimes. If you subtract one datetime from another, the result is an interval. It makes no sense to add two datetimes, so SQL does not allow you to do it.

There are two kinds of intervals: year-month and day-time. This situation is a little messy, but necessary because not all months contain the same number of days. Because a month could be 28, 29, 30, or 31 days long, there is no direct translation from days to months. As a result, when using an interval, you must specify which kind of interval it is. Suppose you expect to take an around-the-world cruise after you retire, starting on June 1, 2045. How many years and months is that from now? An interval value expression gives you the answer.

```
(DATE '2048-06-01' - CURRENT_DATE) YEAR TO MONTH
```

You can add two intervals to obtain an interval result.

```
INTERVAL '30' DAY + INTERVAL '14' DAY
```

However, you cannot do the following:

```
INTERVAL '30' DAY + INTERVAL '14' MONTH
```

The two kinds of intervals do not mix. Besides addition and subtraction, multiplication and division of intervals also are allowed. The expression

```
INTERVAL '7' DAY * 3
```

is valid and gives an interval of 21 days. The expression

```
INTERVAL '12' MONTH / 2
```

is also valid and gives an interval of 6 months. Intervals can also be negative.

```
INTERVAL '-3' DAY
```

gives an interval of -3 days. Aside from the literals I used in the examples above, any value expression or combination of value expressions that evaluates to an interval can be used in an interval value expression.

Boolean value expressions

Only three legal Boolean values exist: TRUE, FALSE, and UNKNOWN. The UNKNOWN value becomes operative when a NULL is involved. Suppose the

Book III
Chapter 1

Values, Variables,
Functions, and
Expressions

Boolean variable Signal1 is TRUE, and the Boolean variable Signal2 is FALSE. The following Boolean value expression evaluates to TRUE.

```
Signal1 IS TRUE
```

So does this one:

```
Signal1 IS TRUE OR Signal2 IS TRUE
```

However, the following Boolean value expression evaluates to FALSE.

```
Signal1 IS TRUE AND Signal2 IS TRUE
```

The AND operator means that both predicates must be true for the result to be true. Because Signal2 is false, the entire expression evaluates to a FALSE value.

Array value expressions

You can use a couple of types of expressions with arrays. The first has to do with cardinality. The maximum number of elements an array can have is called the array's *maximum cardinality*. The actual number of elements in the array at a given time is called its *actual cardinality*. You can combine two arrays by concatenating them, summing their maximum cardinalities in the process. Suppose you want to know the actual cardinality of the concatenation of two array-type columns in a table, where the first element of the first column has a given value. You could execute the following statement:

```
SELECT CARDINALITY (FirstColumn || SecondColumn)
    FROM TARGETTABLE
WHERE FirstColumn[1] = 42 ;
```

The CARDINALITY function gives the combined cardinality of the two arrays, where the first element in the first array has a value of 42.

Note: The first element of an SQL array is considered to be element 1, rather than element 0 as is true for some other languages.

Conditional value expressions

The value of a conditional value expression depends on a condition. SQL offers three variants of conditional value expressions: CASE, NULLIF, and COALESCE. I look at each of these separately.

Handling different cases

The CASE conditional expression was added to SQL to give it some of the functionality that all full-featured computer languages have, the ability to do one thing if a condition holds and another thing if the condition does not hold. Originally conceived as a data sublanguage that was only concerned with managing data, SQL has gradually gained features that enable it to take on more of the functions needed by application programs.

SQL actually has two different CASE structures: the CASE expression described here, and a CASE statement. The CASE expression, like all expressions, evaluates to a single value. You can use a CASE expression anywhere where a value is legal. The CASE statement, on the other hand, doesn't evaluate to a value. Instead, it executes a block of statements.

The CASE expression searches a table, one row at a time, taking on the value of a specified result whenever one of a list of conditions is TRUE. If the first condition is not satisfied for a row, the second condition is tested, and if it is TRUE, the result specified for it is given to the expression, and so on until all conditions are processed. If no match is found, the expression takes on a NULL value. Processing then moves to the next row.

Searching for table rows that satisfy various conditions

You can specify the value to be given to a CASE expression, based on which of several conditions is satisfied. Here's the syntax:

```
CASE
    WHEN condition1 THEN result1
    WHEN condition2 THEN result2
    . . .
    WHEN conditionN THEN resultN
    ELSE resultx
END
```

If, in searching a table, the CASE expression finds a row where condition1 is true, it takes on the value of result1. If condition1 is not true, but condtion2 is true, it takes on the value of result2. This continues for all conditions. If none of the conditions are met and there is no ELSE clause, the expression is given the NULL value. Here's an example of usage:

```
UPDATE MECHANIC
    Set JobTitle = CASE
                        WHEN Specialty = 'Brakes'
                            THEN 'Brake Fixer'
                        WHEN Specialty = 'Engines'
                            THEN 'Motor Master'
                        WHEN Specialty = 'Electrical'
```

```
                        THEN 'Wizard'
               ELSE 'Apprentice'
          END ;
```

The equality condition allows a compact CASE value expression

A shorthand version of the CASE statement can be used when the condition, as in the previous example, is based on equality. The syntax is as follows:

```
CASE valuet
    WHEN value1 THEN result1
    WHEN value2 THEN result2
    . . .
    WHEN valueN THEN resultN
    ELSE resultx
END
```

For the preceding example, this translates to

```
UPDATE MECHANIC
    Set JobTitle = CASE Specialty
                    WHEN 'Brakes' THEN 'Brake Fixer'
                    WHEN 'Engines' THEN 'Motor Master'
                    WHEN 'Electrical' THEN 'Wizard'
                    ELSE 'Apprentice'
             END ;
```

If the condition involves anything other than equality, the first, non-abbreviated form must be used.

The NULLIF special CASE

SQL databases are unusual in that NULL values are allowed. A NULL value can represent an unknown value, a known value that has just not been entered into the database yet, or a value that does not exist. Most other languages that deal with data do not support nulls, so whenever a situation arises in such databases where a value is not known, not yet entered, or nonexistent, the space is filled with a value that would not otherwise occur, such as -1 in a field that never holds a negative value, or *** in a character field in which asterisks are not valid characters.

To migrate data from a database that does not support nulls to an SQL database that does, you can use a CASE statement such as

```
UPDATE MECHANIC
    SET Specialty = CASE Specialty
                    WHEN '***' THEN NULL
                    ELSE Specialty
             END ;
```

You can do the same thing in a shorthand manner, using a `NULLIF` expression, as follows:

```
UPDATE MECHANIC
    SET Specialty = NULLIF(Specialty, '***') ;
```

Admittedly, this looks more cryptic than the `CASE` version, but it does save some tedious typing. You could interpret it as, "Update the MECHANIC table by setting the value of Specialty to NULL if its current value is '***'".

Bypassing null values with COALESCE

The `COALESCE` expression is another shorthand version of `CASE` that deals with null values. It examines a series of values in a table row and assumes the value of the first one that is not `NULL`. If all the listed values are `NULL`, the `COALESCE` expression takes on the `NULL` value. Here's the syntax for a `CASE` expression that does this:

```
CASE
    WHEN value1 IS NOT NULL
        THEN value1
    WHEN value2 IS NOT NULL
        THEN value2
    . . .
    WHEN valueN is NOT NULL
        THEN valueN
    ELSE NULL
END
```

Here's the syntax for the equivalent `COALESCE` expression:

```
COALESCE(value1, value2, . . ., valueN)
```

If you are dealing with a large number of cases, the `COALESCE` version can save you quite a bit of typing.

Converting data types with a CAST expression

In Chapter 6 of Book I, I describe the data types that SQL recognizes. The host languages that SQL statements are often embedded in also recognize data types, and those host language data types are never an exact match for the SQL data types. This could present a problem, except for the fact that, with a `CAST` expression, you can convert data of one type into data of another type. Whereas the first type might not be compatible with the place you want to send the data, the second type is. Of course, not all conversions are possible. If you have a character string such as '2007-08-14', you can convert it to the DATE type with a CAST expression. However, SQL doesn't let you convert a character string such as 'rhinoceros' to the DATE type. The data to be converted must be compatible with the destination type.

Casting one SQL data type to another

The simplest kind of cast is from one SQL data type to another SQL data type. Even for this operation, however, you cannot indiscriminately make any conversion you want. The data you are converting must be compatible with the target data type. For example, suppose you have a table named ENGINEERS with a column named SSN, which is of the NUMERIC type. Perhaps you have another table named MANAGERS that has a column named SocSecNo, which is of the CHAR (9) type. A typical entry in SSN might be 987654321. To find all the engineers who are also managers, you can use the following query. The CAST expression converts the CHAR (9) type to the NUMERIC type so that the operation can proceed.

```
SELECT * FROM ENGINEER
    WHERE ENGINEER.SSN = CAST(MANAGER.SocSecNo AS INTEGER) ;
```

This returns all the rows from the ENGINEER table that have Social Security Numbers that match Social Security Numbers in the MANAGERS table. To do so, it changes the Social Security Number from the MANAGER table from the CHAR (9) type to the INTEGER type, for the purposes of the comparison.

Using CAST to overcome data type incompatibilities between SQL and its host language

Problems arise when you want to send data between SQL and its host language. For example, SQL has the DECIMAL and NUMERIC types, but some host languages, such as Fortran and Pascal, do not. One way around this problem is to use CAST to put a numeric value into a character string, and then put the character string into a host variable that the host language can take in and deal with.

Suppose you maintain salary information as REAL type data in the EMPLOYEE table. You want to make some manipulations on that data that SQL is not well-equipped to perform, but your host language is. You can cast the data into a form the host language can accept, operate on it at the host level, and then cast the result back to a form acceptable to the SQL database.

```
SELECT CAST(Salary AS CHAR (10)) INTO :salary_var
    FROM EMPLOYEE
    WHERE EmpID = :emp_id_var ;
```

That puts the salary value where the host language can grab it and in a form that the host language understands. After the host language is finished operating on the data item, it can return to the SQL database via a similar path:

```
UPDATE EMPLOYEE
    SET Salary = CAST(:salary_var AS DECIMAL(10,2))
        WHERE EmpID = :emp_id_var ;
```

In addition to the conversions shown above, you can do a number of other conversions:

✦ Any numeric type to any other numeric type

✦ Any exact numeric type to a single-component interval, such as INTERVAL DAY

✦ Any DATE to a TIMESTAMP

✦ Any TIME to a TIME with a different fractional seconds precision or a TIMESTAMP

✦ Any TIMESTAMP to a DATE, a TIME, or a TIMESTAMP with a different fractional seconds precision

✦ Any year-month INTERVAL to an exact numeric type

✦ Any day-time INTERVAL to an exact numeric type

✦ Any character string to any other type, where the data makes sense

✦ Any bit string to a character string

✦ A Boolean to a character string

Row value expressions

Row value expressions enable you to deal with the data in an entire table row or a subset of a row. The other expressions that I've shown deal only with a single field in a row at a time. Row value expressions are useful for adding new data to a table a row at a time, or to specify the retrieval of multiple fields from a table row. Here's an example of a row value expression used to enter a new row of data to a table:

```
INSERT INTO CERTIFICATIONS
    (CertificationNo, CertName, MechanicID, Expires)
    VALUES
    (1, 'V8 Engines', 34, 2008-07-31) ;
```

One advantage of using row value expressions is that many SQL implementations can process them faster than the equivalent one-field-at-a-time operations. This could make a significant difference in performance at runtime.

Chapter 2: SELECT Statements and Modifying Clauses

In This Chapter

✔ Retrieving data from a database

✔ Zeroing in on what you want

✔ Optimizing retrieval performance

✔ Using views to optimize performance

The main purpose of storing data on a computer is to be able to retrieve specific elements of the data when you need them. As databases grow in size, the proportion that you are likely to want on any given occasion grows smaller. As a result, SQL provides tools that enable you to make retrievals in a variety of ways. With these tools — SELECT statements and modifying clauses — you can zero in on the precise pieces of information that you want, even though they may be buried among megabytes of data that you're not interested in at the moment.

Finding Needles in Haystacks with the SELECT Statement

SQL's primary tool for retrieving information from a database is the SELECT statement. In its simplest form, with one modifying clause (a FROM clause), it retrieves everything from a table. By adding more modifying clauses, you can whittle down what it retrieves until you are getting exactly what you want, no more and no less.

Suppose you want to display a complete list of all the customers in your CUSTOMER table, including every piece of data that the table stores about each one. That is the simplest retrieval you can do. Here's the syntax:

```
SELECT * FROM CUSTOMER ;
```

The asterisk (*) is a wildcard character that means "all columns." This statement returns all the data held in all the rows of the CUSTOMER table. Sometimes that is what you want. At other times, you may only want *some* of the data on *some* of the customers: those that satisfy one or more conditions. For such refined retrievals, you must use one or more modifying clauses.

Modifying Clauses

In any SELECT statement, the FROM clause is mandatory. You must specify the source of the data you want to retrieve. Other modifying clauses are optional. They serve several different functions:

✦ The WHERE clause specifies a condition. Only those table rows that satisfy the condition are returned.

✦ The GROUP BY clause rearranges the order of the rows returned by placing rows together than have the same value in a grouping column.

✦ The HAVING clause that filters out groups that do not meet a specified condition.

✦ The ORDER BY clause sorts whatever is left after all the other modifying clauses have had a chance to operate.

FROM clauses

The FROM clause is easy to understand if you specify only one table, as in the example above:

```
SELECT * FROM CUSTOMER ;
```

This statement returns all the data in all the rows of every column in the CUSTOMER table. You can, however, specify more than one table in a FROM clause. Consider the following example:

```
SELECT *
   FROM CUSTOMER, INVOICE ;
```

This statement forms a virtual table that combines the data from the CUSTOMER table with the data from the INVOICE table. Each row in the CUSTOMER table combines with every row in the INVOICE table to form the new table. The new virtual table that this combination forms contains the number of rows in the CUSTOMER table multiplied by the number of rows in the INVOICE table. If the CUSTOMER table has 10 rows and the INVOICE table has 100, the new virtual table has 1,000 rows.

This operation is called the *Cartesian product* of the two source tables. The Cartesian product is a type of JOIN. I cover JOIN operations in detail in Chapter 4 of this minibook.

In most applications, the majority of the rows that form as a result of taking the Cartesian product of two tables are meaningless. In the case of the virtual table that forms from the CUSTOMER and INVOICE tables, only the rows where the CustomerID from the CUSTOMER table matches the CustomerID from the INVOICE table are of interest. You can filter out the rest of the rows by using a WHERE clause.

WHERE clauses

I use the WHERE clause many times throughout this book without really explaining it because its meaning and use are obvious: A statement performs an operation (such as a SELECT, DELETE, or UPDATE) only on table rows where a stated condition is True. The syntax of the WHERE clause is as follows:

```
SELECT column_list
    FROM table_name
    WHERE condition ;

DELETE FROM table_name
    WHERE condition ;

UPDATE table_name
    SET column₁=value₁, column₂=value₂, ..., columnₙ=valueₙ
    WHERE condition ;
```

The condition in the WHERE clause may be simple or arbitrarily complex. You may join multiple conditions together by using the logical connectives AND, OR, and NOT (which I discuss later in this chapter) to create a single condition.

The following statements show you some typical examples of WHERE clauses:

```
WHERE CUSTOMER.CustomerID = INVOICE.CustomerID
WHERE MECHANIC.EmployeeID = CERTIFICATION.MechanicID
WHERE PART.QuantityInStock < 10
WHERE PART.QuantityInStock > 100 AND PART.CostBasis > 100.00
```

The conditions that these WHERE clauses express are known as predicates. A *predicate* is an expression that asserts a fact about values.

The predicate PART.QuantityInStock < 10, for example, is True if the value for the current row of the column PART.QuantityInStock is less than 10. If the assertion is True, it satisfies the condition. An assertion may be True, False, or unknown. The unknown case arises if one or more elements in the assertion are null. The *comparison predicates* (=, <, >, <>, <=, and >=) are the most common, but SQL offers several others that greatly increase your capability to distinguish, or "filter out," a desired data item from others in the same column. The following list notes the predicates that give you that filtering capability:

✦ Comparison predicates

✦ BETWEEN

✦ IN [NOT IN]

✦ LIKE [NOT LIKE]

✦ NULL

✦ ALL, SOME, ANY

✦ EXISTS

✦ UNIQUE

✦ OVERLAPS

✦ MATCH

✦ SIMILAR

✦ DISTINCT

Comparison predicates

The examples in the preceding section show typical uses of comparison predicates in which you compare one value to another. For every row in which the comparison evaluates to a TRUE value, that value satisfies the WHERE clause, and the operation (SELECT, UPDATE, DELETE, or whatever) executes upon that row. Rows that the comparison evaluates to FALSE are skipped. Consider the following SQL statement:

```
SELECT * FROM PART
   WHERE QuantityInStock < 10 ;
```

This statement displays all rows from the PART table that have a value of less than 10 in the QuantityInStock column.

Six comparison predicates are listed in Table 2-1.

Table 2-1	SQL's Comparison Predicates
Comparison	*Symbol*
Equal	=
Not equal	<>
Less than	<

Comparison	Symbol
Less than or equal	<=
Greater than	>
Greater than or equal	>=

BETWEEN

Sometimes, you want to select a row if the value in a column falls within a specified range. One way to make this selection is by using comparison predicates. For example, you can formulate a WHERE clause to select all the rows in the PART table that have a value in the QuantityInStock column greater than 10 and less than 100, as follows:

```
WHERE PART.QuantityInStock > 10 AND PART.QuantityInStock < 100
```

This comparison doesn't include parts with a quantity in stock of exactly 10 or 100 — only those values that fall in between these two numbers. To include the end points, you can write the statement as follows:

```
WHERE PART.QuantityInStock >= 10 AND PART.QuantityInStock <= 100
```

Another way of specifying a range that includes the end points is to use a BETWEEN predicate, like this:

```
WHERE PART.QuantityInStock BETWEEN 10 AND 100
```

This clause is functionally identical to the preceding example, which uses comparison predicates. This formulation saves some typing and is a little more intuitive than the one that uses two comparison predicates joined by the logical connective AND.

The BETWEEN keyword may be confusing because it doesn't tell you explicitly whether the clause includes the end points. In fact, the clause *does* include these end points. BETWEEN also fails to tell you explicitly that the first term in the comparison must be equal to or less than the second. If, for example, PART.QuantityInStock contains a value of 50, the following clause returns a True value:

```
WHERE PART.QuantityInStock BETWEEN 10 AND 100
```

However, a clause that you may think is equivalent to the preceding example returns the opposite result, False:

```
WHERE PART.QuantityInStock BETWEEN 100 AND 10
```

If you use BETWEEN, you must be able to guarantee that the first term in your comparison is always equal to or less than the second term.

You can use the BETWEEN predicate with character, bit, and datetime data types as well as with the numeric types. You may see something like the following example:

```
SELECT FirstName, LastName
    FROM CUSTOMER
    WHERE CUSTOMER.LastName BETWEEN 'A' AND 'Mzzz' ;
```

This example returns all customers whose last names are in the first half of the alphabet.

IN and NOT IN

The IN and NOT IN predicates deal with whether specified values (such as GA, AL, and MS) are contained within a particular set of values (such as the states of the United States). You may, for example, have a table that lists suppliers of a commodity that your company purchases on a regular basis. You want to know the phone numbers of those suppliers located in the southern United States. You can find these numbers by using comparison predicates, such as those shown in the following example:

```
SELECT Company, Phone
    FROM SUPPLIER
    WHERE State = 'GA' OR State = 'AL' OR State = 'MS' ;
```

You can also use the IN predicate to perform the same task, as follows:

```
SELECT Company, Phone
    FROM SUPPLIER
    WHERE State IN ('GA', 'AL', 'MS') ;
```

This formulation is more compact than the one using comparison predicates and logical OR.

The NOT IN version of this predicate works the same way. Say that you have locations in New York, New Jersey, and Connecticut, and to avoid paying sales tax, you want to consider using suppliers located anywhere except in those states. Use the following construction:

```
SELECT Company, Phone
    FROM SUPPLIER
    WHERE State NOT IN ('NY', 'NJ', 'CT') ;
```

Using the IN keyword this way saves you a little typing. Saving a little typing, however, isn't that great of an advantage. You can do the same job by using comparison predicates, as shown in this section's first example.

You may have another good reason to use the IN predicate rather than comparison predicates, even if using IN doesn't save much typing. Your DBMS probably implements the two methods differently, and one of the methods may be significantly faster than the other on your system. You may want to run a performance comparison on the two ways of expressing inclusion in (or exclusion from) a group and then use the technique that produces the quicker result. A DBMS with a good optimizer will probably choose the more efficient method, regardless of which kind of predicate you use. A performance comparison gives you some idea of how good your DBMS's optimizer is. If a significant difference between the run times of the two statements exists, the quality of your DBMS's optimizer is called into question.

The IN keyword is valuable in another area, too. If IN is part of a subquery, the keyword enables you to pull information from two tables to obtain results that you can't derive from a single table. I cover subqueries in detail in Chapter 3, but following is an example that shows how a subquery uses the IN keyword.

Suppose that you want to display the names of all customers who've bought the flux capacitor product in the last 30 days. Customer names are in the CUSTOMER table, and sales transaction data is in the PART table. You can use the following query:

Book III
Chapter 2

SELECT Statements
and Modifying
Clauses

```
SELECT FirstName, LastName
  FROM CUSTOMER
  WHERE CustomerID IN
    (SELECT CustomerID
      FROM INVOICE
      WHERE SalesDate >= (CurrentDate - 30) AND InvoiceNo IN
        (SELECT InvoiceNo
          FROM INVOICE_LINE
          WHERE PartNo IN
            (SELECT PartNo
              FROM PART
              WHERE NAME = 'flux capacitor' ) ;
```

The inner SELECT of the INVOICE table nests within the outer SELECT of the CUSTOMER table. The inner SELECT of the INVOICE_LINE table nests within the outer SELECT of the INVOICE table. The inner select of the PART table nests within the outer SELECT of the INVOICE_LINE table. The innermost SELECT finds the CustomerID numbers of all customers who bought the flux capacitor product in the last 30 days. The outermost SELECT displays the first and last names of all customers whose CustomerID is retrieved by the inner SELECT statements.

LIKE and NOT LIKE

You can use the LIKE predicate to compare two character strings for a partial match. Partial matches are valuable if you don't know the exact form of the string for which you're searching. You can also use partial matches to retrieve multiple rows that contain similar strings in one of the table's columns.

To identify partial matches, SQL uses two wildcard characters. The percent sign (%) can stand for any string of characters that have zero or more characters. The underscore (_) stands for any single character. Table 2-2 provides some examples that show how to use LIKE.

Table 2-2	SQL's LIKE Predicate
Statement	*Values Returned*
WHERE String LIKE 'auto%'	auto
	automotive
	automobile
	automatic
	autocracy
WHERE String LIKE '%ode%'	code of conduct
	model citizen
WHERE String LIKE '_o_e'	mope
	tote
	rope
	love
	cone
	node

The NOT LIKE predicate retrieves all rows that don't satisfy a partial match, including one or more wildcard characters, as in the following example:

```
WHERE Email NOT LIKE '%@databasecentral.info'
```

This example returns all the rows in the table where the e-mail address is not hosted at DatabaseCentral.Info.

You may want to search for a string that includes a percent sign or an underscore. In this case, you want SQL to interpret the percent sign as a percent sign and not as a wildcard character. You can conduct such a search by typing an escape character just prior to the character you want SQL to take literally. You can choose any character as the escape character, as long as that character doesn't appear in the string that you're testing, as shown in the following example:

```
SELECT Quote
   FROM BARTLETTS
   WHERE Quote LIKE '20#%'
      ESCAPE '#' ;
```

The % character is escaped by the preceding # sign, so the statement interprets this symbol as a percent sign rather than as a wildcard. You can escape an underscore or the escape character itself, in the same way. The preceding query, for example, would find the following quotation in *Bartlett's Familiar Quotations:*

```
20% of the salespeople produce 80% of the results.
```

The query would also find the following:

```
20%
```

SIMILAR

The SIMILAR predicate offers a more powerful way of finding partial matches than the LIKE predicate provides. With the SIMILAR predicate, you can compare a character string to a regular expression. For example, say you're searching the ChessPiece column of the inventory table of a chess game manufacturer. You could construct a WHERE clause such as the following:

```
WHERE ChessPiece SIMILAR TO
'('Black '(pawn|knight|bishop|rook|queen|king))'
```

This predicate retrieves all rows that contain any of the specified chess pieces. The vertical bar is the OR operator, so any row that has a black pawn, or a black knight, and so on, is retrieved.

NULL

The NULL predicate finds all rows where the value in the selected column is null. In the photographic paper price list table in Chapter 1, several rows have null values in the Size11 column. You can retrieve their names by using a statement such as the following:

```
SELECT (PaperType)
   FROM PAPERS
   WHERE Size11Price IS NULL ;
```

This query returns the following values:

```
Dual-Sided HW Semi-Gloss
Universal 2-Sided Matte
Transparency
```

As you may expect, including the NOT keyword reverses the result, as in the following example:

```
SELECT (PaperType)
    FROM PAPERS
    WHERE Size11Price IS NOT NULL ;
```

This query returns all the rows in the table except the three that the preceding query returns.

The statement Size11Price IS NULL is not the same as Size11Price = NULL. To illustrate this point, assume that, in the current row of the PAPERS table, both Size11Price and Size8Price are null. From this fact, you can draw the following conclusions:

✦ Size11Price IS NULL is True.

✦ Size8Price IS NULL is True.

✦ (Size11Price IS NULL AND Size8Price IS NULL) is True.

✦ Size11Price = Size8Price is unknown.

✦ Size11Price = NULL is an illegal expression.

Using the keyword NULL in a comparison is meaningless because the answer always returns as *unknown*.

Why is Size11Price = Size8Price defined as unknown, even though Size11Price and Size8Price have the same (null) value? Because NULL simply means "I don't know." You don't know what Size11Price is, and you don't know what Size8Price is; therefore, you don't know whether those (unknown) values are the same. Maybe Size11Price is 9.95 and Size8Price is 8.95, or maybe Size11Price is 10.95 and Size8Price is 10.95. If you don't know both the Size 11 value and the Size8 value, you can't say whether the two are the same.

ALL, SOME, ANY

Thousands of years ago, the Greek philosopher Aristotle formulated a system of logic that became the basis for much of Western thought. The essence of this logic is to start with a set of premises that you know to be true, apply valid operations to these premises, and, thereby arrive at new truths. The classic example of this procedure is as follows:

Premise 1: All Greeks are human.

Premise 2: All humans are mortal.

Conclusion: All Greeks are mortal.

Another example:

Premise 1: Some Greeks are women.

Premise 2: All women are human.

Conclusion: Some Greeks are human.

Another way of stating the same logical idea of this second example is as follows:

If any Greeks are women and all women are human, then some Greeks are human.

The first example uses the universal quantifier ALL in both premises, enabling you to make a sound deduction about all Greeks in the conclusion. The second example uses the existential quantifier SOME in one premise, enabling you to make a deduction about some, but not all, Greeks in the conclusion. The third example uses the existential quantifier ANY, which is a synonym for SOME, to reach the same conclusion you reach in the second example.

ANY can be ambiguous

The original SQL used the word ANY for existential quantification. This usage turned out to be confusing and error-prone because the English language connotations of *any* are sometimes universal and sometimes existential:

✔ "Do any of you know where Wilbur Street is?"

✔ "I can eat more pizza than any of you."

The first sentence is probably asking whether at least one person knows where Wilbur Street is. *Any* is used as an existential quantifier. The second sentence, however, is a boast that's stating that I can eat more pizza than the biggest eater among all you people can eat. In this case, *any* is used as a universal quantifier.

Thus, for the SQL-92 standard, the developers retained the word ANY for compatibility with early products but added the word SOME as a less confusing synonym. SQL continues to support both existential quantifiers.

Look at how SOME, ANY, and ALL apply in SQL.

Consider an example in baseball statistics. Baseball is a physically demanding sport, especially for pitchers. A pitcher must throw the baseball from the pitcher's mound, at speeds up to 100 miles per hour, to home plate between 90 and 150 times during a game. This effort can be very tiring, and many times, the pitcher becomes ineffective, and a relief pitcher must replace him before the game ends. Pitching an entire game is an outstanding achievement, regardless of whether the effort results in a victory.

Suppose that you're keeping track of the number of complete games that all major-league pitchers pitch. In one table, you list all the American League pitchers, and in another table, you list all the National League pitchers. Both tables contain the players' first names, last names, and number of complete games pitched.

The American League permits a designated hitter (DH) (who isn't required to play a defensive position) to bat in place of any of the nine players who play defense. Usually the DH bats for the pitcher because pitchers are notoriously poor hitters. (Pitchers must spend so much time and effort on perfecting their pitching that they do not have as much time to practice batting as the other players do.)

Say that you have a theory that, on average, American League starting pitchers throw more complete games than do National League starting pitchers. This is based on your observation that designated hitters enable hard-throwing, but weak-hitting, American League pitchers to stay in close games. Because the DH is already batting for them, the fact that they are poor hitters is not a liability. In the National League, however, a pinch hitter would replace a comparable National League pitcher in a close game because he would have a better chance at getting a hit. To test your theory, you formulate the following query:

```
SELECT FirstName, LastName
   FROM AMERICAN_LEAGUER
   WHERE CompleteGames > ALL
      (SELECT CompleteGames
         FROM NATIONAL_LEAGUER) ;
```

The subquery (the inner SELECT) returns a list, showing for every National League pitcher, the number of complete games he pitched. The outer query returns the first and last names of all American Leaguers who pitched more complete games than ALL of the National Leaguers. The query returns the names of those American League pitchers who pitched more complete games than the pitcher who has thrown the most complete games in the National League.

Consider the following similar statement:

```
SELECT FirstName, LastName
    FROM AMERICAN_LEAGUER
    WHERE CompleteGames > ANY
        (SELECT CompleteGames
            FROM NATIONAL_LEAGUER) ;
```

In this case, you use the existential quantifier ANY instead of the universal quantifier ALL. The subquery (the inner, nested query) is identical to the subquery in the previous example. This subquery retrieves a complete list of the complete game statistics for all the National League pitchers. The outer query returns the first and last names of all American League pitchers who pitched more complete games than ANY National League pitcher. Because you can be virtually certain that at least one National League pitcher hasn't pitched a complete game, the result probably includes all American League pitchers who've pitched at least one complete game.

If you replace the keyword ANY with the equivalent keyword SOME, the result is the same. If the statement that at least one National League pitcher hasn't pitched a complete game is a true statement, you can then say that SOME National League pitcher hasn't pitched a complete game.

EXISTS

You can use the EXISTS predicate in conjunction with a subquery to determine whether the subquery returns any rows. If the subquery returns at least one row, that result satisfies the EXISTS condition, and the outer query executes. Consider the following example:

```
SELECT FirstName, LastName
    FROM CUSTOMER
    WHERE EXISTS
      (SELECT DISTINCT CustomerID
        FROM INVOICE
        WHERE INVOICE.CustomerID = CUSTOMER.CustomerID);
```

The INVOICE table contains all of your company's sales transactions. The table includes the CustomerID of the customer who makes each purchase, as well as other pertinent information. The CUSTOMER table contains each customer's first and last names, but no information about specific transactions.

The subquery in the preceding example returns a row for every customer who has made at least one purchase. The outer query returns the first and last names of the customers who made the purchases that the INVOICE table records.

EXISTS is equivalent to a comparison of COUNT with zero, as the following query shows:

```
SELECT FirstName, LastName
   FROM CUSTOMER
   WHERE 0 <>
     (SELECT COUNT(*)
        FROM INVOICE
        WHERE INVOICE.CustomerID = CUSTOMER.CustomerID);
```

For every row in the INVOICE table that contains a CustomerID that's equal to a CustomerID in the CUSTOMER table, this statement displays the FirstName and LastName columns in the CUSTOMER table. For every sale in the INVOICE table, therefore, the statement displays the name of the customer who made the purchase.

UNIQUE

As you do with the EXISTS predicate, you use the UNIQUE predicate with a subquery. Although the EXISTS predicate evaluates to True only if the subquery returns at least one row, the UNIQUE predicate evaluates to True only if no two rows that the subquery returns are identical. In other words, the UNIQUE predicate evaluates to True *only* if all rows that its subquery returns are unique. Consider the following example:

```
SELECT FirstName, LastName
   FROM CUSTOMER
   WHERE UNIQUE
     (SELECT CustomerID FROM INVOICE
        WHERE INVOICE.CustomerID = CUSTOMER.CustomerID);
```

This statement retrieves the names of all new customers for whom the INVOICE table records only one sale. Two null values are considered to be not equal to each other and thus unique. When the UNIQUE keyword is applied to a result table that only contains two null rows, the UNIQUE predicate evaluates to True.

DISTINCT

The DISTINCT predicate is similar to the UNIQUE predicate, except in the way it treats nulls. If all the values in a result table are UNIQUE, they're also DISTINCT from each other. However, unlike the result for the UNIQUE predicate, if the DISTINCT keyword is applied to a result table that contains only two null rows, the DISTINCT predicate evaluates to False. Two null values are *not* considered distinct from each other, while at the same time they are considered to be unique. This strange situation seems contradictory, but there's a reason for it. In some situations, you may want to treat two null values as different from each other, whereas in other situations, you want to treat them as if they're the same. In the first case, use the UNIQUE predicate. In the second case, use the DISTINCT predicate.

OVERLAPS

You use the OVERLAPS predicate to determine whether two time intervals overlap each other. This predicate is useful for avoiding scheduling conflicts. If the two intervals overlap, the predicate returns a True value. If they don't overlap, the predicate returns a False value.

You can specify an interval in two ways: either as a start time and an end time or as a start time and a duration. Following are a few examples:

```
(TIME '2:55:00', INTERVAL '1' HOUR)
OVERLAPS
(TIME '3:30:00', INTERVAL '2' HOUR)
```

The preceding example returns a True because 3:30 is less than one hour after 2:55.

```
(TIME '9:00:00', TIME '9:30:00')
OVERLAPS
(TIME '9:29:00', TIME '9:31:00')
```

The preceding example returns a True because you have a one-minute overlap between the two intervals.

```
(TIME '9:00:00', TIME '10:00:00')
OVERLAPS
(TIME '10:15:00', INTERVAL '3' HOUR)
```

The preceding example returns a False because the two intervals don't overlap.

```
(TIME '9:00:00', TIME '9:30:00')
OVERLAPS
(TIME '9:30:00', TIME '9:35:00')
```

This example returns a False because even though the two intervals are contiguous, they don't overlap.

MATCH

In Book 2 Chapter 3, I discuss referential integrity, which involves maintaining consistency in a multitable database. You can lose integrity by adding a row to a child table that doesn't have a corresponding row in the child's

Book III
Chapter 2

**SELECT Statements
and Modifying
Clauses**

parent table. You can cause similar problems by deleting a row from a parent table if rows corresponding to that row exist in a child table.

Say that your business has a CUSTOMER table that keeps track of all your customers and a TRANSACT table that records all sales transactions. You don't want to add a row to TRANSACT until after you enter the customer making the purchase into the CUSTOMER table. You also don't want to delete a customer from the CUSTOMER table if that customer made purchases that exist in the TRANSACT table. Before you perform an insertion or deletion, you may want to check the candidate row to make sure that inserting or deleting that row doesn't cause integrity problems. The MATCH predicate can perform such a check.

To examine the MATCH predicate, I use an example that employs the CUSTOMER and TRANSACT tables. CustomerID is the primary key of the CUSTOMER table and acts as a foreign key in the TRANSACT table. Every row in the CUSTOMER table must have a unique, nonnull CustomerID. CustomerID isn't unique in the TRANSACT table because repeat customers buy more than once. This situation is fine and does not threaten integrity because CustomerID is a foreign key rather than a primary key in that table.

Seemingly, CustomerID can be null in the TRANSACT table because someone can walk in off the street, buy something, and walk out before you get a chance to enter his name and address into the CUSTOMER table. This situation can create a row in the child table with no corresponding row in the parent table. To overcome this problem, you can create a generic customer in the CUSTOMER table and assign all such anonymous sales to that customer.

Say that a customer steps up to the cash register and claims that she bought a flux capacitor on May 18, 2007. She now wants to return the device because her Delorean lacks time circuits, and so the flux capacitor is of no use. You can verify her claim by searching your TRANSACT database for a match. First, you must retrieve her CustomerID into the variable vcustid; then you can use the following syntax:

```
... WHERE (:vcustid, 'flux capacitor', '2007-05-18')
         MATCH
         (SELECT CustomerID, ProductName, Date
            FROM TRANSACT)
```

If a sale exists for that customer ID for that product on that date, the MATCH predicate returns a True value. Take back the product and refund the customer's money. (*Note:* If any values in the first argument of the MATCH predicate are null, a True value always returns.)

SQL's developers added the MATCH predicate and the UNIQUE predicate for the same reason — they provide a way to explicitly perform the tests defined for the implicit referential integrity (RI) and UNIQUE constraints.

The general form of the MATCH predicate is as follows:

```
Row_value MATCH  [UNIQUE] [SIMPLE| PARTIAL | FULL ] Subquery
```

The UNIQUE, SIMPLE, PARTIAL, and FULL options relate to rules that come into play if the row value expression R has one or more columns that are null. The rules for the MATCH predicate are a copy of corresponding referential integrity rules.

The MATCH predicate and referential integrity

Referential integrity rules require that the values of a column or columns in one table match the values of a column or columns in another table. You refer to the columns in the first table as the *foreign key* and the columns in the second table as the *primary key* or *unique key*. For example, you may declare the column EmpDeptNo in an EMPLOYEE table as a foreign key that references the DeptNo column of a DEPT table. This matchup ensures that if you record an employee in the EMPLOYEE table as working in department 123, a row appears in the DEPT table where DeptNo is 123.

This situation is fairly straightforward if the foreign key and primary key both consist of a single column. The two keys can, however, consist of multiple columns. The DeptNo value, for example, may be unique only within a Location; therefore, to uniquely identify a DEPT row, you must specify both a Location and a DeptNo. If both the Boston and Tampa offices have a department 123, you need to identify the departments as ('Boston', '123') and ('Tampa', '123'). In this case, the EMPLOYEE table needs two columns to identify a DEPT. Call those columns EmpLoc and EmpDeptNo. If an employee works in department 123 in Boston, the EmpLoc and EmpDeptNo values are 'Boston' and '123'. And the foreign key declaration in EMPLOYEE is as follows:

```
FOREIGN KEY (EmpLoc, EmpDeptNo)
   REFERENCES DEPT (Location, DeptNo)
```

Drawing valid conclusions from your data is complicated immensely if the data contains nulls. Sometimes you want to treat null-containing data one way, and sometimes you want to treat it another way. The UNIQUE, SIMPLE, PARTIAL, and FULL keywords specify different ways of treating data that contains nulls. If your data does not contain any null values, you can save yourself a lot of head-scratching by merely skipping to the section called "Logical

Connectives" later in this chapter. If your data *does* contain null values, drop out of Evelyn Woods speed-reading mode now and read the following paragraphs slowly and carefully. Each paragraph presents a different situation with respect to null values and tells how the MATCH predicate handles it.

If the values of EmpLoc and EmpDeptNo are both nonnull or both null, the referential integrity rules are the same as for single-column keys with values that are null or nonnull. But if EmpLoc is null and EmpDeptNo is nonnull — or EmpLoc is nonnull and EmpDeptNo is null — you need new rules. What should the rules be if you insert or update the EMPLOYEE table with EmpLoc and EmpDeptNo values of (NULL, '123') or ('Boston', NULL)? You have six main alternatives, SIMPLE, PARTIAL, and FULL, each either with or without the UNIQUE keyword. The UNIQUE keyword, if present, means that a matching row in the subquery result table must be unique in order for the predicate to evaluate to a True value. If both components of the row value expression R are null, the MATCH predicate returns a True value regardless of the contents of the subquery result table being compared.

If neither component of the row value expression R is null, SIMPLE is specified, UNIQUE is not specified, and at least one row in the subquery result table matches R, the MATCH predicate returns a True value. Otherwise, it returns a False value.

If neither component of the row value expression R is null, SIMPLE is specified, UNIQUE is specified, and at least one row in the subquery result table is both unique and matches R, the MATCH predicate returns a True value. Otherwise, it returns a False value.

If any component of the row value expression R is null and SIMPLE is specified, the MATCH predicate returns a True value.

If any component of the row value expression R is nonnull, PARTIAL is specified, UNIQUE is not specified, and the nonnull parts of at least one row in the subquery result table matches R, the MATCH predicate returns a True value. Otherwise, it returns a False value.

If any component of the row value expression R is nonnull, PARTIAL is specified, UNIQUE is specified, and the nonnull parts of R match the nonnull parts of at least one unique row in the subquery result table, the MATCH predicate returns a True value. Otherwise, it returns a False value.

If neither component of the row value expression R is null, FULL is specified, UNIQUE is not specified, and at least one row in the subquery result table matches R, the MATCH predicate returns a True value. Otherwise, it returns a False value.

Rule by committee

The SQL-89 version of the standard specified the UNIQUE rule as the default, before anyone proposed or debated the alternatives. During development of the SQL-92 version of the standard, proposals appeared for the alternatives. Some people strongly preferred the PARTIAL rules and argued that they should be the only rules. These people thought that the SQL-89 (UNIQUE) rules were so undesirable that they thought those rules should be considered a bug and the PARTIAL rules specified as a correction. Other people preferred the UNIQUE rules and thought that the PARTIAL rules were obscure, error-prone, and inefficient. Still other people preferred the additional discipline of the FULL rules. The issue was finally settled by providing all three keywords so that users could choose whichever approach they preferred. SQL:1999 added the SIMPLE rules. The proliferation of rules makes dealing with nulls anything but simple. If SIMPLE, PARTIAL, or FULL is not specified, the SIMPLE rules are followed.

If neither component of the row value expression R is null, FULL is specified, UNIQUE is specified, and at least one row in the subquery result table is both unique and matches R, the MATCH predicate returns a True value. Otherwise, it returns a False value.

If any component of the row value expression R is null and FULL is specified, the MATCH predicate returns a False value.

Logical connectives

Often, as a number of previous examples show, applying one condition in a query isn't enough to return the rows that you want from a table. In some cases, the rows must satisfy two or more conditions. In other cases, if a row satisfies any of two or more conditions, it qualifies for retrieval. On other occasions, you want to retrieve only rows that don't satisfy a specified condition. To meet these needs, SQL offers the logical connectives AND, OR, and NOT.

AND

If multiple conditions must all be True before you can retrieve a row, use the AND logical connective. Consider the following example:

```
SELECT InvoiceNo, SaleDate, SalesPerson, TotalSale
    FROM SALES
    WHERE SaleDate >= '2007-05-14'
        AND SaleDate <= '2007-05-21' ;
```

The WHERE clause must meet the following two conditions:

✦ SaleDate must be greater than or equal to May 14, 2007.

✦ SaleDate must be less than or equal to May 22, 2007.

Only rows that record sales occurring during the week of May 14 meet both conditions. The query returns only these rows.

Notice that the AND connective is strictly logical. This restriction can sometimes be confusing because people commonly use the word *and* with a looser meaning. Suppose, for example, that your boss says to you, "I'd like to see the sales for Acheson and Bryant." He said, "Acheson and Bryant," so you may write the following SQL query:

```
SELECT *
   FROM SALES
   WHERE Salesperson = 'Acheson'
      AND Salesperson = 'Bryant';
```

Well, don't take that answer back to your boss. The following query is more like what he had in mind:

```
SELECT *
   FROM SALES
   WHERE Salesperson IN ('Acheson', 'Bryant') ;
```

The first query won't return anything, because none of the sales in the SALES table were made by *both* Acheson and Bryant. The second query returns the information on all sales made by either Acheson or Bryant, which is probably what the boss wanted.

OR

If any one of two or more conditions must be True to qualify a row for retrieval, use the OR logical connective, as in the following example:

```
SELECT InvoiceNo, SaleDate, Salesperson, TotalSale
   FROM SALES
      WHERE Salesperson = 'Bryant'
         OR TotalSale > 200 ;
```

This query retrieves all of Bryant's sales, regardless of how large, as well as all sales of more than $200, regardless of who made the sales.

NOT

The NOT connective negates a condition. If the condition normally returns a True value, adding NOT causes the same condition to return a False value. If a condition normally returns a False value, adding NOT causes the condition to return a True value. Consider the following example:

```
SELECT InvoiceNo, SaleDate, Salesperson, TotalSale
    FROM SALES
        WHERE NOT (Salesperson = 'Bryant') ;
```

This query returns rows for all sales transactions completed by salespeople other than Bryant.

When you use AND, OR, or NOT, sometimes the scope of the connective isn't clear. To be safe, use parentheses to make sure that SQL applies the connective to the predicate you want. In the preceding example, the NOT connective applies to the entire predicate (Salesperson = 'Bryant').

GROUP BY clauses

Sometimes, rather than retrieving individual records, you want to know something about a group of records. The GROUP BY clause is the tool you need.

Suppose you're the sales manager and you want to look at the performance of your sales force. You could do a simple SELECT such as the following:

```
SELECT InvoiceNo, SaleDate, Salesperson, TotalSale
    FROM SALES;
```

You would receive a result similar to that shown in Figure 2-1.

Book III Chapter 2

SELECT Statements and Modifying Clauses

Figure 2-1:
The result set for retrieval of sales from 08/01/2007 to 08/07/2007.

| File | Edit | View | Insert | Format | Records | Tools |
| Window | Help |

| Query1 : Select Query | | | |
InvoiceNo	SaleDate	Salesperson	TotalSale
1	08/01/2007	Acheson	$49.95
2	08/01/2007	Bryant	$24.95
3	08/02/2007	Bennett	$1,710.00
4	08/02/2007	Acheson	$249.95
5	08/03/2007	Bennett	$129.50
6	08/04/2007	Bryant	$75.00
7	08/04/2007	Acheson	$550.00
8	08/05/2007	Acheson	$303.94
9	08/07/2007	Bennett	$12.45
10	08/07/2007	Bryant	$650.00

Datasheet View

This result gives you some idea of how well your salespeople are doing because so few total sales are involved. However, in real life, a company would have many more sales, and it wouldn't be as easy to tell whether sales objectives were being met. To do that, you can combine the GROUP BY clause with one of the aggregate functions (also called set functions) to get a quantitative picture of sales performance. For example, you can see which salesperson is selling more of the profitable high-ticket items by using the average (AVG) function as follows:

```
SELECT Salesperson, AVG(TotalSale)
    FROM SALES
    GROUP BY Salesperson;
```

You would receive a result similar to that shown in Figure 2-2.

Figure 2-2:
Average
sales for
each
salesperson.

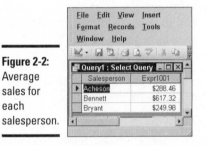

As shown in Figure 2-2, Bennett's average sale is considerably higher than that of the other two salespeople. You compare total sales with a similar query:

```
SELECT Salesperson, SUM(TotalSale)
    FROM SALES
    GROUP BY Salesperson;
```

This gives the result shown in Figure 2-3.

Figure 2-3:
Total sales
for each
salesperson.

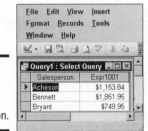

Bennett also has the highest total sales, which is consistent with having the highest average sales.

HAVING clauses

You can analyze the grouped data further by using the HAVING clause. The HAVING clause is a filter that acts similar to a WHERE clause, but on groups of rows rather than on individual rows. To illustrate the function of the HAVING clause, suppose the sales manager considers Bennett to be in a class by himself. His performance distorts the overall data for the other salespeople. You can exclude Bennett's sales from the grouped data by using a HAVING clause as follows:

```
SELECT Salesperson, SUM(TotalSale)
    FROM SALES
    GROUP BY Salesperson
    HAVING Salesperson <> 'Bennett';
```

This gives the result shown in Figure 2-4. Only rows where the salesperson is not Bennett are considered.

Figure 2-4: Total sales for all salespeople except Bennett.

ORDER BY clauses

Use the ORDER BY clause to display the output table of a query in either ascending or descending alphabetical order. Whereas the GROUP BY clause gathers rows into groups and sorts the groups into alphabetical order, ORDER BY sorts individual rows. The ORDER BY clause must be the last clause that you specify in a query. If the query also contains a GROUP BY clause, the clause first arranges the output rows into groups. The ORDER BY clause then sorts the rows within each group. If you have no GROUP BY clause, the statement considers the entire table as a group, and the ORDER BY clause sorts all its rows according to the column (or columns) that the ORDER BY clause specifies.

To illustrate this point, consider the data in the SALES table. The SALES table contains columns for InvoiceNo, SaleDate, Salesperson, and TotalSale. If you use the following example, you see all the SALES data, but in an arbitrary order:

```
SELECT * FROM SALES ;
```

In one implementation, this order may be the one in which you inserted the rows in the table, and in another implementation, the order may be that of the most recent updates. The order can also change unexpectedly if anyone physically reorganizes the database. Usually, you want to specify the order in which you want to display the rows. You may, for example, want to see the rows in order by the SaleDate, as follows:

```
SELECT * FROM SALES ORDER BY SaleDate ;
```

This example returns all the rows in the SALES table, in order by SaleDate.

For rows with the same SaleDate, the default order depends on the implementation. You can, however, specify how to sort the rows that share the same SaleDate. You may want to see the SALES for each SaleDate in order by InvoiceNo, as follows:

```
SELECT * FROM SALES ORDER BY SaleDate, InvoiceNo ;
```

This example first orders the SALES by SaleDate; then for each SaleDate, it orders the SALES by InvoiceNo. But don't confuse that example with the following query:

```
SELECT * FROM SALES ORDER BY InvoiceNo, SaleDate ;
```

This query first orders the SALES by INVOICE_NO. Then for each different INVOICE_NO, the query orders the SALES by SALE_DATE. This probably won't yield the result you want because it is unlikely that multiple sale dates exist for a single invoice number.

The following query is another example of how SQL can return data:

```
SELECT * FROM SALES ORDER BY Salesperson, SaleDate ;
```

This example first orders by SALESPERSON and then by SALE_DATE. After you look at the data in that order, you may want to invert it, as follows:

```
SELECT * FROM SALES ORDER BY SaleDate, Salesperson ;
```

This example orders the rows first by SaleDate and then by Salesperson.

All these ordering examples are ascending (ASC), which is the default sort order. The last SELECT shows earlier SALES first and, within a given date, shows SALES for 'Adams' before 'Baker'. If you prefer descending (DESC) order, you can specify this order for one or more of the order columns, as follows:

```
SELECT * FROM SALES
ORDER BY SaleDate DESC, Salesperson ASC ;
```

This example specifies a descending order for sales date, showing the more recent sales first, and an ascending order for salespeople, putting them in normal alphabetical order.

Tuning Queries

Performance is almost always a top priority for any organizational database system. As usage of the system goes up, if resources such as processor speed, cache memory, and hard disk storage do not go up proportionally, performance starts to suffer and users start to complain. Clearly, one thing that a system administrator can do is increase the resources — install a faster processor, add more cache, buy more hard disks. These solutions may give the needed improvement, and may even be necessary, but you should try a cheaper solution first: improving the efficiency of the queries that are loading down the system.

Generally there are several different ways that you can obtain the information you want from a database; in other words, there are several different ways that you can code a query. Some of those ways are more efficient than others. If one or more queries that are run on a regular basis are bogging down the system, you may be able to bring your system back up to speed without spending a penny on additional hardware. You may just have to recode the queries that are causing the bottleneck.

Popular database management systems have query optimizers that try to eliminate bottlenecks for you, but they don't always do as well as you could do if you tested various alternatives and picked the one with the best performance.

Unfortunately, no general rules apply across the board. The way a database is structured and the columns that are indexed have definite effects. In addition, a coding practice that would be optimal if you use Microsoft SQL Server might result in the worst possible performance if you use Oracle. Because the different DBMSs do things in different ways, what is good for one is not necessarily good for another. There are some things you can do, however, that enable you to find good query plans. In the following sections, I show you some common situations.

SELECT DISTINCT

You use `SELECT DISTINCT` when you want to make sure there are no duplicates in records you retrieve. However, the `DISTINCT` keyword potentially adds overhead to a query that could impact system performance. The impact it may or may not have depends on how it is implemented by the DBMS. Furthermore, including the `DISTINCT` keyword in a `SELECT` operation may not even be needed to assure there are no duplicates. If you are doing a select on a primary key, the result set is guaranteed to contain no duplicates anyway, so adding the `DISTINCT` keyword provides no advantage.

Rather than relying on general rules such as "Avoid using the `DISTINCT` keyword if you can," if you suspect that a query that includes a `DISTINCT` keyword is inefficient, test it to see. First, make a typical query into Microsoft's NorthwindCS sample database. The NorthwindCS database contains records typical of a trading company. There is a Customers table and an Orders table, among others. One thing you might want to do is see what companies in the Customers table have actually placed orders, as recorded in the Orders table. Because a customer may place multiple orders, it makes sense to use the `DISTINCT` keyword, so that only one row is returned for each customer. Here's the code for the query:

```
SELECT DISTINCT Customers.CompanyName
  FROM Customers, Orders
  WHERE Customers.CustomerID = Orders.CustomerID ;
```

The result is shown in Figure 2-5, which shows the first few names of companies that have placed at least one order.

Figure 2-5: Customers who have placed at least one order.

Note that in Object Explorer on the left side, in the Orders table, OrderID is the primary key, and CustomerID is one of several foreign keys. In this query, I used CustomerID to link the Customers table to the Orders table so that I could pull information from both.

It would be interesting to see how efficient this query is. Use Microsoft SQL Server 2005's tools to find out. First, look at the execution plan that was followed to run this query in Figure 2-6.

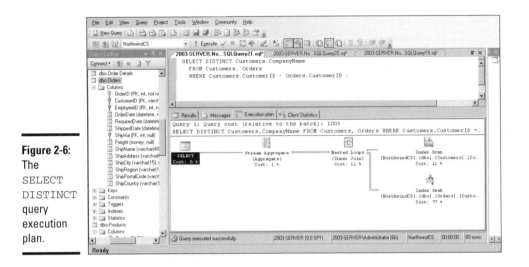

Figure 2-6:
The
`SELECT`
`DISTINCT`
query
execution
plan.

**Book III
Chapter 2**

**SELECT Statements
and Modifying
Clauses**

The execution plan shows that an index seek on the Orders table took 77% of the total time consumed by the query. An index scan of the smaller Customers table took 11% of the time, and the nested loops join took 11%. To see how well or how poorly I'm doing, I look at the client statistics (Figure 2-7).

Total execution time is 80 time units, with client processing time at 30 time units and wait time on server replies at 50 time units.

The execution plan shows that the bulk of the time consumed is due to the index seek on the large Orders table. There is no getting around this operation, and it is doing it about as efficiently as possible. Will rerunning the query deliver better performance due to caching? After rerunning the query, SQL Server gave me the client statistics in Figure 2-8.

The execution plan is the same, but the execution time is less. Small differences in time may be due to other tasks the system is performing during test runs.

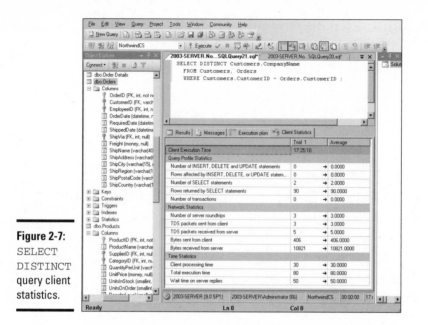

Figure 2-7:
SELECT
DISTINCT
query client
statistics.

Figure 2-8:
SELECT
query client
statistics for
rerun.

Temporary tables

SQL is so feature-rich that there are multiple ways to perform many operations. Not all those ways are equally efficient. Often, the DBMSs optimizer dynamically changes an operation that was coded in a sub-optimal way into a more efficient operation. Sometimes, however, this doesn't happen. To be sure your query is running as fast as possible, code it different ways and test each one. Settle on the one that does the best. Sometimes the best method on one type of query performs poorly on another, so take nothing for granted.

One method of coding a query that has multiple selection conditions is to use temporary tables. Consider an example. Suppose you want to know the names of all the Northwind employees who are residents of the state of Washington and who have been with the company for more than ten years. First you can create a temporary table that holds only Washington residents:

```
SELECT * INTO Temp
  FROM Employees
  WHERE Region = 'WA' ;
```

Then you can find the employees in the Temp table that have more than ten years of service:

```
SELECT EmployeeID, LastName, FirstName
  FROM Temp
  WHERE (Current_Timestamp - HireDate) > 10 ;
```

This gives the result shown in Figure 2-9.

Book III
Chapter 2

**SELECT Statements
and Modifying
Clauses**

Figure 2-9:
Retrieve
ten-year
veterans
who live in
Washington.

Five of Northwind's nine employees have been with the company for more than ten years. Look at the execution plan to see how this retrieval was done (Figure 2-10).

Figure 2-10: SELECT query execution plan using a temporary table.

Creation of the temporary table is one operation, and finding the veterans is another. In the table creation query, scanning the index of the Employees table took 25% of the time used, and creating the temporary table took up the other 75%. The table scan of the temporary table took up all the time of the second query. How did you do performance-wise? Figure 2-11 gives the details.

Total execution time was 180 time units, equally divided between client processing time and wait time on server replies. 488 bytes were sent from the client, and 37,573 bytes were returned by the server.

Now suppose you performed the same operation without using a temporary table. You could do so with the following code:

```
SELECT EmployeeID, LastName, FirstName
  FROM Employees
  Where Region = 'WA'
  AND (Current_Timestamp - HireDate) > 10 ;
```

You get the same result (Figure 2-12) as in Figure 2-9.

Figure 2-11:
SELECT
query
execution
client
statistics
using a
temporary
table.

Book III
Chapter 2

SELECT Statements
and Modifying
Clauses

Figure 2-12:
SELECT
query result
with
compound
condition.

How does the execution plan (Figure 2-13) compare with the one in Figure 2-10?

It's really simple. The clustered index scan on Employees takes up all the time. The real story, however, is in the client statistics (Figure 2-14). How does performance compare with the temporary table version?

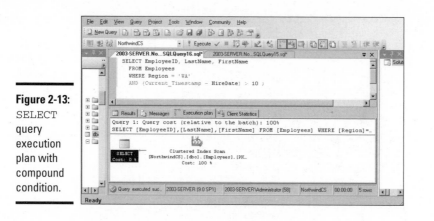

Figure 2-13:
SELECT query execution plan with compound condition.

Figure 2-14:
SELECT query client statistics, with compound condition.

Hmmm. Total execution time is only 40 time units, and that is all due to wait time for server replies. 426 bytes were sent from the client, which is comparable to the upstream traffic in the temporary table case. However, only 8,475 bytes were sent from the server down to the client. That is considerably less than the 37,573 bytes that were downloaded using the temporary table. From both a bandwidth usage standpoint and an execution time standpoint, using a compound condition in this case beats using a temporary table. There may be situations where using a temporary table is better, but using one to avoid a compound condition in a query is generally not one of them.

The ORDER BY clause

The ORDER BY clause can be expensive in terms of both bandwidth between the server and the client and execution time. If you can minimize the number of ORDER BY clauses in a series of queries, you may save resources. This is one place where using a temporary table might actually help. Consider an example. Suppose you want to do a series of retrievals on your Products table, in which you see which products are available in several price ranges. For example, you want one list of products priced between ten dollars and twenty dollars, ordered by unit price. Then you want a list of products priced between twenty dollars and thirty dollars, similarly ordered, and so on. To cover four such price ranges, you could make four queries, all four with an ORDER BY clause. Alternatively, you could create a temporary table with a query that uses an ORDER BY clause, and then draw the data for the ranges in separate queries that do not have ORDER BY clauses. Compare the two approaches. Here's the code for the temporary table approach:

```
SELECT ProductName, UnitPrice INTO Temp
  FROM Products
  WHERE UnitPrice > 10
  AND UnitPrice <= 50
  ORDER BY UnitPrice;
SELECT ProductName, UnitPrice
  FROM Temp
  WHERE UnitPrice > 10
  AND UnitPrice <= 20;
SELECT ProductName, UnitPrice
  FROM Temp
  WHERE UnitPrice > 20
  AND UnitPrice <= 30;
SELECT ProductName, UnitPrice
  FROM Temp
  WHERE UnitPrice > 30
  AND UnitPrice <= 40;
SELECT ProductName, UnitPrice
  FROM Temp
  WHERE UnitPrice > 40
  AND UnitPrice <= 50;
```

**Book III
Chapter 2**

SELECT Statements and Modifying Clauses

The execution plans for this series of queries is shown in Figure 2-15.

The first query, the one that creates the temporary table, has the most complex execution plan. By itself, it takes up 61% of the allotted time, and the other four queries take up the remaining 39%. Figure 2-16 shows the client statistics, measuring resource usage.

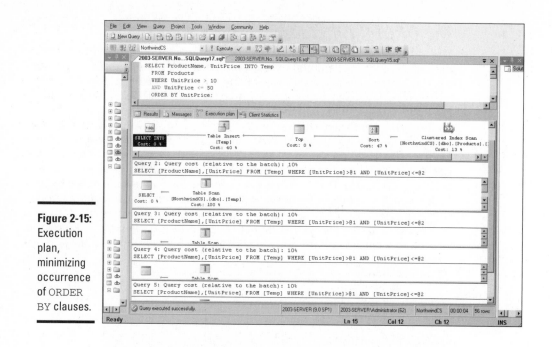

Figure 2-15:
Execution
plan,
minimizing
occurrence
of ORDER
BY clauses.

Figure 2-16:
Client
statistics,
minimizing
occurrence
of ORDER
BY clauses.

Total execution time is 500 time units, and 39,544 bytes were received from the server. Now compare that with no temporary table, but four separate queries, each with its own ORDER BY clause. Here's the code:

```
SELECT ProductName, UnitPrice
   FROM Products
   WHERE UnitPrice > 10
   AND UnitPrice <= 20
   ORDER BY UnitPrice;
SELECT ProductName, UnitPrice
   FROM Products
   WHERE UnitPrice > 20
   AND UnitPrice <= 30
   ORDER BY UnitPrice;
SELECT ProductName, UnitPrice
   FROM Products
   WHERE UnitPrice > 30
   AND UnitPrice <= 40
   ORDER BY UnitPrice;
SELECT ProductName, UnitPrice
   FROM Products
   WHERE UnitPrice > 40
   AND UnitPrice <= 50
   ORDER BY UnitPrice;
```

The resulting execution plan is shown in Figure 2-17.

**Book III
Chapter 2**

**SELECT Statements
and Modifying
Clauses**

Figure 2-17:
Execution
plan,
queries with
separate
ORDER BY
clauses.

Each of the four queries involves a sort. This could be costly. Figure 2-18 shows what the client statistics look like.

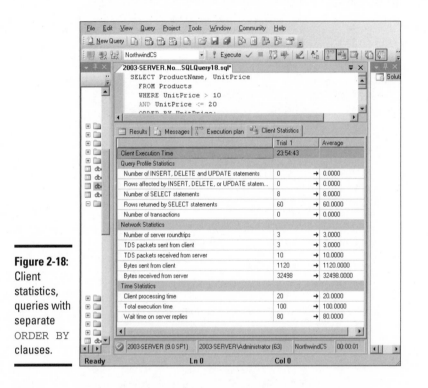

Figure 2-18: Client statistics, queries with separate ORDER BY clauses.

Total execution time is 100 time units, and 32,498 bytes were returned by the server. On both quality metrics, this method performs better than the temporary table method, at least for a database of this size with these characteristics, on SQL Server 2005. As table sizes increase, the time it takes to sort them goes up at an even faster rate. For large tables, the performance advantage tips to the temporary table method as some point.

The HAVING clause

Think about the order in which you do things. Performing operations in the correct order can make a big difference in performance. Whereas the WHERE clause filters out rows that don't meet a search condition, the HAVING clause filters out entire groups that don't meet a search condition. It makes sense to filter first (with a WHERE clause) and group later (with a GROUP BY clause) rather than to group first and filter later (with a HAVING clause). If you group first, you perform the grouping operation on everything. If you filter first, you perform the grouping operation only on what is left after the rows you don't want have been filtered out.

This line of reasoning sounds good. To see if it is borne out in practice, consider this code:

```
SELECT AVG(UnitPrice) AS AvgPrice, CategoryID
  FROM Products
  GROUP BY CategoryID
  HAVING CategoryID = 3 ;
```

It finds the average price of all the products in Category 3 by first grouping the products into categories and then filtering out all except those in Category 3. Figure 2-19 shows what SQL Server returns.

Figure 2-19:
Retrieval with a HAVING clause.

**Book III
Chapter 2**

SELECT Statements and Modifying Clauses

Figure 2-20 shows what the execution plan tells us.

Figure 2-20:
Retrieval with a HAVING clause execution plan.

A clustered index scan takes up most of the time. This is a fairly efficient operation. The client statistics are shown in Figure 2-21.

Figure 2-21: Retrieval with a `HAVING` clause client statistics.

Total execution time is 130 time units, and 11,107 bytes were returned from the server. Now, try filtering first and grouping second.

```
SELECT AVG(UnitPrice) AS AvgPrice
  FROM Products
  WHERE CategoryID = 3 ;
```

There is no need to group because all categories except category 3 are filtered out by the `WHERE` clause. Figure 2-22 shows that the result is the same as in the previous case.

Figure 2-22: Retrieval without a `HAVING` clause.

Figure 2-23 shows how the execution plan differs. Interesting! The execution plan is the same. SQL Server's optimizer has done its job in both cases. Are the client statistics the same too? Check Figure 2-24 to find out.

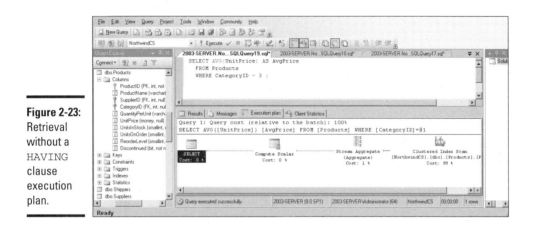

Figure 2-23: Retrieval without a HAVING clause execution plan.

Figure 2-24: Retrieval without a HAVING clause client statistics.

Client processing time is down, total processing time is up slightly due to waiting for the server, and there has been a significant reduction in the number of bytes transferred. Is this a fluke? What if I ran the same query again? Figure 2-25 shows the client statistics for a repeat run.

Figure 2-25:
Repeat run
client
statistics.

Now that the query has been cached, execution times are dramatically lowered. However, the number of bytes transferred is the same. The second formulation actually does reduce the traffic between the server and the client and is thus the better way to code the query, even though the execution plan is the same in both cases.

The OR logical connective

Some systems never use indexes when expressions in a WHERE clause are connected by the OR logical connective. Check your system to see if it does. See how SQL Server handles it.

```
SELECT ProductID, ProductName
  FROM Products
  WHERE UnitPrice < 20
  OR UnitsInStock < 30 ;
```

Check the execution plan to see if SQL Server uses an index (Figure 2-26). SQL Server *does* use an index in this situation, so there is no point in looking for alternative ways to code this type of query.

Figure 2-26:
Query with
OR logical
connective.

Run performance tests such as those shown in this chapter on the exact database you are attempting to tune, rather than on a sample database such as NorthwindCS or even on another production database. Due to differences in table size, indexing, and other factors, conclusions you come to based on one database don't necessarily apply to another.

Chapter 3: Querying Multiple Tables with Subqueries

In This Chapter

✔ Defining subqueries

✔ Discovering how subqueries work

✔ Nesting subqueries

✔ Tuning nested subqueries

✔ Tuning correlation subqueries

*R*elational databases have multiple tables. That's where the word *relational* comes from — multiple tables that relate to each other in some way. One consequence of the distribution of data across multiple tables is that most queries need to pull data from more than one of them. There are a couple of ways to do this. One is to use relational operators, which I cover in the next chapter. The other method is to use subqueries, which is the subject of this chapter.

What Is a Subquery?

A *subquery* is an SQL statement that is embedded within another SQL statement. It's possible for a subquery to be embedded within another subquery, which is in turn embedded within an outermost SQL statement. Theoretically there is no limit to the number of levels of subquery that an SQL statement may include, although any given implementation has a practical limit. A key feature of a subquery is that the table or tables that it references need not be the same as the table or tables referenced by its enclosing query. This has the effect of returning results based on the information in multiple tables.

What Subqueries Do

Subqueries are located within the WHERE clause of their enclosing statement. Their function is to set the search conditions for the WHERE clause. The combination of a subquery and its enclosing query is called a *nested query.* Different kinds of nested queries produce different results. Some subqueries produce a list of values that is then used as input by the enclosing statement. Other subqueries produce a single value that the enclosing statement then evaluates with a comparison operator. A third kind of subquery, called a *correlated subquery,* operates differently, and I discuss it in the "Correlated subqueries" section.

Subqueries that return multiple values

A key concern of many businesses is inventory control. When you are building products that are made up of various parts, you want to make sure that you have an adequate supply of all the parts. If just one part is in short supply, it could bring the entire manufacturing operation to a screeching halt. To see how many products are impacted by the lack of a part they need, you can use a subquery.

Subqueries that retrieve rows satisfying a condition

Suppose your company (Penguin Electronics, Inc.) manufactures a variety of electronic products, such as audio amplifiers, FM radio tuners, and handheld metal detectors. You keep track of your inventory of all your products, as well as all the parts that go into their manufacture, in a relational database. The database has a PRODUCTS table that holds the inventory levels of finished products and a PARTS table that holds the inventory levels of the parts that go into the products.

A part could be included in multiple products, and each product is made up of multiple parts. This means that there is a many-to-many relationship between the PRODUCTS table and the PARTS table. Because this could present problems, you decide to insert an intersection table between PRODUCTS and PARTS, transforming the problematical many-to-many relationship into two easier-to-deal-with one-to-many relationships. The intersection table, named PROD_PARTS, takes the primary keys of PRODUCTS and PARTS as its only attributes. You can create these three tables with the following code:

```
CREATE TABLE PRODUCTS (
   ProductID            INTEGER       PRIMARY KEY,
   ProductName          CHAR (30),
   ProductDescription   CHAR (50),
   ListPrice            NUMERIC (9,2),
   QuantityInStock      INTEGER ) ;

CREATE TABLE PARTS (
   PartID               INTEGER       PRIMARY KEY,
   PartName             CHAR (30),
```

```
    PartDescription        CHAR (50),
    QuantityInStock        INTEGER ) ;

CREATE TABLE PROD_PARTS (
    ProductID              INTEGER       NOT NULL,
    PartID                 INTEGER       NOT NULL ) ;
```

Suppose some of your products include an APM-17 DC analog panel meter. Now you find, to your horror, that you are completely out of the APM-17 part. You can't complete the manufacture of any product that includes it. It is time for management to take some emergency actions. One is to check on the status of any outstanding orders to the supplier of the APM-17 panel meters. Another is to notify the sales department to stop selling all products that include the APM-17, and switch to promoting products that do not include it.

To discover which products include the APM-17, you can use a nested query such as the following:

```
SELECT ProductID
   FROM PROD_PARTS
   WHERE PartID IN
    (SELECT PartID
       FROM PARTS
     WHERE PartDescription = 'APM-17') ;
```

SQL processes the innermost query first, so it queries the PARTS table, returning the PartID of every row in the PARTS table where the PartDescription is APM-17. The outer query uses the IN keyword to find all the rows in the PROD_PARTS table that include a PartID that appears in the result set from the inner query. The outer query then extracts from the PROD_PARTS table the ProductIDs of all the products that include the APM-17 part. These are the products that Sales should stop selling.

Subqueries that retrieve rows that don't satisfy a condition

Because sales are the lifeblood of any business, it is even more important to determine which products the sales team can continue to sell than it is to tell them what not to sell. You can do this with another nested query. Use the query just executed in the preceding section as a base, add one more "layer" of query to it, and return the ProductIDs of all the products that are not affected by the APM-17 shortage.

```
SELECT ProductID
   FROM PROD_PARTS
   WHERE ProductID NOT IN
    (SELECT ProductID
```

```
        FROM PROD_PARTS
        WHERE PartID IN
         (SELECT PartID
            FROM PARTS
            WHERE PartDescription = 'APM-17') ;
```

The two inner queries return the ProductIDs of all the products that include the APM-17 part. The outer query returns all the ProductIDs of all the products that are not included in the result set from the inner queries. This final result set is the list of ProductIDs of products that do not include the APM-17 analog panel meter.

Subqueries that return a single value

Introducing a subquery with one of the six comparison operators (=, <>, <, <=, >, >=) is often useful. In such a case, the expression preceding the operator evaluates to a single value, and the subquery following the operator must also evaluate to a single value. An exception is the case of the *quantified comparison operator,* which is a comparison operator followed by a quantifier (ANY, SOME, or ALL).

To illustrate a case in which a subquery returns a single value, look at another piece of Penguin Electronics' database. It contains a CUSTOMER table that holds information about the companies that buy Penguin products. It also contains a CONTACT table that holds personal data about individuals at each of Penguin's customer organizations. The following code creates Penguin's CUSTOMER and CONTACT tables.

```
CREATE TABLE CUSTOMER (
    CustomerID          INTEGER         PRIMARY KEY,
    Company             CHAR (40),
    Address1            CHAR (50),
    Address2            CHAR (50),
    City                CHAR (25),
    State               CHAR (2),
    PostalCode          CHAR (10),
    Phone               CHAR (13) ) ;

CREATE TABLE CONTACT (
    CustomerID          INTEGER     PRIMARY KEY,
    FirstName           CHAR (15),
    LastName            CHAR (20),
    Phone               CHAR (13),
    Email               CHAR (30),
    Fax                 CHAR (13),
    Notes               CHAR (100),
    CONSTRAINT ContactFK FOREIGN KEY (CustomerID)
        REFERENCES CUSTOMER (CustomerID) ) ;
```

Say that you want to look at the contact information for the customer named Baker Electronic Sales, but you don't remember that company's CustomerID. Use a nested query like this one to recover the information you want:

```
SELECT *
    FROM CONTACT
        WHERE CustomerID =
            (SELECT CustomerID
                FROM CUSTOMER
                    WHERE Company = 'Baker Electronic Sales') ;
```

The result looks something like this:

```
CustomerID FirstName LastName Phone        Notes
---------- --------- -------- ------------ --------------
       767 David     Lee      505-876-3456 Likes to visit
                                           El Pollo Loco
                                           when in Cali.
```

You can now call Dave at Baker and tell him about this month's special sale on metal detectors.

When you use a subquery in an `"="` comparison, the subquery's SELECT list must specify a single column (CustomerID in the example). When the subquery is executed, it must return a single row in order to have a single value for the comparison.

In this example, I assume that the CUSTOMER table has only one row with a Company value of `Baker Electronic Sales`. If the CREATE TABLE statement for CUSTOMER specified a UNIQUE constraint for Company, such a statement guarantees that the subquery in the preceding example returns a single value (or no value). Subqueries like the one in the example, however, are commonly used on columns that are not specified to be UNIQUE. In such cases, you are relying on some other reasons for believing that the column has no duplicates.

If more than one CUSTOMER has a value of `Baker Electronic Sales` in the Company column (perhaps in different states), the subquery raises an error.

If no Customer with such a company name exists, the subquery is treated as if it were null, and the comparison becomes unknown. In this case, the WHERE clause returns no row (because it returns only rows with the condition True and filters rows with the condition False or Unknown). This would probably happen, for example, if someone misspelled the COMPANY as `Baker Electronics Sales`.

Although the equals operator (=) is the most common, you can use any of the other five comparison operators in a similar structure. For every row in the table specified in the enclosing statement's FROM clause, the single value returned by the subquery is compared to the expression in the enclosing statement's WHERE clause. If the comparison gives a True value, a row is added to the result table.

You can guarantee that a subquery returns a single value if you include a set function in it. Set functions, also known as *aggregate* functions, always return a single value. (Set functions are described in Chapter 1.) Of course, this way of returning a single value is helpful only if you want the result of a set function.

Say that you are a Penguin salesperson and you need to earn a big commission check to pay for some unexpected bills. You decide to concentrate on selling Penguin's most expensive product. You can find out what that product is with a nested query:

```
SELECT ProductID, ProductName, ListPrice
    FROM PRODUCT
        WHERE ListPrice =
            (SELECT MAX(ListPrice)
                FROM PRODUCT) ;
```

This is an example of a nested query where both the subquery and the enclosing statement operate on the same table. The subquery returns a single value: the maximum list price in the PRODUCTS table. The outer query retrieves all rows from the PRODUCTS table that have that list price.

The next example shows a comparison subquery that uses a comparison operator other than =:

```
SELECT ProductID, ProductName, ListPrice
    FROM PRODUCTS
        WHERE ListPrice <
            (SELECT AVG(ListPrice)
                FROM PRODUCTS) ;
```

The subquery returns a single value: the average list price in the PRODUCTS table. The outer query retrieves all rows from the PRODUCTS table that have a list price less than the average list price.

In the original SQL standard, a comparison could have only one subquery, and it had to be on the right side of the comparison. SQL:1999 allowed either or both operands of the comparison to be subqueries, and later versions of SQL retain that expanded capability.

Quantified subqueries return a single value

One way to make sure a subquery returns a single value is to introduce it with a quantified comparison operator. The universal quantifier ALL, and the existential quantifiers SOME and ANY, when combined with a comparison operator, process the result set returned by the inner subquery, reducing it to a single value.

Look at an example. From the 1960s through the 1980s, there was fierce competition between Ford and Chevrolet to produce the most powerful cars. Both companies had small block V-8 engines that went into Mustangs, Camaros, and other performance-oriented vehicles.

Power is generally measured in units of horsepower. In general, a larger engine delivers more horsepower, all other things being equal. Because the displacements (sizes) of the engines varied from one model to another, it's unfair to look only at horsepower. A better measure of the efficiency of an engine is horsepower per displacement. Displacement is measured in cubic inches (CID). Table 3-1 shows the year, displacement, and horsepower ratings for Ford small-block V-8s between 1960 and 1980.

Table 3-1	Ford Small-Block V-8s, 1960–1980		
Year	*Displacement (CID)*	*Maximum Horsepower*	*Notes*
1962	221	145	
1963	289	225	4bbl carburetor
1965	289	271	289HP model
1965	289	306	Shelby GT350
1969	351	290	4bbl carburetor
1975	302	140	Emission regulations

The Shelby GT350 was a classic "muscle car" — not a typical car for the weekday commute. Emission regulations taking effect in the early 1970s halved power output and brought an end to the muscle car era. Table 3-2 shows what Chevy put out during the same timeframe.

Table 3-2	Chevy Small-Block V-8s, 1960–1980		
Year	*Displacement (CID)*	*Maximum Horsepower*	*Notes*
1960	283	315	
1962	327	375	

(continued)

Table 3-2 *(continued)*

Year	*Displacement (CID)*	*Maximum Horsepower*	*Notes*
1967	350	295	
1968	302	290	
1968	307	200	
1969	350	370	Corvette
1970	400	265	
1975	262	110	Emission regulations

Here again you see the effect of the emission regulations that kicked in in 1971 — a drastic drop in horsepower per displacement.

Use the following code to create tables to hold these data items:

```
CREATE TABLE FORD (
    EngineID            INTEGER         PRIMARY KEY,
    Year                CHAR (4),
    Displacement        NUMERIC (5,2),
    MaxHP               NUMERIC (5,2),
    Notes               CHAR (30) ) ;

CREATE TABLE CHEVY (
    EngineID            INTEGER         PRIMARY KEY,
    Year                CHAR (4),
    Displacement        NUMERIC (5,2),
    MaxHP               NUMERIC (5,2),
    Notes               CHAR (30) ) ;
```

After filling these tables with the data in Tables 3-1 and 3-2, you can run some queries. Suppose you are a dyed-in-the-wool Chevy fan and are quite certain that the most powerful Chevrolet has a higher horsepower to displacement ratio than any of the Fords. To verify that assumption, enter the following query:

```
SELECT *
  FROM CHEVY
  WHERE (MaxHP/Displacement) > ALL
    (SELECT (MaxHP/Displacement) FROM FORD) ;
```

This returns the result shown in Figure 3-1:

Figure 3-1:
Chevy
muscle
cars with
horsepower
to displace-
ment ratios
higher than
any of the
Fords listed.

The subquery (`SELECT (MaxHP/Displacement) FROM FORD`) returns the
horsepower-to-displacement ratios of all the Ford engines in the FORD table.
The `ALL` quantifier says to return only those records from the CHEVY table
that have horsepower-to-displacement ratios that are higher than all the
ratios returned for the Ford engines. Three different Chevy engines had
higher ratios than any Ford engine of that era, including the highly regarded
Shelby GT350. Ford fans should not be bothered by this result, however.
There's more to what makes a car awesome than just the horsepower-to-
displacement ratio.

What if you had made the opposite assumption? What if you had entered the
following query?

```
SELECT *
  FROM FORD
  WHERE (MaxHP/Displacement) > ALL
    (SELECT (MaxHP/Displacement) FROM CHEVY) ;
```

Because none of the Ford engines has a higher horsepower to displacement
ratio than all of the Chevy engines, the query doesn't return any rows.

Correlated subqueries

In all the nested queries I show in the previous sections, the inner subquery
is executed first, and then its result is applied to the outer enclosing statement. A correlated subquery first finds the table and row specified by the
enclosing statement and then executes the subquery on the row in the subquery's table that correlates with the current row of the enclosing statement's table.

Using a subquery as an existence test

Subqueries introduced with the EXISTS or the NOT EXISTS keyword are examples of correlated subqueries. The subquery either returns one or more rows, or it returns none. If it returns at least one row, the EXISTS predicate succeeds, and the enclosing statement performs its action. In the same circumstances, the NOT EXISTS predicate fails, and the enclosing statement does not perform its action. After one row of the enclosing statement's table is processed, the same operation is performed on the next row. This action is repeated until every row in the enclosing statement's table has been processed.

Testing for existence

Say that you are a salesperson for Penguin Electronics and you want to call your primary contact people at all of Penguin's customer organizations in New Hampshire. Try the following query:

```
SELECT *
    FROM CONTACT
    WHERE EXISTS
        (SELECT *
            FROM CUSTOMER
            WHERE State = 'NH'
                AND CONTACT.CustomerID = CUSTOMER.CustomerID) ;
```

Notice the reference to CONTACT.CustomerID, which is referencing a column from the outer query and comparing it with another column, CUSTOMER. CustomerID, from the inner query. For each candidate row of the outer query, you evaluate the inner query, using the CustomerID value from the current CONTACT row of the outer query in the WHERE clause of the inner query.

The CustomerID column links the CONTACT table to the CUSTOMER table. SQL looks at the first record in the CONTACT table, finds the row in the CUSTOMER table that has the same CustomerID, and checks that row's State field. If CUSTOMER.State = 'NH', the current CONTACT row is added to the result table. The next CONTACT record is then processed in the same way, and so on, until the entire CONTACT table has been processed. Because the query specifies SELECT * FROM CONTACT, all the contact table's fields are returned, including the contact's name and phone number.

Testing for nonexistence

In the previous example, the Penguin salesperson wanted to know the names and numbers of the contact people of all the customers in New Hampshire.

Imagine that a second salesperson is responsible for all of the United States except New Hampshire. She can retrieve her contacts by using NOT EXISTS in a query similar to the preceding one:

```
SELECT *
   FROM CONTACT
   WHERE NOT EXISTS
       (SELECT *
           FROM CUSTOMER
           WHERE State = 'NH'
               AND CONTACT.CustomerID = CUSTOMER.CustomerID) ;
```

Every row in CONTACT for which the subquery does not return a row is added to the result table.

Introducing a correlated subquery with the IN keyword

As I noted in a previous section of this chapter, subqueries introduced by IN or by a comparison operator need not be correlated queries, but they can be. In the "Subqueries that retrieve rows satisfying a condition" section, I give examples of how a non-correlated subquery can be used with the IN predicate. To show how a correlated subquery may use the IN predicate, ask the same question that came up with the EXISTS predicate: What are the names and phone numbers of the contacts at all of Penguin's customers in New Hampshire? You can answer this question with a correlated IN subquery:

```
SELECT *
   FROM CONTACT
   WHERE 'NH' IN
       (SELECT State
           FROM CUSTOMER
           WHERE CONTACT.CustomerID = CUSTOMER.CustomerID) ;
```

The statement is evaluated for each record in the CONTACT table. If, for that record, the CustomerID numbers in CONTACT and CUSTOMER match, the value of CUSTOMER.State is compared to 'NH'. The result of the subquery is a list that contains, at most, one element. If that one element is 'NH', the WHERE clause of the enclosing statement is satisfied, and a row is added to the query's result table.

Introducing a correlated subquery with a comparison operator

A correlated subquery can also be introduced by one of the six comparison operators, as shown in the next example.

Penguin pays bonuses to its salespeople based on their total monthly sales volume. The higher the volume is, the higher the bonus percentage is. The bonus percentage list is kept in the BONUSRATE table:

MinAmount	MaxAmount	BonusPct
0.00	24999.99	0.
25000.00	49999.99	0.01
50000.00	99999.99	0.02
100000.00	249999.99	0.03
250000.00	499999.99	0.04
500000.00	749999.99	0.05
750000.00	999999.99	0.06

If a person's monthly sales are between $100,000.00 and $249,999.99, the bonus is 3% of sales.

Sales are recorded in a transaction master table named TRANSMASTER, which is created as follows:

```
CREATE TABLE TRANSMASTER (
    TransID       INTEGER       PRIMARY KEY,
    CustID        INTEGER       FOREIGN KEY,
    EmpID         INTEGER       FOREIGN KEY,
    TransDate     DATE,
    NetAmount     NUMERIC,
    Freight       NUMERIC,
    Tax           NUMERIC,
    InvoiceTotal  NUMERIC) ;
```

Sales bonuses are based on the sum of the NetAmount field for all of a person's transactions in the month. You can find any person's bonus rate with a correlated subquery that uses comparison operators:

```
SELECT BonusPct
    FROM BONUSRATE
        WHERE MinAmount <=
            (SELECT SUM(NetAmount)
                FROM TRANSMASTER
                    WHERE EmpID = 133)
            AND MaxAmount >=
                (SELECT SUM(NetAmount)
                    FROM TRANSMASTER
                        WHERE EmpID = 133) ;
```

This query is interesting in that it contains two subqueries, making use of the logical connective AND. The subqueries use the SUM aggregate operator, which returns a single value: the total monthly sales of employee number 133. That value is then compared against the MinAmount and the MaxAmount columns in the BONUSRATE table, producing the bonus rate for that employee.

If you had not known the EmpID but had known the person's name, you could arrive at the same answer with a more complex query:

```
SELECT BonusPct
   FROM BONUSRATE
      WHERE MinAmount <=
         (SELECT SUM(NetAmount)
            FROM TRANSMASTER
               WHERE EmpID =
                  (SELECT EmployeeID
                     FROM EMPLOYEE
                        WHERE EmplName = 'Thornton'))
         AND MaxAmount >=
            (SELECT SUM(NetAmount)
               FROM TRANSMASTER
                  WHERE EmpID =
                     (SELECT EmployeeID
                        FROM EMPLOYEE
                           WHERE EmplName = 'Thornton'));
```

This example uses subqueries nested within subqueries, which in turn are nested within an enclosing query, to arrive at the bonus rate for the employee named Thornton. This structure works only if you know for sure that the company has one, and only one, employee whose name is Thornton. If you know that more than one employee is named Thornton, you can add terms to the WHERE clause of the innermost subquery until you're sure that only one row of the EMPLOYEE table is selected.

Correlated subqueries in a HAVING clause

You can have a correlated subquery in a HAVING clause just as you can in a WHERE clause. As I mention in Chapter 2 of this minibook, a HAVING clause is normally preceded by a GROUP BY clause. The HAVING clause acts as a filter to restrict the groups created by the GROUP BY clause. Groups that don't satisfy the condition of the HAVING clause are not included in the result. When used in this way, the HAVING clause is evaluated for each group created by the GROUP BY clause. In the absence of a GROUP BY clause, the HAVING clause is evaluated for the set of rows passed by the WHERE clause, which is considered to be a single group. If neither a WHERE clause nor a GROUP BY clause is present, the HAVING clause is evaluated for the entire table:

```
SELECT TM1.EmpID
   FROM TRANSMASTER TM1
      GROUP BY TM1.EmpID
```

```
HAVING MAX(TM1.NetAmount) >= ALL
    (SELECT 2 * AVG (TM2.NetAmount)
        FROM TRANSMASTER TM2
        WHERE TM1.EmpID <> TM2.EmpID) ;
```

This query uses two aliases for the same table, enabling you to retrieve the EmpID number of all `salespeople` who had a sale of at least twice the average value of all the other salespeople. The query works as follows:

1. The outer query groups TRANSMASTER rows by the EmpID. This is done with the `SELECT`, `FROM`, and `GROUP BY` clauses.

2. The `HAVING` clause filters these groups. For each group, it calculates the `MAX` of the NetAmount column for the rows in that group.

3. The inner query evaluates twice the average NetAmount from all rows of TRANSMASTER whose EmpID is different from the EmpID of the current group of the outer query. Note that in the last line, you need to reference two different EmpID values, so in the `FROM` clauses of the outer and inner queries, you use different aliases for TRANSMASTER.

4. You then use those aliases in the comparison of the query's last line to indicate that you're referencing both the EmpID from the current row of the inner subquery (`TM2.EmpID`) and the EmpID from the current group of the outer subquery (`TM1.EmpID`).

Using Subqueries in INSERT, DELETE, and UPDATE Statements

In addition to `SELECT` statements, `UPDATE`, `DELETE`, and `INSERT` statements can also include `WHERE` clauses. Those `WHERE` clauses can contain subqueries in the same way that `SELECT` statement `WHERE` clauses do.

For example, Penguin has just made a volume purchase deal with Baker Electronic Sales and wants to retroactively provide Baker with a 10-percent credit for all its purchases in the last month. You can give this credit with an `UPDATE` statement:

```
UPDATE TRANSMASTER
    SET NetAmount = NetAmount * 0.9
    WHERE CustID =
        (SELECT CustID
            FROM CUSTOMER
            WHERE Company = 'Baker Electronic Sales') ;
```

You can also have a correlated subquery in an UPDATE statement. Suppose the CUSTOMER table has a column LastMonthsMax, and Penguin wants to give such a credit for purchases that exceed LastMonthsMax for the customer:

```
UPDATE TRANSMASTER TM
    SET NetAmount = NetAmount * 0.9
    WHERE NetAmount >
        (SELECT LastMonthsMax
            FROM CUSTOMER C
            WHERE C.CustID = TM.CustID) ;
```

Note that this subquery is correlated: The WHERE clause in the last line references both the CustID of the CUSTOMER row from the subquery and the CustID of the current TRANSMASTER row that is a candidate for updating.

A subquery in an UPDATE statement can also reference the table that is being updated. Suppose that Penguin wants to give a 10% credit to customers whose purchases have exceeded $10,000:

```
UPDATE TRANSMASTER TM1
    SET NetAmount = NetAmount * 0.9
    WHERE 10000 < (SELECT SUM(NetAmount)
                FROM TRANSMASTER TM2
                    WHERE TM1.CustID = TM2.CustID);
```

The inner subquery calculates the SUM of the NetAmount column for all TRANSMASTER rows for the same customer. What does this mean? Suppose that the customer with CustID = 37 has four rows in TRANSMASTER with values for NetAmount: 3000, 5000, 2000, and 1000. The SUM of NetAmount for this CustID is 11000.

The order in which the UPDATE statement processes the rows is defined by your implementation and is generally not predictable. The order may differ depending on how the rows are arranged on the disk. Assume that the implementation processes the rows for this CustID in this order: first the TRANSMASTER with a NetAmount of 3000, and then the one with NetAmount = 5000, and so on. After the first three rows for CustID 37 have been updated, their NetAmount values are 2700 (90 percent of 3000), 4500 (90 percent of 5000), and 1800 (90 percent of 2000). Then when you process the last TRANSMASTER row for CustID 37, whose NetAmount is 1000, the SUM returned by the subquery would seem to be 10000 — that is, the SUM of the new NetAmount values of the first three rows for CustID 37, and the old NetAmount value of the last row for CustID 37. Thus it would seem that the last row for CustID 37 isn't updated because the comparison with that SUM is not True (10000 is not less than SELECT SUM (NetAmount)). But that is not how the UPDATE statement is defined when a subquery references the table that is being updated. All evaluations of subqueries in an UPDATE statement reference the old values of the table being updated. In the preceding UPDATE for CustID 37, the subquery returns 11000 — the original SUM.

The subquery in an UPDATE statement WHERE clause operates the same as it does in a SELECT statement WHERE clause. The same is true for DELETE and INSERT. To delete all of Baker's transactions, use this statement:

```
DELETE FROM TRANSMASTER
   WHERE CustID =
      (SELECT CustomerID
          FROM CUSTOMER
          WHERE Company = 'Baker Electronic Sales') ;
```

As with UPDATE, DELETE subqueries can also be correlated and can also reference the table being deleted. The rules are similar to the rules for UPDATE subqueries. Suppose you want to delete all rows from TRANSMASTER for customers whose total NetAmount is larger than $10,000:

```
DELETE FROM TRANSMASTER TM1
   WHERE 10000 < (SELECT SUM(NetAmount)
      FROM TRANSMASTER TM2
          WHERE TM1.CustID = TM2.CustID) ;
```

This query deletes all rows from TRANSMASTER that have CustID 37, as well as any other customers with purchases exceeding $10,000. All references to TRANSMASTER in the subquery denote the contents of TRANSMASTER before any deletes by the current statement. So even when you are deleting the last TRANSMASTER row for CustID 37, the subquery is evaluated on the original TRANSMASTER table and returns 11000.

When you update, delete, or insert database records, you risk making a table's data inconsistent with other tables in the database. Such an inconsistency is called a *modification anomaly,* discussed in Chapter 2 of Book II. If you delete TRANSMASTER records and a TRANSDETAIL table depends on TRANSMASTER, you must delete the corresponding records from TRANSDETAIL, too. This operation is called a *cascading delete* because the deletion of a parent record cascades to its associated child records. Otherwise, the undeleted child records become orphans. In this case, they would be invoice detail lines that are in limbo because they are no longer connected to an invoice record.

INSERT can include a SELECT clause. One use for this statement is filling "snapshot" tables. For a table with the contents of TRANSMASTER for October 27, do this:

```
CREATE TABLE TRANSMASTER_1027
    (TransID INTEGER, TransDate DATE,
    ...) ;

INSERT INTO TRANSMASTER_1027
    (SELECT * FROM TRANSMASTER
        WHERE TransDate = 2007-10-27) ;
```

Or you may want to save rows only for large NetAmounts:

```
INSERT INTO TRANSMASTER_1027
    (SELECT * FROM TRANSMASTER TM
        WHERE TM.NetAmount > 10000
            AND TransDate = 2007-10-27) ;
```

Tuning Considerations for Statements Containing Nested Queries

How do you tune a nested query? In some cases, there is no need because the nested query is about as efficient as it can be. In other cases, nested queries are not particularly efficient. Depending on the characteristics of the DBMS you are using, you may want to recode a nested query for higher performance. I mentioned at the beginning of this chapter that many tasks performed by nested queries could also be performed using relational operators. In some cases, using a relational operator yields better performance than a nested query that produces the same result. If performance is an issue in a given application and a nested query seems to be the bottleneck, you might want to try a statement containing a relational operator instead and compare execution times. I discuss relational operations extensively in the next chapter, but for now, take a look at an example.

As I mention earlier in this chapter, there are two kinds of subqueries, uncorrelated and correlated. Use the NorthwindCS database to take a look at a non-correlated subquery without a set function.

```
SELECT OrderID
    FROM [Order Details]
    WHERE ProductID IN
        (SELECT ProductID
            FROM Products
            WHERE UnitsInStock = 0) ;
```

This query takes data from both the Products table and the Order Details table. It returns the OrderIDs of all orders that include products that are out of stock. Figure 3-2 shows the result of the query. Figure 3-3 shows the execution plan, and Figure 3-4 shows the client statistics.

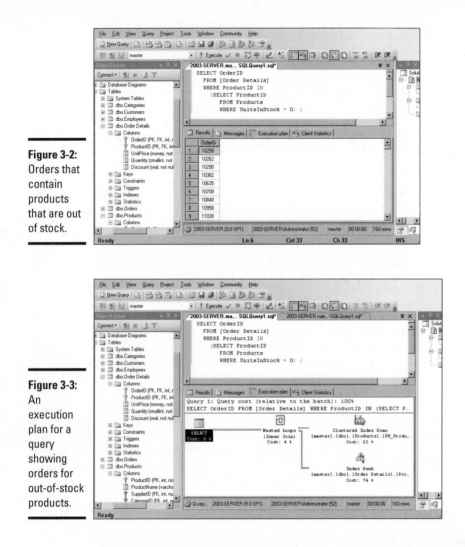

Figure 3-2:
Orders that contain products that are out of stock.

Figure 3-3:
An execution plan for a query showing orders for out-of-stock products.

This was a pretty efficient query. 9070 bytes were transferred from the server, but execution time was only 30 time units. The execution plan shows that an efficient nested loop join was used, which only used 4% of the total time consumed by the query.

How would performance change if the WHERE clause condition was inequality rather than equality?

```
SELECT OrderID
  FROM [Order Details]
  WHERE ProductID IN
```

```
(SELECT ProductID
    FROM Products
    WHERE UnitsInStock < 10) ;
```

Figure 3-4:
Client
statistics for
a query
showing
orders for
out-of-stock
products.

Book III
Chapter 3

Querying Multiple
Tables with
Subqueries

Suppose you don't want to wait until a product is out of stock to see if you have a problem. Take a look at Figures 3-5, 3-6, and 3-7 to see how costly a query is that retrieves orders that include products that are almost out of stock.

Figure 3-5:
A nested
query
showing
orders that
contain
products
that are
almost out
of stock.

Figure 3-6:
An execution plan for a nested query showing orders for almost out-of-stock products.

Figure 3-7:
Client statistics for a nested query showing orders for almost out-of-stock products.

More rows were returned because this query retrieves all the rows the previous one did plus more. The execution plan shows that a merge join was used instead of a nested loop join, and that it consumed proportionally more of the total time. The client statistics show that execution time increased significantly.

Could you achieve the same result more efficiently by recoding with a relational operator? It doesn't seem likely that you could do much better than the query with the equality condition. Take a look at an alternative to the query with the inequality condition:

```
SELECT OrderID
    FROM [Order Details], Products
        WHERE [Order Details].ProductID = Products.ProductID
        AND UnitsInStock < 10 ;
```

Figures 3-8, 3-9, and 3-10 show the results.

Figure 3-8:
A relational query showing orders that contain products that are almost out of stock.

Figure 3-9:
The execution plan for a relational query showing orders for almost out-of-stock products.

Figure 3-10: Client statistics for a relational query showing orders for almost out-of-stock products.

Figure 3-8 shows that the same rows are returned. Figure 3-9 shows that the execution plan is the same as it was for the nested query. Figure 3-10 shows that client processing time is up slightly. In this case, it appears that there is no performance penalty involved with using a nested query as opposed to a relational query. This could be due to the fact that the SQL Server query optimizer is smart enough to choose the best execution plan regardless of how you code the query.

Tuning Correlated Subqueries

Compare a correlated subquery to an equivalent relational query and see if a performance difference shows up:

```
SELECT OD1.OrderID
    FROM [Order Details] OD1
        GROUP BY OD1.OrderID
        HAVING MAX (OD1.UnitPrice) >= ALL
            (SELECT 2 * AVG (OD2.UnitPrice)
                FROM [Order Details] OD2
                WHERE OD1.OrderID <> OD2.OrderID) ;
```

This query into the NorthwindCS database extracts from the Order Details table the order numbers of all the Order Details rows that contain a product whose unit price is greater than or equal to twice the average unit price of all the other products in the table. Figures 3-11, 3-12, and 3-13 show the result.

Figure 3-11:
A correlated subquery showing orders that contain products that are at least twice as costly as the average product.

As shown in the lower-right corner of Figure 3-11, 149 orders contained a product whose unit price is greater than or equal to twice the average unit price of all the other products in the table.

Figure 3-12 shows the biggest execution plan that I show you. Correlated subqueries are intrinsically more complex than are the non-correlated variety. Many parts of the plan have minimal cost, but the clustered index seek takes up 68% of the total and the stream aggregate due to the MAX set function takes up 31%. If you had been dealing with a larger table, the Top N Sort operation would also have become significant.

The client statistics table in Figure 3-13 shows that 37281 bytes were returned by the server and that the total execution time was 3384 time units. Most of the time was taken up by server processing rather than activity on the client side.

Would a relational query do better? You can formulate one, using a temporary table:

```
SELECT 2 * AVG(UnitPrice) AS twiceavgprice INTO Temp
  FROM [Order Details] ;

SELECT OrderID
  FROM [Order Details], Temp
  WHERE UnitPrice >= twiceavgprice ;
```

Figure 3-12:
An execution plan for a correlated subquery showing orders for almost out-of-stock products.

Figure 3-13:
Client statistics for a correlated subquery showing orders for almost out-of-stock products.

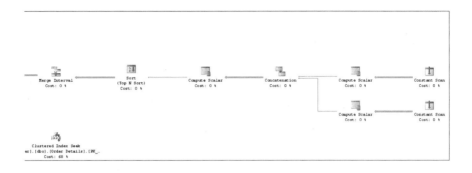

When you run this two-part query, you get the results shown in Figures 3-14, 3-15, and 3-16.

This query is not exactly like the previous one, as evidenced by the fact that it returns 163 rows (see Figure 3-14) rather than 149. The nested query excluded the row being tested from the calculation of the average unit cost, whereas the relational query did not. Depending on what you want the query to show, this may or may not be a significant difference.

Book III
Chapter 3

Querying Multiple
Tables with
Subqueries

Figure 3-14:
Query
showing
orders that
contain
products
that are at
least twice
as costly as
the average
product.

Figure 3-15 shows the execution plans for the two parts of the relational query. In the first part, a clustered index scan and a table insert take up most of the time. In the second part, a clustered index scan and an inner join consume the time.

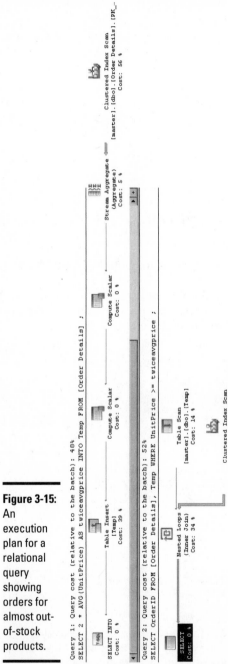

Figure 3-15:
An execution plan for a relational query showing orders for almost out-of-stock products.

Figure 3-16 shows a significant difference in performance. The number of bytes transferred from the server is reduced by almost 50%. Execution time is reduced by an even bigger factor to less than one-sixth the time taken by the nested subquery.

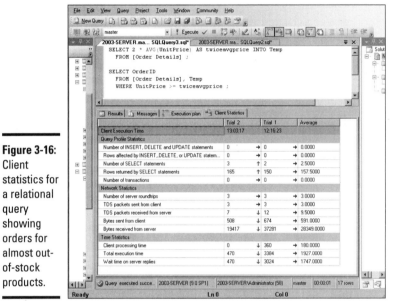

Figure 3-16:
Client statistics for a relational query showing orders for almost out-of-stock products.

Book III
Chapter 3

Querying Multiple
Tables with
Subqueries

Give serious consideration to performing a relational query instead of a correlated subquery if performance is an issue and if an equivalent relational query can be composed.

Chapter 4: Querying Multiple Tables with Relational Operators

In This Chapter

✔ The UNION **statement**

✔ The INTERSECT **statement**

✔ The EXCEPT **statement**

✔ The JOIN **statements**

*I*n Chapter 3 of this minibook, I show you how, by using nested queries, data can be drawn from multiple tables to answer a question that involved different ideas. Another way to collect information from multiple tables is to use the relational operators UNION, INTERSECT, EXCEPT, and JOIN. SQL's UNION, INTERSECT, and EXCEPT operators are modeled after the union, intersect, and except operators of relational algebra. Each one performs a very specific combining operation on the data in two or more tables. The JOIN operator, on the other hand, is considerably more flexible. A number of different joins exist, and each performs a somewhat different operation. Depending on what you want in terms of information retrieved from multiple tables, one or another of the joins or the other relational operators is likely to give it to you. In this chapter, I show you each of SQL's relational operators, cover how it works, and discuss what it can be used for.

UNION

The UNION operator is the SQL implementation of relational algebra's union operator. The UNION operator enables you to draw information from two or more tables that have the same structure. *Same structure* means

♦ The tables must all have the same number of columns.

♦ Corresponding columns must all have identical data types and lengths.

When these criteria are met, the tables are *union-compatible.* The union of two tables returns all the rows that appear in either table and eliminates duplicates.

Suppose you have created a database for a business named Acme Systems that sells and installs computer products. Acme has two warehouses that stock the products, one in Fort Deposit, Alabama, and the other in East Kingston, New Hampshire. It contains two union-compatible tables named DEPOSIT and KINGSTON. Both tables have two columns, and corresponding columns are of the same type. In fact, corresponding columns have identical column names (although this condition isn't required for union compatibility).

DEPOSIT lists the names and quantity in stock of products in the Fort Deposit warehouse. Kingston lists the same information about the East Kingston warehouse. The UNION of the two tables gives you a virtual result table containing all the rows in the first table plus all the rows in the second table. For this example, I put just a few rows in each table to illustrate the operation:

```
SELECT * FROM DEPOSIT ;
```

```
ProductName      QuantityInStock
-----------      ---------------
185_Express             12
505_Express              5
510_Express              6
520_Express              2
550_Express              3
```

```
SELECT * FROM KINGSTON ;
```

```
ProductName      QuantityInStock
-----------      ---------------
185_Express             15
505_Express              7
510_Express              6
520_Express              2
550_Express              1
```

```
SELECT * FROM DEPOSIT
UNION
SELECT * FROM KINGSTON ;
```

```
ProductName      QuantityInStock
-----------      ---------------
185_Express             12
185_Express             15
505_Express              5
505_Express              7
510_Express              6
520_Express              2
550_Express              3
550_Express              1
```

The UNION DISTINCT operator functions identically to the UNION operator without the DISTINCT keyword. In both cases, duplicate rows are eliminated from the result set. In this example, because both warehouses had the same number of 510_Express and 520_Express products, those rows in both tables were exact duplicates, only one of which was returned.

I use the asterisk (*) as shorthand for all the columns in a table. This short-cut is fine most of the time, but it can get you into trouble when you use relational operators in embedded or module-language SQL. What if you add one or more new columns to one table and not to another, or you add different columns to the two tables? The two tables are then no longer union-compatible, and your program is invalid the next time it's recompiled. Even if the same new columns are added to both tables so that they are still union-compatible, your program is probably not prepared to deal with this additional data. So, explicitly listing the columns that you want rather than relying on the * shorthand is generally a good idea. When you're entering ad hoc SQL from the console, the asterisk will probably work fine because you can quickly display table structure to verify union compatibility if your query isn't successful.

UNION ALL

As mentioned previously, the UNION operation normally eliminates any duplicate rows that result from its operation, which is the desired result most of the time. Sometimes, however, you may want to preserve duplicate rows. On those occasions, use UNION ALL.

The following code shows you what UNION ALL produces when it's used with the DEPOSIT and KINGSTON tables:

```
SELECT * FROM DEPOSIT
UNION ALL
SELECT * FROM KINGSTON ;
```

ProductName	QuantityInStock
185_Express	12
505_Express	5
510_Express	6
520_Express	2
550_Express	3
185_Express	15
505_Express	7
510_Express	6
520_Express	2
550_Express	1

UNION CORRESPONDING

You can sometimes form the union of two tables even if they are not union-compatible. If the columns you want in your results table are present and compatible in both tables, you can perform a UNION CORRESPONDING operation. Only the specified columns are considered, and they are the only columns displayed in the result table.

Suppose ACME Systems opens a third warehouse in Jefferson, Maine. A new table named JEFFERSON is added to the database, which includes Product and QuantityInStock columns (as the DEPOSIT and KINGSTON tables do), but also has an additional column named QuantityOnHold. A UNION or UNION ALL of JEFFERSON with either DEPOSIT or KINGSTON would not return any rows because there is not a complete match between all the columns of JEFFERSON and all the columns of the other two tables. However, you can still add the JEFFERSON data to that of either DEPOSIT or KINGSTON by specifying only the columns in JEFFERSON that correspond with the columns in the other table. Here's a sample query:

```
SELECT *
    FROM JEFFERSON
UNION CORRESPONDING BY
    (ProductName, QuantityInStock)
SELECT *
    FROM KINGSTON ;
```

The result table holds the products and the quantities in stock at both warehouses. As with the simple UNION, duplicates are eliminated. Thus, if the Jefferson warehouse happens to have the same quantity of a particular product that the Kingston warehouse has, the UNION CORRESPONDING operation loses one of those rows. To avoid this problem, use UNION ALL CORRESPONDING.

Each column name in the list following the CORRESPONDING keyword must be a name that exists in both unioned tables. If you omit this list of names, an implicit list of all names that appear in both tables is used. But this implicit list of names may change when new columns are added to one or both tables. Therefore, explicitly listing the column names is better than omitting them.

INTERSECT

The UNION operation produces a result table containing all rows that appear in any of the source tables. If you want only rows that appear in all the source tables, you can use the INTERSECT operation, which is the SQL

implementation of relational algebra's intersect operation. I illustrate
INTERSECT by returning to Acme Systems warehouse table:

```
SELECT * FROM DEPOSIT ;

ProductName        QuantityInStock
-----------        ---------------
185_Express             12
505_Express              5
510_Express              6
520_Express              2
550_Express              3


SELECT * FROM KINGSTON ;

ProductName        QuantityInStock
-----------        ---------------
185_Express             15
505_Express              7
510_Express              6
520_Express              2
550_Express              1
```

Only rows that appear in all source tables show up in the INTERSECT operation's result table:

```
SELECT *
    FROM DEPOSIT
INTERSECT
SELECT *
    FROM KINGSTON;

ProductName        QuantityInStock
-----------        ---------------
510_Express              6
520_Express              2
```

The result table tells us that the Fort Deposit and East Kingston warehouses
both have exactly the same number of 510_Express and 520_Express products in stock, a fact of dubious value. Note that, as was the case with UNION,
INTERSECT DISTINCT produces the same result as the INTERSECT operator used alone. In this example, only one of the identical rows displaying
each of two products is returned.

The ALL and CORRESPONDING keywords function in an INTERSECT operation the same way they do in a UNION operation. If you use ALL, duplicates
are retained in the result table. If you use CORRESPONDING, the intersected
tables need not be union-compatible, although the corresponding columns
need to have matching types and lengths.

Consider another example: A municipality keeps track of the cell phones carried by police officers, firefighters, parking enforcement officers, and other city employees. A database table called CELLPHONES contains data on all phones in active use. Another table named OUT, with an identical structure, contains data on all phones that have been taken out of service. No cell phone should ever exist in both tables. With an INTERSECT operation, you can test to see whether such an unwanted duplication has occurred:

```
SELECT *
   FROM CELLPHONES
INTERSECT CORRESPONDING BY (PhoneID)
SELECT *
   FROM OUT ;
```

If the result table contains any rows, you know you have a problem. You should investigate any PhoneID entries that appear in the result table. The corresponding cell phone is either active or out of service; it can't be both. After you detect the problem, you can perform a DELETE operation on one of the two tables to restore database integrity.

EXCEPT

The UNION operation acts on two source tables and returns all rows that appear in either table. The INTERSECT operation returns all rows that appear in both the first and the second table. In contrast, the EXCEPT (or EXCEPT DISTINCT) operation returns all rows that appear in the first table but that *do not* also appear in the second table.

Returning to the municipal cell phone database example, say that a group of phones that had been declared out of service and returned to the vendor for repairs have now been fixed and placed back into service. The CELLPHONES table was updated to reflect the returned phones, but the returned phones were not removed from the OUT table as they should have been. You can display the PhoneID numbers of the phones in the OUT table, with the reactivated ones eliminated, using an EXCEPT operation:

```
SELECT *
   FROM OUT
EXCEPT CORRESPONDING BY (PhoneID)
SELECT *
   FROM CELLPHONES;
```

This query returns all the rows in the OUT table whose PhoneID is not also present in the CELLPHONES table. These are the phones that are still out of service.

JOINS

The UNION, INTERSECT, and EXCEPT operators are valuable in multitable databases in which the tables are union-compatible. In many cases, however, you want to draw data from multiple tables that have very little in common. JOINs are powerful relational operators that combine data from multiple tables into a single result table. The source tables may have little (or even nothing) in common with each other.

SQL supports a number of types of JOINs. The best one to choose in a given situation depends on the result you're trying to achieve.

Cartesian product or cross join

Any multitable query is a type of JOIN. The source tables are joined in the sense that the result table includes information taken from all the source tables. The simplest JOIN is a two-table SELECT that has no WHERE clause qualifiers. Every row of the first table is joined to every row of the second table. The result table is the Cartesian product of the two source tables. The number of rows in the result table is equal to the number of rows in the first source table multiplied by the number of rows in the second source table.

For example, imagine that you're the personnel manager for a company and that part of your job is to maintain employee records. Most employee data, such as home address and telephone number, is not particularly sensitive. But some data, such as current salary, should be available only to authorized personnel. To maintain security of the sensitive information, keep it in a separate table that is password protected. Consider the following pair of tables:

```
EMPLOYEE                          COMPENSATION
--------                          ------------
EmpID                             Employ
FName                             Salary
LName                             Bonus
City
Phone
```

Fill the tables with some sample data:

```
EmpID    FName    LName    City      Phone
-----    -----    -----    ----      -----
    1    Jenny    Smith    Orange    555-1001
    2    Bill     Jones    Newark    555-3221
    3    Val      Brown    Nutley    555-6905
    4    Justin   Time     Passaic   555-8908
```

**Book III
Chapter 4**

**Querying Multiple
Tables with
Relational Operators**

```
Employ   Salary   Bonus
------   ------   -----
     1   63000    10000
     2   48000     2000
     3   54000     5000
     4   52000     7000
```

Create a virtual result table with the following query:

```
SELECT *
    FROM EMPLOYEE, COMPENSATION ;
```

which can also be written

```
SELECT *
    FROM EMPLOYEE CROSS JOIN COMPENSATION ;
```

This query produces

```
EmpID FName   LName   City     Phone     Employ Salary Bonus
----- -----   -----   ----     -----     ------ ------ -----
    1 Jenny   Smith   Orange   555-1001       1  63000 10000
    1 Jenny   Smith   Orange   555-1001       2  48000  2000
    1 Jenny   Smith   Orange   555-1001       3  54000  5000
    1 Jenny   Smith   Orange   555-1001       4  52000  7000
    2 Bill    Jones   Newark   555-3221       1  63000 10000
    2 Bill    Jones   Newark   555-3221       2  48000  2000
    2 Bill    Jones   Newark   555-3221       3  54000  5000
    2 Bill    Jones   Newark   555-3221       4  52000  7000
    3 Val     Brown   Nutley   555-6905       1  63000 10000
    3 Val     Brown   Nutley   555-6905       2  48000  2000
    3 Val     Brown   Nutley   555-6905       3  54000  5000
    3 Val     Brown   Nutley   555-6905       4  52000  7000
    4 Justin  Time    Passaic  555-8908       1  63000 10000
    4 Justin  Time    Passaic  555-8908       2  48000  2000
    4 Justin  Time    Passaic  555-8908       3  54000  5000
    4 Justin  Time    Passaic  555-8908       4  52000  7000
```

The result table, which is the Cartesian product of the EMPLOYEE and COMPENSATION tables, contains considerable redundancy. Furthermore, it doesn't make much sense. It combines every row of EMPLOYEE with every row of COMPENSATION. The only rows that convey meaningful information are those in which the EmpID number that came from EMPLOYEE matches the Employ number that came from COMPENSATION. In those rows, an employee's name and address are associated with that same employee's compensation.

When you're trying to get useful information out of a multitable database, the Cartesian product produced by a cross join is almost never what you want, but it's almost always the first step toward what you want. By applying constraints to the JOIN with a WHERE clause, you can filter out the unwanted rows. The most common JOIN that uses the WHERE clause filter is the equi-join.

Equi-join

An *equi-join* is a cross join with a WHERE clause containing a condition specifying that the value in one column in the first table must be equal to the value of a corresponding column in the second table. Applying an equi-join to the example tables from the previous section brings a more meaningful result:

```
SELECT *
    FROM EMPLOYEE, COMPENSATION
    WHERE EMPLOYEE.EmpID = COMPENSATION.Employ ;
```

This produces the following:

EmpID	FName	LName	City	Phone	Employ	Salary	Bonus
1	Jenny	Smith	Orange	555-1001	1	63000	10000
2	Bill	Jones	Newark	555-3221	2	48000	2000
3	Val	Brown	Nutley	555-6905	3	54000	5000
4	Justin	Time	Passaic	555-8908	4	52000	7000

In this result table, the salaries and bonuses on the right apply to the employees named on the left. The table still has some redundancy because the EmpID column duplicates the Employ column. You can fix this problem with a slight reformulation of the query:

```
SELECT EMPLOYEE.*,COMPENSATION.Salary,COMPENSATION.Bonus
    FROM EMPLOYEE, COMPENSATION
    WHERE EMPLOYEE.EmpID = COMPENSATION.Employ ;
```

This produces the following result:

EmpID	FName	LName	City	Phone	Salary	Bonus
1	Jenny	Smith	Orange	555-1001	63000	10000
2	Bill	Jones	Newark	555-3221	48000	2000
3	Val	Brown	Nutley	555-6905	54000	5000
4	Justin	Time	Passaic	555-8908	52000	7000

**Book III
Chapter 4**

**Querying Multiple
Tables with
Relational Operators**

This table tells you what you want to know, but doesn't burden you with any extraneous data. The query is somewhat tedious to write, however. To avoid ambiguity, it makes good sense to qualify the column names with the names of the tables they came from. However, writing those table names repeatedly can be tiresome.

You can cut down on the amount of typing by using aliases (or *correlation names*). An *alias* is a short name that stands for a table name. If you use aliases in recasting the preceding query, it comes out like this:

```
SELECT E.*, C.Salary, C.Bonus
    FROM EMPLOYEE E, COMPENSATION C
    WHERE E.EmpID = C.Employ ;
```

In this example, E is the alias for EMPLOYEE, and C is the alias for COMPENSATION. The alias is local to the statement it's in. After you declare an alias (in the FROM clause), you must use it throughout the statement. You can't use both the alias and the long form of the table name.

Mixing the long form of table names with aliases creates confusion. Consider the following example, which is confusing:

```
SELECT T1.C, T2.C
    FROM T1 T2, T2 T1
    WHERE T1.C > T2.C ;
```

In this example, the alias for T1 is T2, and the alias for T2 is T1. Admittedly, this isn't a smart selection of aliases, but it isn't forbidden by the rules. If you mix aliases with long-form table names, you can't tell which table is which.

The preceding example with aliases is equivalent to the following SELECT with no aliases:

```
SELECT T2.C, T1.C
    FROM T1, T2
    WHERE T2.C > T1.C ;
```

SQL enables you to join more than two tables. The maximum number varies from one implementation to another. The syntax is analogous to the two-table case:

```
SELECT E.*, C.Salary, C.Bonus, Y.TotalSales
    FROM EMPLOYEE E, COMPENSATION C, YTD_SALES Y
    WHERE E.EmpID = C.Employ
      AND C.Employ = Y.EmpNo ;
```

This statement performs an equi-join on three tables, pulling data from corresponding rows of each one to produce a result table that shows the salespeople's names, the amount of sales they are responsible for, and their compensation. The sales manager can quickly see whether compensation is in line with production.

Storing a salesperson's year-to-date sales in a separate YTD_SALES table ensures better performance and reliability than keeping that data in the EMPLOYEE table. The data in the EMPLOYEE table is relatively static. A person's name, address, and telephone number don't change very often. In contrast, the year-to-date sales change frequently (you hope). Because the YTD_SALES table has fewer columns than EMPLOYEE, you may be able to update it more quickly. If, in the course of updating sales totals, you don't touch the EMPLOYEE table, you decrease the risk of accidentally modifying EMPLOYEE information that should stay the same.

Natural join

The *natural join* is a special case of an equi-join. In the WHERE clause of an equi-join, a column from one source table is compared with a column of a second source table for equality. The two columns must be the same type and length and must have the same name. In fact, in a natural join, *all* columns in one table that have the same names, types, and lengths as corresponding columns in the second table are compared for equality.

Imagine that the COMPENSATION table from the preceding example has columns EmpID, Salary, and Bonus rather than Employ, Salary, and Bonus. In that case, you can perform a natural join of the COMPENSATION table with the EMPLOYEE table. The traditional JOIN syntax looks like this:

```
SELECT E.*, C.Salary, C.Bonus
   FROM EMPLOYEE E, COMPENSATION C
   WHERE E.EmpID = C.EmpID ;
```

This query is a natural join. An alternate syntax for the same operation is the following:

```
SELECT E.*, C.Salary, C.Bonus
   FROM EMPLOYEE E NATURAL JOIN COMPENSATION C ;
```

Condition join

A *condition join* is like an equi-join, except the condition being tested doesn't have to be equality (although it can be). It can be any well-formed predicate. If the condition is satisfied, the corresponding row becomes part of the result table. The syntax is a little different from what you have seen so far, in that the condition is contained in an ON clause rather than a WHERE clause.

Suppose Acme Systems wants to know which products the Fort Deposit warehouse has in larger numbers than does the East Kingston warehouse. This question is a job for a condition join:

```
SELECT *
   FROM DEPOSIT JOIN KINGSTON
   ON DEPOSIT.QuantityInStock > KINGSTON.QuantityInStock ;
```

Column-name join

The *column-name join* is like a natural join, but it's more flexible. In a natural join, all the source table columns that have the same name are compared with each other for equality. With the column-name join, you select which same-name columns to compare. You can choose them all if you want, making the column-name join effectively a natural join. Or you may choose fewer than all same-name columns. In this way, you have a great degree of control over which cross product rows qualify to be placed into your result table.

Suppose you are Acme Systems and you have shipped the exact same number of products to the East Kingston warehouse that you have shipped to the Fort Deposit warehouse. So far, nothing has been sold, so the number of products in inventory in East Kingston should match the number in Fort Deposit. If there are mismatches, it means that something is wrong. Either some products were never delivered to the warehouse, or they were misplaced or stolen after they arrived. With a simple query, you can retrieve the inventory levels at the two warehouses.

```
SELECT * FROM DEPOSIT ;
```

ProductName	QuantityInStock
185_Express	12
505_Express	5
510_Express	6
520_Express	2
550_Express	3

```
SELECT * FROM KINGSTON ;
```

ProductName	QuantityInStock
185_Express	15
505_Express	7
510_Express	6
520_Express	2
550_Express	1

For such small tables, it is fairly easy to see which rows don't match. However, for a table with thousands of rows, it's not so easy. You can use a column name join to see whether any discrepancies exist. I showed only two columns of the DEPOSIT and KINGSTON tables, to make it easy to see how the various relational operators work on them. In any real application, such tables would have additional columns, and the contents of those additional columns would not necessarily match. With a column name join, the join operation only considers the columns specified.

```
SELECT *
    FROM DEPOSIT JOIN KINGSTON
    USING (ProductName, QuantityInStock) ;
```

The result table shows only the rows for which the number of products in stock at Fort Deposit equals the number of products in stock at East Kingston:

```
ProductName QuantityInStock  ProductName QuantityInStock
----------- ---------------  ----------- ---------------
510_Express       6          510_Express        6
520_Express       2          520_Express        2
```

Wow! Only two products match. There is a definite "shrinkage" problem at one or both warehouses. Acme needs to get a handle on security.

Inner join

By now, you're probably getting the idea that joins are pretty esoteric and that it takes an uncommon level of spiritual discernment to deal with them adequately. You may have even heard of the mysterious *inner join* and speculated that it probably represents the core or essence of relational operations. Well, ha! The joke is on you: There's nothing mysterious about inner joins. In fact, all the joins covered so far in this chapter are inner joins. I could have formulated the column-name join in the last example as an inner join by using the following syntax:

```
SELECT *
    FROM DEPOSIT INNER JOIN KINGSTON
    USING (ProductName, QuantityInStock) ;
```

The result is the same.

The inner join is so named to distinguish it from the outer join. An *inner join* discards all rows from the result table that don't have corresponding rows in both source tables. An *outer join* preserves unmatched rows. That's the difference: nothing metaphysical about it.

Outer join

When you're joining two tables, the first one (call it the one on the left) may have rows that don't have matching counterparts in the second table (the one on the right). Conversely, the table on the right may have rows that don't have matching counterparts in the table on the left. If you perform an inner join on those tables, all the unmatched rows are excluded from the output. *Outer joins,* however, don't exclude the unmatched rows. Outer joins come in three types: the left outer join, the right outer join, and the full outer join.

Left outer join

In a query that includes a join, the left table is the one that precedes the keyword JOIN, and the right table is the one that follows it. The *left outer join* preserves unmatched rows from the left table but discards unmatched rows from the right table.

To understand outer joins, consider a corporate database that maintains records of the company's employees, departments, and locations. Tables 4-1, 4-2, and 4-3 contain the database's sample data.

Table 4-1	LOCATION
LocationID	*CITY*
1	Boston
3	Tampa
5	Chicago

Table 4-2		DEPT
DeptID	*LocationID*	*NAME*
21	1	Sales
24	1	Admin
27	5	Repair
29	5	Stock

Table 4-3		EMPLOYEE
EmpID	*DeptID*	*NAME*
61	24	Kirk
63	27	McCoy

Now suppose that you want to see all the data for all employees, including department and location. You get this with an equi-join:

```
SELECT *
    FROM LOCATION L, DEPT D, EMPLOYEE E
    WHERE L.LocationID = D.LocationID
        AND D.DeptID = E.DeptID ;
```

This statement produces the following result:

```
1    Boston    24    1    Admin    61    24    Kirk
5    Chicago   27    5    Repair   63    27    McCoy
```

This results table gives all the data for all the employees, including their location and department. The equi-join works because every employee has a location and a department.

Suppose now that you want the data on the locations, with the related department and employee data. This is a different problem because a location without any associated departments may exist. To get what you want, you have to use an outer join, as in the following example:

```
SELECT *
    FROM LOCATION L LEFT OUTER JOIN DEPT D
        ON (L.LocationID = D.LocationID)
    LEFT OUTER JOIN EMPLOYEE E
        ON (D.DeptID = E.DeptID);
```

This join pulls data from three tables. First, the LOCATION table is joined to the DEPT table. The resulting table is then joined to the EMPLOYEE table. Rows from the table on the left of the LEFT OUTER JOIN operator that have no corresponding row in the table on the right are included in the result. Thus, in the first join, all locations are included, even if no department associated with them exists. In the second join, all departments are included, even if no employee associated with them exists. The result is as follows:

```
1    Boston    24      1      Admin   61      24      Kirk
5    Chicago   27      5      Repair  63      27      McCoy
3    Tampa     NULL    NULL   NULL    NULL    NULL    NULL
5    Chicago   29      5      Stock   NULL    NULL    NULL
1    Boston    21      1      Sales   NULL    NULL    NULL
```

The first two rows are the same as the two result rows in the previous example. The third row (3 Tampa) has nulls in the department and employee columns because no departments are defined for Tampa and no employees are stationed there. The fourth and fifth rows (5 Chicago and 1 Boston) contain data about the Stock and the Sales departments, but the employee columns for these rows contain nulls because these two departments have no employees. This outer join tells you everything that the equi-join told you plus the following:

✦ All the company's locations, whether they have any departments or not

✦ All the company's departments, whether they have any employees or not

The rows returned in the preceding example aren't guaranteed to be in the order you want. The order may vary from one implementation to the next. To make sure that the rows returned are in the order you want, add an ORDER BY clause to your SELECT statement, like this:

```
SELECT *
    FROM LOCATION L LEFT OUTER JOIN DEPT D
        ON (L.LocationID = D.LocationID)
    LEFT OUTER JOIN EMPLOYEE E
        ON (D.DeptID = E.DeptID)
    ORDER BY L.LocationID, D.DeptID, E.EmpID;
```

You can abbreviate the left outer join language as LEFT JOIN because there's no such thing as a left inner join.

Right outer join

I'm sure you have figured out by now how the right outer join behaves. It preserves unmatched rows from the right table but discards unmatched rows from the left table. You can use it on the same tables and get the same result by reversing the order in which you present tables to the join:

```
SELECT *
    FROM EMPLOYEE E RIGHT OUTER JOIN DEPT D
        ON (D.DeptID = E.DeptID)
    RIGHT OUTER JOIN LOCATION L
        ON (L.LocationID = D.LocationID) ;
```

In this formulation, the first join produces a table that contains all departments, whether they have an associated employee or not. The second join produces a table that contains all locations, whether they have an associated department or not.

You can abbreviate the right outer join language as RIGHT JOIN because there's no such thing as a right inner join.

Full outer join

The *full outer join* combines the functions of the left outer join and the right outer join. It retains the unmatched rows from both the left and the right tables. Consider the most general case of the company database used in the preceding examples. It could have

✦ Locations with no departments

✦ Departments with no locations

✦ Departments with no employees

✦ Employees with no departments

To show all locations, departments, and employees, regardless of whether they have corresponding rows in the other tables, use a full outer join in the following form:

```
SELECT *
   FROM LOCATION L FULL OUTER JOIN DEPT D
      ON (L.LocationID = D.LocationID)
   FULL OUTER JOIN EMPLOYEE E
      ON (D.DeptID = E.DeptID) ;
```

You can abbreviate the full outer join language as FULL JOIN because there's no such thing as a full inner join.

ON versus WHERE

The function of the ON and WHERE clauses in the various types of joins is potentially confusing. These facts may help you keep things straight:

✦ The ON clause is part of the inner, left, right, and full joins. The cross join and UNION join don't have an ON clause because neither of them does any filtering of the data.

✦ The ON clause in an inner join is logically equivalent to a WHERE clause; the same condition could be specified either in the ON clause or a WHERE clause.

✦ The ON clauses in outer joins (left, right, and full joins) are different from WHERE clauses. The WHERE clause simply filters the rows that are returned by the FROM clause. Rows that are rejected by the filter are not included in the result. The ON clause in an outer join first filters the rows of a cross product and then includes the rejected rows, extended with nulls.

Join Conditions and Clustering Indexes

The performance of queries that include joins depends, to a large extent, on which columns are indexed, and whether the index is clustering or not. A table can have only one clustering index, where data items that are near each other logically, such as 'Smith' and 'Smithson', are also near each other physically on disk. Using a clustering index to sequentially step through a table speeds up hard disk retrievals and thus maximizes performance.

A clustering index works well with multi-point queries, which look for equality in non-unique columns. This is similar to looking up names in a telephone book. All the Smiths are listed together on consecutive pages. Most or all of them are located on the same hard disk cylinder. You can access multiple Smiths with a single disk seek operation. A non-clustering index, on the other hand, would not have this advantage. Each record typically requires a new disk seek, greatly slowing down operation. Furthermore, you probably have to touch every index to be sure you had not missed one. This is analogous to searching the greater Los Angeles telephone book for every instance of Area Code 626. Most of the numbers are in Area 213, but there will be instances of 626 sprinkled throughout the book.

Consider the following sample query:

```
SELECT Employee.FirstName, Employee.LastName, Student.Major
  FROM Employee, Students
  WHERE Employee.IDNum = Student.IDNum ;
```

This query returns the first and last names and the majors of university employees who are also students. How long it takes to run the query depends on how the tables are indexed. If Employee has a clustering index on IDNum, records searched are on consecutive pages. If Employee and Student both have clustering indexes on IDNum, the DBMS will likely use a merge join, which reads both tables in sorted order, minimizing the number of disk accesses needed. Such clustering often eliminates the need for a costly ORDER BY clause because the records are already sorted in the desired order.

The one disadvantage of clustered indexes is that they can become "tired" after a number of updates have been performed, causing the generation of overflow pages, which require additional disk seeks. Rebuilding the index corrects this problem.

Chapter 5: Cursors

In This Chapter

✔ Declaring a cursor

✔ Opening a cursor

✔ Fetching data from a single row

✔ Closing a cursor

SQL differs from most other computer languages in that it is a non-procedural language. Other languages, such as C, Java, or Basic, are called *procedural languages* because programs written in those languages execute procedures. First they execute one instruction, and then the next one, and so on. They do one thing at a time. When dealing with data, they operate on one table row at a time. SQL, on the other hand, is not restricted to operating on one table row at a time. Its natural mode of operation is to operate on a set of rows. For example, an SQL query may return 42 rows from a database containing thousands of rows. That operation is performed by a single SQL SELECT statement.

Because SQL is a data sublanguage, it does not contain all the features needed to create a database application. It must be used in combination with a procedural language. The SQL portion operates on the data, and the procedural language takes care of the other aspects of the task.

The fact that SQL normally operates on data a set at a time rather than a row at a time constitutes a major incompatibility between SQL and the most popular application development languages. A *cursor* enables SQL to retrieve (or update, or delete) a single row at a time so that you can use SQL in combination with an application written in any of the procedural languages.

A cursor is like a pointer that locates a specific table row. When a cursor is active, you can SELECT, UPDATE, or DELETE the row at which the cursor is pointing.

Cursors are valuable if you want to retrieve selected rows from a table, check their contents, and perform different operations based on those contents. SQL can't perform this sequence of operations by itself. SQL can retrieve the rows, but procedural languages are better at making decisions based on field contents. Cursors enable SQL to retrieve rows from a table one at a time and then feed the result to procedural code for processing. By placing the SQL code in a loop, you can process the entire table row by row.

In a pseudocode representation of embedded SQL, the most common flow of execution looks like this:

```
EXEC SQL DECLARE CURSOR statement
EXEC SQL OPEN statement
Test for end of table
Procedural code
Start loop
    Procedural code
    EXEC SQL FETCH
    Procedural code
    Test for end of table
End loop
EXEC SQL CLOSE statement
Procedural code
```

The SQL statements in this listing are DECLARE, OPEN, FETCH, and CLOSE. Each of these statements is discussed in detail in this chapter.

If you can perform the operation that you want with normal SQL (set-at-a-time) statements, do so. Declare a cursor, retrieve table rows one at a time, and use your system's host language only when normal SQL can't do what you want.

Declaring a Cursor

To use a cursor, you first must declare its existence to the DBMS. You do this with a DECLARE CURSOR statement. The DECLARE CURSOR statement doesn't actually cause anything to happen; it just announces the cursor's name to the DBMS and specifies what query the cursor will operate on. A DECLARE CURSOR statement has the following syntax:

```
DECLARE cursor-name [<cursor sensitivity>]
[<cursor scrollability>]
CURSOR [<cursor holdability>] [<cursor returnability>]
FOR query expression
    [ORDER BY order-by expression]
    [FOR updatability expression] ;
```

Note: The cursor name uniquely identifies a cursor, so it must be unlike that of any other cursor name in the current module or compilation unit.

To make your application more readable, give the cursor a meaningful name. Relate it to the data that the query expression requests or to the operation that your procedural code performs on the data.

Cursor sensitivity may be SENSITIVE, INSENSITIVE, or ASENSITIVE. Cursor scrollability may be either SCROLL or NO SCROLL. Cursor holdability may be either WITH HOLD or WITHOUT HOLD. Cursor returnability may be either WITH RETURN or WITHOUT RETURN.

The query expression

The *query expression* can be any legal SELECT statement. The rows that the SELECT statement retrieves are the ones that the cursor steps through one at a time. These rows are the scope of the cursor.

The query is not actually performed when the DECLARE CURSOR statement is read. You can't retrieve data until you execute the OPEN statement. The row-by-row examination of the data starts after you enter the loop that encloses the FETCH statement.

Ordering the query result set

You may want to process your retrieved data in a particular order, depending on what your procedural code does with the data. You can sort the retrieved rows before processing them by using the optional ORDER BY clause. The clause has the following syntax:

```
ORDER BY sort-specification [ , sort-specification]...
```

You can have multiple sort specifications. Each has the following syntax:

```
(column-name) [COLLATE BY collation-name] [ASC|DESC]
```

You sort by column name, and to do so, the column must be in the select list of the query expression. Columns that are in the table but not in the query select list do not work as sort specifications. For example, you want to perform an operation that is not supported by SQL on selected rows of the CUSTOMER table. You can use a DECLARE CURSOR statement like this:

```
DECLARE cust1 CURSOR FOR
    SELECT CustID, FirstName, LastName, City, State, Phone
      FROM CUSTOMER
    ORDER BY State, LastName, FirstName ;
```

In this example, the SELECT statement retrieves rows sorted first by state, then by last name, and then by first name. The statement retrieves all customers in Alaska (AK) before it retrieves the first customer from Alabama

(AL). The statement then sorts customer records from Alaska by the customer's last name (*Aaron* before *Abbott*). Where the last name is the same, sorting then goes by first name (*George Aaron* before *Henry Aaron*).

Have you ever made 40 copies of a 20-page document on a photocopier without a collator? What a drag! You must make 20 stacks on tables and desks, and then walk by the stacks 40 times, placing a sheet on each stack. This process is called *collation.* A similar process plays a role in SQL.

A collation is a set of rules that determines how strings in a character set compare. A character set has a default collation sequence that defines the order in which elements are sorted. But, you can apply a collation sequence other than the default to a column. To do so, use the optional COLLATE BY clause. Your implementation probably supports several common collations. Pick one and then make the collation ascending or descending by appending an ASC or DESC keyword to the clause.

In a DECLARE CURSOR statement, you can specify a calculated column that doesn't exist in the underlying table. In this case, the calculated column doesn't have a name that you can use in the ORDER BY clause. You can give it a name in the DECLARE CURSOR query expression, which enables you to identify the column later. Consider the following example:

```
DECLARE revenue CURSOR FOR
    SELECT Model, Units, Price,
           Units * Price AS ExtPrice
      FROM TRANSDETAIL
    ORDER BY Model, ExtPrice DESC ;
```

In this example, no COLLATE BY clause is in the ORDER BY clause, so the default collation sequence is used. Notice that the fourth column in the select list comes from a calculation on the data in the second and third columns. The fourth column is an extended price named ExtPrice. In the ORDER BY clause, I first sort by model name and then by ExtPrice. The sort on ExtPrice is descending, as specified by the DESC keyword; transactions with the highest dollar value are processed first.

The default sort order in an ORDER BY clause is ascending. If a sort specification list includes a DESC sort and the next sort should also be in descending order, you must explicitly specify DESC for the next sort. For example:

```
ORDER BY A, B DESC, C, D, E, F
```

is equivalent to

```
ORDER BY A ASC, B DESC, C ASC, D ASC, E ASC, F ASC
```

Updating table rows

Sometimes, you may want to update or delete table rows that you access with a cursor. Other times, you may want to guarantee that such updates or deletions can't be made. SQL gives you control over this issue with the updatability clause of the DECLARE CURSOR statement. If you want to prevent updates and deletions within the scope of the cursor, use this clause:

```
FOR READ ONLY
```

For updates of specified columns only — leaving all others protected — use

```
FOR UPDATE OF column-name [ , column-name]...
```

Any columns listed must appear in the DECLARE CURSOR's query expression. If you don't include an updatability clause, the default assumption is that all columns listed in the query expression are updatable. In that case, an UPDATE statement can update all the columns in the row to which the cursor is pointing, and a DELETE statement can delete that row.

Sensitive versus insensitive cursors

The query expression in the DECLARE CURSOR statement determines the rows that fall within a cursor's scope. Consider this possible problem: What if a statement in your program, located between the OPEN and the CLOSE statements, changes the contents of some of those rows so that they no longer satisfy the query? What if such a statement deletes some of those rows entirely? Does the cursor continue to process all the rows that originally qualified, or does it recognize the new situation and ignore rows that no longer qualify or that have been deleted?

Changing the data in columns that are part of a DECLARE CURSOR query expression after some — but not all — of the query's rows have been processed results in a big mess. Your results are likely to be inconsistent and misleading. To avoid this problem, make your cursor insensitive to any changes that statements within its scope may make. Add the INSENSITIVE keyword to your DECLARE CURSOR statement. As long as your cursor is open, it is insensitive to table changes that otherwise affect rows qualified to be included in the cursor's scope. A cursor can't be both insensitive and updatable. An insensitive cursor must be read-only.

Think of it this way: A normal SQL statement, such as UPDATE, INSERT, or DELETE, operates on a set of rows in a database table (perhaps the entire table). While such a statement is active, SQL's transaction mechanism protects it from interference by other statements acting concurrently on the same data. If you use a cursor, however, your window of vulnerability to harmful interaction is wide open. When you open a cursor, you are at risk until you close it again. If you open one cursor, start processing through a table, and then open a second cursor while the first is still active, the actions you take with the second cursor can affect what the statement controlled by the first cursor sees. For example, suppose that you write these queries:

```
DECLARE C1 CURSOR FOR SELECT * FROM EMPLOYEE
   ORDER BY Salary ;
DECLARE C2 CURSOR FOR SELECT * FROM EMPLOYEE
   FOR UPDATE OF Salary ;
```

Now, suppose you open both cursors and fetch a few rows with C1 and then update a salary with C2 to increase its value. This change can cause a row that you have already fetched with C1 to appear again on a later fetch that uses C1.

The peculiar interactions that are possible with multiple open cursors, or open cursors and set operations, are the sort of concurrency problems that transaction isolation avoids. If you operate this way, you're asking for trouble. So remember: Don't operate with multiple open cursors.

The default condition of cursor sensitivity is ASENSITIVE. The meaning of ASENSITIVE is implementation-dependent. For one implementation, it could be equivalent to SENSITIVE and, for another, it could be equivalent to INSENSITIVE. Check your system documentation for its meaning in your own case.

Scrolling a cursor

Scrollability is a capability that cursors didn't have prior to SQL-92. In implementations adhering to SQL-86 or SQL-89, the only allowed cursor movement was sequential, starting at the first row retrieved by the query expression and ending with the last row. SQL-92's SCROLL keyword in the DECLARE CURSOR statement gives you the capability to access rows in any order that you want. The current version of SQL retains this capability. The syntax of the FETCH statement controls the cursor's movement. I describe the FETCH statement later in this chapter. (See the "Fetching Data from a Single Row" section.)

Opening a Cursor

Although the DECLARE CURSOR statement specifies which rows to include in the cursor, it doesn't actually cause anything to happen because DECLARE is a declaration and not an executable statement. The OPEN statement brings the cursor into existence. It has the following form:

```
OPEN cursor-name ;
```

To open the cursor that I use in the discussion of the ORDER BY clause (earlier in this chapter), use the following:

```
DECLARE revenue CURSOR FOR
    SELECT Model, Units, Price,
           Units * Price AS ExtPrice
        FROM TRANSDETAIL
    ORDER BY Model, ExtPrice DESC ;
OPEN revenue ;
```

You can't fetch rows from a cursor until you open the cursor. When you open a cursor, the values of variables referenced in the DECLARE CURSOR statement become fixed, as do all current date-time functions. Consider the following example of SQL statements embedded in a host language program:

```
EXEC SQL DECLARE CURSOR C1 FOR SELECT * FROM ORDERS
        WHERE ORDERS.Customer = :NAME
        AND DueDate < CURRENT_DATE ;
NAME := 'Acme Co';     //A host language statement
EXEC SQL OPEN C1;
NAME := 'Omega Inc.';  //Another host statement
...
EXEC SQL UPDATE ORDERS SET DueDate = CURRENT_DATE;
```

The fix is in (for date-times)

A similar "fixing" of date-time values exists in set operations. Consider this example:

```
UPDATE ORDERS SET RecheckDate
    = CURRENT_DATE WHERE....;
```

Now suppose that you have a bunch of orders. You begin executing this statement at a minute before midnight. At midnight, the statement is still running, and it doesn't finish executing until five minutes after midnight. It doesn't matter. If a statement has any reference to CURRENT_ DATE (or TIME or TIMESTAMP), the value is fixed when the statement begins, so all the ORDERS rows in the statement get the same RecheckDate. Similarly, if a statement references TIMESTAMP, the whole statement uses

only one timestamp value, no matter how long the statement runs.

Here's an interesting example of an implication of this rule:

```
UPDATE EMPLOYEE SET KEY=
    CURRENT_TIMESTAMP;
```

You may expect that statement to set a unique value in the key column of each EMPLOYEE. You'd be disappointed; it sets the same value in every row.

So when the OPEN statement fixes date-time values for all statements referencing the cursor, it treats all these statements like an extended statement.

The OPEN statement fixes the value of all variables referenced in the declare cursor and also fixes a value for all current date-time functions. Thus the second assignment to the name variable (NAME := 'Omega Inc.') has no effect on the rows that the cursor fetches. (That value of NAME is used the next time you open C1.) And even if the OPEN statement is executed a minute before midnight and the UPDATE statement is executed a minute after midnight, the value of CURRENT_DATE in the UPDATE statement is the value of that function at the time the OPEN statement executed. This is true even if DECLARE CURSOR doesn't reference the date-time function.

Fetching Data from a Single Row

Whereas the DECLARE CURSOR statement specifies the cursor's name and scope, and the OPEN statement collects the table rows selected by the DECLARE CURSOR query expression, the FETCH statement actually retrieves the data. The cursor may point to one of the rows in the cursor's scope, or to the location immediately before the first row in the scope, or to the location immediately after the last row in the scope, or to the empty space between two rows. You can specify where the cursor points with the orientation clause in the FETCH statement.

FETCH syntax

The syntax for the FETCH statement is

```
FETCH [[orientation] FROM] cursor-name
    INTO target-specification [, target-specification]... ;
```

Seven orientation options are available:

◆ NEXT

◆ PRIOR

◆ FIRST

◆ LAST

◆ ABSOLUTE

◆ RELATIVE

◆ <simple value specification>

The default option is NEXT, which was the only orientation available in versions of SQL prior to SQL-92. It moves the cursor from wherever it is to the next row in the set specified by the query expression. If the cursor is located before the first record, it moves to the first record. If it points to record *n,* it moves to record *n*+1. If the cursor points to the last record in the set, it moves beyond that record, and notification of a no data condition is returned in the SQLSTATE system variable. (Chapter 4 of Book IV details SQLSTATE and the rest of SQL's error-handling facilities.)

The target specifications are either host variables or parameters, respectively, depending on whether embedded SQL or module language is using the cursor. The number and types of the target specifications must match the number and types of the columns specified by the query expression in the DECLARE CURSOR. So in the case of embedded SQL, when you fetch a list of five values from a row of a table, five host variables must be there to receive those values, and they must be the right types.

Absolute versus relative fetches

Because the SQL cursor is scrollable, you have other choices besides NEXT. If you specify PRIOR, the pointer moves to the row immediately preceding its current location. If you specify FIRST, it points to the first record in the set, and if you specify LAST, it points to the last record.

An integer value specification must accompany ABSOLUTE and RELATIVE. For example, FETCH ABSOLUTE 7 moves the cursor to the seventh row from the beginning of the set. FETCH RELATIVE 7 moves the cursor seven rows beyond its current position. FETCH RELATIVE 0 doesn't move the cursor.

FETCH RELATIVE 1 has the same effect as FETCH NEXT. FETCH RELATIVE –1 has the same effect as FETCH PRIOR. FETCH ABSOLUTE 1 gives you the first record in the set, FETCH ABSOLUTE 2 gives you the second record in the set, and so on. Similarly, FETCH ABSOLUTE –1 gives you the last record in the set, FETCH ABSOLUTE –2 gives you the next-to-last record, and so on. Specifying FETCH ABSOLUTE 0 returns the no data exception condition code, as does FETCH ABSOLUTE 17 if only 16 rows are in the set. FETCH <simple value specification> gives you the record specified by the simple value specification.

Deleting a row

You can perform delete and update operations on the row that the cursor is currently pointing to. The syntax of the DELETE statement is as follows:

```
DELETE FROM table-name WHERE CURRENT OF cursor-name ;
```

If the cursor doesn't point to a row, the statement returns an error condition. No deletion occurs.

Updating a row

The syntax of the UPDATE statement is as follows:

```
UPDATE table-name
    SET column-name = value [,column-name = value]...
    WHERE CURRENT OF cursor-name ;
```

The value you place into each specified column must be a value expression or the keyword DEFAULT. If an attempted positioned update operation returns an error, the update isn't performed.

Closing a Cursor

After you finish with a cursor, make a habit of closing it immediately. Leaving a cursor open as your application goes on to other issues may cause harm. Also, open cursors use system resources.

If you close a cursor that was insensitive to changes made while it was open, when you reopen it, the reopened cursor reflects any such changes.

The syntax for closing cursor C1 is

```
CLOSE C1 ;
```

Book IV

Data Security

"We take network security here very seriously."

Contents at a Glance

Chapter 1: Protecting Against Hardware Failure and External Threats

In This Chapter

✔ Dealing with trouble in paradise

✔ Maintaining database integrity

✔ Enhancing performance and reliability with RAID

✔ Avoiding disaster with backups

✔ Coping with Internet threats

✔ Piling on layers of protection

Database applications are complex pieces of software that interact with databases, which in turn are complex collections of data that run on computer systems, which in their own right are complex assemblages of hardware components. The more complex something is, the more likely it is to have unanticipated failures. That being the case, a database application is an accident waiting to happen. With complexity piled upon complexity, not only is something sure to go wrong, but when it does, you'll have a hard time telling where the problem lies. However, you can do some things to protect yourself against these threats. Of course, the protections require you to spend time and money. You must evaluate the tradeoff between protection and expense, and find a level of protection you are comfortable with, at an expense you can afford.

What Could Possibly Go Wrong?

Problems can arise in a number of areas. Here are a few:

✦ Your database could be incorrectly structured, making modification anomalies inevitable.

✦ Data-entry errors could introduce bad data into the database.

✦ Users accessing the same data at the same time could interfere with each other.

✦ Changes to database structure could "break" existing database applications.

✦ Upgrading to a new operating system could create problems with existing database applications.

✦ Upgrading system hardware could "break" existing database applications.

✦ Posing a query that has never been asked before could expose a hidden bug.

✦ An operator could accidentally destroy data.

✦ A malicious person could intentionally destroy or steal data.

✦ Hardware could age or wear out and fail permanently.

✦ An environmental condition could cause a "soft" error that exists long enough to alter data, but then disappear. (These are maddening.)

✦ A virus or worm could arrive over the Internet and corrupt data.

From the preceding partial list, you can clearly see that protecting your data can require a significant effort, and as such should be budgeted for adequately during the planning of a database project. In this chapter, I concentrate on hardware issues and malicious threats that arrive over the Internet. I address the other concerns in the next chapter.

Equipment failure

Great strides have been made in recent years in improving the reliability of computer hardware. However, we're still a long way from perfect hardware that will never fail. Anything with moving parts is subject to wear and tear. As a consequence, such devices fail more often than do devices that have no moving parts. Hard disk drives, CD-ROM drives, DVD-ROM drives, and floppy disk drives all depend on mechanical movement, and thus are possible points of failure. So are cooling fans and even on/off switches. Connectors such as USB ports and audio and video jacks that see frequent insertions and extractions are also liable to fail before the non-moving parts do.

Even non-moving parts can fail due to overheating or just from carrying electrical current for too long. Of course, anything can fail if it is physically abused (dropped, shaken, or has coffee spilled into it, for example).

You can do several things to minimize, if not eliminate, problems caused by equipment failure. Here are a few ideas:

✦ Check the specifications of components with moving parts such as hard disk and DVD-ROM drives. Pick components with a high MTBF (Mean Time Between Failures). Do some comparison shopping. You will find a range of values. When shopping for a hard disk, the number of gigabytes per dollar should not be the only thing you look at.

✦ Make sure your computer system has adequate cooling. It is especially important that the processor chips have sufficient cooling. They generate enormous amounts of heat.

✦ Buy memory chips with a high MTBF.

✦ Control the environment where your computer is located. Make sure it gets adequate ventilation and is never subjected to high temperatures. If you cannot control the ambient temperature, turn the system off when the weather gets too hot. Humans can tolerate extreme heat better than computers can.

✦ Isolate your system from shock and vibration.

✦ Establish a policy that prohibits liquids such as coffee, or even water, from being anywhere near the computer.

✦ Restrict access to the computer, so that only those people who agree to your protection rules can come near it.

Platform instability

What's a platform? A platform is the system your database application is running on. It includes the operating system, the basic input/output subsystem (BIOS), the processor, the memory, and all the ancillary and peripheral devices that make up a functioning computer system.

Platform instability is a fancy way of saying that you cannot count on your platform to operate the way it is supposed to. Sometimes this is due to an equipment failure or an impending equipment failure. Other times, it is due to an incompatibility introduced when one or another element in the system is changed.

Because of the danger of platform instability, many database administrators (DBAs) are extremely reluctant to upgrade their system when a new release of the operating system, or a larger, higher-capacity hard disk becomes available. The person who coined the phrase "If it ain't broke, don't fix it" must have been a database administrator. Any change to a happily functioning system is liable to cause platform instability problems, so DBAs resist such changes fiercely, allowing them grudgingly only when it becomes clear that important work cannot be performed without the upgrade.

So how do you protect against platform instability, aside from forbidding any changes to the platform? Here are a few things you can do to protect yourself:

✦ Install the upgrade when nothing important is running and furthermore nothing important is scheduled to be run for several days. Yes, this means coming in on the weekend.

✦ Change only one thing at a time and deal with any issues that arise before making another change that could interact with the first change.

✦ Warn users in advance that you are about to make a configuration change, so they can protect themselves from any possible adverse consequences.

✦ If you can afford it, bring up the new environment on a parallel system and switch over your production work only when it is clear that the new system has stabilized.

Database design flaws

The design of robust, reliable, and high-performing databases is a topic that goes beyond SQL and is worthy of a book in its own right. I recommend my *Database Development For Dummies* (published by Wiley). Many problems that show up long after a database has been placed into service can be traced back to faulty design at the very beginning. It is important to get it right from the start. Give the design phase of every development project the time and consideration it deserves.

Data entry error

It's really hard to draw valid conclusions from information retrieved from a database if faulty data was entered into the database to begin with. Chapter 5 of Book I describes how to enter data into a database with SQL's INSERT statement, and how to modify the data in an existing database record with the UPDATE statement. If a person is entering a series of such statements, keyboarding errors are a real possibility. Even if you're entering records through a form that does validation checks on what you enter, mistypes are still a concern. Entered data can be valid, but nonetheless incorrect. Zero through nine are all valid decimal digits, but if a field is supposed to contain a seven, six is just as wrong as Tuesday. The best defense against data entry errors is to have someone other than the person who entered the data check it against the original source document.

Operator error

People make mistakes. You can minimize the impact of such mistakes by making sure that only intelligent, highly trained, and well-meaning people can get their hands on the database. However, even the most intelligent, highly trained, and well-meaning people make mistakes from time to time. Sometimes those mistakes destroy data or alter it in a way that makes it unusable. Your best defense from such an eventuality is to have a robust and active backup policy, which I discuss in detail later, in the "Backing Up Your System" section.

Taking Advantage of RAID

Equipment failure is one of the things that can go wrong with your database. Of all the pieces of equipment that make up a computer system, the one piece that is most likely to fail is the hard disk drive. A motor is turning a spindle from seven to ten thousand revolutions per minute. Platters holding data are attached to the spindle and spinning with it. Read/write heads on cantilevers are moving in and out across the platter surfaces. Significant heat is generated by the motor and the moving parts. Sooner or later, wear takes it toll and the disk drive fails. When it does, whatever information it contained becomes unrecoverable. Disk failures are inevitable — you just don't know when they will occur. You can do a couple of things to protect yourself from the worst consequences of disk failure. One is to maintain a regular backup discipline that copies production data at intervals and stores it in a safe place offline. The other thing you can do is to put some redundancy into the storage system. This redundancy is accomplished using RAID (Redundant Array of Inexpensive Disks).

RAID technology has two main advantages. The redundancy aspect gives the system a measure of fault tolerance. The inexpensive aspect comes from the fact that several disks with smaller capacities are generally cheaper than a single disk of the same capacity because the large single disk is using the most recent, most advanced technology and is operating on the edge of what is possible. In fact, a RAID array may be configured to have a capacity that is larger than the largest disk drive that is available at any price.

In a RAID array, two or more disks are combined to form a logical disk drive. To the database, the logical disk drive appears to be a single unit, although physically it may be made up of multiple disk drives.

Striping

A key concept of RAID architecture is the idea of *striping*. With striping, data is spread across multiple disks in chunks. One chunk is placed on the first disk; the next chunk is placed on the next disk; and so on. After a chunk is placed on the last disk in the array, the next chunk goes on the first disk, and the cycle starts over. In this way, the data is evenly spread across all the disks in the array, and no single disk contains anything meaningful. In a five-disk array, for example, each disk holds one-fifth of the data. If the chunks are words in a text file, one disk holds every fifth word in the document. You need all of them to put the text back together again in a readable form. Figure 1-1 illustrates the idea of striping.

In Figure 1-1, chunks 1, 2, 3, and 4 constitute one stripe; chunks 5, 6, 7, and 8 constitute the next stripe, and so on. A *stripe* is made up of contiguous chunks on the logical drive, but physically, each chunk is on a different hard disk drive.

RAID levels

There are several levels of RAID, each with its own advantages and disadvantages. Depending on your requirements, you may decide to use one RAID level for some of your data and another RAID level for data that has different characteristics. In the following sections, I briefly discuss the RAID levels that are most commonly used.

RAID 0

RAID 0 is the simplest of the RAID levels. A round robin method distributes data across all the disks in the array in a striped fashion. Striping enhances performance because multiple disks can perform seeks in parallel rather than sequentially, as would be the case with a single large disk. However, RAID 0 offers no fault tolerance. There is no redundancy. If you lose any one disk in the array, you have lost *all* of your data. The data remaining on the disks that are still functioning is of no use without the missing chunks. It's as if, in a five-disk array, every fifth word of a text document is missing, or every fifth reservation in an airline reservation system has disappeared. Actually, it is even worse than that because the chunks typically don't exactly match text words or database records. What remains is unintelligible.

Although it increases performance, RAID 0 provides no benefit over running on a non-RAID disk in terms of fault tolerance. It's not wise to put mission-critical data on a RAID 0 array.

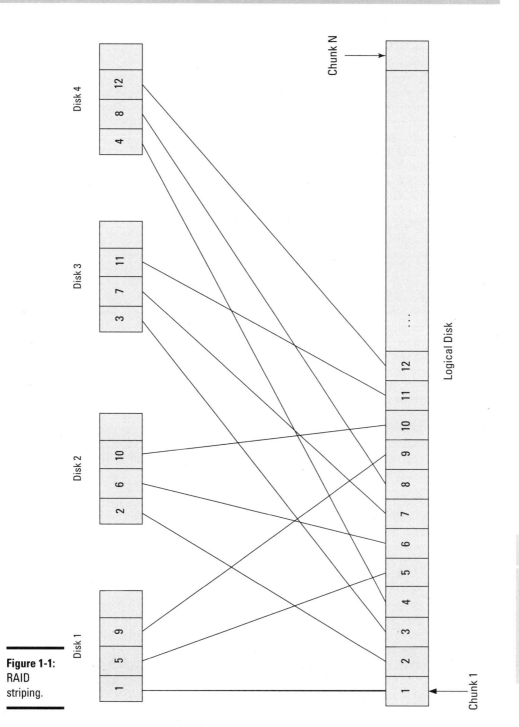

Figure 1-1:
RAID
striping.

RAID 1

RAID 1 is the simplest of the fault-tolerant RAID levels. It does not employ striping. Also known as *disk mirroring*, RAID 1 duplicates the content of one disk on a second disk. Performance is somewhat worse than the performance of a non-RAID disk because every write operation has to go to two disks rather than one. A second disadvantage is that you use two hard disks to hold one hard disk's worth of data — your disk cost is doubled. The benefit of RAID 1 is in the area of fault tolerance. If either of the mirrored disks fails, the other one contains all the data, and performance is unaffected. You can replace the failed disk and fill it up with data to match the surviving disk, to return to the same level of fault tolerance you had at the beginning. RAID 1 is a good choice when both fault tolerance and performance are important, when all your data will fit on a single disk drive, and when cost is not a primary concern.

RAID 5

RAID 5 is a RAID level that uses parity rather than data duplication to achieve fault tolerance. In an array of, say, six physical disks, each stripe consists of five data chunks and one parity chunk. If any one of the physical drives fails, its contents can be deduced from the parity information on the other five drives. The advantage of RAID 5 is that the space available to hold data is $N–1$, where N is the number of disk drives. This compares favorably with RAID 1, where the space available to hold data is N/2. A six-drive RAID 5 array holds up to five disks full of data. Three two-drive RAID 1 arrays only hold up to three disks full of data. You pay a performance penalty for the additional capacity. In a RAID 5 system, every write operation requires four disk accesses: two reads and two writes. Both the target disk stripe and the parity stripe must be read, the parity calculated, and then both stripes must be written.

Because of the performance penalty RAID 5 exacts on writes, RAID 5 isn't a good choice for disks that are often written to. RAID 5 is fine for databases that are read-only or read-mostly. If more than ten percent of disk operations are writes, RAID 5 is probably not the best choice.

RAID 10

RAID 10 combines aspects of RAID 0 and RAID 1. Like RAID 1, RAID 10 mirrors disks. Each disk has an exact duplicate. Like RAID 0, the disks in the array are striped. RAID 10 gives the fault tolerance of RAID 1 and the performance of RAID 0. A RAID 10 array can consist of a large number of disks, so it is a good level to use when a large amount of data is being stored. It is also good from a fault tolerance point of view because it can tolerate the loss of more than one disk, although it cannot handle the loss of both members of a mirror pair.

RAID level comparison

When deciding which RAID level is appropriate for a given database and its associated applications, performance, fault tolerance, and cost are the main considerations. Table 1-1 shows the comparison of these metrics.

Table 1-1		RAID Level Comparison	
RAID Level	*Performance*	*Fault Tolerance*	*Disk Capacity/Data Size*
RAID 0	Best: One disk access/write	Worst: None	Best: 1
RAID 1	Good: Two disk accesses/write	Good: No degradation with single failure	Worst: 2
RAID 5	Fair: Four disk accesses/write	Fair: Full recovery possible	Good: N/(N–1)
RAID 10	Good: Two disk accesses/write	Excellent: No degradation with multiple failures	Worst: 2

Backing Up Your System

Fault tolerance, as described in the section on RAID, and also as implemented with redundant hardware that goes beyond RAID, responds to some, but not all of the threats listed at the top of this chapter. The most effective defense you have against the full spectrum of potential problems is an effective backup procedure. Backing up means making copies of all your important programs and data as often as necessary, so that you can easily and quickly regain full functionality after some misfortune has corrupted or destroyed your system. Depending on the criticality of your application, you should go to greater or lesser lengths to protect your assets.

Preparing for the worst

On September 11, 2001, a terrorist attack destroyed the twin towers of the World Trade Center in lower Manhattan. Along with the lives of thousands of people, the financial hub of the American economy was snuffed out. Virtually all of America's major financial institutions, including the New York Board of Trade (NYBOT), had their center of operations in the World Trade Center. The lives that were lost that day were gone for good. However, within hours, the NYBOT was up and running again, hardly missing a beat. This was possible because it had prepared for the worst. It had implemented the most effective (and most expensive) form of backup. It continuously sent its information off site to a hot site in Queens. The hot site was close enough so that employees who had evacuated the World Trade Center could get to it quickly and start the recovery effort, yet it was far enough away so as not to be affected by a major disaster.

Many companies and government entities can justify the investment in the level of backup employed by the NYBOT. That investment was made because analysis showed that downtime would cost the NYBOT and its clients close to $4,000,000 a day. For enterprises where downtime is not so costly, a lesser investment in backup is justified. However, if loss of your data or programs would cause you any pain at all, some level of backup is called for. This may be no more than copying your active work onto a thumb drive every night after work and taking it home with you. It could mean putting removable hard disks into a fireproof safe in another building. It could mean distributing copies of your data to remote sites over your corporate network. Think carefully about what your threats are, what losses are possible, what the consequences of those losses are, and what investment in backup is justified, in light of those threats, losses, and consequences.

Full or incremental backup

Perhaps you have only one or two megabytes of data that you are actively working on that would cause pain if you were to lose them. Alternatively, you might have a critical database in the terabyte range. In the first case, it won't take much time for you to back up the entire database and remove the backup copy to a safe place. On the other hand, you probably do not want to back up a terabyte database completely several times a day, or even once a day. The size of your database, the speed of your backup procedure, and the cost of your backup medium dictate whether you implement a full backup procedure, or only back up the changes that have been made since the last backup. Backing up only the changes is called *incremental backup*. When a failure occurs, you can go back to your last full backup, and then restore all the incremental backups that followed it, one by one.

Frequency

A big question about backup is, "How often should I do it?" I answer that question with another question, "How much pain are you willing to endure, if you were to suddenly and unexpectedly lose your data?" If you don't mind redoing a couple of hours of work, there is no point in backing up more frequently than every couple of hours. Many organizations perform backups at night after the workers have gone home for the day. These organizations run the risk of losing no more than a day's work. Think carefully about your total situation and what effect data loss could have on you, and then choose an appropriate backup interval. Be sure to adhere to your backup schedule without fail. Long intervals without a failure should not weaken your resolve to maintain your schedule. It is the unexpected that you are defending against.

Backup maintenance

When your latest backup is sent to off site storage or your hot site, don't immediately recycle the backup media from the previous backup. Sometimes problems in the data are not realized right away, and several backup generations are made before anyone recognizes that the data is corrupted. One good discipline, if you are backing up on a daily basis, is to keep a whole week of daily backups, as well as a month's worth of weekly backups, and a year's worth of monthly backups. That should cover most possibilities. The important point is to maintain the number of backups you need, for as long as you need them, to ensure that you will be able to continue operating, with minimum downtime, regardless of what might happen.

Another thing you should do is restore a backup occasionally, just to see if you recover all the data that you backed up. I once went into a company (which shall remain nameless) as a database consultant. They very proudly showed me their backup disks and the fireproof safe they kept them in. There was only one problem. The backup disks were all empty! The employee who dutifully did the backups every night did not have a full understanding of the backup procedure and was actually recording nothing. Luckily, I asked them to do a test restore, and the problem was discovered before they had to do a restoration for real.

Coping with Internet Threats

In addition to all the bad things that can happen to your hardware due to random failures and human mistakes, the Internet is another potential source of major problems. People with malicious intent (called crackers) do not have to get anywhere near your hardware to do great damage to your computer system and your organization. The Internet is your connection to your customers, clients, suppliers, friends, news organizations, and entertainment providers. It is also a connection to people who either want to harm you or to steal the resources of your computer. Attacks on your system can take a number of forms. I briefly discuss a few of the most common ones in the following sections.

Viruses

A *virus* is a self-replicating piece of software that spreads by attaching itself to other programs or to documents. When a human launches the host program, or performs some other action on it, the virus is activated. After it's activated, the virus can propagate by copying itself to other programs. The virus's "payload" can perform other actions, such as erasing disk files, crashing the computer, displaying mocking messages on the user's screen, or commandeering system resources to perform a computation for, and send results back to, the attacker who originated the virus.

At any given time, hundreds of viruses, of varying virulence, are circulating on the Internet. If one happens to infect your computer, it can be an annoyance or a disaster. Consider these options to protect yourself:

✦ **Never connect your computer to the Internet.** This is a very effective technique and a viable idea if none of the work you intend to do on that computer relies on the Internet's resources, and it never exchanges files with any of your computers that *are* connected to the Internet.

✦ **Install antivirus software on your computer and keep it up to date by maintaining a subscription.** New viruses are emerging all the time: To thwart them, you need the latest in antivirus protection.

✦ **Make sure users are aware of virus threats and know how to recognize suspicious e-mails.** This is an important defense against viruses. Caution them not to open e-mail attachments from unknown sources and be careful about visiting Web sites of unknown character. Set their browser settings at a high security level.

Even if you do all of the above recommended actions, your computer still might become infected with a virus. Be on the lookout for any change in the way your computer operates. A sudden slowdown in performance could be a sign that a virus has taken over your system, which is now doing the bidding of some unknown attacker rather than doing what you want it to do.

Worms

Worms are similar to viruses in some respects, and different in others. The defining characteristic of a virus is that it spreads by attaching itself to other programs. The defining characteristic of a worm is that it spreads via networks. Both viruses and worms are self-replicating; however, viruses typically need some action by a human in order to become active. Worms have no such limitation. They can enter an unsuspecting computer via a network connection at any time of day or night, without any action by a human.

Worms can take over thousands of computers in a matter of hours, as an exponentially expanding wave of infection flows out from a single initially infected computer. An infected computer can, for example, send a copy of the worm to every address in the computer's e-mail address book. Each of those computers, which are now infected too, then send the worm on to all the computers in their respective address books. It doesn't take long for the infection to spread around the world. This clogs up communication channels, as bandwidth is consumed by thousands of copies of the worm, which are sent from one computer to another. Depending on the worm's payload, infected computers may start performing a computation, such as password cracking, for the originator of the worm, or they may start erasing files or causing other damage.

You can do a few things to protect yourself from being infected, or failing that, from passing on the infection:

✦ **Employ all patches from the vendors of your software as soon as possible.**

✦ **Harden your system to prevent bad stuff from getting in.** This may involve closing ports that are normally open.

✦ **Block arbitrary outbound connections.** By doing so, if you do get infected, you don't pass on the infection.

If everyone did these things, worms would fizzle out before they got very far.

Denial-of-service attacks

Worms need not actively perform computations or cause damage to the systems they infect. Instead, they can lie dormant, in stealth mode, waiting for a specific time and date, or some other trigger to occur. At the appointed time, thousands of infected computers, now under the control of a malicious cracker, can simultaneously launch a *denial-of-service* attack on some target Web site. The thousands of incoming messages from the worms completely overwhelm the ability of the target site to handle the traffic, preventing legitimate messages from getting through and bringing the Web site down.

Phishing scams

Scammers send out e-mails to thousands or even millions of people, purporting to be from a legitimate bank, or business such as eBay, saying that your account has shown unusual activity and you must update your information. After you input your financial information, the scammer has access to your bank or business account and can transfer your funds to his offshore account in a country that does not monitor financial transactions. The next time you access your account, you receive an unpleasant surprise.

The best defense against a phishing attack is to never respond to an e-mail with sensitive information. Even though the e-mail sends you to a site that looks for all the world like the official Web site of your bank, it is a fake, specifically designed to induce you to surrender your account information and along with it all the money in the account.

Zombie spambots

Zombie spambots are similar to the worms that engage in denial-of-service attacks. However, instead of launching an attack on a single Web site, spambots spew unsolicited advertising messages to lists of e-mail addresses that the spammers have acquired. Rather than being from a single, relatively easy-to-trace source, the spam is produced by thousands of computers that have been taken over by worms to mindlessly pump out spam to their address lists. If you happen to be one of the people whose computer has been taken over, you see an unexplained drop in performance, as a significant fraction of your computational capacity and Internet bandwidth is dedicated to sending spam to unlucky recipients around the world. Such distributed spam attacks are devilishly difficult to trace to their source.

Installing Layers of Protection

The creators of viruses, worms, and bots have become increasingly sophisticated and are perpetually one or two steps ahead of the guys in the white hats who are trying to stamp them out. As a user, you should do everything you can to protect your computers and the sensitive information they contain. Because no one type of protection is totally effective, your best hope is to put several layers of protection between your valuable files and programs and the outside world.

Network layer firewalls

Communication on the Internet consists of packets of data that conform to the TCP/IP protocol. A *network layer firewall* is a packet filter, operating on a low level, that resides on a computer situated between the Internet and a local area network (LAN), in what is called the DMZ (demilitarized zone). The computer that is running the firewall in the DMZ does not contain any sensitive information. Its sole purpose is to protect the LAN. Rules set up by the network administrator (or default values) determine which packets are allowed to pass from the Internet to the LAN and which are rejected.

Application layer firewalls

An *application layer firewall* operates at a higher (more abstract) level than the network layer firewall. It can inspect the contents of network traffic and block traffic that the firewall administrator deems to be inappropriate, such as traffic from known-malicious Web sites, recognized viruses, or attempts to exploit known vulnerabilities in software running on the LAN.

Antivirus software

Considering the hundreds of viruses and worms circulating in the wild, up-to-date antivirus software is a necessity for any computer that is either directly or indirectly connected to the Internet. Even computers that are not connected to the Internet are susceptible to infection, if they can receive software from CD-ROMs, floppy disks, or flash (thumb) drives. Be sure to buy a subscription to one of the popular antivirus programs, such as McAfee or Norton, and then keep the subscription current with regular downloads of updates.

Vulnerabilities, exploits, and patches

Antivirus software can protect you from viruses, worms, and other malware that crackers have created to serve their own nefarious purposes. However, such software cannot protect you from malware that has not yet been released into the wild and detected by the antivirus software vendors.

Existing software may have vulnerabilities that have not yet been exploited by malware developers. New software is almost certain to contain vulnerabilities that are just waiting to be exploited. When exploits for these vulnerabilities appear, all computers are at risk until the vulnerabilities have been patched.

Sometimes exploits (called *zero-day exploits*) are released into the wild on the same day that the vulnerability becomes known. In such cases, the time between the release of the exploit and the release of the patch that shuts it down is a period of time during which there is no effective defense against the exploit.

When a patch *does* become available, install it immediately on all susceptible machines. An ongoing problem is the huge number of naive users who are either not aware of the danger and the associated patch, or who do not realize the importance of hardening their systems against attack. By remaining vulnerable, they endanger not only their own systems, but also others that could be attacked if their machine is compromised.

Education

One of the best defenses against malicious attacks on your systems is for all users to be educated about the threats and the countermeasures that are available to eliminate those threats. Regular training on security should be a part of every organization's defensive arsenal.

Alertness

If you ever sit down at your computer and see something that just strikes you as odd, beware. You could be seeing the evidence that your computer has been compromised. Run some checks. If you don't know what checks to run, ask someone who does know for help. It could be nothing, but then again maybe a stranger is sucking value out of your system. It doesn't hurt to be a little paranoid.

Chapter 2: Protecting Against User Errors and Conflicts

In This Chapter

✔ Discovering even more trouble in paradise

✔ Keeping the garbage out

✔ Taking the ACID test

✔ Preventing mix-ups with transactions

✔ Getting familiar with lock types

✔ Tuning locks

✔ Tuning the recovery system

*A*fter you have done everything you can do to minimize the possibility of problems due to hardware faults and Internet threats, which I discuss in the previous chapter, you still have to worry about yet other things that can damage the data in your database or degrade performance.

Several additional potential sources of error exist. Here are a few of the most important:

✦ The database design could be faulty, leading to modification anomalies or poor performance.

✦ The database application written to access the data in the database could be buggy, leading to database corruption, erroneous results, poor performance, or all of the above.

✦ The data entered into the database could be wrong.

✦ Users accessing the same (or nearby) data at the same time could interfere with each other, impacting performance or even corrupting the data.

Reducing Data Entry Errors

All the things you do to protect your database from harm are to no avail if bad data is entered into it in the first place. Although nowadays quite a bit of data is recorded automatically by instrumentation and delivered to databases electronically, much of the data stored in the world's databases was initially entered by hand by a fallible human at a computer keyboard. Humans are notorious for making typing errors even if they are very conscientious and are excellent spellers. Even data collected automatically could contain errors produced by electronic noise, or a thousand other unpredictable causes. You can't eliminate all these problems before they put bad data into a database, but you can discover and eliminate some of them, at least.

Data types: the first line of defense

SQL is a strongly typed language. That means that if a data entry is supposed to be of a particular type, the database engine will not accept any entry that does not conform to the rules of that type. For example, the BOOLEAN type accepts only values of TRUE and FALSE. It rejects any and all other entries. The INTEGER type accepts only integers, the CHAR type accepts only valid alphanumeric characters, and so on. The strongly typed nature of SQL prevents a lot of bad stuff from being accidentally added to databases. However, strong typing does not prevent data of the correct type but wrong value from being entered.

Constraints: the second line of defense

By applying constraints to your database tables, you can prevent incorrect data that is of the correct type from being accepted. I cover constraints in Chapter 5 of Book I. A number of different kinds of constraints exist, each of which prevents a certain class of problems. Probably the most flexible is the CHECK constraint because it enables you to specify exactly what values are acceptable for entry into a specific database field. Here's another look at an example of the use of a CHECK constraint that first appeared in Chapter 5 of Book I.

```
CREATE TABLE TESTS (
    TestName          CHARACTER (30)        NOT NULL,
    StandardCharge    NUMERIC (6,2)
        CHECK (StandardCharge >= 0.00
          AND StandardCharge <= 200.00)
    ) ;
```

This code guarantees that any entry into the StandardCharge field is of the NUMERIC type with two decimal places, and that the value entered into the StandardCharge field must be no less than zero and no more than 200.00. This kind of protection can prevent many errors due to a slip of the finger or the slip of a decimal point.

Sharp-eyed humans: the third line of defense

Strong typing can assure that data being entered is of the proper type, and constraints can assure that it is in the proper range of values. However, these defenses cannot assure that it is *right*. The only way to make sure that the data that is entered is indeed the data that was supposed to be entered is to have a human who knows what the data should be check it. In most cases, this is too costly and time-consuming, so it is not done. We accept a certain amount of bad data because to have a human check it is not feasible in all but the most critical cases.

Unreliable Database Design

In Book I, I talk quite a bit about modeling a database before you start creating its tables. People who don't put in a full effort at modeling are likely to build databases with inherent design flaws. People who *do* put in a full effort at modeling still might have problems if their models are not adequately normalized. Unnormalized or incompletely normalized models are susceptible to modification anomalies that introduce inconsistencies into the data. Those inconsistencies ultimately lead to incorrect results, which could snowball into disastrous executive decisions. Database design is a topic worthy of a book of its own, and many have been written on the subject.

Programming Errors

Even if a database is carefully modeled and designed in such a way that it accurately and efficiently structures the data, and even if the data entered into it is one hundred percent correct, you still could draw incorrect conclusions based on information you retrieve from that database. How is that so?

Although you can certainly retrieve the information you want from a relational database by entering SQL statements at the system console, this is not the way it is usually done. It is too tedious, time-consuming, and boring, not to mention error-prone, to think up complex SQL queries and enter them on the fly while you sit in front of your computer. Instead, people hire people like you to write database applications that manage and query their databases for them. Those database applications are another potential source of error.

People who write database applications must not only be masters of SQL, but they must also be experts in the procedural language that they embed their SQL statements into. Unfortunately, many people who don't have the

**Book IV
Chapter 2**

**Protecting Against
User Errors and
Conflicts**

requisite background are drafted into writing such applications, with predictable results. The applications never really do all the things that the client expected them to do, and even worse, may even provide misleading results.

Although you can't completely eliminate the chance that your database may have design flaws, or that your database application may contain hidden bugs, you can do one thing to minimize the chance that such problems will do you significant harm: Hire experienced professionals who understand solid database design and database application design, as well as have a good understanding of the system that you want to build. People with this kind of expertise do not come cheap, but, in the long run, they are worth what they cost. You get a system that does what you want it to do and does it reliably and expeditiously.

Conflicts Arising from Concurrent Operation

Suppose your database is well designed and contains correct data, and all the applications that access it are bug-free. You still might have a problem. Databases are typically central repositories of important data for businesses, government agencies, and academic institutions. As such, they are likely to be accessed by multiple people at the same time. If two people attempt to access the same database record at the same time, one could be given precedence, locking out the other. They could even interfere with each other in such a way that both are locked out and neither gets their job done. Even more problematic, they could both be given access, and their operations could be mixed together, corrupting the database.

Protecting the database from corruption is the number-one priority, but after that, making sure that people are able to get their jobs done even when traffic to and from the database is heavy, is also very important. In the upcoming section, I take a look at some of the problems and how they can be solved.

Here's a look at how two perfectly legitimate operations, by two authorized users, can cause a major problem. Suppose you and your friend Calypso have a joint savings account at Medieval Savings and Loan. Currently you have a balance of $47.17 in the account. To meet upcoming expenses, you decide to deposit $100.00 into the account. Coincidentally, Calypso has the same thought at about the same time. You go to the nearest ATM machine and Calypso, who works in another part of the city, goes to a different ATM machine. A problem arises because two operations are being performed on the same account at the same time. Here's what happens:

1. You insert your ATM card into your ATM.

2. Your ATM pulls up your account and notes that you have a balance of $47.17.

3. Calypso inserts her ATM card into her ATM.

4. Calypso's ATM pulls up your account and notes that you have a balance of $47.17.

5. You insert $100.00 in cash into your ATM.

6. Your ATM adds $100.00 to the balance it originally read, giving a total of $147.17.

7. Calypso inserts $100.00 in cash into her ATM.

8. Calypso's ATM adds $100.00 to the balance it originally read, giving a total of $147.17.

If you don't compare notes with Calypso at a later time, you have just been victimized to the tune of $100.00. The write of Calypso's transaction wiped out the fact that you had previously deposited $100.00.

What is the root cause of this problem? The bank tried to handle two operations at once and mixed them up. In this case, the mistake was to the bank's advantage, but it could just as easily have gone the other way. At any rate, any bank that loses its customers' money doesn't keep those customers very long. Problems such as the lost update scenario described here caused database architects to introduce the idea of a transaction. A *transaction* is an indivisible unit of work that cannot be mixed up with anything else the database might be doing. Well-designed transaction architectures have four essential characteristics: atomicity, consistency, isolation, and durability.

Atomicity, Consistency, Isolation, and Durability

The four characteristics of an effective transaction, atomicity, consistency, isolation, and durability, are commonly known by the acronym ACID. To be sure a transaction will protect your data, no matter what unlucky event might occur, it should have ACID. What do those four magic words mean?

✦ **Atomicity:** Database transactions should be atomic, in the classic sense of the word: The entire transaction is treated as an indivisible unit. Either it is executed in its entirety (committed), or the database is restored (rolled back) to the state it would have been in if the transaction had not been executed.

✦ **Consistency:** Oddly enough, the meaning of *consistency* is not consistent; it varies from one application to another. When you transfer funds from one account to another in a banking application, for example, you want the total amount of money in both accounts at the end of the transaction to be the same as it was at the beginning of the transaction. In a different application, your criterion for consistency might be different.

✦ **Isolation:** Ideally, database transactions should be totally isolated from other transactions that execute at the same time. If the transactions are serializable, total isolation is achieved. A serializable set of transactions produces the same results as if they were executed serially, one after another. Serializable transactions do not need to be executed serially — they just need to give the same results that they would give if they had been executed serially. Insisting on serializability can cause performance problems, so if a system has to process transactions at top speed, lower levels of isolation are sometimes used.

✦ **Durability:** After a transaction has committed or rolled back, you should be able to count on the database being in the proper state: well stocked with uncorrupted, reliable, up-to-date data. Even if your system suffers a hard crash after a commit — but before the transaction is stored to disk — a durable DBMS can guarantee that upon recovery from the crash, the database can be restored to its proper state.

Operating with Transactions

Any operation that reads data from or writes data to a database should be enclosed in a transaction. As a result, whenever the database engine encounters an SQL statement that either reads or writes, it automatically starts a transaction, called the *default transaction*. Thus you do not have to explicitly tell the database engine to start a transaction, but you can do so, if you want to modify the default parameters. After you start a transaction, it will either complete successfully or it will not. What happens in either case is discussed in the following sections.

Using the SET TRANSACTION statement

Whatever DBMS you are using has default settings for how the transaction will be run. Although the default settings are perfectly fine most of the time, you can override them if you wish with a SET TRANSACTION statement. Here's the syntax:

```
<set transaction statement> ::=
    SET [ LOCAL ] TRANSACTION <mode> [ , <mode> ] ...

<mode> ::=
```

```
    <isolation level>
  | <access mode>
  | <diagnostics size>

<isolation level> ::=
    READ UNCOMMITTED
  | READ COMMITTED
  | REPEATABLE READ
  | SERIALIZABLE

<access mode> ::=
    READ ONLY
  | READ WRITE

<diagnostics size> ::=
    DIAGNOSTICS SIZE <simple value expression>
```

With the SET TRANSACTION statement, you can set the isolation level, the
access mode, and the diagnostics size. Any one of the modes that you do
not specify assume the default value for that mode. If you specify the READ
ONLY access mode, any statements that change the database, such as
UPDATE, INSERT, and DELETE, cannot execute. The default access mode is
READ WRITE, unless the isolation level is READ UNCOMMITTED. When you
are running at the READ UNCOMMITTED isolation level, the default access
mode is READ ONLY. The default isolation level is SERIALIZABLE. (I cover
isolation levels in more detail later in this chapter. I defer discussion of
DIAGNOSTICS SIZE until Chapter 4 of this minibook.)

You can't start a new transaction while an existing transaction is still active.
If you *do* execute a SET TRANSACTION statement while a transaction is
active, the modes specified in the statement apply only to the *next* transaction, not the current one. The LOCAL keyword restricts the mode settings
specified to the local transaction included in a transaction that encompasses
multiple databases.

Starting a transaction

As I mention earlier, a transaction is automatically started when the database
engine senses that the next statement to execute either reads from or writes
to the database. Default modes are assumed unless a SET TRANSACTION statement has been executed. If one has, the modes specified in it are used instead
of the default modes. The modes specified by a SET TRANSACTION statement
are active only for the next transaction to execute. Any following transactions once again use the default modes, unless another SET TRANSACTION
statement is executed or unless a START TRANSACTION statement is
executed.

**Book IV
Chapter 2**

**Protecting Against
User Errors and
Conflicts**

With a `START TRANSACTION` statement, you can specify modes the same way you can with a `SET TRANSACTION` statement. The difference is that a `START TRANSACTION` statement starts a transaction, whereas a `SET TRANSACTION` statement sets up the modes for a transaction, but does not actually start one.

Access modes

There is not much mystery about the access modes, READ ONLY and READ WRITE. In either mode, you can read the contents of database records, using the `SELECT` statement. However, you can make changes to the database only in READ WRITE mode.

Isolation levels

In the Medieval Savings and Loan example earlier in this chapter, I outline one of the potential problems when two database operations are not sufficiently isolated from each other and interact in an undesirable way. Transactions provide four levels of protection from such harmful interactions, ranging from the fairly weak protection of READ UNCOMMITTED to the level of protection you would get if transactions never ran concurrently (SERIALIZABLE).

READ UNCOMMITTED

The weakest level of isolation is called READ UNCOMMITTED, which allows the sometimes-problematic dirty read. A *dirty read* is a situation in which a change made by one user can be read by a second user before the first user commits (that is, finalizes) the change. The problem arises when the first user aborts and rolls back his transaction. The second user's subsequent operations are now based on an incorrect value. The classic example of this foul-up can appear in an inventory application: One user decrements inventory; a second user reads the new (lower) value. The first user rolls back his transaction (restoring the inventory to its initial value), but the second user, thinking inventory is low, orders more stock and possibly creates a severe overstock. And that's if you're lucky.

Don't use the READ UNCOMMITTED isolation level unless you don't care about accurate results.

You *can* use READ UNCOMMITTED if you want to generate approximate statistical data, such as

✦ Maximum delay in filling orders

✦ Average age of salespeople who don't make quota

✦ Average age of new employees

In many such cases, approximate information is sufficient; the extra (performance) cost of the concurrency control required to give an exact result may not be worthwhile.

READ COMMITTED

The next highest level of isolation is READ COMMITTED: A change made by another transaction isn't visible to your transaction until the other user has committed the other transaction. This level gives you a better result than you can get from READ UNCOMMITTED, but it's still subject to a *nonrepeatable read* — a serious problem that creates a comedy of errors.

To illustrate, consider the classic inventory example. User 1 queries the database to see how many items of a particular product are in stock. The number is ten. At almost the same time, User 2 starts — and then commits — a transaction that records an order for ten units of that same product, decrementing the inventory, leaving none. Now User 1, having seen that ten are available, tries to order five of them. Five are no longer left, however. User 2 has, in effect, raided the pantry. User 1's initial read of the quantity available is not repeatable. The quantity has changed out from under User 1; any assumptions made on the basis of the initial read are not valid.

REPEATABLE READ

An isolation level of REPEATABLE READ guarantees that the nonrepeatable-read problem doesn't happen. This isolation level, however, is still haunted by the phantom read — a problem that arises when the data a user is reading changes in response to another transaction (and does not show the change on-screen) *while the user is reading it.*

Suppose, for example, that User 1 issues a command whose search condition (the WHERE clause or HAVING clause) selects a set of rows, and, immediately afterward, User 2 performs and commits an operation that changes the data in some of those rows. Those data items met User 1's search condition at the start of this snafu, but now they no longer do. Maybe some other rows that first did *not* meet the original search condition now *do* meet it. User 1, whose transaction is still active, has no inkling of these changes; the application behaves as if nothing has happened. The hapless User 1 issues another SQL statement with the same search conditions as the original one, expecting to retrieve the same rows. Instead, the second operation is performed on rows other than those used in the first operation. Reliable results go out the window, spirited away by the phantom read.

SERIALIZABLE

An isolation level of SERIALIZABLE is not subject to any of the problems that beset the other three levels. At this level, concurrent transactions can (in principle) be run serially — one after the other — rather than in parallel, and the results come out the same. If you're running at this isolation level, hardware or software problems can still cause your transaction to fail, but at least you don't have to worry about the validity of your results if you know that your system is functioning properly.

Of course, superior reliability may come at the price of slower performance, so we're back in Tradeoff City. Table 2-1 sums up the tradeoff terms, showing the four isolation levels and the problems they solve.

Table 2-1	Isolation Levels and Problems Solved
Isolation Level	*Problems Solved*
READ UNCOMMITTED	None
READ COMMITTED	Dirty read
REPEATABLE READ	Dirty read
	Nonrepeatable read
SERIALIZABLE	Dirty read
	Nonrepeatable read
	Phantom read

Committing a transaction

Although SQL doesn't require an explicit transaction-starting keyword, it has two that terminate a transaction: COMMIT and ROLLBACK. Use COMMIT when you have come to the end of the transaction and you want to make permanent the changes that you have made to the database (if any). You may include the optional keyword WORK (COMMIT WORK) if you want. If an error is encountered or the system crashes while a COMMIT is in progress, you may have to roll the transaction back and try it again.

Rolling back a transaction

When you come to the end of a transaction, you may decide that you don't want to make permanent the changes that have occurred during the transaction. In fact, you want to restore the database to the state it was in before the transaction began. To do this, issue a ROLLBACK statement. ROLLBACK is a fail-safe mechanism. Even if the system crashes while a ROLLBACK is in progress, you can restart the ROLLBACK after the system is restored, and it restores the database to its pretransaction state.

Why roll back a transaction?

It may be necessary to roll back a transaction if some kind of system failure occurs while the transaction is active. There are a number of possible causes for such a failure. Examples are

+ Power failure

+ Application program crash

+ Operating system crash

+ Failed peripheral device

+ Failed processor

+ System shutdown due to overheating

+ Hurricane or other weather damage

+ Electromagnetic storms due to solar coronal mass ejections

+ Bit flips due to cosmic rays

+ Terrorist attack

In most of the cases cited, although system operation is interrupted and everything in volatile main memory is lost, information stored on non-volatile hard disk is still intact, particularly if it's stored in a RAID array that is physically removed from the main system box. The good information on your hard disk forms the basis for a rollback operation that takes the system back to the condition it was in before the start of any of the transactions that were active when the service interruption occurred.

How can you roll back changes that have already been made? How can you undelete records that you have deleted? How can you restore fields that you have overwritten with new data? How can you remove new records that you have added? The answers to all these questions lie in the log file.

The log file

Because volatile semiconductor memory is so much faster than hard disk storage, when changes are made to a data file, they are not immediately written to hard disk, which is a relatively slow process. Instead, they are written to a page buffer in semiconductor memory. If those same logical memory locations must be accessed again fairly soon, the retrieval is much quicker from the page buffer than it would be from hard disk.

Eventually the page buffer fills up and when a new page is needed, one of the existing pages in the buffer must be swapped out to make room for the new page. During that period of time when information has been written to memory, but is still in the page buffer, it is vulnerable to a failure. When a failure occurs, everything in the page buffer, as well as everything in the system's main memory, is lost. The log file is the primary tool for recovering what has been lost and rendering the system able to redo the incomplete transactions.

The log file, primarily located on disk, but also necessarily partly in the page buffer, records every change that is made to the database. Log file entries pertaining to a transaction are always flushed from the page buffer to disk before the actual changes themselves. If a failure occurs between the time the log file entries are flushed to disk and the time the changes themselves would have been flushed, the changes can be reconstructed from the log file entries. The main idea is to make the window of vulnerability as short as possible. By frequently flushing log file entries to disk, that window is open only a crack. For all but the most ill-timed and severe failures, a minimum of data is lost, and it can be re-entered without too much trouble.

The write-ahead log protocol

The entries in the log file are made according to a formula known as the *write-ahead log protocol*. When a transaction prepares to write to a page containing some target record, it obtains an exclusive lock on the page. I discuss locks extensively later in this chapter. Before the transaction makes the modification to a record, it writes a log record containing the contents of the record both before and after the change. After the log record has been successfully written, the modification itself is written. The change is now sitting in the page buffer, where it is vulnerable to a power outage or other mischance that might require a reboot that erases all volatile storage.

If a failure occurs before the log record and modification are flushed to disk, they are lost. In that case, you must go back to the last good version on disk and redo everything from that point on. If a failure occurs after the log file has been written to disk but before the modification has been, the data in the log file enables full reconstitution of the change.

After a failure, the log file may contain information on

✦ Transactions that were committed, but not yet written to disk

✦ Transactions that were rolled back

✦ Transactions that were still active, and of course not yet written to disk

Transactions that were committed and not yet written to disk need to be redone. Transactions that were rolled back need to be undone. Transactions that were still active need to restarted. You can figure out which of these three actions to do by scanning the log file backwards in time, undoing actions as you go. When you come to a COMMIT statement, put that transaction into the redo list. When you come to a ROLLBACK statement, put that transaction into the undo list. Put the rest of the transactions into the restart list.

When you reach the beginning of the log, you have undone all of the transactions. Now scan forward to redo all the transactions on the redo list. Skip the transactions on the undo list because you have already undone them. Finally, submit the restart list to the DBMS to start those transactions from scratch.

Checkpoints

A log file may accumulate records of transactions for months or years, becoming quite large in the process. Scanning back through the log file can be time-consuming. There is no point in scanning back beyond a point where all transactions are guaranteed to have been safely stored on disk. To shorten the portion of the log that must be scanned, checkpoints are established at intervals. These intervals may be fixed units of time, for example 15 minutes, or they may come after a specific number of entries have been made in the log. In either case, at a checkpoint, all log entries in the page buffer are flushed to disk. This establishes a point beyond which you can be assured that all log entries and all committed transactions are safely on disk.

When a problem occurs that requires recovery, you need only concern yourself with transactions that were active at, or that started later than, the checkpoint. Transactions that were committed prior to the checkpoint will have been flushed to disk at the checkpoint, if not before. The same is true for transactions that were rolled back. Transactions that were active at the checkpoint have to be undone back to the point where they started, and then restarted.

Implementing deferrable constraints

Ensuring the validity of the data in your database means doing more than just making sure the data is of the right type. Perhaps some columns, for example, should never hold a null value — and maybe others should hold only values that fall within a certain range. Such restrictions are *constraints,* as discussed in Book I, Chapter 5.

Constraints are relevant to transactions because they can conceivably prevent you from doing what you want. For example, suppose that you want to add data to a table that contains a column with a NOT NULL constraint. One common method of adding a record is to append a blank row to your table and then insert values into it later. The NOT NULL constraint on one column, however, causes the append operation to fail. SQL doesn't allow you to add a row that has a null value in a column with a NOT NULL constraint, even though you plan to add data to that column before your transaction ends. To address this problem, SQL enables you to designate constraints as either DEFERRABLE or NOT DEFERRABLE.

Constraints that are NOT DEFERRABLE are applied immediately. You can set DEFERRABLE constraints to be either initially DEFERRED or IMMEDIATE. If a DEFERRABLE constraint is set to IMMEDIATE, it acts like a NOT DEFERRABLE constraint — it is applied immediately. If a DEFERRABLE constraint is set to DEFERRED, it is not enforced.

To append blank records or perform other operations that may violate DEFERRABLE constraints, ANSI/ISO standard SQL allows you to use a statement similar to the following:

```
SET CONSTRAINTS ALL DEFERRED ;
```

This statement puts all DEFERRABLE constraints in the DEFERRED condition. It does not affect the NOT DEFERRABLE constraints. After you have performed all operations that could violate your constraints, and the table reaches a state that doesn't violate them, you can reapply them. The statement that reapplies your constraints looks like this:

```
SET CONSTRAINTS ALL IMMEDIATE ;
```

If you made a mistake and any of your constraints are still being violated, you find out as soon as this statement takes effect.

If you do not explicitly set your DEFERRED constraints to IMMEDIATE, SQL does it for you when you attempt to COMMIT your transaction. If a violation is still present at that time, the transaction does not COMMIT; instead, SQL gives you an error message.

SQL's handling of constraints protects you from entering invalid data (or an invalid *absence* of data — which is just as important) while giving you the flexibility to violate constraints temporarily while a transaction is still active.

Consider a payroll example to see why being able to defer the application of constraints is important.

Assume that an EMPLOYEE table has columns EmpNo, EmpName, DeptNo, and Salary. EMPLOYEE.DeptNo is a foreign key referencing the DEPT table. Assume also that the DEPT table has columns DeptNo and DeptName. DEPT.DeptNo is the primary key.

In addition, you want to have a table like DEPT that also contains a Payroll column that holds the sum of the Salary values for employees in each department.

You can create the equivalent of this table with the following view:

```
CREATE VIEW DEPT2 AS
    SELECT D.*, SUM(E.Salary) AS Payroll
        FROM DEPT D, EMPLOYEE E
        WHERE D.DeptNo = E.DeptNo
        GROUP BY D.DeptNo ;
```

You can also define this same view as follows:

```
CREATE VIEW DEPT3 AS
    SELECT D.*,
        (SELECT SUM(E.Salary)
            FROM EMPLOYEE E
            WHERE D.DeptNo = E.DeptNo) AS Payroll
        FROM DEPT D ;
```

But suppose that, for efficiency, you don't want to calculate the sum every time you reference DEPT3.Payroll. Instead, you want to store an actual Payroll column in the DEPT table. You will then update that column every time you change a Salary.

To make sure that the Salary column is accurate, you can include a CONSTRAINT in the table definition:

```
CREATE TABLE DEPT
    (DeptNo CHAR(5),
    DeptName CHAR(20),
    Payroll DECIMAL(15,2),
    CHECK (Payroll = (SELECT SUM(Salary)
            FROM EMPLOYEE E WHERE E.DeptNo= DEPT.DeptNo)));
```

Now, suppose that you want to increase the Salary of employee 123 by 100. You can do it with the following update:

```
UPDATE EMPLOYEE
    SET Salary = Salary + 100
    WHERE EmpNo = '123' ;
```

Book IV
Chapter 2

Protecting Against
User Errors and
Conflicts

And you must remember to do the following as well:

```
UPDATE DEPT D
   SET Payroll = Payroll + 100
   WHERE D.DeptNo = (SELECT E.DeptNo
           FROM EMPLOYEE E
           WHERE E.EmpNo = '123') ;
```

(You use the subquery to reference the DeptNo of employee 123.)

But there's a problem: Constraints are checked after each statement. In principle, *all* constraints are checked. In practice, implementations check only the constraints that reference the values modified by the statement.

After the first preceding UPDATE statement, the implementation checks all constraints that reference values that the statement modifies. This includes the constraint defined in the DEPT table because that constraint references the Salary column of the EMPLOYEE table and the UPDATE statement is modifying that column. After the first UPDATE statement, that constraint is violated. You assume that before you execute the UPDATE statement, the database is correct, and each Payroll value in the DEPT table equals the sum of the Salary values in the corresponding columns of the EMPLOYEE table. When the first UPDATE statement increases a Salary value, this equality is no longer true. The second UPDATE statement corrects this and again leaves the database values in a state for which the constraint is True. Between the two updates, the constraint is False.

The SET CONSTRAINTS DEFERRED statement lets you temporarily disable or suspend all constraints, or only specified constraints. The constraints are deferred until either you execute a SET CONSTRAINTS IMMEDIATE statement, or you execute a COMMIT or ROLLBACK statement. So you surround the previous two UPDATE statements with SET CONSTRAINTS statements. The code looks like this:

```
SET CONSTRAINTS DEFERRED ;
UPDATE EMPLOYEE
   SET Salary = Salary + 100
   WHERE EmpNo = '123' ;
UPDATE DEPT D
   SET Payroll = Payroll + 100
   WHERE D.DeptNo = (SELECT E.DeptNo
           FROM EMPLOYEE E
     WHERE E.EmpNo = '123') ;
SET CONSTRAINTS IMMEDIATE ;
```

This procedure defers all constraints. If you insert new rows into DEPT, the primary keys won't be checked; you have removed protection that you may want to keep. Specifying the constraints that you want to defer is preferable. To do this, name the constraints when you create them:

```
CREATE TABLE DEPT
    (DeptNo CHAR(5),
    DeptName CHAR(20),
    Payroll DECIMAL(15,2),
    CONSTRAINT PayEqSumsal
    CHECK (Payroll = SELECT SUM(Salary)
    FROM EMPLOYEE E     WHERE E.DeptNo = DEPT.DeptNo)) ;
```

With constraint names in place, you can then reference your constraints individually:

```
SET CONSTRAINTS PayEqSumsal DEFERRED;
UPDATE EMPLOYEE
    SET Salary = Salary + 100
    WHERE EmpNo = '123' ;
UPDATE DEPT D
    SET Payroll = Payroll + 100
    WHERE D.DeptNo = (SELECT E.DeptNo
                    FROM EMPLOYEE E
                    WHERE E.EmpNo = '123') ;
SET CONSTRAINTS PayEqSumsal IMMEDIATE;
```

Without a constraint name in the CREATE statement, SQL generates one implicitly. That implicit name is in the schema information (catalog) tables, but specifying the names explicitly is more straightforward.

Now suppose that, in the second UPDATE statement, you mistakenly specified an increment value of 1000. This value is allowed in the UPDATE statement because the constraint has been deferred. But when you execute SET CONSTRAINTS . . . IMMEDIATE, the specified constraints are checked. If they fail, SET CONSTRAINTS raises an exception. If, instead of a SET CONSTRAINTS . . . IMMEDIATE statement, you execute COMMIT, and the constraints are found to be false, COMMIT instead performs a ROLLBACK.

Bottom line: You can defer the constraints only *within* a transaction. When the transaction is terminated by a ROLLBACK or a COMMIT, the constraints are both enabled and checked. The SQL capability of deferring constraints is meant to be used within a transaction. If used properly, it doesn't create any data that violates a constraint available to other transactions.

**Book IV
Chapter 2**

**Protecting Against
User Errors and
Conflicts**

Getting Familiar with Locking

The gold standard for maintaining database integrity is to operate on it with only serializable transactions. There are two major approaches to providing serializability: locking and timestamps. In this section, I look at locking. I cover timestamps in the section later in this chapter, "Enforcing Serializability with Timestamps."

If a transaction is granted a lock on a particular resource, access to that resource by competing transactions is restricted. There are two main kinds of locks:

✦ **Shared locks:** Two or more transactions, each with a shared lock, can concurrently read the contents of a memory location without interfering with each other. As long as none of the transactions attempts to change the data at that location, all of them can proceed without delay. The *lock manager* portion of the DBMS can grant shared locks to all transactions that only want to perform read operations. Shared locks are sometimes called *read locks*.

✦ **Exclusive locks:** In order to perform a write operation on a memory location, a transaction must acquire an exclusive lock. An *exclusive lock* grants to its holder the exclusive right to access the resource being locked. If one transaction holds an exclusive lock on a resource, no competing transaction may acquire either a shared lock or exclusive lock on that resource until the first transaction releases its lock. Exclusive locks are sometimes called *write locks*.

Two-phase locking

Two-phase locking is a protocol designed to guarantee serializability. In the first phase, a transaction can acquire shared and exclusive locks and may also upgrade a shared lock to an exclusive lock. It may not, however, release any locks or downgrade an exclusive lock to a shared lock. In the second phase, the transaction may release shared and exclusive locks and downgrade an exclusive lock to a shared lock, but may not acquire a new shared or exclusive lock, or upgrade a shared lock to an exclusive lock. In the strictest form of two-phase locking, the second phase, in which locks are released or downgraded, cannot occur until the transaction either commits or rolls back. This protects a competing transaction from acquiring a lock on and reading a value from a resource that the original transaction had released before aborting. In such a case the second transaction would potentially read a value that no longer existed in the resource. In fact, after a rollback, it is as if that value never existed.

Granularity

The granularity of a lock determines the size of the resource being locked. Locks that are coarse-grained take rather large resources out of circulation. Fine-grained locks sequester relatively small resources. Course-grained locks deny access to big things, such as tables. Fine-grained locks protect smaller things, such as a row in a table.

This list describes four different types of locks and the granularity of each:

✦ **Database locks:** The database lock is the ultimate in coarse-grained locks. If a transaction puts an exclusive lock on a database, no other transaction can access the database at all until the lock is released. As you might imagine, database locks have a disastrous effect on overall productivity and should be avoided if at all possible. Sometimes a DBA must apply a database lock to prevent other transactions from corrupting the database while she is making alterations to the database structure.

✦ **Table locks:** Table locks, by locking an entire database table, are not as restrictive as a database lock, but are still pretty coarse. Generally, you would only impose a table lock if you were altering the structure of the table or if you were changing data in most or all of the rows in the table.

✦ **Row locks:** Row locks are fine-grained in that they only lock a single row in a table. If you are changing only a value in a single row, there is no point in locking any rows other than that one target row. The only transactions that are impacted by a row lock are those that want to do something to the very same row of the very same table.

✦ **Page locks:** A page lock — which has an intermediate granularity between a table lock and a row lock — locks an entire page in the page buffer. Because information gets transferred between the page buffer and disk a page at a time, some DBMSs provide locks at the page level. As processing proceeds, requiring that pages currently residing in the page buffer be swapped out in favor of pages on disk that are currently needed, the DBMS will resist, if possible, the urge to swap out any page that is locked by an active transaction. Swapping it out, and then swapping it back in again soon, would waste a tremendous amount of time.

Deadlock

Deadlock is not a type of lock, or an example of granularity. It is a problem that can arise in even a well-designed system that uses locking for concurrency control. To illustrate how deadlock can happen, look again at the example where you and your friend Calypso share a bank account. Now that you are using transactions with two-phase locking, you don't have to worry about the lost update problem any more. However, there is still a potential problem. Once again, you and Calypso arrive at two different ATM machines at about the same time.

1. You insert your ATM card into your ATM.

2. The DBMS's lock manager grants you a shared lock on your account record, enabling you to read your balance of $47.17.

3. Calypso inserts her ATM card into her ATM.

4. The DBMS's lock manager grants Calypso a shared lock on your account record, enabling her to read the balance of $47.17.

5. You insert $100.00 in cash into your ATM.

6. The DBMS's lock manager attempts to upgrade your shared lock to an exclusive lock, but cannot because of Calypso's shared lock. It goes into a wait loop, waiting for Calypso's lock to be released.

7. Calypso inserts $100.00 in cash into her ATM.

8. The DBMS's lock manager attempts to upgrade Calypso's shared lock to an exclusive lock, but cannot because of your shared lock. It goes into a wait loop, waiting for your lock to be released.

9. The machine is deadlocked. Neither you nor Calypso can complete your transaction.

10. After some period of time, the DBMS recognizes the deadlock situation and aborts one or both of the deadlocked transactions.

Hopefully instances such as this don't come up too often. By putting your account update into a transaction, you have traded the lost update problem for the deadlock problem. This is an improvement. At least you don't end up with incorrect data in your database. However, it is a hassle to have to redo your ATM transaction. Hopefully you and Calypso don't both try to redo it at the same time.

Tuning Locks

Locks perform an important function in preserving the integrity of transactions. They prevent database corruption by making sure changes by one transaction do not affect the results of another transaction that is operating concurrently. However, they do so at a cost. Locks consume memory and also impact performance because it takes time to acquire a lock. Additional performance is lost while transactions wait for resources that have been locked by another. In some cases, such lockouts prevent data corruption, but, in other cases, locks are needlessly placed when harmful interactions cannot occur.

You can do some things to reduce the overhead burden of locking. Generally, you apply these measures only if performance becomes unsatisfactory. For some of the tuning interventions that I discuss here, you may have to trade off some accuracy in exchange for improved performance.

Measuring performance with throughput

What is performance, anyway? There are many ways of thinking about performance and many system parameters that you can measure to glean information about one aspect of performance or another. In this book, when I talk about performance, I am referring to throughput. *Throughput* is a measure of the amount of work that gets completed per unit time. It is an overall measure that takes into account all the jobs that are running on a system. If one job is running really fast, but its locks are slowing down all the other jobs that are running at the same time, throughput may well be lower than it would be if the first job were reconfigured in such a way that it did not run quite so fast, but held its locks for a shorter period of time.

Eliminating unneeded locks

Locks are designed to prevent concurrently running transactions from interfering with each other. They are applied automatically by the DBMS so the application programmer does not have to worry about whether she should apply a lock. However, at times, such interference is not possible. In those cases, the locking overhead is a burden on the system but there is no corresponding benefit in data integrity.

This is true when only one transaction is running at a time, such as when a database is loading. It is also true when all queries are guaranteed to be read-only; for example, when mining archived information. In such cases, it makes sense to take advantage of the option to suppress the acquisition of locks.

Shortening transactions

Long transactions, which do a lot of things, tend to hold locks for a long time. This, of course, has a negative effect on the performance of all the other transactions that are running at the same time. If everyone followed the discipline of making transactions as short as possible, everyone would benefit by being able to acquire needed locks sooner.

Book IV Chapter 2

Protecting Against User Errors and Conflicts

Albert Einstein once said, with regard to physics, "Make everything as simple as possible, but not simpler." The same logic applies here. Make transactions as short as possible, but not shorter. If you chop up transactions too finely, you could lose serializability, which means you could lose accuracy. For example, if you acquired a shared lock on your bank account, viewed your bank balance, and then dropped your shared lock before acquiring an exclusive lock to make a withdrawal, Calypso might have snuck in while your locks were down and cleaned out your account. This would have been both surprising and disappointing because you just read that there was plenty of money in your account.

Weaken isolation levels (but ver-r-ry carefully)

If you weaken your isolation level from serializable to REPEATABLE READ or perhaps READ COMMITTED, you can increase your throughput. However, there is a good chance that in doing so, bad data will creep into your database. In most cases, weakening your isolation level in that way isn't worth it.

There are a few scenarios where perfect accuracy in data is not required and when system response time is very important. In such cases, weakening the isolation level may be appropriate. Take for instance an airline reservation system.

Suppose an air traveler goes to an airline's online Web site that is running at the READ COMMITTED isolation level and looks up a particular flight. Checking on available seats is a read-only operation that puts a shared lock on the entire airplane. As soon as the cabin image is transmitted, the shared lock is dropped. The traveler decides that she would like to sit in seat 10-C, which shows as available. She clicks on that seat on her screen image to indicate that she wants to reserve that seat. The database attempts to put an exclusive lock on the record for seat 10-C, but fails. In the small interval of time between the database read and the attempted database write, someone else has reserved that seat and it is now unavailable.

This scenario could clearly happen with READ COMMITTED isolation. Is this a problem? Many airlines would think that it is not. Although such a sequence of events is possible, it also tends to be extremely rare. When it does occur, it is not a big deal. The traveler just directs a few choice words at the computer (the universal scapegoat) and successfully selects another seat. In exchange, all the travelers who use the reservation system benefit from faster response to their actions. This might be seen as a reasonable tradeoff.

Be sure to think through the possible problems that could occur if you weaken the isolation level of your database, and the consequences that follow from those problems. If you do decide to weaken the isolation level, it should be with full knowledge of the consequences.

Controlling lock granularity

In most systems, row-level locking, which is fine-grained, is the default. This is the best choice for maximizing throughput in an online transaction environment, such as an airline reservation system or a banking system. However, it's not necessarily the best on a system that runs long transactions that involve most of the rows in a table. In that kind of environment, a table lock, with lower overhead than a large number of row locks, could well deliver better overall throughput. Concurrent transactions could well be delayed to a lesser extent than they would be with row-level locking.

Don't just assume that the finest-grain locking setting is the best. Consider the types of jobs that are typically run and choose lock granularity accordingly.

Don't run DDL statements concurrently with transactions

Data Definition Language (DDL) statements such as CREATE TABLE, DROP INDEX, or ALTER TABLE operate on the system catalog. Because these operations are of such a fundamental nature, ordinary traffic comes to a standstill while they are active. In any normal installation, you are going to need to run some DDL statements from time to time. Just keep in mind the way they monopolize system resources and schedule them at a time when your normal transaction volume is light.

Partitioning insertions

Sequential insertion of records can be a bottleneck. If multiple transactions are inserting records sequentially onto the tail end of a table, they will all be hitting the same buffer page at about the same time and running into page locks. One strategy to relieve the congestion is to partition insertions to the table across different pages or even different disks. One way to achieve this is to set up a clustering index that is not based on time of insertion. This spreads out the inserted records to different pages.

Cooling down hot spots

Hot spots are those records, pages, or tables that everybody wants access to all at once. When a lengthy transaction acquires a lock on a hot item, everybody else suffers. You can do a couple of things to lower the temperature of chronic hot spots. One is to partition transactions as described in the preceding section. Another is to access hot spots as late as possible in a long transaction. This makes the overheated resource unavailable for the shortest amount of time.

Tuning the deadlock interval

Earlier I mention deadlock as a possible problem, even when you are running with a serializable isolation level. The common solution to the deadlock problem starts when the system senses that two or more transactions have not made any progress for an extended period of time. To break the deadlock, the system then forces the abort and rollback of one or perhaps all of the transactions involved. The deadlock interval is the period of time that the system waits before allowing an aborted transaction to restart. Clearly, you don't want to give all the aborted transactions the same deadlock interval. To do so would just be asking for another deadlock. Even if only one transaction is aborted, restarting it too soon could still conflict with a lengthy transaction that is still running.

So how do you choose a good deadlock interval? There is no one good answer, although there should be an element of randomness to it, so that you don't assign the same interval to both participants in a deadlock. Make an educated guess based on the types of transactions that you are running. If excessive deadlocks ensue, try changing the interval or the degree of variance between the deadlock interval of one aborted transaction and the deadlock interval of the other participant in the deadly embrace that started the whole mess.

Enforcing Serializability with Timestamps

Locks aren't the only effective mechanism for keeping concurrent transactions from interfering with each other. Another method involves timestamps. A *timestamp* is a centrally dispensed number assigned to each transaction in strictly increasing order. It could be based on the computer's real-time clock or it could just be a counter that is continually counting up. This method enables the system to determine which active transaction is the oldest, which is the youngest, and the relative positions of all transactions in between. In a conflict situation, the timestamp solution works by designating the younger transaction as the winner. To demonstrate this, look again at the bank account update example:

1. The system sets the timestamp to zero. This is the timestamp for a creating or updating operation.

2. You insert your ATM card into the ATM.

3. Your ATM pulls up your account and notes that you have a balance of $47.17. It sets the timestamp for your transaction to 1, and checks that 1 is greater than or equal to the timestamp of the youngest create or update operation in the system (0). One is greater than zero, so everything is fine.

4. Calypso inserts her ATM card into the ATM.

5. Calypso's ATM pulls up your account and notes that you have a balance of $47.17. It sets the timestamp for her transaction to 2, and checks that 2 is greater than or equal to the youngest create or update operation in the system (0). Two is greater than zero, so everything is fine.

6. You insert $100.00 in cash into your ATM.

7. Your ATM checks your timestamp (1) against the youngest timestamp in the system (2). 1 is not greater than or equal to 2, so you lose. There are no changes to the database to undo, so a new transaction is started for you with timestamp 3.

8. Calypso inserts $100.00 in cash into her ATM.

9. Calypso's ATM checks to see if her timestamp (2) is equal to or greater than the timestamp of the most recent read operation. It, so everything is fine. The ATM registers a balance of $147.17.

10. Your ATM pulls up your account and notes that you have a balance of $147.17. It also notes that your timestamp (3) is equal to or greater than the timestamp of the most recent read (2).

11. Calypso's transaction commits.

12. Your ATM checks that your timestamp (3) is equal to or greater than the timestamp of the most recent read (3). It is, so your update is accomplished and the account balance goes to $247.17.

13. Your transaction commits.

There was a little hitch in the proceedings, but you probably didn't even notice it standing there at the ATM machine. The account updates were performed properly.

The preceding scenario sounds great, but there are potential problems if timing is just a little bit off. Consider the following example:

1. The system sets the timestamp to zero. This is the timestamp for a creating or updating operation.

2. You insert your ATM card into the ATM.

3. Your ATM pulls up your account and notes that you have a balance of $47.17. It sets the timestamp for your transaction to 1 and checks that 1 is greater than or equal to the timestamp of the youngest create or update in the system (0). It is, so everything is fine.

4. Calypso inserts her ATM card into the ATM.

5. Calypso's ATM pulls up your account and notes that you have a balance of $47.17. It sets the timestamp for her transaction to 2 and checks that 2 is greater than or equal to the youngest create or update in the system (0). It is, so everything is fine.

6. You insert $100.00 in cash into your ATM.

7. Your ATM checks your timestamp (1) against the timestamp of the youngest read in the system (2). 1 is not greater than or equal to 2 so you lose. There are no changes to the database to undo, so a new transaction is started for you with timestamp 3.

8. Your new transaction checks your timestamp (3) against the timestamp of the youngest update in the system (0). Three is equal to or greater than zero, so everything is fine. Your transaction reads a balance of $47.17.

9. Calypso inserts $100.00 in cash into her ATM.

10. Calypso's ATM checks to see if her timestamp (2) is equal to or greater than the timestamp of the most recent read operation (3). It is not, so her transaction is aborted, and a new transaction with timestamp 4 is started for her.

11. Calypso's ATM checks to see if her timestamp (4) is equal to or greater than the timestamp of the most recent update operation (0). It is, so everything is fine. Her transaction reads a balance of $47.17.

12. Your ATM checks your timestamp (3) against the timestamp of the youngest read in the system (4). 3 is not greater than or equal to 4, so you lose. There are no changes to the database to undo, so a new transaction is started for you with timestamp 5.

13. And so on, ad infinitum.

This situation is called a *livelock,* as opposed to a deadlock. In a deadlock, two or more transactions are stuck in wait states because they cannot continue without a resource that has been acquired by another one of the deadlocked transactions. A livelock differs in that the participating transactions are continually processing, but are moving no closer to completion. They are stuck in a loop.

One way out of this situation is for the DBMS to keep a list of transactions that have been aborted some fixed number of times. When a transaction goes over the threshold, the DBMS can halt the normal flow of execution and execute the livelocked transactions serially.

Tuning the Recovery System

One thing you can do to maximize performance is to put your database log on a different disk from the disks that contain data. The log is continuously updated with every command that is performed. It just pours its information onto the log disk sequentially. This minimizes the amount of time the disk drive spends seeking because data is written sequentially to a single track, then to other tracks on the same cylinder, and then a short seek is made to an adjacent cylinder and the operation continues. In contrast, the data disks are constantly doing random seeks from one track to another. To mix that operation with the sequential writing of the log would cause a severe hit on performance.

Tuning the recovery system is always a balance between maximizing performance and maintaining system integrity. Although disk failures are rare, they do happen occasionally. Even if your system is protected with a RAID system, you should at intervals take a copy of your database offline. This copy, called a *database dump,* has an effect on performance because it uses resources while it is being run. The dump gives you a starting point if your hard disk system fails catastrophically. You must decide how often to perform database dumps by weighing the performance hit you take while it is running against the pain you would suffer if you didn't run it and a disk failure were to occur.

Similar considerations apply to checkpoints. At a *checkpoint,* all committed transactions are flushed to disk. This is a significant time-consumer because disk operations are orders of magnitude slower than data transfers to solid-state memory. Balanced against this is the time that checkpoints save you when that inevitable failure does occur. A checkpoint limits the distance you have to go back in the log in order to resynchronize the system after a failure. So how frequently should you force a checkpoint? Once again, it is a balance. Compare the overhead cost of a checkpoint to the time it saves you when you have to go to the log to recover consistency after a failure. Set the checkpoint interval at that sweet spot where you save more time in a recovery operation than the overhead of implementing the checkpoints is costing you.

Chapter 3: Assigning Access Privileges

In This Chapter

✓ Controlling operations with SQL

✓ Identifying users and specifying roles

✓ Categorizing users

✓ Granting privileges

✓ Taking privileges away

✓ Granting and revoking roles

*B*ecause databases are among the most valuable assets that any organization has, you must be able to control who has access to them, as well as what level of access to grant. SQL handles access management with the third of its main components, the Data Control Language (DCL). Whereas the Data Definition Language is used to create and maintain the structure of a database and the Data Manipulation Language is use to fill the database structure with data and then operate on that data, the DCL protects the database from unauthorized access and other potential problems.

The SQL Data Control Language

The Data Control Language consists of four SQL statements, and two of them (COMMIT and ROLLBACK) are discussed in Chapter 2 of this minibook. The other two DCL statements (GRANT and REVOKE) control who may access various parts of the database. Before you can grant database access to someone, you must have some way of identifying them. Some parts of that, such as the issuing of passwords and other security measures, are implementation-specific. SQL does however have a standard way of identifying and categorizing users so that the granting and revoking of privileges can be handled relatively easily.

Identifying Authorized Users

Users may be identified individually with a unique identifier, or they may be identified as a member of a group. Individually identified users can be given a customized array of access privileges, whereas group members all receive the same suite of privileges. Groups are defined by the roles the people in them play. People who all perform in the same role have the same access privileges.

User identifiers

SQL does not specify how a user identifier is assigned. In many cases, the operating system's login ID serves the purpose. A user identifier is one of two forms of authorization identifier that enables access to a database system. The other form is a role name, which I discuss in the next section.

Every SQL session is started by a user. That user's user identifier is called the *SQL-session user identifier*. The privileges associated with the SQL-session user identifier determine what privileges that user has and what actions she may perform during the session. When your SQL session starts, your SQL-session user identifier is also the *current user identifier*. The identity of the current user is kept in a special value named CURRENT_USER, which can be queried to find out who is currently in charge of a session.

Getting familiar with Roles

In a small company, identifying users individually does not present any problem. However, in a larger organization, with hundreds of employees doing a variety of different jobs, individually identifying users can become a burden. Every time someone leaves a company or their job responsibilities change or when a new person is hired, database privileges have to be adjusted. This is where roles come in.

Although a company may have hundreds or even thousands of employees, these employees do a limited number of different jobs. If everyone who plays the same role in the company requires the same database access privileges, you can assign those privileges to that group of people based on the roles they play in the organization. For example, one role might be SALES_CLERK. All the sales clerks require the same privileges. All the warehouse workers require different privileges, which is fine, because they play a different role in the company. In this way, the job of maintaining authorizations for everyone is made much simpler. A new sales clerk is added to the SALES_CLERK role name and immediately gains the privileges assigned to that role. A sales clerk leaving the company is deleted from the SALES_CLERK role name and immediately loses all database privileges. An employee changing from one job category to another is deleted from one role name and added to another.

Just as a session initiated by a user is associated with an SQL-session user identifier, it is also associated with an SQL-session *role name.* The value of the current role name is available in the CURRENT_ROLE special value. When an SQL-session is created, the current role name has a null value. At any given instant, either a user identifier is specified and the associated role name has a null value, or a role name is specified and the associated user identifier has a null value. A SET ROLE statement can create a situation where both the user identifier for a session and a role name are both non-null. In such a case, the privileges assigned to both the user identifier and to the role name are available to the user.

Creating roles

You can create a role with a single SQL statement. Here is the syntax:

```
CREATE ROLE <role name>
  [WITH ADMIN {CURRENT_USER | CURRENT_ROLE}] ;
```

When you create a role, the role is automatically granted to you. You are also granted the right to pass the role creation privilege on to others. When creating a role, you may identify yourself either as the current user or the current role. If you identify yourself as the current user, you are the only one who can operate on the new role. If you identify yourself as the current role, anyone who shares your current role with you is also able to operate on the new role.

Destroying roles

The syntax for destroying a role is really easy to understand:

```
DROP ROLE <role name> ;
```

Classifying Users

Aside from the fact that users may be members of a group identified as a role, there are four classes of users. Each of these classes has associated privileges that may supersede the privileges accorded to a user by virtue of her role. The four classes are

+ **The database administrator (DBA):** Every database has at least one and possibly multiple database administrators. It is the responsibility of the DBA to maintain the database, making sure that it is protected from harm and operating at peak efficiency. DBAs have full rights to all the objects in the database. They can create, modify, or destroy any object in the database, including tables and indexes. They can also decide what privileges other users may have.

✦ **Database object owners:** Users who create database objects such as tables and views are automatically the owners of those objects. A database object owner possesses all privileges related to that object. A database object owner's privileges are equal to those of a DBA, but only with respect to the object in question.

✦ **Grantees:** Grantees are users who have been granted selected privileges by either a DBA or database object owner. A grantee may or may not be given the right to grant his privileges to others, who thus also become grantees.

✦ **The public:** All users are considered part of the public, regardless of whether they have specifically been granted any privileges. Thus privileges that are granted to PUBLIC may be exercised by any user.

Granting Privileges

The GRANT statement is the tool you use to grant privileges to users. A fairly large number of privileges may be granted, and they may apply to a fairly large number of objects. As a result, the syntax of the GRANT statement is lengthy. Don't let the length intimidate you! It is all very logical, and fairly simple when you become familiar with it. Here's the syntax:

```
GRANT <privilege list>
  ON <privilege object>
  TO <user list> [WITH GRANT OPTION]
  [GRANTED BY {CURRENT_USER | CURRENT_ROLE}] ;

<privilege list> ::= privilege [ , privilege]...

<privilege> ::=
    SELECT [(<column name> [ , <column name>]...)]
  | SELECT (<method designator> [ , <method designator]...)
  | DELETE
  | INSERT [(<column name> [ , <column name>]...)]
  | UPDATE [(<column name> [ , <column name>]...)]
  | REFERENCES [(<column name> [ , <column name>]...)]
  | USAGE
  | TRIGGER
  | UNDER
  | EXECUTE

<privilege object> ::=
    [TABLE] <table name>
```

```
    | <view name>
    | DOMAIN <domain name>
    | CHARACTER SET <character set name>
    | COLLATION <collation name>
    | TRANSLATION <translation name>
    | TYPE <user-defined type name>
    | <specific routine designator>

    authorizationID [ , authorizationID]...
    | PUBLIC
```

Whew! That's a lot of syntax. Look at it piece by piece, so that it is a little more comprehensible. Not all privileges apply to all privilege objects. The SELECT, DELETE, INSERT, UPDATE, and REFERENCES privileges apply to the table privilege object. The SELECT privilege also applies to views. The USAGE privilege applies to the DOMAIN, CHARACTER SET, COLLATION, and TRANSLATION objects. The TRIGGER privilege applies, logically enough, to triggers. The UNDER privilege applies to user-defined types, and the EXECUTE privilege applies to specific routines.

Looking at data

The first privilege in the privilege list is the privilege of looking at a database object. The SELECT statement retrieves data from database tables and views. To enable a user to execute the SELECT statement, issue a GRANT SELECT statement. For example:

```
GRANT SELECT
   ON CUSTOMER
   TO SALES_MANAGER ;
```

This statement enables the sales manager to query the CUSTOMER table.

Deleting data

In a similar fashion, the GRANT DELETE statement enables a user to delete specified rows from a table.

```
GRANT DELETE
   ON CUSTOMER
   TO SALES_MANAGER ;
```

This enables the sales manager to prune inactive customers from the customer table.

Adding data

With the INSERT statement, you can add a new row of data to a table. The GRANT INSERT statement determines who has the right to perform this operation.

```
GRANT INSERT
   ON CUSTOMER
   TO SALES_MANAGER ;
```

Now the sales manager can add a new customer record to the CUSTOMER table.

Changing data

You can change the contents of a table row with the UPDATE statement. GRANT UPDATE determines who can do it.

```
GRANT UPDATE
   ON RETAIL_PRICE_LIST
   TO SALES_MANAGER ;
```

Now the sales manager can update the retail price list with new pricing information.

Referencing data in another table

You may think that if you can control who does the seeing, creating, modifying, and deleting functions on a table, you're well protected. Against most threats, you are. A knowledgeable hacker, however, can still break in by using an indirect method.

A correctly designed relational database has *referential integrity,* which means that the data in one table in the database is consistent with the data in all the other tables. To ensure referential integrity, database designers apply constraints to tables that restrict what someone can enter into the tables. If you have a database with referential integrity constraints, a user can possibly create a new table that uses a column in your confidential table as a foreign key. That column then serves as a link through which someone can possibly steal confidential information.

Say, for example, that you're a famous Wall Street stock analyst. Many people believe in the accuracy of your stock picks, so whenever you recommend a stock to your subscribers, many people buy that stock, and its value increases. You keep your analysis in a database that contains a table named FOUR_STAR. Your top recommendations for your next newsletter are in that table. Naturally, you restrict access to FOUR_STAR so that word doesn't leak out to the investing public before your paying subscribers receive the newsletter.

You're still vulnerable, however, if anyone other than yourself can create a new table that uses the stock name field of FOUR_STAR as a foreign key, as shown in the following command example:

```
CREATE TABLE HOT_STOCKS (
    Stock CHARACTER (30) REFERENCES FOUR_STAR
    );
```

The hacker can now try to insert the name of every stock on the New York Stock Exchange, American Stock Exchange, and NASDAQ into the table. Those inserts that succeed tell the hacker which stocks match the stocks that you name in your confidential table. It doesn't take long for the hacker to extract your entire list of stocks.

You can protect yourself from hacks such as the one in the preceding example by being very careful about entering statements similar to the following:

```
GRANT REFERENCES (Stock)
  ON FOUR_STAR
  TO SECRET_HACKER;
```

Of course, your hacker will not have a user identifier of SECRET_HACKER. More likely it will be something like JOHN_SMITH. However, beneath that innocent exterior lies a profiteer or agent of a competitor.

Avoid granting privileges to people who may abuse them. True, people don't come with guarantees printed on their foreheads. But if you wouldn't lend your new car to a person for a long trip, you probably shouldn't grant him the REFERENCES privilege on an important table either.

The preceding example offers one good reason for maintaining careful control of the REFERENCES privilege. Here are two other reasons for careful controlling REFERENCES, even if the other person is totally innocent:

+ If the other person specifies a constraint in HOT STOCKS by using a RESTRICT option and you try to delete a row from your table, the DBMS tells you that you can't because doing so violates a referential constraint.

+ If you want to use the DROP command to destroy your table, you find that you must get the other person to first drop his constraint (or his table).

The bottom line is that enabling another person to specify integrity constraints on your table not only introduces a potential security breach, but also means that the other user sometimes gets in your way.

Using certain database facilities

The USAGE privilege applies to domains and user-defined types (UDTs). In order to use or even see a domain or UDT, a user must have the USAGE privilege for that domain or UDT. Suppose Major League Baseball had a domain named MLBTEAMS that consisted of the names of all the Major League Baseball teams. A user holding the role of team owner could be granted usage of that domain as follows:

```
GRANT USAGE
   ON MLBTEAMS
   TO TEAM_OWNER ;
```

Responding to an event

You can grant a user or a role the privilege of creating a trigger that fires when a specified change takes place to a table, such as the renaming of a Major League Baseball team.

```
GRANT TRIGGER
   ON MLBTEAMS
   TO TEAM_OWNER ;
```

Defining new data types

One of the advanced features that was added to SQL in the SQL:1999 version was the ability of users to create structured user-defined types. Naturally, the creator of a UDT has all privileges attached to that UDT. Among those privileges is the USAGE privilege, which allows the type to be used to define columns, routines, and other schema objects. Also included is the UNDER privilege, which permits subtypes of the type to be defined.

```
GRANT UNDER
   ON MLBTEAMS
   TO LEAGUE_VICE_PRESIDENT ;
```

Executing an SQL statement

The EXECUTE privilege enables the grantee to invoke SQL-invoked routines. By restricting the ability to invoke routines, you keep those routines in the hands of those authorized to run them.

```
GRANT EXECUTE
    ON PRICECHANGE
    TO SALES_MANAGER ;
```

Doing it all

For a highly trusted person who has just been given major responsibility, rather than issuing a whole series of GRANT statements, you can take care of everything with just one statement, GRANT ALL:

```
GRANT ALL PRIVILEGES
    ON MLBTEAMS
    TO LEAGUE_VICE_PRESIDENT ;
```

However, GRANT ALL PRIVILEGES is a pretty dangerous statement. In the wrong hands it could cause a lot of damage. For this reason, SQL Server 2005 has deprecated this syntax. That means that although it is still supported, it may be removed in a later release.

Passing on the power

To keep your system secure, you must severely restrict the access privileges you grant and the people to whom you grant these privileges. But people who can't do their work because they lack access are likely to hassle you constantly. To preserve your sanity, you probably need to delegate some of the responsibility for maintaining database security. SQL provides for such delegation through the WITH GRANT OPTION clause. Consider the following example:

```
GRANT UPDATE
    ON RETAIL_PRICE_LIST
    TO SALES_MANAGER WITH GRANT OPTION ;
```

This statement is similar to the previous GRANT UPDATE example in that the statement enables the sales manager to update the retail price list. The statement also gives her the right to grant the update privilege to anyone she wants. If you use this form of the GRANT statement, you must not only trust the grantee to use the privilege wisely, but also trust her to choose wisely in granting the privilege to others.

The ultimate in trust, and therefore the ultimate in vulnerability, is to execute a statement such as the following:

```
GRANT ALL PRIVILEGES
    ON FOUR_STAR
    TO BENEDICT_ARNOLD WITH GRANT OPTION ;
```

Be *extremely* careful about using statements such as this one.

Book IV
Chapter 3

Assigning Access Privileges

Revoking Privileges

If it is possible to grant privileges to users and roles on a database, it better be possible to revoke those privileges too. Things change. People's jobs change, and their need for data changes too. Sometimes people leave the company and go to work for a competitor. You definitely want to revoke privileges in a case like that. The syntax for revoking privileges is similar to the GRANT syntax:

```
REVOKE [GRANT OPTION FOR] <privilege list>
   ON <privilege object>
   FROM <user list>
   [GRANTED BY (CURRENT_USER | CURRENT_ROLE)]
   (RESTRICT | CASCADE) ;
```

The privilege list, privilege object, and user list are the same as they are for GRANT. The major difference for the GRANT syntax is the addition of the RESTRICT and CASCADE keywords. Note that {RESTRICT | CASCADE} is not enclosed in square brackets, meaning that it is not optional. One of the two keywords is required in any REVOKE statement.

If a REVOKE statement includes the RESTRICT keyword, the DBMS checks to see if the privilege being revoked was passed on to one or more other users. If it was, the privilege is not revoked, and you receive an error message instead. If a REVOKE statement includes the CASCADE keyword, the DBMS revokes the privilege as well as any dependent instances of this privilege that were granted by the instance you are revoking.

With the optional GRANT OPTION FOR clause, you can revoke a user's ability to grant a privilege without revoking his ability to use the privilege himself. If you specify GRANT OPTION FOR along with CASCADE, not only is the grant option taken away, but everyone who obtained the privilege through that grant loses the privilege. If you specify GRANT OPTION FOR along with RESTRICT, and anyone had been granted the privilege under consideration, you get an error message, and the grant option is not revoked.

If the optional GRANTED BY clause is present, only those privileges granted by the current user or current role (whichever is specified) are revoked.

If none of the privileges you are trying to revoke actually exist, you get an error message, and nothing is changed. If some of the privileges you are trying to revoke exist, but others don't, you get a warning.

Revoking a user's privileges may not remove those privileges from the user. If you granted the SELECT privilege to Alice WITH GRANT OPTION, and she then granted the privilege to Bob, Bob now has the SELECT privilege. If you, at a later time, grant the SELECT privilege to Bob, he now has that privilege from two sources. If you now revoke the SELECT privilege from Bob, he still has SELECT access to the table in question because of the GRANT SELECT he received from Alice. This situation complicates revocation. If you want to truly be sure that a person no longer has access to a resource, you have to make sure that all grants have been revoked.

Granting Roles

Just as you can grant a privilege to a user, you can also grant a role to a user. Granting a role is a more significant action: When you grant a role to a person, you are granting all the privileges that go along with that role in one action. Here's the syntax:

```
GRANT <role name> [{ , <role name>}...]
  TO <user list>
  [WITH ADMIN OPTION]
  [GRANTED BY {CURRENT_USER | CURRENT_ROLE}] ;
```

As you can see from the syntax, you can grant any number of roles to the names on a list of users with a single GRANT statement. The optional WITH ADMIN OPTION clause is similar to the WITH GRANT OPTION clause that might be a part of a grant of privileges. If you want to grant a role and extend to the grantee the right to grant the same role to others, you do so with the WITH ADMIN OPTION clause. The optional GRANTED BY clause specifies whether you want to record that this GRANT was granted by the current user or by the current role. This distinction may become meaningful when the time comes to revoke the role granted here.

Revoking Roles

The command for revoking a role is very similar to the command for revoking a privilege. Here's what it looks like:

```
REVOKE [ADMIN OPTION FOR] <role name> [{ , <role name>}...]
  FROM <user list>
  [GRANTED BY {CURRENT_USER | CURRENT_ROLE}]
  {RESTRICT | CASCADE}
```

Here you revoke one or more roles from the users in the user list. You can revoke the admin option from a role without revoking the role itself. The GRANTED BY clause requires a little explanation. If a role was specified as being granted by the current user, revoking it with a GRANTED BY

CURRENT_USER clause works, but revoking it with GRANTED BY CURRENT_ROLE clause doesn't. The RESTRICT or CASCADE keywords only apply if the admin option has been used to grant the specified role to other users or roles. If RESTRICT is specified and this role or list of roles has been granted to a sub-grantee, an error message is returned, and the revocation doesn't take effect. If CASCADE is specified and this role or list or roles has been granted to a sub-grantee, the role and all the sub-grantee roles are revoked.

Chapter 4: Error Handling

In This Chapter

✔ **Identifying error conditions**

✔ **Discovering SQLSTATE**

✔ **Handling conditions**

✔ **Using the** WHENEVER **clause**

✔ **The diagnostics areas**

✔ **Examining a constraint violation example**

✔ **Adding constraints to an existing table**

✔ **Interpreting SQLSTATE information**

✔ **Handling exceptions**

Wouldn't it be great if every application you wrote worked perfectly every time? Yeah, and it would also be really cool to win $210 million in the Powerball lottery. Unfortunately, both possibilities are about as likely to happen. Error conditions of one sort or another are inevitable, so it's helpful to know what causes them. SQL's mechanism for returning error information to you is the *status parameter* (or *host variable*) SQLSTATE. Based on the contents of SQLSTATE, you can take different actions to remedy the error condition.

For example, the WHENEVER directive enables you to take a predetermined action whenever a specified condition (if SQLSTATE has a non-zero value, for example) is met. You can also find detailed status information about the SQL statement that you just executed in the diagnostics area. In this chapter, I explain these helpful error-handling facilities and how to use them. First, however, I show you the conditions that might cause those error-handling facilities to be invoked.

Identifying Error Conditions

When people say that a person has a "condition," they usually mean that something is wrong with that person — he is sick or injured. People usually don't bother to mention that a person is in *good* condition; rather, we talk about people who are in serious condition or, even worse, in critical condition. This idea is similar to the way programmers talk about the condition of an SQL statement. The execution of an SQL statement leads to a successful result, a questionable result, or an outright erroneous result. Each of these possible results corresponds to a condition.

Getting to Know SQLSTATE

Every time an SQL statement executes, the database server places a value into the status parameter SQLSTATE. SQLSTATE is a five-character field. It accepts the twenty-six uppercase letters and the numerals 0 through 9. The value that is placed into SQLSTATE indicates whether the preceding SQL statement executed successfully. If it did not execute successfully, the value of SQLSTATE provides some information about the error.

The first two of the five characters of SQLSTATE (the class value) give you the major news as to whether the preceding SQL statement executed successfully, returned a result that may or may not have been successful, or produced an error. Table 4-1 shows the four possible results.

Table 4-1	SQLSTATE Class Values
Class	*Description*
00	Successful completion
01	Warning
02	Not found
Other	Exception

The following list further explains the class values:

✦ **00:** Indicates that the preceding SQL statement executed successfully. This is a very happy and welcome result — most of the time.

✦ **01:** Indicates a warning. This means that something unusual happened during the execution of the SQL statement. This occurrence may or may not be an error — the DBMS can't tell. The warning is a heads-up to the developer, suggesting that perhaps she should check the preceding SQL statement carefully to ensure that it's operating correctly.

✦ **02:** Indicates that no data was returned as a result of the execution of the preceding SQL statement. This may or may not be good news, depending on what the developer was trying to do with the statement. For example, sometimes an empty result table is exactly what the developer wanted the SQL statement to return.

✦ **Any class code other than** 00, 01, **or** 02: Indicates an error condition. An indication of the nature of the error appears in the three characters that hold the subclass value. The two characters of the class code, plus the three characters of the subclass code, together comprise the five characters of SQLSTATE.

The SQL standard defines any class code that starts with the letters *A* through *H* or the numerals 0 through 4; therefore, these class codes mean the same thing in any implementation. Class codes that start with the letters *I* through *Z* or the numerals 5 through 9 are left open for *implementors* (the people who build database management systems) to define because the SQL specification can't anticipate every condition that may come up in every implementation. However, implementors should use these nonstandard class codes as little as possible to avoid migration problems from one DBMS to another. Ideally, implementors should use the standard codes most of the time and the non-standard codes only under the most unusual circumstances.

Because SQLSTATE updates after every SQL operation, you can check it after every statement executes. If SQLSTATE contains 00000 (successful completion), you can proceed with the next operation. If it contains anything else, you may want to branch out of the main line of your code to handle the situation. The specific class code and subclass code that an SQLSTATE contains determines which of several possible actions you should take.

To use SQLSTATE in a module language program, where SQL statements are called from a module by a host program written in a procedural language such as C, include a reference to it in your procedure definitions, as in the following example:

```
PROCEDURE POWERPLANT
    (SQLSTATE, :enginename CHAR (20), :displacement SMALLINT,
        :hp INTEGER, :cylinders INTEGER, :valves INTEGER
INSERT INTO ENGINES
    (EngineName, Displacement, Horsepower, Cylinders, Valves)
    VALUES
    (:enginename, :displacement, :hp, :cylinders, :valves) ;
```

At the appropriate spot in your procedural language program, you can make values available for the parameters (perhaps by soliciting them from the user) and then call up the procedure. The syntax of this operation varies from one language to another, but it looks something like this:

```
enginename = "289HP" ;
displacement = 289 ;
hp = 271 ;
cylinders = 8 ;
valves = 16 ;
POWERPLANT(state, enginename, displacement, hp, cylinders, valves);
```

**Book IV
Chapter 4**

Error Handling

The state of SQLSTATE is returned in the variable state. Your program can examine this variable and then take the appropriate action based on the variable's contents.

Handling Conditions

You can have your program look at SQLSTATE after the execution of every SQL statement. What do you do with the knowledge that you gain?

+ **If you find a class code of 00, you probably don't want to do anything.** You want execution to proceed as you originally planned.

+ **If you find a class code of 01 or 02, you may or may not want to take special action.** If you expected the "Warning" or "Not Found" indication, you probably want to let execution proceed normally. If you didn't expect either of these class codes, you probably want to have execution branch to a procedure that is specifically designed to handle the unexpected, but not totally unanticipated, warning or not found result.

+ **If you receive any other class code, something is wrong.** You should branch to an exception-handling procedure. The specific procedure that you choose to branch to depends on the contents of the three subclass characters, as well as the two class characters of SQLSTATE. If multiple different exceptions are possible, there should be an exception-handling procedure for each one because different exceptions often require different responses. Some errors may be correctable, or you may find a workaround. Other errors may be fatal, calling for termination of the application.

Handler declarations

You can put a condition handler within a compound statement. To create a condition handler, you must first declare the condition that it will handle. The condition declared can be some sort of exception, or it can just be something that is true. Table 4-2 lists the possible conditions and includes a brief description of what causes each type of condition.

Table 4-2	Conditions That May Be Specified in a Condition Handler
Condition	*Description*
SQLSTATE VALUE 'xxyyy'	Specific SQLSTATE value
SQLEXCEPTION	SQLSTATE class other than 00, 01, or 02
SQLWARNING	SQLSTATE class 01
NOT FOUND	SQLSTATE class 02

The following is an example of a condition declaration:

```
DECLARE constraint_violation CONDITION
        FOR SQLSTATE VALUE '23000' ;
```

Handler actions and handler effects

If a condition occurs that invokes a handler, the action specified by the handler executes. This action is an SQL statement, which can be a compound statement. If the handler action completes successfully, the handler effect executes. The following is a list of the three possible handler effects:

✦ **CONTINUE:** Continue execution immediately after the statement that caused the handler to be invoked.

✦ **EXIT:** Continue execution after the compound statement that contains the handler.

✦ **UNDO:** Undo the work of the previous statements in the compound statement, and continue execution after the statement that contains the handler.

If the handler was able to correct whatever problem invoked the handler, the CONTINUE effect may be appropriate. The EXIT effect may be appropriate if the handler didn't fix the problem, but the changes made to the compound statement do not need to be undone. The UNDO effect is appropriate if you want to return the database to the state it was in before the compound statement started execution. Consider the following example:

```
BEGIN ATOMIC
    DECLARE constraint_violation CONDITION
        FOR SQLSTATE VALUE '23000' ;
    DECLARE UNDO HANDLER
        FOR constraint_violation
        RESIGNAL ;
    INSERT INTO students (StudentID, Fname, Lname)
        VALUES (:sid, :sfname, :slname) ;
    INSERT INTO roster (ClassID, Class, StudentID)
        VALUES (:cid, :cname, :sid) ;
END ;
```

If either of the INSERT statements causes a constraint violation, such as adding a record with a primary key that duplicates a primary key already in the table, SQLSTATE assumes a value of 23000, thus setting the constraint_violation condition to a true value. This action causes the handler to undo any changes that have been made to any tables by either INSERT command. The RESIGNAL statement transfers control back to the procedure that called the currently executing procedure.

If both INSERT statements execute successfully, execution continues with the statement following the END keyword.

The ATOMIC keyword is mandatory whenever a handler's effect is UNDO. This is not the case for handlers whose effect is either CONTINUE or EXIT.

Conditions that aren't handled

In the preceding example, consider this possibility: What if an exception occurred that returned an SQLSTATE value other than 23000? Something is definitely wrong, but the exception handler that you coded can't handle it. What happens now? Because the current procedure doesn't know what to do, a RESIGNAL occurs. This bumps the problem up to the next higher level of control. If the problem does not get handled there, it continues to be elevated to higher levels until it is either handled or it causes an error condition in the main application.

The idea that I want to emphasize here is that if you write an SQL statement that may cause exceptions, you should write exception handlers for all such possible exceptions. If you don't, you will have more difficulty isolating the source of the problem when it inevitably occurs.

Dealing with Execution Exceptions: The WHENEVER Clause

What's the point of knowing that an SQL operation didn't execute successfully if you can't do anything about it? If an error occurs, you don't want your application to continue executing as if everything is fine. You need to be able to acknowledge the error and do something to correct it. If you can't correct the error, at the very least you want to inform the user of the problem and bring the application to a graceful termination. The WHENEVER directive is the SQL mechanism for dealing with execution exceptions.

The WHENEVER directive is actually a declaration and is therefore located in your application's SQL declaration section, before the executable SQL code. The syntax is as follows:

```
WHENEVER <condition> <action> ;
```

The condition may be either SQLERROR or NOT FOUND. The action may be either CONTINUE or GOTO address. SQLERROR is True if SQLSTATE has a class code other than 00, 01, or 02. NOT FOUND is True if SQLSTATE is 02000.

If the action is CONTINUE, nothing special happens, and the execution continues normally. If the action is GOTO address (or GO TO address), execution branches to the designated address in the program. At the branch address, you can put a conditional statement that examines SQLSTATE and takes different actions based on what it finds. Here are some examples of this scenario:

```
WHENEVER SQLERROR GO TO error_trap ;
```

or

```
WHENEVER NOT FOUND CONTINUE ;
```

The GO TO option is simply a macro: The implementation (that is, the embedded language precompiler) inserts the following test after every EXEC SQL statement:

```
IF SQLSTATE <> '00000'
   AND SQLSTATE <> '00001'
   AND SQLSTATE <> '00002'
THEN GOTO error_trap;
```

The CONTINUE option is essentially a NO-OP that says "ignore this."

Getting More Information: The Diagnostics Areas

Although SQLSTATE can give you some information about why a particular statement failed, the information is pretty brief. So SQL provides for the capture and retention of additional status information in diagnostics areas. Multiple diagnostics areas are maintained in the form of a last-in-first-out (LIFO) stack. Information on the most recent error can be found at the top of the stack. The additional status information in a diagnostics area can be particularly helpful in cases in which the execution of a single SQL statement generates multiple warnings followed by an error. SQLSTATE only reports the occurrence of one error, but the diagnostics area has the capacity to report on multiple (hopefully all) errors.

The diagnostics area is a DBMS-managed data structure that has two components:

✦ **Header:** The header contains general information about the last SQL statement that was executed.

✦ **Detail area:** The detail area contains information about each code (error, warning, or success) that the statement generated.

The diagnostics header area

In the SET TRANSACTION statement (described in Chapter 2 of this mini-book), you can specify DIAGNOSTICS SIZE. The SIZE that you specify is the number of detail areas allocated for status information. If you don't include a DIAGNOSTICS SIZE clause in your SET TRANSACTION statement, your DBMS assigns its default number of detail areas, whatever that happens to be.

The header area contains ten items, as listed in Table 4-3.

Table 4-3	Diagnostics Header Area
Fields	*Data Type*
NUMBER	Exact numeric with no fractional part
ROW_COUNT	Exact numeric with no fractional part
COMMAND_FUNCTION	VARCHAR (>=128)
COMMAND_FUNCTION_CODE	Exact numeric with no fractional part
DYNAMIC_FUNCTION	VARCHAR (>=128)
DYNAMIC_FUNCTION_CODE	Exact numeric with no fractional part
MORE	Exact numeric with no fractional part
TRANSACTIONS_COMMITTED	Exact numeric with no fractional part
TRANSACTIONS_ROLLED_BACK	Exact numeric with no fractional part
TRANSACTION_ACTIVE	Exact numeric with no fractional part

The following list describes these items in more detail:

✦ The NUMBER field is the number of detail areas that have been filled with diagnostic information about the current exception.

✦ The ROW_COUNT field holds the number of rows affected if the previous SQL statement was an INSERT, UPDATE, or DELETE.

✦ The COMMAND_FUNCTION field describes the SQL statement that was just executed.

✦ The COMMAND_FUNCTION_CODE field gives the code number for the SQL statement that was just executed. Every command function has an associated numeric code.

✦ The DYNAMIC_FUNCTION field contains the dynamic SQL statement.

✦ The DYNAMIC_FUNCTION_CODE field contains a numeric code corresponding to the dynamic SQL statement.

✦ The MORE field may be either a Y or an N. Y indicates that there are more status records than the detail area can hold. N indicates that all the status records generated are present in the detail area. Depending on your implementation, you may be able to expand the number of records you can handle by using the SET TRANSACTION statement.

✦ The TRANSACTIONS_COMMITTED field holds the number of transactions that have been committed.

✦ The TRANSACTIONS_ROLLED_BACK field holds the number of transactions that have been rolled back.

✦ The TRANSACTION_ACTIVE field holds a 1 if a transaction is currently active and a 0 otherwise. A transaction is deemed to be active if a cursor is open or if the DBMS is waiting for a deferred parameter.

The diagnostics detail area

The detail areas contain data on each individual error, warning, or success condition. Each detail area contains 28 items, as Table 4-4 shows.

Table 4-4	Diagnostics Detail Area
Fields	*Data Type*
CONDITION_NUMBER	Exact numeric with no fractional part
RETURNED_SQLSTATE	CHAR (6)
MESSAGE_TEXT	VARCHAR (>=128)
MESSAGE_LENGTH	Exact numeric with no fractional part
MESSAGE_OCTET_LENGTH	Exact numeric with no fractional part
CLASS_ORIGIN	VARCHAR (>=128)
SUBCLASS_ORIGIN	VARCHAR (>=128)
CONNECTION_NAME	VARCHAR (>=128)
SERVER_NAME	VARCHAR (>=128)
CONSTRAINT_CATALOG	VARCHAR (>=128)
CONSTRAINT_SCHEMA	VARCHAR (>=128)
CONSTRAINT_NAME	VARCHAR (>=128)
CATALOG_NAME	VARCHAR (>=128)
SCHEMA_NAME	VARCHAR (>=128)
TABLE_NAME	VARCHAR (>=128)
COLUMN_NAME	VARCHAR (>=128)
CURSOR_NAME	VARCHAR (>=128)

**Book IV
Chapter 4**

Error Handling

(continued)

Table 4-4 *(continued)*

Fields	Data Type
CONDITION_IDENTIFIER	VARCHAR (>=128)
PARAMETER_NAME	VARCHAR (>=128)
PARAMETER_ORDINAL_POSITION	Exact numeric with no fractional part
PARAMETER_MODE	Exact numeric with no fractional part
ROUTINE_CATALOG	VARCHAR (>=128)
ROUTINE_SCHEMA	VARCHAR (>=128)
ROUTINE_NAME	VARCHAR (>=128)
SPECIFIC_NAME	VARCHAR (>=128)
TRIGGER_CATALOG	VARCHAR (>=128)
TRIGGER_SCHEMA	VARCHAR (>=128)
TRIGGER_NAME	VARCHAR (>=128)

CONDITION_NUMBER holds the sequence number of the detail area. If a statement generates five status items that fill up five detail areas, the CONDITION_NUMBER for the fifth detail area is five. To retrieve a specific detail area for examination, use a GET DIAGNOSTICS statement (described later in this chapter in the "Interpreting SQLSTATE Information" section) with the desired CONDITION_NUMBER. RETURNED_SQLSTATE holds the SQLSTATE value that caused this detail area to be filled.

CLASS_ORIGIN tells you the source of the class code value returned in SQLSTATE. If the SQL standard defines the value, the CLASS_ORIGIN is ISO 9075. If your DBMS implementation defines the value, CLASS_ORIGIN holds a string identifying the source of your DBMS. SUBCLASS_ORIGIN tells you the source of the subclass code value returned in SQLSTATE.

CLASS_ORIGIN is important. If you get an SQLSTATE of 22012, for example, the values indicate that it is in the range of standard SQLSTATEs, so you know that it means the same thing in all SQL implementations. However, if the SQLSTATE is 22500, the first two characters are in the standard range and indicate a data exception, but the last three characters are in the implementation-defined range. And if SQLSTATE is 900001, it's completely in the implementation-defined range. SQLSTATE values in the implementation-defined range can mean different things in different implementations, even though the code itself may be the same.

So how do you find out the detailed meaning of 22500 or the meaning of 900001? You must look in the implementor's documentation. Which implementor? If you're using CONNECT, you may be connecting to various products. To determine which one produced the error condition, look at CLASS_ORIGIN and SUBCLASS_ORIGIN: They have values that identify each implementation. You can test the CLASS_ORIGIN and SUBCLASS_ORIGIN to see whether they identify implementors for which you have the SQLSTATE listings. The actual values placed in CLASS_ORIGIN and SUBCLASS_ORIGIN are implementor-defined, but they also are expected to be self-explanatory company names.

If the error reported is a constraint violation, the CONSTRAINT_CATALOG, CONSTRAINT_SCHEMA, and CONSTRAINT_NAME fields identify the constraint being violated.

Examining a Constraint Violation Example

The constraint violation information is probably the most important information that GET DIAGNOSTICS provides. I discuss GET DIAGNOSTICS in the "Interpreting SQLSTATE Information" section, a bit later in this chapter. Consider the following EMPLOYEE table:

```
CREATE TABLE EMPLOYEE (
   ID CHAR(5) CONSTRAINT EmpPK PRIMARY KEY,
   Salary DEC(8,2) CONSTRAINT EmpSal CHECK Salary > 0,
   Dept CHAR(5) CONSTRAINT EmpDept,
   REFERENCES DEPARTMENT) ;
```

And this DEPARTMENT table:

```
CREATE TABLE DEPARTMENT (
   DeptNo CHAR(5),
   Budget DEC(12,2) CONSTRAINT DeptBudget
   CHECK(Budget >= SELECT SUM(Salary) FROM EMPLOYEE,
         WHERE EMPLOYEE.Dept=DEPARTMENT.DeptNo),
   ...);
```

Now consider an INSERT as follows:

```
INSERT INTO EMPLOYEE VALUES(:ID_VAR, :SAL_VAR, :DEPT_VAR);
```

Now suppose that you get an SQLSTATE of 23000. You look it up in your SQL documentation, and it says "integrity constraint violation." Now what? That SQLSTATE value means that one of the following situations is true:

✦ **The value in ID_VAR is a duplicate of an existing ID value:** You have violated the PRIMARY KEY constraint.

✦ **The value in SAL_VAR is negative:** You have violated the CHECK constraint on Salary.

**Book IV
Chapter 4**

Error Handling

✦ **The value in DEPT_VAR isn't a valid key value for any existing row of DEPARTMENT:** You have violated the REFERENCES constraint on Dept.

✦ **The value in SAL_VAR is large enough that the sum of the employees' salaries in this department exceeds the BUDGET:** You have violated the CHECK constraint in the BUDGET column of DEPARTMENT. (Recall that if you change the database, all constraints that may be affected are checked, not just those defined in the immediate table.)

Under normal circumstances, you would need to do a great deal of testing to figure out what is wrong with that INSERT. But you can find out what you need to know by using GET DIAGNOSTICS as follows:

```
DECLARE ConstNameVar CHAR(18) ;
GET DIAGNOSTICS EXCEPTION 1
   ConstNameVar = CONSTRAINT_NAME ;
```

Assuming that SQLSTATE is 23000, this GET DIAGNOSTICS sets ConstNameVar to EmpPK, EmpSal, EmpDept, or DeptBudget. Notice that, in practice, you may also want to obtain the CONSTRAINT_SCHEMA and CONSTRAINT_CATALOG to uniquely identify the constraint given by CONSTRAINT_NAME.

Adding Constraints to an Existing Table

This use of GET DIAGNOSTICS — determining which of several constraints has been violated — is particularly important in the case where ALTER TABLE is used to add constraints that didn't exist when you wrote the program:

```
ALTER TABLE EMPLOYEE
   ADD CONSTRAINT SalLimit CHECK(Salary < 200000) ;
```

Now if you insert data into EMPLOYEE or update the Salary column of EMPLOYEE, you get an SQLSTATE of 23000 if Salary exceeds 200000. You can program your INSERT statement so that, if you get an SQLSTATE of 23000 and you don't recognize the particular constraint name that GET DIAGNOSTICS returns, you can display a helpful message, such as Invalid INSERT: Violated constraint SalLimit.

Interpreting SQLSTATE Information

CONNECTION_NAME and ENVIRONMENT_NAME identify the connection and environment to which you are connected at the time the SQL statement is executed.

If the report deals with a table operation, CATALOG_NAME, SCHEMA_NAME, and TABLE_NAME identify the table. COLUMN_NAME identifies the column within the table that caused the report to be made. If the situation involves a cursor, CURSOR_NAME gives its name.

Sometimes a DBMS produces a string of natural language text to explain a condition. The MESSAGE_TEXT item is for this kind of information. The contents of this item depend on the implementation; the SQL standard doesn't explicitly define them. If you do have something in MESSAGE_TEXT, its length in characters is recorded in MESSAGE_LENGTH, and its length in octets is recorded in MESSAGE_OCTET_LENGTH. If the message is in normal ASCII characters, MESSAGE_LENGTH equals MESSAGE_OCTET_LENGTH. If, on the other hand, the message is in Kanji or some other language whose characters require more than an octet to express, MESSAGE_LENGTH differs from MESSAGE_OCTET_LENGTH.

To retrieve diagnostic information from a diagnostics area header, use the following:

```
GET DIAGNOSTICS status1 = item1 [, status2 = item2]... ;
```

Status*n* is a host variable or parameter; item*n* can be any of the keywords NUMBER, MORE, COMMAND_FUNCTION, DYNAMIC_FUNCTION, or ROW_COUNT.

To retrieve diagnostic information from a diagnostics detail area, the syntax is as follows:

```
GET DIAGNOSTICS EXCEPTION <condition number>
    status1 = item1 [, status2 = item2]... ;
```

Again, status*n* is a host variable or parameter, and item*n* is any of the 28 keywords for the detail items listed in Table 4-4. The condition number is (surprise!) the detail area's CONDITION_NUMBER item.

Handling Exceptions

When SQLSTATE indicates an exception condition by holding a value other than 00000, 00001, or 00002, you may want to handle the situation by

✦ Returning control to the parent procedure that called the subprocedure that raised the exception.

✦ Using a WHENEVER clause to branch to an exception-handling routine or perform some other action.

✦ Handing the exception on the spot with a *compound* SQL statement. A compound SQL statement consists of one or more simple SQL statements, sandwiched between BEGIN and END keywords.

The following is an example of a compound-statement exception handler:

```
BEGIN
    DECLARE ValueOutOfRange EXCEPTION FOR SQLSTATE '74001' ;
    INSERT INTO ENGINES
        (Displacement)
        VALUES
        (:displacement) ;
    SIGNAL ValueOutOfRange ;
    MESSAGE 'Process the next displacement value.'
    EXCEPTION
        WHEN ValueOutOfRange THEN
            MESSAGE 'Handling the displacement range error' ;
        WHEN OTHERS THEN
            RESIGNAL ;
END
```

With one or more DECLARE statements, you can give names to specific SQLSTATE values that you suspect may arise. The INSERT statement is the one that might cause an exception to occur. If the value of :displacement exceeds the maximum value for a SMALLINT data item, SQLSTATE is set to 74001. The SIGNAL statement signals an exception condition. It clears the top diagnostics area. It sets the RETURNED_SQLSTATE field of the diagnostics area to the SQLSTATE for the named exception. If no exception has occurred, the series of statements represented by the MESSAGE 'Process the next displacement value' statement is executed. However, if an exception has occurred, that series of statements is skipped, and the EXCEPTION statement is executed.

If the exception was a ValueOutOfRange exception, the series of statements represented by the MESSAGE 'Handling the displacement range error' statement is executed. If it was any other exception, the RESIGNAL statement is executed. RESIGNAL merely passes control of execution to the calling parent procedure. That procedure may have additional error-handling code to deal with exceptions other than the expected value out-of-range error.

Book V

SQL and Programming

The 5th Wave   By Rich Tennant

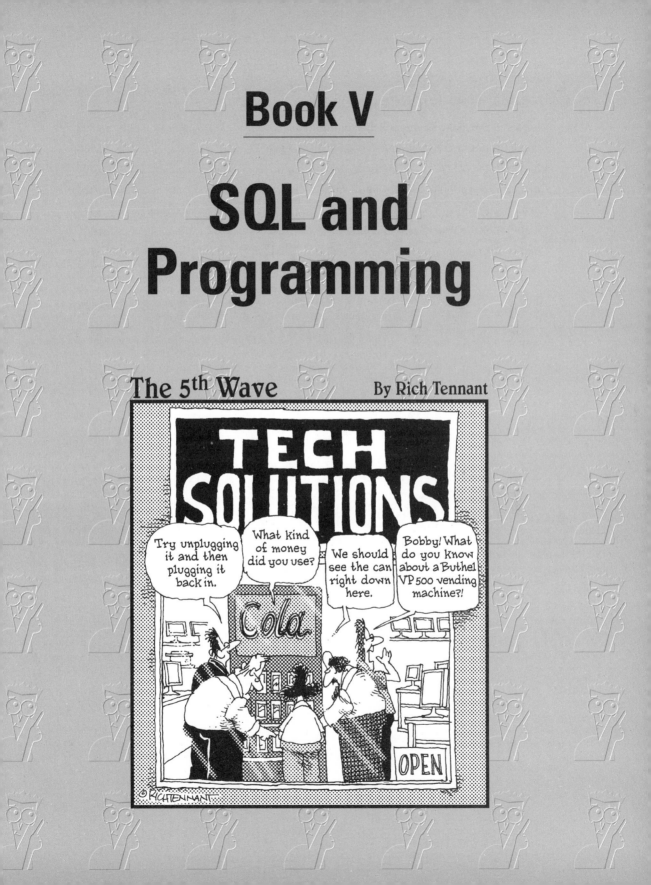

Contents at a Glance

Chapter 1: Database Development Environments

In This Chapter

✓ **Microsoft Access**

✓ **Microsoft SQL Server**

✓ **IBM DB2**

✓ **Oracle 10g**

✓ **MySQL**

*A*side from organizations that locked themselves into a database environment before about 1985, anybody who is using a database system now is probably using a relational database system. Any relational database system that is still around today uses a version of SQL for communication between users and data. Although a number of specialty database products serve specific niche markets, for general use, a relatively small number of DBMS products have significant market share. These products are Access and SQL Server from Microsoft, DB2 from IBM, Oracle from Oracle Corporation, and MySQL from MySQL AB.

In this chapter, I take a brief look at the popular RDBMS products with regard to how they implement SQL.

Microsoft Access

Microsoft Access, like all relational database management systems today, uses SQL for communication between the user and the database. However, it does a really good job of hiding that fact. Access comes with a procedural language called VBA (Visual Basic for Applications). The normal way of writing a data-driven application is to write it in VBA and make use of a library of classes for dealing with the data. The tools for doing that have undergone a massive upheaval in recent years. The back end database engine part of Access, called the Jet Engine, has undergone changes and expanded in flexibility. In addition, the recommended method of 'talking' to the Jet engine has gone through one change after another.

The Jet engine

The Jet engine originated in 1992 as the back end of Access 1.0. Initially it did not support data access via SQL, but in a later version implemented a subset of SQL-92 functionality. In the early days, connecting to native Access .mdb files was done exclusively with DAO (Data Access Objects). ISAM drivers enabled connecting to xBase, Paradox, FoxPro, and Btrieve databases. Later, ODBC made it possible to connect to SQL Server databases, Oracle databases, or any other ODBC-compliant database.

DAO

The DAO (Data Access Objects) interface to the Jet database engine is an object-oriented DLL (Dynamic-Link Library) that creates a workspace object within which all database operations are performed. The DAO DLL, for a number of years used with other products in addition to Access, has been superseded and deprecated for those other uses. However, it remains in the playbook for Access, including Microsoft Office Access 2007.

ADO

ADO (ActiveX Data Objects) was introduced by Microsoft in 1996 as a successor to DAO and as yet another alternative to SQL. Developers can create database applications using ADO without any knowledge of SQL. High-level procedural languages Visual Basic, VBScript, Delphi, and C++ Builder support the ADO interface.

ODBC

ODBC (Open Database Connectivity) is a procedural API (Application Programming Interface) that connects an SQL query to a database. First developed and released by Microsoft in 1992, ODBC has since come to be used by many different programming environments to access many different databases. Hundreds of ODBC drivers exist. Microsoft's version of ODBC ships with every supported version of Windows. Open-source implementations are widely used by Unix and Unix-derived operating systems.

OLE DB

OLE DB (Object Linking and Embedding Database) is a Microsoft API, designed as a successor to ODBC, for accessing a wide variety of data stores, including but not limited to SQL-compliant relational databases. OLE DB interfaces also work with such diverse data sources as object databases, text files, and spreadsheets.

MDB

One of the unusual characteristics of Access databases is that they are entirely contained in a single file. All versions of Access up to and including Access Office 2007 store data, metadata, and everything else in a file with a .mdb extension.

ACCDB

Access Office 2007 has a new database engine that operates on a new file format, with a .accdb extension. This format enables new features, chief among with is interoperability with Microsoft Office SharePoint Server 2007. The .accdb format is not usable by earlier versions of Access, so if you read in a .mdb file, but then write it out in .accdb format, it will no longer run on older versions of Access.

Microsoft SQL Server

SQL Server is Microsoft's primary entry in the database arena. Ranging from the entry-level SQL Server Express 2005 to the unlimited-class SQL Server 2005 Enterprise Edition, SQL Server is based on Microsoft's Transact-SQL, which, in contrast to the SQL in Access, is a full-featured robust implementation of the SQL:1999 international standard that also includes numerous proprietary extensions to the standard syntax. SQL Server runs only under Microsoft operating systems. You can connect to a SQL Server 2005 database via the new SQL Native Client. It is compatible with ODBC, OLE DB, and ADO.NET.

IBM DB2

DB2 is IBM's full-range relational database management system. Scaling from a single user to an unlimited-class enterprise DBMS, DB2 also features a robust implementation of SQL. DB2 operates in a variety of environments, including Microsoft Windows, IBM mainframe z/OS, Unix, and Linux. DB2 supports a wide variety of interfaces, including

- ✦ ODBC
- ✦ OLE DB
- ✦ ADO

+ JDBC (Java-based Database Connectivity)

+ SQLJ (Java-based Embedded SQL)

+ SQL

+ DRDA (X/Open Distributed Database Standard)

+ CLI (X/Open Database Access Standard)

+ EDA/SQL (IBI's EDA SQL Standard)

+ DAL (Apple Relational Database Standard APIs)

+ Net.Data (Internet Database Access)

Oracle 10g

Oracle 10g is the current version of Oracle Corporation's full-range database management system. Oracle Version 2 was the first commercial relational database product when it hit the market in 1979. Oracle has retained a leading position in the marketplace ever since. Oracle's implementation of SQL, called PL/SQL, is a very complete implementation, conforming to the latest version of the ANSI/ISO standard, SQL:2003, as well as offering useful proprietary extensions.

Oracle Database 10g supports all standard relational data types and can be connected to in numerous ways, such as with PL/SQL, JDBC, SQLJ, ODBC.NET, OLE.NET, ODP.NET, XML, XQUERY, and WebDAV. You can write stored procedures in Java, PL/SQL, or using .NET CLR support.

MySQL

MySQL is an open-source DBMS that has grown in capability over the years to the point where it is competitive with the other DBMS products mentioned here in terms of SQL functionality that it supports. MySQL 5.0 is a full-featured implementation of SQL. It offers ODBC, JDBC, and OLE DB connectivity, as well as APIs for most popular languages including C, C++, Python, Tcl, Perl, PHP, and Eiffel.

Chapter 2: Interfacing SQL to a Procedural Language

In This Chapter

✔ **Microsoft Access**

✔ **Microsoft SQL Server**

✔ **MySQL**

✔ **Oracle 10g**

✔ **IBM DB2**

*Y*ou cannot build a user-friendly database application with SQL alone. SQL is a data sublanguage and as such lacks many of the facilities required to build a user interface or even execute a sequence of steps. Building a moderately sophisticated application that involves the data in a database requires a procedural language in addition to SQL. Most DBMSs offer compatibility with several procedural languages. Which ones in particular are offered depends on the source of the DBMS and its history, as well as considerations of what capabilities users are most likely to need. In this chapter, I discuss the most common ways of connecting and interfacing to the most popular DBMS products, Access, SQL Server, MySQL, Oracle 10g, and IBM DB2.

Building an Application with SQL and a Procedural Language

Although languages such as C, Java, and Visual Basic do not intrinsically support database operations, you can use those languages to write procedures that perform such operations. The vendors of database management systems, in order to make their products more usable, make available libraries of such procedures. Some of these procedures perform operations that SQL cannot perform. Others work with SQL to perform a needed function. As a result, in some environments, you can create quite complex database operations without ever having to resort to SQL. Read on to find out how this issue is addressed by the popular database platforms.

Access and VBA

VBA (Visual Basic for Applications) is a subset of Microsoft's Visual Basic language, specifically designed to be the procedural language to go along with Microsoft Access. Hundreds of libraries are available to the VBA database programmer. Figure 2-1 shows the References dialog box, accessible from the Visual Basic Editor's Tools menu, which in turn is accessible from the Access Tools menu, under Macro.

Figure 2-1:
Visual Basic Editor's References dialog box enables you to select libraries to include with your program.

Two of the most important libraries for most applications are the ADODB library and the ADOX library.

The ADODB library

The ADODB library has a small memory footprint and contains basic procedures that just about every application needs. Programs that use this library are not burdened with having to carry along a bunch of procedures that they never use. In keeping with the object-oriented nature of the ADO (ActiveX Data Objects) object model, the library contains objects that perform basic functions. Those functions include

+ Making connections

+ Issuing commands

+ Retrieving recordsets

+ The ability to navigate within a recordset

+ Basic maintenance tasks

Clearly, any application that deals with a database has to connect to it before it can do anything else. The ADODB library gives you that capability with the connection object. In addition the library contains procedures for retrieving data from a data source, specifying a location within the database, and setting the type of locking that will be in force. The command object works with the SQL DML commands to perform SELECT, UPDATE, INSERT, and DELETE operations.

The ADOX library

ADOX is short for ADO Extensions for DDL and Security. DDL is of course SQL's Data Definition Language, which is that part of SQL used to create and destroy database objects. With the ADOX library, you can create tables, indexes, keys, groups, user identities, and views. You can also delete any of those things.

Other libraries

In addition to the general-purpose libraries with broad applicability, there are many specialty libraries that may be of value to your application. Be sure to check on what is available from your DBMS vendor or independent third parties before you go about "reinventing the wheel."

SQL Server and the .NET languages

Microsoft's .NET initiative introduces the idea of "managed code" as a way of eliminating several of the most common sources of programming bugs and as a way to eliminate the chaos and lack of portability that comes when each language has its own API that is not compatible with any other. The .NET languages, such as Visual Basic.NET and C#, among others, all create code that runs under the control of the Common Language Runtime (CLR). The CLR provides just-in-time compilation, memory management, type safety enforcement, exception handling, thread management, and security.

Regardless of what .NET language you write in, your code gets compiled down to Common Intermediate Language (CIL). As a result, the .NET languages are all essentially equivalent and so anything you can do with any one of them, you can do with all of them. If you feel more comfortable writing in Visual Basic.NET, go for it. You can do everything that the people writing in C# or C++.NET can do. When you are programming in the .NET world, you can make use of the thousands of classes, structs, interfaces, enumerations, and delegates in the .NET Framework Class Library. Because every language uses the same API, after you learn the .NET Framework as it applies to one language, you have learned it as it applies to any other.

How does this relate to SQL? Microsoft's implementation of SQL, Transact-SQL, runs on the database server to operate on data stored there. The managed code you write in VB.NET, C#, or any of the other .NET languages can run on either the server or the client. This is welcome flexibility when you want to minimize the computational load on the server. Many of the functions that have traditionally been performed by Transact-SQL can be performed by managed code, in many cases more efficiently. The net result (no pun intended) is a reduction in the overall use of SQL in applications that are written in a .NET language.

MySQL and C++.NET or C#

Although .NET technology was developed by Microsoft, it works with non-Microsoft products such as the open-source database MySQL. You can access MySQL from C++.NET or C# via an ODBC data provider or the MySQL.Data.dll connector. In either case, you have the advantages of managed code, but do not need to use a proprietary DBMS such as SQL Server. All the resources of the .NET Framework are available for you to use against a MySQL database. This might well enable you to do some data manipulations with MySQL that you could not do by using MySQL's implementation of SQL in conjunction with other languages.

MySQL and C

MySQL provides a client library written in C. The library enables you to access a MySQL database from within an application program written in C. The library provides an API that defines how clients establish contact with the database server, and how communication is handled. Other languages, such as Perl, PHP, Java, Python, C++, and Tcl, all have client APIs that are built on top of the C library.

MySQL and Perl

Perl scripts connect to MySQL databases through the Perl interpreter. The Perl interpreter comprises two levels, the database interface (DBI) level and the database driver (DBD) level. The DBI is generic and can direct commands to a MySQL driver, but also to a PostgreSQL driver or drivers that connect to other kinds of databases. Perl, an interpreted scripting language, is probably the most commonly used language for developing MySQL applications.

MySQL and PHP

PHP, like Perl, is an interpreted scripting language, but unlike Perl is especially designed for the development of Web applications. It provides a means of embedding executable scripts into Web pages. The Web page is processed by PHP before being sent to the client for display. This enables the script to generate dynamic content.

Oracle SQL and Java

You can connect to an Oracle database from a Java program using either of two technologies:

✦ **SQLJ:** SQLJ statements may appear anywhere in a Java program where a Java statement may appear. All SQLJ statements begin with #sql to distinguish them from other Java statements. There are two kinds of SQLJ statements:

  • **Declarations:** With a declaration, you can establish a connection to a database. You can also use a declaration to store result sets that come back from the database.

  • **Executable statements:** Executable statements execute embedded SQL statements and PL/SQL blocks. PL/SQL consists of extensions to SQL for performing procedural operations. Executable expressions may also be used to exchange information between the Java program and the database, using variables.

✦ **JDBC:** JDBC is an API, similar to ODBC, for connecting Java programs to a wide variety of database back ends.

DB2 and Java

IBM's DB2 database is accessible to Java application programs via SQLJ and JDBC. JDBC drivers of various types are available on platforms that include Linux, Unix, and Windows, as well as IBM proprietary operating systems such as OS/390, z/OS, and iSeries. SQLJ applets and applications contain embedded SQL statements that are precompiled and bound to a DB2 UDB database. The SQLJ driver translates the embedded SQL code into Java code.

SQL user-defined functions (UDFs) can be in the form of Java modules. Stored procedures can also be created from Java classes. With UDFs, you can extend the functionality of the "plain vanilla" SQL provided by DB2. Putting program logic into stored procedures, which reside on the server improves performance by reducing traffic between the client and the server. Instead of the client issuing a command and receiving a response for each operation, the client merely calls the stored procedure, which performs all the operations and then, at the end, returns the final result to the client.

Chapter 3: Using SQL in an Application Program

In This Chapter

✔ Comparing languages

✔ Determining difficulties getting languages to work with SQL

✔ Embedding SQL in a procedural program

✔ Using SQL modules

*S*QL was originally conceived and implemented with one objective in mind: to create and maintain a structure for data to be stored in a relational database. It was never intended to be a complete language that you could use to create application programs. Application programming was and is the domain of procedural languages such as Fortran, COBOL, Ada, C, and Basic.

Clearly, there is a need for application programs that deal with databases. These require a combination of the features of a procedural language such as C and a data sublanguage such as SQL. Fundamental differences between the architectures and philosophies of procedural languages and of SQL make combining them a challenge. In this chapter, I take a look at the characteristics of and differences between those two very different worlds.

Comparison of SQL to Procedural Languages

SQL is strong in data retrieval. If important information is buried somewhere in a single-table or multitable database, SQL gives you the tools you need to retrieve it. You don't need to know the order of the table's rows or columns because SQL doesn't deal with rows or columns individually. The SQL transaction-processing facilities ensure that your database operations are unaffected by any other users who may be simultaneously accessing the same tables that you are.

A major weakness of SQL is its rudimentary user interface. It has no provision for formatting screens or reports. It accepts command lines from the keyboard and sends retrieved values to the terminal, one row at a time.

Sometimes a strength in one context is a weakness in another. One strength of SQL is that it can operate on an entire table at once. Whether the table has one row, a hundred rows, or a hundred thousand rows, a single SELECT statement can extract the data you want. SQL can't easily operate on one row of a multirow table at a time, however, and sometimes you do want to deal with each row individually. In such cases, you can use SQL's cursor facility, described in Chapter 5 of Book III, or you can use a procedural host language.

Speaking of procedural host languages, what are their strengths and weaknesses? In contrast to SQL, procedural languages are designed for one-row-at-a-time operation, which allows the application developer precise control over the way a table is processed. This detailed control is a great strength of procedural languages. But a corresponding weakness is that the application developer must have detailed knowledge of the way data is stored in the database tables. The order of the database's columns and rows is significant and must be taken into account.

Because of the step-by-step nature of procedural languages, they have the flexibility to produce user-friendly screens for data entry and viewing. You can also produce sophisticated printed reports, with any desired layout.

Classic procedural languages

Classic procedural languages are the first languages used to program computers and their descendants. The very first languages were machine languages, in which both instructions and data were represented as ones and zeros. Digital computers are binary machines and ones and zeros are the only things they understand. Unfortunately, long sequences of ones and zeros are not particularly easy for humans to understand, so it was not long before machine language was superseded by assembly language, and then by compiled high-level languages such as Fortran and COBOL. C and Basic are examples of more recent classic procedural languages.

Classic procedural languages such as C and Basic are complete programming languages. They can implement any procedure that can be represented in algorithmic form. They primarily operate by executing one command after another in sequence, although they also have flow of control structures that enable them to branch, either unconditionally or depending on the value of a condition. They also support loops, which enable a program to execute a section of code repeatedly. SQL, as defined by the SQL-92 international standard, did not have these capabilities. Additions to the standard that became part of SQL:1999 have added some of these capabilities, but not all implementations of SQL have as yet been upgraded to support them.

Object-oriented procedural languages

Object-oriented programming, whose first incarnation was Simula-67 in 1967, came into its own in the 1990s when it became the predominant programming paradigm. Large, complex software projects that would have been very difficult to build with one of the classical procedural languages were more easily accomplished using one or another of the object-oriented languages such as C++, Java, C#, Python, or Visual Basic.NET.

The fundamental unit of a program written in an object-oriented language is the *object,* whereas the *instruction* is the fundamental unit of a classic procedural language program. Each object in an object-oriented program can receive messages sent by other objects, process data, and send messages to other objects.

Object-oriented code is intrinsically modular, which makes object-oriented programs easier to develop, understand, and maintain than programs generated according to the earlier, classic paradigm. Objects are members of classes. A class has associated attributes and methods. Attributes are characteristics of a class, and methods are actions that members of the class can perform.

Non-procedural languages

SQL is an example of a non-procedural language. Rather than dealing with the data in a table one row at a time, it deals with data a set at a time. This means that a query might return a result set containing multiple rows all at once. This is in contrast to procedural languages, both classic and object-oriented, that process tables one row at a time, and return data to the application the same way, one row at a time.

In the early days of relational databases, other non-procedural languages competed with SQL. Among these were QUEL and RDML. QUEL was the data sublanguage of the Ingres database management system that was initially developed at the University of California at Berkeley and later commercialized. It is now sold as an open-source product by Ingres Corporation. Due to the overwhelming acceptance of SQL in the marketplace, SQL syntax has been added to QUEL. RDML is the data sublanguage for Digital Equipment Corporation's Rdb relational database products. Alas, both Rdb and Digital Equipment itself have passed into history.

Although SQL was developed by IBM, it was adopted at a very early stage by the company that was to become Oracle Corporation. Other DBMS vendors followed suit, and SQL became a *de facto* standard. The de facto standard was codified into a recognized "official" standard in 1986. SQL did not beat out QUEL and RDML because of its technical superiority, which was debatable. It won because of IBM's market clout and because Oracle's early adoption of it started a "domino effect" of DBMS vendors joining the club and supporting SQL.

Difficulties in Combining SQL with a Procedural Language

Any time the database and the programming language that is addressing it are using different data models, problems are going to occur. Beyond data models, differences in data types add to the problem. SQL's data types do not match the data types of any of the languages that try to communicate with SQL databases. Despite these challenges, SQL and procedural languages must be made to work together because neither one by itself can do the complete job.

Challenges to using SQL with a classical procedural language

It makes sense to try to combine SQL and procedural languages in such a way that you can benefit from their strengths and not be penalized by their weaknesses. As valuable as such a combination may be, some challenges must be overcome before it can be achieved practically.

Contrasting operating modes

A big problem in combining SQL with a procedural language is that SQL operates on tables a set at a time, whereas procedural languages work on them a row at a time. Sometimes this isn't a big deal. You can separate set operations from row operations, doing each with the appropriate tool. But if you want to search a table for records meeting certain conditions and perform different operations on the records depending on whether they meet the conditions, you may have a problem. Such a process requires both the retrieval power of SQL and the branching capability of a procedural language. Embedded SQL gives you this combination of capabilities by enabling you to *embed* SQL statements at strategic locations within a program that you have written in a conventional procedural language. Other solutions to this problem include proprietary APIs and module language.

Data type incompatibilities

Another hurdle to the smooth integration of SQL with any procedural language is that SQL's data types are different from those of all major procedural languages. This circumstance shouldn't be surprising because the data types defined for any procedural language are different from the types for the other procedural languages. No standardization of data types exists across languages. In releases of SQL prior to SQL-92, data type incompatibility was a major concern. In SQL-92 (and also in subsequent releases of the SQL standard), the CAST statement addresses the problem. Book III, Chapter 1 explains how you can use CAST to convert a data item from the procedural language's data type to one recognized by SQL, as long as the data item itself is compatible with the new data type.

Challenges to using SQL with an object-oriented procedural language

The challenges mentioned above with regard to using SQL with classic procedural languages apply equally when using SQL with object-oriented procedural languages. Added to those however, are additional incompatibilities, often called the impedance mismatch between SQL and object-oriented languages. The original context of the term *impedance mismatch* comes from electrical engineering. Different parts of an electrical circuit may have different impedance values. Connecting two such circuit elements can cause problems. As a simple example, suppose an audio speaker with an intrinsic impedance of 8 ohms is connected to a line with a 50-ohm impedance value. The result is sound that is attenuated, distorted, and noisy. In the context of SQL and object-oriented procedural languages, similar problems occur. The row and column organization of relational tables do not mesh well with the hierarchical class/object paradigm of object-oriented programming.

Database vendors have addressed the impedance mismatch problem by adding object-oriented features to their relational database products, turning their hybrid products into *object-relational* database management systems. The object-oriented features added to such products as DB2, Oracle, and SQL Server were codified in the SQL:1999 international standard.

SQL:1999 notwithstanding, the marriage of SQL to object-oriented languages such as C++, C#, or Visual Basic.NET is not a perfect one. Difficulties remain, but they are manageable ones.

Embedding SQL in an Application

The most common method of mixing SQL with procedural languages is called *embedded SQL*. The name is descriptive: SQL statements are dropped into the middle of a procedural program, wherever they're needed. As you may expect, an SQL statement that suddenly appears in the middle of a C program, for example, can present a challenge for a compiler that isn't expecting it. For that reason, programs containing embedded SQL are usually passed through a preprocessor before being compiled or interpreted. The preprocessor is warned of the imminent appearance of SQL code by a preprocessor directive such as EXEC SQL.

Embedding SQL in an Oracle Pro*C application

As an example of embedded SQL, look at a program written in Oracle's Pro*C version of the C language. The program, which accesses a company's employee table, prompts the user for an employee name and then displays that employee's salary and commission. It then prompts the user for new salary and commission data and updates the employee table with it:

```
EXEC SQL BEGIN DECLARE SECTION;
     VARCHAR uid[20];
     VARCHAR pwd[20];
     VARCHAR ename[10];
     FLOAT salary, comm;
     SHORT salary_ind, comm_ind;
EXEC SQL END DECLARE SECTION;
#include <stdio.h>
main()
{
     int sret;              /* scanf return code */
     /* Log in */
     strcpy(uid.arr,"FRED");    /* copy the user name */
     uid.len=strlen(uid.arr);
     strcpy(pwd.arr,"TOWER");   /* copy the password */
     pwd.len=strlen(pwd.arr);
     EXEC SQL WHENEVER SQLERROR STOP;
     EXEC SQL WHENEVER NOT FOUND STOP;
     EXEC SQL CONNECT :uid;
     printf("Connected to user: percents \n",uid.arr);
     printf("Enter employee name to update:  ");
     scanf("percents",ename.arr);
     ename.len=strlen(ename.arr);
     EXEC SQL SELECT SALARY,COMM INTO :salary,:comm
                FROM EMPLOY
                WHERE ENAME=:ename;
     printf("Employee: percents salary: percent6.2f comm:
percent6.2f \n",
```

```
                   ename.arr, salary, comm);
       printf("Enter new salary:  ");
       sret=scanf("percentf",&salary);
       salary_ind = 0;
       if (sret == EOF !! sret == 0)    /* set indicator */
            salary_ind =-1;     /* Set indicator for NULL */
       printf("Enter new commission:  ");
       sret=scanf("percentf",&comm);
       comm_ind = 0;    /* set indicator */
       if (sret == EOF !! sret == 0)
            comm_ind=-1;           /* Set indicator for NULL */
       EXEC SQL UPDATE EMPLOY
               SET SALARY=:salary:salary_ind
               SET COMM=:comm:comm_ind
               WHERE ENAME=:ename;
       printf("Employee percents updated. \n",ename.arr);
       EXEC SQL COMMIT WORK;
       exit(0);
}
```

You don't have to be an expert in C to understand the essence of what this program is doing and how the program does it. Here's a rundown of the order in which the statements execute:

1. SQL declares host variables.

2. C code controls the user login procedure.

3. SQL sets up error handling and connects to the database.

4. C code solicits an employee name from the user and places it in a variable.

5. An SQL SELECT statement retrieves the named employee's salary and commission data and stores them in the host variables :salary and :comm.

6. C then takes over again and displays the employee's name, salary, and commission and then solicits new values for salary and commission. It also checks to see that an entry has been made, and if one has not, it sets an indicator.

7. SQL updates the database with the new values.

8. C then displays an "operation complete" message.

9. SQL commits the transaction, and C finally exits the program.

You can mix the commands of two languages like this because of the pre-processor. The *preprocessor* separates the SQL statements from the host language commands, placing the SQL statements in a separate external routine. Each SQL statement is replaced with a host language CALL of the corresponding external routine. The language compiler can now do its job. The way the SQL part is passed to the database is implementation-dependent. You, as the application developer, don't have to worry about any of this. The preprocessor takes care of it. You *should* be concerned about a few things, however, that do not appear in interactive SQL — things such as host variables and incompatible data types.

Declaring host variables

Some information must be passed between the host language program and the SQL segments. You do this with *host variables*. In order for SQL to recognize the host variables, you must declare them before you use them. Declarations are included in a declaration segment that precedes the program segment. The declaration segment is announced by the following directive:

```
EXEC SQL BEGIN DECLARE SECTION ;
```

The end of the declaration segment is signaled by

```
EXEC SQL END DECLARE SECTION ;
```

Every SQL statement must be preceded by an EXEC SQL directive. The end of an SQL segment may or may not be signaled by a terminator directive. In COBOL, the terminator directive is END-EXEC; in FORTRAN, it's the end of a line; and in Ada, C, Pascal, and PL/I, it's a semicolon.

Converting data types

Depending on the compatibility of the data types supported by the host language and those supported by SQL, you may have to use CAST to convert certain types. You can use host variables that have been declared in the DECLARE SECTION. Remember to prefix host variable names with a colon (:) when you use them in SQL statements, as in the following example:

```
EXEC SQL INSERT INTO ENGINES
    (EngineName, Displacement, Horsepower, Cylinders, Valves)
    VALUES
    (:engname, :cid, :hp, :cyl, :valves) ;
```

Embedding SQL in an Java application

SQLJ is the tool to use to embed SQL in a Java program. It is similar to the way SQL statements are embedded in an Oracle Pro*C application, but with a slight syntactical difference. Here's an example:

```
#sql (INSERT INTO ENGINES
    (EngineName, Displacement, Horsepower, Cylinders, Valves)
    VALUES
    (:engname, :cid, :hp, :cyl, :valves)) ;
```

`#sql` rather than `EXEC SQL` is the signal to the preprocessor that what follows is an SQL statement.

Using SQL in a Perl application

In a Perl application, the SQL statement is passed to the DBMS as a string rather than embedding an executable statement in the Perl code.

```
my $sql = "INSERT INTO ENGINES
    (EngineName,Displacement,Horsepower,Cylinders, Valves) " .
    "values('$engname','$cid','$hp','$cyl','valves')";
print "SQL => $sql\n" if $DEBUG;
my $sth = $dbh->prepare($sql);
$sth->execute();
```

This code uses the Perl DBI mentioned in Chapter 2 of this minibook. If an error is encountered, the offending SQL statement is printed out. If no error is detected, the SQL statement is prepared, and then the last line actually executes it.

Embedding SQL in a PHP application

Once again, with PHP and a MySQL database, the operation is basically the same as with Perl. Only the syntax has been changed to protect the innocent:

```
$query = "INSERT INTO ENGINES
    (EngineName, Displacement, Horsepower, Cylinders, Valves)
    VALUES
    ('engname', 'cid', 'hp', 'cyl', 'valves')" ;
mysql_query($query) or die('Error, insert query failed');
```

The last line checks to see if the insert was performed successfully. If it was not, an error message is displayed.

Using SQL with a Visual Basic .NET application

Unlike Oracle's Pro*C and Java, but like Perl and PHP, Visual Basic .NET does not support embedded SQL. Instead, it passes a string containing the SQL statement to the ADO.NET data provider to accomplish the same effect as embedded SQL. Here's an example of an SQL operation as Oracle's Pro*C would do it with embedded SQL, followed by the Visual Basic .NET equivalent using ADO.NET. First the Pro*C:

```
EXEC SQL UPDATE VENDOR
SET VendorName = :vendorname
WHERE VendorID = 'PENGUIN';
```

Now the ADO.NET equivalent:

```
Dim strSQL As String
strSQL = "UPDATE VENDOR SET VendorName = @vendorname "& _
"WHERE VendorID = 'PENGUIN'"
Dim cmd As New SqlCommand(strSQL, cn)
Dim par As SqlParameter
Par = cmd.Parameters.Add("@vendorname",SqlDbType.VarChar, 10)
Par.Value = "VendorName"
Dim InsertRecordsAffected As Integer = cmd.ExecuteNonQuery()
```

ADO.NET is a library of data access procedures in the .NET Framework.

Using SQL with other .NET languages

.NET languages besides Visual Basic .NET, such as C#, C++.NET, COBOL.NET, Perl.NET, and so on, all use ADO.NET in the same way that Visual Basic .NET does to provide data access to relational databases. ADO.NET eliminates the need to embed SQL code within a procedural application program.

Using SQL Modules with an Application

Module language provides another method of using SQL with a procedural programming language. With module language, you explicitly put all the SQL statements into a separate SQL module.

An SQL module is simply a list of SQL statements. Each SQL statement is included in an SQL *procedure* and is preceded by a specification of the procedure's name and the number and types of parameters.

Using SQL Modules with an Application **419**

Book V
Chapter 3

Using SQL in an
Application
Program

Each SQL procedure contains only one SQL statement. In the host program, you explicitly call an SQL procedure at whatever point in the host program you want to execute the SQL statement in that procedure. You call the SQL procedure as if it were a host language subprogram.

Thus, an SQL module and the associated host program are essentially a way of explicitly doing what the SQL preprocessor for embedded syntax does.

Embedded SQL is much more common than module language. Most vendors offer some form of module language, but few emphasize it in their documentation. Module language does have several advantages:

✦ Because the SQL is completely separated from the procedural language, you can hire the best SQL programmers available to write your SQL modules, whether they have any experience with your procedural language or not. In fact, you can even defer deciding on which procedural language to use until after your SQL modules are written and debugged.

✦ You can hire the best programmers who work in your procedural language, even if they know nothing about SQL.

✦ Most importantly, no SQL is mixed in with the procedural code, so your procedural language debugger works — which can save you considerable development time.

Once again, what can be looked at as an advantage from one perspective may be a disadvantage from another. Because the SQL modules are separated from the procedural code, following the flow of the logic isn't as easy as it is in embedded SQL when you're trying to understand how the program works.

Module declarations

The syntax for the declarations in a module is as follows:

```
MODULE [module-name]
   [NAMES ARE character-set-name]
   LANGUAGE {ADA|C|COBOL|FORTRAN|MUMPS|PASCAL|PLI|SQL}
   [SCHEMA schema-name]
   [AUTHORIZATION authorization-id]
   [temporary-table-declarations...]
   [cursor-declarations...]
   [dynamic-cursor-declarations...]
   procedures...
```

As indicated by the square brackets, the module name is optional. Naming it anyway is a good idea, to help keep things from getting too confusing. The optional NAMES ARE clause specifies a character set. If you don't include a NAMES ARE clause, the default set of SQL characters for your implementation is used. The LANGUAGE clause tells the module which language it will be called from. The compiler must know what the calling language is because it makes the SQL statements appear to the calling program as if they are subprograms in that program's language.

Although the SCHEMA clause and the AUTHORIZATION clause are both optional, you must specify at least one of them, or both. The SCHEMA clause specifies the default schema, and the AUTHORIZATION clause specifies the authorization identifier. The authorization identifier establishes the privileges you have. If you don't specify an authorization ID, the DBMS uses the authorization ID associated with your session to determine the privileges your module is allowed. If you don't have the privilege to perform the operation your procedure calls for, your procedure isn't executed.

If your procedure requires temporary tables, declare them with the temporary table declaration clause. Declare cursors and dynamic cursors before any procedures that use them. Declaring a cursor after a procedure is permissible as long as that procedure doesn't use the cursor. Doing this for cursors used by later procedures may make sense. You can find more in-depth information on cursors in Chapter 5 of Book III.

Module procedures

Finally, after all these declarations, the functional parts of the module are the procedures. An SQL module language procedure has a name, parameter declarations, and executable SQL statements. The procedural language program calls the procedure by its name and passes values to it through the declared parameters. Procedure syntax is as follows:

```
PROCEDURE procedure-name
   (parameter-declaration [, parameter-declaration ]... )
   SQL statement ;
   [SQL statements] ;
```

The parameter declaration should take the following form:

```
parameter-name data-type
```

or

```
SQLSTATE
```

The parameters you declare may be input parameters, output parameters, or both. SQLSTATE is a status parameter through which errors are reported.

Modules in Oracle

Oracle's implementation of module language, named SQL*Module, is specifically designed to overcome the impedance mismatch between SQL and application programs written in the Ada programming language. SQL*Module compiles SQL standard module language files. A module language file contains parameterized procedures that encapsulate SQL statements. The SQL*Module compiler translates these procedures into calls to the SQL runtime library on the Oracle server. All the SQL code resides in a separate module. SQL*Module defines the interface between the SQL module and the host program written in Ada.

A module is composed of three parts:

✦ A *preamble,* containing introductory material

✦ *Cursor declarations* that queries use to return multiple rows of data

✦ Definitions of *procedures* that are called by the host application

The SQL code that you can put into a module is somewhat restricted. Statements that are not supported by SQL*Module include

✦ DDL statements

✦ DML statements other than SELECT, UPDATE, DELETE, and INSERT

✦ DCL statements other than COMMIT, ROLLBACK, CONNECT, and DISCONNECT

Chapter 4: Designing a Sample Application

In This Chapter

✓ Discovering the client's problem

✓ Approaching the problem

✓ Determining the deliverables

✓ Building an E-R model

✓ Transforming the model

✓ Creating tables

✓ Changing table structure

✓ Removing tables

✓ Designing the user interface

*T*he whole point of learning SQL is to be able to apply that knowledge to solve some problem. Individuals and organizations need information in order to conduct their businesses, whatever they may be. At any given time, the information they need is buried to a huge collection of data that they don't need right now. The key to being able to retrieve the information that you do need is to make sure it is organized in a way that facilitates that retrieval, regardless of what your specific needs are today. In this chapter, I go through the steps of creating an application that gives one (fictitious) organization the information it needs. In the process, you can adapt the ideas explained here to your own situation.

The Client's Problem

After several decades of relatively little activity, interest in the Moon is heating up. Half a dozen nations have expressed interest in or made concrete plans to send spacecraft to the Moon, either to study from lunar orbit, or to land and establish bases. This has opened up opportunities for scholarly organizations that are interested in doing scientific research based on the terabytes of raw data that will start streaming from those spacecraft and bases in the near future. One such organization is the fictitious non-profit

Oregon Lunar Society (OLS) in Portland, Oregon. The OLS has members who may or may not be members of one or more of the Society's several research teams. The research teams do research and produce scholarly papers, which they deliver at conferences and submit to prestigious scientific journals. Members of the teams serve as authors of the papers. The OLS leadership would like to keep track of members, teams, papers, and the authors of the papers.

Approaching the Problem

The first thing a developer needs to do when starting a project is to find out what problem needs to be solved. There must be a problem; otherwise, you would not have been called in to solve it. Of course, the person who called you in feels that he knows what the problem is and what needs to be done to solve it. This person is an important source of information, but not the only one. In most cases, a number of people are affected by the application you produce. You need to get the perspectives of each of those people because they may know things about aspects of the problem that are unknown to the person who initially gave you the assignment. Anyone who may use your application or make decisions based on the results it produces is a stakeholder.

Interviewing the stakeholders

You were called in by the president of the Oregon Lunar Society, a small, independent research organization. As the person who hired you, she is your primary client and probably your best source of information initially. She reveals that the organization presently has two research teams, one focusing on the Moon and the other on Mars. The organization has broadened its focus since it was founded and named to include other bodies in the solar system besides Earth's moon. She is most interested in keeping up-to-date records on the members of the society, and the projects in which they are involved. After telling you her perspective on what is needed, she suggests you talk to the team leaders of each of the research teams, as well as several of the members who have authored papers that have either been delivered at conferences or that have appeared in scholarly journals.

You need to identify and carefully listen to all the stakeholders in the project. Your client, the users, the information technology people (if any), and the recipients of reports all have perspectives and opinions that must be factored into your design.

Your job in drawing out these people is very important. Because the system will be performing a new function, stakeholders probably don't have a well-defined idea of what it should do, as they would in the case of an upgrade of an existing system. They don't have any reference point on which to base their design ideas. They are also more likely to disagree with each other about what is needed. After a first round of interviews, you might have to go back to these people a second time to build a consensus on what is needed.

Drafting a detailed statement of requirements

After you have interviewed all the stakeholders and feel you have a clear idea of what you will need to deliver, when you will need to deliver it, and what it will cost you to deliver it in that timeframe, you need to draft a formal Statement of Requirements. The Statement of Requirements document describes in detail exactly what you will deliver, along with a projected delivery date.

Meet with your client and obtain agreement on the Statement of Requirements. If the client wishes to make revisions to what you have drafted, make sure that the requested revisions are feasible, considering the resources you are able to apply to the project. Generate a revised Statement of Requirements document and have the client sign it, signifying agreement with its contents.

Following up with a proposal

Now that you know exactly what the client wants and when she wants it, decide whether you want to do the job. If you feel the project is not feasible given the time and budget constraints and the resources you can devote to it, politely decline and move on to other things. If the time and budget are adequate, but you do not personally have the expertise to do the job, consider hiring a subcontractor that has the required expertise. This has the benefit of meeting the client's needs, while giving you at least a portion of the income that you would have realized if you had done the job all by yourself.

If you decide to take the job, write a proposal that takes from the Statement of Requirements the things you agree to deliver and when you will deliver them. If you are an outside contractor, include what you will charge to do the job. If you are an employee of the client, include your estimate of the number of hours it will take to complete it, along with any materials and staff required.

If your proposal is accepted by the client, it forms the basis of a contract between the two of you. This contract protects both parties. It protects the client by guaranteeing that she will receive the functionality and performance from the system that she expects. It protects you, the developer, by specifying exactly what you have agreed to deliver.

All too often, after a project is underway, a client thinks of additional features that would enhance the value of the system. She asks you to add them to the project, usually with a statement that the new features will not add significantly to the work. This phenomenon is called *feature creep*. You might agree, the first time this happens, that the added feature would not be much of a burden. After you acknowledge that new features can be added to the scope of the project, however, additional requests are sure to follow. These additional features soak up your time and mental energy, and may even cause you to miss the delivery date on the original project.

Avoid feature creep like the plague! Don't let it get started. When the client comes to you with the first small, innocent-seeming request, refer her to the contract that you both signed. If she wants additional work, it should be considered a separate job, with a separate budget and a separate schedule for completion. This significantly lowers your stress level as well as protects your bottom line. Giving away freebie add-ons to a project can turn a profitable job into a losing proposition.

Determining the Deliverables

The proposal you create in response to the Statement of Requirements should specify exactly what you will deliver, exactly when you will deliver it, and what it will cost, either in dollars or in manpower and resources. There are a few things to keep in mind when you are developing your proposal. They have to do with what the client organization needs now and what it will need in the future.

Finding out what's needed now and later

When you are discussing the assignment with your client after you have interviewed the stakeholders, but prior to formulating the statement of requirements, you are both aware of the current needs of the organization. The project you are planning should meet those needs. It should also provide some of the features that have been identified as valuable, if not absolutely necessary, assuming sufficient time and budget is available to include them.

Sometimes clients are so focused on their current challenges, they do not think ahead to what their needs might be five years, three years, or even one year in the future. One thing that has become clear in recent years is that the business environment is changing rapidly. An organization might succeed beyond expectations and grow in size. Alternatively, the demand for an organization's products or services might diminish drastically or even disappear. In that case, a rapid shift to new products or services might be necessary. In either case, the organization's data handling needs are likely to change. An appreciation of the potential for those changing needs can affect the way you design your system and the particular DBMS that you choose to build it with.

Planning for organization growth

A growth in an organization's business volume can have a major effect on its database needs. If sales increase, more sales need to be tracked. More customers need to be tracked. An expanded product line means more products must be tracked, and more employees are needed to manufacture, sell, and ship them. Those employees need to be tracked. A modest expansion in business volume requires a much larger expansion in data tracking needs. Even a non-profit organization such as the Oregon Lunar Society could have similar growing pains. Research activity could expand dramatically as surprising findings increase government interest and funding. Membership could expand as the public becomes more interested in space.

Most organizations, particularly business endeavors, hope that their business grows. If it does, they probably need expanded database capacity, beyond their current needs. As the developer of their system, you should design it in such a way that it has a reasonable amount of reserve capacity, and will be easily expandable after that reserve is used up.

As a business or other organization grows, more employees are needed to keep things running smoothly. Many of these employees need to access the database at the same time during the workday. This increases contention for database access and other system resources. You will base your application on one of the commercially available database management systems. Some of these are more robust than others under heavy load conditions. An idea of the extent of possible organizational growth may guide you in your choice of DBMS for the project. If substantial growth is possible within the next few years, you should choose a DBMS that can handle the increased load.

Small organizations generally have a relatively informal management structure. The company CEO knows all the employees by name. All-company meetings are held on a regular basis, and everybody has a voice in decisions that are made. Most transactions between individuals are handled verbally.

As an organization grows, this "high touch" environment becomes harder and harder to maintain. Gradually, more and more organizational structure must be put into place. Communication becomes more formal and documented, and more things come to be tracked in company databases. If you are developing for a small organization that has expansion potential, you should design flexibility into your system so that additional functions can be added at a later date without having to make major alterations to what already exists.

Data security becomes an increasingly important issue as an organization expands. When you have hundreds or thousands of employees, it is difficult to have the same level of trust in each and every one of them as you had in your employees when there were only five or six of them. Some files containing sensitive data need to be restricted so that only those with a legitimate need to access them can do so. If the organization you are developing for has the potential to expand significantly beyond its present size, you need to consider using a DBMS that has more robust security than might be warranted by the organization as it currently exists.

As an organization grows, its databases grow in value. It becomes more and more important to protect them from corruption and loss as well as from misuse. A small organization with growth potential should have a database system that is based on a DBMS that has strong data protection features.

Nailing down project scope

One of the most important things that you as a developer must do is accurately determine the scope of the project that you are planning. There are a number of factors that enter into project scope, some obvious and some not so obvious. The obvious factors are

+ How many different things need to be tracked?

+ How much time will the development require?

Some not so obvious factors are

+ How complex are the relationships between the things that are being tracked?

+ What level of expertise is needed to finish the job on time and on budget?

+ What development tools are needed and what do they cost?

+ Where should development be done, at the client site or the developer's facility?

+ What about travel expenses?

+ How available is the client to answer questions?

More non-obvious factors will probably appear after you have started. It is wise to build a contingency factor into your proposed price to cover them.

As an independent developer, accurate project scoping is critical. If you underestimate project scope and underbid the project, you may be forced to spend weeks or months working on a project that is guaranteed to lose you money. If you overestimate project scope, a competing developer with better estimating skill will underbid you and land the job.

If you are an employee of your client organization, accurate scoping is equally important. If you underestimate project scope, you can't deliver what you promised, when you promised to deliver it. If you overestimate project scope, your management may decide to give the project to someone else, and your ability might be called into question. Whether you are an independent developer or an employee of a client organization, your ability to scope projects accurately is crucial to your success.

Building an Entity-Relationship Model

In Book II, Chapter 2, I explain the E-R model. In this section, I show you how to apply that model, based on what you found out by interviewing the stakeholders in the Oregon Lunar Society database. The first step is to determine what the major entities are that need to be tracked. Following that, you must determine how these entities relate to each other.

Determining what the entities are

After talking to all the stakeholders you could find, you come to some conclusions about what the database should contain. There are clearly things you want to track:

- OLS members, along with some personal information on each
- Research teams
- Scholarly papers, both conference and journal
- Authors of papers, whether members or not

Relating the entities to each other

Interviews with Society leaders and other members lead to the construction of the E-R diagram shown in Figure 4-1.

This diagram probably seems confusing at first sight, but a little explanation should make it clearer. First I address the relationships, then the maximum cardinality, and finally the minimum cardinality.

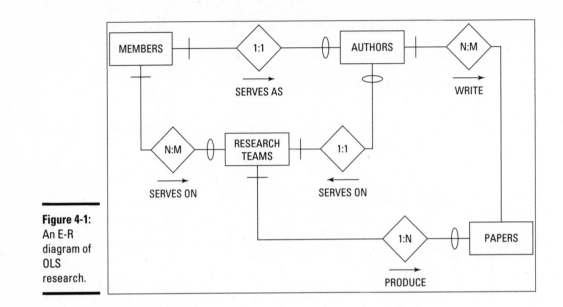

Figure 4-1:
An E-R
diagram of
OLS
research.

Relationships

The relationships define how the important elements of the system are related to each other:

✦ Members serve as Authors

✦ Members serve on Research Teams

✦ Research Teams produce Papers

✦ Authors write Papers

✦ Authors serve on Research Teams

Maximum cardinality

Recall that the *maximum cardinality* of a side of a relationship is the largest number of entity instances that can exist on that side. The relationship between Members and Authors is one-to-one because a Member can only be one Author and an Author can only be one Member. An Author is a Member.

The relationship between Members and Research Teams is many-to-many because a Member can serve on multiple Research Teams and a Research Team may be composed of multiple members.

The relationship between Research Teams and Papers is one-to-many because a Research Team can produce multiple papers, but each Paper is produced by one and only one Research Team.

The relationship between Authors and Papers is many-to-many because an Author may write multiple papers, and a Paper may have multiple Authors.

The relationship between Authors and Research Teams is many-to-many because an Author may serve on multiple Research Teams, and a Research Team may include multiple people who are Authors.

Minimum cardinality

Minimum cardinality of a side of a relationship is the least number of entity instances that can exist on that side. The relationship between Members and Authors is mandatory-to-optional because an Author of an OLS paper must be a Member of OLS, but a Member of OLS need not be an author of a Paper.

The relationship between Members and Research Teams is mandatory-to-optional because all Research Team members must be Members of OLS, but a Member of OLS need not be a member of a Research Team.

The relationship between Research Teams and Papers is mandatory-to-optional because all Papers must be produced by a Research Team, but a Research Team may exist that has not yet produced any Papers.

The relationship between Authors and Papers is mandatory-to-mandatory because a Paper must have a least one Author and a person is not considered to be an Author until she has participated in the writing of a Paper.

The relationship between Authors and Research Teams is optional-to-mandatory because for an Author to serve on a Research Team, the Research Team must exist, but a Research Team can exist that does not include any Authors.

Business rules

In order to accurately model a system, you must do more than determine the relevant entities, the attributes and identifiers of those entities, and the relationships among the entities. You must also capture the business rules that the organization follows for that system. Business rules vary from one organization to another, and they can make a big difference in how you model a system. In an educational context, one school may have a rule that at least eight students must sign up for a class in order for it to be offered. Another school may allow a class to proceed if as few as four students enroll. This would make a difference in the minimum cardinality of the relationship relating courses to students. One airline might cancel a scheduled flight if fewer than five people have bought tickets. Another airline might go ahead with the flight, even if there are no passengers aboard. These are differences in business rules.

As a database developer, it is your job to find out what your client's business rules are. You have to ask probing questions to the people you interview. Their business rules are so much a part of their lives that they probably won't think to mention them to you unless you ask detailed questions about them. Every stakeholder in the client organization has a different perspective on the database system you are building. They are likely to be aware of different business rules too. That is why it is important to talk to everyone involved and make sure you flush out all the rules.

With regard to OLS, investigation uncovers several business rules:

✦ Papers may have multiple coauthors, all of which must be a member of OLS.

✦ An OLS member may be a member of multiple research teams.

✦ Any given paper may be associated with one and only one research team.

Deep thinking

The Oregon Lunar Society example is simple, but it does illustrate the depth of thinking you must do about the entities in a system and how they relate to each other.

Transforming the Model

The first step in converting an E-R model into a relational model is to understand how the terminology used with one relates to the terminology used with the other. In the E-R model, we speak of entities, attributes, identifiers, and relationships. In the relational model, the primary items of concern are relations, attributes, keys, and relationships. How do these two sets of terms relate to each other?

In the E-R model, an entity is something identified as being important. Entities are physical or conceptual objects that you want to keep track of. This sounds a lot like the definition of a relation. The difference is that for something to be a relation, it must satisfy the requirements of First Normal Form (see Book II, Chapter 2). An entity might translate into a relation, but you have to be careful to assure that the resulting relation is in 1NF.

If you can translate an entity into a corresponding relation, the attributes of the entity translate directly into the attributes of the relation. Furthermore, an entity's identifier translates into the corresponding relation's key. The relationships between entities correspond exactly with the relationships between relations. Based on these correspondences, it is not too difficult to translate an E-R model into a relational model. The resulting relational model is not necessarily a good relational model, however. You may have to normalize the relations in it to protect it from modification anomalies. You may also have to decompose any many-to-many relationships to simpler one-to-many relationships. After your relational model is appropriately normalized and decomposed, the translation to a relational database is straightforward.

Eliminating any many-to-many relationships

The E-R model of the OLS database shown in Figure 4-1 contains many-to-many relationships. Such relationships can be problematic when trying to create a reliable database, so the usual practice is to decompose a single many-to-many relationship into two equivalent one-to-many relationships. This decomposition involves the creation of an intersection entity that is located between the two entities that were originally joined by a many-to-many relationship.

To prepare for the decomposition, first look at the entities involved and their identifiers:

Entity	Identifier
MEMBERS	MemberID
AUTHORS	MemberID
RESEARCHTEAMS	TeamID
PAPERS	PaperID

Because there is a one-to-one relationship between MEMBERS and AUTHORS, they can both have the same primary key. MemberID uniquely identifies a member, and it also uniquely identifies an author. TeamID uniquely identifies each of the research teams, and PaperID uniquely identifies each of the papers written under the auspices of the Oregon Lunar Society.

There are three many-to-many relationships:

> MEMBERS:RESEARCHTEAMS
>
> AUTHORS:RESEARCHTEAMS
>
> AUTHORS:PAPERS

You need to place an intersection entity between the two entities of each of these pairs. You could call them, for example, MEM-RES, AUTH-RES, and AUTH-PAP. Figure 4-2 shows the data structure diagram for this relational model.

This relational model includes four entities that correspond to the four entities in Figure 4-1, plus three intersection entities that replace the many-to-many relationships. There is one one-to-one relationship and seven one-to-many relationships. Minimum cardinality is denoted by slashes and ovals. For example, in the MEMBERS:AUTHORS relationship, in order for a person to be an author of an OLS publication, that person needs to be a member of OLS. Thus there is a slash on the MEMBERS side of that relationship. However, a person can be a member of OLS without ever authoring a Society publication. That is why there is an oval on the AUTHORS side of the relationship. Similar logic applies to the slashes and ovals on the other relationship lines.

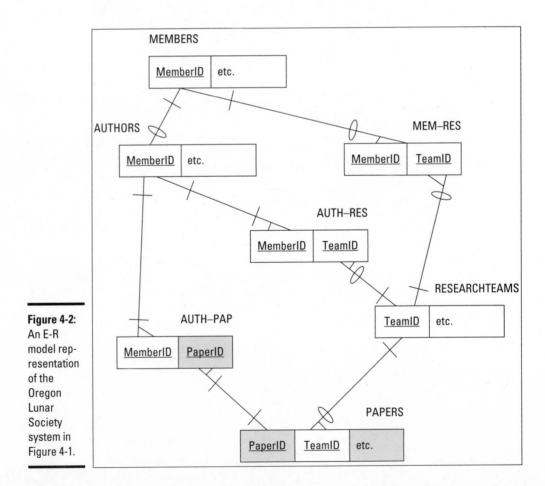

Figure 4-2: An E-R model representation of the Oregon Lunar Society system in Figure 4-1.

The relations are

MEMBERS (<u>MemberID</u>, FirstName, LastName, OfficeHeld, Email, Phone, Street, City, State, ZIP)

AUTHORS (<u>MemberID</u>, FirstName, LastName)

RESEARCHTEAMS (<u>TeamID</u>, TeamName, TeamLeaderFirstName, TeamLeaderLastName, ResearchFocus, MeetingLocation, MeetingSchedule)

PAPERS (<u>PaperID</u>, TeamID, PaperTitle, PrincipalAuthorID, Abstract, WherePublished)

MEM-RES (<u>MemberID</u>, <u>TeamID</u>)

AUTH-RES (<u>MemberID</u>, <u>TeamID</u>)

AUTH-PAP (MemberID, PaperID)

When you have an E-R model that accurately reflects the system being modeled, and contains no many-to-many relationships, the next step is to see that the model is sufficiently normalized.

Normalizing the E-R model

The main reason to normalize a database, as mentioned in Book II, Chapter 2, is to prevent the appearance of modification anomalies in the data. Such anomalies can lead to the loss of needed data or the introduction of spurious data. *Normalization* usually entails splitting up one table into two or more tables that together contain the same information. Each table in a fully normalized database deals with only one idea.

The OLS E-R model has four entities: MEMBERS, AUTHORS, RESEARCHTEAMS, and PAPERS. Look at one of these entities in more detail and consider whether it is sufficiently normalized.

The MEMBERS entity contains all the relatively stable information that OLS keeps on its members. It does not say anything about which research teams they are on or what papers they have written, which could change frequently. It contains only personal information.

Figure 4-3 diagramatically depicts the MEMBERS entity in the E-R model and its corresponding relation in the relational model. On the bottom in Figure 4-3, MemberID is underlined to signify that it is the primary key of the MEMBERS relation. Every member has a unique MemberID.

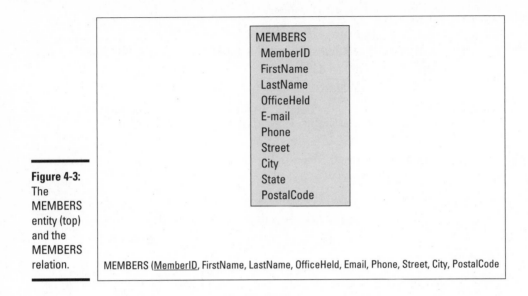

MEMBERS
MemberID
FirstName
LastName
OfficeHeld
E-mail
Phone
Street
City
State
PostalCode

Figure 4-3:
The
MEMBERS
entity (top)
and the
MEMBERS
relation.

MEMBERS (MemberID, FirstName, LastName, OfficeHeld, Email, Phone, Street, City, PostalCode)

The MEMBERS entity maps exactly onto the MEMBERS relation. It is natural to ask whether the MEMBERS relation is in DKNF (see Book II, Chapter 2). Clearly it is not. It is not even in 2NF. State is functionally dependent on PostalCode, which is not a key.

You could normalize the MEMBERS relation by breaking it into two relations as follows:

```
MEMBERS (MemberID, FirstName, LastName, OfficeHeld, Email,
    Phone, Street, City, PostalCode)
POSTAL (PostalCode, State)
```

These two relations are in 2NF and also in DKNF. They also demonstrate a new idea about keys. The two relations are closely related to each other because they share attributes. The PostalCode attribute is contained in both the MEMBERS and the POSTAL relations. MemberID is called the *primary key* of the MEMBERS relation. It must uniquely identify each tuple in the relation. Similarly, PostalCode is the primary key of the POSTAL relation.

In addition to being the primary key of the POSTAL relation, PostalCode is a *foreign key* in the MEMBERS relation. It provides a link between the two relations. An attribute need not be unique in a relation where it is serving as a foreign key, but must be unique on the other end of the relationship where it is the primary key.

After you have normalized a relation into DKNF as we did above with the original MEMBERS relation, it is wise to ask yourself whether full normalization makes sense in this specific case. Depending on how you plan to use the relations, you may want to denormalize somewhat to improve performance. In this example, you probably want to fold the POSTAL relation back into the MEMBERS relation. Generally, if you need any part of a person's address, you need all of it.

Creating Tables

You can create a database, including all its tables from the console, by using interactive SQL statements, by including embedded CREATE statements in a host language program, or by putting the CREATE statements in a module from which they can be called by a procedural language program.

Start building your OLS database by creating the MEMBERS table. Here's the DDL code to do it:

```
CREATE TABLE MEMBERS (
    MemberID    Integer      PRIMARY KEY,
    FirstName   Char (15),
    LastName    Char (20)    NOT NULL,
    OfficeHeld  Char (20),
    Email       Char (50),
    Phone       Char (20),
    Street      Char (25),
    City        Char (20),
    State       Char (2),
    Zip         Char (10) );
```

Note: Notice that each line within the outer parentheses (except the last one) in the statement above is terminated by a comma. The comma tells the DBMS where one field ends and the next one starts. The DBMS does not pay any attention to what line something is printed on. The separation of this single statement onto multiple lines is for the convenience of human readers, not for the DBMS.

The preceding SQL code creates a MEMBERS table. MemberID is the primary key of the table. Applying the NOT NULL constraint to the LastName attribute ensures that you know at least a member's last name even when you might not have complete information on that member. For each Character field, you must explicitly specify the maximum length of an entry in that field. The NOT NULL constraint is an example of a *column constraint*. A column constraint applies only to a single column. In contrast, a *table constraint* applies to an entire table. In the following code, I create the AUTHORS table and illustrate the use of a table constraint in the process:

```
CREATE TABLE AUTHORS (
    MemberID            Integer         PRIMARY KEY,
    FirstName           Char (15),
    LastName            Char (20) NOT NULL,
    CONSTRAINT MemFK FOREIGN KEY (MemberID)
        REFERENCES MEMBERS (MemberID)
        ON DELETE CASCADE );
```

Note: In the preceding code, there is no comma at the end of the CONSTRAINT line because the REFERENCES clause is part of that line. There is no comma at the end of the REFERENCES line because ON DELETE CASCADE is also a part of the CONSTRAINT line.

The PRIMARY KEY constraint is a table constraint. It applies to the entire table. In this case, it says that MemberID is the primary key of the AUTHORS table. I could have applied this constraint to the MEMBERS table too, but I wanted to show you both ways of applying constraints. It is probably better to specify the primary key of a table with the PRIMARY KEY constraint rather than the NOT NULL constraint. That way, there is no doubt which field is the table's primary key.

MemFK is a *foreign key constraint* and is another example of a table constraint. It links the MemberID field in the AUTHORS table to the MemberID field in the MEMBERS table. The ON DELETE CASCADE clause means that if a person is ever deleted from the MEMBERS table, she is automatically deleted from the AUTHORS table too. The reverse is not true. A person can be deleted from the AUTHORS table without affecting her member status.

Note: I have used the convention of naming foreign key constraints by taking the first several letters of the key field and appending FK to them (for example, MemFK). This makes it immediately obvious that we are dealing with a foreign key.

We can create the rest of the tables in a similar manner. Here's the SQL statement that creates the RESEARCHTEAMS table.

```
CREATE TABLE RESEARCHTEAMS (
    TeamID                  Integer         PRIMARY KEY,
    TeamName                Char (30),
    TeamLeaderFirstName     Char (15),
    TeamLeaderLastName      Char (20),
    ResearchFocus           Char (50),
    MeetingLocation         Char (50),
    MeetingSchedule         Char (30) );
```

The PAPERS table is defined in a similar fashion.

```
CREATE TABLE PAPERS (
    PaperID             Integer             PRIMARY KEY,
    TeamID              Integer,
    PaperTitle          Char (50),
    PrincipalAuthorID   Integer,
    Abstract            Char (300),
    WherePublished      Char (30) );
```

The linking tables MEM-RES, AUTH-RES, and AUTH-PAP, derived from the intersection relations with the same names in the relational model, are also defined the same way, but additionally include foreign key constraints.

```
CREATE TABLE MEM-RES (
    MemberID        Integer         NOT NULL,
    Team ID         Integer         NOT NULL,
    CONSTRAINT MemFK FOREIGN KEY (MemberID)
        REFERENCES MEMBERS (MemberID)
        ON DELETE CASCADE,
    CONSTRAINT TeamFK FOREIGN KEY (TeamID)
        REFERENCES RESEARCHTEAMS (TeamID)
        ON DELETE CASCADE );
```

The foreign key constraint MemFK establishes the fact that the MemberID field in the MEM-RES table corresponds to the MemberID field in the MEMBERS tables. Corresponding fields need not have the same names, but it reduces confusion if they do. The ON DELETE CASCADE clause has the effect of removing a person from all research teams when their membership in OLS expires and they are removed from the MEMBERS table.

The TeamFK constraint operates in a similar manner. When a research team is disbanded, all references to that team in MEM-RES are deleted. This has the effect of updating members' information so that they are no longer shown as being members of the disbanded team. Their other team memberships are unaffected.

The final two linking tables are defined in the same way that MEM-RES was defined.

```
CREATE TABLE AUTH-RES (
    MemberID        Integer         NOT NULL,
    Team ID         Integer         NOT NULL,
    CONSTRAINT AuthFK FOREIGN KEY (MemberID)
        REFERENCES AUTHORS (MemberID)
        ON DELETE CASCADE,
    CONSTRAINT TeamFK FOREIGN KEY (TeamID)
```

```
        REFERENCES RESEARCHTEAMS (TeamID)
        ON DELETE CASCADE );

CREATE TABLE AUTH-PAP (
    MemberID          Integer          NOT NULL,
    Paper ID          Integer          NOT NULL,
    CONSTRAINT AuthFK FOREIGN KEY (MemberID)
        REFERENCES AUTHORS (MemberID)
        ON DELETE CASCADE,
    CONSTRAINT PapFK FOREIGN KEY (PaperID)
        REFERENCES PAPERS (PaperID)
        ON DELETE CASCADE );
```

AuthFK is a table constraint, so the fact that a constraint in AUTH-RES and also a constraint in AUTH-PAP both have the same name does not matter. The DBMS will not confuse the two constraints.

At this point, all the tables have been defined, and they are ready to accept data.

Changing Table Structure

Suppose after you have created a table, you decide that you need to add a new column to it, or perhaps remove an existing column that serves no purpose. The DDL ALTER statement is included in SQL for these purposes. For example, if you wanted to add a Fax column to the MEMBERS table, you could do so with the following SQL statement:

```
ALTER TABLE MEMBERS
    ADD COLUMN Fax Char (20) ;
```

You can remove columns using a similar statement:

```
ALTER TABLE MEMBERS
    DROP COLUMN Fax ;
```

Removing Tables

It is really easy to get rid of tables you no longer want — perhaps too easy. For that reason, maintaining a rigorous backup discipline is important. To remove a table from your database, the DROP statement is all you need.

```
DROP TABLE PAPERS ;
```

There's no going back after using the DROP statement. SQL doesn't ask you if you *really* want to perform such a drastic act. It just blows away the table, and then waits for your next instruction.

Designing the User Interface

Every database application has a user interface. This consists of what the user sees on her screen and the key presses and mouse movements and clicks that she performs in order to interact with the application. The screen presents the user with options for actions to perform, queries to process, or reports to view. SQL is not designed to perform any of these user interface tasks. In any relational database application, the part created by the procedural language takes care of these tasks. Your job as the application developer is to make sure that the user interface is intuitive and easy to use, and of course, that it provides access to all of the functionality that the application possesses. Chapter 5 of this minibook gives an example of user interface design.

Chapter 5: Building a Sample Application

In This Chapter

✔ Top-down design

✔ Bottom-up coding

✔ Testing, testing, testing

✔ Fixing the bugs

✔ Bringing on the beta testers

✔ Fixing newly found bugs

✔ Retesting everything

In Chapter 4, I took the idea of a database system for the Oregon Lunar Society from an E-R model, to a relational model, to a relational database. Just as important as the database itself is the user interface. If users cannot get the information they need out of the database, it is not of much value. For a simple application such as the one the OLS needs, after you've designed the user interface, you have, for all intents and purposes, designed the whole application. So, because the database itself is now done, all that is left is designing the user interface and connecting it to the database.

To make sure you don't miss anything important, consider the project as a whole. Think of it as looking down on the project from 20,000 feet. This way, you view not only the project itself, but also the context in which it operates. Taking this view often brings concerns to the surface that you might otherwise not have thought of.

Designing from the Top Down

When you take a top-down approach to design, you consider all the elements of the system and how they relate to each other. You also consider elements external to the system that interact with it. In the case of the OLS system, the primary external element is the users. The user interface should be designed with the users in mind. How familiar are they with computers in general and with the kinds of data stored in the OLS database? If they are fairly sophisticated and comfortable with computers and with OLS, you would design the user interface differently than you would if they were computer novices who were largely unaware of the type of work that the OLS does. Placing considerations of the user interface aside for the moment, the first order of business is to decide what the application should include.

Determining what the application should include

At this point in the process, determining what the application should include is an easy question to answer. Just look at the proposal that was signed by the client, which specified exactly what the deliverables would be. Here's a list of deliverables, taken directly from a signed and agreed-upon proposal:

+ Entry/update/view form for members
+ Membership list
+ Entry/update/view form for authors
+ Author list
+ Entry/update/view form for research teams
+ Research team roster
+ Entry/update/view form for papers
+ Complete papers report
+ Query: Show all papers by a specified author
+ Query: Show all papers by a specified research team

Designing the user interface

After you have determined the forms, reports, and queries that you must support, you can decide how to arrange things so that the user can quickly specify what she wants and ask the application to deliver it. At this point, you should create some mock-ups of screens and present them to the users for feedback. Present two or three alternatives, perhaps one with radio buttons, and a second with list boxes and push buttons, as selection mechanisms for whatever function the user wants. The users feel a greater sense of ownership in the project if they get to choose what it looks like. This helps tremendously in gaining user acceptance. Figure 5-1 shows a mock-up of the main screen, using radio buttons.

One key design criterion here is to keep the screen simple. Sometime designers err by cluttering up screens with too many confusing options.

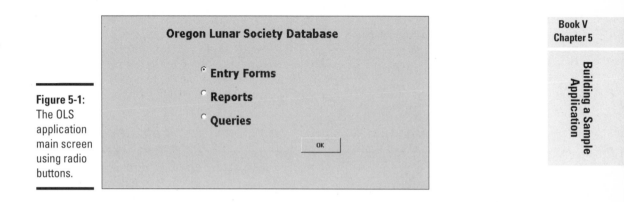

Figure 5-1:
The OLS application main screen using radio buttons.

Figure 5-2 shows the same screen, but this time implemented with command buttons.

Figure 5-2:
The OLS application main screen using command buttons.

After you show the alternatives for the main screen to the users and obtain their feedback, you can proceed to connect the user interface to the database.

Connecting the user interface to the database

Design a menu hierarchy to easily take users to the function they wish to perform. Figure 5-3 shows an example of such a hierarchy for the OLS application.

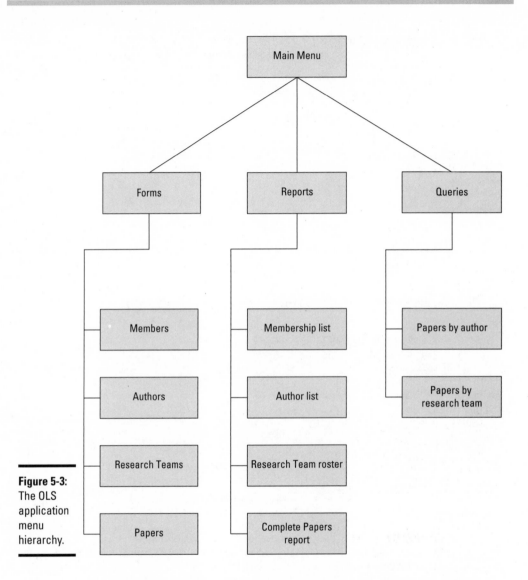

Figure 5-3:
The OLS
application
menu
hierarchy.

The tools for building forms, reports, and queries vary from one DBMS to another, so I won't go into detail on how to do it here. As an example of what one of the forms on the second level of the hierarchy might look like, Figure 5-4 shows one possible form for selecting one of the four forms used to view, enter, modify, or delete records from the MEMBERS, AUTHORS, RESEARCHTEAMS, and PAPERS tables.

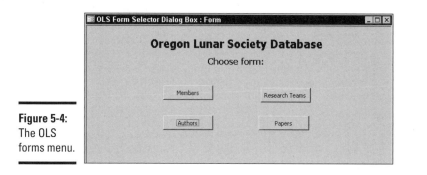

Figure 5-4:
The OLS
forms menu.

Similar forms for reports and queries would also be on the second level.
The third level consists of forms for viewing or editing table information.
Figure 5-5 is an example of what such a form might look like for the
MEMBERS table. Of course, you are free to lay out the form any way you
wish, put your company logo on it, or follow whatever stylistic conventions
are standard in your organization.

Figure 5-5:
The OLS
Members
form.

Coding from the Bottom Up

After you have developed mockups of all the forms in the menu hierarchy, all
the reports, and the query result sets, and have obtained approval from the
stakeholders, the real work can begin. You have created the *appearance* of
an application. Now you must build the substance.

Work to do before starting to build the application

The first thing you must do is build the database itself. The easiest and best
way to do this varies from one DBMS to another. Probably the easiest and
best way will turn out *not* to be using SQL. However, SQL is always an alternative, and it's the same across all platforms.

Create the database

For larger databases, you may want to create catalogs and schemas. You certainly want to create tables, and you may also want to create views. In Book II, Chapter 4, I cover table creation using SQL. You can apply what I discuss there to building tables for the Oregon Lunar Society.

Creating tables

The primary tables of the OLS database are MEMBERS, AUTHORS, RESEARCHTEAMS, and PAPERS. I describe creating them (using the SQL CREATE statement) in Chapter 4 of this minibook. However, you might want to do a little more work in the interest of keeping erroneous data out of the database — you do that by adding constraints, which I discuss in the next section.

Adding constraints to avoid data entry errors

When the MEMBERS table was defined in the previous section, the MemberID attribute was assigned the INTEGER type, and the other attributes were assigned the CHAR type, with various maximum lengths. These assignments constrain the data entered into those fields to some extent, but leave a lot of room for the entry of erroneous data. We can do a better job by applying some constraints to the attributes:

✦ At this time, OLS leadership cannot imagine a membership in excess of 1,000 members, so MemberID could be capped at that level. Any larger number entered must be an error.

✦ Only five offices exist: President, Vice President, Secretary, Treasurer, and Archivist. Any entry in OfficeHeld other than one of those five must be an error.

✦ State may contain only the two-letter abbreviations for Oregon (OR) and the three adjacent states: Washington (WA), Idaho (ID), and California (CA). Membership is restricted to residents of those four states.

✦ ZIP codes for Oregon, Washington, Idaho, and California all start with either 8 or 9.

Applying these constraints to the MEMBERS table eliminates at least some, if not all, data entry errors. If we had thought ahead, we could have applied these constraints when we created MEMBERS with the CREATE statement. If the table has already been created, but data has not yet been entered into it, we can drop the existing empty table and then recreate it, this time applying the constraints. Here's an example:

```
CREATE TABLE MEMBERS (
    MemberID    Integer            PRIMARY KEY,
    FirstName   Character (15),
```

```
LastName     Character (20)    NOT NULL,
OfficeHeld   Character (20),
Email        Character (50),
Phone        Character (20),
Street       Character (25),
City         Character (20),
State        Character (2),
Zip          Character (10),
CONSTRAINT max_size
   CHECK (MemberID BETWEEN 1 AND 1000),
CONSTRAINT offices
   CHECK (OfficeHeld IN ('President', 'Vice President',
          'Secretary', 'Treasurer', 'Archivist')),
CONSTRAINT valid_states
   CHECK (State IN ('OR','WA','ID','CA')),
CONSTRAINT valid_zip
   CHECK (SUBSTRING (Zip FROM 1 FOR 1) = 8
      OR SUBSTRING (Zip FROM 1 FOR 1) = 9)
);
```

If the table has already been created and data has already been added to it, we cannot add constraints after the fact because they could conflict with data that is already in the database.

By examining all the table designs before creating them, we can add appropriate constraints and thereby minimize the problems that inevitably arise when erroneous data enters the database.

Fill database tables with sample data

Every database table starts out empty. After you create a table, either by using SQL's CREATE statement or a DBMS's forms-based tools, that table is nothing but a structured shell containing no data. To make the table useful, you must put some data into it. You may or may not have that data already stored in digital form.

✦ If your data is not already in digital form, someone probably has to enter the data manually, one record at a time. You can also enter data by using optical scanners and voice recognition systems, but the use of such devices for data entry is relatively rare.

✦ If your data is already in digital form but perhaps not in the format of the database tables that you use, you need to translate the data into the appropriate format and then insert the data into the database.

✦ If your data is already in digital form and in the correct format, it's ready for transferring to a new database.

Depending on the current form of the data, you may be able to transfer it to your database in one operation using a bulk loading utility, or you may need to enter the data one record at a time. Each data record that you enter corresponds to a single row in a database table.

Adding data with forms

Most DBMSs support form-based data entry. This feature enables you to create a screen form that has a field for every column in a database table. Field labels on the form enable you to determine easily what data goes into each field. The data-entry operator enters all the data for a single row into the form. After the DBMS accepts the new row, the system clears the form to accept another row. In this way, you can easily add data to a table one row at a time.

Form-based data entry is easy and less susceptible to data-entry errors than is a list of comma-delimited values. The main problem with form-based data entry is that it is nonstandard; each DBMS has its own method of creating forms. This diversity, however, is not a problem for the data-entry operator. You can make the form look generally the same from one DBMS to another. Although this is great for the data entry operator, the application developer must return to the bottom of the learning curve every time he changes development tools. Another possible problem with form-based data entry is that some implementations may not permit a full range of validity checks on the data that you enter.

The best way to maintain a high level of data integrity in a database is to keep bad data out of the database in the first place. You can prevent the entry of some bad data by applying constraints to the fields on a data-entry form. This approach enables you to make sure that the database accepts only data values of the correct type and that fall within a predefined range. Applying such constraints can't prevent all possible errors, but it does catch some of them.

If the form-design tool in your DBMS doesn't enable you to apply all the validity checks that you need to ensure data integrity, you may want to build your own screen, accept data entries into variables, and check the entries by using application program code. After you're sure that all the values entered for a table row are valid, you can then add that row by using the SQL INSERT command.

Entering data with SQL

If you enter the data for a single row into a database table, the INSERT command uses the following syntax:

```
INSERT INTO table_1 [(column_1, column_2, ..., column_n)]
    VALUES (value_1, value_2, ..., value_n) ;
```

As indicated by the square brackets ([ ]), the listing of column names is optional. The default column list order is the order of the columns in the table. If you put the VALUES in the same order as the columns in the table, these elements go into the correct columns — whether you explicitly specify those columns or not. If you want to specify the VALUES in some order other than the order of the columns in the table, you must list the column names, putting the columns in an order that corresponds to the order of the VALUES.

To enter a record into the MEMBERS table, for example, use the following syntax:

```
INSERT INTO MEMBERS (MemberID, FirstName, LastName,
    OfficeHeld, Email, Phone, Street, City, State, Zip)
    VALUES (:vmemid, 'Linda', 'Nguyen', '235 Ion Drive',
    'Titania', 'OR', '97110', '(503) 555-1963') ;
```

The first VALUE, vmemid, is a variable that you increment with your program code after you enter each new row of the table. This approach guarantees that you have no duplication of the MemberID. MemberID is the primary key for this table and, therefore, must be unique. The rest of the values are data items rather than variables that contain data items. Of course, you can hold the data for these columns in variables, too, if you want. The INSERT statement works equally well either with variables or with an explicit copy of the data itself as arguments of the VALUES keyword.

Adding data only to selected columns

Sometimes you want to note the existence of an object, even if you don't have all the facts on it yet. If you have a database table for such objects, you can insert a row for the new object without filling in the data in all the columns. If you want the table in first normal form, you must insert enough data to distinguish the new row from all the other rows in the table. (For a discussion of first normal form, see Book II, Chapter 2.) Inserting the new row's primary key is sufficient for this purpose. In addition to the primary key, insert any other data that you have about the object. Columns in which you enter no data contain nulls.

The following example shows such a partial row entry:

```
INSERT INTO MEMBERS (MemberID, FirstName, LastName)
    VALUES (:vmemid, 'Linda', 'Nguyen') ;
```

You insert only the customer's unique identification number and name into the database table. The other columns in this row contain null values.

Adding a block of rows to a table

Loading a database table one row at a time by using INSERT statements can be tedious, particularly if that's all you do. Even entering the data into a carefully human-engineered ergonomic screen form gets tiring after a while. Clearly, if you have a reliable way to enter the data automatically, you'll find occasions in which automatic entry is better than having a person sit at a keyboard and type.

Automatic data entry is feasible, for example, if the data already exists in electronic form because somebody has already manually entered the data. If so, there is no reason to repeat history. The transfer of data from one data file to another is a task that a computer can perform with a minimum of human involvement. If you know the characteristics of the source data and the desired form of the destination table, a computer can (in principle) perform the data transfer automatically.

Copying from a foreign data file

Suppose that you're building a database for a new application. Some data that you need already exists in a computer file. The file may be a flat file or a table in a database created by a DBMS different from the one you use. The data may be in ASCII or EBCDIC code or in some arcane proprietary format. What do you do?

The first thing you do is hope and pray that the data you want is in a widely used format. If the data is in a popular format, you have a good chance of finding a format conversion utility that can translate the data into one or more other popular formats. Your development environment can probably import at least one of these formats. If you're really lucky, your development environment can handle the data's current format directly. On personal computers, the Access, xBASE, and Paradox formats are probably the most widely used. If the data that you want is in one of these formats, conversion should be easy. If the format of the data is less common, you may need to go through a two-step conversion.

As a last resort, you can turn to one of the professional data-translation services. These businesses specialize in translating computer data from one format to another. They have the capability of dealing with hundreds of formats — most of which nobody has ever heard of. Give one of these services a tape or disk containing the data in its original format, and you get back the same data translated into whatever format you specify.

Transferring all rows between tables

A less severe problem than dealing with foreign data is taking data that already exists in one table in your database and combining that data with compatible data in another table. This process works great if the structure of the second table is identical to the structure of the first table — that is, if every column in the first table has a corresponding column in the second table, and the data types of the corresponding columns match. If so, you can combine the contents of the two tables by using the UNION relational operator. The result is a virtual table containing data from both source tables. I discuss the relational operators, including UNION, in Book III, Chapter 4.

Transferring selected columns and rows between tables

Generally, the structure of the data in the source table isn't identical to the structure of the table into which you want to insert the data. Perhaps only some of the columns match — and these are the columns that you want to transfer. By combining SELECT statements with a UNION, you can specify which columns from the source tables to include in the virtual result table. By including WHERE clauses in the SELECT statements, you can restrict the rows that you place into the result table to those that satisfy specific conditions. I cover WHERE clauses extensively in Book III, Chapter 2.

Suppose that you have two tables, MEMBERS and PROSPECTS, and you want to list everyone living in the state of Idaho who appears in either table. You can create a virtual result table with the desired information by using the following command:

```
SELECT FirstName, LastName
    FROM MEMBERS
    WHERE State = 'ID'
UNION
SELECT FirstName, LastName
    FROM PROSPECTS
    WHERE State = 'ID' ;
```

Here's a closer look:

✦ The SELECT statements specify that the columns included in the result table are FirstName and LastName.

✦ The WHERE clauses restrict the rows included to those with the value 'ID' in the State column.

✦ The State column isn't included in the results table but is present in both the MEMBERS and PROSPECTS tables.

✦ The UNION operator combines the results from the SELECT on MEMBERS with the results of the SELECT on PROSPECTS, deletes any duplicate rows, and then displays the result.

Another way to copy data from one table in a database to another is to nest a SELECT statement within an INSERT statement. This method (a subselect) doesn't create a virtual table but instead duplicates the selected data. You can take all the rows from the MEMBERS table, for example, and insert those rows into the PROSPECTS table. Of course, this only works if the structures of the MEMBERS and PROSPECTs tables are identical. If you want to place only those customers who live in Idaho into the PROSPECTS table, a simple SELECT with one condition in the WHERE clause does the trick, as shown in the following example:

```
INSERT INTO PROSPECTS
   SELECT * FROM MEMBERS
   WHERE State = 'ID' ;
```

Even though this operation creates redundant data (you're now storing member data in both the PROSPECTS table and the MEMBERS table), you may want to do it anyway to improve the performance of retrievals. Be aware of the redundancy, however, and to maintain data consistency, make sure that you don't insert, update, or delete rows in one table without inserting, updating, or deleting the corresponding rows in the other table. Another potential problem is the possibility that the INSERT might generate duplicate primary keys. If even one pre-existing prospect has a primary key ProspectID that matches the corresponding primary key, MemberID, of a member that you are trying to insert into the PROSPECTS table, the insert operation will fail.

Creating the application's building blocks

Although you may use SQL INSERT statements to enter a few rows of sample data to validate that your tables were created correctly, the application that your production people use must be easier to use and less error-prone. Similarly, although you can obtain meaningful results to questions about the data using SQL SELECT statements, doing so is not particularly easy or error-resistant.

You need to build a user-friendly application that features screen forms for data entry, data viewing, data modification, and data deleting. You also need predesigned reports that can be run at regular intervals or whenever desired.

Developing screen forms

Design your screen forms so that users can quickly and easily understand them. Make the placement of items on the forms logical and visible. Group related items together. Make sure that the navigation from one form to another is easy and logical. Create a navigation map similar to Figure 5-3 that shows how forms are linked together. Because user communities can differ widely, have typical users try out your forms and give you feedback on how easy they are to use and whether they provide all the functionality needed.

Developing reports

The discipline required for generating reports is similar to that required for generating screen forms. SQL is not equipped to handle either function. You have to write code in Visual Basic, C, or some other procedural language to create the forms and reports, depend on the tools available in whatever DBMS environment you are operating in, or use a third party report writer such as Crystal Reports from Business Objects, Inc. In any case, when you have completed all the forms and reports that your application needs to provide, the next step is placing them in an integrated structure that presents the users with a unified tool that meets their needs in a convenient way.

Gluing everything together

Some development environments, such as Microsoft Access, give you the integrated structure you need, complete with navigation from one screen to another, without the need for any procedural programming. These applications, however, have limited flexibility, and are unable to handle requirements that are even slightly out of the ordinary. In most cases, you end up having to write some procedural code. If you are developing in the .NET environment, Visual Studio is the tool you use to write the needed procedural code. If you are developing in another environment, you use other tools, but your task is essentially the same. Any analysis of the data beyond what SQL can do requires programming, as do responses to events such as button clicks or error conditions.

Testing, Testing, Testing

After you have finished all your forms, reports, and queries, and written all the code needed to bind the application together, you are still not done. In fact, you may be less than halfway to completion of the project. In most large projects, testing is the most time-consuming part of the entire task — more time-consuming than the design phase or the creation of all the forms, reports, queries, and program code. You need to test your application with the volume and diversity of data that it's likely to encounter after it goes into production. This typically reveals problems that didn't show up when you were working with a few rows of sample data in each of your tables.

You need to deliberately try to "break" the application by making erroneous inputs because you can be sure that after the system goes into production, sooner or later someone will make data entry mistakes. If dates and times are involved, try entering some nonsensical ones and see how the system responds. See what happens if you say, for example, that a product has been delivered before it was ordered. How does the system handle that? How do you *want* the system to handle that?

Fix the bugs

In the course of testing, you inevitably find things that are not as they should be. These may be program bugs, or just inelegancies that, now that you look at them, you know you can improve. Fix them all.

After you have fixed a group of bugs, go back and test the entire application again. If in this second round of testing you discover more bugs, fix them and then test *everything* again. Don't just test whatever it was that you fixed. Test *everything*. Bugs and fixes have a way of interacting in unanticipated ways. Often what you do to fix one bug creates three or four other problems in what you would swear are unrelated areas. The only way to make sure that you have not created additional problems in the course of fixing one is to test everything all over again every time you fix anything. This discipline is called *regression testing* because you regress back to square one every time you fix a bug.

Turn naive users loose

After you can go through your entire suite of tests without encountering a single problem, you are ready to go to the next phase of testing, which is generally called *beta testing*. In a beta test, you give the application to users who are no more technically sophisticated than the end users you are targeting. Actually, the less technically sophisticated your beta testers are, the better. They use your application in ways that you would never think of in a million years. In the process, they uncover bugs that you never came close to finding.

Bring on the hackers

Another good class of beta testers is people with a hacker mentality. These people feel challenged to find the weak spots in your application. They try things that they *know* they are not supposed to do, just to see what happens. In the process, they find problems that neither you nor your unsophisticated beta testers had encountered.

Fix the newly found bugs

As new bugs crop up in the course of beta testing, fix them one by one as they appear. After each fix, run a regression test. If you fix several bugs and then run the regression test, it's hard to determine what caused the 17 new failures that appear. As the hare learned from the tortoise, slow and steady wins the race. Keep things as simple as possible. Fix one thing at a time and then retest everything.

Retest everything

Did I say retest everything? Yes. After you think you have tested the application to death — after you are sure you have squashed all the bugs that could possibly exist, it is time for one final test. This time, rather than running the test yourself, have someone else, someone totally unrelated to the development effort, conduct the entire test suite one more time. After you get a clean run this final time, you can truly say that you are finished. Break out the bubbly!

Chapter 6: SQL's Procedural Capabilities

In This Chapter

✓ Embedding SQL statements in your code

✓ Compound statements

✓ Flow of control statements

✓ Stored procedures

✓ Triggers

✓ Stored functions

✓ Privileges

✓ Stored modules

*I*n its original incarnation, SQL was conceived as a data sublanguage, whose only purpose was interacting with relational databases. It was considered acceptable to embed SQL statements within procedural language code written in some full-featured language in order to create a fully functional database application. However, users have for a long time wanted SQL to have procedural capabilities so that there would be less need to switch back and forth between SQL and some other language in data-driven applications. To solve this problem, vendors started putting procedural capabilities into their implementations of SQL. These non-standard extensions to the language inhibited cross-platform portability until a number of procedural capabilities were standardized with a new section of the ANSI/ISO standard in 1996. That new section is called Persistent Stored Modules (SQL/PSM), although it covers quite a few things in addition to stored modules.

Embedding SQL Statements in Your Code

In Chapter 3, I discussed embedding SQL statements in applications written in one of several procedural languages. Even with the new procedural capabilities that were added to SQL with the Procedural Stored Modules addition, embedding is still necessary, but switches back and forth between languages are much less frequent. In its current version (SQL:2003 with additional functionality added in 2005), the ANSI/ISO SQL standard still describes a language that is not computationally complete.

Introducing Compound Statements

SQL was originally conceived as a non-procedural language that deals with data a set at a time rather than a record at a time. With the addition of the facilities covered in this chapter, however, this statement is not as true as it used to be. SQL has become more procedural, although it still deals with data a set at a time. Because classic SQL (that defined by SQL-92) does not follow the procedural model — where one instruction follows another in a sequence to produce a desired result — early SQL statements were stand-alone entities, perhaps embedded in a C++ or Visual Basic program. With these early versions of SQL, users typically did not pose a query or perform some other operation by executing a series of SQL statements. If users did execute such a series of statements, they suffered a performance penalty. Every SQL statement that is executed requires a message to be sent from the client where the user is located, to the server where the database is located, and then a response must be sent in the reverse direction. This network traffic slows operations as the network becomes congested.

SQL:1999 and all following versions allow compound statements, made up of individual SQL statements, that execute as a unit. This capability eases network congestion because all the individual SQL statements in the compound statement are sent to the server as a unit and executed as a unit, and a single response is sent back to the client.

All the statements included in a compound statement are enclosed between a BEGIN keyword at the beginning of the statement and an END keyword at the end of the statement. For example, to insert data into multiple related tables, you use syntax similar to the following:

```
void main {
    EXEC SQL
        BEGIN
            INSERT INTO STUDENTS (StudentID, Fname, Lname)
                VALUES (:sid, :sfname, :slname) ;
            INSERT INTO ROSTER (ClassID, Class, StudentID)
                VALUES (:cid, :cname, :sid) ;
            INSERT INTO RECEIVABLE (StudentID, Class, Fee)
                VALUES (:sid, :cname, :cfee)
        END ;
/* Check SQLSTATE for errors */
}
```

This little fragment from a C program includes an embedded compound SQL statement. The comment about SQLSTATE deals with error handling. If the compound statement does not execute successfully, an error code is placed in the status parameter SQLSTATE. Of course, placing a comment after the END keyword doesn't correct any errors. The comment is placed there simply to remind you that in a real program, error-handling code belongs in that spot. Error handling is described in detail in Book IV, Chapter 4.

Atomicity

Compound statements introduce a possibility for error that does not exist for simple SQL statements. A simple SQL statement either completes successfully or doesn't. If it doesn't complete successfully, the database is unchanged. This is not necessarily the case for a compound statement.

Consider the example in the preceding section. What if the INSERT to the STUDENTS table and the INSERT to the ROSTER table both took place, but because of interference from another user, the INSERT to the RECEIVABLE table failed? A student would be registered for a class but would not be billed. This kind of error can be hard on a university's finances. The concept that is missing in this scenario is *atomicity*. An atomic statement is indivisible — it either executes completely or not at all. Simple SQL statements are atomic by nature, but compound SQL statements are not. However, you can make a compound SQL statement atomic by specifying it as such. In the following example, the compound SQL statement is safe by introducing atomicity:

```
void main {
     EXEC SQL
         BEGIN ATOMIC
           INSERT INTO STUDENTS (StudentID, Fname, Lname)
               VALUES (:sid, :sfname, :slname) ;
           INSERT INTO ROSTER (ClassID, Class, StudentID)
               VALUES (:cid, :cname, :sid) ;
           INSERT INTO RECEIVABLE (StudentID, Class, Fee)
               VALUES (:sid, :cname, :cfee)
         END ;
/* Check SQLSTATE for errors */
}
```

By adding the keyword ATOMIC after the keyword BEGIN, you can ensure that either the entire statement executes, or — if an error occurs — the entire statement rolls back, leaving the database in the state it was in before the statement began executing.

Variables

One feature that full computer languages such as C or BASIC offer that SQL didn't offer until SQL/PSM is *variables*. Variables are symbols that can take on a value of any given data type. Within a compound statement, you can declare a variable and assign it a value. The variable can then be used within the compound statement. After you exit a compound statement, all the variables declared within it are destroyed. Thus, variables in SQL are local to the compound statement within which they are declared. Here is an example:

```
BEGIN
    DECLARE prezpay NUMERIC ;
    SELECT salary
    INTO prezpay
    FROM EMPLOYEE
    WHERE jobtitle = 'president' ;
END;
```

Cursors

You can declare a cursor within a compound statement. You use cursors to process a table's data one row at a time (see Book III, Chapter 5 for details). Within a compound statement, you can declare a cursor, use it, and then forget it because the cursor is destroyed when you exit the compound statement. Here's an example of this usage:

```
BEGIN
    DECLARE ipocandidate CHAR(30) ;
    DECLARE cursor1 CURSOR FOR
            SELECT company
            FROM biotech ;
    OPEN CURSOR1 ;
    FETCH cursor1 INTO ipocandidate ;
    CLOSE cursor1 ;
END;
```

Conditions

When people say that a person has a "condition," they usually mean that something is wrong with that person — he or she is sick or injured. People usually don't bother to mention that a person is in *good* condition; rather, we talk about people who are in serious condition or, even worse, in critical condition. This idea is similar to the way programmers talk about the condition of an SQL statement. The execution of an SQL statement leads to a successful result, a questionable result, or an outright erroneous result. Each of these possible results corresponds to a condition.

Every time an SQL statement executes, the database server places a value into the status parameter SQLSTATE. SQLSTATE is a five-character field. The value that is placed into SQLSTATE indicates whether the preceding SQL statement executed successfully. If it did not execute successfully, the value of SQLSTATE provides some information about the error.

The first two of the five characters of SQLSTATE (the class value) give you the major news as to whether the preceding SQL statement executed successfully, returned a result that may or may not have been successful, or produced an error. Table 6-1 shows the four possible results. A detailed description of these class values is given in Book IV, Chapter 4.

Table 6-1	SQLSTATE Class Values
Class	**Description**
00	Successful completion
01	Warning
02	Not Found
other	Exception

Assignment

With SQL/PSM, SQL finally gains a function that even the lowliest procedural languages have had since their inception: the ability to assign a value to a variable. Essentially, an assignment statement takes the following form:

```
SET target = source ;
```

In this usage, target is a variable name, and source is an expression. Several examples are

```
SET vfname = 'Brandon' ;

SET varea = 3.1416 * :radius * :radius ;

SET vhiggsmass = NULL ;
```

Following the Flow of Control Statements

Since its original formulation in the SQL-86 standard, one of the main drawbacks that prevented people from using SQL in a procedural manner has been its lack of flow of control statements. Until SQL/PSM was included in the SQL standard, you couldn't branch out of a strict sequential order of execution without reverting to a host language like C or BASIC. SQL/PSM introduces the traditional flow of control structures that other languages provide, thus allowing SQL programs to perform needed functions without switching back and forth between languages.

IF . . . THEN . . . ELSE . . . END IF

The most basic flow of control statement is the IF . . . THEN . . . ELSE . . . END IF statement. It means that if a condition is true, the statements following the THEN keyword should be executed. Otherwise, the statements following the ELSE keyword should be executed. For example:

```
IF
    vfname = 'Brandon'
THEN
    UPDATE students
        SET Fname = 'Brandon'
        WHERE StudentID = 314159 ;
ELSE
    DELETE FROM students
        WHERE StudentID = 314159 ;
END IF
```

In this example, if the variable vfname contains the value Brandon, the record for student 314159 is updated with Brandon in the Fname field. If the variable vfname contains any value other than Brandon, the record for student 314159 is deleted from the students table.

The IF . . . THEN . . . ELSE . . . END IF statement is great if you want to take one of two actions, based on the value of a condition. Often, however, you want to make a selection from more than two choices. At such times, you should probably use a CASE statement.

CASE . . . END CASE

CASE statements come in two forms: the simple CASE statement and the searched CASE statement. Both kinds allow you to take different execution paths, based on the values of conditions.

Simple CASE statement

A simple CASE statement evaluates a single condition. Based on the value of that condition, execution may take one of several branches. For example:

```
CASE vmanufacturer
    WHEN 'General Motors'
    THEN INSERT INTO DOMESTIC (VIN, Make, Model)
            VALUES (:vin, :make, :model) ;
    WHEN 'Ford'
    THEN INSERT INTO DOMESTIC (VIN, Make, Model)
            VALUES (:vin, :make, :model) ;
    WHEN 'Chrysler'
    THEN INSERT INTO DOMESTIC (VIN, Make, Model)
            VALUES (:vin, :make, :model) ;
    WHEN 'Studebaker'
    THEN INSERT INTO DOMESTIC (VIN, Make, Model)
            VALUES (:vin, :make, :model) ;
    ELSE INSERT INTO FOREIGN (VIN, Make, Model)
            VALUES (:vin, :make, :model) ;
END CASE
```

The ELSE clause handles everything that doesn't fall into the explicitly named categories in the THEN clauses.

The ELSE clause is optional. However, if it is not included, and the CASE statement's condition is not handled by any of the THEN clauses, SQL returns an exception.

Searched CASE statement

A searched CASE statement is similar to a simple CASE statement, but it evaluates multiple conditions rather than just one. For example:

```
CASE
    WHEN vmanufacturer  IN ('General Motors','Ford')
    THEN INSERT INTO DOMESTIC (VIN, Make, Model)
            VALUES (:vin, :make, :model) ;
    WHEN vmake IN ('Chrysler','Dodge','Plymouth')
        THEN INSERT INTO DOMESTIC (VIN, Make, Model)
            VALUES (:vin, :make, :model) ;
    WHEN vmodel IN ('Avanti','Lark')
        THEN INSERT INTO DOMESTIC (VIN, Make, Model)
            VALUES (:vin, :make, :model) ;
    ELSE INSERT INTO FOREIGN (VIN, Make, Model)
            VALUES (:vin, :make, :model) ;
END CASE
```

You avoid an exception by putting all cars that are not domestic into the FOREIGN table. Because a car that does not meet any of the stated conditions may still be domestic, this may not be strictly accurate in all cases. If it isn't, you can always add another WHEN clause.

LOOP . . . ENDLOOP

The LOOP statement allows you to execute a sequence of SQL statements multiple times. After the last SQL statement enclosed within the LOOP . . . ENDLOOP statement executes, control loops back to the first such statement and makes another pass through the enclosed statements. The syntax is as follows:

```
SET vcount = 0 ;
LOOP
   SET vcount = vcount + 1 ;
   INSERT INTO asteroid (AsteroidID)
      VALUES (vcount) ;
END LOOP
```

This code fragment preloads your asteroid table with unique identifiers. You can fill in other details about the asteroids as you find them, based on what you see through your telescope when you discover them.

Notice the one little problem with the code fragment in the preceding example: It is an infinite loop. No provision is made for leaving the loop, so it will continue inserting rows into the asteroid table until the DBMS fills all available storage with asteroid table records. If you're lucky, the DBMS raises an exception at that time. If you're unlucky, the system merely crashes.

For the LOOP statement to be useful, you need a way to exit loops before you raise an exception: the LEAVE statement.

LEAVE

The LEAVE statement works just like you might expect it to. When execution encounters a LEAVE statement embedded within a labeled statement, it proceeds to the next statement beyond the labeled statement. For example:

```
AsteroidPreload:
SET vcount = 0 ;
LOOP
   SET vcount = vcount + 1 ;
   IF vcount > 10000
      THEN
         LEAVE AsteroidPreload ;
   END IF ;
   INSERT INTO asteroid (AsteroidID)
      VALUES (vcount) ;
END LOOP AsteroidPreload
```

The preceding code inserts 10,000 sequentially numbered records into the asteroids table, and then passes out of the loop.

WHILE ... DO ... END WHILE

The WHILE statement provides another method for executing a series of SQL statements multiple times. While a designated condition is true, the WHILE loop continues to execute. When the condition becomes false, looping stops. For example:

```
AsteroidPreload2:
SET vcount = 0 ;
WHILE
    vcount < 10000 DO
        SET vcount = vcount + 1 ;
        INSERT INTO asteroid (AsteroidID)
            VALUES (vcount) ;
END WHILE AsteroidPreload2
```

This code does exactly the same thing that AsteroidPreload did in the preceding section. This is just another example of the oft-cited fact that with SQL, you usually have multiple ways to accomplish any given task. Use whichever method you feel most comfortable with, assuming your implementation allows both.

REPEAT ... UNTIL ... END REPEAT

The REPEAT loop is very much like the WHILE loop, except that the condition is checked after the embedded statements execute rather than before. Here's an example:

```
AsteroidPreload3:
SET vcount = 0 ;
REPEAT
    SET vcount = vcount + 1 ;
    INSERT INTO asteroid (AsteroidID)
        VALUES (vcount) ;
    UNTIL X = 10000
END REPEAT AsteroidPreload3
```

Although I perform the same operation three different ways in the preceding example (with LOOP, WHILE, and REPEAT), you will encounter some instances where one of these structures is clearly better than the other two. It is good to have all three methods in your bag of tricks so that when a situation like this arises, you can decide which one is the best tool available for the situation.

FOR . . . DO . . . END FOR

The SQL FOR loop declares and opens a cursor, fetches the rows of the cursor, executes the body of the FOR statement once for each row, and then closes the cursor. This loop makes processing possible entirely within SQL, instead of switching out to a host language. If your implementation supports SQL FOR loops, you can use them as a simple alternative to the cursor processing described in Book III, Chapter 5. Here's an example:

```
FOR vcount AS Curs1 CURSOR FOR
    SELECT AsteroidID FROM asteroid
DO
    UPDATE asteroid SET Description = 'stony iron'
        WHERE CURRENT OF Curs1 ;
END FOR
```

In this example, you update every row in the asteroid table by putting 'stony iron' into the Description field. This is a fast way to identify the compositions of asteroids, but the table may suffer some in the accuracy department. Some asteroids are carbonaceous chondrites, and others are nickel-iron. Perhaps you'd be better off checking the spectral signatures of the asteroids and then entering their types individually.

ITERATE

The ITERATE statement provides a way to change the flow of execution within an iterated SQL statement. The iterated SQL statements are LOOP, WHILE, REPEAT, and FOR. If the iteration condition of the iterated SQL statement is true or not specified, the next iteration of the loop commences immediately after the ITERATE statement executes. If the iteration condition of the iterated SQL statement is false or unknown, iteration ceases after the ITERATE statement executes. For example:

```
AsteroidPreload4:
SET vcount = 0 ;
WHILE vcount < 10000 DO
    SET vcount = vcount + 1 ;
    INSERT INTO asteroid (AsteroidID) VALUES (vcount) ;
    ITERATE AsteroidPreload4 ;
    SET vpreload = 'DONE' ;
END WHILE AsteroidPreload4
```

Execution loops back to the top of the WHILE statement immediately after the ITERATE statement each time through the loop until vcount equals 9999. On that iteration, vcount increments to 10000, the INSERT performs, the ITERATE statement ceases iteration, vpreload is set to DONE, and execution proceeds to the next statement after the loop.

Using Stored Procedures

Stored procedures reside in the database on the server, rather than execute on the client — where all procedures were located before SQL/PSM. After you define a stored procedure, you can invoke it with a CALL statement. Keeping the procedure located on the server rather than the client reduces network traffic, thus speeding performance. The only traffic that needs to pass from the client to the server is the CALL statement. You can create this procedure in the following manner:

```
EXEC SQL
    CREATE PROCEDURE ForeignOrDomestic
        ( IN  manufacturer CHAR (20),
          OUT origin       CHAR (8) )
    BEGIN ATOMIC
        CASE manufacturer
            WHEN 'General Motors' THEN
                SET origin = 'domestic' ;
            WHEN 'Ford' THEN
                SET origin = 'domestic' ;
            WHEN 'Chrysler' THEN
                SET origin = 'domestic' ;
            WHEN 'Studebaker' THEN
                SET origin = 'domestic' ;
            ELSE
                SET origin = 'foreign' ;
        END CASE
    END ;
```

After you have created a stored procedure like the one in this example, you can invoke it with a CALL statement similar to the following statement:

```
CALL ForeignOrDomestic ('Toyota', origin) ;
```

The first argument is the input parameter that is fed to the ForeignOrDomestic procedure. The second argument is the output parameter that the procedure uses to return its result to the calling routine. In this case, it returns foreign.

Working with Triggers

Triggers are useful tools that you can use to execute SQL statements, whenever certain changes are made to a database table. They are analogous to actions that occur in event-driven programming in modern procedural languages. If a predefined change is made to a database table, that event causes an associated trigger to *fire,* which in turn causes an SQL statement or block of SQL statements to execute. The triggered statement could cause another trigger to fire, as well as performing its stated action. There is no limit to the number of levels of nesting for triggers.

One reason you might want to use a trigger is to create an audit trail. If a particular change is made to a table, you may want to record that fact in a log file somewhere. A trigger could cause an SQL statement to make a log entry. Another application of a trigger might be to maintain consistency among tables in a database. A particular change to one table might cause a trigger to fire that causes corresponding changes to be made to other tables. You can even use a trigger to affect something outside of the database. For example, if a new row is inserted into an ORDERS table, you could fire a trigger that wakes up and sets into motion a robot that starts to build the ordered product.

Here's the BNF syntax for the statement that creates a trigger:

```
<trigger definition> ::=
  CREATE TRIGGER <trigger name>
    <trigger action time> <trigger event>
    ON <table name>[REFERENCING old or new values alias list]
    <triggered action>

<trigger action time> ::=
    BEFORE
  | AFTER

<trigger event> ::=
    INSERT
  | DELETE
  | UPDATE [ OF <trigger column list> ]

<trigger column list> ::= <column name list>

<triggered action> ::=
  [ FOR EACH { ROW | STATEMENT } ]
    [ WHEN <left paren> <search condition> <right paren> ]
    <triggered SQL statement>

<triggered SQL statement> ::=
    <SQL procedure statement>
  | BEGIN ATOMIC
      { <SQL procedure statement> <semicolon> }...
    END

<old or new values alias list> ::=
    OLD [ ROW ][ AS ] <old values correlation name>
```

```
| NEW [ ROW ][ AS ] <new values correlation name>
| OLD TABLE [ AS ] <old values table alias>
| NEW TABLE [ AS ] <new values table alias>

<old values correlation name> ::= <correlation name>

<new values correlation name> ::= <correlation name>

<old values table alias> ::= <identifier>

<new values table alias> ::= <identifier>
```

Trigger events

Three different SQL statements, INSERT, DELETE, and UPDATE, can cause
a trigger to fire. A referential action can also cause a trigger to fire. For
example, if a referential integrity constraint is violated, a trigger could
fire, which would then cause some appropriate action to take place. The
optional REFERENCING clause enables you to refer to table values before
the trigger action takes place when the OLD keyword is used, and to refer
to tables values after the trigger action takes place when the NEW keyword
is used.

In the CREATE TRIGGER statement, a table name is specified. If the trigger
event is an INSERT, only an insert operation on the specified table causes
the trigger to fire. Similarly, if the trigger event is a DELETE, only a delete
operation on the specified table causes the trigger to fire. If the trigger event
is an UPDATE on one or more columns in a table, only an UPDATE on those
columns of the specified table causes the trigger to fire.

Trigger action time

A trigger can fire either immediately before the trigger event or immediately
after it, as specified by either the BEFORE or the AFTER keyword.

Triggered actions

There are two kinds of triggers, *row-level* triggers and *statement-level* triggers. A row-level trigger is one whose triggered SQL statement is executed
for every row that is modified by the triggering statement. A statement-level
trigger is one whose triggered SQL statement is executed only once, each
time the triggering statement is executed. The default triggered action is FOR
EACH STATEMENT, if neither FOR EACH ROW nor FOR EACH STATEMENT
is specified. The WHEN clause in a triggered action enables you to specify a
condition. The trigger fires only if the condition evaluates to TRUE.

Triggered SQL statement

The triggered SQL statement can either be a single SQL statement or a BEGIN ATOMIC...END block containing multiple SQL statements. Here's an example:

```
CREATE TRIGGER notify
   AFTER INSERT ON MEMBERS
   FOR EACH STATEMENT
      BEGIN ATOMIC
         CALL send_email ('President', 'New member') ;
         INSERT INTO CHANGE_LOG
            VALUES ('MEMBERS', :vfirstname, :vlastname) ;
      END ;
```

Whenever a new row is inserted into the MEMBERS table, an e-mail message is sent to the organization's president, informing her of the new member. At the same time, a new row is inserted into the CHANGE_LOG table, which records all insertions, deletions, and updates to any table in the database.

Stored Functions

A stored function is similar in many ways to a stored procedure. Collectively, the two are referred to as *stored routines.* They are different in several ways, including the way in which they are invoked. A stored procedure is invoked with a CALL statement, and a stored function is invoked with a function call, which can replace an argument of an SQL statement. The following is an example of a function definition, followed by an example of a call to that function:

```
CREATE FUNCTION Engine (test_engine_ID Integer)
   RETURNS NUMERIC (5,2)

   BEGIN ATOMIC
      DECLARE vdisplacement NUMERIC (5,2)
         DEFAULT '' ;
      SET vdisplacement = (SELECT Displacement FROM FORD
                           WHERE EngineID = test_engine_ID);
   RETURN vdisplacement;
   END ;
```

This function definition returns the displacement of the Ford engine whose engineID is supplied as input. The following SET statement contains a function call to Engine that retrieves the displacement of the engine identified by EngineID = 4004:

```
SET displace = Engine (EngineID)
   WHERE EngineID = 4004 ;
```

Passing Out Privileges

The various privileges that you can grant to users are discussed in Book I, Chapter 4. The database owner can grant the following privileges to other users:

+ The right to DELETE rows from a table

+ The right to INSERT rows into a table

+ The right to UPDATE rows in a table

+ The right to create a table that REFERENCES another table

+ The right of USAGE on a domain

SQL/PSM adds one more privilege that can be granted to a user — the EXECUTE privilege. Here are two examples:

```
GRANT EXECUTE on ForeignOrDomestic to SalesManager ;

GRANT EXECUTE on Engine to Mechanic ;
```

These statements allow the sales manager of the used car dealer to execute the ForeignOrDomestic procedure, and any mechanic in the shop to execute the Engine function. People lacking the EXECUTE privilege for a routine aren't able to use the routine.

Stored Modules

A *stored module* can contain multiple routines (procedures or functions) that can be invoked by SQL. Anyone who has the EXECUTE privilege for a module has access to all the routines in the module. Privileges on routines within a module can't be granted individually. The following is an example of a stored module:

```
CREATE MODULE mod1
   CREATE PROCEDURE ForeignOrDomestic
      ( IN manufacturer CHAR (20),
        OUT origin CHAR (8) )
   BEGIN ATOMIC
      CASE manufacturer
         WHEN 'General Motors' THEN
            SET origin = 'domestic' ;
         WHEN 'Ford' THEN
            SET origin = 'domestic' ;
         WHEN 'Chrysler' THEN
```

```
            SET origin = 'domestic' ;
        WHEN 'Studebaker' THEN
            SET origin = 'domestic' ;
        ELSE
            SET origin = 'foreign' ;
      END CASE
    END ;

    CREATE FUNCTION Engine (test_engine_ID Integer)
    RETURNS NUMERIC (5,2)

    BEGIN ATOMIC
        DECLARE vdisplacement NUMERIC (5,2)
            DEFAULT '' ;
        SET vdisplacement = (SELECT Displacement FROM FORD
                           WHERE EngineID = test_engine_ID);
        RETURN vdisplacement;
        END ;
END MODULE ;
```

The two routines in this module don't have much in common, but they don't have to. You can gather related routines into a single module, or you can stick all the routines you are likely to use into a single module, regardless of whether they have anything in common.

Chapter 7: Connecting to a Remote Database

In This Chapter

✔ Connecting through a remote driver

✔ Connecting through ODBC

✔ What really happens when you make a connection

*W*ith a standalone desktop database system, communication is never an issue. The data-driven application you write has only one place to go for data: the database on your hard disk. Your desktop database management system provides the interface between your application code and the database. This simple situation, once very common, has largely been replaced by client/server database systems that reside on a local area network (LAN) or wide area network (WAN), or Web-based systems that operate over the Internet. In these more complicated configurations, you must communicate with different database back ends in different ways.

In this chapter, I discuss client/server systems. A simple client/server system has one server machine that hosts the database. Multiple client computers are connected to the server over a LAN. Users sit at the client machines, which execute your database application program. Larger systems can have multiple servers, each holding different databases. The part of your program written in a host language such as C++, C#, or Java is executed on the client machine, but the SQL is sent over the network to a server. Before it is sent to the server, the SQL must be translated into something the database understands. Several different methods of doing this exist.

Native Drivers

The simplest form of communication between an application and a database is through a *native driver*. Figure 7-1 shows how a native driver specific to Oracle 10g connects your application to an Oracle 10g database.

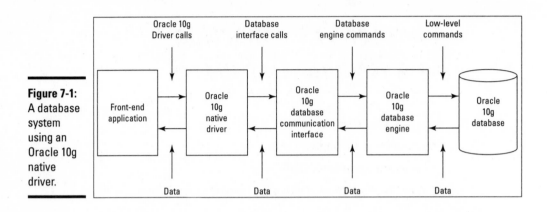

Figure 7-1:
A database
system
using an
Oracle 10g
native
driver.

This arrangement is not much different from that of a standalone desktop database system. The Oracle 10g native driver is specifically designed to take SQL from the application and translate it into Oracle 10g database commands. When the database returns a result set, the native driver translates it into a standard SQL result set and passes it back to the application.

Because native drivers are specifically designed to work with a particular database, they can be highly optimized for that specific situation and thus have very good performance. That specificity, which makes possible the native driver's greatest strength, is also its biggest weakness. When you build a database system that uses a native driver to connect to one type of database, say Oracle 10g, the connection does not work with any other type of database, such as SQL Server.

When you write a database application, the part of the application that communicates with the database is called the Application Programming Interface (API). When you are communicating to databases through native drivers, every native driver is different from all the others, so the API is different for each one, too. This complicates the design and development of applications that must deal with multiple data sources.

Native drivers are great if you know that the application you are writing will have to interface with only one specific data source, both now and in the future. You can't beat the performance of a well-designed native driver. However, if there is a possibility that your application may need to pull data from more than one source, you may want to consider one of the interface options that are not product-specific.

ODBC and Its Major Components

An application may need to access data in multiple databases of incompatible types. Incorporating multiple APIs into your code is not a desirable solution. Happily, there is a better way. ODBC, which stands for Open Database Connectivity, is a widely accepted standard method of communicating with most popular database formats. It accomplishes this by adding an extra layer between the application and the database. Figure 7-2 shows this arrangement. It is unlikely that you would want to connect any realistic application to five different data sources, as shown in Figure 7-2, but with ODBC, you could.

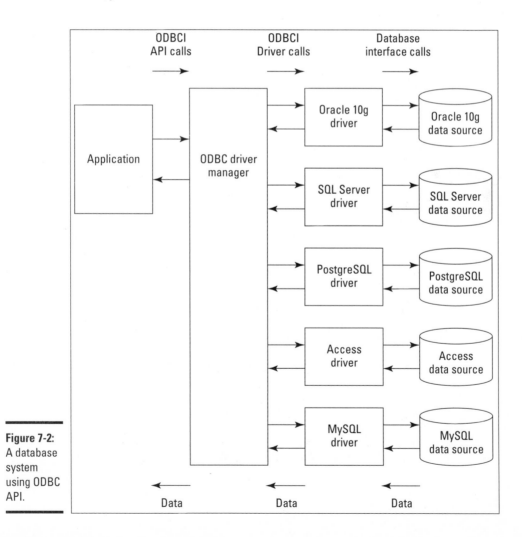

Figure 7-2:
A database system using ODBC API.

The application communicates directly with the driver manager. The front-end of the driver manager always presents the same API to the application. The back end of the driver manager connects to a driver that is specific to the database on the back end. The driver, in turn, connects to the database. This arrangement means that the application programmer never has to worry about the details of how to connect to the database on the back end. All you have to do is make your program compatible with the ODBC API, and you will be successful. The driver manager makes sure that the correct driver is in place to communicate with the database.

ODBC is a direct response to the needs of developers who are designing applications to run on client/server systems. People designing for stand-alone PCs running integrated DBMS systems don't need ODBC. Neither do people designing for proprietary mainframes. The whole point of ODBC is to present a common interface to database applications, so that the application developer does not have to write code specific to whatever platform the data is located on. ODBC translates standard syntax coming from the application into custom syntax specific to the back-end database being accessed. It even allows an application to access multiple different back-end databases at the same time, without getting confused. To provide its function, ODBC can be conceptually (and physically) divided into four major components.

The four major components are the application, the driver manager, the driver, and the data source. The application is the component closest to the user, and the data source is the component that holds the data. Each different type of data source has its own driver. The driver manager manages communication between the application and the data source, through the driver.

Application

The *application* is a piece of software that interacts directly with the user, and that requires access to data. If you are an application programmer, the application is the one ODBC component that you create. It can be a custom program written in a procedural language such as C++ or Visual Basic. It can be a spreadsheet or a word processing package. It can be an interactive query tool. Just about any piece of software that works with data and interacts with a user can be the application portion of an ODBC system. The data accessed by the application can be from a relational database, from an ISAM (Indexed Sequential Access Method) file or from a straight ASCII text file. ODBC provides a lot of flexibility in what kinds of applications can use it and in what kinds of data those applications can access.

Driver manager

The *driver manager* is a library (under Windows it is a Dynamic-Link Library) that provides a common interface to applications, regardless of what data source is being accessed. It performs such functions as

+ Determining which driver to load, based on the data source name supplied by the application

+ Loading and unloading drivers

+ Calling driver functions

+ Implementing some functions itself

+ Performing error checking

A Dynamic-Link Library (DLL) is a library of routines that is linked to an application at runtime. In the case of a driver manager, the routines perform the various functions listed above.

The value of the driver manager is that the application can make function calls to it without regard for which driver or data source is currently in use. After the application identifies the needed driver and data source by sending the driver manager a connection handle, the driver manager loads the driver and builds a table of pointers to the functions in that driver. The application programmer does not need to worry about maintaining a table of pointers to functions in the driver. The driver manager does it under the covers.

Driver managers are written and distributed by the companies that write drivers. Microsoft, Serena, Borland, and OpenLink Software are examples of companies that provide the driver manager component of ODBC systems.

Drivers

Drivers are libraries that implement the functions of the ODBC API. Each driver has a common interface to the driver manager, but its interface to its data source is customized to that particular data source.

Companies that specialize in driver development, such as those listed in the previous section, have developed and made available drivers for most of the popular data sources in use today. As a result, most people never need to write their own drivers. Only those working with unusual data sources, or those requiring functions not supported by standard drivers, need to write their own drivers, using a procedural language such as C or Java.

Two different kinds of drivers exist: file-based drivers and DBMS-based drivers. File-based drivers are used in one-tier configurations, and DBMS-based drivers are used in two-tier configurations.

File-based drivers

File-based drivers are so named because the driver processes the data source directly. A file-based driver must be capable of processing SQL statements and performing the appropriate operations on the database. No DBMS is involved. File-based drivers apply to desktop databases such as FoxPro as well as to spreadsheet files and other flat files. You can use a file-based driver on a standalone PC or on a network. Figure 7-3 shows a typical one-tier configuration.

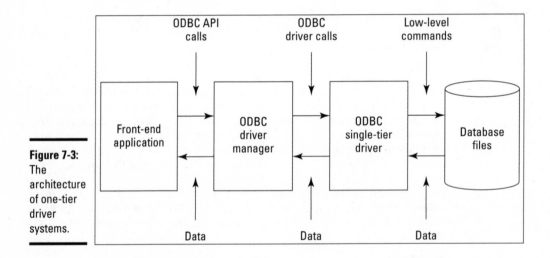

Figure 7-3: The architecture of one-tier driver systems.

In the standalone system, the application, driver manager, driver, and data storage are all on the same system. In the network case, the application, driver manager and the driver are on the client, and only the data source is on the server machine. All the intelligence is on the client.

DBMS-based drivers

DBMS-based drivers operate on multiuser systems operating in true client/server mode. This mode of operation features a balance between the client and server machines. Both do significant processing. The application, driver manager, and driver all reside on the client machine. Together they comprise the "client" part of the client/server system. The data source is composed of the DBMS, such as SQL Server, Oracle, or DB2, and the database itself. These components are located on the server machine. DBMS-based drivers are generally easier to write than file-based drivers because they only need to translate ODBC-compatible SQL statements to commands the database engine understands and handle any results that come back. Figure 7-4 shows the two-tier configuration.

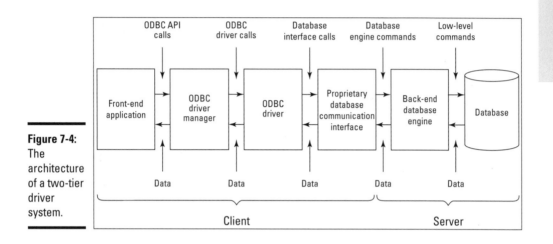

Figure 7-4:
The architecture of a two-tier driver system.

Can ODBC drivers perform as well as native drivers?

You may have heard that ODBC is good because it frees the application developer from having to customize applications to each potential target data source. You may also have heard that ODBC is bad because database access through an ODBC interface is slower than access through a database's native drivers. This criticism makes sense because it seems that going through an extra layer of processing cannot help but slow things down. In fact, database access using ODBC 1.0 *was* significantly slower than the same access through a native driver. Going through an extra layer of processing does slow things down. However, using ODBC does not require you to go through that extra layer.

One big reason ODBC 1.0 access was slow was because the early drivers that implemented it

merely accepted SQL from the application and converted it to the DBMS's native API calls. This has to be slower than a system that generates the native API calls in the first place. Performance of ODBC 2.0 and later drivers has been much better. This is largely due to the fact that these more recent drivers have been written to use the DBMS's underlying data stream protocol rather than the native API. Instead of making an ODBC call that makes a native API call, that uses the data stream protocol, current ODBC drivers use the data stream protocol directly. With this architectural change, ODBC driver performance has become competitive with native driver performance, even exceeding it on some benchmarks.

Data sources

The *data source,* as the name implies, is the source of the data that is accessed by the application. It can be a spreadsheet file, an ASCII file, or a database under the control of a DBMS. The user need not know the technical details of the data source, such as file type, DBMS, operating system, or hardware. The name of the data source is all the user needs to know.

What Happens When the Application Makes a Request

Application development consists of writing, compiling, linking, executing, and debugging. When you get an application to function the way you want it to, you can release it to users. Applications that use ODBC are linked to the Driver Manager's import library at link time. The import library contains those parts of ODBC that deal with importing instructions from the application. Under Windows, the import library is named ODBC32.LIB. In addition to ODBC32.LIB, a running application also makes use of ODBC32.DLL and a driver compatible with the data source. ODBC32.DLL remains loaded in memory as long as any running application requires it. When the last ODBC-enabled application terminates, ODBC32.DLL is unloaded from memory.

Using handles to identify objects

ODBC makes extensive use of the concept of handles. A *handle* is an integer value that identifies an object used by an application. ODBC uses three types of handles that are related to each other in a hierarchical fashion:

+ **Environment handle:** The environment handle is ODBC's global context handle. Every application that uses ODBC must first allocate an environment handle, and, when it finishes, it must free that handle. Every executing application has one and only one environment handle.

+ **Connection handle:** An application connects to one or more data sources. Each such connection is managed by a connection handle. The connection handle identifies the driver used in the connection for the routing of the ODBC function calls. The driver manager keeps a list of all connection handles associated with an environment handle. The application uses the connection handle to establish and also to break the connection to a data source. The connection handle also passes error codes for connection errors back to the application and sets connection options.

+ **Statement handle:** A third kind of handle used by ODBC is the statement handle. Statement handles process SQL statements and catalog functions. When the application sends a function call that contains a statement handle to the driver manager, the driver manager extracts a connection handle from it to route the function call to the correct driver.

An application can have one and only one environment handle. Conversely, each environment handle can be assigned to one and only one application. A single environment handle can "own" multiple connections, each represented by a single connection handle. Each connection can "own" multiple statements, each represented by a single statement handle. Figure 7-5 shows how to use environment handles, connection handles, and statement handles to establish a connection to a data source, execute some SQL statements, and then to break the connection.

Figure 7-5:
Handles
establish
the
connection
between an
application
and a data
source.

The six stages of an ODBC operation

An ODBC operation takes place in distinct stages. Each stage builds on the one that preceded it. Handles provide the mechanism for the exchange of commands and information. First an environment is established. Next a connection between application and data source is built; then an SQL statement is sent to the data source for processing. Results are returned from the data source to the application, and finally the connection is terminated.

Stage 1: The application allocates environment and connection handles in the driver manager

ODBC-enabled applications communicate with the rest of the ODBC system by making function calls. The first step in the process is to allocate an environment handle and a connection handle. Two invocations of the function call `SQLAllocHandle` do the job. The driver manager allocates space in memory for the requested handles and returns the handles to the application. The first invocation of `SQLAllocHandle` initializes the ODBC interface, in addition to allocating memory for global information. If the first `SQLAllocHandle` function executes successfully, execution can proceed to the second `SQLAllocHandle` function. This invocation of `SQLAllocHandle` allocates memory for a connection handle and its associated connection information. `SQLAllocHandle` takes the active environment handle as input and returns a pointer to the newly allocated connection handle as an output. Depending on which development tool they are using, application programmers may or may not have to explicitly allocate environment and connection handles.

Stage 2: The driver manager finds the appropriate driver

After environment and connection handles have established a link between the application and the driver manager, the next step in the process is to link the driver manager to the appropriate driver. There are two functions for accomplishing this task, `SQLConnect` and `SQLDriverConnect`. `SQLConnect` is the simpler of the two, requiring only the connection handle, data source name, user identifier, and user password as input parameters. When the establishment of a connection requires more information than `SQLConnect` provides, `SQLDriverConnect` is used. It passes a connection string to the driver attached to the data source.

Stage 3: The driver manager loads the driver

In a Windows system, after the connection between the driver manager and the driver has been established, the driver manager obtains a library handle for the driver. It then calls the Windows function `GetProcAddress` for each function in the driver. The function addresses are stored in an array associated with the connection handle.

Stage 4: The driver manager allocates environment and connection handles in the driver

Now that the driver has been loaded, environment and connection handles can be called in it. The function SQLAllocHandle can be used for this purpose, as it was used to call the environment and connection handles in the driver manager. If the application uses the function SQLSetConnectOption to set options for the connection, the driver manager calls the driver's SQLSetConnectOption function at this time to enable those options to be set.

Stage 5: The driver manager connects to the data source through the driver

Now at last, the driver manager completes the connection to the data source by calling SQLConnect or SQLDriverConnect. If the driver is a one-tier driver, there is no network connection to make, so this stage is trivial. If it is a multi-tier driver, the driver now calls the network interface software in the client machine, which connects to the server machine that holds the data source. To make this connection, the driver uses information that was stored in the ODBC.INI file when the data source name was created.

After the connection is established in a client/server system, the driver usually sends the user name and password to the server for validation. If the user name and password are valid, the driver returns a standard SQL_ SUCCESS code to the driver manager. If they are not valid, the server returns an error code to the driver. The driver then translates this error code to the standard ODBC error code and returns it to the driver manager as SQLSTATE. The driver manager then returns SQLSTATE to the application.

Stage 6: The data source (finally) executes an SQL statement

With the connection at last established, an SQL statement can be executed. Even this, however, is a multi-stage process. First a statement handle must be allocated. The application does this by issuing an SQLAllocHandle call. When the driver manager receives this call, it allocates a statement handle and then sends an SQLAllocHandle call to the driver. The driver then allocates its own statement handle before returning control to the driver manager, which then returns control to the application.

After the statement handle has been allocated, an SQL statement can be executed. There is more than one way to do this, but the simplest is with the SQLExecDirect function. SQLExecDirect takes a character string as input and sends it to the server. The character string should be a valid SQL statement. If necessary, the driver translates the statement from

ODBC-standard SQL to commands understood by the data source on the server. When the data source receives the request for action, it processes the command and then returns any results to the application via the driver and driver manager. The exact details of this processing and how the results are returned to the client application may differ from one data source (DBMS) to another. These differences are masked by the driver, so that the application always sees standard ODBC responses, regardless of what data source it is communicating with.

The following is a fragment of C code showing the allocation of environment, connection, and statement handles and connection to a data source.

```c
SQLRETURN cliRC = SQL_SUCCESS;
int rc = 0;
SQLHANDLE henv; /* environment handle */
SQLHANDLE hdbc; /* connection handle */
SQLHANDLE hstmt; /* statement handle */

char dbAlias[SQL_MAX_DSN_LENGTH + 1];
char user[MAX_UID_LENGTH + 1];
char pswd[MAX_PWD_LENGTH + 1];

/* check the command line arguments */
rc = CmdLineArgsCheck1(argc, argv, dbAlias, user, pswd);
if (rc != 0)
{
  return 1;
}

/* allocate an environment handle */
cliRC = SQLAllocHandle(SQL_HANDLE_ENV, SQL_NULL_HANDLE,
  &henv);
if (cliRC != SQL_SUCCESS)
{
  printf("\n--ERROR while allocating the environment
  handle.\n");
  printf("  cliRC = %d\n", cliRC);
  printf("  line  = %d\n", __LINE__);
  printf("  file  = %s\n", __FILE__);
  return 1;
}

/* set attribute to enable application to run as ODBC 3.0
  application */
cliRC = SQLSetEnvAttr(henv,
                 SQL_ATTR_ODBC_VERSION,
                 (void *)SQL_OV_ODBC3,
                 0);
```

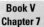

```
ENV_HANDLE_CHECK(henv, cliRC);

/* allocate a database connection handle */
cliRC = SQLAllocHandle(SQL_HANDLE_DBC, henv, &hdbc);
ENV_HANDLE_CHECK(henv, cliRC);

/* connect to the database */
cliRC = SQLConnect(hdbc,
                   (SQLCHAR *)dbAlias, SQL_NTS,
                   (SQLCHAR *)user,
                   SQL_NTS,
                   (SQLCHAR *)pswd,
                   SQL_NTS);
DBC_HANDLE_CHECK(hdbc, cliRC);

/* allocate one or more statement handles */
cliRC = SQLAllocHandle(SQL_HANDLE_STMT, hdbc, &hstmt);
DBC_HANDLE_CHECK(hdbc, cliRC);
```

Book VI

SQL and XML

The 5th Wave   By Rich Tennant

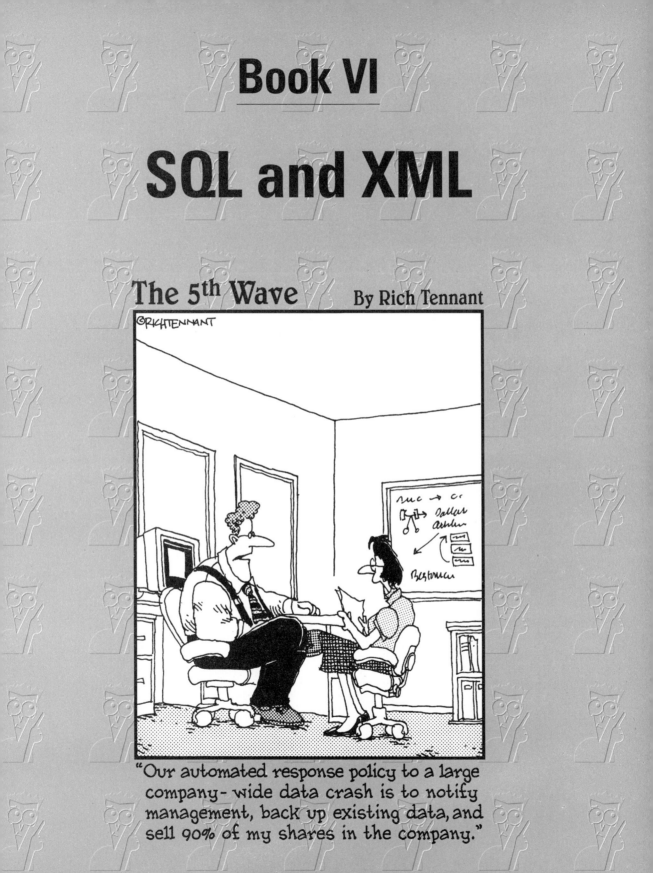

"Our automated response policy to a large company-wide data crash is to notify management, back up existing data, and sell 90% of my shares in the company."

Contents at a Glance

Chapter 1: XML/SQL Basics

In This Chapter

✔ Using XML to bridge communication gaps

✔ Becoming familiar with XML and XML document parts

✔ The XML data type

✔ Mapping SQL to XML

✔ Operating on XML data with SQL functions

XML stands for Extensible Markup Language, a general-purpose markup language that, like HTML, is a subset of SGML (Standard Generalized Markup Language). XML's primary purpose is to serve as a means of sharing information between information systems that could have very different architectures. SQL provides the worldwide standard method for storing data in a highly structured fashion, which enables users to maintain data stores of a wide range of sizes, and to efficiently extract from those data stores the information they want. XML has risen from a de facto standard to an official standard vehicle for transporting data between incompatible systems, particularly over the Internet. By bringing these two powerful methods together, the value of both is greatly increased. SQL can now handle data that doesn't fit nicely into the strict relational paradigm that was originally defined by Dr. Codd. XML can now efficiently take data from SQL databases or send data to them. The result is more readily available information that is easier to share.

XML has come to be a popular means of sharing data over the Internet, particularly over the World Wide Web. A number of derivatives of XML designed to carry specific kinds of data are in use. A few examples are RSS, XHTML, MathML, Scalable Vector Graphics, and MusicML.

Introducing XML

XML is a markup language that marks up text documents with begin and end tags. The tags are in some way descriptive of the meaning of the text that they enclose. Key features are the character data itself, containers called elements, and the attributes of those elements. The data is structured as a tree, with a root element playing host to branch elements, which can in turn give rise to additional branches.

The fundamental unit of XML is a Unicode character. Both eight-bit and sixteen-bit versions of Unicode are required by the international XML specification. When characters are combined, they form an XML document. The document consists of one or more entities, each of which holds a portion of the document's characters.

The XML specification does not specify the names of the elements, the allowable hierarchy, or the meanings of the elements and attributes, as for example, HTML does. XML is much more flexible, leaving the specification of those items to a customizable schema. The XML specification specifies what syntax is legal, and the schema supplements the syntax rules with a set of constraints. Such a constraint can restrict element and attribute names, and the structure of the containment hierarchy. For example, an element named *book* could be restricted to contain no more than ten elements named *chapter*. A different schema could allow up to 20 chapters in a book.

Some of XML's salient characteristics are

+ It is readable by both humans and machines

+ It supports Unicode, so even ideographic languages such as Chinese can be represented

+ It can represent a variety of common data structures, including records, lists, and trees

+ It is self-documenting

+ XML elements have a simple structure and thus are easily parsed

+ It adheres to an international standard

+ It is platform-independent

The Parts of an XML Document

An XML document contains several different parts. I describe them briefly, but first here is some sample XML syntax:

```
<name attribute="value">content</name>
```

Here's a description of the components of a popular game, expressed in XML:

```
<?xml version="1.0" encoding="UTF-8"?>
<game name="chess">
  <title>Chess game</title>
  <gameboard quantity="1">board</gameboard>
```

```
<whitepiece quantity="1">king</whitepiece>
<whitepiece quantity="1">queen</whitepiece>
<whitepiece quantity="2">rook</whitepiece>
<whitepiece quantity="2">bishop</whitepiece>
<whitepiece quantity="2">knight</whitepiece>
<whitepiece quantity="8">pawn</whitepiece>
<blackpiece quantity="1">king</blackpiece>
<blackpiece quantity="1">queen</blackpiece>
<blackpiece quantity="2">rook</blackpiece>
<blackpiece quantity="2">bishop</blackpiece>
<blackpiece quantity="2">knight</blackpiece>
<blackpiece quantity="8">pawn</blackpiece>
<instructions>
  <action>Place pieces on their start squares.</action>
  <action>Play chess, white moving first.</action>
  <action>Play until someone wins or a draw is
declared.</action>
  <action>Shake hands.</action>
</instructions>
</game>
```

XML declaration

The first line of an XML document is usually its *declaration*. The declaration is optional, but informative. It states the version of XML that is being used and may also contain information about character encoding and external objects that the document depends upon. An XML declaration looks something like this:

```
<?xml version "1.0" encoding="UTF-8"?>
```

UTF indicates that a version of Unicode is being used that uses as few as one or as many as four bytes to hold a character. For alphabetic languages such as English, this is fine. Chinese, for example, would use UTF-16, which uses a minimum of two bytes per character.

Elements

After the XML declaration, the rest of an XML document consists of elements. *Elements* may contain attributes and content, and they may be nested. An element starts with a start tag consisting of a name enclosed in angle brackets, and ends with an end tag consisting of the same name preceded by a slash, also enclosed in angle brackets. The element's content is anything that appears between the tags. Here's an example of an element:

```
<action>Place pieces on their start squares.</action>
```

Nested elements

Elements can be *nested* inside other elements:

```
<instructions>
    <action>Place pieces on their start squares.</action>
    <action>Play chess, white moving first.</action>
    <action>Play until someone wins or a draw is
    declared.</action>
    <action>Shake hands.</action>
</instructions>
```

The instructions element contains the four action elements.

The document element

Every XML document must have one and only one top level element, serving as the root of the tree structure, called the *document* element.

Empty elements

An element might exist, but have no content. In such a case it consists of nothing but its start tag and end tag. There are a couple of alternate syntax possibilities for an empty element, using a single tag containing the element name followed by a slash. Here are the three possible syntaxes, which are all equivalent to each other.

```
<nothing></nothing>
<nothing />
<nothing/>
```

Attributes

An element may or may not have attributes. *Attributes* are pairs of names and values that are included in the start tag, after the element name. Attribute values must be enclosed in quotes, either single or double, and each attribute name should appear only once in an element.

```
<blackpiece quantity="2">rook</blackpiece>
```

In this example, the blackpiece element has one attribute, named quantity, which has a value of 2. The quotes show that 2 is a character that represents the number 2, rather than being the number itself.

Entity references

As I discuss later in this chapter, XML is considerably more restrictive than SQL in terms of the characters it recognizes. Whereas SQL recognizes a large number of special characters, XML pretty much only recognizes the upper- and lowercase letters, the integers, and a few punctuation marks. To include special characters in an XML document, you can use *entity references.* An entity reference is a placeholder that represents an entity, typically an unusual character. An entity reference consists of an ampersand (&), the reference, and ends with a semicolon (;). In XML there are five predeclared entity references:

+ & (&)

+ < (<)

+ > (>)

+ ' (')

+ " (")

Here is an example of a predeclared XML entity that uses the entity reference for the ampersand.

```
<company>Smith &amp; Sons, Plumbing, Inc.</company>
```

When viewed in a Web browser, this displays as

Smith & Sons, Plumbing, Inc.

In addition to the five predeclared entity references, you can also create additional ones, using the document's Document Type Definition or XML Schema. Here's an example of the declaration of an entity that has not been predeclared:

```
<?xml version="1.0" encoding=UTF-8"?>
<!DOCTYPE rtm [
  <!ENTITY reg "&#xAE;">
  <!ENTITY registered-TM "ACME&reg; Fireworks, Inc.">
]>
<rtm>
  &registered-TM;
</rtm>
```

AE is the code in hexadecimal for the registered trademark symbol. When displayed in a browser, the rtm document appears as

```
<rtm> ACME(r) Fireworks, Inc. </rtm>
```

Numeric character references

Another way of representing a non-standard character is with a numeric character reference. This method just uses the decimal or hexadecimal code for a character. For decimal, the code is preceded by a # sign. For hexadecimal, the code is preceded by #x. First decimal:

```
<trademark>ACME&#174; Fireworks, Inc.</trademark>
```

and then hexadecimal:

```
<trademark>ACME&#xAE; Fireworks, Inc.</trademark>
```

XML Schema

XML Schema is one of several XML schema languages that are more powerful and flexible than the DTD (Document Type Definition) used in the earlier "Entity references" section. A *schema* is a set of rules that a valid XML document must conform to. XML Schema does that, but goes beyond to the extent of validating information that adheres to specific data types. It is particularly well suited to validating document processing software.

An XML Schema Definition (XSD) is an instance of XML Schema and usually has a filename extension of .xsd. Here's an example of a simple XSD describing a member of the Oregon Lunar Society:

```
<xs:schema
 xmlns:xs=http://www.w3.org/2001/XMLSchema>
 <xs:element name="members" type="Members"/>
 <xs:complexType name="Members">
  <xs:sequence>
   <xs:element name="firstname" type="xs:string"/>
   <xs:element name="lastname" type="xs:string"/>
   <xs:element name="officeheld" type="xs:string"/>
  </xs:sequence>
 </ComplexType>
</xs:schema>
```

An XML document that conforms to this schema might look like the following:

```
<members
 xmlns:xsi=http://www.w3.org/2001/XMLSchema-instance
 xsi:noNameSpaceSchemaLocation="members.xsd">
  <firstname>Bryce</firstname>
  <lastname>Thoreau</lastname>
  <officeheld>Treasurer</officeheld>
</members>
```

An XSD is written in XML Schema and applies constraints on the elements and attributes that may appear in the XML documents to which it applies. It also defines the relationships among the elements and attributes, as well as the types of data that they may contain. XSDs are used to validate XML documents.

Relating SQL to XML

XML, like HTML, is a markup language, which means it's not a full-function language such as C++ or Java. It's not even a data sublanguage such as SQL. However, unlike those languages, it is cognizant of the content of the data it transports. Where HTML deals only with formatting the text and graphics in a document, XML gives structure to the document's content. XML itself does not deal with formatting. To do that, you have to augment XML with a style sheet. As it does with HTML, a style sheet applies formatting to an XML document.

SQL and XML provide two different ways of structuring data so that you can save it and retrieve selected information from it:

✦ SQL is an excellent tool for dealing with numeric and text data that can be categorized by data type and have a well-defined size. SQL was created as a standard way to maintain and operate on data kept in relational databases.

✦ XML is better at dealing with free-form data that cannot be easily categorized. The driving motivations for the creation of XML were to provide a universal standard for transferring data between dissimilar computers and for displaying it on the World Wide Web.

The strengths and goals of SQL and XML are complementary. Each reigns supreme in its own domain and forms alliances with the other to give users the information they want, when they want it, and where they want it.

The XML Data Type

SQL:2003 introduced a new data type to SQL: the XML type. This means that conforming implementations can store and operate on XML-formatted data directly, without first converting to XML from one of the other SQL data types.

The XML data type, including its subtypes, although intrinsic to any implementation that supports it, acts like a user-defined type (UDT). The XML type brings SQL and XML into close contact because it enables applications to perform SQL operations on XML content, and XML operations on SQL content. You can include a column of the XML type with columns of any of the other predefined types covered in Chapter 5 of Book I in a join operation in the WHERE clause of a query. In true relational database fashion, your DBMS determines the optimal way to execute the query, and then does it.

When to use the XML type

Whether you should store data in XML format depends on what you plan to do with that data. Here are some instances where it makes sense to store data in XML format:

+ When you want to store an entire block of data and retrieve the whole block later.

+ When you want to be able to query the whole XML document. Some implementations have expanded the scope of the EXTRACT operator to enable extracting desired content from an XML document.

+ When you need strong typing of data inside SQL statements. Using the XML type guarantees that data values are valid XML values and not just arbitrary text strings.

+ To ensure compatibility with future, as yet unspecified, storage systems that might not support existing types such as CLOB. (See Chapter 5 of Book I for more information on CLOB.)

+ To take advantage of future optimizations that support only the XML type.

Here's an example of how you might use the XML type:

```
CREATE TABLE CLIENT (
     ClientName          CHARACTER (30)        NOT NULL,
     Address1            CHARACTER (30),
     Address2            CHARACTER (30),
     City                CHARACTER (25),
     State               CHARACTER (2),
     PostalCode          CHARACTER (10),
     Phone               CHARACTER (13),
     Fax                 CHARACTER (13),
     ContactPerson       CHARACTER (30),
     Comments            XML(SEQUENCE) ) ;
```

This syntax stores an XML document in the Comments column of the CLIENT table, although not all implementations may support it yet. The document might look something like the following:

```
<Comments>
  <Comment>
    <CommentNo>1</CommentNo>
    <MessageText>Is VetLab equipped to analyze penguin
    blood?</MessageText>
```

```
    <ResponseRequested>Yes</ResponseRequested>
   </Comment>
   <Comment
    <CommentNo>2</CommentNo>
    <MessageText>Thanks for the fast turnaround on the
    leopard seal sputum sample.</MessageText>
    <ResponseRequested>No</ResponseRequested>
   </Comment>
</Comments>
```

When not to use the XML type

On many occasions, it doesn't make sense to use the XML type. Most data in relational databases today is better off in its current format than it is in XML format. Here are a couple of examples of when not to use the XML type:

✦ When the data breaks down naturally into a relational structure with tables, rows, and columns

✦ When you need to update pieces of the document, rather than deal with the document as a whole

Mapping SQL to XML

To exchange data between SQL databases and XML documents, the various elements of an SQL database must be translatable (mapped) into equivalent elements of an XML document, and vice versa. This translation needs to happen for several kinds of things, as described in the following sections.

Mapping character sets to XML

In SQL, the character sets supported are implementation-dependent. This means that IBM's DB2 may support character sets that are not supported by Microsoft's SQL Server. SQL Server may support character sets not supported by Oracle. Although the most common character sets are almost universally supported, using a less common character set may make it difficult to migrate your database and application from one RDBMS platform to another.

XML has no compatibility issue with character sets — it supports only one, Unicode. This is a good thing from the point of view of exchanging data between any given SQL implementation and XML. All the RDBMS vendors have to define a mapping between strings of each of their character sets and Unicode, as well as a reverse mapping from Unicode to each of their character sets. Luckily, XML does not also support multiple character sets. If it did, vendors would have a many-to-many problem, requiring many more mappings and reverse mappings.

Mapping identifiers to XML

XML is much stricter than SQL in the characters it allows in identifiers. Characters that are legal in SQL but illegal in XML must be mapped to something legal before they can become part of an XML document. SQL supports delimited identifiers. This means that all sorts of odd characters such as %, $, and & are legal, as long as they're enclosed within double quotes. Such characters are not legal in XML. Furthermore, XML Names that begin with the characters *XML* in any combination of cases, are reserved and thus cannot be used with impunity. SQL identifiers that begin with those letters have to be changed.

An agreed-upon mapping bridges the identifier gap between SQL and XML. In moving from SQL to XML, all SQL identifiers are converted to Unicode. From there, any SQL identifiers that are also legal XML Names are left unchanged. SQL identifier characters that are not legal XML Names are replaced with a hexadecimal code that either takes the form _xNNNN_ or _xNNNNNNNN_, where *N* represents an uppercase hexadecimal digit. For example, the underscore _ is represented by _x005F_. The colon is represented by _x003A_. These representations are the codes for the Unicode characters for the underscore and colon. The case where an SQL identifier starts with the characters *x, m,* and *l* is handled by prefixing all such instances with a code in the form _xFFFF_.

Conversion from XML to SQL is much easier. All you need to do is scan the characters of an XML name for a sequence of _xNNNN_ or _xNNNNNNNN_. Whenever you find such a sequence, replace it with the character that the Unicode corresponds to. For example, when you come across _x003A_, replace it with :. If an XML Name begins with the characters _xFFFF_, ignore them.

By following these simple rules, you can map an SQL identifier to an XML Name and then back to an SQL identifier again. However, this happy situation does not hold for a mapping from XML Name to SQL identifier and back to XML Name.

Mapping data types to XML

The SQL standard specifies that an SQL data type be mapped to the closest possible XML Schema data type. The designation *closest possible* means that all values allowed by the SQL type are allowed by the XML Schema type, and the fewest possible values not allowed by the SQL type are allowed by the XML Schema type. XML facets, such as `maxInclusive` and `minInclusive`, can restrict the values allowed by the XML Schema type to the values allowed by the corresponding SQL type. For example, if the SQL data type restricts values of the `INTEGER` type to the range –2157483648<value<2157483647, in XML the `maxInclusive` value can be set to 2157483647, and the `minInclusive` value can be set to –2157483648. Here's an example of such a mapping:

```
<xsd:simpleType>
   <xsd:restriction base="xsd:integer">
      <xsd:maxInclusive value="2157483647"/>
      <xsd:minInclusive value="-2157483648"/>
      <xsd:annotation>
         <sqlxml:sqltype name="INTEGER"/>
      </xsd:annotation>
   </xsd:restriction>
</xsd:simpleType>
```

The annotation section retains information from the SQL type definition that is not used by XML but may be of value later if this document is mapped back to SQL.

Mapping non-predefined data types to XML

In the SQL standard, the non-predefined data types include domain, distinct UDT, row, array, and multiset. You can map each of these to XML-formatted data, using appropriate XML code. The next few sections show examples of how to map these types.

Domain

To map an SQL domain to XML, you must first have a domain. For this example, create one by using a CREATE DOMAIN statement.

```
CREATE DOMAIN WestCoast AS CHAR (2)
   CHECK (State IN ('CA', 'OR', 'WA', 'AK')) ;
```

Now, create a table that uses that domain.

```
CREATE TABLE WestRegion (
   ClientName          Character (20)     NOT NULL,
   State               WestCoast          NOT NULL
   ) ;
```

Here's the XML Schema to map the domain into XML:

```
<xsd:simpleType>
   Name="DOMAIN.Sales.WestCoast">

   <xsd:annotation>
      <xsd:appinfo>
```

```
        <sqlxml:sqltype kind="DOMAIN"
           schemaName="Sales"
           typeName="WestCoast"
           mappedType="CHAR_2"
           final="true"/>
      <xsd:appinfo>
    </xsd:annotation>

    <xsd:restriction base="CHAR_2"/>

</xsd:simpleType>
```

When this mapping is applied, it results in an XML document that contains something like the following:

```
<WestRegion>
   <row>
   <ClientName>Nootka Enterprises</ClientName>
   <State>AK</State>
   </row>
   <row>
   <ClientName>Surfin' USA</ClientName>
   <State>CA</State>
   </row>
   <row>
   <ClientName>Cornelius Semiconductor</ClientName>
   <State>OR</State>
   </row>
   <row>
   <ClientName>Orca Inc.</ClientName>
   <State>WA</State>
   </row>
</WestRegion>
```

Distinct UDT

With a distinct UDT, you can do much the same as what you can do with a domain, but with stronger typing. Here's how:

```
CREATE TYPE WestCoast AS Character (2) FINAL ;
```

The XML Schema to map this type to XML is as follows:

```
<xsd:simpleType>
   Name="UDT.Sales.WestCoast">

   <xsd:annotation>
      <xsd:appinfo>
```

```
        <sqlxml:sqltype kind="DISTINCT"
            schemaName="Sales"
            typeName="WestCoast"
            mappedType="CHAR_2"
            final="true"/>
    <xsd:appinfo>
  </xsd:annotation>

    <xsd:restriction base="CHAR_2"/>

</xsd:simpleType>
```

This creates an element that is the same as the one created for the preceding domain.

Row

The ROW type enables you to cram a whole row's worth of information into a single field of a table row. You can create a ROW type as part of the table definition, in the following manner:

```
CREATE TABLE CONTACTINFO (
    Name            CHARACTER (30)
    Phone           ROW (Home CHAR (13), Work CHAR (13))
) ;
```

You can now map this type to XML with the following schema:

```
<xsd:complexType Name="ROW.1">

    <xsd:annotation>
        <xsd:appinfo>
            <sqlxml:sqltype kind="ROW">
                <sqlxml:field name="Home"
                    mappedType="CHAR_13"/>
                <sqlxml:field name="Work"
                    mappedType="CHAR_13"/>
            </sqlxml:sqltype>
        <xsd:appinfo>
    </xsd:annotation>

    <xsd:sequence>
        <xsd:element Name="Home" nillable="true"
            Type="CHAR_13"/>
        <xsd:element Name="Work" nillable="true"
            Type="CHAR_13"/>
    </xsd:sequence>

</xsd:complexType>
```

This mapping could generate the following XML for a column:

```
<Phone>
    <Home>(888)555-1111</Home>
    <Work>(888)555-1212</Work>
</Phone>
```

Array

You can put more than one element in a single field by using an Array rather than the ROW type. For example, in the CONTACTINFO table, declare Phone as an array and then generate the XML Schema that maps the array to XML.

```
CREATE TABLE CONTACTINFO (
    Name            CHARACTER (30),
    Phone           CHARACTER (13) ARRAY [4]
) ;
```

You can now map this type to XML with the following schema:

```
<xsd:complexType Name="ARRAY_4.CHAR_13">

    <xsd:annotation>
       <xsd:appinfo>
          <sqlxml:sqltype kind="ARRAY"
                          maxElements="4"
                          mappedElementType="CHAR_13"/>
       </xsd:appinfo>
    </xsd:annotation>

    <xsd:sequence>
       <xsd:element Name="element"
       minOccurs="0" maxOccurs="4"
       nillable="true" type="CHAR_13"/>
    </xsd:sequence>

</xsd:complexType>
```

This would generate something like this:

```
<Phone>
    <element>(888)555-1111</element>
    <element>xsi:nil="true"/>
    <element>(888)555-3434</element>
</Phone>
```

The element in the array containing `xsi:nil="true"` reflects the fact that the second phone number in the source table contains a null value.

Multiset

The phone numbers in the preceding example could just as well be stored in a multiset as in an array. To map a multiset, use something akin to the following:

```
CREATE TABLE CONTACTINFO (
    Name          CHARACTER (30),
    Phone         CHARACTER (13) MULTISET
) ;
```

You can now map this type to XML with the following schema:

```
<xsd:complexType Name="MULTISET.CHAR_13">

    <xsd:annotation>
       <xsd:appinfo>
          <sqlxml:sqltype kind="MULTISET"
                          mappedElementType="CHAR_13"/>
       </xsd:appinfo>
    </xsd:annotation>

    <xsd:sequence>
       <xsd:element Name="element"
       minOccurs="0" maxOccurs="unbounded"
       nillable="true" type="CHAR_13"/>
    </xsd:sequence>

</xsd:complexType>
```

This would generate something like:

```
<Phone>
    <element>(888)555-1111</element>
    <element>xsi:nil="true"/>
    <element>(888)555-3434</element>
</Phone>
```

Mapping tables to XML

You can map a table to an XML document. Similarly, you can map all the tables in a schema or all the tables in a catalog. Privileges are maintained by the mapping. A person who has the SELECT privilege on only some table columns is allowed to map only those columns to the XML document. The mapping actually produces two documents, one that contains the data in the table and the other that contains the XML Schema that describes the first document. Here's an example of the mapping of an SQL table to an XML data-containing document:

```
<CUSTOMER>
    <row>
        <FirstName>Abe</FirstName>
        <LastName>Abelson</LastName>
        <City>Springfield</City>
        <AreaCode>714</AreaCode>
        <Telephone>555-1111</Telephone>
    </row>
    <row>
        <FirstName>Bill</FirstName>
        <LastName>Bailey</LastName>
        <City>Decatur</City>
        <AreaCode>714</AreaCode>
        <Telephone>555-2222</Telephone>
    </row>
        .
        .
        .
</CUSTOMER>
```

The root element of the document has been given the name of the table. Each table row is contained within a <row> element, and each row element contains a sequence of column elements, each named after the corresponding column in the source table. Each column element contains a data value.

Handling null values

Because SQL data might include null values, you must decide how to represent them in an XML document. You can represent a null value either as nil or absent. If you choose the nil option, the attribute xsi:nil="true" marks the column elements that represent null values. It might be used in the following way:

```
<row>
        <FirstName>Bill</FirstName>
        <LastName>Bailey</LastName>
        <City xsi:nil="true" />
        <AreaCode>714</AreaCode>
        <Telephone>555-2222</Telephone>
</row>
```

If you choose the absent option, you could implement it as follows:

```
<row>
      <FirstName>Bill</FirstName>
      <LastName>Bailey</LastName>
      <AreaCode>714</AreaCode>
      <Telephone>555-2222</Telephone>
</row>
```

In this case, the row containing the null value is absent. There is no reference to it.

Creating an XML schema for an SQL table

When mapping from SQL to XML, the first document generated is the one that contains the data. The second contains the schema information. As an example, consider the schema for the CUSTOMER document shown in the "Mapping tables to XML" section, earlier in this chapter.

```
<xsd:schema>
   <xsd:simpleType name="CHAR_15">
      <xsd:restriction base="xsd:string">
         <xsd:length value = "15"/>
      </xsd:restriction>
   </xsd:simpleType>

   <xsd:simpleType name="CHAR_25">
      <xsd:restriction base="xsd:string">
         <xsd:length value = "25"/>
      </xsd:restriction>
   </xsd:simpleType>

   <xsd:simpleType name="CHAR_3">
      <xsd:restriction base="xsd:string">
         <xsd:length value = "3"/>
      </xsd:restriction>
   </xsd:simpleType>

   <xsd:simpleType name="CHAR_8">
      <xsd:restriction base="xsd:string">
         <xsd:length value = "8"/>
      </xsd:restriction>
   </xsd:simpleType>

   <xsd:sequence>
      <xsd:element name="FirstName" type="CHAR_15"/>
      <xsd:element name="LastName" type="CHAR_25"/>
      <xsd:element
         name="City" type="CHAR_25 nillable="true"/>
```

```
      <xsd:element
         name="AreaCode" type="CHAR_3" nillable="true"/>
      <xsd:element
         name="Telephone" type="CHAR_8" nillable="true"/>
   </xsd:sequence>

</xsd:schema>
```

This schema is appropriate if the nil approach to handling nulls is used. The absent approach requires a slightly different element definition. For example:

```
      <xsd:element
         name="City" type="CHAR_25 minOccurs="0"/>
```

This element specifies that the minimum number of occurrences of City is zero. In other words, the City field need not hold a value.

Operating on XML Data with SQL Functions

The SQL standard defines a number of operators, functions, and pseudo-functions that, when applied to an SQL database, produce an XML result, or when applied to XML data produce a result in standard SQL form. The functions include XMLELEMENT, XMLFOREST, XMLCONCAT, and XMLAGG. I give brief descriptions of these, as well as several others that are frequently used when publishing to the Web. Some of the functions rely heavily on XQuery, a new, standard query language designed specifically for querying XML data. I say more about XQuery in Chapter 3 of this minibook.

XMLELEMENT

The XMLELEMENT operator translates a relational value into an XML element. You can use the operator in a SELECT statement to pull data in XML format from an SQL database and publish it on the Web. Here's an example:

```
SELECT c.LastName
    XMLELEMENT ( NAME "City", c.City ) AS "Result"
FROM CUSTOMER c
WHERE LastName="Abelson" ;
```

Here is the result returned:

LastName	Result
Abelson	<City>Springfield</City>

XMLFOREST

The XMLFOREST operator produces a list, or forest, of XML elements from a list of relational values. Each of the operator's arguments produces a new element. Here's an example of this operator:

```
SELECT c.LastName
    XMLFOREST (c.City,
    c.AreaCode,
    c.Telephone ) AS "Result"
FROM CUSTOMER c
WHERE LastName="Abelson" OR LastName="Bailey" ;
```

This produces the following output:

Book VI
Chapter 1

XML/SQL Basics

LastName	Result
Abelson	`<City>Springfield</City>`
	`<AreaCode>714</AreaCode>`
	`<Telephone>555-1111</Telephone>`
Bailey	`<City>Decatur</City>`
	`<AreaCode>714</AreaCode>`
	`<Telephone>555-2222</Telephone>`

XMLCONCAT

XMLCONCAT provides an alternate way to produce a forest of elements. It does so by concatenating its XML arguments. For example:

```
SELECT c.LastName,
    XMLCONCAT(
        XMLELEMENT ( NAME "first", c.FirstName,
        XMLELEMENT ( NAME "last", c.LastName)
        ) AS "Result"
FROM CUSTOMER c ;
```

This produces:

LastName	Result
Abelson	`<first>Abe</first>`
	`<last>Abelson</last>`
Bailey	`<first>Bill</first>`
	`<last>Bailey</last>`

XMLAGG

XMLAGG, the aggregate function, takes XML documents or fragments of XML documents as input and produces a single XML document as output in GROUP BY queries. The aggregation contains a forest of elements. To illustrate the concept:

```
SELECT XMLELEMENT
    ( NAME "City",
        XMLATTRIBUTES ( c.City AS "name" ) ,
        XMLAGG (XMLELEMENT ( NAME "last" c.LastName )
                )
    ) AS "CityList"
FROM CUSTOMER c
GROUP BY City ;
```

When run against the CUSTOMER table, this query produces:

CityList

```
<City name="Decatur">
    <last>Bailey</last>
</City>
<City name="Philo">
    <last>Stetson</last>
    <last>Stetson</last>
    <last>Wood</last>
</City>
<City name="Springfield">
    <last>Abelson</last>
</City>
```

XMLCOMMENT

The XMLCOMMENT function enables an application to create an XML comment. Its syntax is

```
XMLCOMMENT ( 'comment content'
    [RETURNING
        { CONTENT | SEQUENCE } ] )
```

For example:

```
XMLCOMMENT ('Back up database at 2 am every night.')
```

This would create an XML comment that looks like:

```
<!--Back up database at 2 am every night. -->
```

XMLPARSE

The XMLPARSE function performs a non-validating parse of a string to produce an XML value. You might use it like this:

```
XMLPARSE (DOCUMENT '   GREAT JOB!   '
    PRESERVE WHITESPACE )
```

The preceding code would produce an XML value that is either XML(UNTYPED DOCUMENT) or XML(ANY DOCUMENT). Which of the two subtypes would be chosen is implementation-defined.

XMLPI

The XMLPI function allows applications to create XML processing instructions. The syntax for this function is

```
XMLPI NAME target
    [ , string-expression ]
    [RETURNING
        { CONTENT | SEQUENCE } ] )
```

target identifies the target of the processing instruction. string-expression is the content of the PI. This function creates an XML comment of the form:

```
<? target string-expression ?>
```

XMLQUERY

The XMLQUERY function evaluates an XQuery expression and returns the result to the SQL application. The syntax of XMLQUERY is

```
XMLQUERY ( XQuery-expression
    [ PASSING { By REF | BY VALUE }
      argument-list ]
    RETURNING { CONTENT | SEQUENCE }
    { BY REF | BY VALUE } )
```

Here's an example of the use of XMLQUERY:

```
SELECT max_average,
    XMLQUERY (
        'for $batting_average in
            /player/batting_average
        where /player/lastname = $var1
        return $batting_average'
```

```
        PASSING BY VALUE
            'Mantle' AS var1,
        RETURNING SEQUENCE BY VALUE )
FROM offensive_stats
```

This statement returns the batting average for the New York Yankees star Mickey Mantle stored in the offensive_stats XML document.

XMLCAST

The XMLCAST function is similar to an ordinary SQL CAST function, but has some additional restrictions. XMLCAST enables an application to cast a value from an XML type to either another XML type or an SQL type. Similarly, you can use it to cast a value from an SQL type to an XML type. The restrictions are

+ At least one of the types involved, either the source type or the destination type, must be an XML type.

+ Neither of the types involved may be an SQL collection type, row type, structured type, or reference type.

+ Only values of one of the XML types or the SQL null type may be cast to XML(UNTYPED DOCUMENT) or to XML(ANY DOCUMENT).

Here's an example:

XMLCAST (CLIENT.ClientName AS XML(UNTYPED CONTENT)

The XMLCAST function is transformed into an ordinary SQL CAST. The only reason for using a separate keyword is to enforce the preceding restrictions.

XML Predicates

Predicates return a value of true or false. Some new predicates have been added that specifically relate to XML.

DOCUMENT

The purpose of the DOCUMENT predicate is to determine whether an XML value is an XML document. It tests to see if an XML value is an instance of either XML(ANY DOCUMENT) or XML(UNTYPED DOCUMENT). The syntax is

```
XML-value IS [NOT]
    [ANY | UNTYPED] DOCUMENT
```

If the expression evaluates to a true value, the predicate returns TRUE; otherwise, it returns FALSE, unless the XML value is a null value, in which case it returns an UNKNOWN value. If you don't specify either ANY or UNTYPED, the default assumption is ANY.

CONTENT

You would use the CONTENT predicate to determine whether an XML value is an instance of XML(ANY CONTENT) or XML(UNTYPED CONTENT). The syntax is

```
XML-value IS [NOT]
    [ANY | UNTYPED] CONTENT
```

As is the case with the DOCUMENT predicate, if you don't specify either ANY or UNTYPED, ANY is the default.

XMLEXISTS

As the name implies, you can use this predicate to determine whether a value exists. Here's the syntax:

```
XMLEXISTS ( XQuery-expression
    [ argument-list ])
```

The XQuery expression is evaluated, using the values provided in the argument list. If the value queried by the XQuery expression is the SQL NULL value, the predicate's result is unknown. If the evaluation returns an empty XQuery sequence, the predicate's result is FALSE; otherwise, it is TRUE. You can use this predicate to determine whether an XML document contains some particular content, before using a portion of that content in an expression.

VALID

The VALID predicate is used to evaluate an XML value to see if it is valid in the context of a registered XML schema. The syntax of the VALID predicate is more complex than is the case for most predicates:

```
xml-value IS [NOT] VALID
[XML valid identity constraint option]
[XML valid according-to clause]
```

This predicate checks to see if the XML value is one of the five XML types, that is, XML(SEQUENCE), XML(ANY CONTENT), XML(UNTYPED CONTENT), XML(ANY DOCUMENT), XML(UNTYPED DOCUMENT). Additionally, it might optionally check to see if the validity of the XML value depends on identity constraints, and whether it is valid with respect to a particular XML schema (the validity target).

There are four possibilities for the `identify-constraint-option` component of the syntax:

- ✦ WITHOUT IDENTITY CONSTRAINTS
- ✦ WITH IDENTITY CONSTRAINTS GLOBAL
- ✦ WITH IDENTITY CONSTRAINTS LOCAL
- ✦ DOCUMENT

If the `identify-constraint-option` syntax component isn't specified, WITHOUT IDENTITY CONSTRAINTS is assumed. If DOCUMENT is specified, it acts like a combination of the DOCUMENT predicate and the VALID predicate WITH IDENTITY CONSTRAINTS GLOBAL.

WITH IDENTIY CONSTRAINTS GLOBAL means the value is checked not only against the XML schema, but also against the XML rules for ID/IDREF relationships. ID and IDREF are XML attribute types that identify elements of a document.

WITH IDENTITY CONSTRAINTS LOCAL means the value is checked against the XML schema, but not against the XML rules for ID/IDREF or the XML schema rules for identify constraints.

The XML valid according-to clause identifies the schema that the value will be validated against.

Chapter 2: Storing XML Data in SQL Tables

In This Chapter

✔ Inserting XML data into an SQL pseudo-table

✔ Creating tables that hold XML data

✔ Updating XML documents

✔ Getting to know Oracle's tools for updating tables with XML

✔ Discovering Microsoft's tools for updating tables with XML

*T*he latest update to the ANSI/ISO SQL specification (the 2005 update to SQL:2003) details how to store XML data in an SQL-compliant database and operate on it with SQL. In this chapter, I cover SQL's basic data manipulation operations as applied to XML data. Because the primary focus of this book is SQL, I assume that you are already up to speed on XML.

Inserting XML Data into an SQL Pseudo-Table

Until recently, when thinking about the relationship between SQL and XML, the emphasis has been on converting SQL table data into XML to make it accessible on the Internet. The most recent addition to the SQL standard addresses the complementary problem of converting XML data into SQL tables so that it can be easily queried using standard SQL statements. The XMLTABLE pseudo-function performs this operation. The syntax for XMLTABLE is

```
XMLTABLE ( [namespace-declaration,]
XQuery-expression
[PASSING argument-list]
COLUMNS XMLtbl-column-definitions
```

where argument-list is

```
value-expression AS identifier
```

and `XMLtbl-column-definitions` is a comma-separated list of column definitions, which may contain:

```
column-name FOR ORDINALITY
```

or

```
column-name data-type
[BY REF | BY VALUE]
[default-clause]
[PATH XQuery-expression]
```

Here's an example of how you might use `XMLTABLE` to extract data from an XML document into an SQL pseudo-table. A pseudo-table is not persistent, but in every other respect behaves like a normal SQL table:

```
SELECT clientphone.*
FROM
    clients_xml ,
    XMLTABLE(
        'for $m in
            $col/client
        return
            $m'
    PASSING clients_xml.client AS "col"
    COLUMNS
        "ClientName" CHARACTER (30) PATH 'clientname' ,
        "Phone" CHARACTER (13) PATH 'phone'
    ) AS clientphone
```

When run, the preceding code gives the following result:

```
ClientName                          Phone
----------------------------------- ------------
Abe Abelson                         (714)555-1111
Bill Bailey                         (714)555-2222
Chuck Wood                          (714)555-3333

(3 rows in clientphone)
```

If you want to make it persistent, you can create a table with a CREATE TABLE statement as follows:

```
CREATE TABLE clientphone AS
clients_xml ,
    XMLTABLE(
        'for $m in
```

```
        $col/client
    return
        $m'
PASSING clients_xml.client AS "col"
COLUMNS
    "ClientName" CHARACTER (30) PATH 'clientName' ,
    "Phone" CHARACTER (13) PATH 'phone'
)
```

Creating a Table to Hold XML Data

Although you can create a table to hold XML data using the CREATE TABLE statement wrapped around an XMLTABLE function, as shown in the previous section, you can also create a table the old-fashioned way, specifying one or more columns as having the XML data type, and then, at a later time, inserting XML data into the table. It is just as simple as this:

```
CREATE TABLE CLIENT (
    ClientName          CHARACTER (30)      NOT NULL,
    Address1            CHARACTER (30),
    Address2            CHARACTER (30),
    City                CHARACTER (25),
    State               CHARACTER (2),
    PostalCode          CHARACTER (10),
    Phone               CHARACTER (13),
    Fax                 CHARACTER (13),
    ContactPerson       CHARACTER (30),
    Comments            XML(SEQUENCE) ) ;
```

Tables can hold a mix of data of the XML data type and classic SQL data types, as shown here, or you could create a table in which all columns contain XML data.

Updating XML Documents

At the present time, there is no standard way to update XML documents that are stored in some form of persistent storage, such as an SQL database. There is also no standard way to modify transient XML documents, such as stock tickers. Furthermore, there's no standard way to add new data to an existing XML document. Methods for performing these operations have not been added to the XQuery 1.0 standard because update operations carry some messy baggage. Such operations can cause side effects that complicate operations.

Regardless of whether a standard method exists, you still need to be able to modify XML documents. Some of the required capabilities that you should be able to do include

+ Insert new nodes at specified positions in an instance of a data model

+ Change the value of a node in an instance of a data model

+ Replace nodes in an instance of a data model

+ Modify the properties of nodes in an instance of a data model

+ Delete a node in an instance of a data model

Because you clearly need to be able to update XML documents that reside in SQL databases, and because no universally recognized standard way of doing so exists, DBMS vendors have developed proprietary solutions to the problem. I briefly describe the Oracle and Microsoft solutions.

Discovering Oracle's Tools for Updating XML Data in a Table

Oracle provides three distinct methods of updating XML data in an Oracle database:

+ One method is based on the Document Object Model (DOM) developed by the World Wide Web Consortium (www.w3.org). It provides methods for traversing the DOM representation of an XML document, retrieving values from individual nodes, inserting nodes, deleting nodes, and modifying the values of nodes.

+ Another method uses a Java API that defines a class to represent the XML type, along with methods such as `insertXML()`, `updateXML()`, and `deleteXML()`.

+ The third method is more closely related to SQL/XML. In SQL/XML, applications use ordinary SQL statements to access XML data stored as values of the XML type in tables. The SQL function, `XMLQUERY()`, discussed in Chapter 1 of this minibook, evaluates an XQuery expression and returns the result of that evaluation to an SQL application. Oracle extends SQL/XML with several update functions. There are three functions for inserting new data, one for deleting data, and one for updating existing data.

APPENDCHILDXML

Unlike the row and column structure of an SQL database table, XML documents have a treelike structure. The tree has nodes and branches, with parent nodes branching out to child nodes. The ultimate parent node, called the *root* node, resides at the base of the tree. The APPENDCHILDXML function adds a child node to an existing node. The node it adds is the very last sibling of the existing node's current children. Here's an example, using the CLIENT table created in the "Creating a Table to Hold XML Data" section earlier in this chapter:

```
UPDATE CLIENT SET Comments =
   APPENDCHILDXML(Comments, 'Comments/Comment',
   XMLTYPE('<IssueClosed>Yes</IssueClosed>'))
   WHERE EXTRACTVALUE(Comments,
     '/Comments/Comment/ResponseRequested') = 'No';
```

The second argument of APPENDCHILDXML, 'Comments/Comment', is the XPath expression. It specifies a location within the document. The preceding code makes the following change to the XML document shown in Chapter 1 of this minibook:

**Book VI
Chapter 2**

**Storing XML Data in
SQL Tables**

```
<Comments>
  <Comment>
   <CommentNo>1</CommentNo>
   <MessageText>Is VetLab equipped to analyze penguin
   blood?</MessageText>
    <ResponseRequested>Yes</ResponseRequested>
  </Comment>
  <Comment>
   <CommentNo>2</CommentNo>
   <MessageText>Thanks for the fast turnaround on the leopard
   seal sputum sample.</MessageText>
   <ResponseRequested>No</ResponseRequested>
   <IssueClosed>Yes</IssueClosed>
  </Comment>
</Comments>
```

The IssueClosed node has been added as the last child of the Comment node where ResponseRequested has a value of No.

INSERTCHILDXML

Whereas the APPENDCHILDXML adds a new node to the XML document tree, INSERTCHILDXML inserts a new value into the document at the node specified by the XPath expression. Following is an example:

```
UPDATE CLIENT SET Comments =
   INSERTCHILDXML(Comments, 'Comments/Comment', 'MessageText',
   XMLTYPE('<MessageText>I am only interested in Gentoo
   penguins.</MessageText>'))
   WHERE EXTRACTVALUE(Comments,
     '/Comments/Comment/CommentNo') = 1;
```

This code adds another instance of MessageText to comment number 1. This is the result:

```
<Comments>
  <Comment>
   <CommentNo>1</CommentNo>
   <MessageText>Is VetLab equipped to analyze penguin
   blood?</MessageText>
    <MessageText>I am only interested in Gentoo
   penguins.</MessageText>
    <ResponseRequested>Yes</ResponseRequested>
  </Comment>
  <Comment>
   <CommentNo>2</CommentNo>
   <MessageText>Thanks for the fast turnaround on the leopard
   seal sputum sample.</MessageText>
   <ResponseRequested>No</ResponseRequested>
   <IssueClosed>Yes</IssueClosed>
  </Comment>
</Comments>
```

INSERTXMLBEFORE

The INSERTXMLBEFORE function inserts a new value *before* the node specified by the XPath expression. The following example shows the difference between INSERTXMLBEFORE and INSERTCHILDXML.

```
UPDATE CLIENT SET Comments =
  INSERTXMLBEFORE(Comments, 'Comments/Comment/MessageText[1]',
  XMLTYPE('<MessageText>I am only interested in Gentoo
   penguins.</MessageText>'))
  WHERE EXTRACTVALUE(Comments,
    '/Comments/Comment/CommentNo') = 1;
```

This code adds another instance of MessageText to comment number 1, before the existing instance. The result follows:

```
<Comments>
  <Comment>
   <CommentNo>1</CommentNo>
   <MessageText>I am only interested in Gentoo
   penguins.</MessageText>
<MessageText>Is VetLab equipped to analyze penguin
   blood?</MessageText>
    <ResponseRequested>Yes</ResponseRequested>
  </Comment>
  <Comment>
   <CommentNo>2</CommentNo>
```

```
   <MessageText>Thanks for the fast turnaround on the leopard
   seal sputum sample.</MessageText>
   <ResponseRequested>No</ResponseRequested>
   <IssueClosed>Yes</IssueClosed>
  </Comment>
</Comments>
```

The new addition to Comment Number 1 has been placed ahead of the original message.

DELETEXML

The DELETEXML function deletes the node matched by the XPath expression in the target XML document. As an example, I remove the IssueClosed node from the Comments document. Here's the document before the deletion:

```
<Comments>
  <Comment>
   <CommentNo>1</CommentNo>
   <MessageText>Is VetLab equipped to analyze penguin
   blood?</MessageText>
    <ResponseRequested>Yes</ResponseRequested>
  </Comment>
  <Comment>
   <CommentNo>2</CommentNo>
   <MessageText>Thanks for the fast turnaround on the leopard
   seal sputum sample.</MessageText>
   <ResponseRequested>No</ResponseRequested>
   <IssueClosed>Yes</IssueClosed>
  </Comment>
</Comments>
```

Here's the deletion operation:

```
UPDATE CLIENT SET Comments =
  DELETEXML(Comments, 'Comments/Comment/IssueClosed')
  WHERE EXTRACTVALUE(Comments,
    '/Comments/Comment/ResponseRequested') = 'No';
```

The result is

```
<Comments>
  <Comment>
    <CommentNo>1</CommentNo>
    <MessageText>Is VetLab equipped to analyze penguin
    blood?</MessageText>
    <ResponseRequested>Yes</ResponseRequested>
  </Comment>
```

```
<Comment>
  <CommentNo>2</CommentNo>
  <MessageText>Thanks for the fast turnaround on the leopard
  seal sputum sample.</MessageText>
  <ResponseRequested>No</ResponseRequested>
</Comment>
</Comments>
```

UPDATEXML

The UPDATEXML function updates an existing value in an XML document. To show this in operation, change the ResponseRequested element of the Comments document. First, here's the document before the update:

```
<Comments>
  <Comment>
   <CommentNo>1</CommentNo>
   <MessageText>Is VetLab equipped to analyze penguin
   blood?</MessageText>
    <ResponseRequested>Yes</ResponseRequested>
  </Comment>
  <Comment>
   <CommentNo>2</CommentNo>
   <MessageText>Thanks for the fast turnaround on the leopard
   seal sputum sample.</MessageText>
   <ResponseRequested>No</ResponseRequested>
  </Comment>
</Comments>
```

Next the update operation itself:

```
UPDATE CLIENT SET Comments =
  UPDATEXML(Comments,
    'Comments/Comment/ResponseRequested/text()', Maybe)
  WHERE EXTRACTVALUE(Comments,
    '/Comments/Comment/ResponseRequested') = 'Yes';
```

This causes the following result:

```
<Comments>
  <Comment>
    <CommentNo>1</CommentNo>
    <MessageText>Is VetLab equipped to analyze penguin
   blood?</MessageText>
    <ResponseRequested>Maybe</ResponseRequested>
  </Comment>
  <Comment>
   <CommentNo>2</CommentNo>
   <MessageText>Thanks for the fast turnaround on the leopard
   seal sputum sample.</MessageText>
```

```
<ResponseRequested>No</ResponseRequested>
  </Comment>
</Comments>
```

Oracle's extension functions UPDATEXML, INSERTCHILDXML, INSERTXMLBEFORE, DELETEXML, and UPDATEXML are transformation functions rather than true update functions. They do not update an XML value "in place," but rather return an updated copy of the value they have changed. When used with an SQL UPDATE statement, as shown here, this difference becomes moot.

Introducing Microsoft's Tools for Updating XML Data in a Table

Like Oracle, Microsoft provides more than one way to update XML data in its SQL Server 2005 DBMS:

✦ **Using the modify() method as part of the SET clause of an SQL UPDATE statement:** A parameter determines whether the operation is an insert, an update, or a delete operation.

✦ **Using a set of .NET classes:** Some of these classes provide methods for setting the values of nodes, inserting nodes into specified locations, deleting nodes, and replacing nodes.

✦ **Using the OPENXML function:** This function is part of SQL Server's Transact-SQL implementation of the SQL language. This approach works for inserting data into a table that pulls its data from an XML document that is part of SQL Server's Transact-SQL implementation of the SQL language.

✦ **Using *updategrams:*** With an updategram, you can insert, delete, or update XML data in a database table. An updategram works against the XML views provided by an annotated XSD or XDR schema. One example of such a schema is the mapping schema, which has the information needed to map XML elements and attributes to the corresponding database tables and columns. The updategram uses this mapping information to update the database tables and columns.

Updategram namespace and keywords

An updategram contains three keywords: `<sync>`, `<before>`, and `<after>`. They all exist in the namespace `urn:scehmas-microsoft-com:xml-updategram`. You can use any namespace prefix that you want. For the examples that follow, I use `updg` as a namespace prefix to denote the updategram namespace.

An updategram is a template that contains `<sync>`, `<before>`, and `<after>` blocks. Here's an example of the template:

```
<ROOT xmlns:updg="urn:schemas-microsoft-com:xml-updategram">
  <updg:sync [mapping-schema= "AnnotatedSchemaFile.xml"] >
    <updg:before>
      . . .
    </updg:before>
    <updg:after>
      . . .
    </updg:after>
  </updg:sync>
</ROOT>
```

The code references a mapping-schema named AnnotatedSchemaFile.xml. I discuss mapping schemas in the following section.

The three keywords are defined as follows:

+ **`<before>`:** The state of a record instance before the update.

+ **`<after>`:** The state the record instance is to have after the update.

+ **`<sync>`:** A block that contains the `<before>` and `<after>` blocks. A `<sync>` block may contain more than one set of `<before>` and `<after>` blocks, which are always specified in pairs. A sync block is an atomic item; either all of it is processed or none of it. In that sense, it is similar to a transaction in SQL. If you specify multiple `<sync>` blocks in an updategram and one of them fails, the other `<sync>` blocks proceed normally. They are not affected by the failure. Thus, an updategram is *not* atomic.

You can do an insert, update, or delete with an updategram. Which operation is performed depends on the contents of the `<before>` and `<after>` blocks.

If the `<before>` block is empty, but there is a record instance in the `<after>` block, an insert operation is being performed.

If the `<before>` block contains a record instance, but the `<after>` block is empty, a delete operation is being performed.

If both the `<before>` block and the `<after>` block contain a record instance, the record instance in the `<before>` block is being updated to the record instance in the `<after>` block.

Specifying a mapping schema

Because the structure of an XML document, being a tree, is fundamentally different than the structure of an SQL table with rows and columns, in order for XML data to be placed into an SQL table, and vice versa, there must be a translation from one structure to another. This translation is called a *mapping schema*. In the simplest case, each element in a `<before>` block or `<after>` block maps to a table, and each element's child element or attribute maps to a column in its corresponding table. This situation is called *implicit* or *default* mapping. If such simple correspondence between the XML document and the SQL table does not exist, you must explicitly specify a mapping schema in which the elements and attributes of the updategram match the elements and attributes of the mapping schema.

Implicit mapping

In many cases, an updategram can perform an update without an explicit mapping schema, relying on the default mapping schema instead.

Inserting an element of an XML document into a record in an SQL database

Look at this example of an insert operation, using implicit mapping:

```
<ROOT xmlns:updg="urn:schemas-microsoft-com:xml-updategram">
  <updg:sync >
    <updg:before>
    </updg:before>
    <updg:after>
      <OLS.MEMBERS MemberID="9"
                   FirstName="Sam"
                   LastName="Shovel"
                   OfficeHeld="Investigator"
                   Email="hammett@book.com"
                   Phone="(503)555-8004"
                   Street="154 Polk St."
                   City="Carver"
                   State="OR"
                   Zip="97003"/>
    </updg:after>
  </updg:sync>
</ROOT>
```

This code inserts a new record into the Oregon Lunar Society's MEMBERS table. For this to work without an explicit mapping schema, the MEMBERS element must map to the MEMBERS table in the OLS database, and the attributes specified in the `<after>` block must map to the columns of the MEMBERS table. In an insert operation, the empty `<before>` block is optional. You can leave it out if you want to.

Updating a record in an SQL database from an element of an XML document

Here's an example of using an updategram to modify the information in an existing SQL table:

```
<ROOT xmlns:updg="urn:schemas-microsoft-com:xml-updategram">
  <updg:sync >
    <updg:before>
      <OLS.MEMBERS MemberID="9" />
    </updg:before>
    <updg:after>
      <OLS.MEMBERS Phone="(503)555-5643" />
    </updg:after>
  </updg:sync>
</ROOT>
```

This code updates the phone number for the person with MemberID=9. The updategram uses the columns in the <before> block to find the desired record. Because MemberID is the primary key of the MEMBERS table, by itself, it is sufficient to identify the desired row.

Deleting a record in an SQL database with an updategram

You can also delete one or more records from an SQL table using an updategram. Here's an example that deletes two records from the MEMBERS table.

```
<ROOT xmlns:updg="urn:schemas-microsoft-com:xml-updategram">
  <updg:sync >
    <updg:before>
        <OLS.MEMBERS MemberID="8"/>
        <OLS.MEMBERS MemberID="9"/>
    </updg:before>
    <updg:after>
    </updg:after>
  </updg:sync>
</ROOT>
```

The fact that this updategram has content in its <before> block but an empty <after> block tells you that it is a delete operation.

Explicit mapping

If you are using an updategram to make a simple insertion, update, or deletion, implicit mapping using the default schema works well. However, if you want to perform a complex update, such as inserting records into multiple tables that have a parent-child relationship, you need to specify a mapping schema in order to make sure things end up where you want them to. The mapping schema should be in the same directory as your updategram, or you will need to specify the path to it. Two different kinds of mapping schema are in use, either one of which will work.

Creating an updategram with an XSD schema

XSD stands for XML Schema Definition and is the currently preferred method of specifying a mapping schema. Following is a mapping schema that maps the <MEMBERS> element to the OLS.MEMBERS table:

```
<xsd:schema xmlns:xsd="http://www.w3.org/2001/XMLSchema"
      xmlns:sql="urn:schemas-microsoft-com:mapping-schema">
  <xsd:element name="MEMBERS" sql:relation="OLS.MEMBERS" >
   <xsd:complexType>
       <xsd:attribute name="MemberID"
                      sql:field="MemberID"
                      type="xsd:integer" />
       <xsd:attribute name="FirstName"
                      sql:field="FirstName"
                      type="xsd:string" />
       <xsd:attribute name="LastName"
                      sql:field="LastName"
                      type="xsd:string" />
       <xsd:attribute name="OfficeHeld"
                      sql:field="OfficeHeld"
                      type="xsd:string" />
       <xsd:attribute name="Email"
                      sql:field="Email"
                      type="xsd:string" />
       <xsd:attribute name="Phone"
                      sql:field="Phone"
                      type="xsd:string" />
       <xsd:attribute name="Street"
                      sql:field="Street"
                      type="xsd:string" />
       <xsd:attribute name="City"
                      sql:field="City"
                      type="xsd:string" />
       <xsd:attribute name="State"
                      sql:field="State"
                      type="xsd:string" />
       <xsd:attribute name="Zip"
                      sql:field="Zip"
                      type="xsd:string" />
   </xsd:complexType>
  </xsd:element>
</xsd:schema>
```

**Book VI
Chapter 2**

**Storing XML Data in
SQL Tables**

Save this mapping schema in a file named, for instance, MembersUpdate Schema.xml. Next save the following updategram in a file named Member9Updategram.xml in the same directory.

```
<ROOT xmlns:updg="urn:schemas-microsoft-com:xml-updategram">
  <updg:sync mapping-schema="MembersUpdateSchema.xml">
    <updg:before>
```

```
   </updg:before>
   <updg:after>
     <OLS.MEMBERS MemberID="9"
                  FirstName="Sam"
                  LastName="Shovel"
                  OfficeHeld="Investigator"
                  Email="hammett@book.com"
                  Phone="(503)555-8004"
                  Street="154 Polk St."
                  City="Carver"
                  State="OR"
                  Zip="97003"/>
   </updg:after>
  </updg:sync>
</ROOT>
```

Creating an updategram with an XDR schema

XDR is an older method of specifying a mapping schema and is being gradually replaced by XSD. Here is an XDR schema that is equivalent to the XSD schema given previously:

```
<?xml version="1.0" ?>
  <Schema xmlns="urn:schemas-microsoft-com:xml-data"
        xmlns:dt="urn:schemas-microsoft-com:datatypes"
        xmlns:sql="urn:schemas-microsoft-com:xml-sql">
    <ElementType name="MEMBERS" sql:relation="OLS.MEMBERS" >
      <AttributeType name="MemberID" />
      <AttributeType name="FirstName" />
      <AttributeType name="LastName" />
      <AttributeType name="OfficeHeld" />
      <AttributeType name="Email" />
      <AttributeType name="Phone" />
      <AttributeType name="Street" />
      <AttributeType name="City" />
      <AttributeType name="State" />
      <AttributeType name="Zip" />

      <attribute type="MemberID" sql:field="MemberID" />
      <attribute type="FirstName" sql:field="FirstName" />
      <attribute type="LastName" sql:field="LastName" />
      <attribute type="OfficeHeld" sql:field="OfficeHeld" />
      <attribute type="Email" sql:field="Email" />
      <attribute type="Phone" sql:field="Phone" />
      <attribute type="Street" sql:field="Street" />
      <attribute type="City" sql:field="City" />
      <attribute type="State" sql:field="State" />
      <attribute type="Zip" sql:field="Zip" />
    </ElementType>
  </Schema>
```

In these examples, I have made the attribute names in the schema the same as the corresponding attribute names in the SQL table. This is not necessary. As long as it is clear which attribute corresponds with which, they can have different names. The same updategram that was created to work with the XSD schema will work with this one too.

Creating a mapping schema for tables with a parent-child relationship

In the section on implicit mapping, you don't really need an explicit mapping schema for a simple update such as the one shown previously. However, providing such a schema does no harm. An explicit mapping schema is *required* for a more complex update, such as insertions into two tables that have a parent-child relationship. Here's an example of an XSD schema for such an update:

```
<xsd:schema xmlns:xsd="http://www.w3.org/2001/XMLSchema"
      xmlns:sql="urn:schemas-microsoft-com:mapping-schema">
<xsd:annotation>
  <xsd:appinfo>
    <sql:relationship name="InvoiceToLine"
          parent="Sales.Invoice"
          parent-key="InvoiceNo"
          child="Sales.InvoiceLine"
          child-key="InvoiceNo" />
  </xsd:appinfo>
</xsd:annotation>

  <xsd:element name="Invoice" sql:relation="Sales.Invoice" >
   <xsd:complexType>
     <xsd:sequence>
        <xsd:element name="Line"
              sql:relation="Sales.InvoiceLine"
              sql:relationship="InvoiceToLine" >
          <xsd:complexType>
              <xsd:attribute name="InvoiceNo"
    type="xsd:integer" />
              <xsd:attribute name="ProductID"
    type="xsd:integer" />
              <xsd:attribute name="UnitPrice"
    type="xsd:decimal" />
              <xsd:attribute name="Quantity"
    type="xsd:integer" />

          </xsd:complexType>
        </xsd:element>
     </xsd:sequence>
        <xsd:attribute name="CustomerID" type="xsd:string"/>
        <xsd:attribute name="InvoiceNo"  type="xsd:integer"/>
        <xsd:attribute name="InvoiceDate"  type="xsd:date"/>
```

```
      </xsd:complexType>
    </xsd:element>
</xsd:schema>
```

After you save this schema as InvoiceUpdateSchema.xml, you can reference it with an updategram. The following updategram uses this mapping schema to add a new invoice line record for Invoice Number 1010.

```
<ROOT xmlns:updg="urn:schemas-microsoft-com:xml-updategram">
  <updg:sync mapping-schema="InvoiceUpdateSchema.xml" >
    <updg:before>
       <Invoice InvoiceNo="1010" />
    </updg:before>
    <updg:after>
      <Invoice InvoiceNo="1010" >
          <Line ProductID="17" UnitPrice="$5.95"
              Quantity="2" />
      </Order>
    </updg:after>
  </updg:sync>
</ROOT>
```

An equivalent XDR schema could look like the following:

```
<?xml version="1.0" ?>
<Schema xmlns="urn:schemas-microsoft-com:xml-data"
        xmlns:dt="urn:schemas-microsoft-com:datatypes"
        xmlns:sql="urn:schemas-microsoft-com:xml-sql">

<ElementType name="Line" sql:relation="Sales.InvoiceLine" >
    <AttributeType name="InvoiceNo" />
    <AttributeType name="ProductID" />
    <AttributeType name="UnitPrice"  dt:type="fixed.14.4" />
    <AttributeType name="Quantity" />

    <attribute type="InvoiceNo" />
    <attribute type="ProductID" />
    <attribute type="UnitPrice" />
    <attribute type="Quantity" />
</ElementType>

<ElementType name="Invoice" sql:relation="Sales.Invoice" >
    <AttributeType name="CustomerID" />
    <AttributeType name="InvoiceNo" />
    <AttributeType name="InvoiceDate" />

    <attribute type="CustomerID" />
    <attribute type="InvoiceNo" />
    <attribute type="InvoiceDate" />
```

```
<element type="Line" >
        <sql:relationship
            key-relation="Sales.Invoice"
            key="InvoiceNo"
            foreign-key="InvoiceNo"
            foreign-relation="Sales.InvoiceLine" />
</element>
</ElementType>
</Schema>
```

Element-centric mapping

Element-centric updategrams, as the name implies, code items as elements. Elements contain child elements, which are the properties of the parent element. The parent element maps into a table, and the child elements map into columns in that table. Here's an example from the OLS database:

```
<ROOT xmlns:updg="urn:schemas-microsoft-com:xml-updategram">
<updg:sync >
  <updg:after>
    <OLS.MEMBERS>
        <MemberID>5</MemberID>
        <FirstName>Gus</FirstName>
        <LastName>Roderick</LastName>
        <OfficeHeld>Webmaster</OfficeHeld>
        <Email>hotrod@davenport.net</Email>
        <Phone>(503)555-9976</Phone>
        <Street>43 Ash St.</Street>
        <City>Silverton</City>
        <State>OR</State>
        <Zip>97078</Zip>
    </OLS.MEMBERS>
  </updg:after>
</updg:sync>
</ROOT>
```

Because no mapping schema was specified, this updategram uses implicit mapping.

Attribute-centric mapping

In attribute-centric mapping, the elements have attributes rather than child elements. The following updategram, which also uses implicit mapping, is an example of attribute-centric mapping:

```
<ROOT xmlns:updg="urn:schemas-microsoft-com:xml-updategram">
<updg:sync >
  <updg:before>
```

```
<updg:/before>
<updg:after>
  <OLS.MEMBERS
     MemberID="5"
     FirstName="Gus"
     LastName="Roderick"
     OfficeHeld="Webmaster"
     Email="hotrod@davenport.net"
     Phone="(503)555-9976"
     Street="43 Ash St."
     City="Silverton"
     State="OR"
     Zip="97078"/>
  </OLS.MEMBERS>
</updg:after>
</updg:sync>
</ROOT>
```

Mixed element-centric and attribute-centric mapping

It's possible to mix element-centric and attribute-centric mapping in the same updategram, although why you would want to do so is beyond me. The difference between the two approaches can lead to confusion. Anyway, here's an example:

```
<ROOT xmlns:updg="urn:schemas-microsoft-com:xml-updategram">
<updg:sync >
  <updg:before>
  <updg:/before>
  <updg:after>
    <OLS.MEMBERS
       MemberID="5"
       FirstName="Gus"
       LastName="Roderick"
       OfficeHeld="Webmaster"
       Email="hotrod@davenport.net"
       Phone="(503)555-9976">
       <Street>43 Ash St.</Street>
       <City>Silverton</City>
       <State>OR</State>
       <Zip>97078</Zip>
    </OLS.MEMBERS>
  </updg:after>
</updg:sync>
</ROOT>
```

Once again, this code uses implicit mapping.

Schemas that allow null values

Sometimes the updategram you are using to insert values into an SQL table may not have a value for each of the table's columns. In such a case, you want to put a null value into the columns for which a value is not specified. This is an issue because XML, like most computer languages other than SQL, does not support null values. You can handle this by assigning the xsi:nil attribute to any element in the updategram that might contain a null value. In the corresponding XSD schema, you must specify the XSD *nillable* attribute. Here's an example of such a schema:

```
<xsd:schema xmlns:xsd="http://www.w3.org/2001/XMLSchema"
      xmlns:sql="urn:schemas-microsoft-com:mapping-schema">
  <xsd:element name="MEMBERS" sql:relation="OLS.MEMBERS" >
   <xsd:complexType>
        <xsd:attribute name="MemberID"
                       sql:field="MemberID"
                       type="xsd:integer" />
        <xsd:attribute name="FirstName"
                       sql:field="FirstName"
                       type="xsd:string" />
        <xsd:attribute name="LastName"
                       sql:field="LastName"
                       type="xsd:string" />
        <xsd:all>
          <xsd:element name="OfficeHeld"
                       sql:field="OfficeHeld"
                       type="xsd:string"
                       nillable="true"/>
        </xsd:all>
        <xsd:attribute name="Email"
                       sql:field="Email"
                       type="xsd:string" />
        <xsd:attribute name="Phone"
                       sql:field="Phone"
                       type="xsd:string" />
        <xsd:attribute name="Street"
                       sql:field="Street"
                       type="xsd:string" />
        <xsd:attribute name="City"
                       sql:field="City"
                       type="xsd:string" />
        <xsd:attribute name="State"
                       sql:field="State"
                       type="xsd:string" />
        <xsd:attribute name="Zip"
                       sql:field="Zip"
                       type="xsd:string" />
    </xsd:complexType>
  </xsd:element>
</xsd:schema>
```

**Book VI
Chapter 2**

**Storing XML Data in
SQL Tables**

A member of the Oregon Lunar Society might not hold any office, so the OfficeHeld element is designated as nillable. Here's an example of an update gram that uses this schema:

```
<ROOT xmlns:updg="urn:schemas-microsoft-com:xml-updategram">
  <updg:sync mapping-schema="MembersUpdateSchema.xml">
    <updg:before>
    </updg:before>
    <updg:after>
      <OLS.MEMBERS MemberID="3"
                   FirstName="Tom"
                   LastName="Charges"
                   Email="waldo@magic.com"
                   Phone="(503)555-3211"
                   Street="132 22nd St."
                   City="Portland"
                   State="OR"
                   Zip="97245">
        <OfficeHeld xsi:nil="true">
        </OfficeHeld>
      </OLS.MEMBERS>
    </updg:after>
  </updg:sync>
</ROOT>
```

With the schema used here, records can be inserted into the MEMBERS table from an updategram if the `OfficeHeld` attribute is absent, but that is not true for any of the other attributes. They must all contain definite values.

Chapter 3: Retrieving Data from XML Documents

In This Chapter

✓ Discovering XQuery

✓ Finding out about FLWOR expressions

✓ Comparing XQuery to SQL

*E*arly in the development of XML, one of the primary concerns was the conversion of data stored in SQL databases into XML so that it could be transmitted to other, incompatible data stores or so that it could be displayed on the Web. In Chapter 1 of this minibook, I describe a number of SQL functions whose purposes are to perform such conversions. Converting XML to SQL was also an important endeavor because SQL has traditionally been the premiere tool for extracting the information you want from a collection of data. This conversion usually took the form of "shredding" in which an XML document was torn apart and pieces of it flowed into the columns of tables in an SQL database. Queries could then be made using normal SQL SELECT statements.

Querying XML documents directly, without shredding them into an SQL database, is much more complicated, and thus took a while longer to implement in a standard form. In addition, many common examples of XML documents are not readily shredded. The tree structure of an XML document can be difficult to translate into the row and column structure of a relational database. Consequently, several years of development of XML query facilities have been required to produce the XQuery 1.0 standard. It defines how to query an XML document directly and retrieve the information you want.

XQuery, like XML itself, is a vast topic, which I don't cover in detail here. However, I describe it briefly, and give some examples of its use. These examples are in no way comprehensive, but should give you an idea of what you can do with XQuery. For an in-depth treatment, I recommend *Querying XML* by Jim Melton and Stephen Buxton (published by Morgan Kaufmann Publishers).

XQuery

XQuery is a non-procedural language specifically designed to retrieve desired information from XML documents, just as SQL is a non-procedural language specifically designed to retrieve desired information from relational databases. Whereas relational databases are highly structured, XML documents can be characterized as semi-structured. What an XML document looks like varies a lot more than what a relational database looks like. When I say it's a *non-procedural* language, I mean that a query, whether expressed in SQL or XQuery, describes *what* to do, but not *how* to do it. The "how" is left up to the engines that process the SQL or XQuery code.

Where XQuery came from

XQuery is the result of combining the best parts of several predecessor languages. For a long time, it's been clear that there is great value in being able to query XQL documents directly. Several groups have worked on the problem and have come up with query languages. One of those languages was XQL, written in 1998 by Jonathan Robie, who worked for Software AG at the time. Another, unrelated, language named XQL was developed at Fujitsu Labs at the same time, but never developed beyond the prototype stage.

At about the same time, another language named XML-QL emerged from a collaboration of a number of researchers. Stanford University joined the game with a project named Lore and a language named Lorel, which had object-oriented characteristics. At INRIA, the French National Institute for Research in Computer Science and Control, a research language named YATL was developed. Rounding out the predecessors, a language named Quilt was developed by Don Chamberlin, Jonathan Robie, and Daniela Florescu. Chamberlin had also been one of the authors of SQL.

Although XQuery probably owes more to Quilt than to any of the others, it also takes ideas from the others and benefits from all that has gone before.

What XQuery requires

The XQuery 1.0 Language Specification defines what must be true of a language in order for it to qualify as an XQuery implementation. Actually it defines three different levels. Some things **must** be true, others **should** be true, and some other things **may** be true. This is due to the fact that XQuery is evolving, and it is not yet clear, exactly what will be mandatory in the future.

✦ XQuery is a declarative language, and as such **must** not mandate an evaluation strategy. It describes what the processor should do, not how it should do it.

✦ XQuery **may** have more than one syntax binding, but it **must** have one syntax that is convenient for humans to read and one syntax expressed in XML that reflects the underlying structure of the query.

✦ XQuery **must** define standard error conditions that can occur during execution of a query.

XQuery 1.0 does not have any update capability, which is why vendors such as Oracle and Microsoft offer proprietary update solutions, as shown in the previous chapter.

XQuery functionality

The XQuery Requirements document specifies a number of things that an XQuery implementation **must** do, as well as things that it **should** do, and things that it **may** do. Here are some of those requirements:

✦ XQuery **must** support operations on all data types in the XQuery Data Model.

✦ Queries **must** be able to express simple conditions on text, including on text that spans element boundaries.

✦ Operations on collections **must** include support for universal and existential quantifiers.

✦ XQuery **must** be able to combine related information from different parts of a given document or from multiple documents.

✦ XQuery **must** be able to compute summary information from a group of related document elements (aggregation).

✦ XQuery **must** be able to sort query results.

✦ XQuery **must** support NULL values.

✦ Queries **should** be able to operate on literal data.

✦ Queries **must** be able to perform simple operations on names, such as testing for equality in element names, attribute names, and processing instruction targets. Queries **may** perform more powerful operations on names.

✦ XQuery **should** support the use of externally defined functions on all datatypes of the XML Query Data Model.

✦ XQuery **must** be able to provide access to environmental information, such as current date, time, and time zone.

The requirements I have listed are a partial list. XQuery 1.0 meets all the requirements I have listed as **must** or **should**. Other requirements in the XQuery Requirements may or may not have been met by XQuery 1.0.

Usage scenarios

The World Wide Web Consortium (www.w3.org) has developed a set of 77 use cases that cover nine different categories of queries. In each case, a query is applied to supplied input data, and expected results are given. You can use these use cases as a starting point in testing an XQuery implementation to see if it is more or less working. An exhaustive test suite, which tests every possibility, would take thousands of such cases, but these 77 are a good start. Here, I show you just one such case.

Because this book is about SQL, one category of data that you might want to query using XQuery is data stored in a relational database. Such a case can be found at paragraph 1.4.1 of the XML Query Use Cases document, which is available at www.w3.org/TR/xquery-use-cases/. I reproduce that case here.

This case takes data from a simplified version of an online auction. There are three tables: USERS (see Table 3-1), ITEMS (see Table 3-2), and BIDS (see Table 3-3). The USERS table contains information on buyers and sellers. The ITEMS table lists items that are currently for sale or that have recently been for sale. The BIDS table contains all the bids on record. Here are the tables and the columns they contain:

```
USERS (USERID, NAME, RATING)
ITEMS (ITEMNO, DESCRIPTION, OFFERED_BY, START_DATE, END_DATE,
       RESERVE_PRICE)
BIDS (USERID, ITEMNO, BID, BID_DATE)
```

USERID is the primary key of the USERS table; ITEMNO is the primary key of the ITEMS table, and the combination of USERID and ITEMID is the composite primary key of the BIDS table.

The relational database tables correspond to input documents named users.xml, items.xml, and bids.xml. The correspondence between the tables and the XML documents is specified by the following Document Type Definition (DTD):

```
<!DOCTYPE users [
   <!ELEMENT users (user_tuple*)>
      <!ELEMENT user_tuple (userid, name, rating?)>
         <!ELEMENT userid (#PCDATA)>
         <!ELEMENT name (#PCDATA)>
         <!ELEMENT rating (#PCDATA)> ]>
<!DOCTYPE items [
   <!ELEMENT items (item_tuple*)>
```

```
        <!ELEMENT item_tuple (itemno, description, offered_by,
            start_date?, end_date?, reserve_price?)>
        <!ELEMENT itemno (#PCDATA)>
        <!ELEMENT description (#PCDATA)>
        <!ELEMENT offered_by (#PCDATA)>
        <!ELEMENT start_date (#PCDATA)>
        <!ELEMENT end_date (#PCDATA)>
        <!ELEMENT reserve_price (#PCDATA)> ]>
<!DOCTYPE bids [
    <!ELEMENT bids (bid_tuple*)>
        <!ELEMENT bid_tuple (userid, itemno, bid, bid_date)>
            <!ELEMENT userid (#PCDATA)>
            <!ELEMENT itemno (#PCDATA)>
            <!ELEMENT bid (#PCDATA)>
            <!ELEMENT bid_date (#PCDATA)> ]>
```

The input data is contained in Tables 3-1, 3-2, and 3-3.

Table 3-1   **USERS**

USERID	Name	Rating
U01	Tom Jones	B
U02	Mary Doe	A
U03	Dee Linquent	D
U04	Roger Smith	C
U05	Jack Sprat	B
U06	Rip Van Winkle	B

Table 3-2   **ITEMS**

ITEMID	Description	Offered_By	Start_Date	End_Date	Reserve_Price
1001	Red Bicycle	U01	1999-01-05	1999-01-20	40
1002	Motorcycle	U02	1999-02-11	1999-03-15	500
1003	Old Bicycle	U02	1999-01-10	1999-02-20	25
1004	Tricycle	U01	1999-02-25	1999-03-08	15
1005	Tennis Racquet	U03	1999-03-19	1999-04-30	20
1006	Helicopter	U03	1999-05-05	1999-05-25	50000
1007	Racing Bicycle	U04	1999-01-20	1999-02-20	200
1008	Broken Bicycle	U01	1999-02-05	1999-03-06	25

Table 3-3			BIDS
USERID	**Itemno**	**Bid**	**Bid_Date**
U02	1001	35	1999-01-07
U04	1001	40	1999-01-08
U02	1001	45	1999-01-11
U04	1001	50	1999-01-13
U02	1001	55	1999-01-15
U01	1002	400	1999-02-14
U02	1002	600	1999-02-16
U03	1002	800	1999-02-17
U04	1002	1000	1999-02-25
U02	1002	1200	1999-03-02
U04	1003	15	1999-01-22
U05	1003	20	1999-02-03
U01	1004	40	1999-03-05
U03	1007	175	1999-01-25
U05	1007	200	1999-02-08
U04	1007	225	1999-02-12

The XML representation of this tabular data serves as the input to the query. Following is a truncated version of the XML because the full XML files are lengthy and there is nothing new beyond the first element in each.

```
<items>
  <item_tuple>
    <itemno>1001</itemno>
    <description>Red Bicycle</description>
    <offered_by>U01</offered_by>
    <start_date>1999-01-05</start_date>
    <end_date>1999-01-20</end_date>
    <reserve_price>40</reserve_price>
  </item_tuple>
  <!-- !!! Snip !!! -->

<users>
  <user_tuple>
    <userid>U01</userid>
    <name>Tom Jones</name>
    <rating>B</rating>
  </user_tuple>
  <!-- !!! Snip !!! -->
```

```
<bids>
  <bid_tuple>
    <userid>U02</userid>
    <itemno>1001</itemno>
    <bid>35</bid>
    <bid_date>1999-01-07</bid_date>
    </bid_tuple>
  <bid_tuple>
  <!-- !!! Snip !!! -->
```

Here's one of the queries run against this data: List the item number and description of all bicycles that currently have an auction in progress, ordered by item number.

Book VI
Chapter 3

**Retrieving Data
from XML
Documents**

This query is expressed in XQuery as follows:

```
<result>
  {
    for $i in doc("items.xml")//item_tuple
    where $i/start_date <= current-date()
      and $i/end_date >= current-date()
      and contains($i/description, "Bicycle")
    order by $i/itemno
    return
        <item_tuple>
            { $i/itemno }
            { $i/description }
        </item_tuple>
  }
</result>
```

Assuming that the current date is 1999-01-31, the expected result of the query is

```
<result>
    <item_tuple>
        <itemno>1003</itemno>
        <description>Old Bicycle</description>
    </item_tuple>
    <item_tuple>
        <itemno>1007</itemno>
        <description>Racing Bicycle</description>
    </item_tuple>
</result>
```

The auctions for the old bicycle and the racing bicycle were active on the last day of January 1999.

FLWOR Expressions

FLWOR expressions are to XQuery what SELECT expressions are to SQL. They are the constructs you use to ask questions of an XML document. The acronym FLWOR stands for For, Let, While, Order by, and Return. A FLWOR expression must contain a for clause and a return clause, and may optionally also include let, while, and order by clauses. Here's the syntax of a FLWOR expression:

```
FLWORExpr ::= (ForClause | LetClause)+ WhereClause?
    OrderByClause? "return" ExprSingle

ForClause ::= "for" "$" VarName TypeDeclaration?
    PositionalVar? "in" ExprSingle ("," "$" VarName
    TypeDeclaration? PositionalVar? "in" ExprSingle)*

PositionalVar ::= "at" "$" VarName

LetClause ::= "let" "$" VarName TypeDeclaration? ":="
    ExprSingle ("," "$" VarName TypeDeclaration? ":="
    ExprSingle)*

WhereClause ::= "where" ExprSingle

OrderByClause ::= ("order" "by" | "stable" "order" "by")
    OrderSpecList

OrderSpecList ::= OrderSpec ("," OrderSpec)*

OrderModifier ::= ("ascending" | "descending")? ("empty"
    "greatest" | "empty" "least")? ("collation" URILiteral)?
```

In the preceding code, the following conventions are used:

+ "A?" means that A is optional.

+ "A|B" means either A or B but not both.

+ "A+" means one or more occurrences of A.

+ "A*" means zero or more occurrences of A.

To see how to use a FLWOR expression on an example XML document that corresponds to an SQL table, consider this sample document:

```
<?xml version="1.0" encoding="UTF-8"?>
<customer xmlns:xsi="http://www.w3.org/2001/XMLSchema-
    instance">
    <row>
        <FirstName>Abe</FirstName>
```

```
          <LastName>Abelson</LastName>
          <City>Springfield</City>
          <AreaCode>714</AreaCode>
          <Telephone>555-1111</Telephone>
     </row>
     <row>
          <FirstName>Bill</FirstName>
          <LastName>Bailey</LastName>
          <City>Decatur</City>
          <AreaCode>714</AreaCode>
          <Telephone>555-2222</Telephone>
     </row>
     <row>
          <FirstName>Chuck</FirstName>
          <LastName>Wood</LastName>
          <City>Philo</City>
          <AreaCode>714</AreaCode>
          <Telephone>555-3333</Telephone>
     </row>
</customer>
```

The for clause

A FLWOR expression must have at least a for clause and a return clause. For purposes of illustrating the effect of the for clause, I show a for fragment and the result of that much of a FLWOR expression.

```
for $c in customer/row
```

This selects the row element in the customer XML document. The result is

```
$c:    <row>
          <FirstName>Abe</FirstName>
          <LastName>Abelson</LastName>
          <City>Springfield</City>
          <AreaCode>714</AreaCode>
          <Telephone>555-1111</Telephone>
       </row>
$c:    <row>
          <FirstName>Bill</FirstName>
          <LastName>Bailey</LastName>
          <City>Decatur</City>
          <AreaCode>714</AreaCode>
          <Telephone>555-2222</Telephone>
       </row>
$c:    <row>
          <FirstName>Chuck</FirstName>
          <LastName>Wood</LastName>
          <City>Philo</City>
          <AreaCode>714</AreaCode>
```

```
        <Telephone>555-3333</Telephone>
    </row>
```

The result includes three instances of the variable $c, each one being bound to a separate row element in the binding sequence from the original document. This result is called a *tuple stream*. The for clause iterates over the tuples in the binding sequence, binding the variable to each of the tuples in the sequence in turn.

The let clause

To show the effect of the let clause, I need a second document example to go along with the customers example:

```
<?xml version="1.0" encoding="UTF-8"?>
<product xmlns:xsi="http://www.w3.org/2001/XMLSchema-
    instance">
    <row rating="0">
        <ProdNo>101</ProdNo>
        <Name>Firecracker 1</Name>
        <Size>Big</Size>
    </row>
    <row rating="1">
        <ProdNo>102</ProdNo>
        <Name>Firecracker 2</Name>
        <Size>Huge</Size>
    </row>
    <row rating="3">
        <ProdNo>103</ProdNo>
        <Name>Firecracker 3</Name>
        <Size>Tremendous</Size>
    </row>
</product>
```

Where the for clause iterates over the items in the binding sequence, the let clause binds its variables with the entire sequence. A let clause that binds multiple variables generates a single tuple containing all the variable bindings. Here's an example:

```
let $c := /customer/row, $p := /product/row/ProdNo
```

This produces

```
$c:    <row>                                       $p:   101
           <FirstName>Abe</FirstName>                     102
           <LastName>Abelson</LastName>                   103
           <City>Springfield</City>
           <AreaCode>714</AreaCode>
```

```
            <Telephone>555-1111</Telephone>
        </row>
        <row>
            <FirstName>Bill</FirstName>
            <LastName>Bailey</LastName>
            <City>Decatur</City>
            <AreaCode>714</AreaCode>
            <Telephone>555-2222</Telephone>
        </row>
        <row>
            <FirstName>Chuck</FirstName>
            <LastName>Wood</LastName>
            <City>Philo</City>
            <AreaCode>714</AreaCode>
            <Telephone>555-3333</Telephone>
        </row>
```

The where clause

The result of a `for` clause or a `let` clause contains some data that you want, but likely also contains some irrelevant data that you don't want. You can filter out the data that you don't want with a `where` clause. Consider the following XQuery fragment:

```
for $p at $i in product/row
where $i = $p/@rating
```

This produces the following result:

```
$p:    <row rating="3">                      $i 3
           <ProdNo>103</ProdNo>
           <Name>Firecracker 3</Name>
           <Size>Tremendous</Size>
       </row>
```

Only in the case of the last product does the element counter equal the value of the `rating` attribute.

The order by clause

The `order by` clause, as you would expect, specifies an order for the items in the result, according to the ordering specification (`OrderSpec`). The ordering specification contains a single expression (`ExprSingle`) and an optional ordering modifier (`OrderModifier`). You can add an `order by` clause to one of our previous query fragments and see how it affects the result.

```
for $c in customer/row
order by $c/LastName descending
```

This selects the row element in the customer XML document, listing the tuples in descending order of last name. The result is

```
$c:    <row>
          <FirstName>Chuck</FirstName>
          <LastName>Wood</LastName>
          <City>Philo</City>
          <AreaCode>714</AreaCode>
          <Telephone>555-3333</Telephone>
       </row>
$c:    <row>
          <FirstName>Bill</FirstName>
          <LastName>Bailey</LastName>
          <City>Decatur</City>
          <AreaCode>714</AreaCode>
          <Telephone>555-2222</Telephone>
       </row>
$c:    <row>
          <FirstName>Abe</FirstName>
          <LastName>Abelson</LastName>
          <City>Springfield</City>
          <AreaCode>714</AreaCode>
          <Telephone>555-1111</Telephone>
       </row>
```

Because you are ordering by last name in descending order, the record for Chuck Wood precedes that of Bill Bailey, which comes before the record for Abe Abelson.

The return clause

The return clause specifies what is returned by the FLWOR expression after all the other clauses have had a chance to have an effect. The ExprSingle in the return clause is evaluated once for each tuple produced by the combined activity of the other clauses. The result is a sequence of values. Adding a return clause to the previous query fragment to make a complete query results in the following:

```
<result>
    {
      for $c in doc("customer.xml")
      order by $c/row/LastName descending
      return
          <row>
             { $c/FirstName }
             { $c/LastName }
          </row>
    }
</result>
```

This selects the row element in the customer XML document, listing the tuples in descending order of last name. It then outputs the first and last names in the tuples. The result is

```
<result>
     <row>
         <FirstName>Chuck</FirstName>
         <LastName>Wood</LastName>
     </row>
     <row>
         <FirstName>Bill</FirstName>
         <LastName>Bailey</LastName>

     </row>
     <row>
         <FirstName>Abe</FirstName>
         <LastName>Abelson</LastName>
     </row>
</result>
```

Comparing XQuery to SQL

The data in an XML document is in quite a different form than the data in an SQL table. However, there are some similarities between the two worlds. XQuery's FLWOR expression corresponds to some extent with the SQL SELECT expression. Both are used to retrieve the data you want from a collection of data, most of which you don't want at the moment.

XQuery's FLWOR expression and SQL's SELECT expression

Although XQuery's let clause has no analog in SQL, the XQuery for clause is related to the SQL FROM clause in that both specify the source of the data. XQuery's order by clause serves the same purpose that SQL's ORDER BY clause serves. In both XQuery and SQL, the where clause filters out data that you do not want to include in the final result. SQL's GROUP BY and HAVING clauses have no analog in XQuery.

Relating XQuery data types to SQL data types

Some of XQuery's data types correspond to SQL data types, but others do not. XQuery has some data types that do not correspond to any SQL data types and vice versa. Table 3-4 lists the XQuery data types and, where applicable, the corresponding SQL types. Where there is no corresponding type, a long dash serves as a placeholder.

Table 3-4   **XQuery 1.0 Data Types and Corresponding SQL Data Types**

XQuery 1.0 Data Types	*SQL Data Types*
xs:string	CHARACTER, CHARACTER VARYING, CHARACTER LARGE OBJECT, NATIONAL CHARACTER, NATIONAL CHARACTER VARYING, NATIONAL CHARACTER LARGE OBJECT
xs:normalizedString	--
xs:token	--
xs:language	--
xs:NMTOKEN	--
xs:NMTOKENS	--
xs:Name	--
xs:NCNAME	--
xs:ID	--
xs:IDREF	--
xs:IDREFS	--
xs:ENTITY	--
xs:ENTITIES	--
xs:BOOLEAN	BOOLEAN
xs:decimal	NUMERIC, DECIMAL
xs:integer	INTEGER
xs:nonPositiveInteger	--
xs:negativeInteger	--
xs:long	BIGINT
xs:int	INTEGER
xs:short	SMALLINT
xs:byte	--
xs:nonNegativeInteger	--
xs:unsignedLong	--
xs:unsignedInt	--
xs:unsignedShort	--
xs:unsignedByte	--
xs:positiveInteger	--
xs:float	FLOAT, REAL
xs:double	FLOAT, DOUBLE

XQuery 1.0 Data Types	SQL Data Types
xs:duration	--
xs:dateTime	TIMESTAMP WITH TIME ZONE, TIMESTAMP WITHOUT TIME ZONE
xs:date	DATE WITH TIME ZONE, DATE WITHOUT TIME ZONE
xs:time	TIME WITH TIME ZONE, TIME WITHOUT TIME ZONE
xs:gYearMonth	--
xs:gYear	--
xs:gMonthDay	--
xs:gDay	--
xs:gMonth	--
xs:hexBinary	BINARY LARGE OBJECT
xs:base64Binary	BINARY LARGE OBJECT
xs:anyURI	--
xs:QName	--
xs:NOTATION	--
xdt:dayTimeDuration	INTERVAL (day-time interval)
xdt:yearMonthDuration	INTERVAL (year-month interval)
xs:anyType	XML
xs:anySimpleType	--
xdt:untyped	--
Node types	Structured user-defined types
User-defined complex types	Structured user-defined types
--	ROW
--	REF
List types and sequences	ARRAY
List types and sequences	MULTISET
--	DATALINK

Clearly, there are a lot more XQuery types than SQL types. In most cases, casting an SQL type to an XQuery type is not a problem, but going the other way may be a challenge.

Book VII

Database Tuning Overview

The 5th Wave — By Rich Tennant

"I'll be right there. I just need to do a core dump into my shoe first."

Contents at a Glance

Chapter 1: Tuning the Database

In This Chapter

✓ Analyzing the workload

✓ Contemplating physical design considerations

✓ Choosing and clustering indexes

✓ Co-clustering two relations

✓ Indexing on multiple attributes

✓ Tuning indexes, queries, and transactions

✓ Query tuning in a high-concurrency environment

✓ Benchmarking

✓ Separating user interactions from transactions

✓ Minimizing traffic between application and server

✓ Precompiling frequently used queries

The word *tuning* is generally taken to mean optimizing a system that exists, but is not operating at top capacity. However, tuning doesn't do you much good if your initial design is not at least close to optimal in the first place. Tuning can only take you so far from your starting point. It is a lot easier to tune a slightly off-pitch B-string on your guitar to a perfect B than it is to tune a G-string up to a perfect B. (Also, you're a lot less likely to break the string.) Tuning for optimal performance should start in the initial design stage of a database, not at some later time when design decisions have been cast in concrete.

The performance of a database management system is generally judged by how fast it executes queries. Two types of operations are important, the retrieval of data from a database, and the updating of records in a database. The speed with which records can be accessed is key to both because you must locate a record before you can either retrieve or update the data in it. The users' data model upon which you will base your database design is almost certainly structured in a way that is not the best from a performance standpoint. The users are primarily concerned with functionality and may have little or no idea of how the design of a database affects how well it performs. You must take the users' data model and transform it into a conceptual schema that you actualize in the form of an E-R diagram.

Analyzing the Workload

Optimal design of a database depends largely on how the database will be used. What kinds of queries will it be subjected to? How often will updates be made, compared to how often queries are posed? These kinds of questions try to get at what the workload will be. The answers to such questions have a great bearing on how the database should be structured. In effect, the design of the database is tuned based on how it will typically be used.

To give you a sound foundation for designing your database to best handle the workload to which it will be subjected, draft a *workload description*. The workload description should include the following elements:

✦ A list of all the queries you expect will be run against the database, along with an estimate of the expected frequency of each, compared to the frequencies of all the other queries and update operations.

✦ A list of all the update operations you expect to perform, along with an estimate of the expected frequency of each, compared to the frequencies of all the other updates and queries.

✦ Your goal for the performance of each of the types of queries and updates.

Queries can vary tremendously in complexity, so it is important to determine in advance how complex each is, and how that complexity will affect the overall workload. You can determine query complexity by answering a few questions:

✦ How many relations (tables) are accessed by this query?

✦ Which attributes (columns) are selected?

✦ Which attributes appear in the WHERE clause, and how selective are the WHERE clause conditions likely to be?

Just as queries can vary a great deal, so can update operations. Questions regarding updates should include

✦ Which attributes appear in the WHERE clause, and how selective are the WHERE clause conditions likely to be?

✦ What type of update is it, an INSERT, DELETE, or UPDATE?

✦ In UPDATE statements, which fields will be modified?

Considering the Physical Design

Among the factors that have a major impact on performance, few if any have a greater effect than indexes. On the plus side, indexes point directly to the desired record in a table, thereby bypassing the need to scan down through the table until you come upon the record you want. This can be a tremendous timesaver for a query. On the minus side, every time an insertion update or a deletion update is made to a table, the indexes on that table must be updated too, costing time. When chosen properly, indexes can be a great help. When chosen poorly, indexes can waste resources and slow processing substantially.

Regarding indexes, several questions need to be answered:

✦ Which tables should have indexes and which should not?

✦ For the tables that should have indexes, which columns should be indexed?

✦ For each index, should it be clustered or unclustered?

I address these questions in this chapter.

After you arrive at a conceptual schema and have determined that you need to make changes in order to improve performance, what kinds of modifications can you make?

✦ Often there is more than one way to normalize a schema, and one such way may deliver better performance than others. You may wish to change the way tables are defined in order to take advantage of a schema that gives you better performance than your current schema does.

✦ Although this may sound somewhat heretical, sometimes it pays to denormalize your schema, and accept a risk of modification anomalies, in exchange for a significant performance boost.

✦ Contrary to the preceding point, sometimes it makes sense to take normalization a step further than you otherwise would, in effect to *overnormalize*. This can improve the performance of queries that involve only a few attributes. By giving those attributes a table of their own, retrievals can sometimes be speeded up.

Queries and updates that are run frequently should be examined carefully to see if rewriting them might enable them to execute faster. There is probably not much advantage to applying such scrutiny to queries that are rarely run, but after you have some history and notice the ones that are being run continually, it may pay to give them an extra look to see if they can be improved.

Choosing the Right Indexes

Indexes can dramatically improve the performance of database retrievals. There are several reasons why this is true. One reason is that an index tends to be small compared to the size of the table that it is indexing. This means that the index is likely to be in the cache, which is accessible at semiconductor memory speed rather than on disk. There is a million-to-one performance advantage right there. Other reasons depend on the type of query being performed and on whether the index is clustered. I discuss clustering in the next section.

Avoiding unnecessary indexes

Because there is an overhead cost in maintaining indexes, you do not want to create any indexes that won't improve the performance of any of your retrieval or update queries. To decide which database tables should not be indexed, consult the workload description you created as the first step in the design process. It contains a list of queries and their frequencies.

Here's a no-brainer: If a table has only a small number of rows, there is no point in indexing it. A sequential scan through relatively few rows executes quickly.

For larger tables, the best candidates for indexes are columns that appear in the query's WHERE clause. The WHERE clause determines which table rows are to be selected.

It's likely, particularly in a system where a large number of different queries are run, that some queries are more important than others. Either they are run more often, or they are run against more and larger tables, or getting results quickly is critical for some reason. Whatever the case, prioritize your queries, with the most important first. Create indexes that give the best performance for the most important query. Then move down the line, adding indexes that help the progressively less important queries. Your database management system's query optimizer chooses the best execution plan available to it, based on the indexes that are present.

There are different kinds of indexes, each with its own structure. Whereas one kind of index is better for some retrievals, another kind is better for others. The most common index types are B+ tree, hash, and ISAM. Theoretically, for any given query, the query optimizer chooses the best index type available. Most of the time, practice follows theory.

Choosing a column to index

Any column appearing in a query's WHERE clause is a candidate for indexing. If the WHERE clause contains an exact match selection, such as EMPLOYEE. DepartmentID = DEPARTMENT.DepartmentID, a hash index on EMPLOYEE. DepartmentID usually performs best. The number of rows in the EMPLOYEE table is sure to be larger than the number of rows in the DEPARTMENT table, so the index is of more use if applied to EMPLOYEE than if applied to DEPARTMENT.

If the WHERE clause contains a range selection, such as EMPLOYEE.Age BETWEEN 55 AND 65, a B+ tree index on EMPLOYEE.Age is probably be the best performer. If the table is rarely updated, an ISAM index may be competitive with the B+ tree index.

Multi-column indexes

If a WHERE clause imposes conditions on more than one attribute, such as EMPLOYEE.Age BETWEEN 55 AND 65 AND EMPLOYEE.DeptName = Shipping, a multi-column index should be considered. If the index includes all the columns that the query retrieves (an index-only query), the query could be completed without touching the data table at all. This could dramatically speed the query, and may be sufficient motivation to include a column in the index that you otherwise would not include.

Clustering indexes

A *clustered index* is one that determines the sort order of the table that it is indexing.

Suppose there are several queries of the EMPLOYEE table that have a WHERE clause similar to WHERE EMPLOYEE.LastName = 'Smith'. In such a case, it would be beneficial to have a clustered index on EMPLOYEE.LastName. All the employees named Smith would be clustered together in the index, and they would be retrieved very quickly. Quick retrieval is possible because after you've found the index to the first Smith, you have found them all. Access to the desired records is almost instantaneous. For any given table, there can be only one clustered index. All other indexes on that table must be unclustered. Unclustered indexes can be helpful, but not as helpful as a clustered index. For that reason, if you are going to choose one index to be the clustered index for a table, choose the one that will be used by the most important queries in the list of queries in the workload description.

Consider the following example:

```
SELECT DeptNo
FROM EMPLOYEE
WHERE EMPLOYEE.Age > 29 ;
```

Book VII Chapter 1

Tuning the Database

You can use a B+ tree index on Age to retrieve only the rows where employee age is greater than 29. Whether this is worthwhile depends on the age distribution of the employees. If most employees are 30 or older, the indexed retrieval won't do much better than a sequential scan. Suppose only 10% of the employees are more than 29 years old. If the index on Age is clustered, it will give a substantial improvement over a sequential scan. If it is unclustered, however, as it is likely to be, it could require a buffer page swap for every qualifying employee and will likely be more expensive than a sequential scan. I say that an index on Age is likely to be unclustered based on the assumption that there is probably at least one column in the EMPLOYEE table that would be more deserving of a clustered index than the Age column.

You can see from this example that choosing whether to create an index for a table column is not a simple matter. Doing an effective job of choosing requires detailed knowledge of the data as well as of the queries that are run on it. Figure 1-1 compares the costs of using a clustered index, an unclustered index, and a sequential scan to retrieve rows from a table.

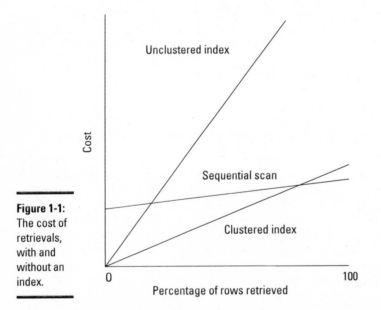

Figure 1-1:
The cost of retrievals, with and without an index.

Figure 1-1 reveals a few things about the cost of indexes.

◆ A clustered index always performs better than an unclustered index.

◆ A clustered index performs better than a sequential scan unless practically all of the rows are retrieved.

✦ When one or very few records are being retrieved, a clustered index performs much better than a sequential scan.

✦ When one or a very few records are being retrieved, an unclustered index performs better than a sequential scan.

✦ When more than about 10% of the records in a table are retrieved, a sequential scan performs better than an unclustered index.

That last point disproves the myth that indexing a retrieval key always improves performance over the performance of a sequential scan.

Choosing index type

In most cases, a B+ tree index is preferred because it does a good job on range queries as well as equality queries. Hash indexes are slightly better than B+ tree indexes in equality queries, but not nearly as good in range queries, so overall, B+ tree indexes are preferred. However, in a couple of cases, a hash join will do better. One is in a nested loop join where the inner table is the indexed table and the index includes the join columns. Because an equality selection is generated for each row in the outer table, the advantage of the hash index over the B+ tree index is multiplied. Another case where the hash join comes out ahead is when there is an important equality query and there are no range queries on a table. You don't need to lose a lot of sleep over choosing an index type. Most database engines make the choice for you, and it will usually be the best choice.

Weighing the cost of index maintenance

Indexes slow update operations because every time a table is updated with either an insertion or a deletion, all its indexes must be updated too. Balance this against the speedup gained by being able to access table rows more quickly than would be possible using a sequential table scan. Even updates are potentially speeded up because a row must first be located before it can be updated. You may find that the net benefit of some indexes does not justify their inclusion in the database. You are better off dropping them.

Composite indexes

Composite indexes are indexes on more than one column. They can give superior performance to queries that have more than one condition in the WHERE clause. Here's an example:

```
SELECT EmployeeID
FROM EMPLOYEES
WHERE Age BETWEEN 55 AND 65
    AND Salary BETWEEN 4000 and 7000 ;
```

Both conditions in the WHERE clause are range conditions. An index based on <Age, Salary> performs about as well as an index based on <Salary, Age>. Either one performs better than an index based only on Age or only on Salary.

Now consider the following example:

```
SELECT EmployeeID
FROM EMPLOYEES
WHERE Age = 57
   AND Salary BETWEEN 4000 and 7000 ;
```

In this case, an index based on <Age, Salary> performs better than an index based on <Salary, Age> because the equality condition on Age means that all the records that have Age = 57 are clustered together by the time the salary evaluation is done.

Tuning Indexes

After the database you have designed has been in operation for a while, you should re-evaluate the decisions you made about indexing. When you created the system, you chose indexes based on what you expected usage to be. Now, after several weeks or months of operation, you have actual usage statistics. Perhaps some of the queries that you thought would be important are not run very often after all. Perhaps you made assumptions about what indexes would be used by the query optimizer, but now you find that limitations of the optimizer prevent it from using them, to the detriment of performance.

Based on the actual performance data that you now have, you can tune your indexes. This may entail dropping indexes that are doing you no good and merely consuming resources. It may mean adding new indexes that speed queries that have turned out to be more important than they at first appeared to be.

For best results, tuning indexes must be an ongoing activity. As time goes on, the nature of the workload is bound to evolve. As it does, the best indexes to support the current workload need to evolve too. The DBA must keep track of performance and respond when it starts to trend downward.

Another problem, which appears after a database has been in operation for an extended period of time, might be called the *tired* index. A tired index is one that is no longer delivering the performance advantage that it did when it was first applied to the database. When an index is fresh and new, whether it is a B+ tree index, an ISAM index, or some other kind, it has an optimal structure. As time goes on, insertions, deletions, and updates are made to the table that the index is associated with. The index must adjust to these changes. In the process of making those adjustments, the structure of the index changes and moves away from optimality. Eventually, performance is affected enough to be noticeable. The best solution to this problem is to drop the index and then rebuild it. The rebuilt index once again has an optimal structure. The only downside to this solution is that the database table must be out of service while its index is being rebuilt. The amount of time it takes to rebuild an index depends on several things, including the speed of the processor and the size of the table being indexed. For some databases, you may not even experience any downside. The database engine will rebuild indexes automatically when needed.

Tuning Queries

After your system has been running a while, you may find that a query is running slower than you expect. There are several possible causes for this, and several possible things you can do to fix it. Because there are generally several different ways to code a query, which all give the same result, perhaps you could recode it, along with an appropriate change of indexes.

Sometimes a query doesn't run as you expect because the query optimizer is not executing the plan that you expect it to. You can check on this with most database management systems by having it display the plan it has generated. It is quite possible that the optimizer is not finding the best plan. Here are some possible causes:

+ Some query optimizers do not handle NULL values well. If the table you are querying contains NULL values in a field that appears in the WHERE clause, this could be the problem.

+ Some query optimizers do not handle expressions well, either arithmetic or string. If one of these appears in the WHERE clause, the optimizer may not handle it correctly.

+ An OR connective in the WHERE clause could cause a problem.

+ If you are expecting the optimizer to select a fast, but sophisticated, plan, you could be disappointed. Sometimes the best plan is beyond the capability of even high-end optimizers to find.

Some database management systems give you some help in overcoming optimizer deficiencies. They give you the power to force the optimizer to use an index that you know will be helpful, or to join tables in an order that you know is the best. For the best results, a thorough knowledge of the capabilities and the deficiencies of your DBMS is essential, as is a good grasp of optimization principles.

Two possible culprits in performance problems are nested queries and correlated queries. Many optimizers do not handle these well. If a query that is either a nested query or a correlated query is not performing up to expectations, recoding it without nesting or correlation is a good thing to try.

Tuning Transactions

In an environment where many users are using a database concurrently, contention for a popular resource can slow performance for everyone. The problem arises because a user locks a resource before using it and releases the lock when she is finished with it. As long as the resource is locked, no one else can access it. Here are several things you can do to minimize the performance impact of locking:

+ **Minimize the amount of time that you hold a lock.** If you are performing a series of operations with a transaction, obtain your locks as late as possible and release them as soon as possible.

+ **Put indexes on a different disk from the one that holds the data files.** This prevents accesses to one from interfering with accesses to the other.

+ **Switch to a hash or ISAM index.** If a table is updated frequently, B+ tree indexes on its columns lose much of their advantage because the root of the tree and the pages just below it must be traversed by every update. They become hot spots, meaning they are locked frequently, becoming a bottleneck. Making the switch might help.

Separating User Interactions from Transactions

Because computer instructions operate in the nanosecond realm and humans operate in the second or even minute realm, one thing that can really slow down a database transaction is any interaction with a human. If that transaction happens to hold a lock on a critical resource, the application the user is interacting with is not the only one to suffer a delay. Every other application that needs that resource is brought to a screeching halt, for an interval of time that could be billions of times longer than necessary. The obvious solution is to separate user interactions from transactions. Never hold a lock on anything while waiting for a human to do something.

Minimizing Traffic between Application and Server

If you have a lot of applications, running on a lot of client machines, all depending on data residing on a server, overall performance is limited by the server's capacity to send and receive messages. The fewer the messages that need to travel between client and server, the better. The smaller the messages that need to travel between client and server, the better. One approach to this problem is to use *stored procedures*. Stored procedures are precompiled application modules that run on the server rather than the client. Their primary purpose is to filter result sets so that only the needed data is transmitted to the client, rather than sending a whole big chunk of the database. This can reduce traffic between the server and client machine dramatically.

Precompiling Frequently Used Queries

If you execute the same query repeatedly, say daily, or even hourly, you can save time by compiling it in advance. At runtime, executing the query is the only thing that needs to be done. The compilation is done only once and never needs to be repeated. The timesaving due to this forethought adds up and becomes significant over the course of weeks and months.

**Book VII
Chapter 1**

Tuning the Database

Chapter 2: Tuning the Environment

In This Chapter

✓ Tuning the recovery system

✓ Tuning the operating system

✓ Making better use of the hardware you have

✓ Adding new hardware

✓ Understanding multiprocessor environments

Computer systems are subject to all kinds of failures — power failures, hardware failures, operating system failures, application program failures, and even DBMS failures. These things happen — you can count on it. The important question you should ask yourself is, "What happens when a failure occurs?" In critical applications, you don't want to lose any data, and you don't want to lose any more time than absolutely necessary.

Failures aside, you want your system to be running as efficiently as possible. Inefficiencies can hamper productivity in many ways, sometimes slowing it to a crawl. In dealing with both failures and inefficiencies, the key to optimizing performance is tuning each of the parts of your total system. Your recovery system is designed to gracefully handle failures. It must be tuned in order to operate at top efficiency. Beyond the recovery system, your operating system and storage subsystem need to be tuned for the work that you are doing. Settings that would be appropriate for one job mix might be terrible for another. If you have multiple computers connected on a network, the way they are connected can have a tremendous impact on performance. All these considerations are important, and they tend to interact, which makes optimizing them even more challenging. I talk about some of the things that you can do to assure that you are getting the best performance out of your system that you can reasonably expect, given the limited budget and staff time that can be devoted to maintaining an acceptable level of performance.

The performance of a database system can vary dramatically: anywhere from lightning-fast to molasses-slow. Where your system sits on that spectrum is largely up to the decisions you make as a developer, the decisions the DBA makes, and the decisions the system administrator makes about how the operating system will run, and what hardware it will run on. All these levels affect the ultimate performance of a database application.

Surviving Failures with Minimum Data Loss

Sooner or later, failures occur. That being the case, planning for those failures can make a big difference. Your plans should be aimed at minimizing the disruption that would be caused by downtime and loss of data. At any given time, the "current" copy of your database resides in two places: on stable storage in the form of hard disk drives, and in a volatile solid-state memory called the page buffer. The page buffer contains the *working set,* which is data that is currently being actively read and written by transactions that have been initiated by the executing program. The pages in the working set are destined to be written to disk, but that has not happened yet. If a failure occurs before a transaction commits or aborts, the recovery system must be able to return the database to a consistent state: either the state the database would have been in if the transaction had committed successfully, or the state the database was in before the transaction started, in the case of an abort.

What happens to transactions where there is no failure?

In the absence of a failure, a transaction can end up in one of two ways — it will either commit or abort. When a transaction commits, it means that it has completed successfully. This does *not* mean that the changes made by the transaction have been written to stable storage, but it does mean that the changes are recoverable in the event of a failure, thanks to the logging feature that is discussed later in this chapter. After the recovery operation is performed, the database is once again in a consistent state.

The other thing that a transaction can do besides committing is aborting. A resource conflict, for example, may prevent a transaction from committing. This is not a failure — nothing is broken. It is just a case of trying to do something at the wrong time. When a transaction aborts, a rollback is initiated. The database transaction log records every operation that takes place in the course of a transaction. The rollback operation consults the log and performs in reverse all the operations listed in it. This restores the database to the state it was in before the transaction started. This is a consistent state. The transaction can be attempted again when conditions are more favorable. In many cases, conditions are favorable just as soon as the rollback completes. Whatever concurrent transaction caused the conflict has either committed or aborted, and the contested resource is now available.

What happens when a failure occurs before a committed or aborted transaction is written to stable storage?

If a failure occurs before a committed or aborted transaction has been written to disk, the database may be left in an inconsistent state. It's up to the recovery system to restore consistency. To do so, it makes use of the transaction log. The log contains a record of what was done up to the point of the failure. This information can be used to restore consistency, either by reconstructing the committed transaction and writing it to disk, or by erasing all record of the aborted transaction, so that it has no effect on the database that exists on disk.

Tuning the Recovery System

Because it's a sure thing that failures will occur, it makes sense to plan ahead for them. A failure that you have not planned for could result in a data loss severe enough to jeopardize the continued survival of your organization. Effective preparation requires that you understand what kinds of failures could possibly happen, what the impact of such failures would be, and what can be done to mitigate that impact.

The most damaging failure is the one that causes the irretrievable loss of data. Data can be irretrievably lost due to a variety of causes, based on the way it is stored. There are two kinds of storage devices in common use today: *volatile* memory and *non-volatile* memory. They are subject to different failure modes. Volatile memory forgets everything if its power is ever interrupted, even for fraction of a second. Thus any kind of power failure can cause all data held in volatile memory to be lost. Non-volatile memory, as I'm sure you have guessed by now, does not lose its contents in the event of a power outage. Another name for non-volatile memory is *persistent* storage. The data persists even in the event of a three-day blackout after a major storm. When power is restored, the data is still there, just waiting for you.

Modern memory systems are hierarchical in nature, with the fastest memory devices at the top of the memory hierarchy and the slowest at the bottom. The fastest devices are also the most expensive in terms of cost per bit stored. For this reason, it is not feasible to populate a memory system completely with the fastest memory available. Here's the hierarchy for a typical database server:

✦ **CPU registers:** CPU registers are the fastest because they are fabricated with the same process as the CPU itself, on the same chip. They are closest to the processing unit, so transit delays between the two are minimized.

+ **Level 1 cache:** Level 1 cache is a little slower than CPU registers.

+ **Level 2 cache:** Level 2 cache is slower yet.

+ **Level 3 cache (if present):** Level 3 cache may or may not be present. If it is, it is a little slower than Level 2 cache.

+ **Main memory:** Main memory is much slower than cache.

+ **Hard disk:** Hard disk is much, much, much slower than main memory.

+ **Magnetic tape:** Magnetic tape is so slow that it is only used for backup and archiving. You would never keep active data on magnetic tape.

CPU registers, cache, and main memory are all examples of *volatile memory.* When you lose power, you also lose all the data stored in those devices. Hard disk and magnetic tape are persistent storage devices. Data stored in such devices survives power outages. This is not to say that persistent storage devices are invulnerable to failure. They just have different failure modes from those of volatile memory devices.

Hard disks and magnetic tape drives are machines that contain moving parts. Such devices fail catastrophically from time to time. If you use them long enough, they are sure to fail. When a hard disk fails, you lose all the data that was stored on it. A regular backup schedule, faithfully followed, can minimize your losses in such an event.

You might wonder why computers have volatile memory at all. Because volatile memory forgets everything after a power interruption or processor reboot, why not use non-volatile persistent storage for all the memory? The answer has to do with performance. Volatile main memory consists of semiconductor RAM chips and non-volatile persistent storage is implemented with hard disk drives. Semiconductor RAM can be as much as a million times faster that hard disks in terms of exchanging data with the processor. With a million-to-one speed advantage, volatile semiconductor RAM earns a place in every computer where speed is a consideration.

Now you might wonder, if volatile RAM is a million times faster than non-volatile hard disk storage, and remedies have been developed for recovering from failures, why would you ever want to use hard disk storage? The answer is cost. The cost to store a bit on hard disk is much lower than the cost to store the same bit in semiconductor RAM. A personal computer might have a 750 GB hard disk, but only 1 GB of RAM. The difference in capacity reflects the difference in cost per bit.

Because volatile and non-volatile memories are both subject to failure, you need strategies to cope with those failures. Because the failure modes are so different, the strategies you use also need to be different. How do you protect data against failures in a volatile memory system? For this discussion, I assume that the non-volatile memory system is operating properly because it's unlikely that both the volatile and non-volatile memory systems would fail at the same time. Such a failure is, of course, possible in the event of a building collapse or other major disaster. There are ways of coping with even those eventualities, but they are beyond the scope of this book.

Putting logs and transactions on different disks

Volatile memory failures, for whatever reason, are inconvenient, but not catastrophic, if the information you need to recover to resume operation is stored on some non-volatile medium such as hard disk. Clearly you can't store the results of your computations directly on hard disk as you perform them. If you did, your processing would be reduced to hard disk speeds rather than the million-times-faster RAM speeds. There are however, things you can do to minimize the amount of time that results spend in RAM before being written to disk. These methods involve transactions and logging.

I discuss transactions and logging in detail in Book IV, Chapter 2. The log is a record of every operation that alters the database in memory. It resides primarily on disk, but part of it, the page buffer, is in RAM. Writes of log entries to disk are made before the results of the corresponding transactions are written to disk. If a system failure or "crash" occurs, you can reconstruct any transactions that were in progress when the crash occurred. If a transaction had committed or aborted but had not yet been flushed to disk, the log on disk holds the information that enables the system to either commit or roll back the transaction as appropriate. By keeping the log on a separate disk from the disk or disks that hold the database, performance during normal operation is maximized because writes to the log are sequential and no time is lost doing disk head seeks. This being the case, frequent writes to the log do not exact the same performance penalty that buffer flushes to the database do.

Put logs and transactions on different disks

To understand why you should put a database's log on its own hard disk drive, you should understand how a hard disk drive is constructed and how it operates.

Hard disk drive construction

A hard disk drive contains a sealed enclosure that is protected from particulates in the air by a very effective air filter. Inside the enclosure, a spindle connected to a motor rotates at speeds on the order of 7,200 revolutions per minute. Attached to the spindle are several circular platters stacked one atop another within the enclosure. The platters are aluminum disks coated with a magnetic material. On each platter a set of more than a thousand concentric tracks are magnetically recorded. These tracks hold the data in the form of magnetic domains that are either magnetized in one direction or the other. For example, if a magnetic north pole is up, it represents a binary one; if a south pole is up, it represents a zero.

An actuator moves an arm, so that its tip, which holds a magnetic read/write head, can hover over any of the tracks. The read/write head, when reading, can sense whether it is flying over a north pole or a south pole and thus reads either a one or a zero. When writing, the head, which is an electromagnet, can flip the polarity of the domains it flies over, thus laying down a pattern of ones and zeros. On the top and the bottom of every platter is an actuator arm and its associated read/write head (except on the very top and bottom platters, which don't have heads on the outside of the stack). The set of corresponding tracks on all the platters, for example, all the track zeros, which are the outermost tracks, constitute a *cylinder*. All the heads in the stack are flying over the same cylinder at any given time.

Hard disk drive performance considerations

Because of the way hard disk drives are constructed, and because mechanical movement is involved, there are limits to how fast a given byte or word can be read or written. The delay involved in a read or write has several components:

+ **Disk drive controller delay:** The time it takes the controller to determine whether it is being asked to do a read or a write and to determine the location that is to be read or written.

+ **Seek time:** The time it takes for the read/write head to move from whatever track it is currently on to the track that it needs to go to next.

+ **Settling time:** The time it takes for the "jiggling" to stop after the read/write head has arrived at the track that it will operate on next.

+ **Rotational latency:** Even at 7,200 RPM, it takes a significant amount of time for a word of data to rotate all the way around the disk and come under the read/write head. If the desired word has just gone by when the head settles over a track, there will be a delay of up to 8 milliseconds before it comes around again.

+ **Read/write time:** The time it takes to actually do the read or write operation.

When you add up all the noted delays, it becomes clear why hard disk storage is so much slower than semiconductor RAM. The natural question that arises is, "What can be done to minimize the delays that are inherent in the operation of hard disks?"

As it happens, a major part of the total delay involved in hard disk operation is due to the combination of seek time, settling time, and rotational latency. Minimizing these dramatically improves performance. The best way to minimize seek time and settling time is to do all your writes on the same cylinder, so that you never have to do a seek. That's not possible, but what you *can* do is make all your writes to the same cylinder until it fills up and then move to an adjacent cylinder. This minimizes both seek time and settling time. Furthermore, if you are writing sequentially along a track, rotational latency is not an issue. You are always writing on the sector that immediately follows the one you have just written.

Because it is critical that log entries be written to disk sooner rather than later, dedicating an entire disk drive to the log is an obvious choice. Sequential writes to the log are as fast as possible because seek time, settling time, and rotational latency are all minimized.

For performance reasons, unless you are dealing with a read-only database, always locate a database's log on its own disk, not sharing the disk with any other function or any other database. This way, log writes are always to sequential sectors on the same disk cylinder, minimizing access time.

It's a given that any reasonable system employs transactions and logging. Transactions and logging are a form of insurance. They protect you from the worst effects of a failure, but you must pay a premium for that protection. Clearly, you want the protection, but you don't want to pay a higher premium for it than you have to. This is where tuning comes in. There is a tradeoff between the time it takes to recover from a failure and performance during normal operation.

To minimize the time to recover from a failure, you should flush log entries from the page buffer located in RAM to hard disk frequently. However, the more often you make disk accesses, the greater the impact on performance. Somehow you must find that "sweet spot" where time to recover from a failure is tolerable and normal operation performance is acceptable. Finding that sweet spot is the DBA's responsibility.

The DBA is the person with the power to determine how often the page buffer is flushed to disk. The specifics of how to do this vary from one DBMS to another. Consult the system administrator documentation for whichever product you are using for details on how to control the timing of buffer flushes. Keep a detailed history of every time your system goes down for any reason, and use that knowledge to estimate the frequency of future failures. Combine that information with the results of the data you have recorded on the amount of time it takes to recover from a failure, in order to decide how to set the buffer flush timing parameters.

Tuning write operations

With a performance difference on the order of a million to one between semi-conductor RAM and hard disk storage, the less frequently you write to disk, the better your performance is. Balancing that consideration is the fact that if you don't write to stable storage, you will lose all your data in the event of a failure.

There is a substantial difference between the amount of time taken by a write to the log disk and a write to the data disk. Because writes to the log disk tend to be sequential writes on the same disk track, with infrequent short seeks to an adjacent track, such writes are much faster than writes to the data disk, which tend to be to random locations, requiring frequent large seeks between distant tracks, and incurring substantial latency delays.

Before a transaction commits, it writes the "after image" of the change to the log disk. It may be quite a while after the change is made before the change is transferred from the buffer, which is in solid-state memory, to the stable storage of the data disk. How long that interval is, affects performance.

If a failure occurs after the log has been updated with the result of a transaction, but before the change has been made to the data disk, recovery is not a problem. Thus you can wait until a convenient time to store the changed data to disk. A convenient time would be when the disk read-write head happened to be located over the track that you want to write to. In such a case, the delay due to seek time and settling time would be avoided.

Different DBMS products have different procedures for determining when it becomes advantageous to start looking for opportunities to make convenient writes. The buffer in solid-state memory is divided into a number of pages. Whenever a change is made to a page, the page is marked as "dirty." There is never a need to write a clean page out to disk because its contents already match the contents of the corresponding disk location. Dirty pages, on the other hand, differ from their corresponding disk locations and eventually have to be written to disk, incurring the performance penalty that such an operation entails. Generally, when the percentage of dirty pages in the page buffer exceeds a certain threshold, the system starts looking for opportunities to make convenient writes.

There is a considerable advantage to delaying writes to the data disk, that goes beyond the difference in speed between a write to buffer and a write to disk. If a memory location is "hot" in the sense that it is being updated frequently, many of those updates may not need to ever be written to disk. Suppose a memory location in the page buffer has a value of 4, for example.

In quick succession, it may be updated to 7, 17, 34, and 54. If the page it is on is not flushed to disk until the last of those writes takes place, the updates to 7, 17, and 34 are never written to disk, and the time that such writes would have taken is never consumed. This consideration strengthens the case for extending the amount of time before dirty pages are written to disk as long as possible, without making recovery from failure unduly onerous.

Dumps

In the preceding sections, I refer to hard disk storage as *stable* storage. It earns that description because it is non-volatile. It doesn't lose its contents when the power goes out. However, it's not immune to destruction. Hard disks *do* fail, and when they do, all the data on them is lost. To address this problem, system administrators do periodic database dumps, in which the entire database is copied to offline media and stored in a safe place.

Database dumps are expensive because it takes a significant amount of time to copy a large database to offline media. In addition, the offline media itself has a cost, as does the space that is taken up by it. For these reasons, you don't want to do dumps too often. On the other hand, you do want to do them often enough. If a hard disk dies, all the changes that have been made to it since the last dump are gone. Can those lost transactions be re-entered? If they are important, there had better be a way. How much of a hassle would re-entering the data be? If it would be more than you are comfortable with, you may need to re-evaluate your dump interval.

If you never dump your database, when your hard disk fails, you will lose all your data. Clearly, that is not an acceptable outcome. At the other extreme, if you perform dumps too frequently, you won't get any work done because your system is spending all its time doing database dumps. That's not acceptable either. Somewhere in the middle is an optimal dump interval.

No perfect dump interval is best for everybody in every situation. There are several points to consider:

+ How "hot" is the database? How many changes are being made to it per second, per hour, per day, or per week?

+ How painful would it be to re-enter updates that had been made since the last dump?

+ How long does a dump take? How much does it impact productivity?

+ Am I using dumps for anything besides insurance against failure? For example, am I data mining dumps? If so, how recent does the information need to be in order to be useful?

✦ How much room for storing dumps do I have?

✦ Can I recycle dump media from several generations back and use it again?

In many cases, doing a dump once per day is sufficient, and can be scheduled at a time when activity is light. In other cases, doing a dump more or less frequently is appropriate. Taking all the above-listed points into consideration, decide on the best dump interval for each of the databases for which you are responsible.

Checkpoints

Hard disk failures are almost always what are called *hard failures*. In a hard failure, something physical is permanently and catastrophically damaged. In the case of a hard disk, this is the infamous disk crash. The term is descriptive, because when a disk crash occurs, you often hear a horrible scraping sound as one of the flying heads slams into its platter at speeds of up to 75 miles per hour.

Luckily, hard failures are relatively rare. Far more common are soft failures. In a *soft failure,* something unexpected has happened and processing has stopped. Perhaps the dreaded "blue screen of death" appears, featuring an indecipherable error message. Maybe the system just freezes and refuses to respond to anything you do. In cases such as this, rebooting the machine often clears the problem. Unfortunately, it also clears all of your volatile, solid state memory. Anything that has not already been flushed to disk is lost. Hopefully the log on disk has been updated recently, and you can reconstruct some of what was lost. That flushing to disk is called *checkpointing*.

There are two different methods of writing data in the page buffer to hard disk stable storage:

✦ **Write the buffer contents to disk one page at a time.** In this case, when a page is needed that is not currently in the buffer is read from disk, it displaces a page that is already in the buffer. If that page is dirty, it must be written to disk before the new page can be read.

✦ **Write the entire contents of the buffer to disk all at once.** This is done at regular intervals called *checkpoints.* The more frequent your checkpoints are, the less data you lose in case of a soft failure, or other failure of any part of the system other than the hard disk subsystem. For this reason, frequent checkpoints are a good idea. However, too-frequent checkpoints are bad because a write to disk of the complete contents of the page buffer takes time that is not being used productively. Here again you have a tradeoff between normal operating performance and the time and effort it would take to recover from a failure.

If you have good statistics on the frequency of failures that cause the loss of the contents of solid-state memory, and the cost, both in lost productivity and extra expense, of recovery from those failures, you can make an informed decision on how frequently you should schedule checkpoints. Checkpoints have a cost in lost productivity, but not as great a cost as a dump. Checkpoints should be performed more frequently than dumps, but not so frequently that multiple checkpoints are likely to occur within the execution time of a typical transaction. Having multiple checkpoints while a transaction is active consumes time, but does not deliver a corresponding reduction in recovery time.

Optimizing batch transactions

A transaction that causes multiple updates is called a *batch* transaction. Batch transactions can be problematical if they are long. If the page buffer fills up while a batch transaction is in progress, it could initiate a rollback, and rolling back a lengthy transaction and then rerunning it can have a major impact on productivity. To address this concern, one option is to break the batch up into smaller minibatches. This, however, must be done carefully. If a batch transaction is rolled back, it undoes every change that was made by the transaction up to the point of the rollback. However, if a batch is broken up into, for example, two minibatches, and a rollback occurs while the second minibatch is executing, the changes made by the first minibatch will not be rolled back. The database is left in an inconsistent state. One solution to this problem is to only allow rollbacks during the first minibatch of a series of minibatches. Doing so, however, severely limits what can be done in the subsequent minibatches. If the minibatches are truly independent of each other, there is no problem, but such independence must be guaranteed in order to preserve the integrity of the database.

Tuning the Operating System

Because your operating system controls an application's access to I/O devices and to hard disk memory, the OS can affect database application performance in many ways. Correspondingly, there are at least an equal number of things you can do to tune the operating system to improve performance. In the following sections, I touch on some of the major areas where you can make a performance difference by acting upon the operating system.

Scheduling threads

Practically all operating systems these days are multi-threaded operating systems. Microsoft Windows is an example of one such operating system. Multi-threading is what makes it possible for you to type text into a Word

**Book VII
Chapter 2**

**Tuning the
Environment**

document while your Excel spreadsheet is recalculating values and your Access database is performing a query. Meanwhile, your media player is piping your favorite song into your headphones. Each one of those tasks is performed by a thread of execution.

Multiple threads of execution do not all operate simultaneously, although they seem to. Instead, they are operating *concurrently*. First a little bit of one task is executed, and then a *context switch* suspends that thread of execution and activates another thread. This swapping goes on so rapidly that to a human observer, it appears as if all the threads are executing at once. Operating systems have moved from single-threaded to multi-threaded because of the great performance boost you get.

Threads improve throughput

You might wonder why multi-threading improves performance. After all, whether you interleave the execution of five tasks or have them run sequentially, you still have to execute all the instructions involved in those five tasks. In fact, it seems that multi-threading should be slower than single threading because there is non-productive overhead involved with every task switch operation.

Despite task switching overhead, multi-threading *does* substantially improve throughput. *Throughput* is the total amount of work that gets done per unit time. Suppose you have a typical organizational database system, with a database server holding the database and multiple client machines making queries or updates to that database. On the server, some of the database is in high-speed cache memory; some is in slower dynamic RAM, and some is stored on very-much-slower hard disk.

If the thread that is currently active needs to access a data item that is neither in cache nor RAM, a long delay occurs before it can proceed. There is no point in stalling everybody while that one thread waits for a response from the hard disk subsystem. As soon as the operating system is asked to go to hard disk for data, it can initiate that operation and then immediately suspend execution of the active thread and activate another thread that is now ready to go. When the needed data becomes available from the hard disk subsystem, the original thread can be reactivated and run at full speed again.

Any one application that is operating in a multi-threaded environment with say, four other applications, is not sped up by the multi-threading process. However, all five applications will finish sooner than they would have if they had been run sequentially because as one application is waiting for a slow operation to complete, the processor can be productively used by another application that is performing fast operations.

The scheduling of threads is a ripe area for tuning. One area where tuning can make a big difference is in context switching.

Context switching

At any given instant, the data that is being acted upon in the processor is the *context* at that instant. All the data in all the processor's user-accessible registers make up the context. An instant later, a computation has been performed, and the context is different.

Before making a context switch, the context of an application must be saved, so that when the application's thread is reactivated, the context can be restored, and execution can proceed as if nothing had happened. A context switch takes time — it takes time to save the context of the thread that is being replaced, and it takes time to restore the context of the thread that is replacing it. Some operating systems are more efficient at context switching than others. That efficiency rating could be a factor in choosing an operating system, depending on the mix of applications that will be running and on the number of applications that will typically be running concurrently.

Round-robin scheduling

Round-robin scheduling is the simplest algorithm for selecting which one of all the threads that are ready to run should run next. The operating system kernel maintains a queue of pointers to threads that are ready to run. It grabs the pointer to the next thread from the head of the queue and places the pointer to the currently executing thread at the tail of the queue. New threads are placed at the tail of the queue when they become ready to run.

Round-robin scheduling treats all threads as if they have equal importance. In a database environment, this is likely to be a valid assumption, so round-robin scheduling is appropriate.

Priority-based scheduling

In priority-based scheduling, each thread is given a priority number, with higher priority threads receiving higher numbers. Higher priority threads are given preference by the scheduler. They run more often and for longer periods of time. The priority assigned to an application, as well as the level of service that a given priority level confers, are quantities subject to tuning.

Priority-based scheduling has a potential pitfall, called *priority inversion*.

Priority inversion

Suppose you have three applications running on three different threads. One has high priority, one has medium priority, and one has low priority. Suppose further that the high-priority thread and the low-priority thread both require the same resource. Here's what could happen:

1. The low-priority thread starts running and acquires an exclusive lock on the key resource.

2. The high-priority thread starts running and tries to acquire the key resource, but fails because the resource is locked by the low-priority thread. This is a priority inversion, but is not too bad. It is called a *bounded priority inversion* because it lasts no longer than the critical section of the low-priority thread, after which the lock is released.

3. The medium-priority thread pre-empts the low-priority thread during the inversion. Now both the high-priority thread and the low-priority thread are idle. The medium-priority thread may even be pre-empted by another, higher-priority thread. This could delay the high-priority thread for an unacceptably long time, causing it to fail. This kind of unbounded priority inversion happened to the Mars Pathfinder spacecraft on Mars in 1997, halting the exploration of the Red Planet by the Sojourner rover until NASA engineers could figure out what had happened and upload a fix to the code.

Here are two possible solutions to the priority inversion:

+ **Priority Inheritance Protocol (PIP):** One solution to the priority inversion problem is to institute the Priority Inheritance Protocol. When a high-priority thread attempts to lock a resource that is already locked by a lower-priority thread, the priority of the lower-priority thread is automatically raised to match the priority of the high-priority thread. In this way, it cannot be pre-empted by a medium priority thread, and the priority inversion is only a bounded one.

+ **Priority Ceiling Protocol (PCP):** Another solution is provided by the Priority Ceiling Protocol. When a thread locks a resource, regardless of what its priority is, it is immediately promoted to having the highest priority. It cannot be pre-empted and thus when it exits its critical section and releases its lock on the resource, the ready thread with the highest priority can now acquire that resource. This is another case of a bounded priority inversion.

Clearly, if priority-based scheduling is used, some scheme such as PIP or PCP should be used also.

Deadlock

Deadlock is another problem related to resource acquisition. Suppose two threads both need the same two resources, A and B:

1. Thread 1 acquires an exclusive lock on resource A.

2. Thread 2 acquires an exclusive lock on resource B.

3. Thread 1 attempts to acquire a lock on resource B, but cannot, so it waits, pending the availability of resource B.

4. Thread 2 attempts to acquire a lock on resource A, but cannot, so it waits, pending the availability of resource A.

5. Neither resource A nor resource B ever becomes available, and both applications 1 and 2 are deadlocked.

A common solution to this problem is for the operating system to notice that neither thread 1 nor thread 2 has made any progress after an interval of time during which progress should have been made. It drops all locks held by both threads and delays them for different intervals of time before allowing them to run again. The delay intervals are tunable quantities. The best intervals are successful at breaking deadlocks practically all of the time.

Determining database buffer size

Earlier in this chapter, I mention that the storage in a computer that runs database applications comes to two varieties, volatile and non-volatile. Volatile memory is considered unstable storage because a power interruption or other failure that causes a machine reboot erases everything in it. Non-volatile memory, in contrast, retains its information when such problems occur. The reason nobody puts all his code and data in non-volatile storage is because it is about a million times slower than the slowest form of volatile storage.

Clearly, the less often you have to go out to the non-volatile storage on hard disk, the better. You enjoy a million-to-one performance advantage if you operate out of semiconductor RAM. For many applications, it is not feasible to retain our entire database in RAM. However, you can afford to keep some of it in RAM (hopefully, that portion of the database that you are most likely to need to access often). The portion of RAM that holds that heavily used portion of the database is called the *database page buffer*. The tuning option that you have is to decide on the size of the page buffer.

If the page buffer is too small, you will be going out to disk more often than you need to, and will suffer serious performance degradation. If the page buffer is larger than it needs to be, you will be paying for expensive RAM when you could be getting the same performance out of dirt-cheap disk. Somewhere in the middle is an optimum.

If your hit rate on the page buffer is between 90% and 95%, you are probably doing about as well as you can expect. That means that nine times out of ten or 19 times out of 20, when you need to access a data item, it is in the buffer. If you are not getting a hit rate in that range, perhaps you could do better with a larger buffer, or perhaps not. Depending on your database, a 70% hit rate may be the best that you can do. You can test the situation by gradually adding more RAM to the buffer until your hit rate plateaus. At that point, you know that adding any additional RAM to the buffer won't improve your performance, but will only add more to your cost.

Tuning page usage factor

The amount of space on a page that is holding data is called the page's *usage factor*. The higher the usage factor, the more data you can store in fast RAM as compared to the amount that must remain on slow hard disk. This is a vote for high usage factors. However, if the usage factor is too high, a problem arises when you make a number of insertions or when you update records by replacing NULL values with data. Tuning is important here. You need to be aware of the kinds of operations that are typically performed on the database. Are insertions common? If so, a lower usage factor is called for. If not, you will get better performance by raising the usage factor. Page usage factor is one of the many places where tuning means trying a setting, taking data, and then trying something else. After you have a good understanding of how your workload performs under the various usage factors, you can pick the one that will serve you the best most of the time.

Maximizing the Hardware You Have

In addition to the tweaks you can make to your recovery system and your operating system, you can do other things to improve performance by making better use of your hardware. I look at just a few of these.

Optimizing placement of code and data on hard disks

You already know from the discussion of hard disk drive construction in the section above on logging that you can improve performance by locating data that will be read or written sequentially in sequential locations on the same track on your hard disk. Keeping the read/write head on the same track eliminates the delay due to seek time and settling time. For data transfers larger than a single track, keeping on the same cylinder on the disk maintains the performance advantage.

When a hard disk is new or has recently been reformatted, you can enjoy good performance by carefully choosing the way in which you copy data to it. As time goes on and updates are made, that beautiful organization is gradually degraded, and your performance is degraded with it. One thing you can do to combat this degradation is to defragment your disks regularly.

Another thing you can do to improve performance is to locate your most frequently used data on the cylinders in the middle of your hard disk. If your disk has cylinders numbered 0 through 1023, you should put the most heavily used data on cylinder 511, or at least near it. This is due to a statistical consideration. If the most heavily used data is clustered in the center of the disk, seeks tend to be short, which also decreases the time it takes for the heads to settle over a track. Furthermore, on those occasions when the heads are over either a high number track or a low numbered track, there is a high probability that they next need to go to one of the heavily used tracks, which is only half the radius of the disk away. Long seeks from say, track 5 to track 1020 are rare.

Tuning the page replacement algorithm

The *page replacement algorithm* is the code that decides which page in the database page buffer to flush to disk when the buffer is full and a new page is needed. You want to flush out a page that is highly unlikely to be needed again soon. The best page to flush is predictable with a high degree of accuracy due to the fact that most applications have a key property, called *temporal locality.* Temporal locality means that a page in the buffer that has been used recently is likely to be needed again soon. The flip side of this coin is that a page that has not been accessed in a long time will probably not be needed any time soon. Such a page is a prime candidate for flushing out to disk. One page replacement algorithm that follows this line of reasoning is the least recently used (LRU) algorithm. Whenever a page must be replaced, the LRU algorithm flushes the page that has been in the buffer the longest time without being either read or written to. The LRU algorithm works very well in most cases. However, depending on what the application is doing, there are other cases where the LRU algorithm is the worst possible one from a performance standpoint. If you monitor performance and notice excessive buffer page swapping, changing the page replacement algorithm may give you a substantial performance enhancement.

Disk controller cache

The disk controller cache is another tunable area. Not only is there a page replacement buffer located in the system's main memory, but there is also a cache located in the hard disk subsystem. How this cache is used can affect performance. The performance of read operations is not affected by which of two protocols you use, but write performance can be affected. These are the two protocols:

✦ **Write-through:** When the write-through protocol is in effect, writes to disk are simultaneously written to both the cache and the disk. This means that every write to the disk subsystem takes as long as a slow, disk write operation rather than as short as a fast cache write operation. When operating under this protocol the cache gives no advantage to write operations, but reads of data in the cache are fast.

✦ **Write-back:** When the write-back protocol is in effect, writes to the disk subsystem go only to the cache, and a "dirty" bit is set to indicate that the contents of the cache differ from the contents of the corresponding locations on disk. Dirty pages are flushed to disk when convenient or when the page replacement algorithm replaces a dirty page with a new page loaded from disk.

For a lightly loaded system, the write-back protocol will usually give better performance because disk accesses are rare. For a heavily loaded system with frequent page swapping and more reading than writing, the write-through protocol may be better. Depending on your job mix, it may pay you to try both protocols, taking statistics for both. After you analyze your statistical data, choose the protocol that performs best.

Adding Hardware

If you hadn't read the material in the preceding sections of this chapter, probably the first thought to come to mind when you determine that your system is not performing the way it should, is "I need new hardware." Perhaps that is true, but it should not be your first option. As demonstrated in the preceding sections, you can try a great many things besides adding new hardware.

When you have exhausted all the possibilities for improvement, using the hardware you have, consider adding hardware. If you add hardware before performing the optimizations discussed above, you could easily be out the money without having addressed the real problem. Performance may not have improved at all because your system's lagging performance was not due to a deficiency in the hardware after all. If your system is optimized to the point that it is doing the best that it can with the hardware it has, and you are still not getting the performance you need, perhaps upgrading your hardware will help.

Faster processor

One obvious choice is to move to a faster processor. This can be an expensive choice because you can't just plug a faster processor chip into your existing motherboard and expect a speedup. The support chips on the motherboard need to match the new processor. This means you probably need to replace the motherboard and may have to move to faster RAM at the same time. You might as well buy a whole new box and give your existing box to your kid to play computer games on. (Wait — that won't work! Today's fast-action computer games with hyper-realistic graphics require the fastest processors on the planet. Your offspring will probably feel dissed if you try to palm off your obsolete processor on him.) At any rate, expensive or not, moving to a faster, more capable CPU may give you a significant performance boost.

More RAM

A less drastic upgrade than a computer switch-out, which may nonetheless make a big difference in performance, is to add RAM to your existing system. Adding RAM may enable you to support a bigger page buffer than you currently have, enabling you to keep more of your data in fast semiconductor memory. If this improves your page buffer hit rate, it could be a very economical way to improve performance.

Faster hard disks

Hard disk drives do not all have the same performance parameters. Seek time, settling time, rotational latency, controller cache size, and disk interface bandwidth are all things to look at. If the disks you currently have are not up to the current state of the art, you might consider replacing them. Think carefully, however, before spending a lot of money on this idea. Although processor performance, RAM densities, and hard disk capacities have been improving at an exponential rate in accordance with Moore's Law, hard disk performance specifications have not scaled nearly as rapidly. Although this year's hard disks have a lot more capacity than last year's, there may be little or no improvement in the speed with which you are able to read from and write to them.

More hard disks

Although trading up to faster hard disk drives may not give you the performance boost you are looking for, adding disk drives that are no faster than the ones you are using now may do it. The advantage of having multiple disks is that while one disk is busy performing one operation, a second disk can be performing a second operation. Because the processor is operating so much faster than the disk drives, in an operation that entails a lot of disk accesses, it can keep multiple disks operating at once. This parallelism could translate into a significant improvement in overall performance.

Performance advantages of RAID arrays

If you are going to spread your database across multiple disks anyway, you might as well configure those disks as a RAID array. RAID is an acronym for Redundant Array of Inexpensive Disks. The disks in a RAID array are inexpensive because at any given point in time, there is a "sweet spot" in the hard disk market. The sweet spot is where you get the most bang for your buck, which in this case means the most megabytes per dollar. If the sweet spot currently happens to be 400 GB, it is cheaper to buy five 400 GB drives and configure them as a RAID array than it would be to buy a single 2 TB drive (if you could even buy a 2 TB drive at any price). The disks in the array are redundant in that your database information is recorded in more than one place. This is an important safety feature for critical databases. If one of your disk drives were to fail and lose all its data, you could keep on operating, using the remaining disks.

There are several different kinds of RAID, some emphasizing redundancy more, and some emphasizing performance more. Here is a brief rundown of the most popular RAID flavors:

+ **RAID 0 is all about performance.** Your data is spread across all the disks in the array in "stripes." The first disk in the array gets a chunk, the second disk gets one, and so on to the last disk in the array. When that stripe is complete, the next chunk starts a new stripe on the first disk. This version of RAID has no fault tolerance. If a disk fails, you have lost the information on it, and the data on all the other disks is useless because it makes no sense without the collection of stripes on the failed disk. RAID 0 is fast because, if you have chosen your stripe widths correctly, a read or a write to the array will engage all or a major fraction of your disk drives in parallel. Because of the lack of fault tolerance, RAID 0 is not a good choice for critical data.

+ **RAID 1 is all about fault tolerance.** It doesn't give you any performance advantage at all. A RAID 1 array consists of exactly two hard disk drives that are in a mirror configuration. Writes to disk go simultaneously to both, so each is a mirror of the other. If one disk fails, the other one contains all the information and operates just as fast as the array did in the first place. RAID 1 gives you a high degree of fault tolerance, but at the cost of doubling the number of disks.

+ **RAID 5 uses parity striping to give you a compromise between the features of RAID 0 and RAID 1.** Your data is striped across multiple disks, but so is parity information. If one of the disks fails, the parity information on the surviving disks can be used to reconstruct the data on the failed disk. This level of fault tolerance is not as good as what RAID 1 gives you because there is performance degradation due to the time taken to reconstruct the failed disk's data on the fly. However, you can keep operating, if at a reduced rate, while replacing the failed disk and flowing the reconstituted data into it. The fact that the data is striped across multiple disks gives you much of the performance advantage of RAID 0, to go along with the fault tolerance that comes from parity striping.

✦ **RAID 10 is a more direct combining of the attributes of RAID 0 and RAID 1 than RAID 5 is.** Half the disks in the array are striped in the manner of RAID 0, and the other half of the disks mirror what is on the first half in the manner of RAID 1. This version of RAID gives you high performance and high fault tolerance, traded off against the requirement to buy a lot of disks.

Multiprocessor Environments

Until now I have been talking primarily about a system that may have multiple client computers engaging in transactions with a database stored on a single database server. For large enough databases where performance is an important consideration, a distributed solution may be called for. This means not only multiple client computers, but multiple servers too. Distributed databases are significantly more complex than single-server databases. I don't go into that complexity much here. Instead, I briefly mention three main architectural choices for such systems. The architecture chosen has a major effect on overall performance. For some types of applications, one architecture is clearly superior to the other two. For another architecture, the advantage goes to one of the other configurations:

✦ **Tightly coupled architecture:** Several processors all share the same main memory and disk farm. The processors all operate in parallel upon the same data.

✦ **Shared-disk architecture:** All the processors in the system each have their own private main memory, but the hard disks are shared.

✦ **Shared-nothing architecture:** All the processors have their own private main memory and their own private hard disks. This architecture is appropriate when the application being run can be divided up into independent subapplications.

Chapter 3: Finding and Eliminating Bottlenecks

In This Chapter

✔ **Identifying the problem**

✔ **Considering possible causes**

✔ **Pondering possible fixes**

✔ **Investigating bottlenecks**

✔ **Judging query efficiency**

✔ **Using resources wisely**

Databases generally start small and grow with time. Operations that could be performed in a reasonable amount of time with a small database gradually take longer as the database grows. This slowdown is probably not due to any general inadequacy of the system, but is probably a specific link in the chain of operations that leads from a request to a result. That specific link is a *bottleneck*. Finding and eliminating bottlenecks is one of the main jobs of any person charged with maintaining a database. The ability to determine the cause of a performance shortfall, and to find a remedy, is valuable in any organization and can be highly rewarding, both intellectually and financially.

Pinpointing the Problem

Have you heard the old backwoods story about the frog in hot water? It goes like this:

> If you throw a frog into a pot of water that is practically boiling, it will jump out right away. However, if you put a frog into a pot that is at a comfortable temperature and gradually turn up the heat, it will not notice anything is amiss, and swim around contentedly until it is too late.

Sometimes database users are like frogs. When they start using a new database application, they let you know right away if it's running slowly. However, if performance is good at first, but then gradually degrades, they may not notice it until the difference is truly dramatic. Some problems manifest themselves right away, whereas others are slow to develop. As you might expect, the causes of the immediate problems tend to be different from the causes of the problems that slowly develop over time. In either case, a database specialist needs to know how to track down the source of the problem, and then take appropriate action to fix it.

After the initial loading of data into a database, only two basic activities are performed on it: Either you are retrieving a selected portion of the data that is there, or you are updating the data that is there. I count adding new data, deleting existing data, or changing existing data all as forms of updates. Some databases experience many more retrievals, called *queries,* than they do updates in a given interval of time. Other databases experience more updates. Some experience about an equal number of queries and updates.

Slow query

Users who are responsible for running queries, like the happily swimming frog, may not notice that their queries are running slower until someone comes by while one is running and remarks on how long it takes for a result to come back. At that point, they call you. You now get the chance to do a little detective work. Somewhere in the application, the DBMS, the network link, the database server, or the storage subsystem, something has maxed out. Your job is to figure out what it is and restore performance to acceptable levels as soon as possible, without replacing or upgrading the parts of the system that are *not* part of the problem. Your job is to find the bottleneck.

Slow update

Perhaps the problem is not with queries, but rather with updates. For a person making adds, changes, or deletes to a database, long waits between entering a change and having the system being ready to accept the next one can be frustrating at best, and intolerable at worst. The causes for delays in updating tend to be different from the causes of slow responses to queries. Although the bottleneck may be different, your job is still the same: Find the source of the problem and then fix it. In the next section, I look at some of the likely causes of bottlenecks.

Determining the Possible Causes of Trouble

The main candidates for causing bottlenecks can be categorized into three areas: indexes, communication, and hardware. In this section, I explore each of these further.

Problems with indexes

Probably the number one cause of less-than-optimal performance is improper indexing. Improper indexing may mean the lack of one or more indexes that should be present, but could also mean the presence of indexes that should not be there.

B+ tree indexes

There are several different kinds of indexes, but the most common is the B+ tree index, also called the B-tree index, where B stands for *balanced*. A B-tree has a tree-like structure, with a root node, from which a row of branch nodes fan out. Another row of branch nodes may fan out from the first row, and so on for as many rows as the tree has. The nodes at the end of the chain of branch nodes are called *leaf nodes*. Leaf nodes have no "children," but instead hold the index values. The root node contains pointers to the first row of branch nodes. The first row of branch nodes contains pointers to the next row of branch nodes. The last row of branch nodes contains pointers to the leaf nodes. The leaf nodes contain pointers to rows in the table being indexed.

Index pluses and minuses

Indexes are valuable because a row in a data table can be found after following a short chain of pointers, as opposed to scanning the table one row at a time until you reach the row you want. The advantage is even greater than it might seem on the surface because indexes tend to be small compared to the size of the data table they are indexing. This means that the index is often entirely contained in cache memory, meaning that the target row in the data table is located at semiconductor RAM speeds rather than mechanical hard disk speeds, as would likely be the case for a full table scan.

However, the advantages are not all on the side of indexing. Indexes tend to degrade in tables with frequent inserts and deletes. Deletes create empty leaf nodes, which fill up space in cache without contributing. This could cause the index to spill out of cache onto the hard disk with the performance penalty that goes along with that. Eliminating the empty leaf cells requires a time-consuming index rebuild, during which no productive processing can take place.

Updates have an even greater impact on performance than delete operations. An update that includes at least one indexed column consists of both a delete and an insert. An index is a table of pointers and updating an index changes the location of that pointer, requiring its deletion from one place and its insertion at another. Indexes on non-key columns that contain values that change frequently cause the worst performance hits. Updates of indexes on primary keys almost never happen, and updates of indexes on foreign keys are rare. Indexes that are not highly selective (for example, indexes on columns that contain many duplicates) often degrade overall performance rather than enhance it.

Index-only queries

Indexes have the ability to speed up queries because they give near-direct access to the rows in a data table from which you want to retrieve data. This is great, but suppose the data you want to retrieve is entirely contained in the columns that comprise the index. In that case, you don't need to access the data table at all: Everything you need is contained in the index. Index-only queries can be very fast indeed. This may make it worthwhile to include in an index a column that you otherwise would not include, just because it is retrieved by a frequently run query. In such a case, the added maintenance cost for the index is overshadowed by the increased speed of retrievals for the frequently run query.

Full table scans versus indexed table access

How do you find the rows you want to retrieve from a database table? The simplest way, called a *full table scan,* is to look at every row in the table, up to the table's "high water mark," grabbing the rows that satisfy your selection condition as you go. The high water mark of a table is the largest number of rows it has ever had. Presently there may be fewer rows because of deletions, but there still may be rows scattered anywhere up to and including the high water mark. The main disadvantage of a full table scan is that it must examine every row in the table up to and including the high water mark. A full table scan may or may not be the most efficient way to retrieve the data you want. The alternative is indexed table access.

As I discussed in the preceding section on the B-tree index, when your retrieval is on an index, you reach the desired rows in the data table after a short walk through a small number of nodes on the tree. Because the index is likely to be cached, such retrievals are much faster than retrievals that must load sequential blocks from the data table into cache before scanning them.

For very small tables, which are as likely to be cached as an index is, a full table scan is about as fast as an indexed table access. This means that indexing small tables is probably a bad idea. It won't gain you significant performance, and adds complexity and size to your database.

Pitfalls in communication

One area where performance may be lost or gained is in the communication between a database server and the client computers that are running the database applications. If the communication channel is too narrow for the traffic, or if it is just not used efficiently, performance can suffer.

ODBC/JDBC versus native drivers

Most databases support more than one way of connecting to client computers running applications. Because these different ways of connecting employ different mechanisms, they have different performance characteristics. The database application, running on a client computer, must be able to send requests to and receive responses from the database, running on the database server. The conduit for this communication is a software driver that translates application requests into a form the database can understand, and database responses into a form the application can understand.

There are two main ways of performing this function. One is to use a native driver, which has been specifically written to interface an application written with a DBMS vendor's application development tools to that same vendor's DBMS back end. The advantage of this approach is that because the driver knows exactly what is required, it performs with a minimum of overhead. The disadvantage is that an application written with one DBMS back end in mind cannot use a native driver to communicate with a database created with a different DBMS.

In practice, there is frequently a need to access a database from an application that was not originally targeted at that database. In such cases, a generalized driver can be used. There are two main types, ODBC and JDBC. ODBC (Open DataBase Connectivity) was originally created by Microsoft, but has been widely adopted by application developers writing in the Visual Basic, C, or C++ programming languages. JDBC (Java DataBase Connectivity) is similar to ODBC, but is designed to be used with the Java programming language.

ODBC consists of a driver manager and the specific driver that is compatible with the target database. The driver performs the ODBC functions and communicates directly with the database server. One feature of the driver manager is its ability to log ODBC calls. This feature can be very helpful in debugging a connection, but slows down communication, so it should be disabled in a production environment. ODBC drivers may provide slower performance than a native driver that has been specifically designed to join a specific client with a specific data source. An ODBC driver may also fail to provide all the functions that a native driver would for a specific data source.

Locking and client performance

Multiple users can perform read operations without interfering with each other, making use of a shared lock. When an update is involved, however, things are different. As long as an update transaction initiated by one client has a resource in the database locked with an exclusive lock, other clients cannot access that resource. Furthermore, an update transaction cannot place an exclusive lock on a resource that currently is held by a shared lock.

This is strong motivation for keeping transactions short. You should consider several factors when you find that a critical resource is being locked too long, slowing performance for everyone. One possibility is that a transaction's SQL code is written in an inefficient manner. This may be due to improper use of indexes, or to poorly written SELECT statements. However, hardware could also be the culprit. Most organizations put their limited IT budget dollars into keeping the servers upgraded because they affect everyone. This is a good idea. However, you cannot ignore the client computers in the process. It only takes one obsolete, slow, client computer to slow processing for everyone by holding locks too long. If response in a multi-user environment seems slow even though you have a fast server, check the clients. For best performance, they should all be operating at comparable performance levels.

Application development tools making suboptimal decisions

Sometimes an application development tool implements a query differently than what you would get if you entered the same query directly from the SQL command prompt. If you suspect lagging performance could be due to your development tool, enter the SQL directly and compare response times. If something the tool is doing is indeed causing the problem, see if you can turn off the feature that is causing extra communication between the client and the server to take place.

Determining whether hardware is robust enough and configured properly

Perhaps your queries are running slowly because your hardware isn't up to the challenge. It could be a matter of a processor that is too slow, insufficient memory, a slow bus clock, or a slow hard disk subsystem. Alternatively, your hardware might be good enough, but is not configured correctly. For example, your database page buffer might not be big enough. You might be running in a mode that is less than optimal, such as flushing the page buffer to disk more often than needed. Perhaps the system is creating checkpoints or database dumps too frequently. These are all configuration issues that, if recognized and addressed, can dramatically improve your performance without touching your equipment budget.

You may well decide that you need to update some aspect of your hardware environment, but before you do, make sure that the hardware that you already have is configured in such a way that you have a proper balance of performance and reliability.

Implementing General Pointers: A First Step Toward Improving Performance

In looking for ways to improve the performance of queries you are running, some general principles almost always apply. If a query is violating any of these principles, you can probably make it run faster by eliminating the violation. Check out the suggestions in this section before expending a lot of effort on other interventions.

Avoid direct user interaction

Among all the components of a database system, the human being sitting at the keyboard is the slowest by far. At almost a thousand times slower than a hard disk and more than a million times slower than semiconductor RAM, nothing brings a system to its knees as fast as putting a human in the loop. Transactions that lock database resources should never require any action by a human. If your application does require such action, changing your application to eliminate it will do more for overall system performance than anything else you can do.

Examine the application/database interaction

One important performance bottleneck is the communication channel between the server and a client machine. This channel has a design capacity that imposes a speed limit on the packets of information that travel back and forth. In addition to the data that gets transmitted, a significant amount of overhead is associated with each packet. Thus one large packet is transmitted significantly faster than numerous small packets that contain the same amount of information. Rather than retrieving a set of rows one at a time, it is better to retrieve the entire set in one shot. Don't put an SQL retrieval statement within a loop in your application program. If you do, you will send a request and receive a response every time through the loop. Instead, grab an entire result set at once and do your processing on the client machine.

Another thing you can do to reduce back and forth traffic is to make use of SQL:2003's flow of control constructs to execute multiple SQL statements in a single transaction. In this case, the number-crunching takes place on the server rather than the client. The result is, however, the same as in the previous paragraph — fewer message packets traveling over the communication channel.

User Defined Functions (UDFs) can also reduce client/server traffic. By including a UDF in a SELECT statement's WHERE clause, processing is localized in the server, and less data needs to be transmitted to the client.

Don't ask for columns that you don't need

It may seem like a no-brainer to not retrieve rows that you don't need. After all, to do so shuttles unneeded information across the communications channel, slowing operations down. However, it's really easy to type the following:

```
SELECT * FROM CUSTOMER ;
```

This retrieves the data you want, along with a lot of unwanted baggage. So work a little harder and list out the columns you want, and *only* the columns you want. If it turns out that all the columns you want are indexed, you can save a lot of time, as the DBMS makes an index-only retrieval. Adding just one unindexed column forces the query to access the data table.

Don't use cursors unless you absolutely have to

Cursors are glacially slow in almost all implementations. If you have a slow-running query that uses cursors, try to find a way to get the same result without cursors. Whatever you come up with is likely to run significantly faster.

Precompile queries

Compiling a query takes time, often more than the time it takes to execute the query. Rather than suffer that extra time every time you execute a query, it's better to suffer it once and then reap the benefit every time you execute the query after the first time. You can do this by putting the query into a stored procedure, which is precompiled by definition:

Precompilation helps most of the time, but it also has its pitfalls:

✦ If an index is added to a column that is important to a query, you should recompile the query so that it will take advantage of the new index.

✦ If a table grows from having relatively few rows to having many rows, you should recompile the query. When compiled with few rows, the optimizer will probably choose a full table scan over using an index because for small tables, indexes offer no advantage. However, after the table has grown to a large size, an index greatly reduces the execution time of the query.

Tracking Down Bottlenecks

Tracking down bottlenecks is the fun part of database maintenance. You get the same charge that a detective gets in solving a mysterious crime. Breaking the bottleneck and watching productivity go through the roof can give you an exhilarating feeling. So where do you start? Your system is crawling when it should be sprinting. It is a complex construction with many elements, both hardware and software. What should you do first?

Isolating performance problems

As long as a wide variety of system elements could potentially be involved in a problem, it is hard to make progress. The first step is to narrow down the possibilities. Do this by finding which parts of the system are performing as they should, thus allowing you to eliminate them as potential sources of the problem. To paraphrase Sherlock Holmes, "When you eliminate all the explanations but one as being not possible, then whatever is left, however unlikely it may seem, must be true."

Performing a top-down analysis

A query is a multi-level operation, and whatever is slowing it down could be at any one of those levels. At the highest level is the query code as implemented in SQL. If the query is written inefficiently, you probably need to look no further for the source of the problem. Rewrite the query more efficiently and check to see if that solves the problem. If it does, great! You don't have to look any further. However, it you don't find an inefficient query, or the rewrite you do doesn't seem to help, you must dig deeper.

Beneath the level of the SQL code is a level where locking, logging, cache management, and query execution take place. These functions are all in the province of the DBMS, and are called into action by the top-level SQL. If there are inefficiencies here, they can certainly slow down operations. Locking more resources than necessary or locking them for too long can slow down operations for everybody. Logging is a vital component of the recovery system, and also helps you determine exactly how the system performs. However, it also absorbs resources. Excessive logging beyond what is needed could be a source of slowdowns. Cache management is a major factor in overall performance. Are the right pages being cached and are they remaining in the cache for the proper amount of time? Finally, at this level, are queries being executed in the most efficient way? Many queries could be executed a variety of different ways and all end up with the same result. However, the different execution plans for these different ways can vary widely in how long they take to execute and in what resources they consume while doing it. All of these possibilities deserve scrutiny when performance is unacceptable and cannot be attributed to poorly written queries.

The lowest level that could contribute to poor performance is the hardware level. Look here after you have confirmed that everything at the higher levels is working as it should. This level includes the hard disk drives, the disk controllers, the processor, and the network. Each one of these could be a bottleneck if its performance does not match that of the other hardware elements.

The performance of hard disk drives tends to degrade over time, as insertions and deletions are made to databases and as files unrelated to database processing are added, changed, or deleted. The disk becomes increasingly fragmented. If you want to copy a large file to disk, but only small chunks of open space are scattered here and there across the disk's cylinders, pieces of the file are copied into those small chunks. In order to read the entire file, the drive's read/write head must move from track to track, slowing down access dramatically. As time goes on, the drive gets increasingly fragmented, imperceptibly at first, and then quite noticeably. The solution to this problem is to run a defragmentation utility. This can take a long time, and because of heavy disk accessing, reduces the system's response time to close to zero. Defragmentation runs should be scheduled at regular intervals when normal traffic is light, in order to maintain reasonable performance. Most modern operating systems include a defragmentation utility that will analyze your hard disk, tell you whether it would benefit from defragmenting, and then, with your consent, perform the defragmentation operation.

The disk controller contains a cache of recently accessed pages. When a page that is already in disk controller cache is requested by the processor, it can be returned much faster than is possible for pages that are only stored on disk. All the considerations I mentioned for optimizing the database page buffer in the processor apply to the disk controller cache as well. The choice of page replacement algorithm can have a major effect on performance, as can cache size.

It goes without saying, but I'll say it anyway, that the processor has a tremendous effect on overall system performance. The processor is the fastest component in the entire system. Processors that are just a few years old are significantly slower than those that are on the market today. Upgrading an older processor, along with all the ancillary circuitry that must be upgraded to support it, can make a significant difference in overall performance. Many organizations have a regular program of replacing computers at regular intervals, such as every three years. The systems that get replaced are moved down to less critical applications. This domino effect of hand-me-down computers ends with donation to charitable organizations. If your computer is more than about three years old, consider replacing it as a possible method of improving your performance, assuming you have already investigated all the other sources of slowdown mentioned above.

The network is the final major subsystem that might be causing performance problems. If the performance of running queries from a client computer on a network is unacceptable, try running the same queries directly on the server. If the queries run significantly faster on the server, this may mean the server's processor is more powerful. However, it also might indicate that the network connection between the server and the client is a bottleneck. There are tools available for analyzing network traffic that can give you some indication whether your network is slowing you down. As is the case with processors, network performance has been steadily increasing also. If your network is starting to get a little old, you might be better served by one with state-of-the-art speed. It is worth looking in to.

Partitioning

Suppose you have done the top-down analysis advocated in the preceding section, and have isolated your performance problem to one of the primary hardware subsystems: the hard disk drive, the disk controller, the processor, or the network. Suppose further that you have done everything you can think of. You have defragmented your hard drives. You have optimized paging in your disk controller. You have optimized paging in your database page buffer. You have analyzed the traffic on your network. Despite all this, the problem persists. Partitioning offers another approach that may break the bottleneck.

**Book VII
Chapter 3**

**Finding and
Eliminating
Bottlenecks**

Partitioning can be helpful if your performance problem is caused by exceeding the capacity of a critical system resource. It is essentially spreading out the work so that the overstretched resource does not get overloaded. You can spread the work either spatially, temporally, or both. Spatial partitioning means doing more things in parallel. This could entail moving to a multi-core processor, adding additional hard disk drives to your RAID array, installing a bigger database page buffer, and so on. You get the idea. Wherever the bottleneck is, widen the neck to increase the flow rate through it.

The other thing to try is to increase temporal partitioning. In this case, you don't make the neck of the bottle any wider. You just schedule workflow so that it is more evenly distributed in time. Don't run large update transactions at the same time that online query activity is high. Give users incentives to use the system across a broader range of times, rather than everybody trying to access the same resources at once.

Locating hotspots

Spreading the work away from an overloaded resource presupposes that you are able to determine which of the many components of your system is causing the bottleneck. Such resources are called *hotspots*. When a resource is hot, it is continually in use. If it is too hot, operations have to wait in line in order to use it. If the waiting takes too long and results in aborts and rollbacks, performance is greatly affected. Happily, a number of tools are available, both at the operating system level and at the database level, that you can use to monitor the performance of various aspects of your system and locate the hotspots. After you have located a hotspot, you are well on your way to solving your performance problem. When you know what the overloaded system component is, you can apply the remedies discussed here to restore performance to an acceptable level.

Analyzing Query Efficiency

Some kinds of problems slow everything that is running on a system. Other kinds of problems impact the performance of only one or a small number of queries. For the class of problems that only seem to affect one or at most a few queries, the major database management systems provide tools that you can use to track down the source of the problem. These tools come in three major categories: query analyzers, performance monitors, and event monitors. Each one of these looks at a different aspect of the way a query is running. Based on what they tell you, you should be able to zero in on whatever is causing your system to perform less well than it should.

Using query analyzers

All the major database management systems offer tools to give the DBA or other person responsible for the efficient operation of the database a way of analyzing how well queries on the database are performing. In versions of Microsoft SQL Server prior to SQL Server 2005, the tool for this job was even named Query Analyzer. However, SQL Server 2005 represents a major break from the past in a number of ways. The functions that had been the province of Query Analyzer are incorporated into the new Microsoft SQL Server Management Studio, along with additional functionality useful for tuning query performance.

Here's a brief introduction to SQL Server 2005's tuning tools (the Database Engine Tuning Advisor and the SQL Server Profiler) to give you an idea of what such tools look like and what they do. It differs in detail from the operation of similar tools for other database management systems, but the overall functions are the same.

Figure 3-1 shows the main screen of Microsoft SQL Server Management Studio.

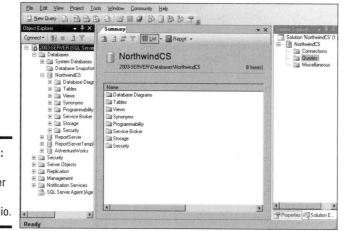

Figure 3-1:
Microsoft
SQL Server
Manage-
ment Studio.

As you can see, I have connected to a database named NorthwindCS. This is a sample SQL Server database provided by Microsoft. If you do not have it already, you can download it from `www.msdn.microsoft.com`. It contains sample data for a fictitious international trading company.

Suppose you are a manager at Northwind and you want to know what customers you have in the USA. You can find out with a simple SQL query. To draft a query in Management Studio, follow these steps:

1. **Click the New Query button at the left end of the Standard toolbar.**

This opens an SQL editor pane in the middle of the Management Studio window, as shown in Figure 3-2.

To remind yourself of the names of the tables in the Northwind database, you can expand the Tables node in the tree in the Object Explorer in the left pane of the Management Studio window.

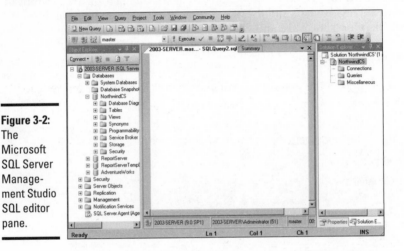

Figure 3-2: The Microsoft SQL Server Management Studio SQL editor pane.

2. **Type your query into the editor pane, as shown in Figure 3-3.**

The tree at the left shows that the Country column is a nullable VARCHAR field, and that the primary key of the Customers table is CustomerID. The Country column is not indexed. There are indexes on City, CompanyName, the primary key PK_Customers, PostalCode, and Region. None of these indexes is of any use for this query. This is an early clue that performance of this query could be improved by tuning.

3. **Execute the query by clicking the Execute button.**

The result of the query shows up in the Results tab, as shown in Figure 3-4.

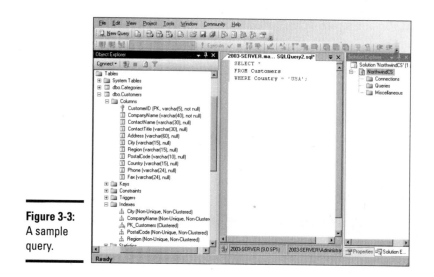

Figure 3-3:
A sample
query.

4. Save your query by name from the File menu.

My example query is named SQLQuery2.sql. You can name yours whatever you wish.

Figure 3-4:
The query
result.

The Database Engine Tuning Advisor

The tool SQL Server provides for tuning queries is the Database Engine Tuning Advisor. To use this tool with the sample query created in the previous section, follow these steps:

1. **From the Management Studio's Tools menu, select, logically enough, Database Engine Tuning Advisor.**

   The Tuning Advisor window, showing the General tab, appears as shown in Figure 3-5.

Figure 3-5:
The
Database
Engine
Tuning
Advisor
window.

The Browse for a Workload File button

2. **When you are asked to connect to the server you are using, do so.**

3. **The system has assigned a default session name, based on your login and the date and time. Change this session name if you want to.**

4. **Under Workload, choose File and then click the Browse for a Workload File button to the right of the long text box.**

5. **Find and select the query file that you just created.**

   I have selected SQLQuery2.sql.

6. **From the Database for workload analysis drop-down list, select your database.**

   I have selected NorthwindCS.

7. Select the check box beside the name of your database in the list of databases toward the bottom of the Tuning Advisor.

8. Make sure the Save Tuning Log check box is selected.

This creates a permanent record of the tuning operation that is about to take place. Figure 3-6 shows what the Tuning Advisor looks like at this point.

Figure 3-6:
I'm ready to tune my query.

9. Click the Tuning Options tab to see what the default tuning options are and possibly to change them.

Figure 3-7 shows the Tuning Advisor's Tuning Options pane.

The Limit Tuning Time check box is selected by default: Tuning can be so time-consuming that it severely impacts normal production operation. To prevent this, you can set a maximum amount of time that a tuning session can take. When that maximum is reached, whatever tuning recommendations have been arrived at so far are shown as the result. If the tuning run had been allowed to run to completion, different recommendations may have been made. If your server is idle or lightly loaded, you may want to uncheck this box to make sure you get the best recommendation.

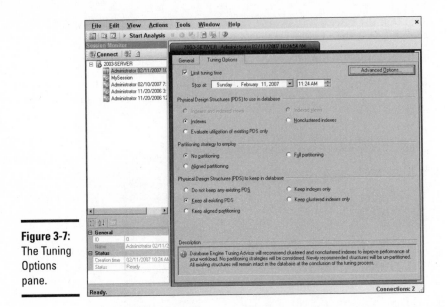

Figure 3-7:
The Tuning
Options
pane.

The three tuning options you can change are

- **Physical Design Structures (PDS) to Use in Database:** The Indexes radio button is selected, and other options are either not selected or not available. For the simple query you are considering, indexes are the only PDS that it makes sense to use.

- **Partitioning Strategy to Employ:** No partitioning is selected. Partitioning means breaking up tables physically across multiple disk drives. This enables multiple read/write heads to be brought into play in a query, speeding access. Depending on the query and the clustering of data in tables, partitioning may enhance performance. Partitioning is, of course, not applicable if the entire database is contained on a single disk drive.

- **Physical Design Structures (PDS) to Keep in Database:** Here you can specify which PDSs to keep. The Tuning Advisor may recommend that other structures, such as indexes or partitioning, which are not contributing to performance, be dropped.

10. **Click the Advanced Options button to see the Advanced Tuning Options dialog box.**

The Advanced Tuning Options dialog box enables you to specify a maximum amount of memory usage for the recommendations (see Figure 3-8). In the process of coming up with a recommendation, the Tuning Advisor can consume considerable memory. If you want to set a limit on the amount it can commandeer, this is the place to do it.

Figure 3-8:
Advanced
tuning
options.

11. **Click OK to return to the General tab and then click the Start Analysis button to commence tuning.**

Depending on the size of the tables involved in the query, this could take a significant amount of time. The Tuning Advisor keeps you apprised on progress as the session runs. Figure 3-9 shows the Progress tab at the end of a successful run. It shows up after a tuning run starts. Figure 3-10 shows the Recommendations tab. It appears after a tuning run completes.

Figure 3-9:
The
Progress
tab after a
successful
run.

**Book VII
Chapter 3**

**Finding and
Eliminating
Bottlenecks**

The Tuning Advisor has concluded that tuning would not improve the performance of this query. This is a "good news/bad news" result. The good news is that the database is already optimally configured to run this query. The bad news is that tuning indexes won't improve the performance of this query. You must have decided to run the Tuning Advisor because you were not satisfied with the performance of the query. Now you find that the perceived poor performance is not due to an indexing problem. You must look elsewhere for the source of the problem.

Figure 3-10:
The Recommendations tab after a successful run.

After you've completed the tuning run, you'll probably want to have a look at the Reports tab, which is shown in Figure 3-11.

Figure 3-11:
The Reports tab after a successful run.

In this report, you see the details of the tuning run. A maximum tuning time of 36 minutes was allocated, and one minute was actually used. The tuning advisor expects a 0.00%improvement if you implement its recommendation to do nothing. Makes sense. A total of 4MB of memory was used, 2MB of it by the recommendation. Luckily, the maximum space for recommendation was 5MB, so the run did not have a memory shortage problem. If the memory allocated originally had been too small, it is a simple matter to raise the limit. Finally, note that 100% of the SELECT statements were in the tuned set. This is a confirmation that the tuning session ran to completion.

SQL Server Profiler

The Database Engine Tuning Advisor is just one tool that SQL Server provides to help you optimize your queries. The SQL Server Profiler is another tool. Rather than operating on SQL scripts, it traces the internal operation of the database engine on a query, showing exactly what SQL statements are submitted to the server, which may differ from the statements written by the SQL programmer, and how the server accesses the database.

After you start a trace in the Profiler by selecting New Trace from the File menu, it traces all DBMS activity until you tell it to stop. Somewhere amongst all the things that are going on, actions relevant to your query are recorded. Figure 3-12 shows the General tab of the Profiler New Trace dialog box you use to set up a trace.

Figure 3-12:
The Profiler
New Trace
dialog box.

Figure 3-13 shows the Events Selection tab of the Profiler New Trace dialog box. In this example, the default selections are shown, selecting almost everything to be recorded. In many cases, this is overkill, and you should deselect the things that do not interest you.

A trace of SQLQuery2.sql dumps everything you ever wanted to know, and much that you didn't, about how the query is run. Figure 3-14 is a brief excerpt from the trace, showing a few recognizable events. Data listed offscreen to the right include CPU usage, number of reads, number or writes, and time consumed by every event represented by a row in the trace file.

Queries aren't the only things that consume system resources. If you are experiencing performance problems, the source of the problem might be somewhere other than in a poorly performing query. Performance monitors are tools that give you a broader view of how a system is performing.

Figure 3-13:
The Events
Selection
tab of the
Profiler
New Trace
dialog box.

Using performance monitors

Whereas a query analyzer reveals the inner workings of a query, hopefully giving you the information you need to make the query perform better, performance monitors give you global information about how your system is running. Primary concerns are

+ What is the processing load on my CPU?

+ How often do I have to go out to sloooow disk, rather than operating out of fast cache?

+ Are disk accesses stacking up, bogging everything down?

Figure 3-14: Excerpt from a trace.

Book VII
Chapter 3

Finding and
Eliminating
Bottlenecks

Figure 3-15 shows the display of SQL Server Management Studio's Performance Monitor before, during, and after a brief SQL query.

Figure 3-15:
Performance
Monitor
display of a
simple
query.

There are three traces in the graph:

✦ The blue trace gives a relative idea of the number of page swaps per second that are made between semiconductor memory and disk storage.

✦ The green trace shows the average disk queue length. This correlates with paging because if you're not paging, your disk queue length goes to zero.

✦ The red trace shows the percentage of utilization of your processor.

Of course, you can't see the colors in this book, but if you follow the steps with your own copy of SQL Server 2005, the Performance Monitor display will look quite festive.

The actual query starts about halfway across the display. Here are some notable things:

✦ Prior to the start of the query, the red CPU-usage trace shows spikes of high activity that correlate with high peaks in the blue page swap trace.

✦ When the query starts, both the blue page swap trace and the green average disk queue length trace hit the roof and stay there until the query is complete. During that time, the red CPU-usage trace fluctuates at a relatively low level.

✦ After the query completes, the blue and green traces drop essentially to zero, and the red trace resumes its normal background behavior.

What does this tell us? It tells us that this particular query hits the disk subsystem pretty hard. If you run this query frequently, you should look for a way to maintain its working set in the database buffer as long as the query is active. One possibility would be to see whether you can convert this to an index-only query. If the only columns you retrieve are indexed and the indexes are in cache, your disk will be hit once and then be able to relax. The action will take place in the buffer.

Finding problem queries

In a poorly performing multi-user, multi-tasking environment, where, at any given moment, multiple queries are being run, tracking down the source of the problem may be difficult. Is it systemic? Are there weaknesses in the server's processor, memory, or the network that are slowing everything down? Or is there one problem query that is gumming up the works for everyone? This is an important question. If you can restore performance to a satisfactory level by tuning a query, it's a lot cheaper than making a major hardware upgrade that may, after all, not solve the problem.

A useful approach is the "divide and conquer" strategy. Find all the jobs that typically run together when performance is slow and run them individually. Use your performance monitoring tools to check for jobs that saturate system resources. Then use your Profiler or other event monitoring tools to find a query that seems to be consuming more time and resources than it should.

When you find a suspicious query, use your query analyzer tools to look inside the query to see exactly where time and resources are being consumed. When you find a "bad actor," you can try a number of things to make matters better. In the next sections, I discuss a few.

Analyzing a query's access plan

A database management system generates an access plan that describes how to execute a query. The details of the access plan depend on what the DBMS knows or can assume about what system resources are available and what the query needs. This knowledge is largely based on statistics that show how the system has been running lately on queries similar to the one for which the access plan is being developed.

Understanding the role of statistics

Up-to-date and accurate statistics are critical to the generation of an efficient access plan. If an access plan is based on statistics that were taken at some time in the dim past, they may bear little relation to the way the system is configured and running today. Most DBMS products have a command similar to SQL Server's UPDATE STATISTICS statement, which generates the latest data on how the system is running. It is a good idea to update statistics before generating an access plan, just to make sure you are giving the query optimizer the best chance to come up with an efficient plan. SQL Server enables you to update statistics for indexed columns in tables, as shown in Figure 3-16.

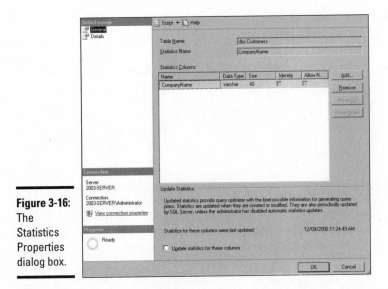

Figure 3-16: The Statistics Properties dialog box.

Checking the access path

After you have run statistics and the query optimizer has generated an access plan, check the plan to see how the query accesses table rows. Is it doing a full table scan? If a full table scan of a large table uploads a big chunk of the table into the database buffer, it could push data out of the buffer that will be needed soon by other queries running concurrently. This won't show up as a performance bottleneck for the query you are looking at, but impacts the performance of the other queries running at the same time. Interactions of this type are devilishly difficult to unravel and fix. Some database management systems are smart enough to recognize this situation and instead of following the normal practice of flushing the least recently used (LRU) pages from the buffer, page out the big chunk instead because it's unlikely to be needed again soon after the scan.

In most situations, unless you are dealing with a very small table, indexed access is better than a full table scan. If your query's access plan specifies a full table scan, examine the plan carefully to see whether indexed access would be better. It may make sense to create a new index, if the appropriate index does not exist.

Here are several reasons why indexed access tends to be better:

✦ The target of an indexed access is almost always cached.

✦ Table blocks reached by an index tend to be "hotter" than other blocks, and consequently are more likely to be cached. These are the rows, after all, that you and possibly other users are hitting.

✦ Full table scans are going to cache a multi-block group, whereas an indexed access retrieves a single block. The single blocks retrieved by indexed access are likelier to contain the rows that you and other users need than blocks in a multi-block group that "came along for the ride" in a full table scan.

✦ Indexed accesses only look at the rows that you want in a retrieved block, rather than every row in the block, saving time.

✦ Indexed accesses scale better than full table scans, which become worse as the table size increases.

Full table scans make sense if you are retrieving 20% or more of the rows in a table. Indexed retrievals are clearly better if you are retrieving a half percent of the rows in the table or fewer. In between those two extremes, the best choice depends on the specific situation.

Filtering selectively

Conditions, such as those in an SQL WHERE clause, act as filters. They exclude the table rows you don't want and pass on for further processing the rows that you might want. If a condition specifies a range of index values for further processing, values outside that range need not be considered and the data table itself need not be accessed as a part of the filtering process. This is the most efficient kind of filter because you only need to look at the index values that correspond to the rows in the data table that you want.

If the desired index range is not determined by the condition, but rows to be retrieved are nonetheless determinable from the index, although index values that are ultimately discarded must be accessed, the underlying data table need not be touched.

Finally, if rows to be retrieved cannot be determined from the index, but require table access, no time is saved in the filtering process, but at least network bandwidth is saved because only the filtered rows need be sent to the requesting client.

Choosing the best join type

In Book III, Chapter 4, I discuss several different join types. Although the SQL code may specify one of the join types discussed there, the join operation that actually is executed is probably one of three basic types: the nested-loops join, the hash join, or the sort-merge join. The Query optimizer chooses one of these join types for you. In most cases, it chooses the type that turns out to be the best. However, you should understand the three types and what distinguishes them from each other, as noted here:

+ **Nested-loops join:** The nested-loops join is a robust method of joining tables, which almost always produces results in close to the shortest possible time. It works by filtering unwanted rows from one table (the driving table) and then joining the result to a second table, filtering out unwanted rows of the result in the process, and then joining the result to the next table, and so on until all tables have been joined, and the fully filtered result is produced.

+ **Hash join:** In some situations, the hash join may perform better than a nested-loops join. This is typically when the smaller of the two tables being joined is small enough to fit entirely into semiconductor memory. Unwanted rows are discarded from the smaller table and the remaining rows are placed into "buckets" according to a hashing algorithm. At the same time, the larger, driving table is filtered, and the remaining rows are then matched to the rows from the smaller table in the hash buckets. Unmatched rows are discarded. The matched rows form the result set.

+ **Sort-merge join:** The sort-merge join reads two tables independently, discarding unwanted rows. First, it presorts both tables on the join key and merges the sorted lists. The presort operation is expensive in terms of time, so unless you can guarantee that both tables will fit into semiconductor memory, this technique performs worse than a hash join of the same tables.

Examining a query's execution profile

Perhaps you have examined an expensive query's access plan and found it to be about as efficient as can be expected. The next step is to look at the query's execution profile. This is the "accounting" information generated by the profiler. Among the pieces of information available are the number of physical and logical reads and the number of physical and logical writes. Logical operations are those that read or write memory. Physical operations are logical operations that go out to disk.

Other information available in the profile includes facts about locking. Of interest are the number of locks held and the length of time they are held. Time spent waiting for locks, as well as deadlocks and timeouts, can tell you a lot about why execution is slow.

Sorts are another performance killer. If the profile shows a high number of sorts or large areas of memory used for sorting, this is a clue that should be pursued.

Resource contention between concurrently running transactions can drag down performance of all involved. This provides excellent motivation to use resources wisely.

Managing Resources Wisely

The physical elements of a database system can play a major role in how efficiently the database functions. A poorly configured system performs well below the performance that is possible if it's configured correctly. In this section, I review the roles played by the various key subsystems.

The disk subsystem

The way data is distributed across the disks in a disk subsystem affects performance. The ideal case is to store contiguous pages on a single cylinder of a disk to support sequential prefetching. Spreading subsequent pages onto other similarly configured disks enables related reads and writes to be made in parallel. A major cause of performance degradation is disk fragmentation caused by deletions opening up free space in the middle of data files that are then filled with unrelated file segments. This causes excessive head seeks, which slow down performance dramatically. Disk fragmentation can accumulate rapidly in transaction-oriented environments, but can become an issue over time even in relatively static systems.

Tools for measuring fragmentation are available at both the operating system and the database level. Operating system defragmentation tools work on the entire disk, whereas database tools measure fragmentation of individual tables. An example of an operating system defragmentation tool is the tool for Microsoft Windows, Disk Defragmenter, which is on the Accessories menu under System Tools. Figure 3-17 shows the result of an analysis of a badly fragmented disk drive.

Figure 3-17: A Windows Disk Defragmenter display of a badly fragmented disk drive.

In addition to being badly fragmented, this drive has very little free space and none of it is in large blocks. This makes it almost impossible to store a new database in a fragment-free manner.

With the Windows Disk Defragmenter, not only can you analyze the fragmentation of a disk drive, but you can also defragment it. Alas, this defragmentation is usually not complete. Files that the defragmenter is unable to relocate continue to impair performance.

Database management systems also have fragmentation analysis tools, but they concentrate on the tables in a database, rather than looking at the entire hard disk. For example, SQL Server offers the `sys.dm_db_index_physical_stats` command. It returns size and fragmentation data for the data and indexes of a specified table or view. It does not fix the fragmentation; it only tells you about it. If you decide that fragmentation is excessive and is impairing performance, you must use other tools, such as the operating system defragmentation utility, to remedy the situation.

The database buffer manager

The job of the buffer manager is to minimize the number of disk accesses made by a query. It does this by keeping hot pages, which have been used recently and are likely to be used again soon, in the database buffer, while at the same time maintaining a good supply of free pages in the buffer. The free pages provide a place for pages that come up from disk, without the need to write a "dirty" page back to disk before the new page can be brought in.

You can see how good a job the buffer manager is doing by looking at the *cache-hit* ratio. This is the number of times a requested page is found in the buffer divided by the total number of page requests. A well-tuned system should have a cache-hit ratio of more than 90%. Another useful metric is the number of free pages. If you check the cache-hit ratio and the number of free pages frequently under a variety of load conditions, you can see a trend developing that could lead to poor performance. Addressing such problems sooner rather than later is wise. With the knowledge you gain with regular monitoring of system health, you can act in a timely manner and maintain a satisfactory level of service.

The logging subsystem

Every transaction that makes an insertion, alteration, or deletion in the database is recorded in the log before the change is actually made to the database. This is a recovery feature that enables a reconstruction of what has occurred prior to a transaction abort or system failure. Because the log must be written to before every action taken on the database, it is a potential source of slowdown, if log writes cannot keep up with the transaction traffic. Use the performance monitoring tools available to you to confirm that there are no holdups due to delays in making log entries.

The locking subsystem

The locking subsystem can impact performance if there is contention by multiple transactions to acquire locks on the same object. If a transaction holds a lock too long, other transactions may time out, necessitating an expensive rollback. You can track down the source of locking problems by checking statistics that are normally kept by the DBMS. Some helpful statistics are

✦ Average lock wait time — the average amount of time a transaction must wait to obtain a lock

✦ Number of transactions waiting for locks

✦ Number of timeouts

✦ Number of deadlocks

Time spent waiting for locks should be low compared to total transaction time. The number of transactions waiting for locks should be low compared to the number of active transactions.

If the metrics cited here point to a problem with locks, you may be able to trace the source of the problem with an event monitor. Things such as time-outs and deadlocks appear in the event log and indicate what was happening when the event occurred.

Book VIII

Appendixes

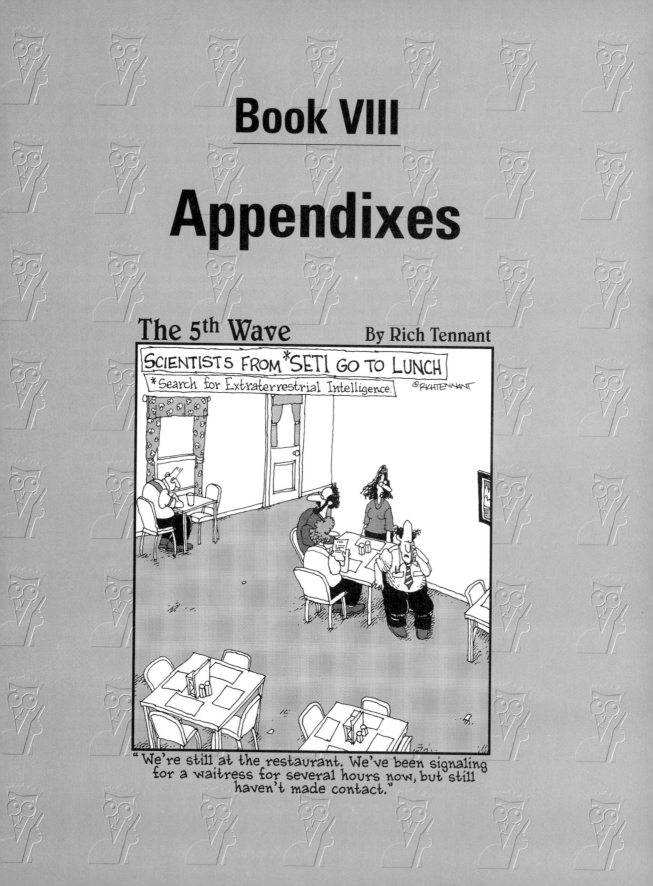

Contents at a Glance

Appendix A: SQL:2003 Reserved Words

ABS	BINARY
ABSENT	BLOB
ALL	BOOLEAN
ALLOCATE	BOTH
ALTER	BY
AND	CALL
ANY	CALLED
ARE	CARDINALITY
ARRAY	CASCADED
AS	CASE
ASENSITIVE	CAST
ASYMMETRIC	CEIL
AT	CEILING
ATOMIC	CHAR
AUTHORIZATION	CHAR_LENGTH
AVG	CHARACTER
BEGIN	CHARACTER_LENGTH
BETWEEN	CHECK
BIGINT	CLOB

CLOSE

COALESCE

COLLATE

COLUMN

COMMIT

CONDITION

CONNECT

CONSTRAINT

CONVERT

CORR

CORRESPONDING

COUNT

COVAR_POP

COVAR_SAMP

CREATE

CROSS

CUBE

CUME_DIST

CURRENT

CURRENT_COLLATION

CURRENT_DATE

CURRENT_DEFAULT_
TRANSFORM_GROUP

CURRENT_PATH

CURRENT_ROLE

CURRENT_TIME

CURRENT_TIMESTAMP

CURRENT_TRANSFORM_GROUP_
FOR_TYPE

CURRENT_USER

CURSOR

CYCLE

DATE

DAY

DEALLOCATE

DEC

DECIMAL

DECLARE

DEFAULT

DELETE

DENSE_RANK

DEREF

DESCRIBE

DETERMINISTIC

DISCONNECT

DISTINCT

DOUBLE	FLOOR
DROP	FOR
DYNAMIC	FOREIGN
EACH	FREE
ELEMENT	FROM
ELSE	FULL
EMPTY	FUNCTION
END	FUSION
END-EXEC	GET
ESCAPE	GLOBAL
EVERY	GRANT
EXCEPT	GROUP
EXEC	GROUPING
EXECUTE	HAVING
EXISTS	HOLD
EXP	HOUR
EXTERNAL	IDENTITY
EXTRACT	IN
FALSE	INDICATOR
FETCH	INNER
FILTER	INOUT
FLOAT	INSENSITIVE

**Book VIII
Appendix A**

**SQL:2003 Reserved
Words**

INSERT	MERGE
INT	METHOD
INTEGER	MIN
INTERSECT	MINUTE
INTERSECTION	MOD
INTERVAL	MODIFIERS
INTO	MODULE
IS	MONTH
JOIN	MULTISET
LANGUAGE	NATIONAL
LARGE	NATURAL
LATERAL	NCHAR
LEADING	NCLOB
LEFT	NEW
LIKE	NIL
LN	NO
LOCAL	NONE
LOCALTIME	NORMALIZE
LOCALTIMESTAMP	NOT
LOWER	NULL
MATCH	NULLIF
MAX	NUMERIC
MEMBER	OCTET_LENGTH

OF	RANGE
OLD	RANK
ON	READS
ONLY	REAL
OPEN	RECURSIVE
OR	REF
ORDER	REFERENCES
OUT	REFERENCING
OUTER	REGR_AVGX
OVER	REGR_AVGY
OVERLAPS	REGR_COUNT
OVERLAY	REGR_INTERCEPT
PARAMETER	REGR_R2
PARTITION	REGR_SLOPE
PERCENT_RANK	REGR_SXX
PERCENTILE_CONT	REGR_SXY
PERCENTILE_DISC	REGR_SYY
POSITION	RELEASE
POWER	RESULT
PRECISION	RETURN
PREPARE	RETURNS
PRIMARY	REVOKE
PROCEDURE	RIGHT

ROLLBACK	SQRT
ROLLUP	START
ROW	STATIC
ROW_NUMBER	STDDEV_POP
ROWS	STDDEV_SAMP
SAVEPOINT	SUBMULTISET
SCOPE	SUBSTRING
SCROLL	SUM
SEARCH	SYMMETRIC
SECOND	SYSTEM
SELECT	SYSTEM_USER
SENSITIVE	TABLE
SESSION_USER	TABLESAMPLE
SET	THEN
SIMILAR	TIME
SMALLINT	TIMESTAMP
SOME	TIMEZONE_HOUR
SPECIFIC	TIMEZONE_MINUTE
SPECIFICTYPE	TO
SQL	TRAILING
SQLEXCEPTION	TRANSLATE
SQLSTATE	TRANSLATION
SQLWARNING	

TREAT	WINDOW
TRIGGER	WITH
TRIM	WITHIN
TRUE	WITHOUT
UNION	XML
UNIQUE	XMLAGG
UNKNOWN	XMLATTRIBUTES
UNNEST	XMLBINARY
UPDATE	XMLCAST
UPPER	XMLCONCAT
USER	XMLCOMMENT
USING	XMLELEMENT
VALUE	XMLEXISTS
VALUES	XMLFOREST
VAR_POP	XMLITERATE
VAR_SAMP	XMLNAMESPACES
VARCHAR	XMLPARSE
VARYING	XMLPI
WHEN	XMLQUERY
WHENEVER	XMLSERIALIZE
WHERE	XMLTABLE
WIDTH_BUCKET	YEAR

Appendix B: Glossary

ActiveX control: A reusable software component that can be added to an application, reducing development time in the process. ActiveX is a Microsoft technology; ActiveX components can be used only by developers who work on Windows development systems.

aggregate function: A function that produces a single result based on the contents of an entire set of table rows. Also called a *set function*.

alias: A short substitute or nickname for a table name.

applet: A small application, written in the *Java* language, stored on a Web server that is downloaded to and executed on a Web client that connects to the server.

application program interface (API): A standard means of communicating between an application and a database or other system resource.

assertion: A constraint that is specified by a CREATE ASSERTION statement (rather than by a clause of a CREATE TABLE statement). Assertions commonly apply to more than one table.

atomic: Incapable of being subdivided.

attribute: A component of a structured type or relation.

back end: That part of a DBMS that interacts directly with the database.

catalog: A named collection of *schemas*.

client: An individual user workstation that represents the *front end* of a DBMS — the part that displays information on a screen and responds to user input.

client/server system: A multiuser system in which a central processor (the server) is connected to multiple intelligent user workstations (the clients).

cluster: A named collection of *catalogs*.

CODASYL DBTG database model: The network database model. *Note:* This use of the term *network* refers to the structuring of the data (*network* as opposed to *hierarchy*), rather than to network communications.

collating sequence: The ordering of characters in a character set. All collating sequences for character sets that have the Latin characters (a, b, c) define the obvious ordering (a, b, c, . . .). They differ, however, in the ordering of special characters (+, -, <, ?, and so on) and in the relative ordering of the digits and the letters.

collection type: A data type that allows a field of a table row to contain multiple objects.

column: A table component that holds a single attribute of the table.

composite key: A key made up of two or more table columns.

conceptual view: The *schema* of a database.

concurrent access: Two or more users operating on the same rows in a database table at the same time.

constraint: A restriction you specify on the data in a database.

constraint, deferred: A constraint that is not applied until you change its status to *immediate* or until you COMMIT the encapsulating transaction.

cursor: An SQL feature that specifies a set of rows, an ordering of those rows, and a current row within that ordering.

Data Control Language (DCL): That part of SQL that protects the database from harm.

Data Definition Language (DDL): That part of SQL used to define, modify, and eradicate database structures.

Data Manipulation Language (DML): That part of SQL that operates on database data.

data redundancy: Having the same data stored in more than one place in a database.

data source: A source of data used by a database application. It may be a database or a flat data file.

data sublanguage: A subset of a complete computer language that deals specifically with data handling. SQL is a data sublanguage.

data type: A set of representable values.

database: A self-describing collection of integrated records.

database, enterprise: A database containing information used by an entire enterprise.

database, personal: A database designed for use by one person on a single computer.

database, workgroup: A database designed to be used by a department or workgroup within an organization.

database administrator (DBA): The person ultimately responsible for the functionality, integrity, and safety of a database.

database engine: That part of a DBMS that directly interacts with the database (serving as part of the *back end*).

database publishing: The act of making the database contents available on the Internet or over an intranet.

database server: The server component of a *client/server* system. It is the place where the database resides.

DB2: A relational database management system marketed by IBM Corporation.

DBMS: A database management system.

deletion anomaly: An inconsistency in a multitable database that occurs when a row is deleted from one of its tables.

descriptor: An area in memory used to pass information between an application's procedural code and its dynamic SQL code.

diagnostics area: A data structure, managed by the DBMS, that contains detailed information about the last SQL statement executed and any errors that occurred during its execution.

distributed data processing: A system in which multiple servers handle data processing.

domain: The set of all values that a database item can assume.

domain integrity: A property of a database table column where all data items in that column fall within the domain of the column.

driver: That part of a database management system that interfaces directly with a database.

driver manager: A component of an *ODBC*-compliant database interface. On Windows machines, the driver manager is a dynamic link library (DLL) that coordinates the linking of data sources with appropriate drivers.

entity integrity: A property of a database table that is entirely consistent with the real-world object that it models.

file server: The server component of a resource-sharing system. It does not contain any database management software.

firewall: A piece of software (or a combination of hardware and software) that isolates an *intranet* from the Internet, allowing only trusted traffic to travel between them.

flat file: A collection of data records that contains only data — no metadata.

foreign key: A column or combination of columns in a database table that references the primary key of another table in the database.

forest: A collection of elements in an XML document.

front end: That part of a DBMS (such as the client in a *client/server* system) that interacts directly with the user.

functional dependency: A relationship between or among attributes of a relation.

hierarchical database model: A tree-structured model of data.

host variable: A variable passed between an application written in a procedural host language and embedded SQL.

HTML (HyperText Markup Language): A standard formatting language for Web documents.

implementation: A particular relational DBMS running on a specific hardware platform.

index: A table of pointers used to locate rows rapidly in a data table.

information schema: The system tables, which hold the database's *metadata*.

insertion anomaly: An inconsistency introduced into a multitable database when a new row is inserted into one of its tables.

Internet: The worldwide network of computers.

intranet: A network that uses World Wide Web hardware and software, but restricts access to users within a single organization.

IPX/SPX: A local area network protocol.

Java: A platform-independent compiled language designed originally for Web application development, but now used in many contexts.

JavaScript: A script language that gives some measure of programmability to HTML-based Web pages.

JDBC (Java DataBase Connectivity): A standard interface between a Java *applet* or application and a database. The JDBC standard is modeled after the ODBC standard.

join: A relational operator that combines data from multiple tables into a single result table.

logical connectives: Used to connect or change the truth value of predicates to produce more complex predicates.

mapping: The translation of data in one format to another format.

metadata: Data about the structure of the data in a database.

modification anomaly: A problem introduced into a database when a modification (insertion, deletion, or update) is made to one of the database tables.

Book VIII
Appendix B

Glossary

module language: A form of SQL in which SQL statements are placed in modules, which are called by an application program written in a host language.

mutator function: A function associated with a user-defined type (UDT), having two parameters whose definition is implied by the definition of some attribute of the type. The first parameter (the result) is of the same type as the UDT. The second parameter has the same type as the defining attribute.

nested query: A statement that contains one or more subqueries.

NetBEUI: A local area network protocol.

Netscape plug-in: A software component downloaded from a Web server to a Web client, where it is integrated with the client's Netscape browser, providing additional functions.

network database model: A way of organizing a database to get minimum redundancy of data items by allowing any data item (node) to be directly connected to any other.

normalization: A technique that reduces or eliminates the possibility that a database is subject to modification anomalies.

object: Any uniquely identifiable thing.

ODBC (Open DataBase Connectivity): A standard interface between a database and an application that is trying to access the data in that database. ODBC is defined by an international (ISO) and a national (ANSI) standard.

Oracle: A relational database management system marketed by Oracle Corporation.

parameter: A variable within an application written in SQL module language.

precision: The maximum number of digits allowed in a numeric data item.

predicate: A statement that may be either logically true or logically false.

primary key: A column or combination of columns in a database table that uniquely identifies each row in the table.

procedural language: A computer language that solves a problem by executing a procedure in the form of a sequence of steps.

query: A question you ask about the data in a database.

rapid application development (RAD) tool: A proprietary, graphically oriented alternative or supplement to SQL. A number of such tools are on the market.

record: A representation of some physical or conceptual object.

reference type: A data type whose values are all potential references to sites of one specified data type.

referential integrity: A state in which all the tables in a database are consistent with each other.

relation: A two-dimensional array of rows and columns, containing single-valued entries and no duplicate rows.

reserved words: Words that have a special significance in SQL and cannot be used as variable names or in any other way that differs from their intended use.

row: A sequence of (field name, value) pairs.

row value expression: A list of value expressions enclosed in parentheses and separated by commas.

scale: The number of digits in the fractional part of a numeric data item.

schema: The structure of an entire database. The information that describes the schema is the database's *metadata*.

schema owner: The person who was designated as the owner when the schema was created.

SEQUEL: A data sublanguage created by IBM that was a precursor of SQL.

set function: A function that produces a single result based on the contents of an entire set of table rows. Also called an *aggregate function*.

SQL: An industry standard data sublanguage, specifically designed to create, manipulate, and control relational databases. **SQL, dynamic:** A means of building compiled applications that does not require all data items to be identifiable at compile time.

SQL, embedded: An application structure in which SQL statements are embedded within programs written in a host language.

SQL, interactive: A real-time conversation with a database.

SQL/DS: A relational database management system marketed by IBM Corporation.

structured type: A user defined type that is expressed as a list of attribute definitions and methods rather than being based on a single predefined source type.

subquery: A query within a query.

subtype: A data type is a subtype of a second data type if every value of the first type is also a value of the second type.

supertype: A data type is a supertype of a second data type if every value of the second type is also a value of the first type.

table: A relation.

TCP/IP (Transmission Control Protocol/Internet Protocol): The network protocol used by the Internet and intranets.

teleprocessing system: A powerful central processor connected to multiple dumb terminals.

transaction: A sequence of SQL statements whose effect is not accessible to other transactions until all the statements are executed.

transitive dependency: A situation in which one attribute of a relation depends on a second attribute, which in turn depends on a third attribute.

translation table: Tool for converting character strings from one character set to another.

trigger: A small piece of code that tells a DBMS what other actions to perform after certain SQL statements have been executed.

update anomaly: A problem introduced into a database when a table row is updated.

user-defined type: A type whose characteristics are defined by a type descriptor specified by the user.

value expression: An expression that combines two or more values.

value expression, conditional: A value expression that assigns different values to arguments, based on whether a condition is logically true.

value expression, datetime: A value expression that deals with DATE, TIME, TIMESTAMP, or INTERVAL data.

value expression, numeric: A value expression that combines numeric values using the addition, subtraction, multiplication, or division operators.

value expression, string: A value expression that combines character strings with the concatenation operator.

value function: A function that performs an operation on a single character string, number, or date/time.

view: A database component that behaves exactly like a table but has no independent existence of its own.

virtual table: A view.

World Wide Web (WWW): An aspect of the Internet that has a graphical user interface. The Web is accessed by applications called *Web browsers,* and information is provided to the Web by installations called *Web servers.*

XML: A widely accepted markup language used as a means of exchanging data between dissimilar systems.

Index

Symbols & Numerics

A

D

O

P

S

U